Lecture Notes in Computer Science 4111

Commenced Publication in 1973
Founding and Former Series Editors:
Gerhard Goos, Juris Hartmanis, and Jan van Leeuwen

Editorial Board

Frank S. de Boer   Marcello M. Bonsangue
Susanne Graf   Willem-Paul de Roever (Eds.)

Formal Methods for Components and Objects

4th International Symposium, FMCO 2005
Amsterdam, The Netherlands, November 1-4, 2005
Revised Lectures

 Springer

Volume Editors

Frank S. de Boer
Centre for Mathematics and Computer Science, CWI
Kruislaan 413, 1098 SJ Amsterdam, The Netherlands
E-mail: F.S.de.Boer@cwi.nl

Marcello M. Bonsangue
Leiden University
Leiden Instiute of Advanced Computer Science
P. O. Box 9512, 2300 RA Leiden, The Netherlands
E-mail: marcello@liacs.nl

Susanne Graf
VERIMAG
2 Avenue de Vignate, Centre Equitation, 38610 Grenoble-Giéres, France
E-mail: Susanne.Graf@imag.fr

Willem-Paul de Roever
University of Kiel
Institute of Computer Science and Applied Mathematics
Hermann-Rodewald-Str. 3, 24118 Kiel, Germany
E-mail: wpr@informatik.uni-kiel.de

Library of Congress Control Number: 2006930291

CR Subject Classification (1998): D.2, D.3, F.3, D.4

LNCS Sublibrary: SL 2 – Programming and Software Engineering

ISSN	0302-9743
ISBN-10	3-540-36749-7 Springer Berlin Heidelberg New York
ISBN-13	978-3-540-36749-9 Springer Berlin Heidelberg New York

Springer is a part of Springer Science+Business Media

springer.com

© Springer-Verlag Berlin Heidelberg 2006
Printed in Germany

Typesetting: Camera-ready by author, data conversion by Scientific Publishing Services, Chennai, India
Printed on acid-free paper   SPIN: 11804192   06/3142   5 4 3 2 1 0

Preface

Large and complex software systems provide the necessary infrastructure in all industries today. In order to construct such large systems in a systematic manner, the focus in the development methodologies has switched in the last two decades from functional issues to structural issues: both data and functions are encapsulated into software units which are integrated into large systems by means of various techniques supporting reusability and modifiability. This encapsulation principle is essential to both the object-oriented and the more recent component-based software engineering paradigms.

Formal methods have been applied successfully to the verification of medium-sized programs in protocol and hardware design. However, their application to the development of large systems requires more emphasis on specification, modeling and validation techniques supporting the concepts of reusability and modifiability and their implementation in new extensions of existing programming languages like Java.

The new format of FMCO 2005 consisted of invited keynote lectures and tutorial lectures selected through a corresponding open call. The latter provide a tutorial perspective on recent developments. In contrast to existing conferences, about half of the program consisted of invited keynote lectures by top researchers sharing their interest in the application or development of formal methods for large-scale software systems (object or component oriented). FMCO does not focus on specific aspects of the use of formal methods, but rather it aims at a systematic and comprehensive account of the expanding body of knowledge on modern software systems.

This volume contains the contributions submitted after the symposium by both invited and selected lecturers. The proceedings of FMCO 2002, FMCO 2003, and FMCO 2004 have already been published as volumes 2852, 3188, and 3657 of Springer's *Lecture Notes in Computer Science*. We believe that these proceedings provide a unique combination of ideas on software engineering and formal methods which reflect the expanding body of knowledge on modern software systems.

June 2006

F.S. de Boer
M.M. Bonsangue
S. Graf
W.-P. de Roever

Organization

The FMCO symposia are organized in the context of the project Mobi-J, a project founded by a bilateral research program of The Dutch Organization for Scientific Research (NWO) and the Central Public Funding Organization for Academic Research in Germany (DFG). The partners of the Mobi-J projects are: the Centrum voor Wiskunde en Informatica, the Leiden Institute of Advanced Computer Science, and the Christian-Albrechts-Universität Kiel.

This project aims at the development of a programming environment which supports component-based design and verification of Java programs annotated with assertions. The overall approach is based on an extension of the Java language with a notion of component that provides for the encapsulation of its internal processing of data and composition in a network by means of mobile asynchronous channels.

Sponsoring Institutions

The Dutch Organization for Scientific Research (NWO)
The Royal Netherlands Academy of Arts and Sciences (KNAW)
The Dutch Institute for Programming research and Algorithmics (IPA)
The Centrum voor Wiskunde en Informatica (CWI), The Netherlands
The Leiden Institute of Advanced Computer Science (LIACS), The Netherlands

Table of Contents

Component and Service Oriented Computing

System Design

Tools

Algebraic Methods

Model Checking

Assertional Methods

Quantitative Analysis

A Software Component Model and Its Preliminary Formalisation

Kung-Kiu Lau[1], Mario Ornaghi[2], and Zheng Wang[1]

[1] School of Computer Science, the University of Manchester
Manchester M13 9PL, United Kingdom
{kung-kiu, zw}@cs.man.ac.uk
[2] Dipartimento di Scienze dell'Informazione,
Universita' degli studi di Milano
Via Comelico 39/41, 20135 Milano, Italy
ornaghi@dsi.unimi.it

Abstract. A software component model should define what components are, and how they can be composed. That is, it should define a theory of components and their composition. Current software component models tend to use objects or port-connector type architectural units as components, with method calls and port-to-port connections as composition mechanisms. However, these models do not provide a proper composition theory, in particular for key underlying concepts such as encapsulation and compositionality. In this paper, we outline our notion of these concepts, and give a preliminary formalisation of a software component model that embodies these concepts.

1 Introduction

The context of this work is Component-based Software Engineering, rather than Component-based Systems. In the latter, the focus is on system properties, and components are typically state machines. Key concerns are issues related to communication, concurrency, processes, protocols, etc. Properties of interest are temporal, non-functional properties such as deadlock-freedom, safety, liveness, etc. In the former, the focus is on software components and middleware for composing them. Usually a software component model, e.g. Enterprise JavaBeans (EJB) [21], provides the underlying framework.

A software component model should define (i) what components are, i.e. their syntax and semantics; and (ii) how to compose components, i.e. the semantics of their composition. Current component models tend to use objects or port-connector type architectural units as components, with method calls and port-to-port connections as composition mechanisms. However, these models do not define a proper theory for composition.

We believe that encapsulation and compositionality are key concepts for such a theory. In this paper, we explain these notions, and their role in a composition theory. Using these concepts, we present a software component model, together with a preliminary formalisation.

F.S. de Boer et al. (Eds.): FMCO 2005, LNCS 4111, pp. 1–21, 2006.

2   Current Component Models

Currently, so-called component models, e.g. EJB and CCM (CORBA Component Model) [24], do not follow a standard terminology or semantics. There are different definitions of what a component is [6], and most of these are not set in the context of a component model. In particular, they do not define composition properly.

For example, a widely used definition of components is the following, due to Szyperski [28]:

> "A software component is a unit of composition with contractually specified interfaces and explicit context dependencies only. A software component can be deployed independently and is subject to composition by third parties."

A different definition is the following by Meyer [20]:

> "A component is a software element (modular unit) satisfying the following conditions:
> 1. It can be used by other software elements, its 'clients'.
> 2. It possesses an official usage description, which is sufficient for a client author to use it.
> 3. It is not tied to any fixed set of clients."

Both these definitions do not mention a component model, in particular how composition is defined.

The following definition given in Heineman and Councill [12] mentions a component model:

> "A [component is a] software element that conforms to a component model and can be independently deployed and composed without modification according to a composition standard."

but it does not define one.

Nevertheless, there is a commonly accepted abstract view of what a component is, viz. a software unit that contains (i) code for performing services, and (ii) an interface for accessing these services (Fig. 1(a)). To provide its services, a component

Fig. 1. A software component

may require some services. So a component is often depicted as in Fig. 1(b), e.g. in CCM and UML2.0 [23].

In current software component models, components are typically objects as in object-oriented languages, and port-connector type architectural units, with method calls and ADL (architecture description languages [26]) connectors as composition mechanisms respectively.

A complete survey of these models is beyond the scope of this paper. It can be found in [17].

3   Our Component Model

In our component model, *components* encapsulate *computation* (and data),[1] and *composition operators* encapsulate *control*. Our components are constructed from (i) computation units and (ii) connectors. A computation unit performs computation within itself, and does not invoke computation in another unit. Connectors are used to build components from computation units, and also as composition operators to compose components into composite components.

3.1   Exogenous Connectors

Our connectors are *exogenous connectors* [16]. The distinguishing characteristic of exogenous connectors is that they encapsulate control. In traditional ADLs, components

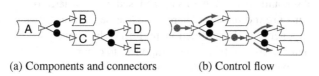

(a) Components and connectors   (b) Control flow

Fig. 2. Traditional ADLs

are supposed to represent *computation*, and connectors *interaction* between components [19] (Fig. 2 (a)). Actually, however, components represent computation as well as *control*, since control originates in components, and is passed on by connectors to other components. This is illustrated by Fig. 2 (b), where the origin of control is denoted by a dot in a component, and the flow of control is denoted by arrows emanating from the dot and arrows following connectors.

In this situation, components are not truly independent, i.e. they are tightly coupled, albeit only indirectly via their ports.

In general, component connection schemes in current component models (including ADLs) use message passing, and fall into two main categories: (i) connection by direct message passing; and (ii) connection by indirect message passing. Direct message

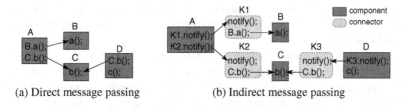

(a) Direct message passing   (b) Indirect message passing

Fig. 3. Connection by message passing

passing corresponds to direct method calls, as exemplified by objects calling methods in other objects (Fig. 3 (a)), using method or event delegation, or remote procedure call (RPC). Software component models that adopt direct message passing schemes as

---

[1] For lack of space, we will not discuss data in this paper.

composition operators are EJB, CCM, COM [5], UML2.0 [23] and KobrA [3]. In these models, there is no explicit code for connectors, since messages are 'hard-wired' into the components, and so connectors are not separate entities.

Indirect message passing corresponds to coordination (e.g. RPC) via connectors, as exemplified by ADLs. Here, connectors are separate entities that are defined explicitly. Typically they are glue code or scripts that pass messages between components indirectly. To connect a component to another component we use a connector that when notified by the former invokes a method in the latter (Fig. 3 (b)). Besides ADLs, other software component models that adopt indirect message passing schemes are JavaBeans [27], Koala [30], SOFA [25], PECOS [22], PIN [14] and Fractal [8].

In connection schemes by message passing, direct or indirect, control originates in and flows from components, as in Fig. 2 (b). This is clearly the case in both Fig. 3 (a) and (b).

A categorical semantics of connectors is proposed in [9], where coordination is modelled through signature morphisms. There is a clear separation between computation, occurring in components, and coordination, performed by connectors. However, shared actions may propagate control from one component to others.

By contrast, in exogenous connection, control originates in and flows from connectors, leaving components to encapsulate only computation. This is illustrated by Fig. 4.

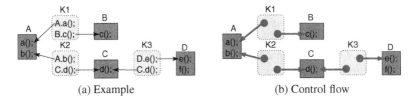

(a) Example   (b) Control flow

Fig. 4. Connection by exogenous connectors

In Fig. 4 (a), components do not call methods in other components. Instead, all method calls are initiated and coordinated by exogenous connectors. The latter's distinguishing feature of control encapsulation is clearly illustrated by Fig. 4 (b), in clear contrast to Fig. 2 (b).

Exogenous connectors thus encapsulate control (and data), i.e. they *initiate* and *coordinate* control (and data). With exogenous connection, components are truly independent and decoupled.

The concept of exogenous connection entails a type hierarchy of exogenous connectors. Because they encapsulate all the control in a system, such connectors have to connect to one another (as well as components) in order to build up a complete control structure for the system. For this to be possible, there must be a type hierarchy for these connectors. Therefore such a hierarchy must be defined for any component model that is based on exogenous connection.

3.2   Components

Our view of a component is that it is not simply a part of the whole system. Rather it is something very different from traditional software units such as code fragments, functions, procedures, subroutines, modules, classes/objects, programs, packages, etc, and equally different from more modern units like DLLs and services.

We define a component as follows:

Definition 1. A *software component* is a software unit with the following defining characteristics: (i) encapsulation and (ii) compositionality.

A component should encapsulate both *data* and *computation*. A component C encapsulates data by making its data private. C encapsulates computation by making sure that its computation happens entirely within itself.

An object can encapsulate data, but it does not encapsulate computation, since objects can call methods in other objects (Fig. 5(a)).

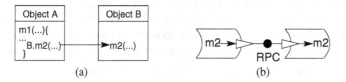

(a)   (b)

Fig. 5. Objects and architectural units

Port-connector type components, as in e.g. ADLs, UML2.0 and Koala, can encapsulate data. However, they usually do not encapsulate computation, since components can call methods in other components by remote procedure call (RPC), albeit only indirectly via connectors (and ports) (Fig. 5(b)).

Components should be *compositional*, i.e. the composition of two components C_1 and C_2 should yield another component C_3, which in turn should also have the defining characteristics of encapsulation and compositionality. Thus compositionality implies that composition preserves or propagates encapsulation.[2]

Classes and objects are not compositional. They can only be 'composed' by method calls, and such a 'composition' does not yield another class or object. Indeed, method calls break encapsulation. Port-connector type components can be composed, but they are not compositional if they do not have (computation) encapsulation.

Encapsulation entails that access to components must be provided by *interfaces*. Classes and objects do not have interfaces. Access to (the methods of) objects, if permitted, is direct, not via interfaces. So-called 'interfaces' in object-oriented languages like Java are themselves classes or objects, so are not interfaces to components. Port-connector type components use their ports as their interfaces.

Our components are constructed from *computation units* and *exogenous connectors*. A computation unit performs just computation within itself and does not invoke computation in another unit. It can be thought of as a class or object with methods, except that these methods do not call methods in other units. Thus it encapsulates computation.

Exogenous connectors encapsulate control, as we have seen in the previous section. The type hierarchy of these connectors in our component model is as follows. At the

---

[2] Compositionality in terms of other (non-functional) properties of sub-components is an open issue, which we do not address here.

lowest level, level 1, because components are not allowed to call methods in other components, we need an exogenous *invocation connector*. This is a *unary* operator that takes a computation unit, invokes one of its methods, and receives the result of the invocation. At the next level of the type hierarchy, to structure the control and data flow in a set of components or a system, we need other connectors for sequencing exogenous method calls to different components. So at level 2, we need *n-ary* connectors for connecting invocation connectors, and at level 3, we need *n-ary* connectors for connecting these connectors, and so on. In other words, we need a hierarchy of connectors of different arities and types. We have defined and implemented such a hierarchy in [16]. Apart from invocation connectors at level 1, our hierarchy includes *pipe* connectors, for sequencing, and *selector* connectors, for branching, at levels $n \geq 2$. These connectors are called *composition connectors* for the obvious reason. Level-1 connectors are invocation connectors, and level-2 composition connectors connect only invocation connectors, but composition connectors at higher levels are polymorphic since they can connect different kinds of connectors at different levels (and with different arities).

We distinguish between (i) *atomic* components and (ii) *composite* components.

Definition 2. An *atomic component* C is a pair $\langle i, u \rangle$ where u is a computation unit, and i is an invocation connector that invokes u's methods. i provides an interface to the component C.

A *composite component* CC is a tuple $\langle k, C_1, C_2, \ldots C_j \rangle$, for some j, where k is a j-ary connector at level $n \geq 2$, and each $C_i, i = 1, \ldots, j$, is either an atomic component or a composite component. k is called a *composition connector*. It provides an interface to the component CC.

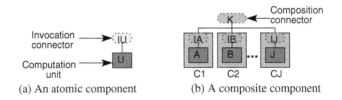

(a) An atomic component   (b) A composite component

Fig. 6. Atomic and composite components

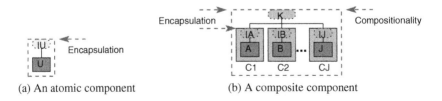

(a) An atomic component   (b) A composite component

Fig. 7. Encapsulation and compositionality

Figure 6 illustrates atomic and composite components. Clearly, an atomic component encapsulates computation, since a computation unit does so, and an invocation connector invokes only methods in the unit (Fig 7(a)). It is easy to see that a composite component also encapsulates computation (Fig 7(b)).

3.3   Composition Operators

To construct systems or composite components, we need composition operators that preserve encapsulation and compositionality. Such composition operators should work only on interfaces, in view of encapsulation.

Glue code is certainly not suitable as composition operators. Neither are object method calls or ADL connectors, as used in current component models. Indeed, these models do not have proper composition operators, in our view, since they do not have the concepts of encapsulation and compositionality.

As in Definition 2, we use exogenous connectors at level $n \geq 2$ as composition operators. These operators are compositional and therefor preserve and propagate encapsulation. As shown in Fig 7(b), a composite component has encapsulation, as a result of encapsulation in its constituent components. Furthermore, the composite component is also compositional. Thus, any component, be it atomic or composite, has a top-most connector that provides an interface, and it can be composed with any other component using a suitable composition operator.

This self-similarity of a composite component is a direct consequence of component encapsulation and compositionality, and provides the basis for a compositional way of constructing systems from components. Fig. 8(b) illustrates self-similarity of a com-

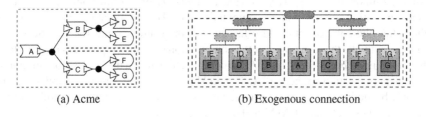

(a) Acme   (b) Exogenous connection

Fig. 8. Self-similarity of a composite component

posite component in a system composed from atomic and composite components. Each dotted box indicates a composite component. Note in particular that the composite at the top level is the entire system itself. Most importantly, every composite component is similar to all its sub-components.

The system in Fig. 8(b) corresponds to the Acme [11] architecture in Fig. 8(a). By comparison, in the Acme system, the composites are different from those in Fig. 8(b). For instance, (D,E) is a composite in (b) but not in (a). Also, in (a) the top-level composite is not similar to the composite (B,D,E) at the next level down. The latter has an interface, but the former does not.

In general, self-similarity provides a compositional approach to system construction, and this is an advance over hierarchical approaches such as ADLs which are not compositional, strictly speaking.

3.4   The Bank Example

Having defined our component model, we illustrate its use in the construction of a simple bank system. The bank system has just one ATM that serves two banks (Bank1 and Bank2) as shown in Fig. 9.

The ATM obtains client details including card number, PIN, and requested services, etc., and locates the bank that the client account belongs to. It then passes client details to the client's bank, which then provides the requested services of withdrawal, deposit, etc.

To construct the bank system, first, two Bank components, Bank1 and Bank2, are assembled by a Selector connector into a BankComposite. Then BankComposite is composed with an ATM component by a Pipe connector into the bank system.

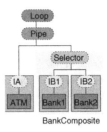

BankComposite

Fig. 9. A simple bank system

All the components in Fig. 9 are well encapsulated. Every atomic component is made up of an invocation connector and a computation unit. The computation unit implements methods that the component could offer, and the invocation connector provides functionalities to invoke those methods of the computation unit; thus it provides the interface to the component. For example, the ATM component is made up of a computation unit ATM and an invocation connector IA. The ATM component encapsulates both data and functions, by defining its data as private and computing its functions entirely within itself. IA invokes methods of ATM and thus serves as its interface.

All the components in Fig. 9 are compositional. The composite component Bank-Composite is itself a component, with the composition connector Selector as its interface. BankComposite also has encapsulation: it encapsulates data and functions of its constituent components, Bank1 and Bank2.

Moreover, the composite component BankComposite in Fig. 9 is self-similar. Bank-Composite has a top-level connector as an interface, and so have its sub-components Bank1 and Bank2.

Finally, in this example, we built the bank system with a loop connector at the outermost level, which iterates and waits for client requests.

4   A Preliminary Formalisation

So far we have defined our component model informally. In this section we present a preliminary formalisation of our model. The formalisation serves as a useful check on the soundness, in the sense of good judgement, of the underlying ideas.

We will assume that our component model provides the basis for a Component-based Software Design System, which we will call DS for convenience. DS should support all the phases of the component life-cycle [18], i.e.:

(i) *Design Phase.* A system or a new component C is designed from the connectors, the computation units, and/or existing components, in a *repository*. If C is a new component, it is added to the repository.

(ii) *Deployment Phase.* Deployment prepares a system or a component C for execution, i.e. turns it into a *binary* b_C and establishes the way of *loading* and instantiating it when it is launched.

(iii) *Run-time Phase.* A binary b_C is launched by loading and instantiating it into a running instance, which provides the services offered by C.

Deployment-phase compositionality should be supported by suitable deployment tools and should follow from design-phase compositionality. For this, a DS should be provided with a composition and run-time infrastructure, implementing deployment-phase composition according to the design-phase semantics of connectors.

Here we outline a first abstract meta-model for the design phase, and discuss functional compositionality and encapsulation. The meta-model is formalised in many-sorted first-order logic with identity. In the explanation we will introduce the signature incrementally and we will explain the intended meaning informally. Axioms are given in the appendix. The purpose is to devise and establish the basic requirements to be satisfied by DS and the design-phase semantics of connectors.

4.1 Components and Their Interfaces

DS should provide a design environment for components with the characteristics of compositionality and encapsulation, as discussed in Section 3.2. Component interfaces play a key role, for two main reasons:

(i) They are the counterpart of encapsulation, i.e., they represent what is made public, while encapsulation represents what is hidden.

(ii) Compositionality requires that the services of a component are defined in terms of those of its sub-components.

To represent components and their interfaces in our general meta-model, we assume that DS has a signature including the following sorts and declarations (Decls):

$$\begin{aligned}
&\text{Sorts: } \textit{Request, Result, ReqType, ResType, OpType, Comp} \\
&\text{Decls: } >> : \textit{ReqType} \times \textit{ResType} \to \textit{OpType} \\
&\qquad :: : \textit{Comp} \times \textit{OpType} \\
&\qquad \in : \textit{Request} \times \textit{ReqType} \mid \textit{Result} \times \textit{ResType}
\end{aligned}$$

Request is the sort of possible requests, and *Result* is that of possible results. *ReqType* is the sort of request types, and *ResType* is that of the result types. By the overloaded membership relation $\in$, each request type $Q : ReqType$ is interpreted as a set of requests, and each result type $R : ReqType$ as a set of results. *Comp* is the sort of possible components. *OpType* is introduced to represent component interfaces. It is freely generated by the constructor $>>$, i.e., its elements are of the form $Q >> R$, with $Q : ReqType$ and $R : ResType$. Interfaces are represented by the interface relation:

$$C :: Q >> R$$

It means that the component C accepts requests $q \in Q$ and yields results $r \in R$. We say that C supports the *operation type* $Q >> R$. The *interface* of C is the set of operation types it supports.

Requests and result types are disjoint. Thus a component cannot answer a request by another request to another component, that is, computation encapsulation is enforced. This will be further discussed in Section 4.3. *Request*, *Result*, *ReqType*, and *ResType* are *open*, i.e., they depend on the DS at hand.

Example 1. In a programming language L, an operation template such as, e.g., $sum(x : int, y : int) : int$ can be represented in our formalism as the operation type

$$sum(x : int, y : int) >> int$$

where the request type $sum(x : int, y : int)$ represents all the call-instances $sum(m, n)$ and the result type is the data type int. That is, *Request* is the set of all possible call-instances of L, *Result* is the set of all the elements of the data types of L, *ReqType* is the set of call-templates, *ResType* is the set of data types of the language, and an operation type $m(x_1 : T_1, \ldots, x_n : T_n) >> T$ corresponds to an operation template $m(x_1 : T_1, \ldots, x_n : T_n) : T$.

Request and result types could also include semantic information, allowing us to use them as specifications and to deal with the correctness issue. Moreover, it may be useful to allow structured information, as illustrated by the following example.

Example 2. We introduce atomic request and result types by templates. A template is of the form $s(x_1 : T_1, \ldots, x_n : T_n)$, where s is the template symbol, $n \geq 0$, and $x_1 : T_1, \ldots, x_n : T_n$ are its parameters. We distinguish between request and result templates. In general, request templates correspond to procedure calls, such as $read()$, $write(x : string)$, etc. Result templates are semantic properties, such as $odd(x : int)$, $x = a + b$, etc. Semantic properties can also be used in requests, as pre-conditions. A request is an instance of a request template, e.g. $read$, $write(4)$, $odd(3)$, and so on. A result is an instance of a result template, e.g. $odd(5)$, $done$, and so on.

An example of an operation type using templates is:

$$sum(x : int, y : int) >> z = x + y$$

The meaning is that for every request $sum(m, n)$ we get a result $z = m + n$.

It may be useful to introduce structured templates, as shown by the following example.

$$read(F : text) >> x : int | not AnInteger$$

expresses the fact that reading from F yields an integer x, unless the characters read do not represent an integer. The use of structured templates is also useful in correspondence with connectors, as will be explained in Section 4.4.

4.2   Composition Operators

Composite components are built by means of composition connectors, starting from atomic components. The latter are built from computation units, by means of invocation connectors. To model this situation, we enrich the signature introduced in the previous section by adding:

Sorts: $Unit, InvConn, CompConn, List(X)$
Decls: The usual operations and relations on lists
$\bullet : InvConn \times Unit \to Comp$
$\bullet : CompConn \times List(Comp) \to Comp$
$ctype : CompConn \times List(OpType) \times OpType$

$Unit$ is the sort of *units*, $InvConn$ that of *invocation connectors*, and $CompConn$ that of *composition connectors*. Parametric lists $List(X)$ are defined as usual, and a list will be represented by the notation $[x_1, \ldots, x_n]$. The overloaded operator $\bullet$ is the composition operator.

Components are defined by *composition terms*. A composition term T indicates how a component is built by connectors starting from units or components already defined and stored in the repository of the DS. Composition terms are generated by the composition $\bullet$: $i \bullet u$ denotes the application of an invocation connector i to a unit u, and $k \bullet [T_1, \ldots, T_n]$ denotes the application of a composition operator k to the sub-terms (denoting sub-components) $T_1, \ldots, T_n$.

Composition connectors are typed by $ctype$. We will write $k : [Op_1, \ldots, Op_n] \to Op$ as a different notation for $ctype(k, [Op_1, \ldots, Op_n], Op)$. If k has a composition type $Op_1, \ldots, Op_n \to Op$, then $k \bullet [T_1, \ldots, T_n]$ has operation type Op whenever it is applied to $T_1 :: Op_1, \ldots, T_n :: Op_n$.

Not all the composition terms represent *components*. Components, together with their interface relation ::, are defined by inductive *composition rules* of the following form:

$$\frac{}{i \bullet u :: Op} r(i, u)$$

$$\frac{T_1 :: Op_1 \quad \ldots \quad T_n :: Op_n}{k \bullet [T_1, \ldots, T_n] :: Op} r(k)$$

For the invocation connector rule $r(i, u)$, the operation type Op is determined by both i and u. For the composition connector rule $r(k)$, Op is determined by the composition type $Op_1, \ldots, Op_n \to Op$ of k. Connectors and the related composition rules are, in general, domain specific and depend on the DS. The components of a DS are defined as follows:

Definition 3. A *composition term* T is a component of a DS with operation type Op iff $T :: Op$ can be derived by the composition rules of the DS.

New composite components can be introduced in the repository of the DS by definitions of the form $C := T$, where C is a new constant symbol and T is a composition term. As usual, the definition $C := T$ expands the current signature by the new constant $C : Conn$ and introduces the definition axiom $C = T$. The interface relation of a component C introduced by a definition $C := T$ is that of T:

$$\text{if } C := T, \text{ then } C :: Q >> R \text{ iff } T :: Q >> R \tag{1}$$

Typed composition connectors have a compositional semantics given by:

- the composition rules of the DS;
- the execution rules explained in Section 4.3, which give the run-time semantics of a component in terms of that of its sub-components.

We distinguish between designing a DS and using it. *Designing* a DS means designing its units and, more importantly, the rules of its connectors, according to the general assumptions of the meta-model. *Using* a DS to design systems and components means using its units and its composition rules. Although, in general, connectors and their composition rules are domain specific, there are general-purpose connectors. Some of them will be shown in Section 4.4. In the following example we show the general-purpose connector *pipe*.

Example 3. A pipe connector $pipe : [Q_1 >> R_1, Q_2 >> R_2] \rightarrow Q_1 >> R_2$ assumes a map $p : Result \rightarrow Request$, to pipe the results $r_1 \in R_1$ of component $C_1 :: Q_1 >> R_1$ into requests $q_2 \in Q_2$ for $C_2 :: Q_2 >> R_2$ (details in Example 4). The composition rule is:

$$\frac{C_1 :: Q_1 >> R_1 \quad C_2 :: Q_2 >> R_2}{pipe \bullet [C_1, C_2] :: Q_1 >> R_2} \, r(pipe).$$

4.3 A Run-Time Semantics

As mentioned before, to run a component represented by a composition term T, we need to compile the units and connectors of T into binaries, to deploy binaries according to T, to load them into the memory and to launch them. This process requires an appropriate infrastructure, that guarantees that the implementation agrees with the *intended run-time semantics* of T. In this section we define the intended run-time semantics in an abstract, i.e. implementation independent, way. To this end, we enrich our signature as follows:

$$
\begin{aligned}
&\text{Sorts: } D, Instance, Step \\
&\text{Decl: } halt, error : D \\
&\qquad \mapsto \; : \; D \times Request \times D \times Result \rightarrow Step; \\
&\qquad \text{i} \; : \; Comp \times D \rightarrow Instance; \\
&\qquad exec \; : \; Comp \times Step
\end{aligned}
$$

Instance is the sort of *run-time instances*, and D is the sort of *data* that can be contained in the memory of instances. We do not model data and their structure in this paper. In the examples we will assume that D is closed with respect to the pairing operation (i.e., if $d_1, d_2 \in D$, then $\langle d_1, d_2 \rangle \in D$). By i$(C, d)$ we represent a running instance of a component C with current memory content $d \in D$. The relation $data(C, d)$ indicates which data are admitted for a component C.

Step is the sort of *execution steps*. It is freely generated by $\mapsto$, i.e., its elements are uniquely represented by terms of the form $\mapsto (d, q, d', r)$. A term $\mapsto (d, q, d', r)$ is also written $[d, q] \mapsto [d', r]$. It indicates an execution step from the current memory content d and request q, into the new memory content d' and result r.

Instances can execute requests. Let $i(C, d)$ be a run-time instance with operation type $C :: QT >> RT$, and let $q \in Q$ be a request. The *execution relation* of a component C

$$exec(C, [d, q] \mapsto [d', r])$$

indicates that when the instance $i(C, d)$ executes a request q, it performs the execution step $[d, q] \mapsto [d', r]$. To treat regular halting and run-time errors, we consider *halt* and *error* as particular memory contents:

$$exec(C, [d, q] \mapsto [halt, r])$$
$$exec(C, [d, q] \mapsto [error, r])$$

We define the run-time semantics of an atomic component $i \bullet u$ by a map $\mathcal{M}(i, u) :$ $D \times Request \to D \times Result$ as follows:

$$exec(i \bullet u, [d, q] \mapsto [d', r]) \leftrightarrow \mathcal{M}(i, u)(d, q) = \langle d', r \rangle$$

We define the run-time semantics of a non-atomic component $k \bullet [T_1, \ldots, T_n]$ by a map $\mathcal{M}(k) : Step^n \to Step$ as follows:

$$exec(k \bullet [T_1, \ldots, T_n], S) \leftrightarrow \wedge_{j=1}^{n} exec(T_j, S_j) \wedge$$
$$S = \mathcal{M}(k)(S_1, \ldots, S_n)$$

Invocation connectors provide *encapsulation* for atomic components through interfaces. The unit u in an atomic component $i \bullet u$ cannot directly call any other unit or component. It can only provide results, i.e., the only way of requiring a service from outside (if needed) is to pass the request as a result through the invocation connector. This "request-result" is then managed by the other connectors, that is, control is performed by connectors. The semantics of composition connectors is compositional. Indeed: (a) it preserves encapsulation through interfaces and (b) $\mathcal{M}(k)$ indicates how the resulting step S is obtained from the computation steps S_j of the sub-components, in a way that does not depend on the specific features of the sub-components, but only on their operation types $Op_1, \ldots, Op_n$ and on the connector $k : [Op_1, \ldots, Op_n] \to Op$.

An abstract compositional run-time semantics is useful for two main reasons. The first one is that a compositional semantics supports "predictability", since the result of a composition is also a component and its services are defined in terms of those of the sub-components. The second reason is that it abstracts from the implementation details, related to the compilation of composition terms into runnable binaries. The correctness of different implementations with respect to the abstract run-time semantics fixed for composition terms supports interoperability. Thus, *designing* the abstract run-time semantics of connectors and units means defining the maps $\mathcal{M}(i, u)$ and $\mathcal{M}(k)$ according to the general requirements explained above. *Implementing* it means implementing a run-time infrastructure that is correct with respect to the abstract semantics.

The correctness of an implementation is with respect to the abstract execution semantics. With the step $[d, q] \mapsto [d', r]$ we associate the *observable step* $q \mapsto r$. An implementation is correct if the observable steps obtained by running it coincide with those defined by the abstract run-time semantics. That is, we abstract from the internal representation of data, and we are only interested in observable requests and results.

Example 4. Here we show the run-time semantics of the *pipe* rule of Example 3.

$$
\begin{aligned}
exec(pipe \bullet [C_1, C_2], [\langle d_1, d_2 \rangle, q_1], [\langle d'_1, d'_2 \rangle, r_2]) &\leftrightarrow exec(C_1, [d_1, q_1] \mapsto [d'_1, r_1]) \wedge \\
&\quad exec(C_2, [d_2, q_2] \mapsto [d'_2, r_2]) \wedge \\
&\quad q_2 = p(r_1)
\end{aligned}
$$

In this rule, results $r_1 \in R_1$ are piped into requests $p(r_1) \in Q_2$, the sub-component C_1 has data d_1 and the sub-component C_2 has separate data d_2, and the whole component has data $\langle d_1, d_2 \rangle$ (i.e., $data(pipe \bullet [C_1, C_2], d)$ holds iff $d = \langle d_1, d_2 \rangle$, with $data(C_1, d_1)$ and $data(C_2, d_2)$). We may have different kinds of pipe, e.g., the piping mechanism could also depend on the request q_1.

4.4 The Bank Example

In this section, we illustrate our general model. Firstly we outline part of a possible DS, and then we apply it to the bank example (Section 3.4).

The DS defines interfaces through structured templates, as in Example 2. Here we consider the structuring operators $|$, sel and $*$, defined as follows.

- A request/result of a type $A_1 | \cdots | A_n$ is a pair $\langle k, a \rangle$, with $1 \le k \le n$ and $a \in A_k$.
- A request/result of type $sel(p \in S : A(p))$ is a pair $\langle v, a \rangle$, where S is a finite set of values, $v \in S$ and $a \in A(v)$.
- A request/result of type A^* is a sequence $[a_1, \ldots, a_n]$ such that $a_i \in A$.

The composition rules for the connectors related to the above structures are:

$$
\frac{C :: Q >> R}{loop \bullet [C] :: Q^* >> R^*} r(loop) \qquad \frac{C_1 :: Q_1 >> R_1 \quad \ldots \quad C_n :: Q_n >> R_n}{case \bullet [C_1, \ldots, C_n] :: Q_1 | \cdots | Q_n >> R} r(case)
$$

$$
\frac{C(v_1) :: Q(v_1) >> R \quad \ldots \quad C(v_n) :: Q(v_n) >> R}{sel \bullet [C(v_1), \ldots, C(v_n)] :: sel(p \in \{v_1, \ldots, v_n\} : Q(p) >> R)} r(sel)
$$

The execution semantics is:

$$
\begin{aligned}
exec(case \bullet [C_1, \ldots, C_n], [d, \langle j, q \rangle] \mapsto [d', r]) &\leftrightarrow exec(C_j, [d_j, q] \mapsto [d'_j, r']) \wedge \\
&\quad (\wedge_{k \ne j} \ d'_k = d_k) \wedge r' \stackrel{R_j, R}{\mapsto} r \\
exec(sel \bullet [C(v_1), \ldots, C(v_m)], [d, \langle v_j, q \rangle] \mapsto [d', r]) &\leftrightarrow exec(C(v_j), [d_j, q] \mapsto [d'_j, r]) \\
&\quad \wedge (\wedge_{k \ne j} \ d'_k = d_k) \\
exec(loop \bullet C, [d, [q|\underline{q}]] \mapsto [d', [r|\underline{r}]]) &\leftrightarrow exec(C, [d, q] \mapsto [d_1, q_1]) \wedge \\
&\quad exec(loop \bullet C, [d_1, \underline{q}], [d', \underline{r}])
\end{aligned}
$$

The *case* component has $data(case \bullet [C_1, \ldots, C_n], \langle d_1, \ldots, d_n \rangle)$, with $data(C_j, d_j)$ (similarly for the *sel* component). The connector *case* requires that there is a map $r' \stackrel{R_j, R}{\mapsto} r$ from $r' \in R_j$ into $r \in R$, depending on the result types R_j and R. In particular:

$$
a \stackrel{A, A|B}{\mapsto} \langle 1, a \rangle
$$
$$
b \stackrel{B, A|B}{\mapsto} \langle 2, b \rangle
$$

The connector *sel* applies to n instances of a parametric component $C(p) :: Q(p) >> R$ and executes the one indicated by v_j. The *loop* connector iterates C over a sequence of requests. Besides these connectors, we also have the pipe connector explained above.

Now we sketch a possible construction of the bank system (Section 3.4) using the DS partially outlined above.

In Fig. 9, the invocation connectors for the ATM and bank computation units encapsulate them into atomic components with the following operation types:

$$atmC := IA \bullet ATM :: choose() >> (chosen(n, Acc, Op)|notOkPin)$$
$$b(n) := IB_n \bullet Bank_n :: do(n, Acc, Op) >> amount(Acc, A)|refusedOp$$

Firstly, we informally explain the semantics of the atomic components.

In the operation type of $atmC$, $choose()$ indicates that the user inputs a PIN and an operation choice. If the PIN is not recognised, the result is $notOkPin$, otherwise it is $chosen(n, Acc, Op)$, indicating that the PIN corresponds to the account Acc of the bank number n, and Op is the operation chosen.

In the operation type of $b(n)$, $do(n, Acc, Op)$ indicates that an operation Op has been requested on the account Acc of bank n. The operation Op may be accepted or refused, as indicated by the result type of $amount(Acc, A)|refusedOp$. If accepted, the result $amount(Acc, A)$ indicates that A is the amount of Acc after the operation. The operation (when not refused) may update the current amount.

Now we compose the atomic components by connectors, to obtain our system. We firstly build the *banks* composite of the two banks and sending a requested operation to the target bank n, by means of a selector connector:

$$banks := sel \bullet [b(1), b(2)] ::$$
$$sel(n \in \{1, 2\} : do(n, Acc, Op)) >> (amount(Acc, A)|refusedOp)$$

By a *pipe*, we build the component $atmOp$, performing a single ATM request and, by a *loop*, the component *system*, looping on ATM requests, as follows.

$$atmOp := pipe \bullet [atmC, case \bullet [banks, noOperation]] ::$$
$$choice() >> (amount(Acc, A)|refusedOp)|notOkPin$$
$$system := loop \bullet atmOp :: choice()^* >> ((amount(Acc, A)|refusedOp)|notOkPin)^*$$

The internal connector $case \bullet [C, \ noOperation]$ is to be considered as a part of the *pipe* connector, and the $noOperation$ branch is not a sub-component. It maps results into results and is used to bypass C. In our example, the request type of $case \bullet [banks, noOperation]$ is $sel(n \in \{1, 2\} : do(n, Acc, Op))|notOkPin$. If the result of $atmC$ is $\langle 2, notOkPin \rangle$, we pipe it into $\langle 2, notOkPin \rangle$ itself, so that $case$ passes the result $notOkPin$ to the $noOperation$ branch. If the result of $atmC$ is $\langle 1, chosen(n, Acc, Op \ ) \rangle$, we pipe it into $\langle 1, \langle n, do(n, Acc, Op) \rangle \rangle$, so that the request $\langle n, do(n, Acc, Op) \rangle$ is passed to *banks*.

To illustrate the run-time semantics of connectors, we show the execution of a request. The whole system has the following data:

– a database $atmdb$, associating each valid PIN to a bank and an account number;
– databases db_i (with $i = 1$ or $i = 2$), containing the accounts of bank i.

The data-components association should be decided in the deployment phase. Since here we abstract from it, data are triples $d = \langle atmdb, db_1, db_2 \rangle$, where $atmdb$ is used by $atmC$, db_1 by $b(1)$, and db_2 by $b(2)$.

By the semantics of *loop*, the computation step corresponding to a sequence of requests of length n has the form

$$[[d_0, [choice(), choice(), \ldots, choice()]] \mapsto [d_n, [Res_1, Res_2, \ldots, Res_n]]]$$

where each $[d_{n-1}, choice()] \mapsto [d_n, Res_n]$ is performed by $atmOp$. We consider the first step $[d_0, choice()] \mapsto [d_1, Res_1]$, and we assume that the the user inputs a correct PIN and requires a withdrawal of £50, and that the (correct) PIN input is related to the bank $b(2)$ and the account number $Acc = 2341$. We assume that the total amount of the account (stored in db_2) is £5170.

By the semantics of the pipe connector, we have two sub-steps:

$$[d_0, choice()] \overset{atmC}{\mapsto} [d_0, \langle 1, chosen(2, 2341, withdraw(50)) \rangle]$$
$$[d_0, \langle 1, \langle 2, op(2, 2341, withdraw(50)) \rangle \rangle \rangle] \overset{case \bullet [banks, noOperation]}{\mapsto} [d_1, Res_1]$$

where we indicate on the top of $\mapsto$ the sub-component performing the step. The first step corresponds to the semantics of the atomic component $atmC$ informally explained above, and its result $\langle 1, chosen(2, 2341, withdraw(50)) \rangle$ is piped into the request for the second step. By the semantics of *case*, the second step is obtained from the sub-step:

$$[d_0, \langle 2, op(2, 2341, withdraw(50)) \rangle] \overset{sel \bullet [b(1), b(2)]}{\mapsto} [d_1, Res_1]$$

By the semantics of *sel*, the latter is obtained from the step

$$[d_0, op(2, 2341, withdraw(50))] \overset{b(2)}{\mapsto} [d_1, \langle 1, amount(2341, 5120) \rangle]$$

performed by the atomic component $b(2)$, which updates the current amount of the account 2341 stored in the database db_2. By the semantics of *case*, the result Res_1 is obtained by the mapping $\overset{R_2, R}{\mapsto}$. Here R_2 is $amount(Acc, A)|refusedOp$, and R is $(amount\ (Acc, A)|refusedOp)|notOkPin$. Thus, the mapping is:

$$\langle 1, amount(2341, 5120)) \rangle \overset{R_2, R}{\mapsto} Res_1 = \langle 1, \langle 1, amount(2341, 5120) \rangle \rangle$$

The result $Res_1 : (amount(Acc, A)|refusedOp)|notOkPin$ indicates that the *pin* is okay, the operation has been performed successfully and the new amount is £5120.

5   Discussion

In our component model, exogenous connectors play a fundamental role, not only for constructing atomic components but also for composing components into composites, whilst providing interfaces to all these (atomic and composite) components. Independently, exogenous connection has been defined as exogenous coordination in coordination languages for concurrent computation [2]. Also independently, in object-oriented programming, the courier patter [10] uses the idea of exogenous connection. There are also similarities with Service Oriented Architectures [29], where business processes accessing (independent) services can be specified by means of an orchestration language. However, no current model relies on encapsulation requirements as strong as ours. We believe that strong encapsulation is a key feature to obtain truly independent and reusable components.

The preliminary formalisation of our component model provides a semantic framework for our approach to component-based software development. Our model and formalisation highlight the basic ideas and fix the minimal requirements for a component system based on exogenous connectors, whilst leaving completely open the choice of the specific connectors and of the interface language. The possibility of designing connectors and interfaces in our model is illustrated by the example of Section 4.4, which outlines part of a possible DS. The example shows that an interface language tailored to the structural properties of connectors allows us to link the meaning of data involved in computation to the structure of components. In this way, the semantic framework of our model should enable us to reason formally not only about the correctness of individual atomic components, but also about the correctness of any composite component, and therefore the correctness of any system built from components.

Consequently, two benefits should accrue, viz. *predictable assembly* of component-based systems, and *verified software* built from pre-verified components. Predictable assembly is the ultimate goal of Component-based Software Engineering, whilst verified software has remained a grand challenge for a long time [13]. We believe that our component model can contribute to predictable assembly because it allows us to generate interfaces to any composite component (or system) we build, directly from the interfaces of its constituent (sub)components.

By the same token, our model can contribute to the verified software challenge by breaking the problem down into smaller sub-problems, and in particular by enabling proof reuse, i.e. using proofs of sub-components directly in the proof of a composite or system. To realise these benefits, we are implementing our component model in the Spark [4] language, which has proof tools which can support verification of components.

Our formalisation (and model) is only preliminary at present however. Many issues still need to be investigated, e.g. what kinds of connectors are useful in practice, considering the constructs introduced in other approaches, e.g. in web service orchestration languages such as BPEL [1]. The problem is to establish whether particular connectors are compositional and preserve strong encapsulation.

For instance, in the bank example, we have used a loop connector at the outer-most level, simply because it is natural to use such a connector to handle continuous inputs from clients. This connector, as defined here, is compositional because it iterates on a finite sequence of requests. Ideally, however, it should allow an infinite stream of inputs, but unfortunately such a loop connector is not compositional. Clearly whether a loop terminates is usually only known at run-time. So whether it can ever be used as a composition connector at design time remains a moot point. Equally, a non-terminating loop connector may be acceptable, even desirable, at the outer-most level. It would be interesting to study the possibility of introducing infinite streams into our approach while maintaining a notion of control encapsulation, by using general formal contexts, such as FOCUS [7].

6   Conclusion

In this paper, we have presented a software component model and its preliminary formalisation. Encapsulation and compositionality are the key concepts that underlie our model. In contrast, existing component models tend to use either objects or architectural units as components, which are neither well encapsulated nor compositional.

Our component model is based on exogenous connectors. Using these connectors to construct and compose components is the key to achieving encapsulation and compositionality. Composite components constructed by exogenous connectors are self-similar, which makes a compositional approach to system construction possible. In contrast to existing software component models, our self-similar components are also encapsulated and compositional.

Another benefit of exogenous connection is that components are loosely coupled, since control is originated and encapsulated by connectors, unlike ADL connectors that do not originate or encapsulate control. As a result, systems are modular and therefore easier to maintain and re-configure.

References

1. T. Andrews, F. Curbera, H. Dholakia, Y. Goland, J. Klein, F. Leymann, K. Liu, D. Roller, D. Smith, S. Thatte, I. Trickovic, and S. Weerawarana. *Business Process Execution Language for Web Services(BPEL4S) - Version 1.1.* IBM, http://www-106.ibm.com/developerworks/library/ws-bpel/, 2004.
2. F. Arbab. The IWIM model for coordination of concurrent activities. In P. Ciancarini and C. Hankin, editors, *LNCS 1061*, pages 34–56. Springer-Verlag, 1996.
3. C. Atkinson, J. Bayer, C. Bunse, E. Kamsties, O. Laitenberger, R. Laqua, D. Muthig, B. Paech, J. Wüst, and J. Zettel. *Component-based Product Line Engineering with UML*. Addison-Wesley, 2001.
4. J. Barnes. *High Integrity Software: The SPARK Approach to Safety and Security*. Addison-Wesley, 2003.
5. D. Box. *Essential COM*. Addison-Wesley, 1998.
6. M. Broy, A. Deimel, J. Henn, K. Koskimies, F. Plasil, G. Pomberger, W. Pree, M. Stal, and C. Szyperski. What characterizes a software component? *Software – Concepts and Tools*, 19(1):49–56, 1998.
7. M. Broy and K. Stølen. *Specification and Development of Interactive Systems: Focus on Streams, Interfaces, and Refinement*. Springer, 2001.
8. E. Bruneton, T. Coupaye, and M. Leclercq. An open component model and its support in Java. In *Proc. 7th Int. Symp. on Component-based Software Engineering*, pages 7–22. Springer-Verlag, 2004.
9. J.L. Fiadeiro, A.Lopes, and M.Wermelinger. A mathematical semantics for architectural connectors. LNCS 2793, pages 178-221, 2003.
10. E. Gamma, R. Helm, R. Johnson, and J. Vlissides. The Courier pattern. *Dr. Dobb's Journal*, Feburary 1996.
11. D. Garlan, R.T. Monroe, and D. Wile. Acme: Architectural description of component-based systems. In G.T. Leavens and M. Sitaraman, editors, *Foundations of Component-Based Systems*, pages 47–68. Cambridge University Press, 2000.
12. G.T. Heineman and W.T. Councill, editors. *Component-Based Software Engineering: Putting the Pieces Together*. Addison-Wesley, 2001.

13. IFIP TC2 working conference on Verified Software: Theories, Tools, Experiments, 10-13 October 2005, ETH Zürich, Switzerland. http://vstte.ethz.ch/.
14. J. Ivers, N. Sinha, and K.C Wallnau. A Basis for Composition Language CL. Technical Report CMU/SEI-2002-TN-026, CMU SEI, 2002.
15. K.-K. Lau and M. Ornaghi. Specifying compositional units for correct program development in computational logic. In M. Bruynooghe and K.-K. Lau, editor, *Program Development in Computational Logic, Lecture Notes in Computer Science 3049*, pages 1–29. Springer-Verlag, 2004.
16. K.-K. Lau, P. Velasco Elizondo, and Z. Wang. Exogenous connectors for software components. In *Proc. 8th Int. SIGSOFT Symp. on Component-based Software Engineering, LNCS 3489*, pages 90–106, 2005.
17. K.-K. Lau and Z. Wang. A survey of software component models. Pre-print CSPP-30, School of Computer Science, The University of Manchester, April 2005. http://www.cs.man.ac.uk/cspreprints/PrePrints/cspp30.pdf.
18. K.-K. Lau and Z. Wang. A taxonomy of software component models. In *Proc. 31st Euromicro Conference*, pages 88–95. IEEE Computer Society Press, 2005.
19. N.R. Mehta, N. Medvidovic, and S. Phadke. Towards a taxonomy of software connectors. In *Proc. 22nd Int. Conf. on Software Engineering*, pages 178–187. ACM Press, 2000.
20. B. Meyer. The grand challenge of trusted components. In *Proc. ICSE 2003*, pages 660–667. IEEE, 2003.
21. Sun Microsystems. Enterprise Java Beans Specification, Version 3.0, 2005.
22. O. Nierstrasz, G. Arévalo, S. Ducasse, R. Wuyts, A. Black, P. Müller, C. Zeidler, T. Genssler, and R. van den Born. A component model for field devices. In *Proc. 1st Int. IFIP/ACM Working Conference on Component Deployment*, pages 200–209. ACM Press, 2002.
23. OMG. *UML 2.0 Superstructure Specification.* http://www.omg.org/cgi-bin/doc?ptc/2003-08-02.
24. OMG. *CORBA Component Model, V3.0*, 2002. http://www.omg.org/technology/documents/formal/components.htm
25. F. Plasil, D. Balek, and R. Janecek. SOFA/DCUP: Architecture for component trading and dynamic updating. In *Proc. ICCDS98*, pages 43–52. IEEE Press, 1998.
26. M. Shaw and D. Garlan. *Software Architecture: Perspectives on an Emerging Discipline.* Prentice Hall, 1996.
27. Sun Microsystems. *JavaBeans Specification*, 1997. http://java.sun.com/products/javabeans/docs/spec.html.
28. C. Szyperski, D. Gruntz, and S. Murer. *Component Software: Beyond Object-Oriented Programming.* Addison-Wesley, second edition, 2002.
29. E. Thomas. *Service-Oriented Architecture: Concepts, Technology, and Design.* Prentice Hall, 2005.
30. R. van Ommering, F. van der Linden, J. Kramer, and J. Magee. The Koala component model for consumer electronics software. *IEEE Computer*, pages 78–85, March 2000.

Appendix

We formalise our model as an open specification framework [15]. We distinguish between *open* and *defined* symbols. The meaning of the defined symbols is established by the definition axioms, in terms of the open ones. The open symbols are to be axiomatised when designing a specific DS based on exogenous connectors. The constraint axioms represent proof obligations to be satisfied when axiomatising a DS. The axiomatisation presented here contains the minimal requirements and has a loose semantics.

The signature is the one explained in Section 4. We import the parametric abstract data type $List(X)$. The defined sorts are $OpType$, $List(X)$, $Comp$, $Instance$, and $Step$. They are freely generated from the open sorts, according to the following constructor axioms (see [15]):

$$
\begin{aligned}
OpType &\quad \text{constructed by} \quad >>: ReqType \times ResType \to OpType; \\
Comp &\quad \text{constructed by} \quad \bullet : InvConn \times Unit \to Comp, \\
&\qquad\qquad\qquad\qquad\ \bullet : CompConn \times List(Comp) \to Comp; \\
Instance &\quad \text{constructed by} \quad \text{i} : Comp \times D \to Instance; \\
Step &\quad \text{constructed by} \quad \mapsto: D \times Request \times D \times Result \to Step;
\end{aligned}
$$

In Section 4.3 we have informally introduced the semantic function $\mathcal{M}$. Here we introduce it in the signature by the declaration

$$\mathcal{M} : InvConn \times Unit \times Step \mid CompConn \times List(Step) \times Step$$

and we axiomatise $exec$ by mutual recursion (axioms $dax_{1,j}$), using the auxiliary (overloaded) predicate $exec : List(Comp) \times List(Step)$. The other axioms introduce auxiliary predicates used later, in the constraint axioms: dax_2 extend the overloaded interface relation to sequences of components ($[C_1, \ldots, C_n] :: [Op_1, \ldots, Op_n]$ indicates that $C_i :: Op_i$); $dax_{3,k}$ introduce the relations $domain$, $range$ and $stype$, indicating the expected types of requests, data and results in computation steps; $dax_{4,1}$ introduce $total(C, Op)$, indicating that $C :: Op$ computes a total input-output relation, and the axiom $dax_{4,2}$ extends $total$ to lists of components. In the axioms we will use the following typed variables: $i : InvConn$, $k : CompConn$, $u : Unit$, $S : Step$, $LC : List(Comp)$, $LS : List(Step)$, $LO : List(Op)$, $Q : ReqType$, $R : ResType$, $q : Request$, $r : Result$, $d : D$, $Op : OpType$, and we will leave the most external quantification understood.

Definition Axioms:

$dax_{1,1}$ $exec(i \bullet u, S) \;\leftrightarrow\; \mathcal{M}(i, u, S)$

$dax_{1,2}$ $exec(k \bullet LC, S) \;\leftrightarrow\; \exists LS(exec(LC, LS) \wedge \mathcal{M}(k, LS, S))$

$dax_{1,3}$ $exec([], []) \;\wedge\; (exec([C|LC], [S|LS]) \;\leftrightarrow\; exec(C, S) \wedge exec(LC, LS))$

dax_2 $[] :: [] \;\wedge\; ([C|LC] :: [Op|LO] \;\leftrightarrow\; C :: Op \wedge LC :: LO)$

$dax_{3,1}$ $domain(d, q, C, Q >> R) \;\leftrightarrow\; C :: Q >> R \wedge q \in Q \wedge data(C, d)$

$dax_{3,2}$ $range(d, r, C, Q >> R) \;\leftrightarrow\; C :: Q >> R \wedge r \in R \wedge (data(C, d) \vee d = halt)$

$dax_{3,3}$ $stype([d, q] \mapsto [d', r], C, Op) \;\leftrightarrow\; domain(d, q, C, Op) \wedge range(d', r, C, Op)$

$dax_{3,4}$ $stype([], [], [])\wedge$
$\qquad\quad\ (stype([S|LS], [C|LC], [Op|LO]) \leftrightarrow stype(S, C, Op) \wedge stype(LS, LC, LO))$

$dax_{4,1}$ $total(C, Op) \;\leftrightarrow\; C :: Op \;\wedge$
$\qquad\quad\ \forall d, q(domain(d, q, C, Op) \to \exists d', r\ exec(C, [d, q] \mapsto [d', r]))$

$dax_{4,2}$ $total([], []) \;\wedge\; (total([C|LC], [Op|LO]) \;\leftrightarrow\; total(C, Op) \wedge total(LC, LO))$

In the following, instead of $ctype(k, LO, O)$ and $stype(S, C, Op)$ we will use the more intuitive notation $k : LO \to Op$ and $S : (C :: OP)$. Now we give the constraint axioms. By c_1 we require that a composition term $k \bullet [T_1, \ldots, T_n]$ is a component with operation type Op only if the subcomponents $T_1, \ldots, T_n$ agree with the type of k. The if part is left open and has to be fixed by the composition rules of the specific DS

(see Definition 3). By $c_{2,i}$ we require that the semantic relation $\mathcal{M}$ conforms to the domain and range types of components. The other constraints allow us to prove Theorem 1, which states that each component terminates.

Constraints:

c_1 $(k \bullet L) :: Op \rightarrow \exists\, LO(L :: LO \wedge k : LO \rightarrow Op)$

$c_{2,1}$ $(i \bullet u) :: Op \rightarrow \forall\, S(\mathcal{M}(i, u, S) \rightarrow S : (i \bullet u :: Op))$

$c_{2,2}$ $(k \bullet LC :: Op) \wedge LS : (LC :: LO) \rightarrow \forall S(\mathcal{M}(k, LS, S) \rightarrow S : (k \bullet LS :: Op))$

$c_{3,1}$ $(i \bullet u) :: Op \rightarrow \forall\, d, q(domain(d, q, i \bullet u, Op) \rightarrow \exists\, d', r\, \mathcal{M}(i, u, [d, q] \mapsto [d', r]))$

$c_{3,2}$ $(k \bullet LC :: Op) \wedge total(LC, LO) \rightarrow \forall\, d, q\, (domain(d, q, k \bullet LC, Op)$
$\rightarrow \exists\, d', r(exec(k \bullet LC, [d, q] \mapsto [d', r])))$

Theorem 1. *The following sentences can be proved from the above axioms:*
$\forall C, Op(C :: Op \rightarrow total(C, Op))$

It is worthwhile to remark that constraints are proof obligations when a specific DS is axiomatised. In particular, c_1 is a proof obligation for the composition rules, and the other constraints are proof obligations for the relation $\mathcal{M}$ defining the run-time semantics. We show how such proof obligations work by proving, as an example, that the semantics for $pipe(Q_1 >> R_1, Q_2 >> R_2)$ satisfies $c_{3,2}$.

Let $pipe \bullet [C_1, C_2]$ be a generic pipe component, and $[\langle d_1, d_2 \rangle, q_1]$ be a generic element of its domain. We have to prove that there is a step

$$exec(pipe \bullet [C_1, C_2], [\langle d_1, d_2 \rangle, q_1] \mapsto [\langle d'_1, d'_2 \rangle, r_2])$$

By the assumption $total([C_1, C_2] :: [Q_1 >> R_1, Q_2 >> R_2])$ of $c_{3,2}$, we get $total(C_1 :: Q_1 >> R_1)$ and $total(C_2 :: Q_2 >> R_2)$. By $total(C_1 :: Q_1 >> R_1)$, there is $[d'_1, r_1]$ such that $exec(C_1, [d_1, q_1] \mapsto [d'_1, r_1])$. By the pipe operation we can build $q_2 = p(r_1)$, and we get $[d_2, q_2]$ in the domain of C_2. Finally, by $total(C_2 :: Q_2 >> R_2)$, we can conclude that the required result $[\langle d'_1, d'_2 \rangle, r_2]$ exists. Thus, the semantics of $pipe$ is well defined in our model.

Synchronised Hyperedge Replacement as a Model for Service Oriented Computing⋆

Gian Luigi Ferrari[1], Dan Hirsch[2], Ivan Lanese[3], Ugo Montanari[1], and Emilio Tuosto[4]

[1] Computer Science Department, University of Pisa, Italy
{giangi, ugo}@di.unipi.it
[2] Computer Science Department, University of Pisa, Italy and Department of Computing,
Imperial College, London, UK
dhirsch@doc.ic.ac.uk
[3] Computer Science Department, University of Bologna, Italy
lanese@cs.unibo.it
[4] Computer Science Department, University of Leicester, UK
et52@mcs.le.ac.uk

Abstract. This tutorial paper describes a framework for modelling several aspects of distributed computing based on *Synchronised Hyperedge Replacement* (SHR), a graph rewriting formalism. Components are represented as edges and they rewrite themselves by synchronising with neighbour components the *productions* that specify their behaviour. The SHR framework has been equipped with many formal devices for representing complex synchronisation mechanisms which can tackle mobility, heterogeneous synchronisations and non-functional aspects, key factors of Service Oriented Computing (SOC). We revise the SHR family as a suitable model for contributing to the formalisation of SOC systems.

1 Introduction

Modern distributed inter-networking systems are very complex and constituted by a varied flora of architectures and communicating infrastructures. Such systems are heterogeneous, geographically distributed and highly dynamic since the communication topology can vary and the components can, at any moment, connect to or detach from the system. Recently, *Service Oriented Computing* (SOC) has emerged as a suitable paradigm for specifying such global systems and applications. Engineering issues are tackled by exploiting the concept of *services*, which are the building blocks of systems. Services are autonomous, platform-independent, mobile/stationary computational entities. In the deployment phase, services can be independently described, published and categorised. At runtime they are searched/discovered and dynamically assembled for building wide area distributed systems.

All this requires, on the one hand, the development of foundational theories to cope with the requirements imposed by the global computing context, and, on the other hand, the application of these theories for their integration in a pragmatic software engineering approach. At the architectural level, the fundamental features to take into account for the description of components and their interactions include: dynamic (possibly self

---

⋆ Partially supported by the Project EC FET – Global Computing 2, IST-2005-16004 SENSORIA.

organising) reconfiguration, mobility, coordination, complex synchronisation mechanisms, and awareness of *Quality of Service* (QoS).

Process calculi are among the most successful models for concurrency and, in the last years, CSP [19], CCS [26] and π-calculus [27] gained paramount relevance and helped to understand many of the phenomena arising in distributed computing. Many of the recent proposals like Ambient [2], Klaim [8], Join [12] and D-π [30] (to cite a few) have been deeply inspired by the work on CSP, CCS and π-calculus. Also, distributed systems can be naturally modelled by means of graph-based techniques [32]. Among those, we choose *Synchronised Hyperedge Replacement* (SHR) where systems are modelled as *hypergraphs*, that is graphs where each (hyper)edge can be connected to any number of nodes (instead of just two). Edges represent components connected via shared nodes (representing communication ports).

Originally, SHR aimed at modelling distributed systems and software architectures, however, it turns out to be expressive enough to model many process calculi. In fact, it can naturally encode π-calculus [14], Ambient and Klaim [33] or Fusion [23]. In our opinion, SHR conjugates the ability of expressing various forms of synchronisation and communication features (typical of process calculi) with a suggestive visual representation of systems' topology (typical of graph models). In SHR, constraint satisfaction is exploited to guide rewriting by synchronising context-free *productions* that specify the behaviour of single edges. Productions define how an edge can be rewritten into a generic graph and the conditions that this rewriting imposes on adjacent nodes. Global transitions are obtained by parallel application of productions with "*compatible*" conditions. What "compatible" exactly means depends on the chosen synchronisation model. The Hoare model (so called since it extends CSP synchronisation [19]), for instance, requires that all edges connected to the same node execute the same action on it. Instead, the Milner model (extending the model of CCS [26]) requires exactly two edges to interact by performing complementary actions while the other edges must stay idle on that node. SHR, and in particular its variant SHR-HS [25] (outlined in § 7), allows also different synchronisation policies to live together in a single framework.

Aims and structure of the paper. A number of published results (see the brief bibliographic note at the end of this section) is here collected with the main goal to give a systematic presentation of the SHR approach. A relevant effort has indeed been put on giving a uniform and incremental presentation. Also, we tried to help intuition by showing how the various synchronisation mechanisms actually extend the basic model discussed in § 3. It might be useful to have the many versions of SHR harmonised within a common formal context and we hope to have been able to clearly introduce the SHR family by rephrasing it in simpler, yet rigorous, definitions.

Preliminary definitions and notations for graphs are reported in § 2. We introduce *basic Milner SHR* (bMSHR for short) in § 3, where the mathematical basis of SHR are discussed in the simpler framework based on Milner synchronisation without considering name mobility and name fusion. These aspects are added in § 4, giving rise to MSHR. This extension allows to substantially increase the expressivity of the approach for modelling both architectural and programming aspects of mobile and reconfigurable distributed applications. In § 5 we define *Synchronisation Algebras with Mobility* (SAMs for short), an abstract formalisation of the concept of synchronisation model, extending Winskel's synchronisation algebras (SAs) [35] to cope with mobility and handling of local resources. SAMs are exploited in § 6, where we present *parametric SHR* [24,22] which permits to abstract from the synchronisation model by choosing each time the most adequate SAM (whose primitives correspond to the ones used in the modelled system). Parametric SHR smoothly adapts SHR to various interaction mechanisms; for instance, it can uniformly represent MSHR and SHR with Hoare synchronisation. A first SAM-based SHR is *SHR for heterogeneous systems* (SHR-HS) [25,21] in § 7 where different SAMs can be associated to different nodes. SHR-HS has been devised to model systems where heterogeneity concerns both applications and their underlying middlewares so that different synchronisation policies can be used and dynamically changed (and, hence, negotiated) within systems. This feature is fundamental to model coordination at the application level, where interaction patterns are dynamically determined. Another SAM-based SHR proposal is SHReQ [17] (§ 8), an SHR framework for handling abstract high-level QoS requirements expressed as *constraint-semirings* (c-semirings) [1], algebraic structures suitable for multi-criteria QoS [6]. We exploit the algebraic features of c-semirings by embedding them in the SHR synchronisation mechanism: interactions among components are ruled by synchronising them on actions that are c-semiring values, expressing QoS constraints imposed by all components participating to the synchronisation. Finally, in § 9 we outline our plans for future investigations.

Brief SHR bibliography. Various facets of SHR have been studied w.r.t. issues related to distributed systems. SHR has been introduced in [3] with the name of "Grammars for Distributed Systems". Here Hoare synchronisation was used, and the emphasis was on analysing the history of the computation, explicitly represented as part of the graph. Infinite computations and concurrency issues have been considered in [9] while [4] extends SHR by allowing to merge and split nodes. In [31] there is a presentation of SHR inside the Tile Model [13], and an approach to find the allowed transitions using constraint solving techniques is also proposed. A main extension is given in [15], where *node mobility* is added. This is obtained by allowing actions to carry tuples of nodes. When actions synchronise the carried tuples of nodes are merged. This allows to create new connections at runtime. In literature, inference rules (in the SOS style [29]) based on a notation for representing graphs as *syntactic judgements* are defined for different mobile synchronisation mechanisms, presenting SHR as a general model for mobile process calculi. However, SHR extends process algebras to allow synchronisations of any number of partners and on any number of channels at the same time. In [15] only newly created nodes can be communicated and merged. In [20] a mapping into the Tile Model [13] is used to prove that an ad hoc bisimilarity is a congruence. Another important step is made in [16], where also old nodes can be communicated, but they can be merged only with new nodes. This kind of SHR, with Milner synchronisation, is shown to be strictly related [16] to π-calculus [27]. A later improvement is presented in [10], where fusions of arbitrary nodes are allowed. These are exploited [10,23] to give semantics to the Ambient Calculus [2] and to the Fusion Calculus [28]. Finally, in [24,22] the SHR synchronisation mechanism is generalised allowing a complete parametrisation of SHR w.r.t. the synchronisation and mobility policies. Many applications of SHR can be found in literature, in particular in the field of process calculi [33], of software architectures [14,15,5] and QoS [17].

2   Hypergraphs

In this section we introduce a presentation of (hyper)graphs as (syntactic) judgments, which is convenient to write the rules for describing SHR behaviour. We first introduce some mathematical notations.

Notation. Given a set V, we let V^* be the set of tuples on V. We denote a tuple as $\mathbf{v} = \langle v_1, \ldots, v_n \rangle$, the empty tuple as $\langle \rangle$, the i-th element of $\mathbf{v}$ as $\mathbf{v}[i]$, and write $|\mathbf{v}|$ for the length of $\mathbf{v}$.

Given a function f, $\mathrm{dom}(f)$ is its domain, and function $f|_S$ is the restriction of f to S, namely $f|_S(x) = f(x)$ if $x \in S$, $f|_S(x)$ is undefined otherwise. We denote with $f \circ g$ the composition of f and g, namely $(f \circ g)(x) = f(g(x))$.

For a syntactic structure s with names and binders, $\mathrm{fn}(s)$ is the set of its free names.

A graph is composed by a set of nodes and a set of *(hyper)edges* which connect nodes. Set $\mathcal{N}$ is a countable infinite set of node names while set $\mathcal{L}$ is the set of edge labels. A label $L \in \mathcal{L}$ is assigned a *rank*, i.e., a natural number (denoted as $\mathrm{rank}(L)$). An edge labelled by L connects $\mathrm{rank}(L)$ nodes and a node connected to an edge is said to be an *attachment node* of that edge.

A *syntactic judgment* specifies a graph along with its interface, i.e., its *free nodes*.

Definition 2.1 (Graphs as judgements). *A judgment has form $\Gamma \vdash G$ where:*

1. *$\Gamma \subseteq \mathcal{N}$ is a finite set of names (the free nodes of the graph);*
2. *G is a graph term generated by the grammar*

$$G ::= L(\mathbf{x}) \quad | \quad G|G \quad | \quad \mathsf{v}y\,G \quad | \quad nil$$

where $\mathbf{x}$ is a tuple of names, $L \in \mathcal{L}$, $\mathrm{rank}(L) = |\mathbf{x}|$ and y is a name.

In $\mathsf{v}y\,G$, restriction operator v binds y in G, $\mathrm{fn}(G)$ is defined accordingly as usual and we demand that $\mathrm{fn}(G) \subseteq \Gamma$.

Graph *nil* is the empty graph, $|$ is the parallel composition operator of graphs (merging nodes with the same name) and $\mathsf{v}y$ is the restriction operator of nodes; free/bound nodes correspond to free/bound names. Edges are terms of the form $L(x_1, \ldots, x_n)$, where the x_i are arbitrary names and $\mathrm{rank}(L) = n$. Condition $\mathrm{fn}(G) \subseteq \Gamma$ accounts for having free isolated nodes in G (e.g., $\{x\} \vdash nil$ is graph with only the isolated node x).

We assume that restriction has lower priority than parallel composition. For conciseness, curly brackets are dropped from interfaces Γ in judgements and Γ_1, Γ_2 denotes $\Gamma_1 \cup \Gamma_2$, provided that $\Gamma_1 \cap \Gamma_2 = \emptyset$ (e.g., $\Gamma, x = \Gamma \cup \{x\}$, if $x \notin \Gamma$).

Example 2.2. Consider the judgment

$$u \vdash \mathsf{v}z_1, \ldots, z_n\ B_n(u, z_1, \ldots, z_n)|S_1(z_1)|\ldots|S_n(z_n)$$

which describes a system where many servers S_i are connected to the network via a manager B_n and can be graphically represented as:

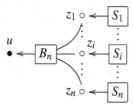

Edges are drawn as rectangles and nodes are bullets (empty for bound nodes and solid for free nodes). A connection between a node and an edge is represented by a line, called *tentacle*; an arrowed tentacle indicates the first attachment node of the edge. The other nodes are determined by numbering tentacles clockwise (e.g., for B_n, u is the first attachment node, z_1 is the second and so on).

Definition 2.3 (Structural congruence on graph judgements). *Graph terms are considered up to axioms* $(AG1 \div 7)$ *below:*

$$(\text{AG1}) \ (G_1|G_2)|G_3 \equiv G_1|(G_2|G_3) \quad (\text{AG2}) \ G_1|G_2 \equiv G_2|G_1 \quad (\text{AG3}) \ G|nil \equiv G$$

$$(\text{AG4}) \ \nu x \, \nu y \, G \equiv \nu y \, \nu x \, G \quad (\text{AG5}) \ \nu x \, G \equiv G \ if \ x \notin \text{fn}(G)$$

$$(\text{AG6}) \ \nu x \, G \equiv \nu y \, G\{y/x\}, \ if \ y \notin \text{fn}(G) \quad (\text{AG7}) \ \nu x \, G_1|G_2 \equiv G_1|\nu x \, G_2, \ if \ x \notin \text{fn}(G_1)$$

For judgments, we define $\Gamma_1 \vdash G_1 \equiv \Gamma_2 \vdash G_2$ *iff* $\Gamma_1 = \Gamma_2$ *and* $G_1 \equiv G_2$.

Axioms (AG1), (AG2) and (AG3) define respectively the associativity, commutativity and identity over *nil* for operator $|$. Axioms (AG4) and (AG5) state that nodes can be restricted only once and in any order. Axiom (AG6) defines α-conversion of a graph w.r.t its bound names. Axiom (AG7) defines the interaction between restriction and parallel composition (note that function fn is well-defined on equivalence classes). We consider judgements for graphs up to structural congruence which amounts to consider graphs up to graph isomorphisms that preserve free nodes, labels of edges, and tentacles [14].

3 Basic Milner SHR

The simplest version of SHR is *basic Milner SHR* (bMSHR), where "basic" refers to the absence of mobility and "Milner" is reminiscent of the CCS synchronisation. Later, bMSHR will be extended with mobility and more complex synchronisation policies.

Milner synchronisation models two-parties synchronisation and requires that actions are partitioned into normal actions a and co-actions $\bar{a}$ (where $\bar{\bar{a}} = a$). Furthermore, there are two special actions: an action ε standing for "not taking part to the synchronisation" and an action τ representing a complete binary synchronisation. Thus, Milner synchro-nisation on a node x requires two complementary actions to interact, while other con-nected edges must stay idle on x (i.e., they all exhibit action ε on x). The final result of the synchronisation is τ.

Notation. A *renaming* is a function $\sigma : \mathcal{N} \to \mathcal{N}$, $x\sigma$ is the application of σ to $x \in \text{dom}(\sigma)$ and yields $\sigma(x)$. If $\sigma \circ \sigma = \sigma$, the renaming is said *idempotent* and is *injective* when σ is injective. Renaming $\{x/y\}$ is such that $\{x/y\}(y) = x$ and $\{x/y\}(z) = z$ for all $z \neq y$ in the domain of $\{x/y\}$.

We use $\{(x,y) \mid x \in \text{dom}(f) \ \wedge \ y = f(x)\}$ as a set-theoretic representation of a function f.

We can now define *transitions*, and then we show some inference rules to derive them from *productions*.

Definition 3.1 (SHR transitions). *A relation* $\Gamma \vdash G \xrightarrow{\Lambda} \Gamma \vdash G'$ *is an SHR transition if* $\Gamma \vdash G$ *and* $\Gamma \vdash G'$ *are judgments for graphs, and* $\Lambda : \Gamma \to Act$ *is a total function, where Act is a set of actions.*

Intuitively transition $\Gamma \vdash G \xrightarrow{\Lambda} \Gamma \vdash G'$ specifies that graph $\Gamma \vdash G$ is rewritten into $\Gamma \vdash G'$ and, while doing this, the action $\Lambda(x)$ is performed on each node x in the interface Γ. Notice that the starting and the final graph share the same interface.

Productions are special transitions specifying the behaviour of a single edge.

Definition 3.2 (Productions). *A production is an SHR transition of the form:*

$$x_1, \ldots, x_n \vdash L(x_1, \ldots, x_n) \xrightarrow{\Lambda} x_1, \ldots, x_n \vdash G \tag{1}$$

where $\text{rank}(L) = n$ *and* $x_1, \ldots, x_n$ *are all distinct. Production (1) is* idle *iff* $\Lambda(x_i) = \varepsilon$ *for each i and G is $L(x_1, \ldots, x_n)$.*

A transition is obtained by composing productions in a set $\mathcal{P}$ that contains any idle production and is closed under all injective renamings (that is, the application of an injective renaming to a productions in $\mathcal{P}$ yields productions in $\mathcal{P}$).

Composition is performed by merging nodes and thus connecting the edges. Synchronisation conditions as specified in productions must be satisfied.

Definition 3.3 (Inference rules for bMSHR). *The admissible behaviours of bMSHR are defined by the following inference rules.*

$$(par\text{-}b) \quad \frac{\Gamma \vdash G_1 \xrightarrow{\Lambda} \Gamma \vdash G_2 \qquad \Gamma' \vdash G_1' \xrightarrow{\Lambda'} \Gamma' \vdash G_2' \qquad \Gamma \cap \Gamma' = \emptyset}{\Gamma, \Gamma' \vdash G_1 | G_1' \xrightarrow{\Lambda \cup \Lambda'} \Gamma, \Gamma' \vdash G_2 | G_2'}$$

$$(merge\text{-}b) \quad \frac{\Gamma \vdash G_1 \xrightarrow{\Lambda} \Gamma \vdash G_2}{\Gamma\sigma \vdash G_1\sigma \xrightarrow{\Lambda'} \Gamma\sigma \vdash G_2\sigma}$$

where $\sigma : \Gamma \to \Gamma$ *is an idempotent renaming and:*

1. *for all* $x, y \in \Gamma$ *such that* $x \neq y$, *if* $x\sigma = y\sigma$, $\Lambda(x) \neq \varepsilon$ *and* $\Lambda(y) \neq \varepsilon$ *then*
   $(\forall z \in \Gamma \setminus \{x, y\}.z\sigma = x\sigma \Rightarrow \Lambda(z) = \varepsilon) \wedge \Lambda(x) = a \wedge \Lambda(y) = \bar{a} \wedge a \neq \tau$

2. $\Lambda'(z) = \begin{cases} \tau & \text{if } x\sigma = y\sigma = z \wedge x \neq y \wedge \Lambda(x) \neq \varepsilon \wedge \Lambda(y) \neq \varepsilon \\ \Lambda(x) & \text{if } x\sigma = z \wedge \Lambda(x) \neq \varepsilon \\ \varepsilon & \text{otherwise} \end{cases}$

$$(res\text{-}b) \quad \frac{\Gamma, x \vdash G_1 \xrightarrow{\Lambda} \Gamma, x \vdash G_2 \qquad \Lambda(x) = \varepsilon \vee \Lambda(x) = \tau}{\Gamma \vdash \nu x\, G_1 \xrightarrow{\Lambda|_\Gamma} \Gamma \vdash \nu x\, G_2}$$

$$(new\text{-}b) \quad \frac{\Gamma \vdash G_1 \xrightarrow{\Lambda} \Gamma \vdash G_2 \qquad x \notin \Gamma}{\Gamma, x \vdash G_1 \xrightarrow{\Lambda \cup \{(x,\varepsilon)\}} \Gamma, x \vdash G_2}$$

Rule (par-b) deals with the composition of transitions which have disjoint sets of nodes and rule (merge-b) allows to merge nodes. Condition 1 requires that at most two non ε actions are performed on nodes to be merged. If they are exactly two then they have to be complementary, and the resulting action is τ (condition 2). Since σ is required to be idempotent, it yields an equivalence relation on Γ and a choice of a standard representative. In fact, $x, y \in \Gamma$ are equivalent under σ iff $x\sigma = y\sigma$; the representative element of the equivalence class of x is $x\sigma$. Rule (res-b) binds node x. This is allowed only if either τ or ε actions are performed on x, forcing either a complete synchronisation (τ) or no synchronisation (ε). Rule (new-b) allows to add to the source graph an isolated free node where an action ε is performed.

Example 3.4. Consider an instance of the system in Example 2.2 where edge $B_2(u,z_1,z_2)$ takes requests on node u and broadcasts them to $S_1(z_1)$ and $S_2(z_2)$ by synchronising on nodes z_1 and z_2, respectively. The productions for B_2 and S_i ($i \in \{1,2\}$) are:

$$u,z_1',z_2' \vdash B_2(u,z_1',z_2') \xrightarrow{(u,\mathrm{req}),(z_1',\overline{\mathrm{req}}),(z_2',\overline{\mathrm{req}})} u,z_1',z_2' \vdash B_2(u,z_1',z_2') \qquad (2)$$

$$z_i \vdash S_i(z_i) \xrightarrow{(z_i,\mathrm{req})} z_i \vdash S_i'(z_i) \qquad (3)$$

The inference rules for bMSHR can be used to derive transition

$$u,z_1,z_2 \vdash B_2(u,z_1,z_2)|S_1(z_1)|S_2(z_2) \xrightarrow{(u,\mathrm{req})} u \vdash \nu z_1,z_2\, B_2(u,z_1,z_2)|S_1'(z_1)|S_2'(z_2)$$

a proof of which can be as follows. First, rule (par-b) is applied to productions (2) and (3) for S_1 and then applied again the production (3) for S_2. This yields a transition whose target graph is $u,z_1',z_2',z_1,z_2 \vdash B_2(u,z_1',z_2')|S_1(z_1)|S_2(z_2)$. Then, synchronisation is obtained by applying rule (merge-b) with substitution $\{z_1/z_1',z_2/z_2'\}$ so that, on node z_1 (resp. z_2), complementary actions $\overline{\mathrm{req}}$ by B_2 and req by S_1 (resp. S_2) are performed, producing a τ. Finally, z_1 and z_2 can be restricted using rule (res-b).

4   Milner SHR

This extension introduces a main feature of SHR, namely mobility. In the SHR framework mobility is intended as node mobility: nodes can be created and communicated together with actions, and when two actions interact corresponding nodes are merged. This allows to change the graph topology by creating new links during the computation.

We extend the definition of SHR transitions (Definition 3.1), adding the mobility part according to the approach of [10], which allows to send and merge both already existent and newly created nodes. We first formalise our alphabet of actions.

Definition 4.1 (Action signature). *An* action signature *is a triple* $(Act, \mathrm{ar}, \varepsilon)$ *where Act is the set of actions,* $\varepsilon \in Act$, *and* $\mathrm{ar} : Act \to \mathbb{N}$ *is the arity function satisfying* $\mathrm{ar}(\varepsilon) = 0$.

The action signature $(Act_{Mil}, \mathrm{ar}, \varepsilon)$ for Milner synchronisation has further structure. In fact, $Act_{Mil} = \mathcal{A} \cup \overline{\mathcal{A}} \cup \{\tau,\varepsilon\}$ where $\mathcal{A}$ is the set of (input) actions and $\overline{\mathcal{A}} = \{\overline{a} \mid a \in \mathcal{A}\}$ is the set of *co-actions*, τ is a special action with $\mathrm{ar}(\tau) = 0$. Finally, for each $a \in \mathcal{A}$ we have the constraint that $\mathrm{ar}(a) = \mathrm{ar}(\overline{a})$.

Mobility is modelled by letting function Λ in transitions to carry tuples of nodes. Hereafter, $\Lambda : \Gamma \to (Act \times \mathcal{N}^*)$ is a total function assigning, to each node $x \in \Gamma$, an action $a \in Act$ and a tuple $\mathbf{y}$ of node references sent to x such that $\mathrm{ar}(a) = |\mathbf{y}|$. We let $\mathrm{act}_\Lambda(x) = a$ and $\mathrm{n}_\Lambda(x) = \mathbf{y}$ when $\Lambda(x) = (a,\mathbf{y})$. Finally, the *set of communicated (resp. fresh) names* of Λ is $\mathrm{n}(\Lambda) = \{z \mid \exists x.z \in \mathrm{n}_\Lambda(x)\}$ (resp. $\Gamma_\Lambda = \mathrm{n}(\Lambda) \setminus \Gamma$).

Definition 4.2 (SHR transitions with mobility). *Given an action signature* (Act, ar, ε) *as described above, a SHR transition with mobility is a relation of the form:*

$$\Gamma \vdash G \xrightarrow{\Lambda, \pi} \Phi \vdash G'$$

where $\pi : \Gamma \to \Gamma$ *is an idempotent renaming accounting for node merging such that* $\forall x \in n(\Lambda). \ x\pi = x.$ *Finally,* $\Phi = \Gamma\pi \cup \Gamma_\Lambda.$

As for σ in Definition 3.3, idempotency of π introduces equivalence classes on nodes and maps every node into a standard representative. By condition $\forall x \in n(\Lambda). \ x\pi = x$, only references to representatives can be sent while $\Phi = \Gamma\pi \cup \Gamma_\Lambda$ states that free nodes are never erased ($\supseteq$) and new nodes are bound unless communicated ($\subseteq$).

Note that Φ is fully determined by Λ and π (since $\Gamma = \text{dom}(\Lambda)$) and that, unlike in bMSHR, it might be $\Phi \neq \Gamma$.

The definition of productions is extended as follows.

Definition 4.3 (Productions). *A production is now an SHR transition of the form:*

$$x_1, \ldots, x_n \vdash L(x_1, \ldots, x_n) \xrightarrow{\Lambda, \pi} \Phi \vdash G \qquad (4)$$

where $\text{rank}(L) = n$ *and* $x_1, \ldots, x_n$ *are all distinct. Production (4) is idle if* $\Lambda(x_i) = (\varepsilon, \langle\rangle)$ *for each* i, $\pi = id$ *and* $\Phi \vdash G = x_1, \ldots, x_n \vdash L(x_1, \ldots, x_n).$

As before, sets of productions include all the idle productions and are closed under injective renamings.

MSHR semantics (and the successive extensions) exploits a *most general unifier* *(mgu)* accounting for name fusions. The result of the application of the mgu is the fusion of nodes (new and old ones) changing the topology of graph (i.e. mobility).

The rules for MSHR presented below extend the ones for bMSHR with the machinery to deal with mobility.

Definition 4.4 (Inference rules for MSHR). *The admissible behaviours of MSHR are defined by the following inference rules.*

$$(par\text{-}M) \quad \frac{\Gamma \vdash G_1 \xrightarrow{\Lambda, \pi} \Phi \vdash G_2 \qquad \Gamma' \vdash G'_1 \xrightarrow{\Lambda', \pi'} \Phi' \vdash G'_2 \qquad (\Gamma \cup \Phi) \cap (\Gamma' \cup \Phi') = \emptyset}{\Gamma, \Gamma' \vdash G_1 | G'_1 \xrightarrow{\Lambda \cup \Lambda', \pi \cup \pi'} \Phi, \Phi' \vdash G_2 | G'_2}$$

$$(merge\text{-}M) \quad \frac{\Gamma \vdash G_1 \xrightarrow{\Lambda, \pi} \Phi \vdash G_2}{\Gamma\sigma \vdash G_1\sigma \xrightarrow{\Lambda', \pi'} \Phi' \vdash \nu U \ G_2\sigma\rho}$$

where $\sigma : \Gamma \to \Gamma$ *is an idempotent renaming and:*

1. *for all* $x, y \in \Gamma$ *such that* $x \neq y$, *if* $x\sigma = y\sigma \wedge \Lambda(x) \neq \varepsilon \wedge \Lambda(y) \neq \varepsilon$ *then* $(\forall z \in \Gamma \setminus \{x, y\}. z\sigma = x\sigma \Rightarrow \Lambda(z) = \varepsilon) \wedge \Lambda(x) = a \wedge \Lambda(y) = \bar{a} \wedge a \neq \tau$
2. $S_1 = \{n_\Lambda(x) = n_\Lambda(y) \mid x\sigma = y\sigma\}$
3. $S_2 = \{x = y \mid x\pi = y\pi\})$
4. $\rho = \text{mgu}((S_1 \cup S_2)\sigma)$ *and* ρ *maps names to representatives in* $\Gamma\sigma$ *whenever possible*

5. $\Lambda'(z) = \begin{cases} (\tau, \langle\rangle) & \text{if } x\sigma = y\sigma = z \wedge x \neq y \wedge \text{act}_\Lambda(x) \neq \varepsilon \wedge \text{act}_\Lambda(y) \neq \varepsilon \\ (\Lambda(x))\sigma\rho & \text{if } x\sigma = z \wedge \text{act}_\Lambda(x) \neq \varepsilon \\ (\varepsilon, \langle\rangle) & \text{otherwise} \end{cases}$

6. $\pi' = \rho\lfloor_{\Gamma\sigma}$

7. $U = (\Phi\sigma\rho) \setminus \Phi'$

$$(\textit{res-M}) \quad \frac{\Gamma, x \vdash G_1 \xrightarrow{\Lambda, \pi} \Phi \vdash G_2}{\Gamma \vdash \nu x\, G_1 \xrightarrow{\Lambda\lfloor_\Gamma, \pi\lfloor_\Gamma} \Phi' \vdash \nu Z\, G_2}$$

where:

6. $(\exists y \in \Gamma . x\pi = y\pi) \Rightarrow x\pi \neq x$

7. $\text{act}_\Lambda(x) = \varepsilon \vee \text{act}_\Lambda(x) = \tau$

8. $Z = \{x\}$ *if* $x \notin n(\Lambda\lfloor_\Gamma), Z = \emptyset$ *otherwise*

$$(\textit{new-M}) \quad \frac{\Gamma \vdash G_1 \xrightarrow{\Lambda, \pi} \Phi \vdash G_2 \quad x \notin \Gamma \cup \Phi}{\Gamma, x \vdash G_1 \xrightarrow{\Lambda \cup \{(x, \varepsilon, \langle\rangle)\}, \pi} \Phi, x \vdash G_2}$$

Rules (par-M) and (new-M) are essentially as before. In rule (merge-M) now mobility must be handled. In particular, when actions and co-actions synchronise, parameters in corresponding positions are merged. This set of merges is computed in S_1 (condition 2), while S_2 (condition 3) describes old merges traced by π. Condition 4 combines the two sets of equations, updates them with σ and then chooses a representative for each equivalence class using a mgu. Among the possible equivalent mgus we choose one of those where nodes in $\Gamma\sigma$ are chosen as representatives (if they are in the equivalence class). This is necessary to avoid unexpected renamings of nodes because of fusions with new nodes which may then disappear. Note that (condition 5) Λ is updated with the merges specified by ρ and that (condition 6) π' is ρ restricted to the nodes of the graph which is the source of the transition. We may have to reintroduce restrictions (condition 7) if some nodes were extruded by the synchronised actions, since they will no more appear in the label. In rule (res-M) the bound node x must not be a representative if it belongs to a non trivial equivalence class.

Example 4.5. Consider the system in Example 3.4 with two servers S_1 and S_2, but where a client C must be first authenticated by an authority A. The graph representing the system is as follows:

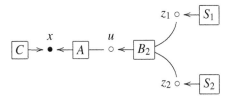

We can model the fact that C is allowed to access the services by letting it move from node x to node u, namely by extruding the private node u to C. The productions for C and A are as follows:

$$x \vdash C(x) \xrightarrow{(x,\overline{\text{auth}},\langle y \rangle)} x,y \vdash C'(y) \qquad\qquad x,u \vdash A(x,u) \xrightarrow{(x,\text{auth},\langle u \rangle)} x,u \vdash A(x,u)$$

where, in the first production the client becomes attached to the received node y after the transition. In fact, when synchronisation is performed, new node y and node u are merged, with u as representative. Note that the restriction on u is reintroduced. Starting from $x \vdash \nu u\, C(x) \mid A(x,u)$ we will obtain $x \vdash \nu u\, C'(u) \mid A(x,u)$.

5 Synchronisation Algebras with Mobility

Synchronisation Algebras with Mobility (SAMs) allow us to parameterise SHR w.r.t. synchronisation models, e.g., MSHR will come out as just a particular instance of the general framework. SAMs extend synchronisation algebras (SAs), introduced in the framework of calculi for interaction such as CCS in [35]. Specifically, SAMs allow us to deal with mobility and to handle local resources (i.e., restriction), as they are used in SHR and more generally in mobile calculi. In general, SAMs must be able to express the synchronisation among any number of actions, each carrying its tuple of parameters. Actions from a multiset $\{|a_1, \ldots, a_n|\}$ can interact, and either they express compatible constraints, thus the system can perform a transition where these actions are executed on the same node, or they express incompatible constraints. For instance, in Milner synchronisation, a synchronisation among a, $\bar{a}$ and ε is allowed, while one involving a and b is not. With respect to [35], SAMs require to manage nodes carried by the actions.

A main ingredient in the formalisation of SAMs is the action synchronisation, which specifies an allowed pattern of interaction between two components. Before giving the definition, some notations are required.

Notation. The disjoint union of sets A and B is denoted as $A \uplus B$ and $\text{inj}_1 : A \to A \uplus B$ (resp. $\text{inj}_2 : B \to A \uplus B$) is the left (resp. right) inclusion. When no confusion arises, $\text{inj}_i(x)$ is written as x. Given $\text{inj}_i(x) \in A \uplus B$, $comp(\text{inj}_i(x))$ is element $\text{inj}_{3-i}(x)$ in $B \uplus A$. The set $\{1, \ldots, n\}$ is denoted by $\underline{n}$ (where $\underline{0} \overset{\text{def}}{=} \emptyset$) and id_n is the identity function on it. Finally, given two functions $f : A \to C$ and $g : B \to D$, $[f,g] : A \uplus B \to C \uplus D$ is the pairing of f and g, namely, $[f,g]$ applies f to elements in A and g to those in B.

Definition 5.1 (Action synchronisation). *Given an action signature* $\mathbf{A} = (Act, \text{ar}, \varepsilon)$, *an* action synchronisation *on* $\mathbf{A}$ *is a triple* $(a, b, (c, \text{Mob}, \doteq))$ *where* $a, b, c \in Act$, Mob $:$ $\underline{\text{ar}(c)} \to \underline{\text{ar}(a)} \uplus \underline{\text{ar}(b)}$ *and* $\doteq$ *is an equivalence relation on* $\underline{\text{ar}(a)} \uplus \underline{\text{ar}(b)}$.

An action synchronisation $(a, b, (c, \text{Mob}, \doteq))$ relates two synchronising actions a and b to a triple $(c, \text{Mob}, \doteq)$, representing the results of the synchronisation of a and b. Action c is the out-coming action, Mob is a communication function that tells how the parameters of c are taken from those of a and b and $\doteq$ is an equivalence relation on the parameters of a and b which generalises set S_1 in rule (merge-M) of Definition 4.4. Since actual parameters are not known at SAM-definition time, Mob and $\doteq$ are defined according to the positions of the parameters in the tuples: for instance

$\text{Mob}(1) = \text{inj}_2(3)$ means that the first parameter of c comes from the third parameter of the second action.

In order to finitely specify interactions among an unbound number of components, a compositional approach is needed. The intuition is that action synchronisation specifies how two components interact. The result of a synchronisation of many actions must be independent of the order of composition, hence composition of action synchronisations must be associative and commutative. The formalisation of this requirement is rather technical, thus we refer the interested reader to [22].

Action synchronisation relations impose conditions on action synchronisations.

Definition 5.2 (Action synchronisation relation). *An action synchronisation relation on an action signature* $\mathbf{A} = (Act, \text{ar}, \varepsilon)$ *is a set ActSyn of action synchronisations s.t.:*

1. $(a, b, (c, \text{Mob}, \doteq)) \in ActSyn \Rightarrow (c = \varepsilon \Leftrightarrow a = b = \varepsilon)$;
2. *composition of action synchronisations is associative and commutative.*

Condition 1 states that action ε can arise only as combination of actions ε. Note that condition 2 must be enforced not only as far as actions are concerned, but also for the part related to communication (Mob) and fusions ($\doteq$). It amounts to say that when all the actions in a tuple are composed, the result is independent on the order of composition. This can be formalised as a condition on the used SAM.

Having multiple action synchronisations for the same pair of interacting actions allows nondeterminism. In particular, the result of the synchronisation is nondeterministically chosen among the allowed alternatives.

As last step toward SAMs, we introduce a commonly used communication function and a related equivalence relation. The two definitions jointly define message passing, in the sense that they merge parameters in the same position and they make the result available as parameter of the composed action.

Definition 5.3 (Communication function for message passing). *The communication function for message passing* $MP_{i,j}$ *with* $i, j \in \mathbb{N}$ *is the function from* $\max(i, j)$ *to (any superset of)* $\underline{i} \uplus \underline{j}$ *such that* $MP_{i,j}(m) = \text{inj}_1(m)$ *if* $m \leq i$, $MP_{i,j}(m) = \overline{\text{inj}_2(m)}$ *otherwise.*

Definition 5.4 (Equivalence relation for message passing). *The equivalence relation for message passing* EQ_i *with* $i \in \mathbb{N}$ *is the equivalence relation on any superset S of* $\underline{i} \uplus \underline{i}$ *given by* $id_S \cup \{(\text{inj}_1(m), \text{inj}_2(m)) \mid m \leq i\}$.

Example 5.5. A synchronisation between two actions a and b of arity 2 and 4, giving an action c of arity 3, with $\text{Mob} = MP_{2,3}$ and $\doteq = EQ_2$ can be depicted as

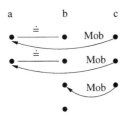

The first two parameters of c are obtained by merging the ones from a and b, while the third one is taken from b. The fourth parameter of b is simply discarded.

Definition 5.6 (SAM). *A quintuple* $(\mathfrak{I}, \mathbf{A}, Init, Fin, ActSyn)$ *is a* Synchronisation Algebra with Mobility *over the action signature* $\mathbf{A}$ *where* $\mathfrak{I}$ *is an identifier, $Init, Fin \subseteq Act$ are the* initial actions *and* final actions *respectively and $ActSyn$ is an action synchronisation relation on* $\mathbf{A}$. *We require that* $\varepsilon \in Init$ *and*

1. $\forall i \in Init, a \in Act \setminus \{\varepsilon\}.(i, a, (c, \mathrm{Mob}, \doteq)) \in ActSyn \implies c = a \wedge \mathrm{Mob} = MP_{ar(i), ar(a)}$
   $\wedge \doteq \subseteq EQ_{ar(a)}$*;*
2. $\forall a \in Act.\exists i \in Init.(i, a, (a, MP_{ar(i), ar(a)}, \doteq)) \in ActSyn$ *with* $\doteq \subseteq EQ_{ar(a)}$.

Identifier $\mathfrak{I}$ is used to distinguish SAMs with the same structure but that can be composed in different ways (this will be used in SHR-HS, see § 7). Set $Init$ contains ε and some trivial actions that can be executed by nodes themselves, and they are a technical trick to deal with isolated nodes. Condition 1 specifies that the synchronisation of an initial action i with any action $a \neq \varepsilon$, if allowed, preserves a and its parameters. Condition 2 requires that each action a has an action i to synchronise with.

Finally, the set Fin of final actions contains the actions that are considered complete, and which thus do not require any further interaction in order to be meaningful. From a technical point of view, these are the actions allowed on bound channels, and they allow to deal with local resources.

Remark 5.7. From now on, to simplify the presentation, we will not write explicitly the action synchronisations obtained by commutativity; furthermore, given a SAM $A = (\mathfrak{I}, \mathbf{A}, Init, Fin, ActSyn)$, $(a, b, (c, \mathrm{Mob}, \doteq)) \in A$ denotes $(a, b, (c, \mathrm{Mob}, \doteq)) \in ActSyn$.

We present some examples of SAMs over a parametric set inp of input actions.

Definition 5.8 (Milner SAM). *For SAM $Milner_{inp}$, $Init = \{\varepsilon\}$, $Fin = \{\tau, \varepsilon\}$ where*

- $Act = \{\tau, \varepsilon\} \cup \bigcup_{a \in inp}\{a, \bar{a}\}$ *with* $ar(\bar{a}) = ar(a)$ *for each $a \in inp$, $ar(\tau) = 0$;*
- $(\lambda, \varepsilon, (\lambda, MP_{ar(\lambda), 0}, EQ_0)) \in ActSyn$ *for each $\lambda \in Act$,*
  $(a, \bar{a}, (\tau, MP_{0,0}, EQ_{ar(a)})) \in ActSyn$ *for each $a \in inp$.*

The first action synchronisation specifies that an action synchronising with ε is just propagated, together with its parameters. The second action synchronisation formalises the reaction of an action and the corresponding co-action. As expected, corresponding parameters are merged by $EQ_{ar(a)}$.

Definition 5.9 (Hoare SAM). *SAM $Hoare_{inp}$ is given by:*

- $Act = Init = Fin = \{\varepsilon\} \cup inp$;
- $(\lambda, \lambda, (\lambda, MP_{ar(\lambda), ar(\lambda)}, EQ_{ar(\lambda)})) \in ActSyn$ *for each $\lambda \in Act$.*

The only (schema of) action synchronisation in Hoare SAM models the agreement among the participants on the action to perform. During synchronisation corresponding parameters are merged and the results are propagated.

Definition 5.10 (Broadcast SAM). *For SAM Bdc_{inp}, $Init = \{\varepsilon\} \cup inp$, $Fin = \{\varepsilon\} \cup \bigcup_{a \in inp}\{\overline{a}\}$ and*

- $Act = \{\varepsilon\} \cup \bigcup_{a \in inp}\{a, \overline{a}\}$ *with* $ar(\overline{a}) = ar(a)$ *for each* $a \in inp$;
- $(a, \overline{a}, (\overline{a}, MP_{ar(a),ar(\overline{a})}, EQ_{ar(a)})) \in ActSyn$ *for each* $a \in inp$,
  $(a, a, (a, MP_{ar(a),ar(a)}, EQ_{ar(a)})) \in ActSyn$ *for each* $a \in inp \cup \{\varepsilon\}$.

The main difference w.r.t. Milner SAM is that here an output can synchronise with more than one input, thus when synchronisation is performed the result is the output itself, which can thus interact with further inputs. Notice also that two inputs can interact (this is required to ensure associativity), thus when an output is finally met, its parameters are merged with the ones of all the inputs. If no output is met then the resulting action is an input, which is not allowed on a bound channel. Also, broadcast SAM forces all the connected edges to interact with an output, in fact they cannot perform an action ε. Thus this SAM models secure broadcast, where a check is made to ensure that the broadcasted message is received by all the listeners. Multicast SAM Mul_{inp} can be easily obtained from Bdc_{inp} by adding $(\lambda, \varepsilon, (\lambda, MP_{ar(\lambda),0}, EQ_0))$ to $ActSyn$, for each $\lambda \in Act$.

6 Parametric SHR

We outline *parametric SHR*, an SHR framework where the synchronisation policy can be freely chosen. The main ingredients of this model are a SAM, which specifies the synchronisation model used, and a set of inference rules, parametric on the above SAM, used to derive transitions from productions. Clearly, productions for parametric SHR must use actions in the set of actions Act_A of the SAM A used as parameter.

For space constraints we show just the rule (merge-p), and we outline the main differences between the other rules and the corresponding ones for Milner synchronisation. For a full formal account of the topic see [24,22].

Definition 6.1 (Merge rule for parametric SHR). *Let $\sigma = \{x/y\}$,*

$$(merge\text{-}p) \quad \frac{\Gamma, x, y \vdash G_1 \xrightarrow{\Lambda, \pi} \Phi \vdash G_2}{\Gamma, x \vdash G_1\sigma \xrightarrow{\Lambda', \pi'} \Phi' \vdash \nu U \; G_2\sigma\rho}$$

1. $\Lambda(x) = (a_1, \mathbf{v}_1), \Lambda(y) = (a_2, \mathbf{v}_2)$
2. $(a_1, a_2, (c, \text{Mob}, \doteq)) \in ActSyn$
3. $S_1 = \{\mathbf{v}_{i_1}[j_1] = \mathbf{v}_{i_2}[j_2] \mid \text{inj}_{i_1}(j_1) \doteq \text{inj}_{i_2}(j_2)\}$
4. $S_2 = \{t = u \mid t\pi = u\pi\}$
5. $\rho = \text{mgu}((S_1 \cup S_2)\sigma)$ *and ρ maps names to representatives in Γ, x whenever possible*
6. $\mathbf{w}[i] = (\mathbf{v}_j[k])\sigma\rho$ *if* $\text{Mob}(i) = \text{inj}_j(k)$
7. $\Lambda'(z) = \begin{cases} (c, \mathbf{w}) & \text{if } z = x \\ (\text{act}_\Lambda(z), (\text{n}_\Lambda(z))\sigma\rho) & \text{for each } z \in \Gamma \end{cases}$
8. $\pi' = \rho|_{\Gamma,x}$
9. $U = \Phi\sigma\rho \setminus \Phi'$

The main difference between the parametric inference rules and the ones in Definition 4.4 is that the parametric ones can be instantiated to model systems using a chosen synchronisation model.

To make the presentation clearer, rule (merge-p) uses a renaming $\sigma = \{x/y\}$ instead of a generic idempotent renaming. Synchronisation between two actions a_1 and a_2 is allowed iff there is an action synchronisation in *ActSyn* with a_1 and a_2 as first and second field respectively (condition 2). Also, the component Mob is used to compute the parameters of the resulting action (condition 6), while $\doteq$ is used to compute the first set of equalities (condition 3) which contributes to ρ.

In the rule for restriction, the action performed on the bound node must belong to *Fin*, while only actions in *Init* (with a tuple of fresh names as parameters) can be performed on a new node.

Parametric SHR fully recovers Milner SHR, in fact it is enough to instantiate it using the Milner SAM, see [24,22] for a formal statement. Naturally, parametric SHR can do more, as shown by the following example.

Example 6.2. We can exploit parametric SHR to improve the modelling of the system in Example 4.5. In fact, if we consider parametric SHR instantiated with Milner SAM, the example can be fully recovered. The synchronisation is obtained using rule (merge-p), which produces the same effect as the one in Example 4.5. Moreover, if we consider the SAM for broadcast synchronisation (Definition 5.10) instead of Milner, then the edge B_2, which is part of the infrastructure for communication, can be deleted. The graph for the new system with broadcast is:

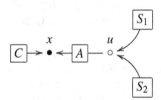

In fact, broadcast synchronisation obtains the desired effect, by allowing an action $\overline{req}$ to interact with two actions *req*. The result of the broadcast synchronisation gives $\overline{req}$ that is in set *Fin*, thus u can be restricted.

7   SHR for Heterogeneous Systems

An *heterogeneous system* is a system where different subsystems exploit different synchronisation protocols. A further generalisation of SHR is *SHR for heterogeneous systems* (SHR-HS) [25,22] where heterogeneity is introduced by labelling nodes with SAMs that specify the synchronisation policy used on them. Hence, SHR-HS focuses on the management of the primitives available on nodes. Depending on circumstances, different strategies have to be followed. Specifically, at the network level the labelling is quite static, since it depends on hardware features, while at the application level it can change dynamically as a result of negotiations among different components. In fact, services that differ (e.g., w.r.t. their QoS aspects) can be conveniently described by different SAMs.

In SHR-HS this is modelled by allowing SAMs labelling a node to dynamically change as a result of a synchronisation among different parties. Technically, this corresponds to update the labelling when nodes are merged or created. Therefore, a set $\mathcal{A}lg$ of SAMs is assumed together with an operator $\diamond$ of SAM composition. Also, $\langle \mathcal{A}lg, \diamond, A_\varepsilon \rangle$ is assumed to be a commutative monoid. Associativity and commutativity are needed so that the result of the composition of SAMs does not depend on the order of composition. The requirement of having a neutral element is not restrictive since one can always add an unused element and set it as neutral element of the composition. A neutral element is useful when one wants to ensure that the label of a node x is preserved when x is merged with another node, e.g., with a parameter of an initial action. The main definitions of SHR are extended to deal with nodes labelled by SAMs, introduced by turning Γ into a function from nodes to SAMs.

Definition 7.1 (Labelled graphs). *A labelled graph is a judgement $\Gamma \vdash G$ where Γ is a finite function from $\mathcal{N}$ to $\mathcal{A}lg$; G is like before, but now restricted nodes are labelled, e.g., $\nu y : A.G$ where $y \in \mathcal{N}$ and $A \in \mathcal{A}lg$.*

Extending previous notation, $x_1 : A_1, \ldots, x_n : A_n$ denotes a function mapping $x_i \in \mathcal{N}$ to $A_i \in \mathcal{A}lg$, for $i \in \{1, \ldots, n\}$. Structural congruence and isomorphisms of graphs are as in Definition 2.3 but, now, they must preserve SAMs labelling nodes.

Transitions $\Gamma \vdash G \xrightarrow{\Lambda, \pi} \Gamma \vdash G'$ are extended accordingly with the additional requirement that $act_\Lambda(x) \in \Gamma(x)$. Moreover, productions $\Gamma \vdash L(\mathbf{x}) \xrightarrow{\Lambda, \pi} \Phi \vdash G$ impose some requirements on how the labels in the target graph are chosen. Any SAM can be used to label nodes not in $dom(\Gamma)$, i.e., generated in the production, while for a node $x \in dom(\Gamma)$, $\Phi(x\pi)$ is $\Gamma(x_1) \diamond \ldots \diamond \Gamma(x_n)$ where $x_1, \ldots, x_n$ are all the nodes that π maps to $x\pi$.

In the inference rules, a production can be applied to an edge only if it specifies correct labels for the attached nodes. To specify SAMs applicable in different circumstances, suitable meta-notations can be used. Moreover, since now contexts are functions, both their domains (i.e., the sets of nodes) and their labelling SAMs must be kept into account. As an example, we give the merge rule (the others can straightforwardly be adapted from rules in Definition 4.4 and can be found in [25,22]).

Definition 7.2 (Merge rule for SHR-HS). *Let $\sigma = \{x/y\}$,*

$$(merge\text{-}HS) \quad \frac{\Gamma, x : A, y : A \vdash G_1 \xrightarrow{\Lambda, \pi} \Phi \vdash G_2}{\Gamma, x : A \vdash G_1\sigma \xrightarrow{\Lambda', \pi'} \Phi' \vdash \nu U \, G_2\sigma\rho}$$

1. $\Lambda(x) = (a_1, \mathbf{v}_1), \Lambda(y) = (a_2, \mathbf{v}_2)$
2. $(a_1, a_2, (c, Mob, \doteq)) \in A$
3. $S_1 = \{\mathbf{v}_{i_1}[j_1] = \mathbf{v}_{i_2}[j_2] \mid inj_{i_1}(j_1) \doteq inj_{i_2}(j_2)\}$
4. $S_2 = \{t = u \mid t\pi = u\pi\}$
5. $\rho = mgu((S_1 \cup S_2)\sigma)$ *and ρ maps names to representatives in $dom(\Gamma) \cup \{x\}$ whenever possible*
6. $\mathbf{w}[i] = (\mathbf{v}_j[k])\sigma\rho$ *if* $Mob(i) = inj_j(k)$
7. $\Lambda'(z) = \begin{cases} (c, \mathbf{w}) \text{ if } z = x \\ (act_\Lambda(z), (n_\Lambda(z))\sigma\rho) \text{ for each } z \in \Gamma \end{cases}$

8. $\pi' = \rho \lfloor_{\text{dom}(\Gamma) \cup \{x\}}$
9. $\text{dom}(U) = \text{dom}(\Phi)\sigma\rho \setminus \text{dom}(\Phi')$
10. *the label of each node $x \in \text{dom}(U) \cup \text{dom}(\Phi')$ is computed as follows: x is the representative according to $\sigma\rho$ of an equivalence class $\{x_1, \ldots, x_n\}$ of nodes which have in Φ labels $A_1, \ldots, A_n$. Then the label of x is $A_1 \diamond \ldots \diamond A_n$*

Nodes x and y can be merged only if they have the same label A, and the interaction is performed according to one of the action synchronisations in its action synchronisation relation. The node resulting from the merge of x and y is also labelled with A. Nodes not involved in the merging preserve their label while the others get their labels as resulting from the application of $\diamond$.

Example 7.3. The system of Example 6.2 can be now more accurately modelled by simultaneously using a SAM for Milner synchronisation on actions for authorisation, and one for broadcast of requests. Thus on each node only the desired actions are available. This avoids undesired executions caused by malicious clients. Available synchronisations are exploited by the authority to ensure that clients can issue only authorised requests. Also, actions can specify the synchronisation policy (e.g, Milner or broadcast synchronisation) so that clients dynamically choose what protocol to use.

At a first sight, it might be argued that parametric SHR can model heterogeneous systems. However, parametric SHR does not fit with heterogeneous systems because it makes each synchronisation policy available on each node, which is not what heterogeneous systems (as we consider them here) require. On the other hand, parametric SHR is a special case of SHR-HS where a unique SAM is used (as shown in [22]).

8   SHReQ: Coordinating Application Level QoS

Awareness of *Quality of Service* (QoS) is an emergent exigency in SOC which is no longer considered only as a low-level aspect of systems. The ability of formally specifying and programming QoS requirements may represent a significant added-value of the SOC paradigm. Moreover, QoS information can drive the design and development of programming interfaces and languages for QoS-aware middlewares as well as to drive the search-bind cycle of SOC.

In SHReQ, a calculus based on SHR, abstract high-level QoS requirements are expressed as *constraint-semiring* [1] and embedded in the rewriting mechanism which is parameterised with respect to a given c-semiring. Basically, values of c-semirings are synchronisation actions so that synchronising corresponds to the product operation of c-semirings that can be regarded as the simultaneous satisfaction of the QoS requirements of the participants to the synchronisation.

Definition 8.1 (C-semiring). *An algebraic structure $\langle S, +, \cdot, 0, 1 \rangle$ is a constraint semiring if S is a set with $0, 1 \in S$, and $+$ and $\cdot$ are binary operations on S such that:*

- *$+$ is commutative, associative, idempotent, 0 is its unit element and 1 is its absorbing element (i.e., $a + 1 = 1$, for any $a \in S$);*
- *$\cdot$ is commutative, associative, distributes over $+$, 1 is its unit element, and 0 is its absorbing element (i.e., $a \cdot 0 = 0$, for any $a \in S$).*

The additive operation $(+)$ of a c-semiring induces a partial order on S defined as $a \leq_S b \iff \exists c : a + c = b$. The minimum is thus $\mathbf{0}$ and the maximum is $\mathbf{1}$. C-semirings have two distinguished features that result very useful for modelling abstract QoS. First, the cartesian product of c-semirings is still a c-semiring, hence we can uniformly deal with many different quantities simultaneously. Second, partial order $\leq_S$ provides a mechanism of choice. These features make c-semirings suitable for reasoning about multi-criteria QoS issues [6,7]. The fact that c-semiring structure is preserved by cartesian product is here exploited to compose synchronisation policies.

Example 8.2. The following examples introduce some c-semirings together with their intended application to model QoS attributes. A more complete list can be found in [1].

- The boolean c-semiring $\langle \{true, false\}, \vee, \wedge, false, true \rangle$ can be used to model network and service availability.
- The optimisation c-semiring $\langle Real, min, +, +\infty, 0 \rangle$ applies to a wide range of cases, like prices or propagation delay.
- The max/min c-semiring $\langle Real, max, min, 0, +\infty \rangle$ can be used to formalise bandwidth, while the corresponding c-semiring over the naturals $\langle \mathbb{N}, max, min, 0, +\infty \rangle$ can be applied for resource availability.
- Performance can be represented by the probabilistic c-semiring $\langle [0, 1], max, \cdot, 0, 1 \rangle$.
- Security degrees are modelled via the c-semiring $\langle [0, 1, \ldots, n], max, min, 0, n \rangle$, where n is the maximal security level (unknown) and 0 is the minimal one (public).

Hereafter, given a c-semiring $\langle S, +, \cdot, \mathbf{0}, \mathbf{1} \rangle$, $\text{ar}_S : S \to \mathbb{N}$ is an arity function assigning arities to values in S. Graphs in SHReQ are called *weighted graphs* because values is S are used as weights and record quantitative information on the computation of the system.

Syntactically, SHReQ graphs are as those in SHR-HS where SAMs are replaced by c-semiring values. We write $x_1 : s_1, \ldots, x_n : s_n \vdash G$ for the weighted graph whose weighting function maps x_i to s_i, for $i \in \{1, \ldots, n\}$.

SHReQ rewriting mechanism relies on c-semirings where additional structure is defined. More precisely, we assume sets *Sync*, *Fin* and *NoSync* such that

- *Sync* $\subseteq$ *Fin* $\subseteq S$, $\mathbf{1} \in$ *Sync* and $\text{ar}_S(s) = 0$ if $s \in$ *Sync*;
- *NoSync* $\subseteq S \setminus$ *Fin*, $\mathbf{0} \in$ *NoSync* and $\forall s \in S. \forall t \in$ *NoSync*.$s \cdot t \in$ *NoSync*.

The intuition follows the SAM approach (Definition 5.6) and it is that *Fin* contains those values of S representing events of complete synchronisations. Among the actions in *Fin* we can select a subset of "pure" synchronisation actions, namely complete synchronisations that do not expose nodes. Set *NoSync*, on the contrary, contains the values that represent "impossible" synchronisations.

SHReQ productions follow the lines of Definition 4.3 and 4.4, but have a slightly different interpretation. For simplicity, we avoid the π component in SHReQ transitions and require that free nodes cannot be merged. Technically, this is obtained by considering undefined the most general unifier operation when it yields the fusion of two free nodes. In [18] the general unification is defined for SHReQ.

Definition 8.3 (SHReQ productions). *Let S be a c-semiring $\langle S,+,\cdot,\mathbf{0},\mathbf{1}\rangle$. A SHReQ production is a production*

$$\Gamma \vdash L(x_1,\ldots,x_n) \xrightarrow{\Lambda} \Phi \vdash G \qquad (5)$$

built on top of the action signature $(S,\text{ar}_S,\mathbf{1})$ where Γ maps nodes in $\{x_1,\ldots,x_n\}$ to S.

Production (5) states that, in order to replace L with G in a graph H, applicability conditions expressed by the function Γ on the attachment nodes of L must be satisfied in H and, henceforth, L "contributes" to the rewriting by offering Λ in the synchronisation with adjacent edges. Function Γ expresses the *minimal* QoS requirements on the environment in order to apply the production, i.e., given $x \in \text{dom}(\Gamma)$, the weight w on the node corresponding to x must satisfy $\Gamma(x) \leq w$. As before, function Φ is fully determined by Γ and Λ, where the weight of new nodes is set to $\mathbf{1}$ (i.e., $\Phi(y) = \mathbf{1}$ if $y \in \Gamma_\Lambda$), while for old nodes it traces the result of the synchronisation performed on them.

In production (5), c-semiring values play different roles in Γ and Λ: in Γ, they are interpreted as the minimal requirements to be fulfilled by the environment; in Λ they are the "contribution" that L yields to the synchronisation with the surrounding edges.

For space limitations, we only give the inference rule (merge-s) for merging nodes, the other rules being a simple rephrasing of those seen in previous sections. Rule (merge-s) is an adaptation of (merge-p) in Definition 6.1:

$$(\text{merge-s}) \quad \frac{\Gamma,x:r,y:s \vdash G_1 \xrightarrow{\Lambda \cup \{(x,s_1,\mathbf{v}_1),(y,s_2,\mathbf{v}_2)\}} \Phi \vdash G_2}{\Gamma,x:r+s \vdash G_1\sigma \xrightarrow{\Lambda'} \Phi' \vdash \nu U\, G_2\sigma\rho}$$

with $\sigma = \{x/y\}$ and Λ', Φ', ρ and U computed as in Definition 6.1, where action synchronisation on x is given by the c-semiring multiplication and its result is saved as the new weight of the synchronising node (i.e., $x : s_1 \cdot s_2$) both for free nodes and for nodes in U. In order to ensure applicability of productions also when there are more resources available than required, the following rule is introduced.

$$(\text{order-s}) \quad \frac{\Gamma,x:r \vdash G_1 \xrightarrow{\Lambda} \Phi \vdash G_2 \qquad r \leq t}{\Gamma,x:t \vdash G_1 \xrightarrow{\Lambda} \Phi \vdash G_2}$$

The other rules are similar to the ones in Definition 4.4.

Example 8.4. Let us consider Example 6.2. We can model the authority choosing the server that offers the cheapest service. To this aim, we use the cartesian product of two c-semirings. The first c-semiring is: $\langle R^+,max,min,0,\infty\rangle$, for the price of the service. The second c-semiring is used for synchronisation. In this way, we are able to define a general synchronisation policy as a unique c-semiring combining a classical synchronisation algebra with QoS requirements. The second c-semiring corresponds to multicast synchronisation. Assume $W = \{\text{req},\text{auth},\overline{\text{req}},\overline{\text{auth}},\mathbf{1}_W,\mathbf{0}_W,\bot\}$. Set W can be equipped with a c-semiring structure $\langle W,+,\cdot,\mathbf{0}_W,\mathbf{1}_W\rangle$, where:

$$\text{req}\cdot\overline{\text{req}} = \overline{\text{req}}, \quad \text{auth}\cdot\overline{\text{auth}} = \overline{\text{auth}}, \quad \text{req}\cdot\text{req} = \text{req}, \quad \text{auth}\cdot\text{auth} = \text{auth},$$

$$a,b \in W \setminus \{\mathbf{0}_W,\mathbf{1}_W\} \wedge a \neq b \wedge b \neq \overline{a} \implies a\cdot b = \bot$$

plus rules obtained by commutativity and the ones for $\mathbf{0}_W$ and $\mathbf{1}_W$.

The operation $+$ is obtained by extending the c-semiring axioms for the additive operation with $a + a = a$ and $a, b \notin \{0_W, 1_W\} \wedge a \neq b \implies a + b = \bot$, for all $a, b \in W$.

Below we show a graphical representation of a two steps derivation. Instead of reporting productions for each rewriting step, tentacles are decorated with actions. For the sake of clarity, in each step we only write actions and weights of the relevant nodes.

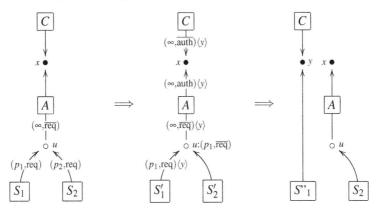

The first step selects the server with the lowest price where p_i is the price for S_i (in this step no names are communicated). This is obtained as the result of the synchronisation in u, i.e., $((\overline{\text{req}} \cdot \text{req}) \cdot \text{req}, \min(\infty, p_1, p_2))$. Assuming p_1 less than p_2 the new weight of u is $(\overline{\text{req}}, p_1)$. The second step shows the client connecting to the cheapest server S_1 (informed by A) by connecting to a new node y. After the first synchronisation, the cheapest server is identified by the authority using the new weight on node u. This guides the behaviour of S_1 and of the authority to produce the new connection to the client. In particular, the applicability condition of server rule requires its price to be less than or equal to the price on the node, and this can be satisfied only by the cheapest one (we suppose for simplicity that server costs are unique).

9   Concluding Remarks

In this tutorial paper we introduced SHR as a basic metalanguage with strong theoretical foundations for describing distributed systems within the SOC paradigm. We have addressed the key issues of the SHR model describing features like mobility, heterogeneity and Quality of Service. A great deal of future work remains. At the experimental level, more experience in specifying and designing service oriented applications is needed. The problem of supporting the development of highly decentralised applications (from requirement and design to implementation and maintenance) is at the edge of research in software engineering. Indeed, software engineering technologies must support the shift from the client-server interaction model to other models which better accommodate the constraints posed by the SOC paradigm. We argue that the SHR model fosters a declarative approach by identifying the interaction borders of services where satisfaction of certain properties (e.g. Quality of Service) has a strong impact on the behaviours. Some preliminary results on the exploitation of the SHR model in specifying and designing internetworking systems can be found in [11]. In this perspective the development of tool support for the SHR framework would be of great value. In the short term, we plan to experiment our framework to model workflow among services (e.g. by extending the Petri Nets translation developed in [34]).

At the foundational level, future work will be focused on the definition of abstract semantics for the SHR model. A basic question is "what is the appropriate notion of semantic equivalence for SHR?". Bisimulation-based equivalences have been proved to be a powerful basis for semantic equivalence of process calculi. Bisimulation semantics has the main advantage of capturing the idea of interaction within arbitrary contexts thus providing the semantic machinery for compositional reasoning. Hence, a main problem is understanding whether bisimilarity is a congruence w.r.t. the operators of system composition or not, i.e. whether the compositions of bisimilar systems are bisimilar or not. If they are, then the observational properties of a complex system can be derived by composing the results obtained on their components. The development of a compositional bisimulation semantics for SHR is not straightforward, since it requires to define a suitable algebra of graphs and exploit bialgebraic techniques in a non trivial way. Some preliminary results can be found in [22]. A further line of future research concerns the development of a "true concurrent" semantics for SHR where the notions of causality and independence are explicitly represented. The ability of reasoning on the causality flow could be particularly useful to manage the complexity of service oriented applications. For instance the analysis of service workflows can benefit from knowledge about causality: it suffices to focus on the causal dependencies among service invocations to understand the properties of the business interactions. We plan to extend the techniques introduced in [9] to equip SHR with a truly concurrent semantics.

Acknowledgements. The authors thank the anonymous reviewers for their valuable comments and suggestions.

References

1. S. Bistarelli, U. Montanari, and F. Rossi. Semiring-based constraint satisfaction and optimization. *Journal of the ACM*, 44(2):201–236, 1997.
2. L. Cardelli and A. D. Gordon. Mobile ambients. In *Proc. of FoSSaCS'98*, volume 1378 of *LNCS*, pages 140–155. Springer, 1998.
3. I. Castellani and U. Montanari. Graph grammars for distributed systems. In *Graph-Grammars and Their Application to Computer Science*, volume 153 of *LNCS*, pages 20–38. Springer, 1983.
4. A. Corradini, P. Degano, and U. Montanari. Specifying highly concurrent data structure manipulation. In *Proc. of Computing 85*. Elsevier Science, 1985.
5. A. Corradini and D. Hirsch. An operational semantics of CommUnity based on graph transformation systems. In *Proc. of GT-VMT 2004*, volume 109 of *Elect. Notes in Th. Comput. Sci.*, pages 111–124. Elsevier Science, 2004.
6. R. De Nicola, G. Ferrari, U. Montanari, R. Pugliese, and E. Tuosto. A Formal Basis for Reasoning on Programmable QoS. In *International Symposium on Verification – Theory and Practice*, volume 2772 of *LNCS*, pages 436–479. Springer, 2003.
7. R. De Nicola, G. Ferrari, U. Montanari, R. Pugliese, and E. Tuosto. A process calculus for qos-aware applications. In *Proc. of Coordination'05*, volume 3454 of *LNCS*, pages 33–48. Springer, 2003.

8. R. De Nicola, G. Ferrari, and R. Pugliese. KLAIM: A kernel language for agents interaction and mobility. *IEEE Trans. Software Eng.*, 24(5):315–330, 1998.
9. P. Degano and U. Montanari. A model for distributed systems based on graph rewriting. *Journal of the ACM*, 34(2):411–449, 1987.
10. G. Ferrari, U. Montanari, and E. Tuosto. A LTS semantics of ambients via graph synchronization with mobility. In *ICTCS'01*, volume 2202 of *LNCS*, pages 1–16. Springer, 2001.
11. G. Ferrari, U. Montanari, and E. Tuosto. Graph-based models of internetworking systems. In *Formal Methods at the Crossroads: From Panacea to Foundational Support*, volume 2757 of *LNCS*, pages 242–266. Springer, 2003.
12. C. Fournet and G. Gonthier. The reflexive CHAM and the join-calculus. In *Proc. of POPL '96*, pages 372–385, 1996.
13. F. Gadducci and U. Montanari. The tile model. In *Proof, Language and Interaction: Essays in Honour of Robin Milner*. MIT Press, 2000.
14. D. Hirsch. *Graph Transformation Models for Software Architecture Styles*. PhD thesis, Departamento de Computación, Facultad de Ciencias Exactas y Naturales, U.B.A., 2003.
15. D. Hirsch, P. Inverardi, and U. Montanari. Reconfiguration of software architecture styles with name mobility. In *Proc. of Coordination '00*, volume 1906 of *LNCS*, 2000.
16. D. Hirsch and U. Montanari. Synchronized hyperedge replacement with name mobility. In *Proc. of CONCUR'01*, volume 2154 of *LNCS*. Springer, 2001.
17. D. Hirsch and E. Tuosto. SHReQ: A framework for coordinating application level QoS. In *Proc. of SEFM'05*, pages 425–434. IEEE Computer Society Press, 2005.
18. D. Hirsch and E. Tuosto. Coordinating Application Level QoS with SHReQ. *Journal of Software and Systems Modelling*, 2006. Submitted.
19. C. A. R. Hoare. A model for communicating sequential processes. In *On the Construction of Programs*. Cambridge University Press, 1980.
20. B. König and U. Montanari. Observational equivalence for synchronized graph rewriting. In *Proc. of TACS'01*, volume 2215 of *LNCS*, pages 145–164. Springer, 2001.
21. I. Lanese. Exploiting user-definable synchronizations in graph transformation. In *Proc. of GT-VMT'06*, Elect. Notes in Th. Comput. Sci. ES, 2006. To appear.
22. I. Lanese. *Synchronization Strategies for Global Computing Models*. PhD thesis, Computer Science Department, University of Pisa, Pisa, Italy, 2006. Forthcoming.
23. I. Lanese and U. Montanari. A graphical fusion calculus. In *Proceedings of the Workshop of the COMETA Project on Computational Metamodels*, volume 104 of *Elect. Notes in Th. Comput. Sci.*, pages 199–215. Elsevier Science, 2004.
24. I. Lanese and U. Montanari. Synchronization algebras with mobility for graph transformations. In *Proc. of FGUC'04 – Foundations of Global Ubiquitous Computing*, volume 138 of *Elect. Notes in Th. Comput. Sci.*, pages 43–60. Elsevier Science, 2004.
25. I. Lanese and E. Tuosto. Synchronized hyperedge replacement for heterogeneous systems. In *Proc. of Coordination'05*, volume 3454 of *LNCS*, pages 220–235. Springer, 2005.
26. R. Milner. *A Calculus of Communicating Systems*, volume 92 of *LNCS*. Springer, 1982.
27. R. Milner, J. Parrow, and J. Walker. A calculus of mobile processes, I and II. *Inform. and Comput.*, 100(1):1–40,41–77, 1992.
28. J. Parrow and B. Victor. The fusion calculus: Expressiveness and symmetry in mobile processes. In *Proc. of LICS'98*, pages 176–185. IEEE Computer Society Press, 1998.
29. G. D. Plotkin. A structural approach to operational semantics. *J. Log. Algebr. Program.*, 60-61:17–139, 2004.
30. J. Riely and M. Hennessy. Distributed processes and location failures. *TCS*, 266(1–2):693–735, 2001.

31. F. Rossi and U. Montanari. Graph rewriting, constraint solving and tiles for coordinating distributed systems. *Applied Categorical Structures*, 7(4):333–370, 1999.
32. G. Rozenberg, editor. *Handbook of graph grammars and computing by graph transformations, vol. 1: Foundations*. World Scientific, 1997.
33. E. Tuosto. *Non-Functional Aspects of Wide Area Network Programming*. PhD thesis, Computer Science Department, University of Pisa, Italy, 2003.
34. W. M. P. van der Aalst and K. B. Lassen. Translating workflow nets to BPEL4WS. Technical Report WP 145, Eindhoven University of Technology, 2005.
35. G. Winskel. Synchronization trees. *TCS*, 34:33–82, 1984.

Control of Modular and Distributed Discrete-Event Systems

Jan Komenda[1] and Jan H. van Schuppen[2]

[1] Institute of Mathematics - Brno Branch, Czech Academy of Sciences,
Žižkova 22, 616 62 Brno, Czech Republic
komenda@ipm.cz
[2] CWI, P.O. Box 94079, 1090 GB Amsterdam, The Netherlands
J.H.van.Schuppen@cwi.nl

Abstract. Control of modular and distributed discrete-event systems appears as an approach to handle computational complexity of synthesizing supervisory controllers for large scale systems. For both modular and distributed discrete-event systems sufficient and necessary conditions are derived for modular control synthesis to equal global control synthesis for the supremal controllable sublanguage, for the supremal normal sublanguage, and for the supremal controllalble and normal sublanguage. The modular control synthesis has a much lower computational complexity than the corresponding global control synthesis for the respective sublanguages.

1 Introduction

The purpose of the paper is to present an overview of recent results together with new results on control of modular (concurrent) and distributed discrete-event systems. Discrete-event systems (DES) are dynamical systems which are studied in computer science with applications in manufacturing, communication networks, but also in software engineering (automated system design). In particular the various types of state transition systems (automata, Petri Nets, process algebras) are typical instances of DES. The topic of modular DES arises because of an increasing complexity of engineering systems, in particular of computer and communication networks. There is a strong need for system theoretical treatment of modular DES motivated by these emerging application fields. Control of discrete-event systems is a natural generalization of their verification that is now very well established for both finite and infinite state transition systems.

In computer science the problems of supervisory control synthesis are studied as automated synthesis. In control theory for DES the goal is not to verify the specification, but to impose it by means of a supervisor that runs in parallel with the original system. The supervisor is chosen such that the composed system meets the specification. In the Ramadge-Wonham framework it is an automaton which runs in parallel with the original system and the parallel composition of the original system with the supervisor (called closed-loop or controlled system)

F.S. de Boer et al. (Eds.): FMCO 2005, LNCS 4111, pp. 44–63, 2006.
© Springer-Verlag Berlin Heidelberg 2006

meets the specification given mostly by a language or a logical formula. In this way the specification is imposed on the controlled system.

Although most of the verification and control problems for finite-state transition systems are decidable, the high complexity of most control and verification problems makes them practically difficult. Moreover, there are undecidable control problems for decentralized DES [10], [16]. In order to limit the high computational complexity of (global) control synthesis efficient methods for component-based control synthesis are developed. Synthesis of modular and distributed systems has also been treated by computer scientists, see for example [13].

A discrete-event system is said to have *complete observations* if all events are observed and are available for the supervisory control. A discrete-event system is said to have *partial observations* if only a strict subset of the events are observed and are available for the supervisory control. A *modular discrete-event system* is a system consisting of a composition of two or more subsystems where each subsystem or module has complete observations of its (local) events. A *distributed discrete-event system* is a system consisting of a composition of two or more subsystems where at least one subsystem has only partial observations of its events.

The novelty of the paper is in the following results: The necessary conditions for commutativity between parallel composition and supremal sublanguages (Theorems 3, 4, and 5; supremal controllable sublanguages, supremal normal sublanguages, and supremal controllable and normal sublanguages), necessary conditions in case of indecomposable specifications (Theorems 7, 8, and 9), and necessary and sufficient conditions for closed-loop languages with respect to the antipermissive control policy in case of global specification (Theorems 6 and 10).

Because this paper appears in a proceedings of a theoretical computer science symposium, there is an additional tutorial text in Section 2 for computer scientists on the concepts and results of control theory for discrete-event systems.

The paper has the following structure. The next section is an introduction to supervisory control. Section 3 is devoted to modular control with complete observations and with decomposable specification languages. In Section 4 the case of a distributed DES and a decomposable specification is treated. In Section 5 the case is discussed of a modular DES with an indecomposable specification. Finaly in Section 6 the case of a distributed system with an indecomposable specification is treated. In Section 7 concluding remarks are proposed.

2   Control of Discrete-Event Systems - Introduction

In this section basic notation and terminology of supervisory control is recalled. The notation used in this paper is mostly taken from the lecture notes of W.M. Wonham [19] and the book [1].

A (deterministic) *generator*

$$G = (Q, A, f, q_0, Q_m),$$

is an algebraic structure consisting of a *state set* Q, an *event set* A, a *partial transition function* $f : Q \times A \rightarrow Q$, an *initial state* $q_0 \in Q$, and a *subset of marked states* $Q_m \subseteq Q$. A transition is also denoted as $q \overset{a}{\mapsto} q^+ = f(q, a)$. If a transition is defined then this is denoted by $f(q, a)!$ Denote by A^* the set of all finite strings of elements of the alphabet A and the empty string. Extend the transition function f to $f : Q \times A^* \rightarrow Q$ by induction. Define respectively the *language* and the *marked language* of the generator as,

$$L(G) = \{s \in A^* | f(q_0, s)!\}, \quad L_m(G) = \{s \in L(G) | f(q_0, s) \in Q_m\}.$$

Note that unlike $L_m(G)$, $L(G)$ is always prefix-closed. The prefix closure of a language $K \subseteq A^*$ is denoted by prefix(K). We often abuse notation and write L instead of $L(G)$. The tuple of languages $(L_m(G), L(G))$ will be called the *behavior* of the generator. The system is said to be *nonblocking* if the the prefix closure of the marked language $L_m(G)$ equals the language $L(G)$. This is equivalent to the property that every string of the system, $s \in L(G)$, can be extended to a marked string, thus there exists a string $v \in A^*$ such that $sv \in L_m(G)$.

A *controlled generator* is a structure

$$(G, A_c, \Gamma_c), \text{ where,}$$

$\quad G \quad$ is a generator,

$\quad A_c \subseteq A \quad$ is the subset of *controllable events*,

$A_{uc} = A \setminus A_c \quad$ is the subset of *uncontrollable events*, and

$\quad \Gamma_c = \{S \subseteq A | A_{uc} \subseteq S\}, \text{ is called the *set of control patterns*.}$

The set of control patterns $S(s)$ is the subset of events that the supervisor enables after string s has been generated by G. A *supervisory control* or a *supervisor* for the controlled generator is map $S : L(G) \rightarrow \Gamma_c$. The *closed-loop system* associated with a controllable generator and a supervisory control as denoted above is defined as the language $L(S/G) \subseteq A^*$ and the marked language $L_m(S/G) \subseteq L(S/G)$ which satisfy respectively,

$\quad (1) \quad \epsilon \in L(S/G),$

$\quad (2) \quad$ if $s \in L(S/G)$ and if $a \in S(s)$ such that $sa \in L(G)$

$\quad\quad\quad$ then $sa \in L(S/G);$

$\quad L_m(S/G) = L(S/G) \cap L_m(G).$

Note that at the automata level the supervision is implemented by a parallel composition of the generator and the supervisor. This composition is a special form of the synchronous product (with priorities), in order to ensure that a supervisor never disables uncontrollable events.

Problem 1. Supervisory control problem. Consider a controlled generator (G, A_c, Γ_c) and a specification sublanguage $K \subset L_m(G)$. Does there exist a supervisor S such that the closed-loop system satisfies (1) $L_m(S/G) \subseteq K$ and (2) $L(S/G)$ is nonblocking?

Because often the subset of the specification sublanguage K contains only the safe strings, thus the unsafe strings are excluded, the control objective (1) of the above problem is called the *safety control objective*. Not every language can be exactly achieved by a supervisor. The property called controllability is needed.

Definition 1. *A language $K \subseteq A^*$ is said to be* controllable *with respect to plant language $L = L(G)$ and alphabet A_{uc} if $\forall s \in \mathrm{prefix}(K)$ and $\forall a \in A_{uc}$ such that $sa \in L$ we have that $sa \in \mathrm{prefix}(K)$. Equivalently,*

$$\mathrm{prefix}(K)A_{uc} \cap L \subseteq \mathrm{prefix}(K). \tag{1}$$

Theorem 1. *(Due to Ramadge, Wonham, see [14].) There exists a nonblocking supervisory control S for a generator G such that $L_m(S/G) = K$ and $L(S/G) = \mathrm{prefix}(K)$ if and only if*

1. *K is controllable with respect to $L(G)$ and A_{uc} and*
2. *$K = \mathrm{prefix}(K) \cap L_m(G)$ (then one says that K is $L_m(G)$−closed.).*

As a corollary for prefix-closed specifications:

Corollary 1. *Let $\emptyset \neq K \subseteq L(G)$ be prefix closed. There exists a supervisory control S for G such that $L_m(S/G) = K$ and $L(S/G) = K$ if and only if K is controllable with respect to $L(G)$ and A_{uc}.*

The corresponding supervisory control $S : L(G) \to \Gamma_c$ is:

$$S(s) = A_{uc} \cup \{a \in A_c : sa \in \mathrm{prefix}(K)\}.$$

Note the abuse of notaton, where the same symbol is used to denote a supervisor and a control law. This is justified by the fact that, considering a supervisor, the control law is described by the transition function of the supervisor in the form of the set of active events after string s has been processed by the supervisor. Most often one is concerned only with the safety issue, i.e. the controlled behavior must be included in the specification language. This is why for specifications which are not controllable, supremal controllable sublanguages are considered. The notation $\sup \mathrm{C}(K, L, A_u)$ is chosen for the supremal controllable sublanguage of K with respect to L and A_u. This language always exists, it is the union of all controllable sublanguages because controllability is preserved by language unions.

In the presence of partial observations additional issues appear. A *generator with partial observations* is a structure (G, A_o) where G is a generator, $A_o \subseteq A$ is called the subset of *observable events*, and $A_{uo} = A \setminus A_o$ is called the subset of *unobservable events*. In this case define the *natural projection* $P : A^* \to A_o^*$ such that $P(\epsilon) = \epsilon$ and P erases only the unobservable events. Note that the supervisor cannot distinguish between two strings with the same projections, i.e. after two such strings the same control law must be applied. Therefore, a supervisor with partial observations is a map $S : P(L(G)) \to \Gamma_c$. Define also the inverse projection $P_i^{-1} : \mathrm{Pwr}(A_i^*) \to \mathrm{Pwr}(A^*)$ on subsets of strings or languages.

Let K be a specification language. The supervisory control with partial observations is:

$$S(s) = A_{uc} \cup \tag{2}$$
$$\{a \in A_c : \exists s' \in \text{prefix}(K) \text{ with } P(s') = P(s) \text{ and } s'a \in \text{prefix}(K)\}.$$

The additional property needed to exactly achieve a specification language by a supervisor with partial observations is called observability.

Definition 2. *The sublanguage $K \subseteq P(L)$ is said to be* observable *with respect to the plant language L and the projection P if*

$$\forall s \in \text{prefix}(K), \ \forall a \in A_c,$$
$$sa \in L, \ s'a \in \text{prefix}(K), \text{ and } P(s) = P(s') \ \Rightarrow \ sa \in \text{prefix}(K). \tag{3}$$

Theorem 2. *(Due to F. Lin and W.M. Wonham, see [11].) Consider a generator with partial observations. There exists a nonblocking supervisory control S with partial observations such that $L_m(S/G) = K$ and $L(S/G) = \text{prefix}(K)$ if and only if*

1. *K is controllable with respect to $L(G)$ and A_{uc},*
2. *K is observable with respect to $L(G)$ and P, and*
3. *$K = \text{prefix}(K) \cap L_m(G)$. ($K$ is $L_m(G)-$closed.)*

Unfortunately, unlike controllability, observability is not preserved by language unions. This is why a stronger property, called normality, has been introduced.

Definition 3. *[1] Consider a controlled generator with partial observations and a specification sublanguage $K \subseteq L_m(G)$. Call the specification sublanguage K $(L, P)-$ normal if*

$$\text{prefix}(K) = P^{-1}P(\text{prefix}(K)) \cap L. \tag{4}$$

It is known that normal languages are closed with respect to unions, hence the supremal normal sublanguage of K always exists, it is the union of all normal sublanguages of K and it is denoted by $\sup N(K, L, P)$.

Recall finally that in the case $A_c \subseteq A_o$ normality coincides with observability. This assumption is widely accepted in the computer science community, where only uncontrollable actions might be internal (silent).

For control problems with partial observations and a safety control objective, *supremal controllable and normal sublanguages* are important.

Recall that the synchronous product (also called the parallel composition) of languages $L_1 \subseteq A_1^*$ and $L_2 \subseteq A_2^*$ is defined by $L = L_1 \parallel L_2 = \cap_{i=1}^2 P_i^{-1}(L_i)$, where $P_i : A^* \to A_i^*$, $i = 1, 2$ are natural projections to local event sets.

Definition 4. *Consider two generators,*

$$G_1 = (Q_1, A_1, f_1, q_{1,0}, Q_{1,m}), \ G_2 = (Q_2, A_2, f_2, q_{2,0}, Q_{2,m}).$$

Their synchronous product *is the generator*

$$G_1\|G_2 = (Q_1 \times Q_2, A_1 \cup A_2, f, q_0, Q_m),$$

$$q_0 = (q_{1,0}, q_{2,0}), \quad Q_m = Q_{1,m} \times Q_{2,m},$$

$$f((q_1, q_2), a) = \begin{cases} (f_1(q_1, a), f_2(q_2, a)) & \text{if } a \in A_1 \cap A_2, \\ & \quad i = 1, 2, \ f_i(q_i, a)! \\ (f_1(q_1, a), q_2), & \text{if } a \in A_1 \setminus A_2, \ f_1(q_1, a)! \\ (q_1, f_2(q_2, a)), & \text{if } a \in A_2 \setminus A_1 \ f_2(q_2, a)! \\ \text{undefined}, & \text{otherwise.} \end{cases}$$

It can then be proven that,

$$L(G_1\|G_2) = L(G_1)\|L(G_2), \ L_m(G_1\|G_2) = L_m(G_1)\|L_m(G_2).$$

Denote for $n \in \mathbb{Z}$ the set of the first n integers by $\mathbb{Z}_n = \{1, 2, \ldots, n\}$.

Definition 5. *A* modular discrete-event system *(also called a concurrent discrete-event system) is the synchronous product of two or more modules or local subsystems in which each module has complete observations of the state of its own module but does not have observations of the states of other modules unless it shares observable events with these other modules. Mathematically, a modular discrete-event system with $n \in \mathbb{Z}$ modules is a structure $\{G_i, A_{i,c}, A_{i,o}, \Gamma_{i,c}, i \in \mathbb{Z}_n\}$ consisting of n controlled generators. The associated* global system *is the synchronous product of the modules or the local subsystems, $\|_{i=1}^n G_i$. Denote the natural projections by $P_i : (\cup_{i=1}^n A_i)^* \to A_i^*$.*

A distributed discrete-event system *is a structure as above consisting of n controlled generators where at least one of the modules has only partial observations of that module.*

3 Modular Supervisory Control with a Decomposable Specification

In this section the concurrent behavior of the modules $\{G_i, i \in \mathbb{Z}_n\}$ is considered. Consider the local alphabets of these subplants, $\{A_i, i \in \mathbb{Z}_n\}$, which are not necessarily pairwise disjoint. Denote the partition of the local alphabet into the subset of controllable events, A_{ic}, and the subset of uncontrollable events, A_{iu}, by $A_i = A_{iu} \cup A_{ic}$ for all $i \in \mathbb{Z}_n$.

Definition 6. *Consider a modular DES. The local plants $\{G_i, i \in \mathbb{Z}_n\}$ agree on the controllability of their common events if*

$$A_{iu} \cap A_j = A_i \cap A_{ju}, \ \forall i, j \in \mathbb{Z}_n. \tag{5}$$

This definition stemming from [18] means that the events shared by two modules or local subsystems must have the same control status for both controllers associated to these subsystems. In the following it will often be assumed that the modules satisfy the condition of agreement on the controllability of their common events. Denote $A_c = \cup_{i=1}^n A_{ic}$. The assumption on the agreement on common events implies that $A_{ic} = A_c \cap A_i$. Also, if we denote $A_u = \cup_{i=1}^n A_{iu}$ then we still have the disjoint union $A = A_c \cup A_u$ due to the assumption of agreement on the controllability of their common events. Denote by $A = \cup_{i=1}^n A_i$ the global alphabet and by $P_i : A \to A_i$ the projections to the local alphabets. The concept of inverse projection $P_i^{-1} : \mathrm{Pwr}(A_i) \to \mathrm{Pwr}(A)$ is also used.

The local plant languages or the languages of the modules will be denoted by $\{L_i, i \in \mathbb{Z}_n\}$ and the local specification languages by $\{K_i, i \in \mathbb{Z}_n\}$. We assume in this section that the global plant L and the specification K languages are decomposable into local plant and local specification languages: $L = \|_{i=1}^n L_i$ and $K = \|_{i=1}^n K_i$. This formulation is equivalent to the following definition.

Definition 7. *Consider a modular DES. One says that $L \subseteq A^*$ is* decomposable *with respect to $\{P_i, \ i \in \mathbb{Z}_n\}$ if $L = \|_{i=1}^n P_i(L)$.*

Proposition 1. *Consider a modular DES. $L \subseteq A^*$ is decomposable with respect to $\{P_i, \ i \in \mathbb{Z}_n\}$ if and only if there exists $\{L_i \subseteq A_i^*, i \in \mathbb{Z}_n\}$ such that*

$$L = \|_{i=1}^n L_i = \cap_{i=1}^n (P_i)^{-1}(L_i). \tag{6}$$

Proof. ($\Rightarrow$) It is sufficient to consider $L_i := P_i(L)$.
($\Leftarrow$) If $L = \|_{i=1}^n L_i = \cap_{i=1}^n (P_i)^{-1}(L_i)$, then it follows from properties of projections that

$$P_i(L) \subseteq L_i \cap \cap_{j \neq i} P_i P_j^{-1}(L_j) \subseteq L_i, \ \forall i \in \mathbb{Z}_n. \text{ Thus we have that,}$$
$$\|_{i=1}^n P_i(L) = \cap_{i=1}^n (P_i)^{-1} P_i(L) \ \subseteq \ \cap_{i=1}^n P_i^{-1}(L_i) = L,$$

by our assumption. The first inclusion follows from the fact that $P_i(P_i)^{-1}$ is identity and that projection of an intersection is contained in the intersection of projections. The inclusion $L \subseteq \cap_{i=1}^n P_i^{-1}(P_i(L))$ is obvious.

Note that $P_i(L) \subseteq L_i$ means that for any tuple of languages $\{L_i' \subseteq A_i^*, \forall i \in \mathbb{Z}_n\}$ such that $L = \|_{i=1}^n L_i'$ we have $P_i(L) \subseteq L_i'$, i.e. $\{P_i(L), \ i \in \mathbb{Z}_n\}$ is the smallest possible decomposition of L into local languages.

Definition 8. *Consider a modular discrete-event system and either a global specification language or a family of local specifications. From the local specifications one can always compute the global specification as described above.*

Global control synthesis of a modular discrete-event system is the procedure by which first all modules are combined into the global plant and then control synthesis is carried out as described in Section 2. This can refer to either construction of a supervisor which meets the specification or to the supremal supervisor.

Modular control synthesis of a modular discrete-event system is the procedure by which control synthesis is carried out for each module or local subsystem. The global supervisor formally consists of the synchronous product of the local supervisors though that product is not computed in practice.

In terms of behaviors, the optimal global control synthesis is represented by the closed-loop language

$$\sup C(K, L, A_u) = \sup C(\|_{i=1}^n K_i, \|_{i=1}^n L_i, A_u),$$

using the operation supremal controllable sublanguage $\sup C(K, L, A_u)$ defined in the last section. Similarly, modular control synthesis yields in terms of behaviors the partial language

$$\|_{i=1}^n \sup C(K_i, L_i, A_{iu}).$$

Problem 2. Consider a modular discrete-event system and a decomposable specification language. Determine necessary and sufficient conditions with respect to which modular control synthesis equals global control synthesis for the supremal controllable sublanguage within the specification language. Equivalently, if,

$$\|_{i=1}^n \sup C(K_i, L_i, A_{iu}) = \sup C(\|_{i=1}^n K_i, \|_{i=1}^n L_i, A_u). \tag{7}$$

Later in the paper also the problems are investigated of when modular control synthesis equals global control synthesis for the supremal normal sublanguage, for the supremal controllable and normal sublanguage, and for the closed-loop language in case of an antipermissive control policy.

There exists an example which establishes that modular control synthesis does not equal global control synthesis in general. Theorem 3 provides necessary and sufficient conditions for modular control synthesis to equal global control synthesis. This problem has been studied algebraically in [18]. The concept of mutual controllability ([18]) plays the key role.

Definition 9. *Consider a modular DES. The modular plant languages $\{L_i \subseteq A_i^*, \ i \in Z_n\}$ are called* mutually controllable *if*

$$\text{prefix}(L_j)(A_{ju} \cap A_i) \cap P_j(P_i)^{-1}\text{prefix}(L_i) \subseteq \text{prefix}(L_j), \ \forall i, j \in Z_n, \ i \neq j. \tag{8}$$

Note that both local and global plant languages are typically prefix closed, hence the prefix closures above can be removed.

Mutual controllability can be viewed as local controllability of the modular plant languages with respect to the shared uncontrollable events; thus, for all $i, j \in Z_n$ with $i \neq j$, the modular language L_j is controllable with respect to the shared uncontrallable events $(A_{ju} \cap A_i)$ and the local view of the other module $(P_i(P_j)^{-1}(L_j))$ as the new plant. This condition is important for modular computation of global supremal controllable sublanguages.

The computational complexity of checking mutual controllability is much lower than that of checking controllability of a sublanguage over the global alphabet.

The sufficiency part of Theorem 3 is due to K.C. Wong and S.-H. Lee, see [18]. We have presented in [3] a coalgebraic version of the proof for commutativity of supremal controllable sublanguages with the synchronous product:

Theorem 3. Modular control synthesis equals global control synthesis for the supremal controllable sublanguage in case of a modular DES. *Assume that the local plants agree on the controllability of their common events.*
If the local plant languages $\{L_i \subseteq A_i^*, \ i \in Z_n\}$ *are mutually controllable then*

$$\|_{i=1}^n \sup C(K_i, L_i, A_{iu}) \sup C(\|_{i=1}^n K_i, \|_{i=1}^n L_i, A_u). \tag{9}$$

Conversely, if for fixed local plant languages $\{L_i, \ i \in Z_n\}$ *equation (9) holds true for any* $\{K_i \subseteq L_i, i \in \mathbb{Z}_n\}$ *then, for all* $i \in \mathbb{Z}_n$, $P_i(L)$ *is controllable with respect to* L_i *and* A_{iu}; *equivalently, then*

$$P_i(L)A_{iu} \cap L_i \subseteq P_i(L), \ \forall i \in \mathbb{Z}_n. \tag{10}$$

Proof. We have shown the first part of the theorem in [3], the proof is stated in [6]. Note that an algebraic proof of sufficiency is stated in [18].

It remains to prove the necessity part of the theorem. Assume now that for fixed local plant languages $\{L_i, \ i \in Z_n\}$ equation (9) holds true for any local specification languages $K_i \subseteq L_i$. Then it holds true in particular for $K_i := P_i(L)$. Since L and K are decomposable we have

$$L = \bigcap_{i=1}^n P_i^{-1} P_i(L) = \bigcap_{i=1}^n P_i^{-1} K_i = K, \ (\text{cf. Proposition 1}). \tag{11}$$

$$L = K = \sup C(L, L, A_u) = \|_{i=1}^n \sup C(P_i(L), L_i, A_{iu})$$
$$\subseteq \cap_{i=1}^n P_i^{-1}(\sup C(P_i(L), L_i, A_{iu})),$$
$$L \subseteq (P_i)^{-1}(\sup C(P_i(L), L_i, A_{iu}), \ \forall i \in \mathbb{Z}_n; \tag{12}$$

Note that $P_i(L) \subseteq L_i, \ \forall i \in \mathbb{Z}_n$, because L is decomposable. Indeed

$$P_i(L) = P_i(\bigcap_{i=1}^n P_i^{-1}(L_i)) \subseteq P_i(P_i)^{-1}(L_i) \cap \cap_{j \neq i} P_i(P_j)^{-1}(L_j) \subseteq L_i,$$

where the last inclusion follows from $P_i(P_i)^{-1}(L_i) = L_i$.

By applying the projection on both sides of inclusion (12)

it follows from the monotonicity of projections that

$$P_i(L) \subseteq P_i(P_i)^{-1} \sup C(P_i(L), L_i, A_{iu}) = \sup C(P_i(L), L_i, A_{iu}) \subseteq P_i(L),$$

from the definition of supremal controllable sublanguages. Hence,

$$P_i(L) = \sup C(P_i(L), L_i, A_{iu}),$$

which means that for all $i \in \mathbb{Z}_n$, $P_i(L)$ is controllable with respect to L_i and A_{iu}.

4   Distributed Supervisory Control with a Decomposable Specification

In this section we consider the situation of a distributed plant, thus for which at least one module or subsystem does not have complete observations but only partial observations. For each local plant, the local alphabet admits a partition, denoted by $A_i = A_{o,i} \cup A_{uo,i}, \forall i \in \mathbb{Z}_n$ into locally observable and locally unobservable event sets. The global system has observation set $A_o = \cup_{i=1}^n A_{o,i} \subseteq A = \cup_{i=1}^n A_i$. Globally unobservable events are denoted by $A_{uo} = A \setminus A_o$ and locally unobservable events by $A_{uo,i} = A_i \setminus A_{o,i}$. The projections of the global alphabet into the local ones are denoted by $P_i : A^* \to A_{o,i}^*$, $i = 1, 2$. Partial observations in individual modules are expressed via local projections $P_i^{loc} : A_i^* \to A_{o,i}^*$, while the global projection is denoted by $P : A^* \to A_o^*$.

Definition 10. *Consider a distributed DES. The local plants are said to* agree *on the observability of their common events* if

$$A_{o,i} \cap A_j = A_i \cap A_{o,j}, \ \forall i,j \in \mathbb{Z}_n. \tag{13}$$

The problem is to determine necessary and sufficient conditions for modular control synthesis to equal global control synthesis for a distributed control system. In Theorem 4 a condition similar to mutual controllability is needed. By analogy it is called mutual normality.

Definition 11. *Consider a distributed DES. Local plant languages* $\{L_i \subseteq A_i^*, i \in \mathbb{Z}_n\}$ *are called* mutually normal *if*

$$(P_i^{loc})^{-1} P_i^{loc}(L_i) \cap P_i(P_j)^{-1}(L_j) \subseteq L_i, \ \forall i,j \in \mathbb{Z}_n, \ i \neq j. \tag{14}$$

Mutual normality can be viewed as normality of the local plant languages with respect to the local views of the other plant languages.

Theorem 4. *Modular control synthesis equals global control synthesis for supremal normal sublanguages in case of a distributed DES. Assume that the local plants agree on the observability of their common events.*
If $\{L_i \subseteq A_i^*, \ i \in Z_n\}$ *are mutually normal then*

$$\sup \mathrm{N}(\|_{i=1}^n K_i, \|_{i=1}^n L_i, P) = \|_{i=1}^n \sup \mathrm{N}(K_i, L_i, P_i^{loc}). \tag{15}$$

Conversely, if for fixed local plant languages $\{L_i, \ i \in Z_n\}$ *equation (15) holds true for any* $\{K_i \subseteq L_i, i \in \mathbb{Z}_n\}$, *then*

$$P_i(L) \text{ are normal with respect to } L_i \text{ and } P_i^{loc}, \ \forall i \in \mathbb{Z}_n. \tag{16}$$

Proof. The sufficiency part has been shown in [6], where the coinductive proof principle has been used. Now we show the necessity part of the theorem. Assume now that for fixed local plant languages $\{L_i \ i \in \mathbb{Z}_n\}$ equation (15) holds true. Consider any $i \in \mathbb{Z}_n$ and any local specification languages $K_i \subseteq L_i$. Then it holds true in particular for $K_i := P_i(L)$. Since L is decomposable we have

$$L = \bigcap_{i=1}^n P_i^{-1} P_i(L) = K;$$

$$L = \sup \mathrm{N}(L, L, A_u) = \|_{i=1}^n \sup \mathrm{N}(P_i(L), L_i, P_i^{loc}).$$
$$L \subseteq (P_i)^{-1} \sup \mathrm{N}(P_i(L), L_i, P_i^{loc}), \ \forall i \in \mathbb{Z}_n. \text{ Recall that} \tag{17}$$

$P_i(L) \subseteq L_i$, because L is decomposable. (18)

By applying the projection P_i on both sides of the inclusion (17)
it follows from the monotonicity of projections that

$P_i(L) \subseteq P_i(P_i)^{-1} \sup \mathrm{N}(P_i(L), L_i, P_i^{loc}) = \sup \mathrm{N}(P_i(L), L_i, P_i^{loc})$.

$\sup \mathrm{N}(P_i(L), L_i, P_i^{loc}) \subseteq P_i(L)$,

from the definition of supremal normal sublanguages.

$P_i(L) = \sup \mathrm{N}(P_i(L), L_i, P_i^{loc})$,

which means that for all $i \in \mathbb{Z}_n$, $P_i(L)$ is normal with respect to L_i and P_i^{loc}.

The proof of the above theorem for one direction depends only on the assumption that the local plants agree on the observability of their common events. Hence the following corollary is obtained.

Corollary 2. *If the local plants agree on the observability of their common events then we have*

$$\sup \mathrm{N}(\|_{i=1}^n K_i, \|_{i=1}^n L_i, P) \supseteq \|_{i=1}^n \sup \mathrm{N}(K_i, L_i, P_i^{loc}). \quad (19)$$

Theorem 4 is useful for the computation of (global) supremal normal sublanguages of large distributed plants. If the conditions of the theorem are satisfied, then it is sufficient to compute local supremal normal sublanguages and to synchronize them.

The interest of this theorem should be clear: Under the conditions which are stated it is possible to do the optimal (least restrictive) control synthesis with partial observations locally, and this represents an exponential savings on the computational complexity and makes in fact the optimal control synthesis of large distributed plants feasible.

Let us introduce the notation $\sup \mathrm{CN}(K, L, P, A_u)$ for the supremal (L, P)−normal and controllable sublanguage of K with respect to A_u. Using a single-step algorithm for computation of supremal controllable and normal sublanguages ([8]), we have proven in [4] the sufficiency part of the following theorem:

Theorem 5. *Modular control synthesis equals global control synthesis for supremal controllable and normal sublanguage in case of a distributed DES. Assume that the local plants agree on the controllability of their common events and on the observability of their common events.*

If the local plant languages $\{L_i \subseteq A_i^*,\ i \in Z_n\}$ are mutually controllable and mutually normal then

$$\|_{i=1}^n \sup \mathrm{CN}(K_i, L_i, P_i^{loc}, A_{iu}) = \sup \mathrm{CN}(\|_{i=1}^n K_i, \|_{i=1}^n L_i, P, A_u). \quad (20)$$

Conversely, if for fixed local plant languages $\{L_i\ i \in Z_n\}$ equation (20) holds true for any $\{K_i \subseteq L_i, i \in \mathbb{Z}_n\}$, then for any $i, j \in \mathbb{Z}_n$ with $i \neq j$, $\{P_i(L),\ i \in \mathbb{Z}_n\}$ are (1) normal with respect to L_i and P_i^{loc} and (2) controllable with respect to L_i and A_{iu}.

Proof. The sufficiency was shown in [4]. In view of the preceding theorems for sup C and sup N the necessity part follows.

In [18] there is a procedure to change a plant which does not satisfy the mutual controllability condition to one that satisfies it. It may be that a similar procedure can be found in the future for mutual normality. Nevertheless one cannot hope to find a universal procedure how to make a set of local plant languages mutually normal. Indeed, in the shuffle case mutual normality cannot hold as we show in the next section. However specific methods exist for this simpler case.

Example and Verification of Sufficient Conditions

The purpose of this section is mainly to illustrate our results with an example. Before starting with concrete examples we consider several extreme cases of distributed DES. First of all, if all event alphabets are disjoint, the so called shuffe case, we notice that $P_i(P_j)^{-1}(L_j) = A_i^*$ for any $L_j \subseteq A_j^*$. This means that the condition of mutual normality cannot be satisfied. The intuitive reason is that there is no relation between local subsystems in this case. This is not surprising, because the observations of local agents are in this case completely independent and therefore there is a huge gap between local and global observations.

On the other hand, it is obvious from the definition of mutual normality that in the case of full local observations (all P_i^{loc}'s become identity mappings), mutual normality is trivially satisfied. Another extreme case occurs when all subsystems have the same event alphabets. Then all the P_i's are identity mappings, i.e. the mutual normality becomes usual normality between two languages in a slightly more general sense (the assumption is lifted that one of the languages is a sublanguage of the other). This might justify why we call our condition mutual normality, it is a symmetric notion of normality.

We show an example of a plant composed of two modules, where the commutativity between the supremal normal sublanguages and parallel product does not hold. Therefore mutual normality does not hold either.

Example 1. Let $A = \{a, a_1, a_2, \tau, \tau_1, \tau_2\}$, $A_1 = \{a_1, \tau_1, a, \tau\}$, $A_2 = \{a_2, \tau_2, a, \tau\}$, $A_o = \{a_1, a_2, a\}$, $A_{o,1} = \{a_1, a\}$, and $A_{o,2} = \{a_2, a\}$. Consider the following plant languages and specification sublanguages (the marked languages are not considered):

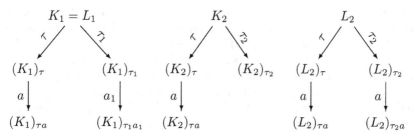

We use the notation $U_1 = \sup N(K_1, L_1, P_1^{loc})$, $U_2 = \sup N(K_2, L_2, P_2^{loc})$, $U = \sup N(K_1, L_1, P_1^{loc}) \parallel \sup N(K_2, L_2, P_2^{loc})$, and $V = \sup N(K_1 \parallel K_2, L_1 \parallel L_2, P)$.

We have trivially that $U_1 = K_1 = L_1$. It is easy to see that $U_2 = \sup \mathrm{N}(K_2, L_2, P_2^{loc}) = \{\varepsilon, \tau, \tau_2\}$. Computing the parallel products $K = K_1 \parallel K_2$ and $L = L_1 \parallel L_2$ yields $K = L$, i.e. we obtain trivially $K = L = V$ as is shown in the diagram below, where $U = U_1 \parallel U_2$ is also computed:

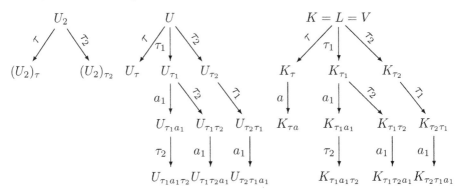

Thus, $U \neq V$, because $U_\tau \overset{a}{\nrightarrow}$, while $V_\tau \overset{a}{\rightarrow}$. Therefore we only have the strict inclusion $U \subset V$ and the commutativity studied in this paper does not hold for this example. According to Theorem 4 mutual normality cannot hold. Indeed, we have

$$(P_1^{loc})^{-1} P_1^{loc}(L_1) \cap P_1(P_2)^{-1}(L_2) = \tau_1^*(\tau\tau_1^* a_1 + a_1\tau_1^*\tau)\tau_1^*,$$

but we have e.g. $(\tau_1)^n \notin L_1$ for $n \geq 2$.

Antipermissive Control Policy

The standard permissive control law is useful for safety control problems only if the specification is observable, otherwise it yields infimal coobservable and controllable superlanguages of K. If K represents safety specifications then these are violated if permissive control policy is applied.

There exists a dual control policy for DES with partial observations, called *antipermissive*. For the supervisor to enable event $a \in A$ it is necessary that all indistinguishable events corresponding to this trace can be prolongated within K (in permissive control policy it is sufficient that one of those strings can be prolongated within K). The interest of the antipermissive control policy is in its safety and the fact that the synthesized languages are observable languages in general larger then supremal normal sublanguages.

Denote by V the supervisor associated with a partial automaton S, and the corresponding antipermissive control policy by $S_A : P(L(G)) \rightarrow \Gamma_c$, where Γ_c is the class of enabled events, also called control patterns (i.e. supersets of the event subset A_u that are always enabled). Algebraically, the antipermissive control policy is defined as follows:

$$S_A(s) = A_{uc} \cup \left\{ \begin{array}{l} a \in A_c : \forall s' \in \mathrm{prefix}(K) \cap P^{-1}P(s) \\ (s'a \in L \Rightarrow s'a \in \mathrm{prefix}(K)) \end{array} \right\}. \tag{21}$$

Similarly as for the permissive control policy the supervisor marks all states that have been marked in the plant and that 'survive' under supervision.

We have formulated in [8] a single-step algorithm for computation of closed-loop languages with respect to the antipermissive control policy. This algorithm has been used in [5] for deriving sufficient conditions under which these languages are preserved by modular (local) control synthesis.

Denote for all $i \in \mathbb{Z}_n$ by $\mathrm{AP}(K_i, L_i, P_i^{loc})$ the closed-loop language corresponding to the local antipermissive control synthesis (with local projection P_i^{loc}, local DES L_i, and local specification K_i). Similarly, $\mathrm{AP}(\|_{i=1}^n K_i, \|_{i=1}^n L_i, P)$ stands for closed-loop language corresponding to the global antipermissive control synthesis.

In Theorem 6 a condition similar to mutual controllability (Wong and Lee, 2002) is used. By analogy it is called mutual observability.

Definition 12. *Consider a distributed DES. Local plant languages* $\{L_i \subseteq A_i^*$, $i \in \mathbb{Z}_n\}$ *are called* mutually observable *if*

$$\forall i, j \in \mathbb{Z}_n, \ i \neq j, \ \forall s, s' \in L_i \ and \ a \in A_{ic}:$$
$$(sa \in P_i(P_j)^{-1}(L_j) \ and \ P_i^{loc}(s) = P_i^{loc}(s') \ and \ s'a \in L_i)$$
$$\Rightarrow \ sa \in L_i. \tag{22}$$

Now we extend the main result of [5] where only sufficient conditions were presented.

Theorem 6. *Modular control synthesis equals global control synthesis for the closed-loop language in case of a completely-observed DES using an antipermissive control policy. Assume that the modular plants agree on the observability of their common events.*

If the local plant languages $\{L_i \subseteq A_i^*, \ i \in Z_n\}$ *are mutually observable then*

$$\mathrm{AP}(\|_{i=1}^n K_i, \|_{i=1}^n L_i, P) = \|_{i=1}^n \mathrm{AP}(K_i, L_i, P_i^{loc}). \tag{23}$$

Conversely, if for fixed local plant languages $\{L_i \ i \in Z_n\}$ *equation (23) holds true for any* $\{K_i \subseteq L_i, i \in \mathbb{Z}_n\}$*, then, for any* $i \neq j$*,* $\{P_i(L), \ i \in \mathbb{Z}_n\}$ *are observable with respect to* L_i *and* $A_{o,i}$*.*

In view of our previous results it is straightforward to show that a neccesary structural condition for local antipermissive control policy to equal global antipermissive control policy is that $\mathrm{AP}(P_i(L), L_i, P_i^{loc}) = P_i(L)$, which means that for all $i \in \mathbb{Z}_n$, $P_i(L)$ is observable with respect to L_i and $A_{i,o}$.

The interest of this theorem should be clear: under the conditions that are stated it is possible to perform the antipermissive control synthesis with partial observations locally, which represents an exponential save on the computational complexity and makes in fact the antipermissive control synthesis of large distributed plants feasible. Recall that under very general conditions we have one inclusion meaning that global antipermissive control synthesis yields in general a larger language that the local antipermissive control synthesis.

5 Modular Supervisory Control with an Indecomposable Specification

In many engineering problems the specification is only defined globally and is not decomposable unlike the plant language. An example is the specification for a communication protocol of a wireless network. In this section the case of general specification languages that are neither necessarily decomposable nor contained in the global plant language is studied. Necessary and sufficient conditions are found with respect to which handling of the global plant is avoided for the computation of supremal controllable sublanguages of (global) indecomposable specification languages.

Consider a modular discrete-event system and assume that the local plants agree on the controllability of their common events. Denote the global plant and the specification languages by L and K, respectively. In our setting, L is decomposable into local plant languages: $L = L_1 \parallel \cdots \parallel L_n$ (note that the L_i may have different alphabets). In most of the works on this topic K is similarly decomposable into local specification languages and $K \subseteq L$. The general case is when this condition is not satisfied and, moreover, K may not be included in L. This case has been studied in [2], where the assumption that all shared events are controllable is used. A condition on K called $G-$observability was needed for local synthesis of the supremal controllable sublanguage.

Instead of local specifications, languages $K_i := K \cap P_i^{-1}(L_i)$ are considered. These will play the role of local components of specification languages, although their alphabet is the global alphabet A. They can be considered as local over-approximations of $K \cap L$, because clearly $K \cap L = \cap_{i=1}^n K_i$.

Definition 13. *Consider a modular DES. The modular plant languages* $\{L_i, \ i \in Z_n\}$ *are called* globally mutually controllable *if*

$$P_j^{-1}(L_j)(A_{ju}) \cap P_i^{-1}(L_i) \subseteq P_j^{-1}(L_j), \ \forall i, j \in \mathbb{Z}_\mathrm{n}, \ i \neq j. \tag{24}$$

Proposition 2. *Consider a modular DES. Global mutual controllability (GMC) is equivalent to the following property:*

$$P_j^{-1}(L_j)A_u \cap P_i^{-1}(L_i) \subseteq P_j^{-1}(L_j), \ \forall i, j \in \mathbb{Z}_\mathrm{n}, \ i \neq j. \tag{25}$$

Proof. Note that the only difference is that A_{ju} in GMC is replaced by A_u. Therefore the new property is clearly stronger then GMC. Maybe surprisingly the converse implication is satisfied as well. Let GMC hold true, $s \in P_j^{-1}(L_j)$, $u \in A_u$, and $su \in P_i^{-1}(L_i)$. Then we have two cases: either $u \in A_j$ or $u \notin A_j$. The former case entails that $u \in A_{ju}$ due to the shared event controllability status assumption. Using GMC we conclude $su \in P_j^{-1}(L_j)$. In the latter case we notice that $P_j(u) = \varepsilon$, i.e. $P_j(su) = P_j(s)$, which means that $P_j(su) \in L_j$, i.e. $s \in P_j^{-1}(L_j)$.

Definition 14. *Consider a modular DES. The modular plant languages* $\{L_i, \ i \in Z_n\}$ *are called* modularly controllable *if*

$$(LA_u) \cap P_i^{-1}(L_i) \subseteq L, \ \forall i \in \mathbb{Z}_\mathrm{n}. \tag{26}$$

Modular controllability is in general weaker than global mutual controllability and it will play the role of a necessary condition.

Proposition 3. *Consider a modular DES. Global mutual controllability (GMC) implies modular controllability.*

Proof. Let for any $i \neq j \in Z_n$:

$$P_j^{-1}(L_j)A_u \cap P_i^{-1}(L_i) \subseteq P_j^{-1}(L_j).$$

Since for $j = i$ the inclusion is trivially true, we have the inclusion for any $i, j \in Z_n$. Then, by taking intersection for j over Z_n we obtain:

$$\bigcap_{j=1}^{n}[P_j^{-1}(L_j)A_u \cap P_i^{-1}(L_i)] \subseteq \bigcap_{i=1}^{n}[P_j^{-1}(L_j).A_u]$$

Since $[\bigcap_{i=1}^{n} P_j^{-1}(L_j)]A_u \subseteq \bigcap_{i=1}^{n}[P_j^{-1}(L_j).A_u]$ we obtain finally, $LA_u \cap P_i^{-1}(L_i) \subseteq L$, i.e. modular controllability (MC).

The next theorem provides novel necesary and sufficient conditions for modular control synthesis to equal global control synthesis. In [9] it was shown only that global mutual controllability is a sufficient condition.

Theorem 7. *Modular control synthesis equals global control synthesis for the supremal controllable sublanguage in case of complete observations and of indecomposable specifications. Consider a modular discrete-event system. Assume that the local plants agree on the controllability of their common events.*

If the local plants $\{L_i, i \in Z_n\}$ are modularly controllable then

$$\sup C(K \cap L, L, A_u) = \bigcap_{i=1}^{n} \sup C(K_i, P_i^{-1}(L_i), A_u). \tag{27}$$

Conversely, if for a given modular plant equality (27) holds true for any global specification K then the local plant languages, $\{L_i, i \in Z_n\}$ are modularly controllable.

6   Distributed Supervisory Control with an Indecomposable Specification

In this section the case is studied of control of a distributed discrete-event system, thus for which one or more of the local plants has only partial observations, and of an indecomposable specification. First a structural condition called global mutual normality is introduced. It is similar to mutual normality in the case of decomposable specification ([3]), but it concerns $P_i^{-1}(L_i)$ instead of L_i.

Definition 15. *Consider a distributed DES. The modular plant languages $\{L_i \subseteq A_i^*, i \in Z_n\}$ are called globally mutually normal if*

$$(P^{-1}PP_j^{-1})(L_j) \cap P_i^{-1}L_i \subseteq P_j^{-1}L_j, \ \forall i, j \in \mathbb{Z}_n, \ i \neq j. \tag{28}$$

Definition 16. *Consider a distributed DES. Modular plant languages* $\{L_i, \ i \in Z_n\}$ *are called* modularly normal *if L is* $(P_i^{-1}(L_i), P)-normal;$ *or, equivalently,*

$$P^{-1}P(L) \cap P_i^{-1}(L_i) \subseteq L, \ \forall i \in \mathbb{Z}_n. \tag{29}$$

Modular normality is in general weaker than global mutual normality (GMN).

Proposition 4. *Consider a distributed DES. Global mutual normality (GMN) implies modular normality (MN).*

Proof. Let GMN holds true, or, equivalently,

$$(P^{-1}PP_j^{-1})(L_j) \cap P_i^{-1}L_i \subseteq P_j^{-1}L_j, \forall i, j \in \mathbb{Z}_n, \ i \neq j.$$

Since for $i = j$ the inclusion becomes trivial, we may assume that the inclusion is satisfied for any $i, j \in Z_n$. We obtain: $P^{-1}PL \cap P_i^{-1}L_i = P^{-1}P(\cap_{i=1}^n P_j^{-1}L_j) \subseteq \cap_{j=1}^n (P^{-1}PP_j^{-1})(L_j) \cap P_i^{-1}L_i \subseteq \cap_{i=1}^n P_j^{-1}L_j = L$, where the last inclusion follows from intersecting both sides of the first inclusion (GMN) for j ranging over Z_n. Thus MN holds true.

Theorem 8. Modular control synthesis equals global control synthesis for the supremal normal sublanguage in case of a distributed DES and of an indecomposable specification. *Consider a distributed DES. Assume that the local plants agree on the observability of their common events.*
If the local plant languages $\{L_i, \ i \in Z_n\}$ *are modularly normal then*

$$\sup N(K \cap L, L, P) = \bigcap_{i=1}^{n} \sup N(K_i, P_i^{-1}(L_i), P). \tag{30}$$

Conversely, if for a given modular plant equality (30) holds true for any global specification $K \subseteq A^*$ *then the local plant (partial) languages* $\{L_i, \ i \in Z_n\}$ *are modularly normal.*

Now we present an example, where it is shown that global mutual normality (GMN) is not a necessary condition.

Example 2. Let $A = \{a, a_1, a_2, \tau, \tau_1, \tau_2\}$, $A_1 = \{a_1, \tau_1, a, \tau\}$, $A_2 = \{a_2, \tau_2, a, \tau\}$, $A_o = \{a_1, a_2, a\}$, $A_{o,1} = \{a_1, a\}$, and $A_{o,2} = \{a_2, a\}$. Consider the following local plant languages (the marked languages are not considered): Let prefix$(K) = \{\varepsilon, a, a_1, a_1 a_2\}$. One can easily verify that K is not decomposable. Indeed, the inclusion prefix$(K) \subset P_1^{-1}P_1(\text{prefix}(K)) \cap P_2^{-1}P_2(\text{prefix}(K))$ is strict, i.e. prefix$(K) \neq P_1^{-1}P_1(\text{prefix}(K)) \cap P_2^{-1}P_2(\text{prefix}(K))$. Computing further the parallel product $L = L_1 \parallel L_2$ yields:

$$\sup N(K \cap L, L, P) = \{\varepsilon\}.$$

Note that in this example $K_i = K \cap P_i^{-1}L_i = K$ for $i = 1, 2$. It is also easy to see that $\sup N(K_i, P_i^{-1}(L_i), P) = \{\varepsilon\}$ as well for $i = 1, 2$. i.e. the commutativity holds trivially true.

On the other hand, global mutual normality does not hold. We have e.g.

$$\tau_1 \in (P^{-1}PP_1^{-1})(L_1) \cap (P_2)^{-1}(L_2) \setminus P_1^{-1}(L_1).$$

Modular Computation of Supremal Controllable and Normal Sublanguages

Theorem 9. Modular control synthesis equals global control synthesis for the supremal controllable and normal sublanguage in case of a distributed DES and of an indecomposable specification. *Consider a distributed DES. Assume that the local plants (1) agree on the controllability of their common events and (2) agree on the observability of their common events.*

If the local plant languages $\{L_i,\ i \in Z_n\}$ are modularly controllable and modularly normal, then

$$\sup CN(K \cap L, L, P, A_u) = \bigcap_{i=1}^{n} \sup CN(K_i, P_i^{-1}(L_i), P, A_u). \tag{31}$$

Conversely, if for a given modular plant equality (31) holds true for any global specification K then local plant languages $\{L_i,\ i \in Z_n\}$ are modularly controllable and modularly normal.

Proof. The proof of sufficiency relies on a coinduction-like algorithm for compuation of $\sup CN$ from [8] and the coinduction proof principle. The proof for necessity is the same as in the previous theorems.

Note that global mutual controllability together with global mutual normality imply modular controllability and modular normality, and the former notions are easier to verify than the latter ones, because they do not include the global plant. In fact, although modular controllability and modular normality can be checked in polynomial time (but in size of global DES!), their verification requires the construction of the global system, which contradicts the modular approach, because the size of global system grows exponentially with the number of components. On the other hand verification of global mutual controllability and global mutual normality is polynomial in the size of the local components.

Antipermissive Control Policy

In this subsection our intention is to generalize the results concerning modular computation of supremal normal sublanguages of global specifications to modular computation of closed-loop languages using the antipermissive control policy. This will be done in the very same way as was done in section 4 for local specification. Unlike the setting of section 4 we will work with $P_i^{-1}(L_i)$ instead of L_i. Since we work with the global alphabet, synchronous composition coincides with intersection. The concept of modular observability using Definition 2 is needed:

Definition 17. *Consider a distributed DES. The modular plant languages $\{L_i,\ i \in Z_n\}$ are called* modularly observable *if for any $i \in Z_n$ we have that L is observable with respect to $P_i^{-1}(L_i)$ and A_o.*

Theorem 10. Modular control synthesis equals global control synthesis for the closed-loop language in case of a distributed DES, of an indecomposable specification, and of an antipermissive control policy. *Consider a distributed discrete-event system. Assume that the local plants (1) agree on the controllability of their common events and (2) agree on the observability of their common events.*

If $\{L_i,\ i \in Z_n\}$ are modularly observable then

$$\mathrm{AP}(K \cap L, L, P) = \bigcap_{i=1}^{n} \mathrm{AP}(K_i, P_i^{-1}(L_i), P). \tag{32}$$

Conversely, if for a given modular plant equality (32) holds true for any global specification K then the local plant (partial) languages $\{L_i,\ i \in Z_n\}$ are modularly observable.

7   Conclusion

An overview has been presented of different methods for modular control of DES together with new methods and conditions. Most of the possible special cases of modular and distributed control have been covered (both fully and partially observed systems, both local and global specifications). Among the new results we provided for all presented cases necessary conditions for modular control synthesis to equal global control synthesis. Antipermissive control policy was proposed for the global specification and necessary and sufficient conditions have been presented for local antipermissive control policy to yield the same result as computationally much more efficient local antipermissive control policy.

These results are important for the optimal supervisory control of large distributed plants, because with respect to the derived conditions control synthesis can be implemented modularly. All the sufficient conditions we have presented are easier to check than their counterparts for global systems. The structural condition do not depend on a particular specification, which is very important for global (indecomposable) specifications.

Acknowledgements. Partial financial support of the Grant GA AV No. B100190609 and of the Academy of Sciences of the Czech Republic, Institutional Research Plan No. AV0Z10190503 is gratefully acknowledged.

References

1. S.G. Cassandras and S. Lafortune. *Introduction to Discrete Event Systems*, Kluwer Academic Publishers, Dordrecht 1999.
2. B. Gaudin and H. Marchand. Modular Supervisory Control of a Class of Concurrent Discrete Event Systems. Proceedings *WODES'04*, Workshop on Discrete-Event Systems, pp. 181-186, Reims, September 22-24, 2004.

3. J. Komenda and J.H. van Schuppen. Supremal Normal Sublanguages of Large Distributed Discrete-Event Systems. Proceedings *WODES'04*, Workshop on Discrete-Event Systems, Reims, September 22-24, 2004.
4. J. Komenda. Modular Control of Large Distributed Discrete-Event Systems with Partial Observations. In Proceedings of the 15th International Conference on Systems Science, Vol. II, pp. 175-184, Wroclaw, Poland, September 2004.
5. J. Komenda and J. H. van Schuppen. Modular antipermissive control of discrete-event systems. Proceedings of IFAC World Congress 2005, Prague, July 2005.
6. J. Komenda and J. H. van Schuppen. Supremal Sublanguages of General Specification Languages Arising in Modular Control of Discrete-Event Systems. Proceedings of Joint 44th IEEE Conference on Decision and Control and European Control Conference, Sevilla, pp. 2775-2780, December 2005.
7. J. Komenda, J. H. van Schuppen. Modular control of discrete-event systems with coalgebra. Submitted, August 2005.
8. J. Komenda and J. H. van Schuppen. Control of Discrete-Event Systems with Partial Observations Using Coalgebra and Coinduction. Discrete Event Dynamical Systems: Theory and Applications 15(3), 257-315, 2005.
9. J. Komenda and J. H. van Schuppen. Optimal Solutions of Modular Supervisory Control Problems with Indecomposable Specification Languages. Proceedings International Workshop on Discrete Event Systems (WODES), 2006, to appear.
10. M. Lamouchi and J.G. Thistle. Effective Control Synthesis For Discrete Event Systems Under Partial Observations. In Proceedings of the IEEE Conference on Decision and Control, 2000.
11. F. Lin and W.M. Wonham, On Observability of Discrete-Event Systems, *Information Sciences*,44: 173-198, 1988.
12. R. Milner. Communication and Concurrency. *Prentice Hall International Series in Computer Science*. Prentice Hall International, New York, 1989.
13. A. Pnueli and R. Rosner. Distributed reactive systems are hard to synthesize, *Proceedings of the 1990 IEEE Symposium on the Foundations of Computer Science*, IEEE, New York, 1990, 746–757.
14. P.J. Ramadge and W.M. Wonham. The Control of Discrete-Event Systems. *Proc. IEEE*, 77:81-98, 1989.
15. J.J.M.M. Rutten. Universal Coalgebra: A Theory of Systems. *Theoretical Computer Science* 249(1):3-80, 2000.
16. S. Tripakis. Undecidable Problems of Decentralized Observation and Control. In Proceedings of the IEEE Conference on Decision and Control, 2001.
17. J.N. Tsitsiklis. On the Control of Discrete-Event Dynamical Systems, *Mathematics of Control, Signal, and Systems*, 95-107, 1989.
18. K.C. Wong and S. Lee. Structural Decentralized Control of Concurrent Discrete-Event Systems. *European Journal of Control*, 8:477-491, 2002.
19. W.M. Wonham. Lecture notes on control of discrete-event systems, University of Toronto, Department ECE, Toronto, 2005.
http://www.control.toronto.edu/people/profs/wonham/wonham.html
20. W.M. Wonham and P.J. Ramadge. On the Supremal Controllable Sublanguage of a Given Language, *SIAM J. Control Optim.*, 25:637-659, 1987.

Model-Based Security Engineering with UML: Introducing Security Aspects

Jan Jürjens*

Dep. of Informatics, TU Munich, Germany

Abstract. Developing security-critical systems is difficult and there are many well-known examples of security weaknesses exploited in practice. Thus a sound methodology supporting secure systems development is urgently needed.

Our aim is to aid the difficult task of developing security-critical systems in a formally based approach using the notation of the Unified Modeling Language. We present the extension UMLsec of UML that allows one to express security-relevant information within the diagrams in a system specification. UMLsec is defined in form of a UML profile using the standard UML extension mechanisms. In particular, the associated constraints give criteria to evaluate the security aspects of a system design, by referring to a formal semantics of a simplified fragment of UML. In this tutorial exposition, we concentrate on an approach to develop and analyze security-critical specifications and implementations using aspect-oriented modeling.

1   Introduction

Constructing security-critical systems in a sound and well-founded way poses high challenges. To support this task, we defined the extension UMLsec of the UML [Jür01, Jür02, Jür04]. Various recurring security requirements (such as secrecy, integrity, authenticity and others), as well as assumptions on the security of the system environment, are offered as stereotypes and tags by the UMLsec definition. These can be included in UML diagrams firstly to keep track of the information. Using the associated constraints that refer to a formal semantics of the used simplified fragment of UML, the properties can be used to evaluate diagrams of various kinds and to indicate possible vulnerabilities. One can thus verify that the stated security requirements, if fulfilled, enforce a given security policy. One can also ensure that the requirements are actually met by the given UML specification of the system. This way we can encapsulate knowledge on prudent security engineering and thereby make it available to developers which may not be specialized in security. One can also go further by checking whether the constraints associated with the UMLsec stereotypes are fulfilled in a given specification, if desired by performing an automated formal security verification using automated theorem provers for first order logic or model-checkers. In

---

* http://www4.in.tum.de/~juerjens

F.S. de Boer et al. (Eds.): FMCO 2005, LNCS 4111, pp. 64–87, 2006.

this tutorial exposition, we present in particular an Aspect-Oriented Modeling approach which separates complex security mechanisms (which implement the security aspect model) from the core functionality of the system (the primary model) in order to allow a security verification of the particularly security-critical parts, and also of the composed model.

We explain how to formally evaluate UML specifications for security requirements in Sect. 2. We introduce a fragment of the UMLsec notation in Sect. 3 and explain the various stereotypes with examples. In Sect. 4, we explain how one can specify security aspects in UMLsec models and how these are woven into the primary model using our approach. Sect. 5 explains our code analysis framework. Throughout the paper we demonstrate our approach using a variant of the Internet protocol Transport Layer Security (TLS). In Sect. 6, we report on experiences from using our approach in an industrial setting. After comparing our research with related work, we close with a discussion and an outlook on ongoing research.

2   Security Evaluation of UML Diagrams

A UMLsec diagram is essentially a UML diagram where security properties and requirements are inserted as stereotypes with tags and constraints, although certain restrictions apply to enable automated formal verification. UML offers three main "light-weight" language extension mechanisms: stereotypes, tagged values, and constraints [UML03].[1] Stereotypes define new types of modeling elements extending the semantics of existing types or classes in the UML metamodel. Their notation consists of the name of the stereotype written in double angle brackets « », attached to the extended model element. This model element is then interpreted according to the meaning ascribed to the stereotype. One way of explicitly defining a property is by attaching a tagged value to a model element. A tagged value is a name-value pair, where the name is referred to as the *tag*. The corresponding notation is {*tag* = *value*} with the tag name *tag* and a corresponding *value* to be assigned to the tag. If the value is of type Boolean, one usually omits {*tag* = *false*}, and writes {*tag*} instead of {*tag* = *true*}. Another way of adding information to a model element is by attaching logical *constraints* to refine its semantics (for example written in first-order predicate logic).

To construct an extension of the UML one collects the relevant definitions of stereotypes, tagged values, and constraints into a so-called profile [UML03]. For UMLsec, we give validation rules that evaluate a model with respect to listed security requirements. Many security requirements are formulated regarding the behavior of a system in interaction with its environment (in particular, with potential adversaries). To verify these requirements, we use the formal semantics defined below.

---

[1] In the following, we use UML 1.5 since the official DTD for UML 2.0, which would be needed by our tools, has not yet been released at the time of writing.

2.1   Outline of Formal Semantics

For some of the constraints used to define the UMLsec extensions we need to refer to a precisely defined semantics of behavioral aspects, because verifying whether they hold for a given UML model may be mathematically non-trivial. Firstly, the semantics is used to define these constraints in a mathematically precise way. Secondly, we have developed mechanical tool support for analyzing UML specifications for security requirements using model-checkers and automated theorem provers for first-order logic [Jür05b]. For this, a precise definition of the meaning of the specifications is necessary. For security analysis, the security-relevant information from the security-oriented stereotypes is then incorporated (cf. Sect. 2.3).

The semantics for the fragment of UML used for UMLsec is defined formally in [Jür04] using so-called *UML Machines*, which is a kind of state machine with input/output interfaces similar to the Focus model [BS01], whose behavior can be specified in a notation similar to that of Abstract State Machines [Gur00], and which is equipped with UML-type communication mechanisms. Because of space restrictions, we cannot recall the definition of UML Machines nor the formal semantics here completely. Instead, we use an abstraction of UML Machines in terms of their associated input/output functions to define precisely and explain the interfaces of the that part of our UML semantics that we need here to define the UMLsec profile. Our semantics includes simplified versions of the following kinds of diagrams:

Class diagrams define the static class structure of the system: classes with attributes, operations, and signals and relationships between classes. On the instance level, the corresponding diagrams are called *object diagrams.*

Statechart diagrams (or *state diagrams*) give the dynamic behavior of an individual object or component: events may cause a change in state or an execution of actions. For our approach to be as widely applicable as possible and for the purposes of the current paper, we use a general definition of the notion of a component by which a component is a part of the system which interacts with the rest of the system (and possibly the system environment) through a well-defined interface (this definition is inspired for example by the view taken in [BS01]).

Sequence diagrams describe interaction between objects or system components via message exchange.

Activity diagrams specify the control flow between several components within the system, usually at a higher degree of abstraction than statecharts and sequence diagrams. They can be used to put objects or components in the context of overall system behavior or to explain use cases in more detail.

Deployment diagrams describe the physical layer on which the system is to be implemented.

Subsystems (a certain kind of *packages*) integrate the information between the different kinds of diagrams and between different parts of the system specification.

There is another kind of diagrams, the use case diagrams, which describe typical interactions between a user and a computer system. They are often used in an informal way for negotiation with a customer before a system is designed. We will not use it in the following. Additionally to sequence diagrams, there are *collaboration diagrams*, which present similar information. Also, there are *component diagrams*, presenting part of the information contained in deployment diagrams.

The used fragment of UML is simplified to keep automated formal verification that is necessary for some of the more subtle security requirements feasible. Note that in our approach we identify system objects with UML objects, which is suitable for our purposes. Also, we are mainly concerned with instance-based models. Although simplified, our choice of a subset of UML is reasonable for our needs, as we have demonstrated in several industrial case-studies (some of which are documented in [Jür04]).

The formal semantics for subsystems incorporates the formal semantics of the diagrams contained in a subsystem. It

- models actions and internal activities explicitly (rather than treating them as atomic given events), in particular the operations and the parameters employed in them,
- provides passing of messages with their parameters between objects or components specified in different diagrams, including a dispatching mechanism for events and the handling of actions, and thus
- allows in principle whole specification documents to be based on a formal foundation.

In particular, we can compose subsystems by including them into other subsystems.

Objects, and more generally system components, can communicate by exchanging messages. These consist of the message name, and possibly arguments to the message (which will be assumed to be elements of the set **Exp** defined in Sect. 2.2). Message names may be prefixed with object or subsystem instance names. Each object or component may receive messages received in an input queue and release messages to an output queue.

In our model, every object or subsystem instance O has associated multi-sets inQu_O and outQu_O (*event queues*). Our formal semantics models sending a message $msg = op(exp_1, \ldots, exp_n) \in$ **Events** from an object or subsystem instance S to an object or subsystem instance R as follows:

(1) S places the message $R.msg$ into its multi-set outQu_S.
(2) A scheduler distributes the messages from out-queues to the intended in-queues (while removing the message head); in particular, $R.msg$ is removed from outQu_S and msg added to inQu_R.
(3) R removes msg from its in-queue and processes its content.

In the case of operation calls, we also need to keep track of the sender to allow sending return signals. This way of modeling communication allows for a very flexible treatment; for example, we can modify the behavior of the scheduler to take account of knowledge on the underlying communication layer (for example regarding security issues, see Sect. 2.3).

At the level of single objects, behavior is modeled using statecharts, or (in special cases such as protocols) possibly as using sequence diagrams. The internal activities contained at states of these statecharts can again be defined each as a statechart, or alternatively, they can be defined directly using UML Machines.

Using subsystems, one can then define the behavior of a system component C by including the behavior of each of the objects or components directly contained in C, and by including an activity diagram that coordinates the respective activities of the various components and objects.

Thus for each object or component C of a given system, our semantics defines a function $[\![C]\!]()$ which

- takes a multi-set I of input messages and a component state S and
- outputs a set $[\![C]\!](I, S)$ of pairs (O, T) where O is a multi-set of output messages and T the new component state (it is a *set* of pairs because of the non-determinism that may arise)

together with an *initial state* S_0 of the component.

Specifically, the behavioral semantics $[\![D]\!]()$ of a statechart diagram D models the run-to-completion semantics of UML statecharts. As a special case, this gives us the semantics for activity diagrams. Any sequence diagram $\mathcal{S}$ gives us the behavior $[\![\mathcal{S}.C]\!]()$ of each contained component C.

Subsystems group together diagrams describing different parts of a system: a system component $\mathcal{C}$ given by a subsystem $\mathcal{S}$ may contain subcomponents $\mathcal{C}_1, \ldots, \mathcal{C}_n$. The behavioral interpretation $[\![\mathcal{S}]\!]()$ of $\mathcal{S}$ is defined as follows:

(1) It takes a multi-set of input events.
(2) The events are distributed from the input multi-set and the link queues connecting the subcomponents and given as arguments to the functions defining the behavior of the intended recipients in $\mathcal{S}$.
(3) The output messages from these functions are distributed to the link queues of the links connecting the sender of a message to the receiver, or given as the output from $[\![\mathcal{S}]\!]()$ when the receiver is not part of $\mathcal{S}$.

When performing security analysis, after the last step, the adversary model may modify the contents of the link queues in a certain way explained in Sect. 2.3.

2.2 Modeling Cryptography

We introduce some sets to be used in modeling cryptographic data in a UML specification and its security analysis.

We assume a set **Keys** with a partial injective map $(\ )^{-1} : \textbf{Keys} \to \textbf{Keys}$. The elements in its domain (which may be public) can be used for encryption and for verifying signatures, those in its range (usually assumed to be secret) for decryption and signing. We assume that every key is either an encryption or decryption key, or both: Any key k satisfying $k^{-1} = k$ is called *symmetric*,

- _ :: _   (concatenation)
- **head**(_) and **tail**(_)   (head and tail of a concatenation)
- {_}_   (encryption)
- $\mathcal{D}ec\__(\_)$ (decryption)
- $\mathcal{S}ign\__(\_)$ (signing)
- $\mathcal{E}xt\__(\_)$ (extracting from signature)
- $\mathcal{H}ash(\_)$ (hashing)

Fig. 1. Abstract Crypto Operations

the others are called *asymmetric*. We assume that the numbers of symmetric and asymmetric keys are both infinite. We fix infinite sets **Var** of *variables* and **Data** of *data values*. We assume that **Keys**, **Var**, and **Data** are mutually disjoint. **Data** may also include *nonces* and other secrets.

To define the *algebra of cryptographic expressions* **Exp** one considers a term algebra generated from ground data in **Var**∪**Keys**∪**Data** using the symbolic operations in Fig. 1. In that term algebra, one defines the equations $\mathcal{D}ec_{K^{-1}}(\{E\}_K)$ $= E$ and $\mathcal{E}xt_K(\mathcal{S}ign_{K^{-1}}(E)) = E$ (for all $E \in$ **Exp** and $K \in$ **Keys**) and the usual laws regarding concatenation, head(), and tail(). We write $\mathbf{fst}(E) \overset{\text{def}}{=} \mathbf{head}(E)$, $\mathbf{snd}(E) \overset{\text{def}}{=} \mathbf{head}(\mathbf{tail}(E))$, and $\mathbf{thd}(E) \overset{\text{def}}{=} \mathbf{head}(\mathbf{tail}(\mathbf{tail}(E)))$ for each $E \in$ **Exp**.

This symbolic model for cryptographic operations implies that we assume cryptography to be perfect, in the sense that an adversary cannot "guess" an encrypted value without knowing the decryption key. Also, we assume that one can detect whether an attempted decryption is successful. See for example [AJ01] for a formal discussion of these assumptions.

Based on this formalization of cryptographical operations, important conditions on security-critical data (such as freshness, secrecy, integrity) can then be formulated at the level of UML diagrams in a mathematically precise way (see Sect. 3).

In the following, we will often consider *subalgebras* of **Exp**. These are subsets of **Exp** which are closed under the operations used to define **Exp** (such as concatenation, encryption, decryption etc.). For each subset E of **Exp** there exists a unique smallest (wrt. subset inclusion) **Exp**-subalgebra containing E, which we call **Exp**-*subalgebra generated by E*. Intuitively, it can be constructed from E by iteratively adding all elements in **Exp** reachable by applying the operations used to define **Exp** above. It can be seen as the knowledge one can obtain from a given set E of data by iteratively applying publicly available operations to it (such as concatenation and encryption etc.) and will be used to model the knowledge an attacker may gain from a set E of data obtained for example by eavesdropping on Internet connections.

2.3   Security Analysis of UML Diagrams

Our modular UML semantics allows a rather natural modeling of potential adversary behavior. We can model specific types of adversaries that can attack different parts of the system in a specified way. For example, an attacker of type *insider* may be able to intercept the communication links in a company-wide local area network. Several such adversary types are predefined in UMLsec and can be used directly (see Sect. 3). Advanced users can also define adversary types themselves by making use of threat sets defined below. If it is unknown which adversary type should be considered, one can use the most general adversary that has the capabilities of all possible adverary types. We model the actual behavior of the adversary by defining a class of UML Machines that can access the communication links of the system in a specified way. To evaluate the security of the system with respect to the given type of adversary, we consider the joint execution of the system with any UML Machine in this class. This way of reasoning allows an intuitive formulation of many security properties. Since the actual verification is rather indirect this way, we also give alternative intrinsic ways of defining security properties below, which are more manageable, and show that they are equivalent to the earlier ones.

Thus for a security analysis of a given UMLsec subsystem specification $\mathcal{S}$, we need to model potential adversary behavior. We model specific types of adversaries that can attack different parts of the system in a specified way. For this we assume a function $\mathsf{Threats}_A(s)$ which takes an *adversary type* A and a stereotype s and returns a subset of $\{\mathsf{delete}, \mathsf{read}, \mathsf{insert}, \mathsf{access}\}$ (*abstract threats*). These functions arise from the specification of the physical layer of the system under consideration using deployment diagrams. They are predefined for the standard UMLsec adversary types, as explained in Sect. 3, but can also be defined by the advanced users themselves. For a link l in a deployment diagram in $\mathcal{S}$, we then define the set $\mathsf{threats}_A^{\mathcal{S}}(l)$ of *concrete threats* to be the smallest set satisfying the following conditions:

If each node n that l is contained in[2] carries a stereotype s_n with $\mathsf{access} \in \mathsf{Threats}_A(s_n)$ then:

- If l carries a stereotype s with $\mathsf{delete} \in \mathsf{Threats}_A(s)$ then $\mathsf{delete} \in \mathsf{threats}_A^{\mathcal{S}}(l)$.
- If l carries a stereotype s with $\mathsf{insert} \in \mathsf{Threats}_A(s)$ then $\mathsf{insert} \in \mathsf{threats}_A^{\mathcal{S}}(l)$.
- If l carries a stereotype s with $\mathsf{read} \in \mathsf{Threats}_A(s)$ then $\mathsf{read} \in \mathsf{threats}_A^{\mathcal{S}}(l)$.
- If l is connected to a node that carries a stereotype t with $\mathsf{access} \in \mathsf{Threats}_A(t)$ then $\{\mathsf{delete}, \mathsf{insert}, \mathsf{read}\} \subseteq \mathsf{threats}_A^{\mathcal{S}}(l)$.

The idea is that $\mathsf{threats}_A^{\mathcal{A}}(x)$ specifies the *threat scenario* against a component or link x in the UML Machine System $\mathcal{A}$ that is associated with an adversary type A. On the one hand, the threat scenario determines, which data the adversary can obtain by *accessing* components, on the other hand, it determines, which actions the adversary is permitted by the threat scenario to apply to the concerned links. delete means that the adversary may delete the messages in the corresponding link queue, read allows him to read the messages in the link queue, and insert allows him to insert messages in the link queue.

Then we model the actual behavior of an adversary of type A as a *type A adversary machine*. This is a state machine which has the following data:

---

[2] Note that nodes and subsystems may be nested one in another.

- a control state control $\in$ State,
- a set of *current adversary knowledge* $\mathcal{K} \subseteq \mathbf{Exp}$, and
- for each possible control state $c \in$ State and set of knowledge $K \subseteq \mathbf{Exp}$, we have
  - a set $\mathsf{Delete}_{c,K}$ which may contain the name of any link l with delete $\in$ threats$_A^S(l)$
  - a set $\mathsf{Insert}_{c,K}$ which may contain any pair (l, E) where l is the name of a link with insert $\in$ threats$_A^S(l)$, and $E \in \mathcal{K}$, and
  - a set $\mathsf{newState}_{c,k} \subseteq$ State of states.

The machine is executed from a specified initial state control $:=$ control$_0$ with a specified *initial knowledge* $\mathcal{K} := \mathcal{K}_0$ iteratively, where each iteration proceeds according to the following steps:

(1) The contents of all link queues belonging to a link l with read $\in$ threats$_A^S(l)$ are added to $\mathcal{K}$.
(2) The content of any link queue belonging to a link $l \in \mathsf{Delete}_{\mathsf{control},\mathcal{K}}$ is mapped to $\emptyset$.
(3) The content of any link queue belonging to a link l is enlarged with all expressions E where $(l, E) \in \mathsf{Insert}_{\mathsf{control},\mathcal{K}}$.
(4) The next control state is chosen non-deterministically from the set $\mathsf{newState}_{\mathsf{control},\mathcal{K}}$.

The set $\mathcal{K}_0$ of initial knowledge contains all data values v given in the UML specification under consideration for which each node n containing v carries a stereotype s_n with access $\in$ Threats$_A(s_n)$. In a given situation, $\mathcal{K}_0$ may also be specified to contain additional data (for example, public encryption keys).

Note that an adversary A able to remove all values sent over the link l (that it, delete$_l \in$ threats$_A^S(l)$) may not be able to selectively remove a value e with known meaning from l: For example, the messages sent over the Internet within a virtual private network are encrypted. Thus, an adversary who is unable to break the encryption may be able to delete all messages undiscrimatorily, but not a single message whose meaning would be known to him.

To evaluate the security of the system with respect to the given type of adversary, we then define the *execution of the subsystem $\mathcal{S}$ in presence of an adversary of type A* to be the function $[\![\mathcal{S}]\!]_A()$ defined from $[\![\mathcal{S}]\!]()$ by applying the modifications from the adversary machine to the link queues as a fourth step in the definition of $[\![\mathcal{S}]\!]()$ as follows:

(4) The type A adversary machine is applied to the link queues as detailed above.

Thus after each iteration of the system execution, the adversary may non-deterministically change the contents of link queues in a way depending on the level of physical security as described in the deployment diagram (see Sect. 3).

There are results which simplify the analysis of the adversary behavior defined above, which are useful for developing mechanical tool support, for example to check whether the security properties secrecy and integrity (see below) are provided by a given specification. These are beyond the scope of the current paper and can be found in [Jür04].

One possibility to specify security requirements is to define an idealized system model where the required security property evidently holds (for example, because all links and components are guaranteed to be secure by the physical layer specified in the deployment diagram), and to prove that the system model under consideration is behaviorally equivalent to the idealized one, using a notion of behavioral equivalence of UML models. This is explained in detail in [Jür04].

In the following subsection, we consider alternative ways of specifying the important security properties secrecy and integrity which do not require one to explicitly construct such an idealized system and which are used in the remaining parts of this paper.

2.4 Important Security Properties

As an example, the formal definitions of the important security property secrecy is considered in this section following the standard approach of [DY83]. The formalization of secrecy used in the following relies on the idea that a process specification preserves the secrecy of a piece of data d if the process never sends out any information from which d could be derived, even in interaction with an adversary. More precisely, d is leaked if there is an adversary of the type arising from the given threat scenario that does not initially know d and an input sequence to the system such that after the execution of the system given the input in presence of the adversary, the adversary knows d (where "knowledge", "execution" etc. have to be formalized). Otherwise, d is said to be kept secret.

Thus we come to the following definition.

Definition 1. *We say that a subsystem S preserves the secrecy of an expression E from adversaries of type A if E never appears in the knowledge set $\mathcal{K}$ of A during execution of $[\![S]\!]_A()$.*

This definition is especially convenient to verify if one can give an upper bound for the set of knowledge $\mathcal{K}$, which is often possible when the security-relevant part of the specification of the system S is given as a sequence of command schemata of the form *await event e – check condition g – output event e'* (for example when using UML sequence diagrams or statecharts for specifying security protocols, see Sect. 3).

3 The UMLsec Extension

We can only shortly recall part of the UMLsec notation here for space reasons. A complete account can be found in [Jür04]. In Table 1 we give some of the stereotypes from UMLsec, in Table 2 the associated tags, and in Table 3 the threats corresponding to the default adversary (which define the "security semantics" of the UMLsec models). The constraints connected to the stereotypes

Table 1. UMLsec stereotypes (excerpt)

Stereotype	Base Class	Tags	Constraints	Description
Internet	link			Internet connection
encrypted	link			encrypted connection
LAN	link			LAN connection
secure links	subsystem		dependency security matched by links	enforces secure communication links
secrecy	dependency			assumes secrecy
integrity	dependency			assumes integrity
secure dependency	subsystem		《call》, 《send》 respect data security	structural interaction data security
critical	object	secrecy, integrity		critical object
data security	subsystem		provides secrecy	basic datasecurity requirements

Table 2. UMLsec tags (excerpt)

Tag	Stereotype	Type	Multipl.	Description
secrecy	critical	String	*	data secrecy
integrity	critical	String	*	data integrity

are explained in detail below. They can be formalized in first-order logic and thus verified by an automated first-order logic theorem prover, which is part of our UML analysis tool suite.

The primary model is a set of UML models and the dynamic aspect are weaved in by including the stereotypes defined above.

Internet, encrypted, LAN: These stereotypes on links (resp. nodes) in deployment diagrams denote the corresponding requirements on communication links (resp. system nodes), namely that they are implemented as Internet links, encrypted Internet links, resp. as LAN links. We require that each link or node carries at most one of these stereotypes. For each adversary type A, we have a function $\mathsf{Threats}_A(s)$ from each stereotype

$$s \in \{\langle\!\langle \mathsf{Internet} \rangle\!\rangle, \langle\!\langle \mathsf{encrypted} \rangle\!\rangle, \langle\!\langle \mathsf{LAN} \rangle\!\rangle\}$$

to a set of strings $\mathsf{Threats}_A(s) \subseteq \{\mathsf{delete}, \mathsf{read}, \mathsf{insert}, \mathsf{access}\}$ under the following conditions:

- for a node stereotype s, we have $\mathsf{Threats}_A(s) \subseteq \{\mathsf{access}\}$ and
- for a link stereotype s, we have $\mathsf{Threats}_A(s) \subseteq \{\mathsf{delete}, \mathsf{read}, \mathsf{insert}\}$.

Thus $\mathsf{Threats}_A(s)$ specifies which kinds of actions an adversary of type A can apply to node or links stereotyped s. This way we can evaluate UML specifications using the approach explained in Sect. 2.1. We make use of this for the constraints of the remaining stereotypes of the profile.

Table 3. Some threats from the *default* attacker

Stereotype	Threats$_{default}$()
Internet	{delete,read,insert}
encrypted	{delete}
LAN	∅

As an example the threat sets associated with the default adversary type are given in Table 3.

secure links: This stereotype, which may label (instances of) subsystems, is used to ensure that security requirements on the communication are met by the physical layer. More precisely, the constraint enforces that for each dependency d with stereotype $s \in \{\text{«secrecy»}, \text{«integrity»}\}$ between subsystems or objects on different nodes n, m, we have a communication link l between n and m with stereotype t such that

- in the case of $s = \text{«secrecy»}$, we have read $\notin$ Threats$_A(t)$, and
- in the case of $s = \text{«integrity»}$, we have insert $\notin$ Threats$_A(t)$.

Example. In Fig. 2, given the *default* adversary type, the constraint for the stereotype «secure links» is violated: The model does not provide communication secrecy against the *default* adversary, because the Internet communication link between web-server and client does not give the needed security level according to the Threats$_{default}(Internet)$ scenario. Intuitively, the reason is that Internet connections do not provide secrecy against default adversaries. Technically, the constraint is violated, because the dependency carries the stereotype «secrecy», but for the stereotype «Internet» of corresponding link we have read $\in$ Threats$_{default}(Internet)$.

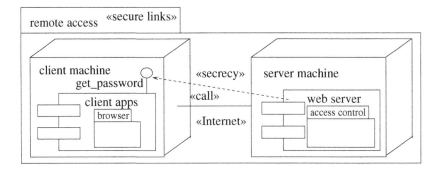

Fig. 2. Example *secure links* usage

secrecy, integrity: « call » or « send » dependencies in object or component diagrams stereotyped « secrecy » (resp. « integrity ») are supposed to provide secrecy (resp. integrity) for the data that is sent along them as arguments or return values of operations or signals. This stereotype is used in the constraint for the stereotype « secure links ».

secure dependency: This stereotype, used to label subsystems containing object diagrams or static structure diagrams, ensures that the « call » and « send » dependencies between objects or subsystems respect the security requirements on the data that may be communicated along them, as given by the tags {secrecy} and {integrity} of the stereotype « critical ». More exactly, the constraint enforced by this stereotype is that if there is a « call » or « send » dependency from an object (or subsystem) C to an interface I of an object (or subsystem) D then the following conditions are fulfilled.

- For any message name n in I, n appears in the tag {secrecy} (resp. {integrity}) in C if and only if it does so in D.
- If a message name in I appears in the tag {secrecy} (resp. {integrity}) in C then the dependency is stereotyped « secrecy » (resp. « integrity »).

If the dependency goes directly to another object (or subsystem) without involving an interface, the same requirement applies to the trivial interface containing all messages of the server object.

Example. Figure 3 shows a key generation subsystem stereotyped with the requirement « secure dependency ». The given specification violates the constraint for this stereotype, since the Random generator and the « call » dependency do not provide the security levels for random() required by Key generator. More precisely, the constraint is violated, because the message *random* is required to be secret by Key generator (by the tag {secrecy} in Key generator), but it is not guaranteed to be secret by Random generator (in fact there are no secret messages in Random generator and so the tag {secrecy} is missing), and also the

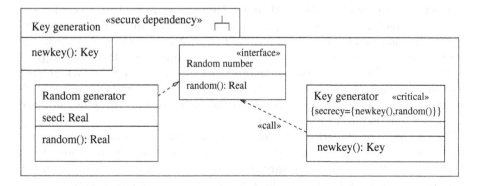

Fig. 3. Key generation subsystem

communication dependency is not guaranteed to preserve secrecy. Note that the {secrecy} tag is used at the key generator to both require and assure secrecy (for the random() method called at the random generator resp. the newkey() method offered by the key generator).

critical: This stereotype labels objects or subsystem instances containing data that is critical in some way, which is specified in more detail using the corresponding tags. These tags include {secrecy} and {integrity}. Their values are the names of expressions or variables (that is, attributes or message arguments) of the current object the secrecy (resp. integrity) of which is supposed to be protected. These requirements are enforced by the constraint of the stereotype « data security » which labels (instances of) subsystems that contain « critical » objects (see there for an explanation).

data security: This stereotype labeling (instances of) subsystems has the following constraint. The subsystem behavior respects the data security requirements given by the stereotypes « critical » and the associated tags contained in the subsystem, with respect to the threat scenario arising from the deployment diagram.

More precisely, the constraint is given by the following conditions that use the concepts of preservation of secrecy resp. integrity defined in Sect. 2.3.

secrecy. The subsystem preserves the secrecy of the data designated by the tag {secrecy} against adversaries of type A.
integrity. The subsystem preserves the integrity of the data designated by the tag {integrity} against adversaries of type A.

Note that it is enough for data to be listed with a security requirement in *one* of the objects or subsystem instances contained in the subsystem to be required to fulfill the above conditions.

Thus the properties of secrecy and integrity are taken relative to the type of adversary under consideration. In case of the default adversary, this is a principal external to the system; one may, however, consider adversaries that are part of the system under consideration, by giving the adversary access to the relevant system components (by defining $\text{Threats}_A(s)$ to contain access for the relevant stereotype s). For example, in an e-commerce protocol involving customer, merchant and bank, one might want to say that the identity of the goods being purchased is a secret known only to the customer and the merchant (and not the bank). This can be formulated by marking the relevant data as "secret" and by performing a security analysis relative to the adversary model "bank" (that is, the adversary is given access to the bank component by defining the Threats() function in a suitable way).

The secrecy and integrity tags can be used for data values as well as variable and message names (as permitted by the definitions of secrecy and integrity in Sect. 2.3). Note that the adversary does not always have access to the input and output queues of the system (for example, if the system under consideration is part of a larger system it is connected through a secure connection). Therefore it may make sense to use the secrecy tag on variables that are assigned

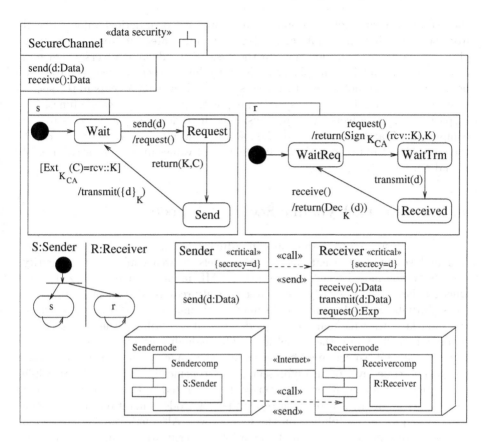

Fig. 4. Security protocol

values received by the system; that is, effectively, one may require values that are received to be secret. Of course, the above condition only ensures that the component under consideration keeps the values received by the environment secret; additionally, one has to make sure that the environment (for example, the rest of the system apart from the component under consideration) does not make these values available to the adversary.

Example. The example in Fig. 4 shows the specification of a very simple security protocol. The sender requests the public key K together with the certificate $Sign_{K_{CA}}(rcv :: K)$ certifying authenticity of the key from the receiver and sends the data d back encrypted under K (here $\{M\}_K$ is the encryption of the message M with the key K, $Dec_K(C)$ is the decryption of the ciphertext C using K, $Sign_K(M)$ is the signature of the message M with K, and $Ext_K(S)$ is the extraction of the data from the signature using K). Assuming the *default* adversary type and by referring to the adversary model outlined in Sect. 2.3 and by using the formal semantics defined in [Jür04], one can establish that the secrecy of d is preserved. (Note that the protocol only serves as a simple example for the use of patterns, not to propose a new protocol of practical value.) Recall from Sect. 2.4 that the requirements {secrecy} and {integrity} refer to the type of adversary under consideration. In the case of the default adversary, in this example this is an adversary that has access to the Internet link between the two nodes only. It does not have direct access to any of the components in the specification (this would have to be specified explicitly using the Threats() function). In particular, the adversary to be considered here does not have access to the components R and S (if it would, then secrecy and integrity would fail because the adversary could read and modify the critical values directly as attributes of R and S).

4   Introducing Dynamic Security Aspects

Aspects encapsulate properties (often non-functional ones) which crosscut a system, and we use transformations of UML models to "weave in" dynamic security aspects on the model level. The resulting UML models can be analyzed as to whether they actually satisfy the desired security requirements using automated tools [Jür05b]. Secondly, one should make sure that the code constructed from the models (either manually or by code generation) still satisfies the security requirements shown on the model level. This is highly non-trivial, for example because different aspects may be woven into the same system which may interfere on the code level in an unforeseen way. To achieve it, one has in principle two options: One can either again verify the generated code against the desired security requirements, or one can prove that the code generation preserves the security requirements fulfilled on the model level. Although the second option would be conceptually more satisfying, a formal verification of a code generator of industrially relevant strength seems to be infeasible for the foreseeable future. Also, in many cases, completely automated code generation may not be practical anyway. We therefore followed the first option and extended our UML security analysis techniques from [UML04] to the code level (presently C code, while the analysis of Java code is in development). The analysis approach (of which early ideas were sketched in [JH05]) now takes the generated code and automatically verifies it against the intended security requirement, which has been woven in as dynamic aspects. This is explained in Sect. 5. This verification thus amounts to a *translation validation* of the weaving and code construction process. Note that performing the analysis both at the model and the code level is not overly redundant: the security analysis on the model level has the advantage that problem found can be corrected earlier when this requires less effort, and the security analysis on the code level is still necessary as argued above. Also, in practice generated code is very rarely be used without any changes, which again requires verification on the code level.

The model transformation resulting from the "weaving in" of a dynamic security aspect p corresponds to a function f_p which takes a UML specification S and returns a UML specification, namely the one obtained when applying p to S. Technically, such a function can be presented by defining how it should act on certain subsystem instances[3], and by extending it to all possible UML specifications in a compositional way. Suppose that we have a set S of subsystem instances such that none of the subsystem instances in S is contained in any other subsystem instance in S. Suppose that for every subsystem instance $\mathcal{S} \in S$ we are given a subsystem instance $f_p(\mathcal{S})$. Then for any UML specification $\mathcal{U}$, we can define $f_p(\mathcal{U})$ by substituting each occurrence of a subsystem instance $\mathcal{S} \in S$ in $\mathcal{U}$ by $f_p(\mathcal{S})$. We demonstrate this by an example.

We consider the data secrecy aspect in the situation of communication over untrusted networks, as specified in Fig. 5. In the subsystem, the Sender object is supposed to accept a value in the variable d as an argument of the operation send and send it over the « encrypted » Internet link to the Receiver object, which delivers the value as a return value of the operation receive. According to the stereotype « critical » and the associated tag {secrecy}, the subsystem is supposed to preserve the secrecy of the variable d.

A well-known implementation of this aspect is to encrypt the traffic over the untrusted link using a key exchange protocol. As an example, we consider a simplified variant of the handshake protocol of the Internet protocol TLS in Fig. 6. This can be seen as a refinement of the generic scenario in Fig. 5 and is a similar but different protocol from the one in Fig. 4. The notation for the cryptographic algorithms was defined in Sect. 2.2.

The goal of the protocol is to let a sender send a secret over an untrusted communication link to a receiver in a way that provides secrecy, by using symmetric session keys.[4] The sender S initiates the protocol by sending the message $request(N, K_S, Sign_{K_S^{-1}}(S :: K_S))$ to the receiver R. If the condition $[\mathbf{snd}(\mathcal{E}xt_{K'}(c_S))=K']$ holds, where K' and c_S are the second and third arguments of the message received earlier (that is, if the key K_S contained in the signature matches the one transmitted in the clear), R sends the return message $return(\{Sign_{K_R^{-1}}(K :: N')\}_{K'}, Sign_{K_{CA}^{-1}}(R :: K_R))$ back to S (where N' is the first argument of the message received earlier). Then if the condition

$$[\mathbf{fst}(\mathcal{E}xt_{K_{CA}}(c_R))=R \wedge \mathbf{snd}(\mathcal{E}xt_{K''}(\mathcal{D}ec_{K_S^{-1}}(c_k)))=N]$$

holds, where c_R and c_k are the two arguments of the message received by the sender, and $K'' ::= \mathbf{snd}(\mathcal{E}xt_{K_{CA}}(c_R))$ (that is, the certificate is actually for R and the correct nonce is returned), S sends $transmit(\{d\}_k)$ to R, where $k ::= \mathbf{fst}(\mathcal{E}xt_{K''}(\mathcal{D}ec_{K_S^{-1}}(c_k)))$. If any of the checks fail, the respective protocol participant stops the execution of the protocol.

Note that the receiver sends two return messages - the first matches the return trigger at the sender, the other is the return message for the receive message with which the receiver object was called by the receiving application at the receiver node.

---

[3] Although one could also define this on the type level, we prefer to remain on the instance level, since having access to instances gives us more fine-grained control.

[4] Note that in this simplified example, which should mainly demonstrate the idea of dynamic security aspect weaving, authentication is out of scope of our considerations.

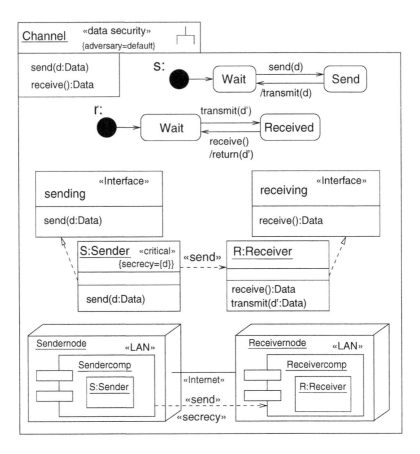

Fig. 5. Aspect weaving example: sender and receiver

To weave in this aspect p in a formal way, we consider the set S of subsystems derived from the subsystem in Fig. 5 by renaming: This means, we substitute any message, data, state, subsystem instance, node, or component name n by a name m at each occurrence, in a way such that name clashes are avoided. Then f_p maps any subsystem instance $\mathcal{S} \in S$ to the subsystem instance derived from that given in Fig. 6 by the same renaming. This gives us a presentation of f_p from which the definition of f_p on any UML specification can be derived as indicated above.

One can do the weaving by defining the transformation explained above using the model transformation framework BOTL developed at our group [BM03]. The overall tool-suite supporting our aspect-oriented modeling approach is given in Fig. 7. The tool-flow proceeds as follows. The developer creates a primary UML model and stores it in the XMI file format. The static checker checks that the security aspects formulated in the static views of the model are consistent. The dynamic checker weaves in the security aspects with the dynamic model. One can then verify the resulting UML model against the security requirements using

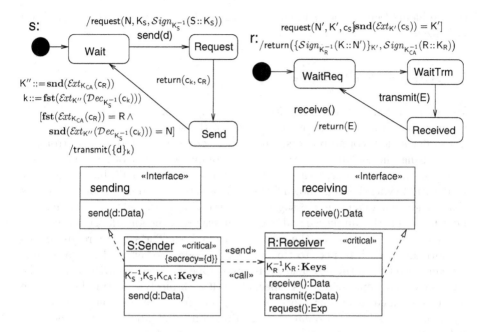

Fig. 6. Aspect weaving example: secure channel

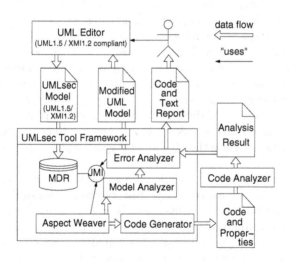

Fig. 7. UML verification framework: usage

the analysis engine (an automated theorem prover for first-order logic). One then constructs the code and also verify it against the security requirements using the theorem prover. The error analyzer uses the information received from the static and dynamic checkers to produce a text report for the developer describing the problems found, and a modified UML model, where the errors found are visualized.

5 Analyzing the Code

We define the translation of security protocol implementations to first-order logic formulas which allows automated analysis of the source code using automated first-order logic theorem provers. The source code is extracted as a control flow graph using the aiCall tool [Abs04]. It is compiled to first-order logic axioms giving an abstract interpretation of the system behavior suitable for security analysis following the well-known Dolev-Yao adversary model [DY83]. The idea is that an adversary can read messages sent over the network and collect them in his knowledge set. He can merge and extract messages in the knowledge set and can delete or insert messages on the communication links. The security requirements are formalized with respect to this adversary model. For example, a data value remains secret from the adversary if it never appears in the knowledge set of the adversary. Our approach works especially well with nicely structured code, such as that obtained using our aspect weaving tool from the previous section. For example, we apply an automated transformation which abstracts from pointers before applying our security analysis (which is a standard technique in C code verification, see e.g. [DHH02]).

We explain the transformation from the control flow graph generated from the C program to first-order logic, which is given as input to the automated theorem prover. For space restrictions, we restrict our explanation to the analysis for secrecy of data. The idea here is to use a predicate knows which defines a bound on the knowledge an adversary may obtain by reading, deleting and inserting messages on vulnerable communication lines (such as the Internet) in interaction with the protocol participants. Precisely, knows(E) means that the adversary may get to know E during the execution of the protocol. For any data value s supposed to remain confidential, one thus has to check whether one can derive knows(s). Here we use the algebra of cryptographic expressions defined in Sect. 2.2.

The set of predicates defined to hold for a given program is defined as follows. For each publicly known expression E, the statement knows(E) is derived. To model the fact that the adversary may enlarge his set of knowledge by constructing new expressions from the ones he knows, including the use of cryptographic operations, formulas are generated which axiomatize these operations.

We now define how a control flow graph generated from a C program gives rise to a logical formula characterizing the interaction between the adversary and the protocol participants. We observe that the graph can be transformed to consist of transitions of the form trans(state, inpattern, condition, action, truestate), where inpattern is empty and condition equals true where they are not needed, and where action is a logical expression of the form localvar = value resp. outpattern in case of a local assignment resp. output command (and leaving it empty if not needed). If needed, there may be additionally another transition corresponding to the negation of the given condition, where we safely abstract from the negated condition (for logical reasons beyond this exposition).

Now assume that the source code gives rise to a transition $TR1 = \text{trans}(s1, i1, c1, a1, t1)$ such that there is a second transition $TR2 = \text{trans}(s2, i2, c2, a2, t2)$ where $s2 = t1$. If there is no such transition $TR2$, we define $TR2 = \text{trans}(t1, [], \text{true}, [], t1)$ to simplify our presentation, where $[]$ is the empty input or output pattern. Suppose that $c1$ is of the form $\text{cond}(arg_1, \ldots, arg_n)$. For $i1$, we define $\bar{i1} = \text{knows}(i1)$ in case $i1$ is non-empty and otherwise $\bar{i1} = \text{true}$. For $a1$, we define $\bar{a1} = a1$ in case $a1$ is of the form $\text{localvar} = \text{value}$ and $\bar{a1} = \text{knows}(\text{outpattern})$ in case $a1 = \text{outpattern}$ (and $\bar{a1} = \text{true}$ in case $a1$ is empty). Then for $TR1$ we define the following predicate:

$$\text{PRED}(TR1) \equiv \bar{i1}\&c1 \Rightarrow \bar{a1}\&\text{PRED}(TR2) \tag{1}$$

The formula formalizes the fact that, if the adversary knows an expression he can assign to the variable $i1$ such that the condition $c1$ holds, then this implies that $\bar{a1}$ will hold according to the protocol, which means that either the equation $\text{localvar} = \text{value}$ holds in case of an assignment, or the adversary gets to know outpattern, in case it is send out in $a1$. Also then the predicate for the succeeding transition $TR2$ will hold.

To construct the recursive definition above, we assume that the control flow graph is finite and cycle-free. As usual in static code analysis, loops are unfolded over a number of iterations provided by the user. The predicates $\text{PRED}(TR)$ for all such transitions TR are then joined together using logical conjunctions and closed by forall-quantification over all free variables contained. It is interesting to note that the resulting formula is a Horn formula. Previous investigations of the

```
void TLS_Client (char* secret)
{   char Resp_1 [MSG_MAXLEN];
    char Resp_2 [MSG_MAXLEN];
    // allocate and prepare buffers
    memset (Resp1, 0x00, MSG_MAXLEN);
    memset (Resp2, 0x00, MSG_MAXLEN);
    // C->S: Init
    send (n, k_c, sign(conc(c, k_c), inv(k_c)));
    // S->C: Receive Server's respond
    recv (Resp_1, Resp_2);
    // Check Guards
    if ( (memcmp(fst(ext(Resp_2, k_ca)), s, MSG_MAXLEN) == 0) &&
         (memcmp(snd(ext(dec(Resp_1, inv(k_c)),
              snd(ext(Resp_2, k_ca)))), n, MSG_MAXLEN) == 0) )
    { // C->S: Send Secret
        send (symenc(secret, fst(ext(dec(Resp_1,
          inv(k_c)), snd(ext(Resp_2, k_ca))))))); }}
```

Fig. 8. Fragment of abstracted client code

```
input_formula(protocol,axiom,(
  ![Resp_1, Resp_2] : (
    ((knows(conc(n, conc(k_c,sign(conc(c,conc(k_c,eol)),inv(k_c))))))
    & ((knows(Resp_1) & knows(Resp_2)
    & equal(fst(ext(Resp_2,k_ca)),s)
    & equal(snd(ext(dec(Resp_1,inv(k_c)),snd(ext(Resp_2,k_ca)))),n))
      => knows(enc(secret,fst(ext(dec(Resp_1,inv(k_c)),
                          snd(ext(Resp_2,k_ca))))))))))).
```

Fig. 9. Core protocol axiom for client

interplay between Horn formulas and control flow have been done in [dBKPR89], although with a different motivation.

Figure 8 gives a simplified C implementation of the client side of the TLS variant considered earlier. From this, the control flow graph is generated automatically. The main part of the transformation of the client to the e-SETHEO input format TPTP is given in Fig. 9. We use the TPTP notation for the first-order logic formulas, which is the input notation for many automated theorem provers including the one we use (e-SETHEO). Here & means logical conjunction and ![E1, E2] forall-quantification over E1, E2. The protocol itself is expressed by a for-all quantification over the variables which store the message arguments received.

Given this translation of the C code to first-order logic, one can now check using the automated theorem prover that the code constructed from the UMLsec aspect model still satisfies the desired security requirements. For example, if the prover can derive knows(secret) from the formulas generated by the protocol, the adversary may potentially get to know secret. Details on how to perform this analysis given the first-order logic formula are explained in [Jür05b] and on how to use this approach to analyze crypto-based Java implementations in [Jür06].

6   Industrial Application

We have applied our method in several project with industrial partners. In one of them, the goal was the correct development of a security-critical biometric authentication system which is supposed to control access to a protected resource. Because the correct design of such cryptographic protocols and the correct use within the surrounding system is very difficult, our method was chosen to support the development of the biometric authentication system. Our approach has been applied at the specification level in [Jür05b] where several severe security flaws had been found. We have also applied the approach presented here to the source-code level for a prototypical implementation we constructed from the specification [Jür05a]. The security analaysis results achieved so far are obtained with the automated theorem prover within less than a minute computing time on an AMD Athlon processor with 1533 MHz. tact frequency and 1024 MB RAM.

7   Related Work

So far, there seems to be no comparable approach which allows one to include a comparable variety of security requirements in a UML specification which is then, based on a formal semantics, formally verified for these requirements using tools such as automated theorem provers and model-checkers, and which comes with a transition to the source code level where automated formal verification can also be applied.

There has, however, been a substantial amount of work regarding some of the topics we address here (for example formal verification of security-critical systems or secure systems development with UML). Work on logical foundations for object-oriented design in general and UML in particular includes for example [FELR98, HS03, ABdBS04, dBBSA04, OGO04, FSKdR05]. There has been a lot of work on formal methods for secure systems, for an overview we have to refer to [Jür04].

[HLN04] represents threats as crosscutting concerns to help determining the effect of security requirements on functional requirements. The approach analysis the interaction between assets and functional requirements to expose vulnerabilities to security threats against the security requirements. In [FRGG04], aspect models are used to describe crosscutting solutions that address quality or non-functional concerns on the model level. It is explained how to identify and compose multiple concerns, such as security and fault tolerance, and how to identify and solve conflicts between competing concerns.

A more complete discussion of related work has to be omitted for space reasons but can be found in [Jür04].

8   Conclusion and Future Perspectives

We gave an overview over the extension UMLsec of UML for secure systems development, in the form of a UML profile using the standard UML extension mechanisms. Recurring security requirements are written as stereotypes, the associated constraints ensure the security requirements on the level of the formal semantics, by referring to the threat scenario also given as a stereotype. Thus one may evaluate UML specifications to indicate possible vulnerabilities. One can thus verify that the stated security requirements, if fulfilled, enforce a given security policy. At the hand of small examples, we demonstrated how to use UMLsec to model security requirements, threat scenarios, security concepts, security mechanisms, security primitives, underlying physical security, and security management.

In this tutorial exposition, we concentrated on an approach to develop and analyze security-critical specifications and implementations using aspect-oriented modeling. As demonstrated, UMLsec can be used to encapsulate established rules on prudent security engineering, also by applying security patterns, and thereby makes them available to developers not specialized in security. We also explained how to analyze the source code resulting in the aspect-oriented development approach from the UMLsec diagrams against security requirements with respect to its dynamic behavior, using automated theorem provers for first-order logic. The definition and evolvement of the UMLsec notation has been based on experiences from in industrial application projects. We reported on the use of UMLsec and its tool-support in one such application, the formal security verification of a biometric authentication system, where several security weaknesses were found and corrected using our approach during its development. For space restrictions, we could only present a brief overview over a fragment of UMLsec. The complete notation with many more examples and applications can be found in [Jür04].

Acknowledgements. The research summarized in this chapter has benefitted from the help of too many people to be able to include here; they are listed in [Jür04]. Helpful comments from the reviewers to improve the presentation are gratefully acknowledged.

References

[ABdBS04] E. Ábráham, M.M. Bonsangue, F.S. de Boer, and M. Steffen. Object connectivity and full abstraction for a concurrent calculus of classes. In *ICTAC 2004*, pages 37–51, 2004.

[Abs04] AbsInt. aicall. http://www.aicall.de/, 2004.

[AJ01] M. Abadi and J. Jürjens. Formal eavesdropping and its computational interpretation. In N. Kobayashi and B. C. Pierce, editors, *Theoretical Aspects of Computer Software (4th International Symposium, TACS 2001)*, volume 2215 of *LNCS*, pages 82–94. Springer, 2001.

[BM03] P. Braun and F. Marschall. The BOTL tool. http://www4.in.tum.de/˜marschal/botl, 2003.

[BS01] M. Broy and K. Stølen. *Specification and Development of Interactive Systems*. Springer, 2001.

[dBBSA04] F.S. de Boer, M.M. Bonsangue, M. Steffen, and E. Ábráham. A fully abstract semantics for UML components. In *FMCO 2004*, pages 49–69, 2004.

[dBKPR89] F.S. de Boer, J.N. Koek, C. Palamidessi, and J.J.M.M. Rutten. Control flow versus logic: a denotational and a declarative model for guarded Horn clauses. In *MFCS 1989*, pages 165–176, 1989.

[DHH02] D. Dams, W. Hesse, and G.J. Holzmann. Abstracting C with abC. In *CAV 2002*, pages 515–520, 2002.

[DY83] D. Dolev and A. Yao. On the security of public key protocols. *IEEE Transactions on Information Theory*, IT-29(2):198–208, 1983.

[FELR98] R. B. France, A. Evans, K. Lano, and B. Rumpe. The UML as a formal modeling notation. *Computer Standards & Interfaces*, 19:325–334, 1998.

[FRGG04] R.B. France, I. Ray, G. Georg, and S. Ghosh. Aspect-oriented approach to early design modelling. *IEE Proceedings - Software*, 151(4):173–186, 2004.

[FSKdR05] H. Fecher, J. Schönborn, M. Kyas, and W.P. de Roever. 29 new unclarities in the semantics of UML 2.0 state machines. In *ICFEM 2005*, pages 52–65, 2005.

[Gur00]   Y. Gurevich. Abstract state machines. In T. Rus, editor, *8th International Conference on Algebraic Methodology and Software Technology (AMAST 2000)*, volume 1816 of *LNCS*. Springer, 2000.

[HLN04]   C. Haley, R. Laney, and B. Nuseibeh. Deriving security requirements from crosscutting threat descriptions. In *3rd International Conference on Aspect Oriented Software Development (AOSD'04)*. ACM, 2004.

[HS03]   Ø. Haugen and K. Stølen. STAIRS – steps to analyze interactions with refinement semantics. In P. Stevens, editor, *The Unified Modeling Language (UML 2003)*, volume 2863 of *LNCS*, pages 388–402. Springer, 2003. 6th International Conference.

[JH05]   J. Jürjens and S.H. Houmb. Dynamic secure aspect modeling with UML: From models to code. In *ACM / IEEE 8th International Conference on Model Driven Engineering Languages and Systems (MoDELS / UML 2005)*, LNCS. Springer, 2005.

[Jür01]   J. Jürjens. Towards development of secure systems using UMLsec. In H. Hußmann, editor, *4th International Conference on Fundamental Approaches to Software Engineering (FASE)*, volume 2029 of *LNCS*, pages 187–200. Springer, 2001.

[Jür02]   J. Jürjens. UMLsec: Extending UML for secure systems development. In J.-M. Jézéquel, H. Hußmann, and S. Cook, editors, *5th International Conference on the Unified Modeling Language (UML 2002)*, volume 2460 of *LNCS*, pages 412–425. Springer, 2002.

[Jür04]   J. Jürjens. *Secure Systems Development with UML*. Springer, 2004.

[Jür05a]   J. Jürjens. Code security analysis of a biometric authentication system using automated theorem provers. In *21st Annual Computer Security Applications Conference (ACSAC 2005)*. IEEE, 2005.

[Jür05b]   J. Jürjens. Sound methods and effective tools for model-based security engineering with UML. In *27th International Conference on Software Engineering (ICSE 2005)*. IEEE, 2005.

[Jür06]   J. Jürjens. Security analysis of crypto-based Java programs using automated theorem provers. In S. Easterbrook and S. Uchitel, editors, *21st IEEE/ACM International Conference on Automated Software Engineering (ASE 2006)*. ACM, 2006.

[OGO04]   Iu. Ober, S. Graf, and Il. Ober. Validation of UML models via a mapping to communicating extended timed automata. In *SPIN 2004*, pages 127–145, 2004.

[UML03]   UML Revision Task Force. OMG UML Specification v. 1.5. OMG Document formal/03-03-01. Available at http://www.omg.org/uml, March 2003.

[UML04]   UMLsec group. Security analysis tool, 2004. http://www.umlsec.org.

The Pragmatics of STAIRS

Ragnhild Kobro Runde[1], Øystein Haugen[1], and Ketil Stølen[1,2]

[1] Department of Informatics, University of Oslo, Norway
[2] SINTEF ICT, Norway

Abstract. STAIRS is a method for the compositional development of interactions in the setting of UML 2.0. In addition to defining denotational trace semantics for the main aspects of interactions, STAIRS focuses on how interactions may be developed through successive refinement steps. In this tutorial paper, we concentrate on explaining the practical relevance of STAIRS. Guidelines are given on how to create interactions using the different STAIRS operators, and how these may be refined. The pragmatics is illustrated by a running example.

1 Introduction

STAIRS [HHRS05a] is a method for the compositional development of interactions in the setting of UML 2.0 [OMG05]. In contrast to e.g. UML state machines and Java programs, interactions are usually incomplete specifications, typically describing example runs of the system. STAIRS is designed to deal with this incompleteness. Another important feature of STAIRS is the possibility to distinguish between alternative behaviours representing underspecification and alternative behaviours that must all be present in an implementation, for instance due to inherent nondeterminism.

STAIRS is not intended to be a complete methodology for system development, but should rather be seen as a supplement to methodologies like e.g. RUP [Kru04]. In particular, STAIRS focuses on refinement, which is a development step where the specification is made more complete by information being added to it in such a way that any valid implementation of the refined specification will also be a valid implementation of the original specification.

In this paper we focus on refinement relations. We define general refinement, which in turn has four special cases referred to as narrowing, supplementing, detailing and limited refinement. Narrowing means to reduce the set of possible system behaviours, thus reducing underspecification. Supplementing, on the other hand, means to add new behaviours to the specification, taking into account the incomplete nature of interactions, while detailing means to add more details to the specification by decomposing lifelines. By general refinement, the nondeterminism required of an implementation may be increased freely, while limited refinement is a special case restricting this possibility.

Previous work on STAIRS has focused on its basic ideas, explaining the various concepts such as the distinction between underspecification and inherent nondeterminism [HHRS05a, RHS05b], time [HHRS05b], and negation [RHS05a], as

F.S. de Boer et al. (Eds.): FMCO 2005, LNCS 4111, pp. 88–114, 2006.
© Springer-Verlag Berlin Heidelberg 2006

well as how these are formalized. In this paper, we take the theory of STAIRS one step further, focusing on its practical consequences by giving practical guidelines on how to use STAIRS. In particular, we explain how to use the various STAIRS operators when creating specifications in the form of interactions, and how these specifications may be further developed through valid refinement steps.

The paper is organized as follows: In Sect. 2 we give a brief introduction to interactions and their semantic model as we have defined it in STAIRS. Section 3 is an exampleguided walkthrough of the main STAIRS operators for creating interactions, particularly focusing on alternatives and negation. For each operator we give both its formal definition and guidelines for its practical usage. Section 4 gives the pragmatics of refining interactions. In Sect. 5 we explain how STAIRS relates to other similar approaches, in particular UML 2.0, while we give some concluding remarks in Sect. 6.

2   The Semantic Model of STAIRS

In this section we give a brief introduction to interactions and their trace semantics as defined in STAIRS. The focus here is on the semantic model. Definitions of concrete syntactical operators will mainly be presented together with the discussion of these operators later in this paper. For a thorough account of the STAIRS semantics, see [HHRS05b] and the extension with data in [RHS05b].

An interaction describes one or more positive (i.e. valid) and/or negative (i.e. invalid) behaviours. As a very simple example, the sequence diagram in Fig. 1 specifies a scenario in which a client sends the message cancel(appointment) to an appointment system, which subsequently sends the message appointment-Cancelled back to the client, together with a suggestion for a new appointment to which the client answers with the message yes. The client finally receives the message appointmentMade.

Formally, we use denotational trace semantics to explain the meaning of a single interaction. A trace is a sequence of events, representing a system run. The most typical examples of events are the sending and the reception of a message, where a message is a triple (s, tr, re) consisting of a signal s, a transmitter lifeline tr and a receiver lifeline re. For a message m, we let $!m$ and $?m$ denote the sending and the reception of m, respectively. As will be explained in Sect. 3.2, we also have some special events representing the use of data in e.g. constraints and guards.

The diagram in Fig. 1 includes ten events, two for each message. These are combined by the implicit weak sequencing operator seq, which will be formally defined at the end of this section. Informally, the set of traces described by such a diagram is the set of all possible sequences consisting of its events such that the send event is ordered before the corresponding receive event, and events on the same lifeline are ordered from top down. Shortening each message to the first and the capitalized letter of its signal, we thus get that Fig. 1 specifies two positive traces $\langle !c, ?c, !aC, ?aC, !aS, ?aS, !y, ?y, !aM, ?aM \rangle$ and $\langle !c, ?c, !aC, !aS, ?aC, ?aS, !y, ?y, !aM, ?aM \rangle$, where the only difference is the

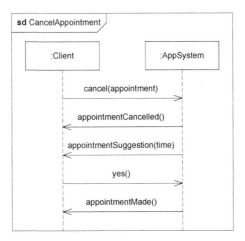

Fig. 1. Example interaction: CancelAppointment

relative ordering of the two events $?aC$ and $!aS$. Figure 1 gives no negative traces.

Formally, we let $\mathcal{H}$ denote the set of all well-formed traces. A trace is well-formed if, for each message, the send event is ordered before the corresponding receive event. An *interaction obligation* (p, n) is a pair of trace-sets which gives a classification of all of the traces in $\mathcal{H}$ into three categories: the positive traces p, the negative traces n and the inconclusive traces $\mathcal{H} \setminus (p \cup n)$. The inconclusive traces result from the incompleteness of interactions, representing traces that are not described as positive or negative by the current interaction. We say that the interaction obligation is contradictory if the same trace is both positive and negative, i.e. if $p \cap n \neq \emptyset$. To give a visual presentation of an interaction obligation, we use an oval divided into three regions as shown in Fig. 2.

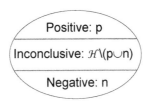

Fig. 2. Illustrating an interaction obligation

As explained in the introduction, one of the main advantages of STAIRS is its ability to distinguish between traces that an implementation *may* exhibit (e.g. due to underspecification), and traces that it *must* exhibit (e.g. due to inherent nondeterminism). Semantically, this distinction is captured by stating that the semantics of an interaction d is a *set* of m interaction obligations,

$[\![\,d\,]\!] = \{(p_1, n_1), \ldots, (p_m, n_m)\}$. Intuitively, the traces allowed by an interaction obligation (i.e. its positive and inconclusive traces) represent potential alternatives, where being able to produce only one of these traces is sufficient for an implementation. On the other hand, the different interaction obligations represent mandatory alternatives, in the sense that each obligation specifies traces of which at least one must be possible for a correct implementation of the specification.

We are now ready to give the formal definition of seq. First, weak sequencing of trace sets is defined by:

$$s_1 \succeq s_2 \overset{\text{def}}{=} \{h \in \mathcal{H} \mid \exists h_1 \in s_1, h_2 \in s_2 : \forall l \in \mathcal{L} : h \lceil l = h_1 \lceil l \frown h_2 \lceil l\} \quad (1)$$

where $\mathcal{L}$ is the set of all lifelines, $\frown$ is the concatenation operator on sequences, and $h \lceil l$ is the trace h with all events not taking place on the lifeline l removed. Basically, this definition gives all traces that may be constructed by selecting one trace from each operand and combining them in such a way that the events from the first operand must come before the events from the second operand (i.e. the events are ordered from top down) for all lifelines. Events from different operands may come in any order, as long as sending comes before reception for each message (as required by $h \in \mathcal{H}$). Notice that weak sequencing with an empty set as one of the operands yields the empty set.

Weak sequencing of interaction obligations is defined by:

$$(p_1, n_1) \succeq (p_2, n_2) \overset{\text{def}}{=} (p_1 \succeq p_2, (n_1 \succeq p_2) \cup (n_1 \succeq n_2) \cup (p_1 \succeq n_2)) \quad (2)$$

Finally, seq is defined by

$$\begin{aligned} [\![\,\text{seq}\,[d]\,]\!] &\overset{\text{def}}{=} [\![\,d\,]\!] \\ [\![\,\text{seq}\,[D, d]\,]\!] &\overset{\text{def}}{=} \{o_1 \succeq o_2 \mid o_1 \in [\![\,\text{seq}\,[D]\,]\!] \wedge o_2 \in [\![\,d\,]\!]\} \end{aligned} \quad (3)$$

where d is a single interaction and D a list of one or more interactions. For a further discussion of seq, see Sect. 3.4.

3   The Pragmatics of Creating Interactions

In this section, we focus on the different syntactical constructs of interactions in order to explain the main theory of STAIRS and how these constructs should be used in practical development. For each construct, we demonstrate its usage in a practical example, to motivate its formal semantics and the pragmatic rules and guidelines that conclude each subsection.

As our example, we will use a system for appointment booking to be used by e.g. doctors and dentists. The appointment system should have the following functionality:

- MakeAppointment: The client may ask for an appointment.
- CancelAppointment: The client may cancel an appointment.

– Payment: The system may send an invoice message asking the client to pay for the previous or an unused appointment.

The interactions specifying this system will be developed in a stepwise manner. In Sect. 4 we will justify that all of these development steps are valid refinement steps in STAIRS.

3.1 The Use of alt Versus xalt

Consider again the interaction in Fig. 1. As explained in Sect. 2, this interaction specifies two different traces, depending on whether the client receives the message appointmentCancelled before or after the system sends the message appointmentSuggestion. Which one of these we actually get when running the final system, will typically depend on the kind of communication used between the client and our system. If the communication is performed via SMS or over the internet, we may have little or no delay, meaning that the first of these messages may be received before the second is sent. On the other hand, if communication is performed by sending letters via ordinary mail, both messages (i.e. letters) will probably be sent before the first one arrives at the client.

Seeing that the means of communication is not specified in the interaction, all of these are acceptable implementations. Also, it is sufficient for an implementation to have only one of these available. Hence, the two traces of Fig. 1 exemplify underspecification. In the semantics, this is represented by the two traces being grouped together in the same interaction obligation.

The underspecification in Fig. 1 is an implicit consequence of weak sequencing. Alternatives representing underspecification may also be specified explicitly by using the operator alt, as in the specification of MakeAppointment in Fig. 3. In this interaction, when requesting a new appointment the client may ask for either

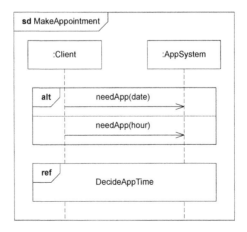

Fig. 3. MakeAppointment

a specific date or a specific hour of the day (for instance if the client prefers his appointments to be after work or during the lunch break). As we do not require the system to offer both of these alternatives, they are specified using alt. After the client has asked for an appointment, the appointment is set up according to the referenced interaction DecideAppTime.

The specification of DecideAppTime is given in Fig. 4. Here, the system starts with suggesting an appointment, and the client then answers either yes or no. Finally, the client gets a receipt according to his answer. As the system must be able to handle both yes and no as reply messages, these alternatives are *not* instances of underspecification. Specifying these by using alt would therefore be insufficient. Instead, they are specified by the xalt operator (first introduced in [HS03]) in order to capture alternative traces where an implementation must be able to perform all alternatives.

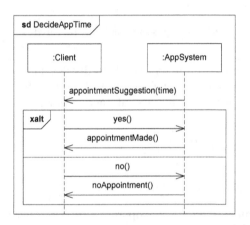

Fig. 4. DecideAppTime

In Fig. 5, which gives a revised version of CancelAppointment from Fig. 1, another use of xalt is demonstrated. In this case, xalt is used to model alternatives where the conditions under which each of them may be chosen is not known. This interaction specifies that if a client tries to cancel an appointment, he may either get an error message or he may get a confirmation of the cancellation, after which the system tries to schedule another appointment (in DecideAppTime). In Sect. 3.2 we demonstrate how guards may be added as a means to constrain the applicability of the two alternatives in this example.

A third use of xalt is to specify inherent nondeterminism, as in a coin toss where both heads and tails should be possible outcomes. More examples, and a discussion of the relationship between alt and xalt, may be found in [RHS05b] and [RRS06].

The crucial question when specifying alternatives is: Do these alternatives represent similar traces in the sense that implementing only one is sufficient? If yes, use alt. Otherwise, use xalt.

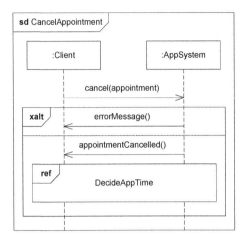

Fig. 5. CancelAppointment revisited

Formally, the operands of an xalt result in distinct interaction obligations in order to model the situation that they must all be possible for an implementation. On the other hand, alt combines interaction obligations in order to model underspecification:

$$[\![\, \mathsf{xalt}\ [d_1, \ldots d_m]\,]\!] \stackrel{\text{def}}{=} \bigcup_{i \in [1,m]} [\![\, d_i\,]\!] \tag{4}$$

$$[\![\, \mathsf{alt}\ [d_1, \ldots, d_m]\,]\!] \stackrel{\text{def}}{=} \{\, \biguplus \{o_1, \ldots, o_m\} \mid \forall i \in [1, m] : o_i \in [\![\, d_i\,]\!]\, \} \tag{5}$$

where m is the number of interaction operands and the inner union of interaction obligations, $\biguplus$, is defined as:

$$\biguplus_{i \in [1,m]} (p_i, n_i) \stackrel{\text{def}}{=} (\bigcup_{i \in [1,m]} p_i, \bigcup_{i \in [1,m]} n_i) \tag{6}$$

The difference between alt and xalt is also illustrated in Fig. 6, which is an informal illustration of the semantics of Fig. 3. The dotted lines should be interpreted as parentheses grouping the semantics of sub-interactions, and the second seq-operand is the semantics of the referenced interaction DecideApp-Time. In each interaction obligation of Fig. 6, every trace that is not positive is inconclusive, as Fig. 3 gives no negative traces.

Every interaction using the STAIRS-operators except for infinite loop is equivalent to an interaction having xalt as the top-level operator. This is because xalt describes mandatory alternatives. If there are only finitely many alternatives (which is the case if there is no infinite loop) they may be listed one by one. In particular, we have that all of these operators distribute over xalt. For instance, we have that the interaction alt [xalt $[d_1, d_2], d_3$] is equivalent to the interaction xalt [alt $[d_1, d_3]$, alt $[d_2, d_3]$], and similarly for interactions with more than two operands and for the other operators.

The pragmatics of alt vs xalt
- Use alt to specify alternatives that represent similar traces, i.e. to model
  - underspecification.
- Use xalt to specify alternatives that must all be present in an implementation, i.e. to model
  - inherent nondeterminism, as in the specification of a coin toss.
  - alternative traces due to different inputs that the system must be able to handle (as in Fig. 4);
  - alternative traces where the conditions for these being positive are abstracted away (as in Fig. 5).

3.2 The Use of Guards

In Fig. 5, xalt was used in order to specify that the system should be able to respond with either an error message or with the receipt message appointment-Cancelled (followed by DecideAppTime), if a client wants to cancel an appointment. With the current specification, the choice between these alternatives may be performed nondeterministically, but as suggested in the previous section, it is more likely that there exist some conditions for when each of the alternatives may be chosen. In Fig. 7 these conditions are made explicit by adding them to the specification in the form of guards as a step in the development process.

For the first alternative, the guard is used to specify that if the client wants to cancel an appointment less than 24 hours in advance, he will get an error message. In general, the guard else may be used as a short-hand for the conjunction of the negation of all the other guards. This means that for the second alternative of Fig. 7, the appointment will be cancelled and the system will try to schedule a new appointment only if the appointment is at least 24 hours away.

Similarly, in Fig. 8, guards are added to the alt-construct of Fig. 3 in order to constrain the situations in which each of the alternatives needApp(date) and needApp(hour) is positive. The guards specify that the client may only ask for an appointment at today or at a later date, or between the hours of 7 A.M. and 5 P.M. We recommend that one always makes sure that the guards of an alt-construct are exhaustive. Therefore, Fig. 8 also adds an alternative where the client asks for an appointment without specifying either date or hour. This alternative has the guard true, and may always be chosen. As this example demonstrates, the guards of an alt-construct may be overlapping. This is also the case for xalt.

In order to capture guards and more general constraints in the semantics, the semantics is extended with the notion of a state. A state σ is a total function assigning a value (in the set Val) to each variable (in the set Var). Formally, $\sigma \in Var \rightarrow Val$. Semantically, a constraint is represented by the special event $check(\sigma)$, where σ is the state in which the constraint is evaluated:

$$[\![\text{ constr}(c)]\!] \stackrel{\text{def}}{=} \{ (\{\langle check(\sigma)\rangle \mid c(\sigma)\}, \{\langle check(\sigma)\rangle \mid \neg c(\sigma)\}) \} \quad (7)$$

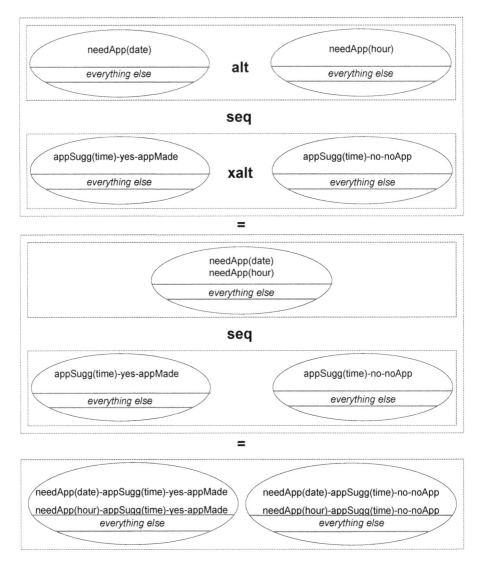

Fig. 6. IllustratingMakeAppointment

The semantics of guarded xalt is defined by:

$$\llbracket \text{ xalt } [c_1 \rightarrow d_1, \ldots, c_m \rightarrow d_m] \rrbracket \stackrel{\text{def}}{=} \bigcup_{i \in [1,m]} \llbracket \text{ seq } [\text{constr}(c_i), d_i] \rrbracket \qquad (8)$$

Notice that for all states, a constraint is either true and the trace $\langle check(\sigma) \rangle$ is positive, or the constraint is false and the trace $\langle check(\sigma) \rangle$ is negative. For guarded xalt (and similarly for alt defined below), this has the consequence that a guard must cover *all* possible situations in which the specified traces are positive,

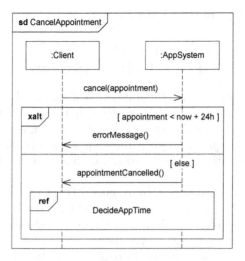

Fig. 7. CancelAppointment revisited

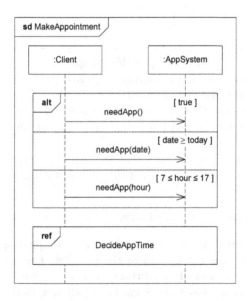

Fig. 8. MakeAppointment revisited

since a false guard means that the traces described by this alternative are negative. When relating specifications with and without guards, an alt/xalt-operand
without a guard is interpreted as having the guard true. This interpretation,
together with the use of constr in the definition of guards, ensures that adding
guards to a specification (as in the examples above) is a valid refinement step as
will be explained in Sect. 4.

The semantics of guarded alt is defined by:

$$[\![\text{alt } [c_1 \to d_1, \ldots, c_m \to d_m]]\!] \overset{\text{def}}{=} \tag{9}$$
$$\{ \uplus\{o_1, \ldots, o_m\} \mid \forall i \in [1, m] : o_i \in [\![\text{seq } [\text{constr}(c_i), d_i]]\!] \}$$

The UML 2.0 standard ([OMG05]) states that if all guards in an alt-construct are false then the empty trace $\langle\rangle$ (i.e. doing nothing) should be positive. In [RHS05b], we gave a definition of guarded alt which was consistent with the standard. However, implicitly adding the empty trace as positive implies that alt is no longer associative. For this reason, we have omitted this implicit trace from definition (9).

Definition (9) is consistent with our general belief that everything which is not explicitly described in an interaction should be regarded as inconclusive for that diagram. If all guards are false, all of the described traces are negative and the interaction has an empty set of positive traces. To avoid confusion between our definition and that of UML, we recommend to always make sure that the guards of an alt-construct are exhaustive. If desired, one of the alternatives may be the empty diagram, skip, defining the empty trace as positive:

$$[\![\text{skip}]\!] \overset{\text{def}}{=} \{(\{\langle\rangle\}, \emptyset)\} \tag{10}$$

The pragmatics of guards

- Use guards in an alt/xalt-construct to constrain the situations in which the different alternatives are positive.
- Always make sure that for each alternative, the guard is sufficiently general to capture all possible situations in which the described traces are positive.
- In an alt-construct, make sure that the guards are exhaustive. If doing nothing is valid, specify this by using the empty diagram, skip.

3.3   The Use of refuse, veto and assert

As explained in the introduction, interactions are incomplete specifications, specifying only example runs as opposed to the complete behaviour of the system. In this setting, it is particularly important to specify not only positive, but also negative traces, stating what the system is *not* allowed to do. In STAIRS, negative traces are defined by using one of the operators refuse, veto, or assert. The operators refuse and veto are both used to specify that the traces of its operand should be considered negative. They differ only in that veto has the empty trace as positive, while refuse does not have any positive traces at all. The importance of this difference will be explained later in this section, after the formal definitions. The assert operator specifies that only the traces in its operand are positive and that all other traces are negative.

In the revised version of DecideAppTime given in Fig. 9, these three operators are used in order to add negative traces to the specification in Fig. 4. Figure 9

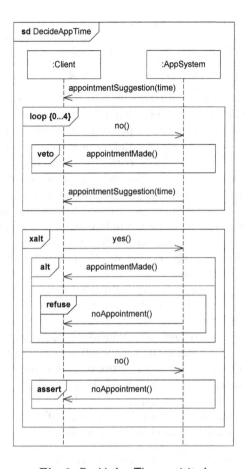

Fig. 9. DecideAppTime revisited

also adds some positive traces via the loop-construct, which may be interpreted as an alt between performing the contents of the loop 0, 1, 2, 3, or 4 times. For a formal definition of loop, see [RHS05b].

Inside the loop, veto is used to specify that after the client has answered no to the suggested appointment, the system should not send the message AppointmentMade before suggesting another appointment. In the first xalt-operand, alt in combination with refuse is used to specify that the client should get the receipt message AppointmentMade when he accepts the suggested appointment, and that it would be negative if he instead got the message noAppointment. In the second xalt-operand, assert is used to specify that the system should send the message noAppointment after the client has answered with the final no, and that no other traces are allowed. This is in contrast to the first xalt-operand, which defines one positive and one negative trace, but leaves all other traces inconclusive.

Formally, refuse and veto are defined by:

$$[\![\, \text{refuse}\,[d]\,]\!] \stackrel{\text{def}}{=} \{(\emptyset, p \cup n) \mid (p, n) \in [\![\, d\,]\!]\} \tag{11}$$

$$[\![\, \text{veto}\,[d]\,]\!] \stackrel{\text{def}}{=} \text{alt}\,[\, \text{skip}, \text{refuse}\,[d]\,] \tag{12}$$

Both operators define that all traces described by its operand should be considered negative. The difference between refuse and veto is that while refuse has *no* positive traces, veto has the empty trace as positive, meaning that doing nothing is positive for veto. To understand the importance of this difference, it is useful to imagine that for each lifeline, each interaction fragment is implemented as a subroutine. Entering a new interaction fragment will then correspond to calling the subroutine that implements this fragment. For an interaction fragment with refuse as its main operator, no such subroutine may exist, as there are no positive traces. Hence, the program fails to continue in such a case. However, an interaction fragment with veto as its main operator, corresponds to an empty routine that immediately returns and the program may continue with the interaction fragment that follows.

The choice of operator for a concrete situation, will then depend on the question: Should doing nothing be possible in this otherwise negative situation? If yes, use veto. If no, use refuse.

Consider again Fig. 9. Here, veto is used inside the loop construct as sending the message no (then doing nothing), and then sending AppointmentSuggestion(time) should be positive. On the other hand, refuse is used in the first xalt operand, as we did not want to specify the message yes followed by doing nothing as positive.

Using assert ensures that for each interaction obligation of its operand, at least one of the described positive traces will be implemented by the final system, as all inconclusive traces are redefined as negative. Formally:

$$[\![\, \text{assert}\,[d]\,]\!] \stackrel{\text{def}}{=} \{(p, n \cup (\mathcal{H} \setminus p)) \mid (p, n) \in [\![\, d\,]\!]\} \tag{13}$$

The pragmatics of negation
- To effectively constrain the implementation, the specification should include a reasonable set of negative traces.
- Use refuse when specifying that one of the alternatives in an alt-construct represents negative traces.
- Use veto when the empty trace (i.e. doing nothing) should be positive, as when specifying a negative message in an otherwise positive scenario.
- Use assert on an interaction fragment when all possible positive traces for that fragment have been described.

3.4 The Use of seq

As explained in Sect. 2, the weak sequencing operator seq is the implicit composition operator for interactions, defined by the following invariants:

- The ordering of events within each of the operands is maintained in the result.
- Events on different lifelines from different operands may come in any order.
- Events on the same lifeline from different operands are ordered such that an event of the first operand comes before that of the second operand, and so on.

Consider again the revised specification of CancelAppointment in Fig. 7. In the second xalt-operand, the system sends the message appointmentCancelled to the client, and subsequently the referenced interaction DecideAppTime is performed. Here, the first thing to happen is that the system sends the message AppointmentSuggestion to the client (as specified in Fig. 9).

As seq is the operator used for sequencing interaction fragments, this means that in general *no* synchronization takes place at the beginning of an interaction fragment, i.e. that different lifelines may enter the fragment at different points in time. In the context of Fig. 7, this means that there is no ordering between the reception of the message appointmentCancelled and the sending of the message AppointmentSuggestion, in exactly the same way as there would have been no ordering between these if the specification had been written in one single diagram instead of using a referenced interaction.

In Fig. 10, traces are added to the specification of CancelAppointment in the case where the client wants to cancel an appointment less than 24 hours before it is supposed to take place.

The first alt-operand specifies that the system may give an error message (as before). The second operand specifies that the sending of the message appointmentCancelled alone is negative, while the third operand specifies that sending the message appointmentCancelled and then performing (the positive traces of) Payment (specified in Fig. 11) is positive.

This example demonstrates that a trace (e.g. appointmentCancelled followed by Payment) is not necessarily negative even if a prefix of it (e.g. appointmentCancelled) is. This means that the total trace must be considered when categorizing it as positive, negative or inconclusive. Another consequence is that every trace which is not explicitly shown in the interaction should be inconclusive. For instance, in Fig. 10 all traces where the message appointmentCancelled is followed by something other than Payment, are still inconclusive.

The formal definition of seq was given in Sect. 2. As no synchronization takes place at the beginning of each seq-operand, it follows from the definitions that i.e. seq $[d_1, \text{alt } [d_2, d_3]] = \text{alt } [\text{seq } [d_1, d_2], \text{seq } [d_1, d_3]]$ and that loop $\{2\}$ $[d] = \text{seq } [d, d]$ as could be expected.

The pragmatics of weak sequencing

- Be aware that by weak sequencing,
  - a positive sub-trace followed by a positive sub-trace is positive.
  - a positive sub-trace followed by a negative sub-trace is negative.
  - a negative sub-trace followed by a positive sub-trace is negative.
  - a negative sub-trace followed by a negative sub-trace is negative.
  - the remaining trace combinations are inconclusive.

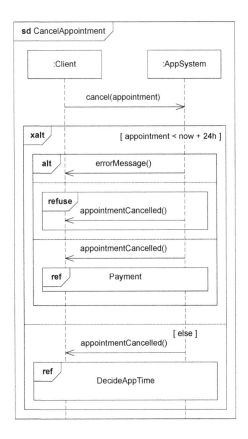

Fig. 10. CancelAppointment revisited

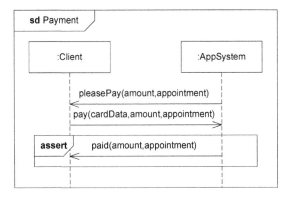

Fig. 11. Payment

4   The Pragmatics of Refining Interactions

In a development process, specifications may be changed for several reasons, including capturing new user requirements, giving a more detailed design, or correcting errors. STAIRS focuses on those changes which may be defined as refinements. In this section, we explain some main kinds of refinement in STAIRS, and demonstrate how each of the development steps taken in the example in Sect. 3 are valid refinement steps.

Figure 12 illustrates how the different refinement notions presented in this paper are related. Supplementing, narrowing and detailing are all special cases of the general refinement notion. Limited refinement is a restricted version of general refinement, which limits the possibility to increase the nondeterminism required of an implementation. In Fig. 12, we have also illustrated what refinement relation is used for each of the development steps in our running example. For instance, the placement of $1 \rightarrow 5$ means that Fig. 5 is a supplementing and general refinement of Fig. 1, but not a limited refinement.

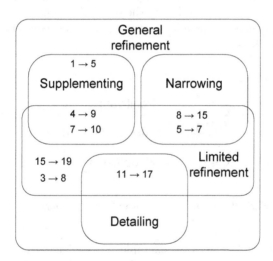

Fig. 12. The refinement relations of STAIRS

In the discussion of each of the five refinement notions, we will refer to the following definition of compositionality:

Definition 1 (Compositionality). *A refinement operator $\rightsquigarrow$ is compositional if it is*

- *reflexive: $d \rightsquigarrow d$*
- *transitive: $d \rightsquigarrow d' \wedge d' \rightsquigarrow d'' \Rightarrow d \rightsquigarrow d''$*
- *monotonic with respect to* refuse, veto, *(guarded)* alt, *(guarded)* xalt *and* seq*:*

$$d \rightsquigarrow d' \Rightarrow \text{refuse } [d] \rightsquigarrow \text{refuse } [d']$$
$$d \rightsquigarrow d' \Rightarrow \text{veto } [d] \rightsquigarrow \text{veto } [d']$$
$$d_1 \rightsquigarrow d'_1, \ldots, d_m \rightsquigarrow d'_m \Rightarrow \text{alt } [d_1, \ldots, d_m] \rightsquigarrow \text{alt } [d'_1, \ldots, d'_m]$$
$$d_1 \rightsquigarrow d'_1, \ldots, d_m \rightsquigarrow d'_m \Rightarrow \text{xalt } [d_1, \ldots, d_m] \rightsquigarrow \text{xalt } [d'_1, \ldots, d'_m]$$
$$d_1 \rightsquigarrow d'_1, \ldots, d_m \rightsquigarrow d'_m \Rightarrow \text{seq } [d_1, \ldots, d_m] \rightsquigarrow \text{seq } [d'_1, \ldots, d'_m]$$

Transitivity enables the stepwise development of interactions, while monotonicity is important as it means that the different parts of an interaction may be refined separately.

4.1   The Use of Supplementing

As interactions are incomplete specifications typically describing only example runs, we may usually find many possible traces that are inconclusive in a given interaction obligation. By supplementing, inconclusive traces are re-categorized as either positive or negative as illustrated for a single interaction obligation in Fig. 13. Supplementing is an activity where new situations are considered, and will most typically be used during the early phases of system development. Examples of supplementing includes capturing new user requirements and adding fault tolerance to the system.

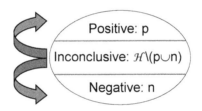

Fig. 13. Supplementing of interaction obligations

DecideAppTime in Fig. 9 is an example of supplementing, as it adds both positive and negative traces to the specification in Fig. 4. All traces that were positive in the original specification, are still positive in the refinement. Another example of supplementing is CancelAppointment in Fig. 10, which adds traces to the specification in Fig. 7. Again, all traces that were positive in the original specification remain positive in the refinement, and the negative traces remain negative.

Formally, supplementing of interaction obligations is defined by:

$$(p, n) \rightsquigarrow_s (p', n') \stackrel{\text{def}}{=} p \subseteq p' \ \wedge \ n \subseteq n' \tag{14}$$

For an interaction with a set of interaction obligations as its semantics, we require that each obligation for the original interaction must have a refining obligation in the semantics of the refined interaction. This ensures that the alternative traces (e.g. the inherent nondeterminism) required by an interaction are also required by the refinement. Formally:

$$d \rightsquigarrow_s d' \overset{\text{def}}{=} \forall o \in [\![\, d \,]\!] : \exists o' \in [\![\, d' \,]\!] : o \rightsquigarrow_s o' \tag{15}$$

Supplementing is compositional as defined by Definition 1.

The pragmatics of supplementing
- Use supplementing to add positive or negative traces to the specification.
- When supplementing, all of the original positive traces must remain positive and all of the original negative traces must remain negative.
- Do not use supplementing on the operand of an **assert**.

4.2   The Use of Narrowing

Narrowing means to reduce underspecification by redefining positive traces as negative, as illustrated in Fig. 14. As for supplementing, negative traces must remain negative in the refinement.

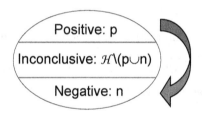

Fig. 14. Narrowing of interaction obligations

One example of narrowing, is adding guards to CancelAppointment in Fig. 7. In the original specification in Fig. 5, we had for instance no constraint on the alternative with the message appointmentCancelled, while in the refinement this alternative is negative if it occurs less than 24 hours prior the appointment.

In general, adding guards to an alt/xalt-construct is a valid refinement through narrowing. Seeing that an operand without a guard is interpreted as having true as guard, this is a special case of a more general rule, stating that a valid refinement may limit a guard as long as the refined condition implies the original one. This ensures that all of the positive traces of the refinement were also positive (and not negative) in the original specification.

Another example of narrowing is given in MakeAppointment in Fig. 15. Here, the refuse-operator is used to specify that the client may *not* ask for an appointment at a specific hour. This means that even though these traces were positive in the specification in Fig. 8, they are now considered negative in the sense that asking for a specific hour is not an option in the final implementation.

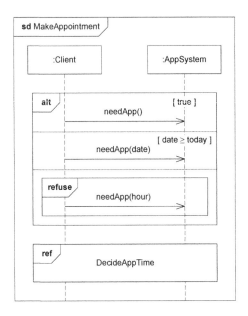

Fig. 15. MakeAppointment revisited

Formally, narrowing of interaction obligations is defined by:

$$(p, n) \rightsquigarrow_n (p', n') \overset{\text{def}}{=} p' \subseteq p \; \wedge \; n' = n \cup p \setminus p' \qquad (16)$$

and narrowing of interactions by:

$$d \rightsquigarrow_n d' \overset{\text{def}}{=} \forall o \in [\![\, d \,]\!] : \exists o' \in [\![\, d' \,]\!] : o \rightsquigarrow_n o' \qquad (17)$$

Narrowing is compositional as defined by Definition 1. In addition, the narrowing operator $\rightsquigarrow_n$ is monotonic with respect to **assert**.

The pragmatics of narrowing

- Use narrowing to remove underspecification by redefining positive traces as negative.
- In cases of narrowing, all of the original negative traces must remain negative.
- Guards may be added to an alt-construct as a legal narrowing step.
- Guards may be added to an xalt-construct as a legal narrowing step.
- Guards may be narrowed, i.e. the refined condition must imply the original one.

4.3   The Use of Detailing

Detailing means reducing the level of abstraction by decomposing one or more lifelines, i.e. by structural decomposition. As illustrated in Fig. 16, positive traces remain positive and negative traces remain negative in relation to detailing. The only change is that the traces of the refinement may include more details, for instance internal messages that are not visible in the more abstract specification.

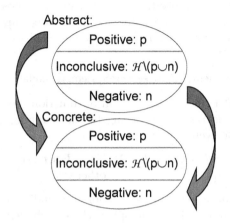

Fig. 16. Detailing of interaction obligations

Figure 17 is a detailing refinement of Payment in Fig. 11. In this case, the lifeline AppSystem is decomposed into the two lifelines Calendar, taking care of appointments, and Billing, handling payments. This decomposition has two effects with respect to the traces of the original specification. First of all, internal communication between Billing and Calendar is revealed (i.e. the messages need-Pay and paymentReceived), and secondly, Billing has replaced AppSystem as the

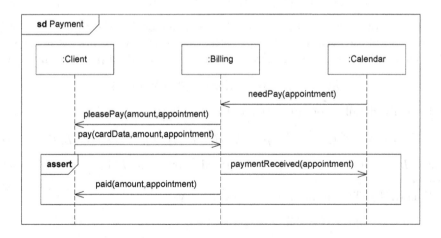

Fig. 17. Payment with decomposition

sender/receiver of messages to and from the client. In general, some of the client's messages could also have been sent to/from Calendar.

We say that an interaction is a detailing refinement if we get the same positive and negative traces as in the original specification when both hiding the internal communication in the decomposition and allowing for a possible change in the sender/receiver of a message. Formally, the lifeline decomposition will in each case be described by a mapping L from concrete to abstract lifelines. For the above example, we get

$$L = \{\text{Client} \mapsto \text{Client}, \text{Billing} \mapsto \text{AppSystem}, \text{Calendar} \mapsto \text{AppSystem}\}$$

Formally, we need to define a substitution function $subst(t, L)$, which substitutes lifelines in the trace t according to the mapping L. First, we define substitution on single events:

$$subst(e, L) \overset{\text{def}}{=} \begin{cases} k(s, L(tr), L(re)) & \text{if } e = k(s, tr, re), k \in \{!, ?\} \\ e & \text{otherwise} \end{cases} \quad (18)$$

In general, a trace t may be seen as a function from indices to events. This trace function may be represented as a mapping where each element $i \mapsto e$ indicates that e is the i'th element in the trace, and we define the substitution function on traces by:

$$subst(t, L) \overset{\text{def}}{=} \{i \mapsto subst(t[i], L) \mid i \in [1 \ldots \#t]\} \quad (19)$$

where $\#t$ and $t[i]$ denotes the length and the i'th element of the trace t, respectively.

We then define an abstraction function $abstr(t, L, E)$, which transforms a concrete trace into an abstract trace by removing all internal events (with respect to L) that are not present in the set of abstract events E:

$$abstr(t, L, E) \overset{\text{def}}{=} \{e \in \mathcal{E} \mid tr.e \neq re.e \vee e \in E\} \circledS (subst(t, L)) \quad (20)$$

where $\mathcal{E}$ denotes the set of all events, $tr.e$ and $re.e$ denote the transmitter and the receiver of the event e, and $A \circledS t$ is the trace t with all events not in the set A removed. We also overload $abstr$ to trace sets in standard pointwise manner:

$$abstr(s, L, E) \overset{\text{def}}{=} \{abstr(t, L, E) \mid t \in s\} \quad (21)$$

Formally, detailing of interaction obligations is then defined by:

$$(p, n) \rightsquigarrow_c^{L,E} (p', n') \overset{\text{def}}{=} p = abstr(p', L, E) \wedge n = abstr(n', L, E) \quad (22)$$

where L is a lifeline mapping as described above, and E is a set of abstract events.

Finally, detailing of interactions is defined by:

$$d \rightsquigarrow_c^{L,E} d' \overset{\text{def}}{=} \forall o \in [\![d]\!] : \exists o' \in [\![d']\!] : o \rightsquigarrow_c^{L,E} o' \quad (23)$$

Detailing is compositional as defined by Definition 1. In addition, the detailing operator $\rightsquigarrow_c^{L,E}$ is monotonic with respect to assert.

> **The pragmatics of detailing**
> - Use detailing to increase the level of granularity of the specification by decomposing lifelines.
> - When detailing, document the decomposition by creating a mapping L from the concrete to the abstract lifelines.
> - When detailing, make sure that the refined traces are equal to the original ones when abstracting away internal communication and taking the lifeline mapping into account.

4.4   The Use of General Refinement

Supplementing, narrowing and detailing are all important refinement steps when developing interactions. Often, it is useful to combine two or three of these activites into a single refinement step. We therefore define a general refinement notion, of which supplementing, narrowing and detailing are all special cases. This general notion is illustrated for one interaction obligation in Fig. 18.

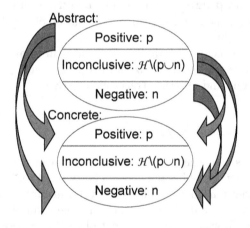

Fig. 18. General refinement of interaction obligations

As an example of general refinement, MakeAppointment in Fig. 8 combines supplementing and narrowing in order to be a refinement of the interaction in Fig. 3. Adding an operand to the alt-construct is an example of supplementing, and is not covered by the definition of narrowing. On the other hand, adding guards is an example of narrowing, and is not covered by the definition of supplementing. For this to be a valid refinement step, we therefore need the general refinement notion, formally defined by:

$$d \leadsto_r^{L,E} d' \stackrel{\text{def}}{=} \forall o \in [\![\, d \,]\!] : \exists o' \in [\![\, d' \,]\!] : o \leadsto_r^{L,E} o' \tag{24}$$

where general refinement of interaction obligations is defined by:

$$(p, n) \rightsquigarrow_r^{L,E} (p', n') \overset{\text{def}}{=} n \subseteq abstr(n', L, E) \ \wedge \tag{25}$$
$$p \subseteq abstr(p', L, E) \cup abstr(n', L, E)$$

Note that L may be the identity mapping, in which case the refinement does not include any lifeline decompositions (as in the case of MakeAppointment described above). Also, E may be the set of all events, $\mathcal{E}$, meaning that all events are considered when relating the traces of the refinement to the original traces. General refinement is compositional as defined by Definition 1.

Combining narrowing and supplementing may in general result in previously inconclusive traces being supplemented as positive, and the original positive traces made negative by narrowing. In order to specify that a trace *must* be present in the final implementation, and not removed by narrowing, we need to specify an obligation with this trace as the only positive, and all other traces as negative. The only legal refinement of this operand will then be redefining the trace as negative (by narrowing), leaving an empty set of positive traces and a specification that is not implementable.

The pragmatics of general refinement
- Use general refinement to perform a combination of supplementing, narrowing and detailing in a single step.
- To define that a particular trace *must* be present in an implementation use xalt and assert to characterize an obligation with this trace as the only positive one and all other traces as negative.

4.5   The Use of Limited Refinement

Limited refinement is a special case of general refinement, with less possibilities for adding new interactions obligations. By definition (24) of general refinement, new interaction obligations may be added freely, for instance in order to increase the nondeterminism required of an interaction. One example of this is CancelAppointment in Fig. 5, which is a refinement of the interaction given in Fig. 1. While the original specification only gave one interaction obligation with two positive traces, the refinement gives both this interaction obligation and also two new interaction obligations that are not refinements of the original one.

At some point during the development process, it is natural to limit the possibilities for creating new interaction obligations with fundamentally new traces. This is achieved by limited refinement, which has the additional requirement that each obligation of the refined interaction must have a corresponding obligation in the original interaction.

In STAIRS, stepwise development of interactions will be performed by first using general refinement to specify the main traces of the system, before switching to limited refinement which will then be used for the rest of the development process. Typically, but not necessarily, assert on the complete specification will be used at the same time as switching to limited refinement. This ensures that new traces may neither be added to the existing obligations, nor be added to the specification in the form of new interaction obligations. Note that using assert on the complete specification is not the same as restricting further refinements to be limited, as assert considers each interaction obligation separately.

Note also that limited refinement allows a refinement to have more interaction obligations than the original specification, as long as each obligation is a refinement of one of the original ones. One example is given in Fig. 19, which is a limited refinement of MakeAppointment in Fig. 15. In Fig. 19, alt has been replaced by xalt in order to specify that the client *must* be offered the choice of specifying a preferred date when asking for an appointment, while assert has been added to specify that there should be no other alternatives. In this particular case, we have not included the referenced interaction DecideAppTime in the scope of the assert-construct, as we want the possibility of supplementing more traces here. Transforming alt to xalt means in this example that each of the interaction obligations for Fig. 15 (there are two due to the xalt in DecideApp-Time) has two refining obligations in the semantics of Fig. 19. As all obligations in Fig. 19 have a corresponding obligation in Fig. 15, this is a valid instance of limited refinement.

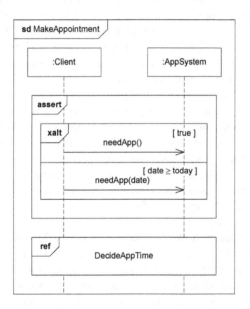

Fig. 19. MakeAppointment revisited

Formally, limited refinement is defined by:

$$d \leadsto_l^{L,E} d' \stackrel{\text{def}}{=} d \leadsto_r^{L,E} d' \land \forall o' \in [\![\, d' \,]\!] : \exists o \in [\![\, d \,]\!] : o \leadsto_r^{L,E} o' \qquad (26)$$

Limited refinement is compositional as defined by Definition 1.

The pragmatics of limited refinement
- Use assert and switch to limited refinement in order to avoid fundamentally new traces being added to the specification.
- To specify globally negative traces, define these as negative in all operands of xalt, and switch to limited refinement.

---

5   Related Work

The basis of STAIRS is interactions and sequence diagrams as defined in UML 2.0 [OMG05]. Not all of the UML 2.0 operators are defined by STAIRS, but we believe that those covered are the most useful ones in practical system development. The STAIRS operator xalt is added to this set as UML 2.0 does not distinguish between alternatives that represent underspecification and alternatives that must all be present in an implementation, but uses the alt operator in both cases.

For guarded alt, we have in our semantics chosen not to follow UML 2.0 in that the empty trace is positive if no guard is true. Instead, we recommend to make all specifications with guarded alt so that the guards are exhaustive, ensuring that this will never be a problem in practice. The UML 2.0 standard [OMG05] is vague with respect to whether the traces with a false guard should be negative or not. As we have argued, classifying these as negative is fruitful as adding guards to a specification will then be a valid refinement step.

For defining negative behaviour, UML 2.0 uses the operators neg and assert. In [RHS05a], we investigated several possible formal definitions of neg, trying to capture how it was being used on the basis of experience. However, we concluded that one operator for negation is not sufficient, which is why STAIRS defines the two operators refuse and veto to be used instead of neg.

Decomposition in UML 2.0 is the same as detailing in STAIRS, but with a more involved syntax using the concepts of interaction use and gates. With the UML 2.0 syntax, the mapping from concrete to abstract lifelines is given explicitly in the diagram.

In [GS05], Grosu and Smolka give semantics for UML sequence diagrams in the form of two Büchi automata, one for the positive and one for the negative behaviours. Refinement then corresponds to language inclusion. Their refinement notion is compositional and covers supplementing and narrowing, but not detailing. All alternatives are interpreted as underspecification, and there is no means to capture inherent nondeterminism as with xalt in STAIRS.

In [CK04], the semantics of UML interactions are defined by the notions of positive and negative satisfaction. This approach is in many ways similar to STAIRS, but does not distinguish between underspecification and inherent nondeterminism. Their definition of the UML operator neg corresponds to the STAIRS operator veto, where the empty trace is taken as positive. [CK04] defines that for alternatives specified by alt, a trace is negative only if it is negative in both operands. Also, a trace is regarded as negative if a prefix of it is described as negative, while we in STAIRS define it as inconclusive as long as the complete trace is not described by the diagram.

Another variant of sequence diagrams is Message Sequence Charts (MSCs) [ITU99]. The important distinction between different kinds of alternatives is not made for MSCs either. As in our approach, a trace is negative if its guard is false in an MSC. Refinement of MSCs is considered by Krüger in [Krü00]. Narrowing in STAIRS corresponds closely to property refinement, while detailing corresponds to structural refinement. As there is no notion of inconclusive traces in [Krü00], refinement in the form of supplementing is not considered.

Live Sequence Charts (LSCs) [DH99, HM03] is an extension of MSCs, where charts, messages, locations and conditions are specified as either universal (mandatory) or existential (optional). An existential chart specifies a behaviour (one or more traces) that must be satisfied by at least one system run, while a universal chart is a specification that must be satisfied at all times. As a universal chart specifies all allowed traces, this is not the same as inherent nondeterminism in STAIRS, which only specifies some of the traces that must be present in an implementation. In contrast to STAIRS and UML 2.0, LSC synchronizes the lifelines at the beginning of each interaction fragment. This reduces the set of possible traces, and makes it easier to implement their operational semantics.

6   Conclusions and Future Work

In this paper we have focused on giving practical guidelines for the use of STAIRS in the development of interactions. For each concept, these guidelines have been summarized in paragraphs entitled "The Pragmatics of. . . ". We have focused on situations in which STAIRS extends or expands interactions as defined in UML 2.0 [OMG05]. This includes how to define negative behaviours and how to distinguish between alternatives that represent the same behaviour and alternatives that must all be present in an implementation. STAIRS is particularly concerned with refinement, and we have given guidelines on how to refine interactions by adding behaviours (supplementing), removing underspecification (narrowing) or by decomposition (detailing).

In [RHS05b], we gave a brief explanation of what it means for an implementation to be correct with respect to a STAIRS specification. We are currently working on extending this work, leading to "the pragmatics of implementations".

The research on which this paper reports has been partly carried out within the context of the IKT-2010 project SARDAS (15295/431). We thank the other members of the SARDAS project for useful discussions related to this work. We thank Iselin Engan for helpful comments on the final draft of this paper. We also thank the anonymous reviewers for constructive feedback.

References

[CK04]   Mara Victoria Cengarle and Alexander Knapp. UML 2.0 interactions: Semantics and refinement. In *Proc. 3rd Int. Wsh. Critical Systems Development with UML (CSDUML'04)*, Technical report TUM-I0415, pages 85–99. Institut für Informatik, Technische Universität München, 2004.

[DH99]   Werner Damm and David Harel. LSC's: Breathing life into message sequence charts. In *Proc. 3rd IFIP Int. Conf. on Formal Methods for Open Object-Based Distributed Systems (FMOODS'99)*, 1999.

[GS05]   Radu Grosu and Scott A. Smolka. Safety-liveness semantics for UML sequence diagrams. In *Proc. 5th Int. Conf. on Applications of Concurrency to System Design (ACSD'05)*, pages 6–14, 2005.

[HHRS05a]   Øystein Haugen, Knut Eilif Husa, Ragnhild Kobro Runde, and Ketil Stølen. STAIRS towards formal design with sequence diagrams. *Journal of Software and Systems Modeling*, 22(4):349–458, 2005.

[HHRS05b]   Øystein Haugen, Knut Eilif Husa, Ragnhild Kobro Runde, and Ketil Stølen. Why timed sequence diagrams require three-event semantics. In *Scenarios: Models, Transformations and Tools*, volume 3466 of *LNCS*, pages 1–25. Springer, 2005.

[HM03]   David Harel and Rami Marelly. *Come, Let's Play.: Scenario-Based Programming Using LSCs and the Play-Engine*. Springer, 2003.

[HS03]   Øystein Haugen and Ketil Stølen. STAIRS — Steps to analyze interactions with refinement semantics. In *Proc. International Conference on UML (UML'2003)*, volume 2863 of *LNCS*, pages 388–402. Springer, 2003.

[ITU99]   International Telecommunication Union. *Recommendation Z.120 — Message Sequence Chart (MSC)*, 1999.

[Krü00]   Ingolf Heiko Krüger. *Distributed System Design with Message Sequence Charts*. PhD thesis, Technische Universität München, 2000.

[Kru04]   Philippe Kruchten. *The Rational Unified Process*. Addison-Wesley, third edition, 2004.

[OMG05]   Object Management Group. *UML Superstructure Specification, v. 2.0*, document: formal/05-07-04 edition, 2005.

[RHS05a]   Ragnhild Kobro Runde, Øystein Haugen, and Ketil Stølen. How to transform UML neg into a useful construct. In *Norsk Informatikkonferanse NIK'2005*, pages 55–66. Tapir, 2005.

[RHS05b]   Ragnhild Kobro Runde, Øystein Haugen, and Ketil Stølen. Refining UML interactions with underspecification and nondeterminism. *Nordic Journal of Computing*, 12(2):157–188, 2005.

[RRS06]   Atle Refsdal, Ragnhild Kobro Runde, and Ketil Stølen. Underspecification, inherent nondeterminism and probability in sequence diagrams. In *Proc. 8th IFIP Int. Conf. on Formal Methods for Open Object-Based Distributed Systems (FMOODS'06)*, volume 4037 of *LNCS*, pages 138–155. Springer, 2006.

Smallfoot: Modular Automatic Assertion Checking with Separation Logic

Josh Berdine[1], Cristiano Calcagno[2], and Peter W. O'Hearn[3]

[1] Microsoft Research
[2] Imperial College, London
[3] Queen Mary, University of London

Abstract. Separation logic is a program logic for reasoning about programs that manipulate pointer data structures. We describe Smallfoot, a tool for checking certain lightweight separation logic specifications. The assertions describe the shapes of data structures rather than their detailed contents, and this allows reasoning to be fully automatic. The presentation in the paper is tutorial in style. We illustrate what the tool can do via examples which are oriented toward novel aspects of separation logic, namely: avoidance of frame axioms (which say what a procedure does not change); embracement of "dirty" features such as memory disposal and address arithmetic; information hiding in the presence of pointers; and modular reasoning about concurrent programs.

1 Introduction

Separation logic is a program logic geared toward specifying and verifying properties of dynamically-allocated linked data structures [35], which has lead to much simpler by-hand specifications and program proofs than previous formalisms. Specifications in separation logic are "small", in that a specification of a program component concentrates on the resources relevant to its correct operation (its "footprint"), not mentioning the resources of other components at all [32]. In this paper we describe Smallfoot, an experimental tool for checking certain separation logic specifications.

The aim of the tool was simple: we wanted to see whether the simplicity of the by-hand proofs in separation logic could be transferred to an automatic setting. Smallfoot uses lightweight assertions that describe the shapes of data structures rather than their detailed contents; this restriction allows the reasoning to be fully automatic. The input language allows first-order procedures with reference and value parameters, essentially as in [17], together with operations for allocating, deallocating, mutating and reading heap cells. Smallfoot requires pre- and post-conditions for the procedures, and loop invariants. It also supports annotations for concurrency, following a concurrent extension of separation logic [31,11].

In [5] we defined the symbolic execution mechanism and proof procedure that lie at the heart of Smallfoot, but we did not there show how they could be used to prove programs. The purpose of this paper is the opposite: to show what the

F.S. de Boer et al. (Eds.): FMCO 2005, LNCS 4111, pp. 115–137, 2006.
© Springer-Verlag Berlin Heidelberg 2006

tool can do, without exposing its innards. We proceed in a tutorial style. We describe in an informal way how the proof rules of [32,35,31] are used in the tool, in conjunction with the execution mechanism, but we do not give a fully formal description or a repeat of the techniques of [5]. For a full understanding of exactly how Smallfoot works familiarity with [32,35,31,5] is essential. But we have tried to make the presentation relatively self-contained, and we hope that many of the main points can be gleaned from our examples and the discussion surrounding them.

We begin in the next section by introducing Smallfoot with three examples. The purpose of this work is to explore separation logic's modularity in an automatic setting, and that is the subject of all three examples. We will discuss some of the features of Smallfoot as we go through the examples, and highlight some of the issues for automation that guided its design. A description of the input language and some central points in the verification condition mechanism is then given in Sections 3 and 4. Several further examples are given in Section 5, and we conclude with a discussion of related and future work.

We stress that Smallfoot is limited in various ways. Its input language has been designed to match the theoretical work on separation logic, rather than an existing widely-used language; our purpose was to experiment with the logic, rather than to produce a mature end-user tool. Beyond the basic primitives of separation logic, Smallfoot at this point includes several hardwired predicates for singly-, doubly-, and xor-linked lists, and for trees, but not (yet) a mechanism for arbitrary inductive definitions of data structures. We included xor lists just to illustrate how reachability does not feature in separation logic; we have not incorporated more general address arithmetic. Smallfoot cannot handle all of the more advanced algorithms that have been the subject of by-hand proofs in separation logic, particularly graph algorithms [40,6,7]. Further, it does not have specifications for full functional correctness. Extensions in some of these directions would necessitate abandoning the automatic aspect, relying on interactive proof. Those are areas for further work.

2   Smallfoot in Three Nutshells

We begin with a warning: you should suspend thinking about the global heap when reading separation logic specifications, otherwise the logic can seem counterintuitive. Rather than global heaps you can think of heaplets, portions of heap. An assertion talks about a heaplet rather than the global heap, and a spec $[P] C [Q]$ says that if C is given a heaplet satisfying P then it will never try to access heap outside of P (other than cells allocated during execution) and it will deliver a heaplet satisfying Q if it terminates. (Of course, this has implications for how C acts on the global heap.) This heaplet reading may seem a simple point, but we have found that separation logic's "local way of thinking" can lead to confusions, which arise from reverting to thinking in terms of the global heap. So we will return to this point several times below.

2.1   Local Specifications and Framing

Consider a procedure for disposing a tree:

```
disp_tree(p) [tree(p)] {
  local i,j;
  if (p = nil) {} else {
    i := p→l; j := p→r; disp_tree(i); disp_tree(j); dispose(p); }
} [emp]
```

This is the expected procedure that walks a tree, recursively disposing left and right subtrees and then the root pointer. It uses a representation of tree nodes with left and right fields, and the empty tree is represented by nil.

This Smallfoot program includes a precondition and postcondition, corresponding to a partial correctness specification:

$$[\text{tree}(p)] \quad \texttt{disp\_tree}(p) \quad [\text{emp}]$$

(We use square instead of curly brackets, despite treating partial correctness, to maintain consistency with Smallfoot's concrete syntax.) This is an example of the small specifications supported by separation logic: it talks only about the portion of heap relevant to the correct operation of the procedure. In particular, $\text{tree}(p)$ describes a heaplet where p points to a tree, *and where there are no junk cells, cells not in the tree.* This "no junk cells" part is necessary to be able to conclude emp, that the heaplet on termination is empty.

Smallfoot discovers a proof of this program by symbolic execution. The proof in the else branch corresponds to the proof steps:

$$[(p \mapsto l\!: x, r\!: y) * \text{tree}(x) * \text{tree}(y)]$$
$$i := p{\to}l; \; j := p{\to}r;$$
$$[(p \mapsto l\!: i, r\!: j) * \text{tree}(i) * \text{tree}(j)]$$
$$\texttt{disp\_tree}(i);$$
$$[(p \mapsto l\!: i, r\!: j) * \text{tree}(j)]$$
$$\texttt{disp\_tree}(j);$$
$$[p \mapsto l\!: i, r\!: j]$$
$$\texttt{dispose}(p);$$
$$[\text{emp}]$$

After we enter the else branch we know that $p{\neq}$nil so that, by unrolling, p is an allocated node that points to left and right subtrees occupying separate storage. Then the roots of the two subtrees are loaded into i and j. Notice how the next proof steps follow operational intuition. The first recursive call removes the left subtree, the second call removes the right subtree, and the final instruction removes the root pointer p. The occurrences of the separating conjunction $*$ in these assertions ensure that the structures described, the two subtrees and root pointer, occupy separate memory, as is necessary if an operation that removes one of them is not to affect one of the others. This verification is carried out using the specification of `disp_tree` as an assumption, as in the usual treatment of recursive procedures in Hoare logic [17].

In the if branch we use an implication $\text{tree}(p) \wedge p{=}\text{nil} \Rightarrow \text{emp}$, which relies on the "no junk" character of the tree predicate.

The assertions in this proof use very little of separation logic; they are all of the form $\Pi \wedge \Sigma$ where Π is a pure boolean condition and Σ is a $*$-combination of heap predicates. All of the assertions in Smallfoot are of this special form (together with conditionals over them), and this enables a symbolic execution mechanism where $*$-conjuncts are updated in-place.

There is a hidden part in the proof outline just given: in the two procedure calls the preconditions at the call sites do not match the preconditions for the overall specification of `disp_tree`. For example, for the second call the assertion at the call site is $(p{\mapsto}l{:}i, r{:}j){*}\text{tree}(j)$ while the procedure spec would suggest that the precondition should just be $\text{tree}(j)$ (after renaming of the parameter). This is where the local way of thinking comes in. The specification of `disp_tree` says that a heaplet satisfying $\text{tree}(j)$ is transformed into one satisfying emp. The input heaplet need not be the whole heap, we can effect this transformation on a heaplet that lives inside a larger heap, and then slot the result into that larger heap.

In separation logic, this pulling out and slotting in is described using the $*$ connective. Generally, a heaplet h satisfies $P * Q$ if it can be split into two disjoint heaplets h_P and h_Q that satisfy P and Q. The above narrative for the call `disp_tree`(j) tells us to take $(p{\mapsto}l{:}i, r{:}j){*}\text{tree}(j)$, pull out the heaplet description $\text{tree}(j)$, transform it to emp, and slot that back in, obtaining $(p{\mapsto}l{:}i, r{:}j) * \text{emp}$. Then, we can use an identity $P * \text{emp} \Leftrightarrow P$.

Separation logic has an inference rule (the frame rule)

$$\frac{[P]\,C\,[Q]}{[R * P]\,C\,[R * Q]}$$

(where C doesn't assign to R's free variables) which lets us do "pull out, perform local surgery, slot in" in a proof. To automatically generate proofs using this rule, which was implicitly applied in the steps in the proof for the else branch above, we need a way to infer frame axioms. If we are given an assertion at a call site and a procedure precondition, we must find the leftover part (which lets us do the "pull out" step). Often, this leftover part can be found by simple pattern matching, as is the case in the `disp_tree` example, but there are other cases where pattern matching will not do. Technically, Smallfoot uses a method of extracting frame axioms from incomplete proofs in a proof theory for entailments [5].

2.2 Processes That Mind Their Own Business

Concurrent separation logic [31] has the following rule for parallel composition:

$$\frac{[P]\,C\,[Q] \qquad [P']\,C'\,[Q']}{[P * P']\,C \parallel C'\,[Q * Q']}$$

where C does not change variables free in P', C', Q', and vice versa. The idea of this rule is that the specifications $[P]\,C\,[Q]$ and $[P']\,C'\,[Q']$ describe all the resources that C and C' might access, that they mind their own business; so, if we know that the resources are separate in the precondition, then we can reason about the concurrent processes independently. A simple example of this is a parallel composition of two heap alterations on different cells, where the $*$ in the precondition guarantees that x and y are not aliases:

$$[x \mapsto c: 3 \; * \; y \mapsto c: 3]$$

$$
\begin{array}{c|c}
[x \mapsto c: 3] & [y \mapsto c: 3] \\
x \rightarrow c := 4 & y \rightarrow c := 5 \\
[x \mapsto c: 4] & [y \mapsto c: 5]
\end{array}
$$

$$[x \mapsto c: 4 \; * \; y \mapsto c: 5]$$

The local thinking is exercised more strongly in concurrent than in sequential separation logic. A points-to fact $x \mapsto c: 3$ describes a heaplet with a single cell x that is a record with a c field whose value is 3. As far as the left process is concerned, reasoning is carried out for a heaplet with a single cell, its heaplet, and similarly for the right. In the global heap, though, it is not the case that there is only one cell; there are at least two! The two views, local and more global, are reconciled by the form of the concurrency rule.

To apply the concurrency rule automatically we need a way to get our hands on the preconditions of the constituent processes. We could do this in several ways, such as by requiring an annotation with each $\|$, or by introducing a "named process" concept which requires a precondition but no postcondition. We settled on requiring the constituents of a $\|$ to be procedure calls; because procedures come with pre/post specs we can use their preconditions when applying the concurrency rule. The postconditions are not strictly necessary for automating the concurrency rule. We made this choice just to avoid multiplying annotation forms. A Smallfoot program corresponding to the above example, but where we create the two separate cells, is:

```
upd(x, y) [x↦] {x→c := y;} [x↦c: y]

main() {
    x := new(); y := new(); x→c := 3; y→c := 3;
    upd(x,4) || upd(y,5);
} [x↦c: 4 * y↦c: 5]
```

In the precondition of upd the assertion $x \mapsto$ indicates that x points to something. It denotes a singleton heaplet in which x is the only allocated or defined cell. The postcondition describes a singleton heaplet where the c field of location x has y as its contents.

When a pre- or post-condition is left out, as the pre for main is in this program, it defaults to emp. Also, Smallfoot accepts a collection of procedures as input, one optionally "main".

In contrast, when we change the main program to

```
main() {
    x := new(); x→c := 3; y := x;
    upd(x,4) || upd(y,4);
} [y=x ∧ x↦c: 4]
```

then Smallfoot flags an error; since x and y are aliases, there is no way to split the heap into two parts, giving one symbolic cell to each of the constituent processes. In general, if a Smallfoot program has a race — where two processes may attempt to access the same cell at the same time — then an error is reported. (More precisely, any such attempted parallel accesses must be wrapped in critical sections which specify atomicity assumptions for accesses.)

Our description of how the proof is found for sequential `disp_tree` is almost the same for a parallel variant, which Smallfoot proves using the concurrency rule:

```
par_disp_tree(p) [tree(p)] {
  local i,j;
  if (p = nil) {} else {
    i := p→l;  j := p→r;
    par_disp_tree(i) || par_disp_tree(j);
    dispose(p); }
} [emp]
```

The reader's reaction to `disp_tree` and `par_disp_tree` might be: aren't they rather trivial? Well, yes, and that is part of the point. For contrast, consider `par_disp_tree` in the rely/guarantee formalism [21,27], which is rightly celebrated for providing compositional reasoning about concurrency. In addition to a precondition and a postcondition saying that the nodes in the tree are deallocated, we would have to formalize two additional assertions:

Rely. No other process touches my tree $tree(p)$; and
Guarantee. I do not touch any storage outside my tree.

Although compositional, as this example demonstrates the relies and guarantees can be rather global, and can complicate specifications even in simple examples when no interference is present. The Smallfoot specification for this procedure is certainly simpler.

2.3   Process Interaction and Heaplet Transfer

Process interaction in Smallfoot is done with conditional critical regions (CCRs) [18]. The programming model is based on "resources" r and CCR statements with r when(B) $\{C\}$. CCRs for common resource r must be executed with mutual exclusion, and each has a guard which must hold before execution.

Data abstractions can be protected with CCRs by wrapping critical regions around code that accesses a data structure. A more daring form of concurrency is when several processes access the same piece of state outside of critical sections [31]. In separation logic it is possible to show that daring programming idioms are used consistently. An example is a pointer-transferring buffer: instead of copying a (perhaps large) portion of data from one process to another, a pointer to the data is sent. Typically, the sending and receiving processes access the pointer without synchronization.

A toy version of this scenario is the following code snippet using buffer operations put and get:

$$x := \text{new}(); \quad \| \quad \text{get}(y;);$$
$$\text{put}(x); \quad\quad\quad \text{dispose}(y);$$

This creates a new pointer in the left process and then places it in the buffer. The right process then reads out the pointer and disposes it. We would typically want to fill the pointer contents in the left process before sending it, and to do something with those contents in the right. The point is that to reason about the dispose in the right process we must know that y is not dangling after we do the get operation. It is useful to use the intuition of "permission to access" to describe this [9,8]: the permission to access the pointer moves from the first to the second process along with the pointer value. Further, when permission transfers it must disappear from the left process or else we could mistakenly justify a further dispose(x) in the left process, after the put. In conjunction with the dispose(y) in the right process that would disastrously lead to a double-disposal that we must rule out.

This is where the local way of thinking helps. An assertion at a program point describes a heaplet, which represents a local permission to access, instead of a global heap. put(x) will have precondition $x \mapsto$ and postcondition emp, the idea being that the heaplet for x flows out of the left process and into the buffer. The emp postcondition ensures that, even if the value of x remains unchanged, the local knowledge that x is not dangling (the permission) is given up, thus preventing further disposal. At this point the global heap is not empty, but the heaplet/permission for the left process is. get($y;$) will have precondition emp and postcondition $y \mapsto$, connoting that the heaplet (the permission) materializes in the second process.

A Smallfoot program encoding this scenario is:

```
resource buf (c) [if c=nil then emp else c↦]

init() { c := nil; }

put(x) [x↦] { with buf when(c=nil) { c := x; } } [emp]

get(y;) [emp] { with buf when(c≠nil) { y := c; c := nil; } } [y↦]

putter() { x := new(); put(x); putter(); }

getter() { get(y;); /* use y */ dispose(y); getter(); }

main() { putter() || getter(); }
```

In the CCR model resource names are used to determine units of mutual exclusion. Different CCRs with r when(B) $\{C\}$ for the same resource name r cannot overlap in their executions. A CCR can proceed with its body C only when its boolean condition B holds. A resource declaration indicates some private variables associated with the resource (in this case c) and an invariant that describes its internal state.

When we have resource declarations as here an `init` procedure is needed for initialization; when we do not have a resource declaration, the initialization can be omitted. The `init` procedure is run before `main`; it's job is to set up the state that is protected by the named resource, by establishing the resource invariant.

In this code the omitted preconditions and postconditions are all (by default) `emp`, except the post of `init` which is (by default) the resource invariant (the assertion in the resource declaration). The `put` and `get` operations are encoded using little critical regions. The resource *buf* has an invariant which describes its heaplet: it says that if *c*=nil then the buffer has no permission, else it holds permission to access *c*. The `put` operation can fire only when *c*=nil, and so because of the invariant we will know at that point that *buf*'s heaplet is `emp`. The assignment *c*:= *x* changes the *buf* state so that the only way for the invariant to be true is if *c*↦; the permission to access the pointer (at this point denoted by both *c* and *x*) flows into the buffer. Furthermore, the `put` operation cannot have *x*↦ as its postcondition because separation is maintained between the resource invariant and the heaplet assertions for the two processes. A similar narrative can be given about how `get` effects a transfer from the buffer to the `getter` process.

In fact, the annotations in this code are more than is strictly needed. If we were to inline `put` and `get`, then Smallfoot would verify the resulting code. We separated out these operations only to display what their specifications are.

What makes this all work is an inference rule

$$\frac{[(P * R_r) \wedge B] \, C \, [Q * R_r]}{[P] \, \texttt{with } r \, \texttt{when}(B) \, \{C\} \, [Q]}$$

where R_r is an invariant formula associated with resource r. This rule is used to verify the `put` and `get` procedures, and the concurrency rule is then used for the composition of `putter` and `getter`. Even though the program loops, the fact that it gets past Smallfoot ensures that no pointer is ever disposed twice (without an intervening allocation), that there is no race condition, and that the resource invariant is true when not in the middle of a critical section.

Besides the separation between resource and process enforced using *, this rule (which stems originally from [18]) is wonderfully modular: the precondition and postcondition P and Q of a CCR do not mention the invariant R_r at all. This allows reasoning about processes in isolation, even in the presence of interaction.

3   The Input Language

3.1   Annotated Programs

A Smallfoot program consists of sets of resource declarations

$$\texttt{resource } r(\vec{x}_r) R_r$$

where $\vec{x}_r$ and R_r are resource r's protected variables and invariant; and procedure declarations

$$f(\vec{p}\, ; \vec{v})[P_f] \, C_f \, [Q_f]$$

where procedure f's parameters $\vec{p}$ are passed by reference and $\vec{v}$ by value, and assertions P_f and Q_f are f's pre- and post-conditions. In this formal description the preconditions and postconditions have to be included, but we repeat that in the tool if a pre or post is left out then it is emp by default. Assertions are described later; commands are generated by:

$$E ::= x \mid \text{nil} \mid c \mid E \,\text{xor}\, E$$
$$B ::= E{=}E \mid E{\neq}E$$
$$S ::= x{:=}E \mid x{:=}E{\to}t \mid E{\to}t{:=}E \mid x{:=}\text{new}() \mid \text{dispose}(E)$$
$$C ::= S \mid C\,;C \mid \text{if}(B)\,\{C\}\,\text{else}\,\{C\} \mid \text{while}(B)\,[I]\,\{C\}$$
$$\mid\ f(\vec{x}\,;\vec{E}) \mid f(\vec{x}\,;\vec{E}) \parallel f(\vec{x}\,;\vec{E}) \mid \text{with}\ r\ \text{when}(B)\,\{C\}$$

There is the additional evident constraint on a program that in any procedure call $f(\vec{y}\,;\vec{E})$ or region with r when(B) $\{C\}$ the variable f/r must be defined in a procedure/resource declaration.

Smallfoot programs are subject to certain variable restrictions, which are needed for the soundness of Hoare logic rules; for example, that variable aliasing and concurrent races for variables (not heap cells) are ruled out. These conditions are, in general, complex and unmemorable; they may be found in [4].

3.2   Assertions and Specifications

The assertions are *-combinations of heap predicates and $\wedge$-combinations of pure boolean facts, together with conditionals over these. Conditionals are used rather than disjunctions because they preserve the "preciseness" property that is needed for soundness of concurrent separation logic [11]. The heap predicates include the points-to relation, the tree predicate, a predicate for singly-linked list segments and one for xor-linked lists. (We also have conventional doubly-linked lists in Smallfoot, but do not include any examples for them in this paper.)

$$P,Q,R,I ::= \Pi \wedge \Sigma \mid \text{if } B \text{ then } P \text{ else } P \qquad H ::= E{\mapsto}\rho \mid \text{tree}(E) \mid \text{ls}(E,E)$$
$$\Pi ::= B_1 \wedge \cdots \wedge B_n \mid \text{true} \mid \text{false} \qquad\qquad \mid\ \text{xlseg}(E,E,E,E)$$
$$\Sigma ::= H_1 * \cdots * H_n \mid \text{emp} \qquad\qquad \rho ::= t_1{:}E_1,\ldots,t_n{:}E_n$$

The model assumes a finite collection Fields (from which the t_i are drawn), and disjoint sets Loc of locations and Values of non-addressable values, with nil $\in$ Values. We then set:

$$\text{Heaps} \stackrel{\text{def}}{=} \text{Loc} \stackrel{\text{fin}}{\rightharpoonup} (\text{Fields} \to \text{Values} \cup \text{Loc})$$

$$\text{Stacks} \stackrel{\text{def}}{=} \text{Variables} \to \text{Values} \cup \text{Loc}$$

In this heap model a location maps to a record of values. The formula $E{\mapsto}\rho$ can mention any number of fields in ρ, and the values of the remaining fields are implicitly existentially quantified.

For $s \in$ Stacks, $h \in$ Heaps, the key clauses in the satisfaction relation for assertions are as follows:

$$s \vDash E{=}F \qquad\qquad \overset{\text{def}}{\text{iff}}\ [\![E]\!]s = [\![F]\!]s$$

$$s \vDash E{\neq}F \qquad\qquad \overset{\text{def}}{\text{iff}}\ [\![E]\!]s \neq [\![F]\!]s$$

$$s \vDash \Pi_0 \wedge \Pi_1 \qquad\qquad \overset{\text{def}}{\text{iff}}\ s \vDash \Pi_0 \text{ and } s \vDash \Pi_1$$

$$s, h \vDash E_0 \mapsto t_1 {:}\, E_1, \ldots, t_k {:}\, E_k \ \overset{\text{def}}{\text{iff}}\ h = [[\![E_0]\!]s{\rightarrow}r] \text{ where } r(t_i) = [\![E_i]\!]s \text{ for } i \in 1..k$$

$$s, h \vDash \mathsf{emp} \qquad\qquad \overset{\text{def}}{\text{iff}}\ h = \varnothing$$

$$s, h \vDash \Sigma_0 * \Sigma_1 \qquad\qquad \overset{\text{def}}{\text{iff}}\ \exists h_0, h_1.\ h = h_0{*}h_1 \text{ and } s, h_0 \vDash \Sigma_0 \text{ and } s, h_1 \vDash \Sigma_1$$

$$s, h \vDash \Pi \wedge \Sigma \qquad\qquad \overset{\text{def}}{\text{iff}}\ s \vDash \Pi \text{ and } s, h \vDash \Sigma$$

For pure assertions Π we do not need the heap component in the satisfaction relation. $h = h_0{*}h_1$ indicates that the domains of h_0 and h_1 are disjoint, and that h is their graph union. The semantics $[\![E]\!]s \in$ Values of expressions is as expected. We will not provide semantic definitions of the predicates for trees and lists now, but give inductive characterizations of them later.

Each command C determines a relation:

$$[\![C]\!] \colon (\text{Stacks} \times \text{Heaps}) \longleftrightarrow (\text{Stacks} \times \text{Heaps}) \cup \{\text{fault}\}$$

The fault output occurs when a command attempts to dereference a dangling pointer. For example, $x{\rightarrow}tl := y$ produces a fault when applied to state s, h, where $s(x)$ is not a location in the domain of h. We will not give a formal definition of $[\![C]\!]$; when considering concurrency it is especially intricate [11]. The interpretation of Hoare triples is:

> $[P] \, C \, [Q]$ holds if, whenever given a state satisfying P, C will not produce a fault and, if it terminates, will deliver a state satisfying Q. More mathematically: $s, h \vDash P \wedge (s, h)[\![C]\!]\sigma \implies \sigma \neq \text{fault} \wedge \sigma \vDash Q$

This interpretation guarantees that C can only access heap which is guaranteed to exist by P. For, if C were to alter heap outside of an assertion P, then it would fault when that heap was deleted, and that would falsify $[P] \, C \, [Q]$.

4   Verification Condition Generation

Smallfoot chops an annotated program into Hoare triples for certain symbolic instructions, that are then decided using the symbolic execution mechanism of [5]. Execution reduces these triples to entailments $P \vdash Q$. These entailments are usually called verification conditions; we will use the same terminology for the output of the chopping phase, before the execution phase.

4.1   Verification Conditions

A verification condition is a triple $[P] \, SI \, [Q]$ where SI is a "symbolic instruction":

$$SI ::= \epsilon \mid S \mid [P]\mathsf{jsr}_{\vec{x}}\,[Q] \mid \text{if } B \text{ then } SI \text{ else } SI \mid SI \,;\, SI$$

A symbolic instruction is a piece of loop-free sequential code where all procedure calls have been instantiated to jsr instructions of the form $[P]\,\mathsf{jsr}_{\bar{x}}\,[Q]$. This form plays a central role in Smallfoot. We use it not only to handle procedure calls, but also for concurrency and for entry to and exit from a critical region.

Semantically, $[P]\,\mathsf{jsr}_{\bar{x}}\,[Q]$ is a "generic command" in the sense of [38]. It is the greatest relation satisfying the pre- and post-condition, and subject to the constraint that only the variables in $\bar{x}$ are modified. An adaptation of generic commands which requires the relation to agree on local and pull out/slot in interpretations of triples, can be found in [33].

Overall, what the execution mechanism does for $[P]\,SI\,[Q]$ is start with P and run over statements in SI generating postconditions. For each postcondition P' thus obtained, it checks an entailment $P' \vdash Q$ using a terminating proof theory.

We will not give a detailed description of the symbolic execution mechanism, referring to [5] for the details. (We remark that the presentation there does not include conditional assertions if B then P else Q, but these are easily dealt with.) Instead, we will describe how the mechanism works in a particular case, in the else branch of the disp_tree program.

When we take that branch we have to establish a triple

$$[p{\neq}\mathrm{nil} \wedge \mathsf{tree}(p)]\,C\,[\mathsf{emp}]$$

where C is the command in the else branch, with procedure calls instantiated to jsr instructions. Applying the tree unroll rule yields

$$[p{\neq}\mathrm{nil} \wedge (p{\mapsto}l{:}\,i',r{:}\,j') * \mathsf{tree}(i') * \mathsf{tree}(j')]\,C\,[\mathsf{emp}]$$

for fresh variables i' and j'. After the first two assignment statements in C we are left with:

$$[p{\neq}\mathrm{nil} \wedge (p{\mapsto}l{:}\,i,r{:}\,j) * \mathsf{tree}(i) * \mathsf{tree}(j)]$$
$$([\mathsf{tree}(i)]\,\mathsf{jsr}\,[\mathsf{emp}])\,;([\mathsf{tree}(j)]\,\mathsf{jsr}\,[\mathsf{emp}])\,;\,\mathtt{dispose}(p)\,[\mathsf{emp}]$$

To apply $[\mathsf{tree}(i)]\,\mathsf{jsr}\,[\mathsf{emp}]$ we have to find a frame axiom, using the frame rule from earlier, and it is just $(p{\mapsto}l{:}\,i,r{:}\,j) * \mathsf{tree}(j)$. Similarly, in the next step we obtain $p{\mapsto}l{:}\,i,r{:}\,j$ as the frame axiom, and finally we dispose p. (Frame inference is not always so easy; for example, CCR examples later require a certain amount of logical reasoning beyond pattern matching.) This leaves us with an easy entailment:

$$p{\neq}\mathrm{nil} \wedge \mathsf{emp} \vdash \mathsf{emp}$$

4.2   VCGen

For each procedure declaration $f(\vec{p};\vec{v})[P]\,C\,[Q]$ we generate a set of verification conditions $vcg(f,[P]\,C\,[Q])$. The formal definition can be found in [4], and here we illustrate how it applies to the par_disp_tree and heaplet transfer examples presented in Sections 2.2 and 2.3.

Recall the specification of `par_disp_tree`: $[\text{tree}(p)]\,\texttt{par\_disp\_tree}(p)\,[\text{emp}]$. So for a call `par_disp_tree`$(i)$, *vcg* considers a single generic command:

$$[\text{tree}(i)]\,\mathsf{jsr}\,[\text{emp}]$$

which indicates that the net effect of calling `par_disp_tree` on i is to consume a tree starting from i, produce no heap, and modify no (nonlocal) variables in the process. Using this straight-line command, and the similar one for the call `par_disp_tree`(j), the net effect of the recursive parallel function calls `par_disp_tree`(i) ∥ `par_disp_tree`(j) is to consume trees starting at i and j, produce no heap, and modify no variables. This is the core of the verification condition of `par_disp_tree`, and is expressed by the straight-line command:

$$[\text{tree}(i) * \text{tree}(j)]\,\mathsf{jsr}\,[\text{emp}]$$

With this, the whole body of `par_disp_tree` is expressed by a conditional command, and so `par_disp_tree`'s single VC is obtained by tacking on the pre- and post-conditions:

$[\text{tree}(p)]$
if $p{=}0$ then ϵ else $i := p{\to}l;\, j := p{\to}r;([\text{tree}(i) * \text{tree}(j)]\,\mathsf{jsr}\,[\text{emp}])\,;\texttt{dispose}(p)$
$[\text{emp}]$

This VC is then discharged by symbolic execution, which propagates the precondition forward through the command and then checks (for each branch of the execution) that the computed postcondition entails the specified one.

For the heaplet transfer example, the `init` procedure must establish the resource invariant from precondition emp, yielding VC:

$$[\text{emp}]\,\mathsf{jsr}\,[\text{if } c{=}\text{nil then emp else } c{\mapsto}]$$

For brevity, if we inline `put` and `get` in `putter` and `getter`:

```
putter() [emp] {              getter() [emp] {
  local x;                      local y;
  x := new();                   with buf when(c≠nil) {
  with buf when(c=nil) {          y := c;  c := nil; }
    c := x; }                   dispose(y);
  putter();                     getter();
} [emp]                       } [emp]
```

The crux of the VCs of these functions is the straight-line command which expresses the CCR commands. For `getter` this is:

$[\text{emp}]\,\mathsf{jsr}\,[(\text{if } c{=}\text{nil then emp else } c{\mapsto}) \wedge c{\neq}\text{nil}]\,;$
$y := c\,;c := \text{nil}$
$[\text{if } c{=}\text{nil then emp else } c{\mapsto}]\,\mathsf{jsr}_c\,[\text{emp}]$

The generic commands for CCR entry and exit act as resource transformers. Recalling that the resource invariant for *buf* is (if $c=$nil then emp else $c\mapsto$), the initial generic command expresses that upon entry into the CCR, the guard holds and resource invariant is made available to the body. Notice how the invariant is obtained starting from emp as a precondition, "materializing" inside the CCR as it were. Then the body runs, and the final generic command expresses that the body must reestablish the resource invariant prior to exiting the CCR.

The CCR in `putter` works similarly, but illustrates resource transfer on exit:

$$[\text{emp}]\,\text{jsr}\,[(\text{if } c=\text{nil then emp else } c\mapsto) \wedge c=\text{nil}]\,;$$

$$c := x$$

$$[\text{if } c=\text{nil then emp else } c\mapsto]\,\text{jsr}_c\,[\text{emp}]$$

The use of emp in the postcondition, considering that $x\neq$nil since x will have just been allocated, effectively deletes the invariant $c\mapsto$ from consideration, and the cell pointed-to by c will not be accessible to the code following the CCR.

The VCs for `putter` and `getter` are then:

[emp]
  $x := \text{new}()$;
  [emp]
    jsr
  [(if $c=$nil then emp else $c\mapsto$) $\wedge c=$nil];
  $c := x$;
  [if $c=$nil then emp else $c\mapsto$]jsr_c [emp];
  [emp]jsr [emp]
[emp]

[emp]
  [emp]
    jsr
  [(if $c=$nil then emp else $c\mapsto$) $\wedge c\neq$nil];
  $y := c$;
  $c := \text{nil}$;
  [if $c=$nil then emp else $c\mapsto$]jsr_c [emp];
  $\text{dispose}(y)$;
  [emp]jsr [emp]
[emp]

Note that, as usual, when verifying a recursive procedure, the procedure's specification is assumed. Here, this means that each recursive call is replaced by a generic command with the procedure's pre- and post-conditions.

The main command is then a parallel function call:

$$\texttt{putter}();\quad \| \quad \texttt{getter}();$$

which gives the additional verification condition:

$$[\text{emp}]\,([\text{emp}]\,\text{jsr}\,[\text{emp}])\,[\text{emp}]$$

Note that in both of these examples, no analysis of potential interleavings of the executions of parallel commands is needed. Given the resource invariants, the concurrent separation logic treatment of CCRs allows us to just verify a few triples for simple sequential commands.

5 Further Examples

5.1 More on Trees

The specification of `disp_tree` does not use $*$, even though the proof does. An example that uses $*$ in its spec is:

```
copy_tree(q; p) [tree(p)] {
  local i, j, i', j';
  if (p = nil) { q := p; }
  else {
    i := p→l;  j := p→r;
    copy_tree(i'; i);  copy_tree(j'; j);
    q := new();  q→l := i';  q→r := j'; }
} [tree(q) * tree(p)]
```

The tree predicate that we use is not sensitive to the contents of the tree, only the fact that it is a tree. So, if in `copy_tree` the final two steps were

$$q \rightarrow l := j'; \quad q \rightarrow r := i';$$

then we would actually have an algorithm for rotating the tree, though it would satisfy the same spec. If, on the other hand, we mistakenly point back into the old tree

$$q \rightarrow l := i; \quad q \rightarrow r := j;$$

then an error is reported; we do not have separation on termination.

The tree predicate that we have used here is one that satisfies

$$\text{tree}(E) \iff (E{=}\text{nil} \land \text{emp}) \lor (\exists x, y. (E \mapsto l{:}\, x, r{:}\, y) * \text{tree}(x) * \text{tree}(y))$$

where x and y are fresh. The use of the $*$ between $E \mapsto l{:}\, x, r{:}\, y$ and the two subtrees ensures that there are no cycles, the $*$ between the subtrees ensures that there is no sharing (it is not a DAG), and the use of emp in the base case ensures that there are no cells in a memory satisfying $\text{tree}(E)$ other than those in the tree. The fact that the specification does not mention any data field is what makes this a shape specification, insensitive to the particular data.

This definition of $\text{tree}(E)$ is not something that the user of Smallfoot sees; it is outside the fragment used by the tool (it has a quantifier). Reasoning inside the tool essentially uses rolling and unrolling of this definition. For instance, the proof step where we entered the else branch uses an entailment

$$p{\neq}\text{nil} \land \text{tree}(p) \vdash \exists x, y. (p \mapsto l{:}\, x, r{:}\, y) * \text{tree}(x) * \text{tree}(y)$$

together with stripping the existential (generating fresh variables) when the right-hand side is subsequently used as a precondition.

5.2   Linked Lists

We now give an example, using lists, that cannot be handled using simple (un)rolling of an inductive definition. We work with linked lists that use field tl for the next element. The predicate for linked-list segments is the least satisfying the following specification.

$$\text{ls}(E, F) \iff (E{=}F \land \text{emp}) \lor (E{\neq}F \land \exists y. E \mapsto tl{:}\, y * \text{ls}(y, F))$$

A complete linked list is one that satisfies $\text{ls}(E, \text{nil})$.

Consider the following Smallfoot program, where the pre and post use complete lists only, but the loop invariant requires a genuine segment $\mathsf{ls}(x,t)$. (One would use genuine segments in pres and posts for, e.g., queues.):

```
append_list(x; y)  [ls(x, nil) * ls(y, nil)] {
    if (x = nil) { x := y; }
    else {
        t := x;  u := t→tl;
        while (u ≠nil)  [ls(x, t) * t↦tl: u * ls(u, nil)] {
            t := u;  u := t→tl; }
        t→tl := y; }
} [ls(x, nil)]
```

The most subtle part of reasoning in this example comes in the last step, which involves a triple

$$[\mathsf{ls}(x,t) * t{\mapsto}tl\colon \mathrm{nil} * \mathsf{ls}(y,\mathrm{nil})]\ \ t{\to}tl := y;\ \ [\mathsf{ls}(x,\mathrm{nil})]$$

We use a symbolic execution axiom

$$[A * x{\mapsto}f\colon y]\, x{\to}f\!:= z\, [A * x{\mapsto}f\colon z]$$

to alter the precondition in-place, and then we use the rule of consequence with the entailment

$$\mathsf{ls}(x,t) * t{\mapsto}tl\colon y * \mathsf{ls}(y,\mathrm{nil}) \vdash \mathsf{ls}(x,\mathrm{nil})$$

of the postcondition. This entailment does not itself follow from simple unrolling of the definition of list segments, but is proven in the proof theory used within Smallfoot by applying the inductive definition to conclude $\mathsf{ls}(t,\mathrm{nil})$ from $t{\mapsto}tl\colon y *$ $\mathsf{ls}(y,\mathrm{nil})$, and then applying a rule that encodes the axiom

$$\mathsf{ls}(E_1, E_2) * \mathsf{ls}(E_2, \mathrm{nil}) \vdash \mathsf{ls}(E_1, \mathrm{nil})$$

It is this axiom that does not follow at once from list rolling and unrolling; in the metatheory it would require a proof by induction.

Generally, for each hardwired inductive predicate Smallfoot uses a collection of such rules that are consequences of induction, but that can be formulated in a way that does not require enumeration of inductive hypotheses. The proof theory we have obtained in this manner is complete as well as terminating for entailments involving lists and trees [5].

This ability to prove inductive properties is one of the characteristics which sets this approach apart from Alias Types [39] and its descendants. Alias Types includes coercions to roll and unroll inductive types, but (as far as we understand) consequences of induction must be witnessed by loops.

A final comment on this example. In the loop invariant we did not include a *-conjunct $\mathsf{ls}(y,\mathrm{nil})$, which would indicate that the loop preserves the listness of y. The reason we did not include this is that y's list is outside the footprint of the loop; Smallfoot discovers it as a frame axiom.

5.3   Information Hiding

The following describes a toy memory manager, which maintains binary cons cells in a free list. When the list is empty, the `alloc(x;)` operation calls `new` in a way similar to how `malloc()` might call a system routine `sbrk()` to request additional memory.

```
resource mm (f) [ls(f, nil)]

init() { f := nil; }

alloc(x;) [emp] {
  with mm when(true) {
    if(f = nil) { x := new(); } else { x := f; f := x→tl; } }
} [x↦]

dealloc(y) [y↦] { with mm when(true) { y→tl := f; f := y; } } [emp]
```

The use of CCRs provides mutual exclusion, so that several calls to `alloc` or `dealloc` in different process will not interfere. The real point of the example, though, is information hiding. Because of the modularity of the CCR rule, the interface specifications for `alloc` and `dealloc` do not mention the free list at all. Furthermore, the specification of `dealloc` forces permission to access a deallocated cell to be given up, and this is essential to prevent incorrect usage.

For example, the little main program

$$\texttt{main() \{ alloc}(z;); \texttt{ dealloc}(z); \ z→tl := z; \ \}$$

is flagged as an error by Smallfoot, because the precondition to $z→tl := z$ will be emp; we must know that z points to something to do a dereference, this program would tie a cycle in the free list.

However, the reason that this program is ruled out is not just because the invariant it violated, it is because the cell z (now in the free list) cannot be touched at all after `dealloc(z)`. For example, if we were to replace $z→tl := z$ by $z→tl := \text{nil}$ then the free list would not be corrupted in the global state, but the example still would not pass Smallfoot; it breaks abstraction by dereferencing a cross-boundary pointer, into the free list abstraction.

The effect of this information hiding can be seen more strongly by replacing the occurrences of `new` and `dispose` in the pointer-transferring buffer with calls to the homegrown memory manager.

$$\texttt{putter() \{ alloc}(x;); \texttt{ put}(x); \texttt{ putter(); \}}$$

$$\texttt{getter() \{ get}(y;); \ \texttt{/* use y */ dealloc}(y); \texttt{ getter(); \}}$$

If we replace the `putter` and `getter` procedures from Section 2.3 with these, include joint initialization of the two resources

$$\texttt{init() \{ } f := \text{nil}; \ c := \text{nil}; \ \}$$

and leave everything else the same, then the code verifies. If we did not use the CCR rule to hide resource invariants, we would have to "thread" the free list through the buffer code, forcing us to alter the specifications of `put` and `get` by including $\mathsf{ls}(f, \mathrm{nil})$ in their preconditions and postconditions.

5.4   XOR-deqs

For our final example we consider DEQs – double-ended queues – implemented using an xor-linked list. Recall that an xor-linked list is a compact representation of doubly-linked lists where, instead of using separate fields to store previous and next nodes, their bitwise exclusive or is stored in one field [23]. Besides their entertainment value, using xor lists here demonstrates how Smallfoot does not depend on reachability. The fact that the separation logic triple $[P]\,C\,[Q]$ asserts that execution of C in states described by P will not access any other locations (except possibly locations newly allocated by C) does not depend on whether other such locations are reachable or not. We will also allow concurrent access to the DEQ, though that aspect is of secondary importance for the example.

The following predicate describes xor-linked list segments:

$$\mathsf{xlseg}(E_1, F_1, E_2, F_2)$$
$$\overset{\text{def}}{\text{iff}}\ (E_1{=}F_1 \wedge E_2{=}F_2 \wedge \mathsf{emp})$$
$$\vee\,(E_1{\neq}F_1 \wedge E_2{\neq}F_2 \wedge \exists x.\,(E_1{\mapsto}l{:}\,(E_2\,\mathtt{xor}\,x)) * \mathsf{xlseg}(x, F_1, E_1, F_2))$$

In reading this definition it helps to think of a picture:

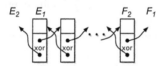

The basic idea is that a resource will own the DEQ represented as an xor list, while processes accessing the two ends will hold dummy nodes *back* and *front* which will be used for putting elements in the DEQ. Operations for getting from the DEQ will release nodes into the calling processes. The resource declaration and invariant are as follows; additionally, an initialization is needed (code omitted) which sets up the pictured postcondition.

> **resource** $xdeq(n, p)$ $[\mathit{front}{=}p \wedge \mathit{back}{=}n \wedge \mathsf{xlseg}(f, n, p, b)]$
>
> **init()** { ... } $[(\mathit{front}{\mapsto}l{:}\,\mathit{prev}\,\mathtt{xor}\,f) * (\mathit{back}{\mapsto}l{:}\,\mathit{next}\,\mathtt{xor}\,b)]$

In this invariant it helps to consider the picture above: heaps cells corresponding to the nodes n and p (and hence *front* and *back*) are not held in the DEQ, but rather are pointers into the processes that hold them as dummy nodes.

There are four procedures for accessing the DEQ: in Table 1 we show the code for putting on the back and getting from the front, and the specifications only for the other two (their code is similar).

What the `getf` procedure does is dispose the dummy node *front* it currently has, replacing it with the first node f that is in the DEQ. This is done by an

Table 1. xor-linked DEQ accessors

```
getf(x;) [front↦l: prev xor f] {
  local t, old_f;
  t := front→l;
  old_f := prev xor t;
  dispose(front);
  prev := front;
  /* split new dummy link
     off front */
  with xdeq when(old_f≠n) {
    t := f→l;
    f := t xor p;
    p := old_f;
    front := p;
  }
  x := front→d;
} [front↦l: prev xor f]

getb(x;) [back↦l: next xor b] {
  ...
} [back↦l: next xor b]
```

```
putb(x) [back↦l: next xor b] {
  local t, new_n, old_p;
  /* allocate new dummy link */
  new_n := new();
  new_n→l := next xor back;
  /* store datum in previous dummy,
     link to new dummy */
  back→d := x;
  t := back→l;
  old_b := t xor next;
  back→l := new_n xor old_b;
  /* move previous dummy link
     into DEQ */
  with xdeq when(p≠back) {
    b := back;
    n := new_n;
    back := n;
  }
} [back↦l: next xor b]

putf(x) [front↦l: prev xor f] {
  ...
} [front↦l: prev xor f]
```

---

ownership transfer, within a critical region, similar to what was done in the pointer-transferring buffer in Section 2.3. Note that, although $front↦l: prev$ xor f is true at the beginning and end of the procedure, it is false at intermediate points. Similarly, the putb procedure stores a new item in the d field of its dummy node $back$, and then effects an ownership transfer where this node gets swallowed into the DEQ data structure. The crucial point is that the accesses $x:= front→d$ and $back→d:= x$ of the data fields occur outside of critical sections. It is this that allows these accesses to be done in parallel.

[Aside: There is one limitation of Smallfoot that this example shows: in the putb procedure we include a test $(p≠back)$ which happens to be true in any execution. This condition is an additional annotation that Smallfoot needs to verify the code. The difficulty is that two processes may be allocating nodes concurrently, and the allocated nodes will indeed be different, but our current assertions do not allow us to say so, locally. We say "current" because if we change the memory model to allow "existence permissions" [7,8] then it is possible to do away with the extra annotation in a by-hand proof; we have not, though, incorporated existence permissions into Smallfoot as of yet.]

To show these procedures working, we set up two parallel processes procf and procb which nondeterministically choose whether to do a put or get operation on the two ends of the DEQ. (The `nondet` keyword was not in the formal grammar for Smallfoot before, but it is in the tool and is implemented by talking both branches of a conditional in symbolic execution.)

```
procf (x) [front↦l: prev xor f] {        procb (x) [back↦l: next xor b] {
  if(nondet) {                              if(nondet) {
    getf(x;); /* use x */ }                   getb(x;); /* use x */ }
  else {                                    else {
    /* produce an x */ putf(x); }             /* produce an x */ putb(x); }
  procf(x);                                 procb(x);
} [false]                                 } [false]
```

$$ \text{main() procf(42) || procb(13);} $$

Smallfoot verifies the resulting program using a terminating proof theory for facts about xor lists. It involves basic identities for xor, together with adaptations of the rules in [5] for list segments. Again, this example could not be verified without consequences of induction that go beyond rolling and unrolling of an inductive definition, and Smallfoot uses several such for xor lists, akin to the axiom described in Section 5.2.

This is a variant of classic algorithms which allow concurrent access to two ends of a queue. As usual, we could allow multiple processes at each end of the queue by using mutexes to rule out concurrent accesses from the same end.

6   Conclusions and Related Work

Before discussing related work we mention some of Smallfoot's limitations.

First, even when a program's preconditions and postconditions can be expressed using Smallfoot assertions, we will not be able to verify it if its (loop and resource) invariants cannot be expressed. An example of this is Parkinson and Bornat's proof [34] of the non-blocking stack of Michael [26]. (Parkinson has verified a different non-blocking algorithm which is included amongst the examples on our web pages, but we are unable to express the invariant for Michael's algorithm.)

Incidentally, although Brookes has shown that concurrent separation logic rules out races [11], this should not be taken to mean that it cannot be used on programs that are normally considered racy. Generally, one can use little CCRs to explicitly notate statements that are considered atomic, or one could use some other notation (e.g., "atomic") with the same proof methodology, and that is what Parkinson and Bornat have done in [34].

Second, Smallfoot uses a strict separation model, which does not allow sharing of read access. As a consequence it cannot handle, e.g., a readers and writers program, which is proven in [8] using a less strict "counting permissions" model of separation logic. Adding permission accounting is on our to-do list.

Third, it would be straightforward to include inductive definitions, if we were content to just roll and unroll them. However, then very many interesting programs would not verify. Several examples in this paper involving linked lists required properties to be proven at both ends, and these would not be verifiable using rolling and unrolling alone. A direction for future research is to find a class of inductive definitions and to classify consequences of induction that can be included in a terminating proof theory.

The most closely related works to Smallfoot are the Pointer Assertion Logic Engine [28] and Alias Types [39] and its relatives (e.g. [13,9]). PALE is stronger than Smallfoot in the range of predicates it considers, based on graph types. The state of development of Smallfoot is more directly comparable to the first version of PALE [20], which was for linked lists only, and we hope to encompasses some graph structures in the future. Conversely, PALE does not check frame conditions on recursive calls, and this (intentionally) leads to unsoundness, whereas the treatment of framing is a focus of Smallfoot. Also, PALE does not deal with concurrency. Early on in the Smallfoot development we considered whether we could translate a fragment of separation logic into the fragment of monadic second-order logic that PALE is based on. For some specific assertions it is possible but we were unable to find a general scheme. The decidability of fragments of monadic second-order logic is brittle, and can be broken by adding features. Most importantly, we were unable to see how to give a compositional interpretation of *.

With regard to Alias Types, there are many similarities. Most importantly, both approaches use a substructural logic or type theory for heaps. We believe it is fair to say that the annotation burden in Smallfoot is considerably less than in Alias Types, owing mainly to inference of frame axioms. Alias Types were aimed at intermediate languages, so that is not a criticism of them. Another difference is that Alias Types use a range of inductive predicates, while we only use several specific predicates. However, our proof theory uses strong and sometimes complete inductive properties, such as are needed when working at both ends of a linked list.

The shape analysis of Sagiv, Reps and Wilhelm [37] provides a powerful verification technique for heaps. The biggest problem with the approach is that it is non-modular, in that an update to a single abstract heap cell can necessitate changing the whole abstract heap (some steps to build in modularity have been taken in [36]). We considered whether we could use ideas from shape analysis within a single procedure, and leverage *'s modularity for interprocedural and concurrent analysis. Again, we had great difficulty dealing with * compositionally, and further difficulties with the dispose instruction. But investigations continue; if this direction worked out it would give us access to a much wider range of abstractions (using "canonical abstraction" [37]).

We are often asked: why did you not just give a deep (semantic) embedding of separation logic in a predicate logic, and then use a general theorem prover, instead of constructing your own proof method? The short answer is that the deep embedding leads to nested quantifiers in the interpretation of *, and this is an impediment to automation; attempts so far along these lines have proven to be highly non-automatic. Of course it would be valuable to construct a deep embedding and develop a range of tactics and make use of general purpose provers, but that is for separate work.

Work on ESC and Spec# has resulted in important advances on modular heap verification [16,3]. Ideas of ownership and inclusion have been used to classify objects, and give a way of avoiding frame axioms, intuitively related to work on ownership types and semantics [12,1]. Methods based on fixed ownership structures have been described (e.g., [25,14]), but fixed structures are inflexible, e.g., having difficulty dealing with ownership transfer examples (like our pointer-transferring buffer or memory manager), except possibly under draconian restrictions (such as unique-pointer restrictions). A recent emphasis has been on using ownership assertions that refer to auxiliary fields that may be altered, and this leads to added flexibility [2,24], including transfer. New schemes are being invented to extend the basic idea, such as a "friends" concept that lets invariants reach across hierarchical ownership domain [30]. We refer to David Naumann's survey paper for a fuller account of and further references to research in this area [29].

In contrast, separation logic does not require a hierarchical ownership structure to ensure locality or encapsulation. Assertions just describe heaplets, portions of state, and an assertion encapsulates all of the state that a command is allowed to change. Still, there appear to be some similarities between the owner-ship assertion approaches and the reasons for why separation logic works modularly [41,33]; there seem to be, in particular, remarkably similar intuitions underlying a recent ownership-invariant system for concurrency [19] and concurrent separation logic [31]. A careful comparison of their models could be worthwhile.

Modular reasoning about concurrent programs has also received much attention, often based on the fundamental work of Jones, Misra and Chandy [21,27]. Our remarks at the end of Section 2.2 apply also in any comparison between Smallfoot and tools based on rely/guarantee (e.g. [15]). Our remarks should not be taken to be an ultimate argument for separation logic over rely/guarantee, and it would be interesting to attempt to marry their strong points (easy treatment of independence, powerful treatment of dependence). We should add that the criticisms we made echo comments made by Jones himself [22].

Smallfoot is written in OCaml, and all of the examples in this paper verified in a few milliseconds on an ordinary laptop. We have not included a timing table or other experimental results, because for the small examples we have considered the interpretation of such results would be questionable, except that if the verifications had taken minutes or hours and not milliseconds then that would have been a negative indication. The source code for the current version of Smallfoot (v0.1), together with the examples from this paper and several others, is available for download from the address given in reference [4].

Acknowledgments. Thanks to Matthew Parkinson, who wrote lots of little programs that tested the tool and pointed out a number of bugs. All three authors were partially supported by the EPSRC. During Berdine's stay at Carnegie Mellon University during 2003, his research was sponsored by National Science Foundation Grant CCR-0204242.

References

1. A. Banerjee and D.A. Naumann. Ownership confinement ensures representation independence for object-oriented programs. *Journal of the ACM*, 52(6):894–960, 2005. Preliminary version in POPL'02.
2. M. Barnett, R. DeLine, M. Fahndrich, K.R.M. Leino, and W. Schulte. Verification of object-oriented programs with invariants. *Journal of Object Technology*, 3(6):27–56, 2004.
3. M. Barnett, K.R.M. Leino, and W. Schulte. The Spec# programming system: An overview. In *CASSIS'04 post-proceedings*, 2004.
4. J. Berdine, C. Calcagno, and P.W. O'Hearn. Verification condition generation and variable conditions in Smallfoot. Available from
   http://www.dcs.qmul.ac.uk/research/logic/theory/projects/smallfoot/index.html.
5. J. Berdine, C. Calcagno, and P.W. O'Hearn. Symbolic execution with separation logic. In *3rd APLAS*, pages 52–68, 2005.
6. L. Birkedal, N. Torp-Smith, and J.C. Reynolds. Local reasoning about a copying garbage collector. In *31st POPL*, pages 220–231, 2004.
7. R. Bornat, C. Calcagno, and P. O'Hearn. Local reasoning, separation, and aliasing. Presented at *2nd SPACE Workshop*, 2004.
8. R. Bornat, C. Calcagno, P. O'Hearn, and M. Parkinson. Permission accounting in separation logic. *32nd POPL*, 59–70, 2005.
9. J. Boyland. Checking interference with fractional permissions. In *10th SAS*, pages 55–72, 2003.
10. P. Brinch-Hansen, editor. *The Origin of Concurrent Programming*. Springer-Verlag, 2002.
11. S.D. Brookes. A semantics for concurrent separation logic. *Theoretical Computer Science, to appear*. Preliminary version in *CONCUR'04*, 2006.
12. D. Clarke, J. Noble, and J. Potter. Simple ownership types for object containment. In *15th ECOOP*, pages 53–76, 2001.
13. R. DeLine and M. Fähndrich. Enforcing high-level protocols in low-level software. In *8th PLDI*, pages 59-69, 2001.
14. W. Dietl and P. Müller. Universes: Lightweight ownership for JML. *Journal of Object Technology*, 2006.
15. C. Flanagan, S.N. Freund, and S. Qadeer. Thread-modular verification for shared-memory programs. In *11th ESOP*, pages 262-277, 2002.
16. C. Flanagan, K.R.M. Leino, M. Lillibridge, G. Nelson, J.B. Saxe, and R. Stata. Extended static checking for Java. In *9th PLDI*, pages 234 - 245, 2002.
17. C.A.R. Hoare. Procedures and parameters: An axiomatic approach. In E. Engeler, editor, *Symposium on the Semantics of Algorithmic Languages*, volume 188 of *Lecture Notes in Mathematics*, pages 102–116. Springer-Verlag, 1971.
18. C.A.R. Hoare. Towards a theory of parallel programming. In *Operating Systems Techniques*, Acad. Press, pages 61-71. Reprinted in [10], 1972.
19. B. Jacobs, K.R.M. Leino, F. Piessens, and W. Schulte. Safe concurrency for aggregate objects with invariants. In *3rd SEFM*, 2005.
20. J. Jenson, M. Jorgensen, N. Klarkund, and M. Schwartzback. Automatic verification of pointer programs using monadic second-order logic. In *4th PLDI*, pages 225-236, 1997.
21. C.B. Jones. Specification and design of (parallel) programs. *IFIP Conf.*, 1983.
22. C.B. Jones. Wanted: A compositional approach to concurrency. In A. McIver and C. Morgan, editors, *Programming Methodology*, pages 1–15, 2003. Springer-Verlag.

23. D.E. Knuth. *The Art of Computer Programming, Volume I: Fundamental Algorithms.* Addison Wesley, 2nd edition, 1973.
24. K.R.M. Leino and P. Müller. Object invariants in dynamic contexts. In *18th ECOOP*, pages 491-516, 2004.
25. K.R.M. Leino, A. Poetzsch-Heffter, and Y. Zhou. Using data groups to specify and check side effects. In *9th PLDI*, pages 246 - 257, 2002.
26. M.M. Michael. Hazard pointers: Safe memory reclamation for lock-free objects. *IEEE TPDS*, 15(6):491–504, 2004.
27. J. Misra and K.M. Chandy. Proofs of networks of processes. *IEEE Trans. Software Eng.*, 7(4):417–426, 1981.
28. A. Möller and M.I. Schwartzbach. The pointer assertion logic engine. In *8th PLDI*, pages 221-231, 2001.
29. D.A. Naumann. Assertion-based encapsulation, invariants and simulations. In *3rd FMCO*, pages 251-273, 2005.
30. D.A. Naumann and M. Barnett. Friends need a bit more: Maintaining invariants over shared state. In *7th MPC*, pages 54-84, 2004.
31. P.W. O'Hearn. Resources, concurrency and local reasoning. *Theoretical Computer Science, to appear.* Preliminary version in *CONCUR'04*, 2006.
32. P.W. O'Hearn, J.C. Reynolds, and H. Yang. Local reasoning about programs that alter data structures. In *15th CSL.* pages 1-19, 2001.
33. P.W. O'Hearn, H. Yang, and J.C. Reynolds. Separation and information hiding. In *31st POPL*, pages 268-280, 2004.
34. M. Parkinson and R. Bornat. Exploiting linearisability in program logic. Draft paper, 2005.
35. J.C. Reynolds. Separation logic: A logic for shared mutable data structures. In *17th LICS*, pages 55-74.
36. N. Rinetzky, J. Bauer, T. Reps, M. Sagiv, and R. Wilhelm. A semantics for procedure local heaps and its abstractions. In *32nd POPL*, pages 296–309, 2005.
37. M. Sagiv, T. Reps, and R. Wilhelm. Parametric shape analysis via 3-valued logic. *ACM TOPLAS*, 24(3):217–298, 2002.
38. J. Schwarz. Generic commands—A tool for partial correctness formalisms. *The Computer Journal*, 20(2):151–155, 1977.
39. D. Walker and J.G. Morrisett. Alias types for recursive data structures. In *3rd Types in Compilation* Workshop, pages 177-206, 2001.
40. H. Yang. An example of local reasoning in BI pointer logic: the Schorr-Waite graph marking algorithm. Presented at *1st SPACE Workshop*, 2001.
41. H. Yang and P.W. O'Hearn. A semantic basis for local reasoning. In *5th FOSSACS*, pages 402–416, 2002.

Orion: High-Precision Methods for Static Error Analysis of C and C++ Programs

Dennis R. Dams and Kedar S. Namjoshi

Bell Labs, Lucent Technologies, 600 Mountain Ave., Murray Hill, NJ 07974,
{dennis, kedar}@research.bell-labs.com

Abstract. We describe the algorithmic and implementation ideas behind a tool, *Orion*, for finding common programming errors in C and C++ programs using static code analysis. We aim to explore the fundamental trade-off between the cost and the precision of such analyses. Analysis methods that use simple dataflow domains run the risk of producing a high number of false error reports. On the other hand, the use of complex domains reduces the number of false errors, but limits the size of code that can be analyzed.

Orion employs a two-level approach: potential errors are identified by an efficient search based on a simple domain; each discovered error path is then scrutinized by a high-precision feasibility analysis aimed at filtering out as many false errors as possible.

We describe the algorithms used and their implementation in a GCC-based tool. Experimental results on a number of software programs bear out the expectation that this approach results in a high signal-to-noise ratio of reported errors, at an acceptable cost.

1   Introduction

We consider the use of data-flow analysis (DFA) as a *debugging aid*, as implemented in tools like Flexelint [1], Coverity [2], Fortify [3] and Uno [4]. The inherent approximate nature of DFA leads in this context to *false alarms*: bogus error messages, which often are far more numerous than genuine ones. Such poor *signal-to-noise ratios* may be the reason why DFA-based debugging aids are not routinely used. If this problem can be overcome, static error checks can become a standard element of the regular build process, much like the type checking that is already performed by compilers. A prerequisite is that the additional time taken by the analysis remains acceptable.

The standard answer of DFA to the false-alarm problem is to track more dataflow facts, or, in terms of Abstract Interpretation, to use more precise *abstract domains*. For example, by tracking known and inferred ranges for boolean and other variables, many false alarms can be avoided. However, the added precision may render the analysis forbiddingly expensive. A new generation of tools, including SLAM [5] and BANDERA [6], take an incremental approach in that they add additional precision only as needed, as identified by e.g. "Counter-Example Guided Abstraction Refinement" (CEGAR, [7]). The BLAST [8] tool

F.S. de Boer et al. (Eds.): FMCO 2005, LNCS 4111, pp. 138–160, 2006.
© Springer-Verlag Berlin Heidelberg 2006

takes this even further by increasing the precision only for certain regions of the analyzed code. Still, these tools are limited in terms of the size of code that can be handled in a reasonable amount of time: usually in the order of 10-20KLoC (KLoC=1000 lines of source code), although there have been applications to larger code bases [9]. The reason is that these are software *verifiers*, targeted towards producing a yes/no answer for a particular query. This forces them to apply *sound* abstractions, and to make a substantial effort, in terms of using complex abstract domains, in order to prove correctness.

The aim of static error checkers, on the other hand, is to find errors with a high degree of accuracy within a reasonable amount of time and memory resources. Specifically, it is acceptable to sacrifice soundness, and miss a few errors, to the benefit of the signal-to-noise ratio and analysis time. We aim at a ratio of 3:1 or higher — meaning at least 3 out of every 4 reported errors have to be real ones. This number has been suggested by software developers as being acceptable. Furthermore, analysis time should be in the same order of magnitude as build time.

1.1   Path-Oriented, Two-Level Analysis

Orion is a static error checker that achieves an excellent signal-to-noise ratio within a favorable analysis time. It reconciles these conflicting aims by using two precision levels for its analysis, as follows. It performs a DFA with *light-weight abstract domains* (level 1). Unlike traditional DFA, this is done with an automaton-based model checking algorithm. The advantage is that the search is *path-oriented*, meaning that it readily produces execution paths corresponding to potential errors. To bring down the high ratio of false error paths that would result, each of the potential-error paths found is then submitted to a separate, more precise analysis (level 2). Scrutinizing a single path acts as a *feasibility check*. If the path is infeasible, it is suppressed; otherwise it is reported as a potential error. The scope of this additional precision remains limited to the individual path, however, and does not get communicated back to any part of the level-1 analysis, as would be the case with the software verifiers mentioned above.

We note two consequences of this scheme. First, reasoning about a single ("straight-line") path is much easier than about code fragments that may contain branch/merge points and loops. As a result, we can afford to use very precise domains for level 2. Second, the overall two-level approach exploits the fact that we accept unsoundness of the analysis. This point will be discussed in Section 3.2.

Level 1: Path-Oriented, Light-Weight DFA. The level-1 data-flow analysis performs a depth-first search on the product of the control-flow graph and an observer automaton based on a light-weight abstract domain. This observer automaton, in turn, is represented by a product of automata, each representing a particular, usually simple, data-flow fact being tracked. The depth-first search scheme allows error paths to be produced instantly. The abstract domain keeps track of any information that is necessary for Orion's defect detection.

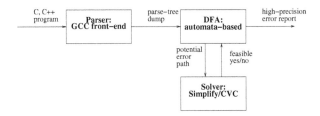

Fig. 1. Orion tool architecture

For example, in order to identify uses of uninitialized variables (use-before-def analysis), it needs to be known which variables have not been assigned a value along each path being explored. We sometimes refer to the automaton that tracks this information as the *error automaton*. In addition, by tracking a small amount of additional information, e.g. known and inferred ranges for boolean and other variables, many infeasible paths can be weeded out without reliance on level 2 checks. Such additional automata are called *information automata*. The automata, including the control-flow graph, typically depend on each other. For example, an error automaton that flags out-of-bounds array accesses depends on an information automaton that tracks variable ranges.

While the path exploration is based on a depth-first search, we have developed a number of optimizations to it. Our algorithm utilizes the notion of *covering*, known from the area of Petri Nets [10], to shortcut the search. In addition, we propose a novel idea called *differencing* to further optimize the algorithm.

Level 2: Tunable Feasibility Checking. The feasibility check that determines whether a path can actually occur under some run-time valuation of data variables makes use of theorem-provers. Theorem-provers are powerful but require human interaction and patience. However, Orion uses them in an "incomplete" way, resulting in an approach that is fully automatic and fast. Namely, the prover is allowed a predetermined amount of time; only if it finds within this time that the path is infeasible, that path is ignored. This crude, but effective, approach provides a simple way to *tune* Orion's precision by trading the signal-to-noise ratio for analysis time. In addition, the architecture of Orion allows one to plug in different provers so as to experiment with alternatives and profit from advances in the field.

1.2 Tool Architecture

There are three main parts to Orion: the parser, the data-flow analyzer (for level 1), and the solvers (for level 2), see Figure 1. The parser being used is the front-end of GCC, the Gnu Compiler Collection. Relying on this open source compiler has several advantages: it supports multiple languages, is widely used, and is being actively developed. The GCC version used is `3.5-tree-ssa`, a development branch that offers a uniform, simplified parse tree for C and C++, and is intended to be the basis for future code transformations and static analyses to be built by GCC developers [11].

GCC can dump the parse tree to a text file, which then forms the starting point for the analysis. The data-flow analyzer, together with several utilities, forms the core of Orion. This is written mostly in Objective Caml, about 18K lines of code altogether. The GCC dump is parsed into an OCaml data structure, from which a control-flow graph is constructed that is the main object of the path exploration. At every step of this search, each of a collection of automata is updated. Every automaton can be viewed as an *observer* of the sequences of statements being traversed in the path exploration, keeping track of the data-flow facts of a particular kind that hold at each control location that is reached. This modular set-up allows for an easy selection and combination of abstract domains in effect during the data-flow analysis.

Error paths, as flagged by one of the observer automata, are sent off to a solver during the path exploration. These solvers are theorem provers based mainly on decision procedures, aimed at providing automatic proofs for most questions submitted. Currently, two such provers have been interfaced to Orion: Simplify [12] and CVC [13].

1.3   Paper Outline

Section 2 gives details of the model-checking based abstract state space exploration of level 1. In particular, it gives general formulations of the covering and differencing algorithms together with several theoretical results, and discusses their relation to standard data-flow algorithms. These algorithms are then specialized to the setting of automata-based analysis of control-flow graphs, and another optimization, *state aggregation*, is briefly discussed. Section 3 is concerned with the level 2 feasibility checking. It also explains how the interaction between depth-first search and feasibility may affect completeness of the approach. The experimental results on several programs are presented in Section 4. Section 5 discusses the contributions in the perspective of related work, and Section 6 concludes.

2   Path Exploration, Covering, and Differencing

The approach to DFA sketched above, namely an exploration of a graph in search for error states, is an instance of the view of *DFA as model checking of an abstract interpretation* [14]. In this view, the error automaton represents the (negation of the) property being checked, while the product of the flow graph and the information automata represents the abstract interpretation over which the property is checked. That is, each state of this abstract interpretation represents an overapproximation of the set of all run-time states that may be reached at the corresponding flow graph location. Traversing the overall product (of abstract interpretation and error automaton) state by state, in search for

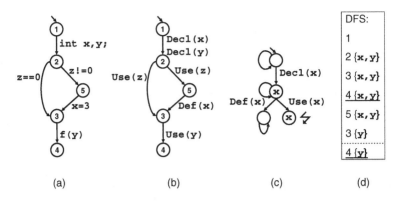

Fig. 2. Use-before-def checking

reachable error states (product states in which the error-automaton component is an error state), amounts to performing an explicit-state model check of a safety property.

While this view is conceptually appealing, applying it naively may lead to algorithms that are inferior to the traditional approach to DFA, in which a solution to a set of flow equations is computed iteratively. We illustrate this point by an example. Figure 2, part (a), shows a small C program as a control-flow graph whose edges are labeled with the program statements. Part (c) shows an error automaton that checks for use-before-def errors of the variable x (unmarked edges are taken when no other transitions are enabled). A similar automaton, not shown, is assumed that checks y. We think of these as a single error automaton defined by their product, whose states are thus subsets of $\{x, y\}$; e.g., the state $\{x\}$ represents all run-time states in which x has been declared but not yet defined. Thus, if a variable v is an element of some state automaton s, the automaton moves to an error state if a transition is taken that is labeled with Use(v). As its transitions depend on information about whether variables are declared, defined, and used in the program, we need the abstract interpretation of the program that is shown in part (b). The overall product graph to be explored has states (n, s) where n is the location in the graph of part (b) and s is the state of the product error automata.

Part (d) shows a sequence of states that is visited in a typical depth-first traversal; the error states are underlined. The point to note is that the use-before-def error of y (in the statement $f(y)$) is found twice along this sequence: once from state $(3, \{x, y\})$, where both x and y are tracked as being declared but not yet defined, and another time when only y is tracked, from state $(3, \{y\})$. This is an inefficiency: clearly, after having checked for use-before-def errors, "below" location 3, of any variable in $\{x, y\}$, when the search hits location 3 again with a *subset* of these variables, it could have backtracked safely, without missing any errors. In Figure 2 this is indicated by a dashed line, showing that state $(4, \{y\})$ does not need to be visited. In general, the savings from such early backtracking may be much more significant than in this example.

In an equation-solving approach this effect would not occur due to the fact that the first data-flow set to be associated with location 3 is $\{x, y\}$; when the set $\{y\}$ is then merged with it, it does not change $(\{x, y\} \cup \{y\} = \{x, y\})$, so no further propagation is needed [15]. In this section, we fix this shortcoming of the model-checking based approach to DFA by combining it with a notion of *covering*. In the example above, the search can backtrack from state $(3, \{y\})$ because, intuitively, it is "covered" by the already-visited state $(3, \{x, y\})$. While the addition of covering restores the efficiency of the algorithm in comparison to the equation-solving approach, we present a second optimization, called *differencing*, that may result in an additional performance improvement, and which has not been proposed in the context of the equation-solving approach, to the best of our knowledge. Both notions are formalized as extensions of a highly non-deterministic White-Grey-Black coloring search [16]. Depth-first search, as well as other strategies, can be obtained by restricting the non-determinism in this algorithm.

2.1 General Search with Covering and Differencing

The goal is to search a finite graph for the presence of a reachable error state. Throughout, let $G = (S, I, R)$ be the graph being searched, where S is a finite set of states, $I \subseteq S$ is a set of initial states, and $R \subseteq S \times S$ is a transition relation. Let $E \subseteq S$ be a set of error states. We say that a state t is reachable in G from a state s, and denote it by $s \xrightarrow{*} t$, iff either $s = t$, or there is a finite sequence (a *path*) $s_0, s_1, \ldots, s_n$ with $n > 0$, where $s_0 = s$, $s_n = t$, and $(s_i, s_{i+1}) \in R$ for all i, $0 \leq i < n$. The set of reachable states, *Reach*, is given by $\{t \mid (\exists s : I(s) \wedge s \xrightarrow{*} t)\}$.

Algorithm I: Basic White-Grey-Black Search. We first describe the very general search strategy, attributable to Edsger W. Dijkstra, which starts with all states colored white, and re-colors states as grey or black during execution. The intuition is that white states are unexplored, grey states are the "frontier" of partially explored states, and black states are fully explored. The program is given below. The color of a state is given by its entry in the array "color". We abbreviate $(color[s] = W)$ by $white(s)$, and similarly for $grey(s)$ and $black(s)$. We use upper case symbols, e.g., *Grey*, *Black*, to indicate the set of states with that color. Actions are non-deterministically chosen (indicated by []) guarded commands, where each guarded command has the form $guard \longrightarrow assignment$. The notation $([]s, t : \ldots)$ indicates a set of actions indexed by variables s, t of the appropriate types.

var color: array [S] of (W,G,B)
initially $(\forall s : white(s))$
actions
    $([]s : I(s) \wedge white(s) \longrightarrow color[s] := G)$
[] $([]s, t : grey(s) \wedge R(s, t) \wedge white(t) \longrightarrow color[t] := G)$
[] $([]s : grey(s) \wedge (\forall t : R(s, t) \Rightarrow \neg white(t)) \longrightarrow color[s] := B)$

The key properties are: (a) invariantly, $Grey \cup Black$ is a subset of $Reach$, and (b) if $Grey$ cannot increase, then $(Grey \cup Black)$ is the set of reachable states, and the size of $Grey$ must decrease through the last action. Hence, we obtain the well-known theorem below.

Theorem 1. *Algorithm I terminates with* $Black = Reach$.

Algorithm II: Covering-based Search. The basic WGB search terminates with $Black = Reach$, so to determine whether there is a reachable error state, one can check if $Black \cap E$ is non-empty. (Of course, this check could be made during the execution of the algorithm, but in the worst-case, the algorithm may have to explore all reachable states.) The goal of a covering-based search is to explore *fewer* than all reachable states, while still determining the exact answer. This is done by exploiting a "covering" relation between states where, informally, if a state s covers state t, then any path to an error state from t has a "matching" path to an error from s. Thus, there is no harm in stopping the exploration from t if it is covered by an already explored state.

Formally, a *subset-covering* relation (usually a pre-order), $\sqsupseteq \subseteq 2^S \times 2^S$, is required to have the following property: for all subsets X, Y of S, if $X \sqsupseteq Y$ (read as X *covers* Y), then: for every $k > 0$, and every y in Y that has a path of length k to an error state, there is x in X that has a path of length *at most* k to an error state. We also introduce an additional color, Red (R), to label states that have been covered. The new algorithm is given below – it extends the WGB algorithm with the final indexed action.

var color: array [S] of (W,G,B,R)
initially $(\forall s : white(s))$
actions
   $([]s : I(s) \wedge white(s) \longrightarrow color[s] := G)$
[] $([]s, t : grey(s) \wedge R(s, t) \wedge white(t) \longrightarrow color[t] := G)$
[] $([]s : grey(s) \wedge (\forall t : R(s, t) \Rightarrow \neg white(t)) \longrightarrow color[s] := B)$
[] $([]s : grey(s) \wedge ((Grey \setminus \{s\}) \cup Black) \sqsupseteq \{s\} \longrightarrow color[s] := R)$

The new action colors s red if it is covered by the other explored, but *uncovered* (i.e., non-red), set of states. Once a state is colored red, exploration is stopped from that state, as if it is colored black, but with the difference that red states cannot be used as part of a covering set. Both path matching and the distinction between red and black states are important: there are simple examples showing that dropping either one leads to an unsound or incomplete search method. As the algorithm proceeds, all white initial states are examined and turn grey, and grey states turn red or black. Thus, the final result is given by the following theorem. Note that $(Black \cup Red)$ is generally a *strict subset* of the reachable states, yet it suffices to detect errors.

Theorem 2. *Algorithm II terminates, and there is a reachable error state iff one of the states in* $(Black \cup Red)$ *is an error state.*

Algorithm III: Adding Differencing Mechanisms. In the previous algorithm, a state s is covered, intuitively, because *all* error paths from s have matching paths from the set of states that covers $\{s\}$. It may, however, be the case that for some states s' that remain uncovered, *most*, but not all, of the error paths from s' are matched by already explored states, while the remainder can be matched from a small set of as yet unexplored states. These new states represent, in a sense, the small "difference" of the error behavior of s' and that of the already explored states. One may then choose to stop exploring s', and explore the difference states instead. We modify the last action of the previous program to enable this choice, with *Diff* being the choice of the difference set. (The previous action can be recovered by setting *Diff* to the empty set; note that $T \sqsupseteq \emptyset$ is true for all T.)

$$([]s, Diff : grey(s) \wedge (Diff \subseteq White) \wedge$$
$$((Grey \setminus \{s\}) \cup Black \cup Diff) \sqsupseteq \{s\} \wedge \{s\} \sqsupseteq Diff$$
$$\longrightarrow color[s] := R; (\textbf{foreach } t : t \in Diff : color[t] := G))$$

The new action chooses a difference set *Diff* for some grey node s, and uses it to provide a covering. Then s is colored red, and all the states in *Diff* are colored grey. The choice of a difference set cannot, however, be completely arbitrary: it includes only white states, and $\{s\}$ must cover *Diff*. This last constraint ensures that, even though Diff may contain unreachable states, any errors found from Diff states are also errors from $\{s\}$ and, inductively, from a reachable state. The full proof of correctness takes this into account, and otherwise is essentially identical to the proof for the covering only search.

Theorem 3. *Algorithm III terminates, and there is a reachable error state iff one of the states in* $(Black \cup Red)$ *is an error state.*

2.2 Application to Control-Flow Graphs

In Orion, the differencing-based algorithm is applied in the level-1 analysis to control flow graphs of individual functions. Formally, a control flow graph (CFG) is a tuple (V, V_0, Σ, E), where V is a finite set of *control locations*, $V_0 \subseteq V$ is a set of *entry locations*, Σ is a set of *program statements*, and $E \subseteq V \times \Sigma \times V$ is a finite set of *program transitions*, where a transition (n, a, n') can be viewed as a control flow transition from n to n', labeled with statement a. Orion adopts the model checking approach to analysis: thus, analysis properties are represented by finite state automata, which operate on Σ, and reject if an erroneous execution is found. An analysis automaton is a tuple $(S, I, \Sigma, \Delta, F)$, where S is a finite set of states, $I \subseteq S$ is a set of *initial states*, Σ, as above, is the *alphabet*, $\Delta \subseteq S \times \Sigma \times S$, is the *transition relation*, and $F \subseteq S$ is the set of *rejecting states*. The (synchronous) composition of K such automata, $A_1, \ldots, A_K$, with a CFG (V, V_0, Σ, E) can be viewed as the single automaton with: $V \times S_1 \times \ldots \times S_K$ as the state set, $V_0 \times I_1 \times \ldots \times I_K$ as the initial states, Σ as the alphabet, with a transition relation Δ defined by $((n, s_1, \ldots, s_K), a, (n', s'_1, \ldots, s'_K)) \in \Delta$ iff $(n, a, n') \in E$, and $(s_i, a, s'_i) \in \Delta_i$ *for all* i in $[1, K]$, and $(n, s_1, \ldots, s_K)$ being a rejecting state iff *for some* i in $[1, K]$, s_i is in F_i. This definition implies that the language of the combined automaton is the union of the (rejecting) languages of the components. While the automata can be run individually on the CFG, combining them can sometimes saves analysis time, while requiring more space. Moreover, the automata are sometimes combined in more complex ways, where the state of one automaton is used as an input to the other (this is referred to as the *cascade* or *wreath* product). For instance, array bounds checking is carried out by a combination of two automata: one that tracks upper and lower bounds on the values of program variables (this information is also used to filter out infeasible paths), the other simply applies the computed bounds to each array indexing operation.

The model checking problem is to determine whether there is a path in this product to a rejecting state (recall that rejecting automaton states signal program errors). Note that we focus on safety properties, which can be analyzed by checking reachability. In order to use covering and differencing during the search, we need a general mechanism by which covering and differencing operations for individual automata are combined to provide such operations for a tuple of automata. We show how this can be done below.

We assume the existence of individual covering relations, $\sqsupseteq_i$, for each automaton, and construct the *point-wise global covering* relation: $(n, s_1, \ldots, s_K) \sqsupseteq (n', s'_1, \ldots, s'_K)$ if and only if $n = n'$ and $s_i \sqsupseteq_i s'_i$ for all i in $[1, K]$. For example, one automaton could keep track of the current set of uninitialized variables, U, in its internal state. This can be done by letting each state of the automaton be one such set, and including a transition from a state U to a state U' on program action a, if U' results from U by removing variables defined in a and adding variables newly declared in a (e.g., local scope declarations). Another automaton could, similarly, keep track of an estimate, B, of upper and lower bounds for each defined variable. For the first automaton, $U \sqsupseteq_1 U'$ may be defined as $U \supseteq U'$. If there is a sequence of program actions that results in a use-before-def error because a variable, say x, in U' is accessed by the last action without being defined along the sequence, then the same sequence causes an error from U, as x is included in U (note that the same sequence is possible because $n = n'$). Similarly, $B \sqsupseteq_2 B'$ iff the bounds information in B' denotes a subset of the run-time states denoted by the information in B. Any error path from B' can be enabled from B, as the information in B is more approximate than that in B'. E.g., the joint covering relation ensures that $(\{a, b\}, (c > 0))$ covers $(\{a\}, (c > 1))$, since $\{a\}$ is a subset of $\{a, b\}$, and $(c > 1)$ implies $(c > 0)$.

Similarly, given functions $diff_i$ that choose an appropriate difference set for each automaton, we can define a *point-wise global differencing* function as follows: $diff((n, s_1, \ldots, s_K), (n', s'_1, \ldots, s'_K))$ is defined only if $n = n'$ (i.e., same control location), and is given by the set $\{(n, s) \mid (\exists i, d : d \in diff_i(s_i, s'_i) \land s = (s_1, \ldots, s_{i-1}, d, s_{i+1}, \ldots, s_K))\}$. I.e., for the common control location, the difference set is obtained by taking, in turn, the difference of one of the component automaton states, while keeping the others the same. For the example above, the difference function for uninitialized variable sets is just set difference, while that for bounds information is bounds difference. Thus, the global difference of $(\{a, b\}, (c > 0))$ relative to $(\{a, d\}, (c > 10))$ at control location n is given by the set $\{(n, \{b\}, (c > 0)), (n, \{a, b\}, (c > 0 \land c \le 10))\}$.

Aggregating States. An optimization made in Orion to enable fast covering and differencing calculations is to merge the set of currently reached automata states for each control location in an approximate, but conservative manner. This is done by defining merge functions per automaton domain, and applying them point-wise to states with the same control location. Thus, if $merge_i$ is the merge function for automaton i, then the *point-wise global merge* is defined as $merge((n, s_1, \ldots, s_K), (n, s'_1, \ldots, s'_K)) = (n, merge_1(s_1, s'_1), \ldots, merge_i(s_K, s'_K))$. In our example, the merge of uninitialized variable sets is done through set union, and that of bounds by widening bounds. Thus, $merge((n, \{a, b\}, (c > 0)), (n, \{a, d\}, (c > 10)))$ gives $(n, \{a, b, d\}, (c > 0))$. While the merge operator can be quite approximate, we have not observed it to lead to many false error reports, and furthermore, it does indeed considerably speed up the covering and differencing operations. An approximate merge may lead to missed errors due to early covering, this issue is discussed further in Section 3.2.

3 Feasibility Checking

As explained in the introduction, a potential finite error path detected at level 1 is subjected to further analysis by a feasibility check, which determines whether it can correspond to a real execution. By integrating bounds information in the abstract state at level 1 some error paths can already be ruled out at an early stage. The level-2 feasibility check described here is applied to other error paths that are generated at level 1. In this section we describe the manner in which this check is performed, optimizations, and some consequences for the completeness of the error detection strategy.

3.1 Checking for Feasibility with Weakest Preconditions

Any finite path through a control flow graph of a function is a sequence formed from assignment statements, function calls, and boolean tests. For example, $read(\&x); (x < 0); y = x; (y > 3); z = f(x, y)$ could be such a path, where x, y, z are integer valued variables, and f is a function. This path is infeasible: from the first three actions, one may infer that the value of y is negative; hence, the subsequent test $(y > 3)$ fails. Such inference can be formalized in many equivalent ways; we do so primarily through the use of *weakest liberal preconditions* for statements, as introduced by Dijkstra in [17].

The weakest liberal precondition for statement S to establish property ϕ after execution, denoted by $wlp(S, \phi)$, is that set of states from which every terminating execution of S makes the program enter a state satisfying ϕ. Letting $s \xrightarrow{S} t$ denote the fact that execution of statement S from state s can result in state t, this set is formally defined as $wlp(S, \phi) = \{s \mid (\forall t : s \xrightarrow{S} t \Rightarrow \phi(t))\}$. The weakest precondition can be calculated by substitution for simple assignments $(wlp(x = e, \phi(x)) = \phi(e))$, and by implication for tests $(wlp(g, \phi) = (g \Rightarrow \phi))$, and inductively for sequences of actions $(wlp((S_1; S_2), \phi) = wlp(S_1, wlp(S_2, \phi)))$. Its relationship to feasibility checking is given by the following theorem.

Theorem 4. *A finite path π is feasible if and only if $wlp(\pi, false)$ is not valid.*

Proof. From the inductive definition of wlp for paths, one obtains the following set-based characterization of $wlp(\pi, \phi)$: it is the set $\{s \mid (\forall t : s \xrightarrow{\pi} t \Rightarrow \phi(t))\}$. A path π is feasible iff (by definition) there are program states s, t such that $s \xrightarrow{\pi} t$ holds. By the prior characterization of wlp, this is equivalent to saying that there exists a state s such that s is not in $wlp(\pi, false)$; i.e., that $wlp(\pi, false)$ is not a validity.

For the example above, the wlp calculation proceeds as follows: $wlp(z = f(x, y), false) = false$; $wlp((y > 3), false) = ((y > 3) \Rightarrow false) = (y \leq 3)$; $wlp(y = x, (y \leq 3)) = (x \leq 3)$; $wlp((x < 0), (x \leq 3)) = ((x < 0) \Rightarrow (x \leq 3)) = true$; and $wlp(read(\&x), true) = true$. But $true$ is trivially valid: hence, by the theorem above, this path is infeasible. Notice that as $wlp(\pi, true) = true$ holds for all π, infeasibility can be detected early, and the $read$ statement does not really need to be examined. The weakest precondition calculates backwards; its dual is the strongest postcondition, sp, which calculates forwards, and is defined as follows: $sp(S, \phi) = \{t \mid (\exists s : \phi(s) \wedge s \xrightarrow{S} t)\}$. Their duality leads to the following theorem.

Theorem 5. *A finite path π is feasible if and only if $sp(\pi, true)$ is satisfiable.*

Proof. It is well known that wlp and sp are near-inverses (formally, adjoints in a Galois connection). Thus, $(\psi \Rightarrow wlp(\pi, \phi))$ is valid iff $(sp(\pi, \psi) \Rightarrow \phi)$ is valid. Substituting $\psi = true, \phi = false$, we obtain that $wlp(\pi, false)$ is valid iff $\neg(sp(\pi, true))$ is valid; thus, $wlp(\pi, false)$ is not valid iff $sp(\pi, true)$ is satisfiable.

We thus have two equivalent ways of calculating feasibility: either perform a forwards, symbolic calculation of $sp(\pi, true)$ and apply a satisfiability solver, or perform a backwards, substitution-based calculation for $wlp(\pi, false)$ and apply a validity checker. The approach we have implemented in Orion is somewhat of a hybrid: we calculate aliasing and points-to information along π in the forward direction, and use it to reduce the intermediate results of the wlp calculation. A key point is that aliasing information is quite accurate along a single path, more so than when it is calculated for a control flow graph, where accuracy is lost when merging information for incoming edges at a CFG node. The need for such points-to information is due to the fact that wlp, when applied to assignments through pointer variables, results in a case explosion. For instance, computing $wlp(*p = e, \phi(x, y))$ requires a case split on whether p points to x, to y, or to neither. Formally, it is given by the expression below, where $pt(p, x)$ is a predicate that is true iff p holds the address of x.

if $pt(p, x)$ then (if $pt(p, y)$ then $\phi(e, e)$ else $\phi(e, y)$)

else (if $pt(p, y)$ then $\phi(x, e)$ else $\phi(x, y)$)

Without points-to information to contain this case splitting, the *wlp* expressions at intermediate points on the path can grow exponentially, resulting in a slowdown. Orion can also use bounds information gathered for this path during the first phase analysis of the control flow graph to similarly reduce arithmetic expressions early in the *wlp* calculation.

Orion sends the expressions that represent *wlp*'s of paths to a validity checker — we currently use either Simplify [12] or CVC [13] as the checkers. An interesting observation is that the use of *wlp* automatically provides a *slicing* [18] of the path relative to the feasibility check, since an assignment that does not affect variables in the current post-condition is treated as a no-op by the *wlp* substitution mechanism (e.g., $wlp(z = e, \phi(x)) = \phi(x)$).

An example of the effect of Orion's feasibility check is shown in Figure 3. When run on the source code shown on the left, without feasibility check the error path on the right is produced. With feasibility checking enabled, no errors are reported. The example is somewhat contrived to demonstrate several aspects of Orion's reasoning power on a few lines of code.

```
int f(int i)       // line 1
{                  // 2
  int r, a, *p = &a;  // 3
  int m = 1;       // 4
                   // 5
  if (i<2)         // 6
    r = m*i;       // 7
  else             // 8
    m++;           // 9
  a = m*(i+1);     // 10
  if (*p>=6)       // 11
    r = m*6;       // 12
  return r;        // 13
}
```

```
example.c:13 (function f) ::
  use of un-initialized
  variable(s): r

Possibly feasible error path:
example.c:3:   p=(&a)
example.c:4:   m=1
example.c:6:   !((i<=1))
example.c:9:   m=(m+1)
example.c:10:  a=(m*(i+1))
example.c:11:  !(((*p)>5))
example.c:11:  ((void)0)
example.c:13:  return_value=r
```

Fig. 3. With feasibility checking, the error path (on the right) is suppressed

3.2   Implications for Completeness

Orion is focussed on finding errors. Two important correctness (i.e., non-performance) aspects in this context[1] are (i) *soundness*: is every reported error feasible? and (ii) *completeness*: does the procedure find *all* real errors?

Although Orion uses feasibility checking, as described above, to filter out false error reports, soundness is weakened due to fundamental limitations in decision procedures. These include the exponential complexity of some decision procedures and, indeed, the non-computability of validity for certain logics (e.g., arithmetic with multiplication). To achieve a reasonable analysis time, Orion

---

[1] Note that the notions of soundness and completeness are defined opposite from those in the context of program *verification*.

limits the time allowed for the solvers, inevitably permitting in some false error paths to be reported. Orion thus aims to achieve a high degree of – but not perfect – precision in its error reports.

An analysis algorithm can obtain perfect completeness by reporting all potential errors: all real errors are contained in this report. However, this comes at the expense of soundness. Conversely, an algorithm can achieve perfect soundness by not reporting any errors but, of course, at the cost of completeness. Thus, there appears to be a balance between the two aspects: it may be necessary to sacrifice some completeness in order to achieve a high degree of soundness. In what follows, we point out two such tradeoffs in Orion.

State-based vs. Path-based Search. In the previous section, we argued that path-based search was impractical, and presented three state-based search algorithms. While these are indeed more efficient, they may compromise completeness, when combined with feasibility checking. Consider, for instance, the program below.

```
int foo(int x)
{
    int u,v;
L1:   if (x > 0) v=x; else v=x+1;
L2:   if (x < 0)
L3:         return u;
L4:   else return x;
}
```

The return statement at L3 is a candidate for an uninitialized variable error, and there are two possible paths to L3: $P_1 :: (x > 0); v = x; (x < 0); return\ u$, and $P_2 :: (x \leq 0); v = x + 1; (x < 0); return\ u$. A search that tries all paths will consider both, and point out P_2 as a feasible error path. But now consider a depth-first search that only keeps track of the current set of uninitialized variables. If the search tries path P_1 first, it will find the potential error, but a feasibility check will reject the path as being infeasible. Backtracking to L1, the search tries the else-branch at L1. However, it enters L2 with the same set of uninitialized variables, $\{u\}$, as before, and must backtrack without exploring P_2 in full. Hence, the real error goes unreported, a failure of completeness!

Notice that the failure is due to the feasibility check: dropping the check will cause an error report to be generated, with a path that is infeasible — but, of course, at the cost of soundness. The fundamental problem is that *any* state-based search that uses a finite abstract domain can be "fooled" into not distinguishing between some of the possibly infinitely many different paths that reach a control point. Orion actually avoids the problem for this example, since it also keeps track of upper and lower bounds on variable values, which can distinguish the prefixes of P_1 and P_2 at L2. However, it may be possible for a complex enough program to fool the bounds tracking procedure into considering distinct prefixes as indistinguishable from one another: [19] has a discussion of this phenomenon in the more general context of abstraction methods.

Covering vs. Depth-first Search. As described in the previous section, a covering-based search is far more efficient than pure depth-first search. However, this too, may come with a completeness cost. The covering property preserves the existence of error paths, but not specific errors: i.e., if state t covers state s, and there is a path to an error from s, there must be a matching path from t, but not necessarily to the *same* error location. This general problem does not hold for the case of control-flow graphs, since covering states share a common control location. However, we have observed that a covering based search can miss reporting some errors in our tests of Orion. In this case, it is due to a different, but related phenomenon: the potentially over-approximate aggregation. Such an over-approximation enables some states to be covered, while this would not have been the case with an exact aggregation — such false covering, if it occurs, leaves some paths unexplored. However, in our tests, the number of missed errors is small (usually one or two) and, in all the cases we encountered, the missed error paths are infeasible. There is a tradeoff here that can be exploited. For instance, one can try Orion with the fast covering-based search for initial testing, but once all reported real errors have been fixed, one may try Orion with the more comprehensive, but slower depth-first search to expose any missed errors.

4 Experimental Evaluation

Covering and Differencing. Experiments with the covering and differencing algorithms show a clear advantage in execution times relative to pure depth-first search: at least 3-fold, usually more. The intuition behind the differencing method is that it can speed up the search by: (i) potentially covering more states, thus exploring fewer states overall, and (ii) faster computations, as difference states are generally smaller than the original (e.g., a subset). Experiments so far show, however, that for the properties we check for with Orion, the speedup obtained with smaller representations is nearly matched by the cost of the differencing operation. The benefit in run times is marginal, with a maximum speedup of about 10%. We continue to explore this issue, however, and to look for more efficient differencing implementations.

Feasibility. The table in Figure 4 summarizes the result of running Orion on various publicly available software packages. The experiments were run on an AMD Opteron 2.6GHz dual core, 8GB, under Linux, except for the first (emacs-21.3), which had to be run on a considerably slower machine due to OS incompatibility issues. In any case, the measurements are not directly comparable over the different entries, as they were collected in multi-user mode. The errors being checked are use-before-def of variables variables, null-pointer dereferencing, and out-of-bounds indexing of arrays. These checks are made for individual functions in the program, making no assumptions about the context in which a function is called. The first three columns in the table show the name and version of the program analyzed, the number (in 1000s) of lines of code that were analyzed (this need not be the total amount of C code in the package, due to configuration options),

Source	KLoC	compile time (s)	compile + analyze time (s)	errs.	infeas.	real errs.
emacs-21.3	25.9	199	412	3	5	3
jpeg-6b	28.8	7	35	0	25	0
libxslt-1.1.12	31.2	27	103	2	1	0
sendmail-8.11.6	76.2	9	82	5	16	2
libxml-2.6.16	200.1	97	295	3	12	2

Fig. 4. Results on some open source packages

and the compilation time, in seconds, when Orion is not used. The next three columns give the results of compilation with the Orion checks enabled. The column "errs." lists the number of errors as reported by Orion, i.e., the number of error paths (as identified at level 1) that are determined to be *feasible* by Orion's feasibility check (at level 2). The column "infeas." lists the number of paths that show up as potential errors at level 1, but that are determined to be infeasible at level 2, and are thus not reported. The last column lists the number of real errors, among those reported by Orion, as determined by a manual inspection, see below. The analyses are run with precision 2, meaning that the time allotted for every feasibility check is 2 seconds. Increasing this time-out value does not show a significant decrease in the number of errors reported for these examples, while with precision 1 and lower, Orion does not invoke external validity checkers for feasibility checking, which leads to significantly more false alarms. For sendmail, jpeg, and emacs, a few additional customized options were given to indicate that certain functions should be considered as "exit functions" that do not return. This helped suppress a couple of false alarms.

The numbers of errors that are reported versus infeasible paths that are suppressed witness the effectiveness of the feasibility checking. An indication of the signal-to-noise ratio that is achieved may be derived by comparing the number of reported errors (column "errs.") to the number of those that are deemed real (column "real errs."). For the manual checks, we considered an error to be real if it was feasible locally within a procedure. It may be that some of these "real" errors are infeasible when considered in their interprocedural context. Still, arguably such cases indicate a lack of defensive coding (in no case did we find comments or assertions in the code that indicated the assumptions made).

5   Related Work

Run-time Checking and Dynamic Analysis. An alternative way to detect programming errors is to monitor the code during execution. Tools such as Purify (from Rational/IBM) and CCured [20] insert checks into the code to this effect, that get compiled and executed along with the program. VeriSoft [21], DART [22], and JPF [23] on the other hand do not insert checking code, but can be seen as advanced schedulers that perform various checks on the underlying code. Since they have full control over the scheduling, several different executions can be tested, i.e. they can be viewed as bounded model checkers. What run-time checkers and dynamic analyzers have in common is that they explore an *under-approximation* of a program's run-time state space. In this sense they are orthogonal to the DFA approach.

Static Analyzers. Tools that approach Orion most closely in terms of usage, purpose, and underlying techniques are Uno [4], MC/Coverity [24], PolySpace [25], klocwork [26], ESP [27], FlexeLint [1], and BEAM [28]. The distinguishing features of Orion are:

- Its 2-level, tunable approach, which results in excellent signal-to-noise ratios without serious time penalties. At the same time it gives the user control over the desired precision: High precision can be achieved by allowing the solvers more time to perform a deep semantic analysis of the error paths returned at the first, more superficial level. The experimental results reported show that this reduces the amount of false alarms in a significant way, without excessively burdening the analysis time.
- The application of the covering and differencing optimizations uniformly for all abstract domains. MC/Coverity uses similar techniques to handle aggregate state machines produced by the per-variable check paradigm adopted in that tool (cf. the handling of block summaries by the tool). Uno implements a form of covering and differencing as well. Our general treatment allows us to prove the correctness of covering and differencing independently of the search scheme and the covering relation used. The current implementation of Orion uses a covering relation over a combined domain for tracking uninitialized variables and bounds information, as explained in Section 2.2. We are considering adding points-to information as well; such extensions are easy to add thanks to the generality of the implementation.

The roots of the covering algorithm go back at least to work by Karp and Miller [10], but it has been reformulated several times in connection with various abstract domains (cf. [29,30,8]).

While the high degree of automation offered by all these tools increases their acceptance by software developers, there will always be errors that escape such static analyses — this is due to the undecidability of the problem of showing the absence of errors. If correctness is a serious concern, like in case of safety-critical applications, tools that require *annotations* can offer more certainty. ESC [31] and LClint [32] are examples of such tools. Orion also allows insertion of a limited form of user-annotations, but this feature has not been used in the experiments.

Several alternative approaches exist to ameliorate the signal-to-noise ratio. One is to *rank* the errors reported, based on heuristic rules and history information, such that errors with a high probability of being real occur first. This idea is e.g. implemented in Microsoft's PREfix and PREfast defect detection tools [33], and also in MC/Coverity [24]. The drawback is that in order to be effective, such rules must be partly specific to the area of application, and consequently it may take a domain expert to devise effective heuristics. Another technique used in the above-mentioned tools is to suppress certain errors based on similarity to previously reported ones. Orion's distinguishing features are orthogonal to these techniques, and can be combined to get the best of worlds.

Software Verification Tools. The introduction already discussed the relation of Orion to software verification tools based on symbolic processing, such as SLAM [5], BLAST [8], and BANDERA [6], stressing the difference between *error checking* and *verification*. Orion can be seen as an effort to apply techniques from the model checking and verification field to the problem of improving the precision of static error analysis to acceptable levels. Our experimental results appear to bear out the hypothesis that the 2-level analysis procedure discussed in this paper is effective at performing high-precision static error analysis. Some of the technical details of Orion's implementation differ from, or extend, the algorithms used in the verification tools mentioned above. The covering search algorithm presented here is more general than the one used in BLAST, and the addition of differencing is novel. Orion analyzes paths using weakest preconditions, as in BLAST, but with a forward, path-specific, points-to analysis (SLAM uses symbolic processing—i.e., strongest postconditions—to analyze for feasibility). On the other hand, these verifiers include methods for automatic refinement of the initial abstraction, based on hints obtained from the infeasibility proofs for false error paths; such refinement is necessary to show correctness. So far, we have not found a need to add such abstraction refinement: the feasibility checking mechanism appears to do a good enough job of filtering out false errors.

6   Conclusions and Ongoing Work

We have presented the static error checker Orion, which is aimed at producing error reports with a low false-alarm rate in reasonable analysis time. The approach that enables this is an automaton-based, path-oriented, two-level data-flow analysis, that uses powerful external solvers in a tunable fashion, and is optimized by the use of covering, differencing, and state aggregation schemes.

Depth-first search can be seen as a particular scheduling of the general chaotic iteration scheme for data flow analyses. However, our covering and differencing algorithms presented earlier are more general than DFA, since they do not require a control flow graph skeleton on which to execute the algorithm.

Experiments on several programs shows that in most cases the targeted signal-to-noise ratio of 3:1 is achieved. A detailed inspection of the reasons that some infeasible paths are still reported as errors suggest two priorities for further work.

First, it turns out that the computation of expressions that represent weakest preconditions, tends to run out of the allocated resources in cases where the paths are very long (hundreds of statements). Orion can perform an interprocedural analysis for uses of uninitialized global pointer variables[2], and since interprocedural paths tend to be very long, no feasibility checks are performed in this case. We are currently investigating alternative solvers such as CVC-Lite

---

[2] The implementation is based on standard techniques for model checking of recursive state machines [34,35], and thus can deal with recursive functions in C and C++.

[36], and also looking into other approaches to feasibility checking such as the use of a SAT-based symbolic model checker (CBMC, see [37]) and of a testing-based tool (DART, see [22]).

Another source of false alarms is the out-of-bounds array check. We are currently working on an improved and generalized buffer-overflow checking module for Orion.

It has been pointed out that Orion is not a complete method for error detection. The interaction between the level-1 and level-2 checks may cause errors to be missed as explained in Section 3. Furthermore, when encountering certain language features such as long-jumps and function pointers, Orion favors analysis speed over completeness. The fact that it still finds a significant amount of errors in code that may be considered well-tested, confirms that such sacrifices are justified. Nevertheless, it is our intention to address the various sources of incompleteness by offering options to run Orion in a stricter mode, or at least to warn of the occurrence of language constructs that are not treated conservatively. In comparison, note that a static analyzer like Astrée [38], which is aimed at proving the *absence* of certain types of errors, comes with rather drastic restrictions on the allowed language constructs in order to guarantee its claims.

While the analysis times reported in our experiments are reasonable, in some cases they are an order of magnitude more than the time required to compile a program without error analysis by Orion. In addition, when software is analyzed that less well-tested, the number of errors can be significantly higher, leading to an increased analysis time due to more numerous feasibility checks. In order to address this, we have implemented an *incremental* algorithm in Orion; the results are reported elsewhere, see [39].

Acknowledgements. We would like to thank Gerard Holzmann for sharing insights into the implementation of Uno. We would also like to thank Glenn Bruns, Nils Klarlund, and the anonymous referees for suggesting several improvements to the presentation. This work is supported in part by grant CCR-0341658 from the National Science Foundation.

References

1. (FlexeLint) http://www.gimpel.com.
2. (Coverity) http://www.coverity.com.
3. (Fortify) http://www.fortifysoftware.com/products/sca.jsp.
4. Holzmann, G.: Static source code checking for user-defined properties. In: Proc. IDPT 2002, Pasadena, CA, USA (2002)
   http://www.cs.bell-labs.com/what/uno/index.html.
5. Ball, T., Rajamani, S.: The SLAM toolkit. In: CAV. Volume 2102 of LNCS. (2001)
6. Corbett, J., Dwyer, M., Hatcliff, J., Pasareanu, C., Robby, Laubach, S., H.Zheng: Bandera: extracting finite-state models from Java source code. In: ICSE. (2001)
   http://www.cis.ksu.edu/santos/bandera.
7. Clarke, E.M., Grumberg, O., Jha, S., Lu, Y., Veith, H.: Counterexample-guided abstraction refinement for symbolic model checking. J. ACM **50**(5) (2003) 752–794

8. Henzinger, T.A., Jhala, R., Majumdar, R., Necula, G.C., Sutre, G., Weimer, W.: Temporal-safety proofs for systems code. In: CAV. Volume 2404 of LNCS. (2002)
9. Henzinger, T.A., Jhala, R., Majumdar, R., McMillan, K.L.: Abstractions from proofs. In: POPL. (2004) 232–244
10. Karp, R., Miller, R.: Parallel program schemata. J.CSS **3**(2) (1969)
11. Merrill, J.: GENERIC and GIMPLE: A new tree representation for entire functions. In: First GCC Developers Summit. (2003) at `www.gcc.gnu.org`.
12. (Simplify) `http://research.compaq.com/SRC/esc/Simplify.html`.
13. Stump, A., Barrett, C., Dill, D.: CVC: a Cooperating Validity Checker. In: 14th International Conference on Computer-Aided Verification. (2002)
14. Schmidt, D., Steffen, B.: Program analysis *as* model checking of abstract interpretations. In: SAS. Volume 1503 of LNCS., Springer Verlag (1998)
15. Aho, A.V., Sethi, R., Ullman, J.D.: Compilers: Principles, Techniques, and Tools. Addison–Wesley (1987)
16. Dijkstra, E., Lamport, L., Martin, A., Scholten, C., Steffens, E.: On-the-fly garbage collection: An excercise in cooperation. C.ACM **21**(11) (1978)
17. Dijkstra, E.: Guarded commands, nondeterminacy, and formal derivation of programs. CACM **18**(8) (1975)
18. Tip, F.: A survey of program slicing techniques. Journal of programming languages **3** (1995) 121–189
19. Dams, D.: Comparing abstraction refinement algorithms. In: SoftMC: Workshop on Software Model Checking. (2003)
20. Necula, G., McPeak, S., Weimer, W.: CCured: type-safe retrofitting of legacy code. In: POPL. (2002)
21. Godefroid, P.: Model checking for programming languages using Verisoft. In: POPL. (1997)
22. Godefroid, P., Klarlund, N., Sen, K.: Dart: Directed automated random testing. In: Proc. of the ACM SIGPLAN. (2005)
23. Visser, W., Havelund, K., Brat, G., Park, S.: Model checking programs. In: ICSE. (2000) `http://ase.arc.nasa.gov/visser/jpf`.
24. Hallem, S., Chelf, B., Xie, Y., Engler, D.: A system and language for building system-specific, static analyses. In: PLDI. (2002)
25. (PolySpace) `http://www.polyspace.com`.
26. (Klocwork) `http://www.klocwork.com`.
27. Das, M., Lerner, S., Seigle, M.: ESP: Path-sensitive program verification in polynomial time. In: PLDI. (2002)
28. Brand, D.: A software falsifier. In: International symposium on Software Reliability Engineering. (2000) 174–185
29. Finkel, A.: Reduction and covering of infinite reachability trees. Information and Computation **89**(2) (1990)
30. Emerson, E., Namjoshi, K.S.: On model checking for non-deterministic infinite-state systems. In: LICS. (1998)
31. Flanagan, C., Leino, K.M., Lillibridge, M., Nelson, G., Saxe, J., Stata, R.: Extended static checking for Java. In: PLDI. (2002)
32. Larochelle, D., Evans, D.: Statically detecting likely buffer overflow vulnerabilities. In: USENIX Security Symposium. (2001)
33. Bush, W., Pincus, J., Sielaff, D.: A static analyzer for finding dynamic programming errors. Software: Practice and Experience **30**(7) (2000) 775–802
34. Benedikt, M., Godefroid, P., Reps, T.: Model checking of unrestricted hierarchical state machines. icalp 2001: 652-666. In: ICALP. Volume 2076 of LNCS. (2001)

35. Alur, R., Etessami, K., Yannakakis, M.: Analysis of recursive state machines. In: CAV. Volume 2102 of LNCS. (2001)

36. (CVC Lite) http://chicory.stanford.edu/CVCL/.

37. (CBMC) http://www.cs.cmu.edu/~modelcheck/cbmc/.

38. Cousot, P., Cousot, R., Feret, J., Mauborgne, L., Miné, A., Monniaux, D., Rival, X.: The ASTRÉE Analyser. In Sagiv, M., ed.: Proceedings of the European Symposium on Programming (ESOP'05). Volume 3444 of Lecture Notes in Computer Science., Edinburgh, Scotland, © Springer (2005) 21–30

39. Conway, C.L., Namjoshi, K.S., Dams, D., Edwards, S.A.: Incremental algorithms for inter-procedural analysis of safety properties. In Etessami, K., Rajamani, S.K., eds.: Computer Aided Verification. Number 3576 in LNCS (2005) 449–461

Appendix

We present detailed proofs of theorems in this section.

Algorithm I: White-Grey-Black Search

The algorithm is reproduced below.

var color: array [S] of (W,G,B)
initially $(\forall s : white(s))$
actions
$$([]s : I(s) \wedge white(s) \longrightarrow color[s] := G)$$
$[]$ $([]s,t : grey(s) \wedge R(s,t) \wedge white(t) \longrightarrow color[t] := G)$
$[]$ $([]s : grey(s) \wedge (\forall t : R(s,t) \Rightarrow \neg white(t)) \longrightarrow color[s] := B)$

Theorem 1. *Algorithm I terminates with Black = Reach.*

Proof. 1. Termination: to show termination, consider the progress measure $\rho = (|White|, |Grey|)$ under lexicographic ordering. As the graph is finite, this measure is finite, and the lexicographic order is well-founded. Notice that the first two actions, if executed, strictly decrease $|White|$, while the third action, if executed, keeps $|White|$ constant, but strictly decreases $|Grey|$. Thus, ρ decreases strictly for every executed action; hence, the program terminates.

2. Correctness: we show some auxiliary invariants first.

2a. $(Grey \cup Black) \subseteq Reach$ is invariant. (proof) this is true initially as the sets on the left are empty. The first action turns a white initial state grey, thus preserving the invariant. The second action turns a white successor of a grey state (reachable, by induction) grey, thus preserving the invariant. The third action changes the color of a grey state to black, thus keeping the union constant. (endproof)

2b. $post(Black) \subseteq (Grey \cup Black)$ is invariant. (proof) this is true initially as $Black$ is empty. The first two actions increase only $Grey$, thus they preserve the invariant. The last action moves a state from grey to black, but the newly blackened state satisfies this condition. (endproof)

At termination, all actions are disabled. Thus: (i) from the disabling of the first action, all initial states are non-white, so $I \subseteq (Grey \cup Black)$; (ii) from the disabling of the second action, all grey states have non-white successors, so $post(Grey) \subseteq (Grey \cup Black)$; (iii) from the disabling of the third action, all grey states have at least one white successor. The second and third consequences together imply that $Grey = \emptyset$. Hence, from (i), $I \subseteq Black$, and from (2b), $post(Black) \subseteq Black$. Thus, $Black$ is a solution to the fixpoint equation for the set of reachable states. Since $Reach$ is the least solution, and from (2a) we have that $Black \subseteq Reach$, we get that $Black = Reach$.

Algorithm II: Covering-Based Search

The algorithm is given below.

var color: array [S] of (W,G,B,R)
initially $(\forall s : white(s))$
actions
   $([]s : I(s) \wedge white(s) \longrightarrow color[s] := G)$
$[]$ $([]s, t : grey(s) \wedge R(s,t) \wedge white(t) \longrightarrow color[t] := G)$
$[]$ $([]s : grey(s) \wedge (\forall t : R(s,t) \Rightarrow \neg white(t)) \longrightarrow color[s] := B)$
$[]$ $([]s : grey(s) \wedge ((Grey \setminus \{s\}) \cup Black) \sqsupseteq \{s\} \longrightarrow color[s] := R)$

Theorem 2. *Algorithm II terminates, and there is a reachable error state iff one of the states in $(Black \cup Red)$ is an error state.*

Proof. 1. Termination: We use the same progress measure, $\rho = (|White|, |Grey|)$, as before. This decreases strictly for the first three actions, which are identical to those of the previous algorithm. The fourth action keeps $|White|$ unchanged while decreasing $|Grey|$.

2. Correctness:

2a. $(Grey \cup Black \cup Red) \subseteq Reach$ is invariant. (proof) this is true initially as the sets on the left are empty. The first action turns a white initial state grey, thus preserving the invariant. The second action turns a white successor of a grey state (reachable, by induction) grey, thus preserving the invariant. The third action changes the color of a grey state to black, while the last one changes the color of a grey state to red, thus keeping the union constant. (endproof)

2b. $post(Black) \subseteq (Grey \cup Black \cup Red)$ is invariant. (proof) this is true initially as $Black$ is empty. The first two actions increase only $Grey$, thus they preserve the invariant. The third action moves a state from grey to black, but the newly blackened state satisfies this condition. The fourth action only moves a state from grey to red. (endproof)

At termination, all actions are disabled. Thus: (i) from the disabling of the first action, all initial states are non-white, so $I \subseteq (Grey \cup Black \cup Red)$; (ii) from the disabling of the second action, all grey states have non-white successors, so $post(Grey) \subseteq (Grey \cup Black \cup Red)$; (iii) from the disabling of the third action, all grey states have at least one white successor. The second and third consequences together imply that $Grey = \emptyset$. Hence, from (i), $I \subseteq (Black \cup Red)$, and from (2b), $post(Black) \subseteq (Black \cup Red)$.

However, we cannot claim, as in the previous proof, that $Black \cup Red$ satisfies the fixpoint equation. Indeed, we hope it does not, since this would mean that $Black \cup Red = Reach$, and we want this set of states to be a strict subset of the reachable states. At termination, red states can have successors that are any color except grey, as there are no grey states left. What we would like to claim is that $Reach \cap E \neq \emptyset$ if, and only if, $(Black \cup Red) \cap E \neq \emptyset$. To do so, we prove the stronger invariant below.

3. Invariantly, $Reach \cap E \neq \emptyset$ iff $(Grey \cup Black \cup Red \cup (I \cap White)) \xrightarrow{*} E$.
(proof) [right-to-left] by contrapositive. Suppose that there is no reachable error state. By (2a), it is not possible to reach an error state from $(Grey \cup Black \cup Red \cup (I \cap White))$, which is a subset of the reachable states.

[left-to-right] suppose that there is a reachable error state. We have to show that the right-hand expression is an invariant. The property is true initially as all initial states are white. The first transition only moves a state from $(I \cap White)$ to $Grey$, so error reachability is invariant. The second adds a $Grey$ state, hence reachability to an error state is preserved. The third moves a state from $Grey$ to $Black$, while the last moves a state from $Grey$ to Red, so again, reachability to error states is preserved. (endproof)

At termination, this invariant implies, as $Grey$ is empty, and all initial states are non-white (condition (i) above), that $Reach \cap E \neq \emptyset$ iff $(Black \cup Red) \xrightarrow{*} E$. This is not enough to imply the equivalence of $Reach \cap E \neq \emptyset$ and $(Black \cup Red) \cap E \neq \emptyset$: though the successors of a black state are colored only red or black, the error may be in a white successor of a red state, which remains unexplored on termination. We use the path-length constraint on the covering relation to show that this situation can occur only if a red/black state is itself an error state.

4. Invariantly, for any $k > 0$, if $Red \xrightarrow{=k} E$, then $(Grey \cup Black) \xrightarrow{\leq k} E$.
(proof) This is true initially as there are no red states, so the antecedent is false for all k. Assuming the claim to be true, we show that it is preserved by every transition. The first three transitions can only increase the set $(Grey \cup Black)$, without affecting red states, thus the property, being monotonic in $(Grey \cup Black)$, continues to hold. The last transition moves a state s from grey to red. By the path-length constraint on the covering relation, the implication holds for the newly red state s after the transition. Consider any other red state t and any k for which there is a path to error of length k. By the induction hypothesis, before the transition, there is a path from a grey/black state, t', of length k', where $k' \leq k$, to a state in E. If this path cannot be used as a witness after the transition, it must be because t' turns red after the transition; hence, $t' = s$. But then, by the covering property for s, there must be a path of length at most k' from one of the grey/black states after the transition to a state in E. (endproof)

Now we argue that $(Black \cup Red) \xrightarrow{*} E$ holds iff $(Black \cup Red) \cap E \neq \emptyset$. The direction from right to left is trivial. For the other direction, let k be the length of the shortest path to an E-node from $(Black \cup Red)$. If $k = 0$, we are done. If $k > 0$, the start state of the path must be in *Red*, otherwise there is a shorter path by (2b) and the assumption that *Grey* $\neq \emptyset$. However, in that case, by (4) and the assumption that *Grey* $\neq \emptyset$, there is a path of length at most k from a black node to E; hence, again, there is a shorter path by (2b). Thus, k must be 0.

Algorithm III: Adding Differencing Mechanisms

The algorithm is identical to that presented before, but for a modified final action.

$$([]s, Diff : grey(s) \land (Diff \subseteq White) \land$$
$$((Grey \setminus \{s\}) \cup Black \cup Diff) \sqsupseteq \{s\} \land \{s\} \sqsupseteq Diff$$
$$\longrightarrow color[s] := R; ([]t : t \in Diff : color[t] := G))$$

Theorem 3. *Algorithm III terminates, and there is a reachable error state iff one of the states in $(Black \cup Red)$ is an error state.*

Proof. Surprisingly, the proof of correctness is essentially identical to the one for the covering-only search.

1. Termination: this holds with reasoning identical to that in the previous proof.

2. Correctness: The only difference is that since Diff can include unreachable states, so (2a) no longer holds, so we have to adjust the proof of the right-to-left direction of (3). We give the new proof below; the rest of the argument is identical.

3. Invariantly, *Reach* $\cap E \neq \emptyset$ iff $(Grey \cup Black \cup Red \cup (I \cap White)) \xrightarrow{*} E$.

[right-to-left proof] Suppose that there is no reachable E-state. We have to show that the r.h.s. is invariantly false. The r.h.s. is false initially as it reduces to $I \xrightarrow{*} E$, which is false by assumption.

Suppose that it is false, we show that no action can make it true. The first action only colors a white initial state grey, so the r.h.s. stays false. Since there is no path to error from grey states, marking white successors of grey states as grey (the second action) cannot introduce a path to error. Similarly, the third action only colors a grey state black, so it does not make the r.h.s. true.

The fourth action, however, turns a grey state red *and* adds a set of — perhaps unreachable — states, *Diff*, to *Grey*. So the only way in which the property can be true after the transition is if *Diff* $\xrightarrow{*} E$ holds. But the constraint $\{s\} \sqsupseteq$ *Diff* in the guard, together with the path-matching constraint on the covering relation, implies that $s \xrightarrow{*} E$ is true. But this is known to be false, as s is a grey state before the transition. Hence, the property remains false after the transition.

Beyond Bisimulation: The "up-to" Techniques

Davide Sangiorgi

Università di Bologna, Italy
http://www.cs.unibo.it/~sangio/

Abstract. We consider the bisimulation proof method – an instance of the co-induction proof method – that is at the heart of the success of bisimulation. We discuss a number of enhancements of the method and some open problems.

1 Bisimulation

Bisimulation (and, more generally, co-induction) can be regarded as one of the most important contributions of Concurrency Theory to Computer Science. Nowadays, bisimulation and the co-inductive techniques developed from the idea of bisimulation are widely used, not only in Concurrency, but, more broadly, in Computer Science, in a number of areas: functional languages, object-oriented languages, type theory, data types, domains, databases, compiler optimisations, program analysis, verification tools, etc.. For instance, in type theory bisimulation and co-inductive techniques have been used: to prove soundness of type systems; to define the meaning of equality between (recursive) types and then to axiomatise and prove such equalities; to define co-inductive types and manipulate infinite proofs in theorem provers. Also, the development of Final Semantics, an area of Mathematics based on co-algebras and category theory and that gives us a rich and deep perspective on the meaning of co-induction and its duality with induction, has been largely motivated by the interest in bisimulation.

In this paper we consider the bisimulation proof method – an instance of the co-induction proof method – that is at the heart of the success of bisimulation. More precisely, we discuss enhancements of the method, motivate them, and hint at some related open problems. This is not supposed to be a comprehensive paper, but rather a quick guide to the state of the art in the topic, which the interested reader could also use to search for more details.

We consider bisimilarity on standard labelled transition systems. Their transitions are of the form $P \xrightarrow{\mu} Q$, where P and Q are *processes*, and label μ is drawn from some alphabet of *actions*.

Definition 1. A relation $\mathcal{R}$ on processes is an *bisimulation* if whenever $(P, Q) \in \mathcal{R}$,

1. $P \xrightarrow{\alpha} P'$ implies $Q \xrightarrow{\alpha} Q'$ and $(P', Q') \in \mathcal{R}$, for some Q'
2. the converse, on the actions from Q.

P and Q are *bisimilar*, written $P \sim Q$, if $(P, Q) \in \mathcal{R}$ for some bisimulation $\mathcal{R}$.

F.S. de Boer et al. (Eds.): FMCO 2005, LNCS 4111, pp. 161–171, 2006.

($\sim$ can also be viewed as the greatest fixed-point of a certain monotone function on relations, whose definition closely follows the bisimulation clauses above.) By definition of $\sim$, a bisimulation relation is contained in $\sim$, and hence it consists of only pairs of bisimilar processes. This immediately suggests a proof method for $\sim$, by far the most popular one: to demonstrate that $(P, Q) \in \sim$ holds, find a bisimulation relation containing the pair (P, Q).

2   An Example of Redundancy

In the clauses of definition (1) the same relation $\mathcal{S}$ is mentioned in the hypothesis and in the thesis. In other words, when we check the bisimilarity clause on a pair (P, Q), all needed pairs of derivatives, like (P', Q'), must be present in $\mathcal{S}$. We cannot discard any such pair of derivatives from $\mathcal{S}$, or even "manipulate" its process components. In this way, a bisimulation relation often contains many pairs strongly related with each other, in the sense that, at least, the bisimilarity between the processes in some of these pairs implies that between the processes in other pairs. For instance, in a process algebra a bisimulation relation might contain pairs of processes obtainable from other pairs through application of algebraic laws for bisimilarity, or obtainable as combinations of other pairs and of the operators of the language. These redundancies can make both the definition and the verification of a bisimulation relation annoyingly heavy and tedious: it is difficult at the beginning to guess all pairs which are needed; and the bisimulation clauses must be checked on all pairs introduced.

As an example, let P be a non-deadlocked process from a CCS-like language, and $!P$ the process recursively defined thus: $!P \stackrel{\text{def}}{=} P \mid !P$. Process $!P$ represents the *replication* of P, i.e., a countable number of copies of P in parallel. (In certain process algebras, e.g., the π-calculus, replication is the only form of recursion allowed, since it gives enough expressive power and enjoys interesting algebraic properties.) A property that we naturally expect to hold is that duplication of replication has no behavioural effect, i.e, $!P \mid !P \sim !P$. To prove this, we would like to use the *singleton* relation

$$\mathcal{S} \stackrel{\text{def}}{=} \{(!P \mid !P, !P)\}\,.$$

But $\mathcal{S}$ is easily seen not to be a bisimulation relation. For instance, if $P \stackrel{\mu}{\longrightarrow} P'$, then we have

$$!P \mid !P \stackrel{\mu}{\longrightarrow} !P \mid P' \mid !P$$

The derivative process does not appear in the processes of $\mathcal{S}$, hence $!P$ cannot possibly match the transition from $!P \mid !P$ in a way that would close the bisimulation diagram.

If we add pairs of processes to $\mathcal{S}$ so as to make it into a bisimulation relation, then we might find that the simplest solution is to take the *infinite* relation

$$\mathcal{R} \stackrel{\text{def}}{=} \{(Q_1, Q_2) \; : \; \text{for some } R, \\ Q_1 \sim R \mid !P \mid !P \text{ and } Q_2 \sim R \mid !P\}\,.$$

The size augmentation in passing from $\mathcal{S}$ to $\mathcal{R}$ is rather discouraging. But it does somehow seem unnecessary, for the bisimilarity between the two processes in $\mathcal{S}$ already implies that between the processes of all pairs of $\mathcal{R}$. In this sense we can consider the added pairs *redundant*, because they can be derived from the original pair using the laws of $\sim$.

3   Enhancements of the Bisimulation Proof Method

The objective of enhancements of the bisimulation proof method is to prove bisimilarity results using relations smaller than bisimulations; that is, relations in which some redundant pairs have been omitted. To write this formally, we introduce the notion of progression, and set some terminology.

We let $\mathcal{R}$ and $\mathcal{S}$ range over binary relations on processes. The union of relations $\mathcal{R}$ and $\mathcal{S}$ is $\mathcal{R} \cup \mathcal{S}$, and their composition is $\mathcal{R}\mathcal{S}$ (i.e., $(P, P') \in \mathcal{R}\mathcal{S}$ holds if for some P'', both $(P, P'') \in \mathcal{R}$ and $(P'', P') \in \mathcal{S}$ hold). We often use the infix notation for relations; hence $P \, \mathcal{R} \, Q$ means $(P, Q) \in \mathcal{R}$.

Definition 2 (progression). *Given two relations $\mathcal{R}$ and $\mathcal{S}$, we say that $\mathcal{R}$ progresses to $\mathcal{S}$, written $\mathcal{R} \rightarrowtail \mathcal{S}$, if $P \, \mathcal{R} \, Q$ implies:*

1. *whenever $P \xrightarrow{\mu} P'$, there is Q' such that $Q \xrightarrow{\mu} Q'$ and $P' \, \mathcal{S} \, Q'$;*
2. *the converse, i.e., whenever $Q \xrightarrow{\mu} Q'$, there is P' such that $P \xrightarrow{\mu} P'$ and $P' \, \mathcal{S} \, Q'$.*

When $\mathcal{R}$ and $\mathcal{S}$ coincide, the above clauses are the ordinary ones of the definition of a bisimulation relation. By "enhancement of the bisimulation proof method" we refer to a technique that, for a given relation $\mathcal{R}$, allows us to infer $\mathcal{R} \subseteq \sim$ if

$$\mathcal{R} \rightarrowtail \mathcal{R} \cup \{\text{some redundant pairs}\}$$

holds; that is, in the bisimulation diagrams we allow the derivative processes to belong to a relation larger than the original one.

Such enhancements relieve the work involved with the bisimulation proof method, because fewer diagrams have to be proved (one works with relations that are included in bisimulations but need not be bisimulations themselves). They can also make it simpler to find the relation $\mathcal{R}$ to work with.

4   Examples of Enhancements

Some enhancement techniques were proposed shortly after the discovery of bisimulation. The best known example is Milner's *bisimulation up to bisimilarity* technique [Mil89], in which the closure of a bisimulation relation is achieved up to bisimilarity itself. Precisely, this technique allows us to prove bisimilarities using progressions of the form $\mathcal{R} \rightarrowtail \sim \mathcal{R} \sim$, in which one requires that $(P, Q) \in \mathcal{R}$ and $P \xrightarrow{\mu} P'$ imply that

there are processes P'', Q', Q'' such that
$$P' \sim P'', \; Q \xrightarrow{\mu} Q' \sim Q'' \text{ and } (P'', Q'') \in \mathcal{R}.$$

Intuitively, the technique is sound because $\sim$ is transitive; hence from the bisimilarity between P'' and Q'' we can also infer the bisimilarity between the derivatives P' and Q'.

A different form of enhancement is the *up-to-contexts* [San98, San96, BS98], which allows us to cut a common context in matching derivatives. Now progressions are of the form $\mathcal{R} \longmapsto \mathcal{C}(\mathcal{R})$, where

$$\mathcal{C}(\mathcal{R}) \stackrel{\text{def}}{=} \{(C[P], C[Q]) \; : \; P \, \mathcal{R} \, Q\}$$

Here we are assuming – without getting into the mathematical details – that the process language is defined by means of a grammar, and $C[\cdot]$ represents a process context for such grammar (precisely, a monadic context, meaning that the hole appears at most once). With up-to-contexts, the bisimulation clause becomes: $(P, Q) \in \mathcal{R}$ and $P \xrightarrow{\mu} P'$ imply that

there are processes P'', Q'' and a context $C[\cdot]$ such that
$$P' = C[P''], \; Q \xrightarrow{\mu} C[Q''] \text{ and } (P'', Q'') \in \mathcal{R}.$$

In this case, the technique would seem sound if $\sim$ is preserved by contexts. Hence from the bisimilarity between P'' and Q'' we can infer that between the derivatives $C[P'']$ and $C[Q'']$.

Yet another technique is *up to injective substitutions*, widely used in π-calculus and related formalisms (see [SW01]). This technique allows us to apply injective substitutions on names to the derivatives of two processes, which is very handy when dealing with languages whose transition system make use of substitutions on names. Progressions are of the form $\mathcal{R} \longmapsto Inj(\mathcal{R})$, where

$$Inj(\mathcal{R}) \stackrel{\text{def}}{=} \{(P\sigma, Q\sigma) \; : \; P \, \mathcal{R} \, Q \, , \; \sigma \text{ injective on names}\}$$

The soundness of the technique would seem to rely on the invariance of bisimilarity with respect to injective substitutions.

Sometimes it can also be useful to compose different techniques to obtain more powerful forms of enhancements. For instance, one can think of combining the three techniques above into an *up to bisimilarity, contexts, and injective substitutions*, in which progressions are of the form $\mathcal{R} \longmapsto \sim \mathcal{C}(Inj(\mathcal{R})) \sim$ (the three constituent techniques could even be combined in a different way). Thus, the bisimulation clause becomes: $(P, Q) \in \mathcal{R}$ and $P \xrightarrow{\mu} P'$ imply that

there are processes P'', Q'', a context $C[\cdot]$,
and an injective substitution σ on names such that
$$P' \sim C[P''\sigma], \; Q \xrightarrow{\mu} \sim C[Q''\sigma] \text{ and } (P'', Q'') \in \mathcal{R}.$$

We can apply the technique above to our example about replication in Section 2 to show that $\mathcal{S}$ is a bisimulation up to bisimilarity and contexts (up-to-injective-substitutions in this case is not necessary). We do not present the full proof; we only sketch a representative case of the proof. Thus suppose $P \xrightarrow{\mu} P'$ and therefore $!P \mid !P \xrightarrow{\mu} !P \mid P' \mid !P$. We show that this transition can be matched by $!P$. We can use the corresponding transition $!P \xrightarrow{\mu} P' \mid !P$. We have

$$!P \mid P' \mid !P \sim P' \mid !P \mid !P,$$

and

$$P' \mid !P \sim P' \mid !P.$$

Now, from the pair $(P' \mid !P \mid !P, P' \mid !P)$ we get back to the original pair $(!P \mid !P, !P)$ of $\mathcal{S}$ by removing the common context $P' \mid [\cdot]$. In summary, we have:

$$
\begin{array}{ccc}
!P \mid !P & & !P \\
\mu \downarrow & & \mu \downarrow \\
!P \mid P' \mid !P \sim P' \mid !P \mid !P & \mathcal{C}(\mathcal{S}) & P' \mid !P \sim P' \mid !P
\end{array}
$$

which closes the diagram, up to $\sim$ and contexts.

Enhancements of the bisimulation proof methods are sometimes extremely useful; they seem to be even *essential* in calculi for mobility such as the π-calculus, and higher-order languages such Ambients [CG98] or Higher-Order π-calculus [San92, SW01]. See for instance Merro and Zappa Nardelli's proof of the Ambient perfect firewall equation, one of the basic laws for Ambients [MZN05].

To be able to use an enhancement we first have to prove its soundness. This can be a difficult task. The difficulty tends to increase as the technique itself, or the language onto which it is applied, become more powerful or sophisticated. For instance, the proof of soundness of the technique that we above called "up to bisimilarity, contexts, and injective substitutions" can be far from trivial. Indeed, it is quite challenging if the language is higher order, meaning that terms of the language can be communicated or move about.

In summary, we look for a general theory of enhancements that, most notably, would allow us to understand what an enhancement is, how enhancements can be composed, and how to prove their soundness. We discuss below some of the difficulties that one encounters in this direction, and some (partial) solutions that have been proposed.

5   What Is a Redundant Pair?

First, one would need to understand what a redundant pair is. The intuition that we gave at the end of Section 2 – a pair is redundant if it can be derived from the remaining pairs using laws for bisimilarity – is not quite right (in the sense that the condition is important but, as it stands, it is not sufficient).

Here is a counterexample, in CCS. The following is a valid inference rule for $\sim$ (i.e., if the pair in the premise is in $\sim$ then also the pair in the conclusion is so):

$$\texttt{Pref-inv} \frac{(a.P, a.Q)}{(P, Q)}$$

Consider now relation

$$\mathcal{R} \stackrel{\text{def}}{=} \{(a.\,b, a.\,c)\}$$

The pair (b, c) would thus be redundant in $\mathcal{R} \cup \{(b, c)\}$, since (b, c) can be derived from the other pair $(a.\,b, a.\,c)$ via rule `Pref-inv`. However, we have

$$\mathcal{R} \rightarrowtail \mathcal{R} \cup \{(b, c)\},$$

and yet $a.\,b \not\sim a.\,c$. This shows that this definition of redundant pair is unsound: from the progression $\mathcal{R} \rightarrowtail \mathcal{R} \cup \{(b, c)\}$ we cannot derive $\mathcal{R} \subseteq \sim$.

Even for the techniques discussed in Section 4, stating when they are sound (i.e., which languages, which forms of bisimilarity) is difficult. For instance, consider the up-to-bisimilarity-and-contexts technique. We hinted in Section 4 that its soundness would seem to derive from the properties that bisimilarity is transitive and preserved by contexts. Again, surprisingly, this condition alone is not sufficient (and, again, we do not know at present how to refine the condition). Consider the simple process language

$$P := f(P) \;\bigm|\; a.\,P \;\bigm|\; \mathbf{0}$$

where $a.\,-$ is a CCS-like prefix, $\mathbf{0}$ is the inactive process and f is an operator whose behaviour is given by the rule

$$\frac{X \stackrel{a}{\longrightarrow} X' \quad X' \stackrel{a}{\longrightarrow} X''}{f(X) \stackrel{a}{\longrightarrow} X''}$$

That is, in order to release some action, f requires the release of two actions from its argument. On this language it is easy to show that bisimilarity is transitive and preserved by all contexts (in fact, we can infer that bisimilarity is a congruence from the fact that the transition rules of the operators are in *tyft* format [GV92]). Despite this, the up-to-bisimilarity-and-contexts technique is not sound. To see this, take

$$\mathcal{R} \stackrel{\text{def}}{=} \{(a.\,\mathbf{0}, a.\,a.\,\mathbf{0})\}$$

Processes $a.\,\mathbf{0}$ and $a.\,a.\,\mathbf{0}$ are not bisimilar. But the diagram

$$
\begin{array}{ccccc}
a.\,\mathbf{0} & & \mathcal{R} & & a.\,a.\,\mathbf{0} \\
a \downarrow & & & & a \downarrow \\
\mathbf{0} & \sim f(a.\,\mathbf{0}) & \mathcal{C}(\mathcal{R}) & f(a.\,a.\,\mathbf{0}) \sim & a.\,\mathbf{0}
\end{array}
$$

shows that $\mathcal{R} \rightarrowtail \sim \mathcal{C}(\mathcal{R}) \sim$ holds. In this diagram, $\mathbf{0} \sim f(a.\,\mathbf{0})$ and $f(a.\,a.\,\mathbf{0}) \sim a.\,\mathbf{0}$ hold because the operator f transforms two consecutive a transitions into a single one.

Below is another counterexample, in this case showing that the *form* of the bisimilarity matters. So far we have used *strong* bisimilarity, in which all actions are treated equally. Other forms of bisimilarity have been proposed, such as *weak bisimilarity* and *branching bisimilarity*. In weak bisimilarity, for instance, internal actions (indicated as τ) are partially ignored. Weak transitions are introduced thus: first, $P \Longrightarrow P'$ holds if P can evolve into P' with a – possibly empty – sequence of τ-steps; then $P \stackrel{\mu}{\Longrightarrow} P'$ stands for $P \Longrightarrow \stackrel{\mu}{\longrightarrow} \Longrightarrow P'$ (where $\Longrightarrow \stackrel{\mu}{\longrightarrow} \Longrightarrow$ is the composition of relations). In weak bisimulation, the bisimulation clauses become:

1. if $(P, Q) \in \mathcal{R}$ and $P \stackrel{\mu}{\longrightarrow} P'$ with $\mu \neq \tau$, then there is Q' such that $Q \stackrel{\mu}{\Longrightarrow} Q'$ and $(P', Q') \in \mathcal{R}$;
2. if $(P, Q) \in \mathcal{R}$ and $P \longrightarrow P'$, then there is Q' such that $Q \Longrightarrow Q'$ and $(P', Q') \in \mathcal{R}$.
3. the converse of (1) and (2), on the actions from Q.

Weak bisimilarity, written $\approx$, is transitive; yet, the up-to-bisimilarity technique fails. To see this, take

$$\mathcal{R} \stackrel{\text{def}}{=} \{(\tau. a. \mathbf{0}, \mathbf{0})\}$$

The processes in this pair can match each other's transitions, up to $\approx$. For instance, the transition $\tau. a. \mathbf{0} \stackrel{\tau}{\longrightarrow} a. \mathbf{0}$ is matched by $\mathbf{0} \Longrightarrow \mathbf{0}$, using the equalities $a. \mathbf{0} \approx \tau. a. \mathbf{0}$ and $\mathbf{0} \approx \mathbf{0}$. However, $\tau. a. \mathbf{0} \approx \mathbf{0}$ is obviously false.

6   Towards an Algebra of Enhancements

We mention here an attempt towards an algebra of enhancements, proposed in [San98] and that focuses on the properties of composition of techniques.

The progressions used in [San98] are of the form $\mathcal{R} \rightarrowtail \mathcal{F}(\mathcal{R})$, where $\mathcal{F}$ is a function from relations to relations. One is interested in functions $\mathcal{F}$ that are *sound* with respect to $\sim$, i.e. such that $\mathcal{R} \rightarrowtail \mathcal{F}(\mathcal{R})$ implies $\mathcal{R} \subseteq \sim$. Relevant questions are: Which conditions ensure soundness of functions? Which interesting functions are sound? Which interesting properties are satisfied by the class of sound functions?

A simple functorial-like condition, called *respectfulness*, is suggested to guarantee the soundness of $\mathcal{F}$. This condition requires that if $\mathcal{R} \subseteq \mathcal{S}$ and $\mathcal{R} \rightarrowtail \mathcal{S}$ hold, then $\mathcal{F}(\mathcal{R}) \subseteq \mathcal{F}(\mathcal{S})$ and $\mathcal{F}(\mathcal{R}) \rightarrowtail \mathcal{F}(\mathcal{S})$ must hold too. A useful property about the class of respectful functions is that it is closed under important function constructors like composition, union, iteration, and chaining (chaining gives us relational composition). Consequently, it suffices to define a few primitive respectful functions: more complex functions can then be derived via combinations of the primitive ones, and the soundness of the former follows from that of the latter.

Among the primitive functions there is the identity function and the constant-to-$\sim$ function, which maps every relation onto $\sim$. Another primitive function is the function $\mathcal{C}$ of the up-to-contexts technique. (More precisely, the paper shows that when the transition relation among processes is defined structurally on the operators of the language, certain conditions on the form of the transition rules ensure the respectfulness of $\mathcal{C}$; these conditions are met in familiar process algebras like ACP [BK84], CCS [Mil89], and the π-calculus [Mil99, SW01].)

Examples of respectful functions easily derivable from the above primitive ones are: the function which returns the transitive closure of a relation; the function which returns the closure of a relation under polyadic contexts (i.e., contexts which might have more than one hole, and each of these hole can appear more than once); the function mapping a relation $\mathcal{R}$ onto $\sim\mathcal{R}\sim$, where $\sim\mathcal{R}\sim$ is the composition of the three relations (this function gives us Milner's bisimulation up to bisimilarity technique; in this setting, it is recovered as a combination of the identity and constant-to-$\sim$ functions). Again, more sophisticated functions – and hence proof techniques for $\sim$ – can in turn be derived from these ones; for instance, the function that gives us the "up to bisimilarity, contexts, and injective substitutions" technique that we defined and used in Section 4.

Hirschkoff [Hir99, Hir98] has proved the theory of respectful functions in Coq, and has used the theory to develop a prototype for mechanically verifying bisimilarity results.

However, the present theory of respectful functions can only be a preliminary attempt towards a more general and robust theory. To begin with, the definition of respectfulness looks very ad hoc; we do not have abstract mathematical characterisations of it as in the case of the bisimulation proof method (notably using Final Semantics and co-algebras). Further, *chaining*, one of the key constructors for composing techniques according to the theory of respectfulness for strong bisimilarity, is not sound with weak bisimilarity. Therefore, when in comes to composing different techniques for weak bisimilarity, the theory of respectfulness might not help.

7   Weak Bisimilarity and Expansion

We mentioned above that chaining, one of the key constructors in the theory of respectfulness, is not sound for weak bisimilarity. For strong bisimilarity, chaining is mainly used to make top-compositions with the up-to-bisimilarity technique, that is, to add this technique on top of others. For instance, chaining allows us to add 'up to bisimilarity" on top of "up to contexts" and therefore infer that the progression $\mathcal{R} \longmapsto \sim \mathcal{C}(\mathcal{R}) \sim$ is sound. The theory of respectfulness for weak bisimilarity prevent us from making similar inferences precisely because of the problems with chaining.

Therefore, at present, if one wants to use similar compositions of techniques for weak bisimilarity one has to prove *directly* that the specific compositions of interest are sound. The analogue in the strong case would be proving directly that, for example, the up-to-bisimilarity-and-contexts technique is sound.

A further problem with weak bisimilarity is that we cannot use, alone or in compositions, the up-to-bisimilarity technique, which, as shown in Section 5, is not sound. In its place, a number of variations have been proposed; for instance, allowing only uses of strong bisimilarity within the up to bisimilarity [Mil89]. The most important variation, however, involves a relation called *expansion* [AKH92, SM92]. Expansion is a preorder derived from weak bisimilarity by, essentially, comparing the number of silent actions. The idea underlying expansion is roughly that if Q expands P, then P and Q are bisimilar, except that in mimicking Q's behaviour, P cannot perform more τ transitions than Q. We can think of P as being at least as fast as Q, or more generally, we can think that Q uses at least as many resources as P. An interest of expansion derives from the fact that, in practice, most of the uses of weak bisimilarity are indeed instances of expansion. Expansion enjoys an elegant mathematical theory, explored in [AKH92]. Expansion is preserved by all CCS operators but sum, and has a complete proof system for finite terms based on a modification of the standard τ laws for CCS. Expansion is also a powerful auxiliary relation for up-to techniques involving weak forms of behavioural equivalence.

To define expansion we need the following notation.

1. $P \xrightarrow{\hat{\tau}} P'$ holds if $P \xrightarrow{\tau} P'$ or $P' = P$.
2. If $\alpha \neq \tau$ then $P \xrightarrow{\hat{\alpha}} P'$ if $P \xrightarrow{\alpha} P'$.

Definition 3. A relation $\mathcal{S}$ is an *expansion* if whenever $(P, Q) \in \mathcal{S}$,

1. $P \xrightarrow{\alpha} P'$ implies $Q \xRightarrow{\alpha} Q'$ and $(P', Q') \in \mathcal{S}$ for some Q'
2. $Q \xrightarrow{\alpha} Q'$ implies $P \xrightarrow{\hat{\alpha}} P'$ and $(P', Q') \in \mathcal{S}$ for some P'.

Q *expands* P, written $P \preceq Q$ or $Q \succeq P$, if $(P, Q) \in \mathcal{S}$ for some expansion $\mathcal{S}$.

In the bisimulation up to expansion, the requirement is: $(P, Q) \in \mathcal{R}$ and $P \xrightarrow{\mu} P'$ imply that

$$\text{there is a process } Q' \text{ such that}$$
$$Q \xRightarrow{\mu} Q' \text{ and } P' \succeq \mathcal{R} \preceq Q';$$

"Up to expansion" can be added on top of other techniques; thus, in "up-to expansion and contexts", the bisimulation clause becomes: $(P, Q) \in \mathcal{R}$ and $P \xrightarrow{\mu} P'$ imply that

$$\text{there are processes } P'', Q', Q'' \text{ and a context } C[\cdot] \text{ such that}$$
$$P' \succeq C[P''], \text{ and } Q \xrightarrow{\mu} Q' \succeq C[Q''], \text{ and } (P'', Q'') \in \mathcal{R}.$$

Two major problems still remain:

1. How to integrate a relation such as expansion in a general theory of bisimulation enhancements.
2. Expansion is sometimes too rigid.

The second problem arises because, in the definition of expansion, at *every* step the same comparison between the two processes is maintained; that is, if $P \preceq Q$ then P should be "better" than Q in every matching transitions. This requirement can sometimes be too strong. For instance, P may be globally more efficient than Q and yet in a few places P may require some more internal work than Q. An example of this situation can be found in [HPS05], where two abstract machines for an implementation of (a variant of) Ambients are compared. One of the machines is an optimisation of the other, and is therefore more efficient. However its efficiency is obtained partly by employing more sophisticated data structures, which require an initialisation phase. As a consequence, when the data structures are created, the optimised machine can be slower; as the two machines continue to execute, however, the choice of better data structures produces a gain. Thus neither machine is an expansion of the other. Further, because of similar technical details, one cannot even use expansion as an auxiliary up-to-relation in a prove of weak bisimilarity between the two machines. Indeed, the proof of correctness of the optimised abstract machine in [HPS05] makes use of a full weak bisimulation, which makes the relation to use, and the proof that this relation is a weak bisimulation, long and complex.

Very recently, Damien Pous [Pou05] has proposed refinements of the expansion relation that can be integrated into the theory of respectful functions of Section 6 and that could overcome the problems of expansion indicated above. A possible drawback of these refinements is that they might be difficult to use (i.e., it might be difficult to establish the existence of such a refinement between two given processes). However, more experiments are needed to prove or disprove such claims.

8   Conclusions

We need to understand better what is an enhancement of the bisimulation proof method: what makes an enhancement sound and why, and how it can be used. It would be highly desirable to have general results, applicable to different languages and different forms of bisimulation.

References

[AKH92]   S. Arun-Kumar and M. Hennessy. An efficiency preorder for processes. *Acta Informatica*, 29:737–760, 1992.

[BK84]   J.A. Bergstra and J.W. Klop. Process algebra for synchronous communication. *Information and Computation*, 60:109–137, 1984.

[BS98]   M. Boreale and D. Sangiorgi. A fully abstract semantics for causality in the π-calculus. *Acta Informatica*, 35:353–400, 1998.

[CG98]   L. Cardelli and A.D. Gordon. Mobile ambients. In Nivat. M., editor, *Proc. FoSSaCS '98*, volume 1378 of *Lecture Notes in Computer Science*, pages 140–155. Springer Verlag, 1998.

[GV92]   J.F. Groote and F.W. Vaandrager. Structured operational semantics and bisimulation as a congruence. *Information and Computation*, 100:202–260, 1992.

[Hir98]   D. Hirschkoff. Automatically proving up to bisimulation. In Petr Jancar and Mojmir Kretinsky, editors, *Proceedings of MFCS '98 Workshop on Concurrency (Brno, Czech Republic, 27-29 August 1998)*, volume 18 of *entcs*. Elsevier Science Publishers, 1998.

[Hir99]   D. Hirschkoff. *Mise en oeuvre de preuves de bisimulation*. PhD thesis, Phd Thesis, Ecole Nationale des Ponts et Chausses, 1999.

[HPS05]   Daniel Hirschkoff, Damien Pous, and Davide Sangiorgi. A correct abstract machine for safe ambients. In *COORDINATION*, pages 17–32, 2005.

[Mil89]   R. Milner. *Communication and Concurrency*. Prentice Hall, 1989.

[Mil99]   R. Milner. *Communicating and Mobile Systems: the π-Calculus*. Cambridge University Press, 1999.

[MZN05]   M. Merro and F. Zappa Nardelli. Behavioural theory for mobile ambients. Journal of the ACM. To appear, 2005.

[Pou05]   Damien Pous. Up-to techniques for weak bisimulation. In *ICALP*, pages 730–741, 2005.

[San92]   D. Sangiorgi. *Expressing Mobility in Process Algebras: First-Order and Higher-Order Paradigms*. PhD thesis CST–99–93, Department of Computer Science, University of Edinburgh, 1992.

[San96]   D. Sangiorgi. Locality and non-interleaving semantics in calculi for mobile processes. *Theoretical Computer Science*, 155:39–83, 1996.

[San98]   D. Sangiorgi. On the bisimulation proof method. *Journal of Mathematical Structures in Computer Science*, 8:447–479, 1998.

[SM92]   D. Sangiorgi and R. Milner. The problem of "Weak Bisimulation up to". In W.R. Cleveland, editor, *Proc. CONCUR '92*, volume 630 of *Lecture Notes in Computer Science*, pages 32–46. Springer Verlag, 1992.

[SW01]   D. Sangiorgi and D. Walker. *The π-calculus: a Theory of Mobile Processes*. Cambridge University Press, 2001.

Separation Results Via Leader Election Problems

Maria Grazia Vigliotti[1,3], Iain Phillips[2], and Catuscia Palamidessi[3,4]

[1] INRIA Sophia-Antipolis, France
[2] Department of Computing, Imperial College London, England
[3] INRIA Futurs, France
[4] LIX Polytechnique, France

Abstract. We compare the expressive power of process calculi by study-
ing the problem of electing a leader in a symmetric network of processes.
We consider the π-calculus with mixed choice and with separate choice,
value-passing CCS and Mobile Ambients. We provide a unified approach
for all these calculi using reduction semantics.

1 Introduction

Expressiveness results, in formal languages, deal primarily with the question of
the power of the underpinning formal model. Different models of computation
can be compared using the notion of *encoding*. A typical example comes from
classical computability theory: Turing machines, Unlimited Register Machines
and Lambda Calculus are considered to be *equally powerful* since they can be
reciprocally *encoded*.

In this tutorial we consider expressiveness results about concurrent models of
computation. In the last twenty years, many different concurrent calculi have
been developed, and most of them are Turing complete, that is, they can compute the same functions as Turing machines. However, function computability
is only one possible way to evaluate the power of a concurrent language: other
aspects, related to the concurrent nature of the model, should also be taken into
account. Our focus is on the synchronisation capabilities of a calculus, and more
precisely on the mechanisms that allow remote processes to achieve an agreement. Agreement is considered an important problem in Distributed Computing
and a lot of research has been devoted to finding algorithms to achieve it, or,
depending on the model of computation, proving its impossibility. Apart from
the theoretical interest, the problem has important implications of a practical
nature in the field of Distributed Systems, where the design of the operating
system has to ensure the correct interaction between remote processes in a distributed setting, when a central coordinator is not available or not feasible. Also,
in the implementation of (concurrent) languages one has to face the problem of
whether certain interaction primitives are too expressive to be implemented in
a given distributed architecture.

One approach to comparing two calculi is to exhibit an encoding or to show
that such an encoding cannot exist. The notion of encoding is, naturally, subject to specific conditions. For instance, the encoding should not itself solve the

F.S. de Boer et al. (Eds.): FMCO 2005, LNCS 4111, pp. 172–194, 2006.
© Springer-Verlag Berlin Heidelberg 2006

problem of synchronisation: it would be like mapping Turing machines into finite automata by using a translation which adds an oracle.

To show that an encoding does not exist, one way of proceeding is to show that there is a problem that can be solved in one calculus, but not in the other. In the field of distributed algorithms [11, 30], various models of computation have been compared via the *symmetric leader election problem*, which consists in requiring the members of a symmetric network to elect one of them as their leader. The difficulty consists in breaking the initial symmetry to achieve a situation which is inherently asymmetric (one is the leader and the others are not). This method has proved rather successful also for the comparison of various process calculi [3, 20, 7, 22, 21, 24, 23, 25, 31]. In the case of process calculi, actually, some of the symmetry-breaking arguments are rather sophisticated and use additional discriminations that are related to the topology of the network. In other words, some calculi admit a solution to leader election problems only if the network has a specific topology, such as a fully connected graph.

In this tutorial we shall collect, present, systematise and interpret a collection of results regarding expressiveness in process calculi obtained by means of the *symmetric leader election problem*. We shall provide a uniform presentation by the use of reduction semantics, and we shall highlight the similarities and differences between the various approaches to leader election problems. In particular, we shall focus on the following calculi: Communicating Concurrent Systems (CCS), the π-calculus with mixed choice (π_m) and with separate choice (π_s), and Mobile Ambients (MA).

CCS [12, 14] is a simple calculus, that aims to represent concurrency with synchronous communication. Based on the concept of channels, it contains two primitives for sending and receiving which can synchronise by handshaking on the same channel. In this paper we shall consider *value-passing* CCS, where input and output primitives carry value parameters. However, for the sake of simplicity, we shall call it CCS throughout the paper.

The π-calculus [15] enhances the CCS model by allowing processes to communicate channel names, which can also be used as channels for communication, allowing the dynamic creation of new links between processes (link mobility). In this paper we do not consider the full π-calculus as originally presented; we omit the matching operator and require choices to be guarded, as in [14]. We call this version the *mixed-choice* π-calculus, which we denote by π_m; here the word "mixed" signifies that a choice can contain both input and output guards. CCS as we shall present it can be seen as a subset of π_m.

The asynchronous π-calculus [10, 2] has become particularly popular as a model for asynchronous communication. In this fragment there is no explicit choice, and outputs have no continuation. However output prefixing and separate choice can be encoded in the asynchronous π-calculus [2, 19]; separate choice is guarded choice with the restriction that input and output guards cannot be mixed in the same choice. In this tutorial we look at the *separate-choice* π-calculus, which we denote by π_s, rather than the asynchronous π-calculus; however the results valid for π_s also hold for the asynchronous π-calculus.

Finally, we shall deal with Mobile Ambients. MA [5] has been proposed to model features of computation over the Internet. This calculus is based on the simple unifying concept of *ambient*. Computation is no longer defined as exchanging values, but it is the result of ambients moving into and out of other ambients bringing along active processes and possibly other ambients.

Several relations among the above calculi are obvious or have been proved in the literature, addressing at least partially the issue of expressiveness. However, questions about their expressive power can still be asked:

- π_s is a subcalculus of π_m. *Is π_m strictly more expressive?*
- CCS with value passing can be viewed as a subcalculus of π_m. Thus π_m is as least as expressive as CCS. *Does an encoding exist from π_m into CCS?*
- The asynchronous π-calculus can be encoded into MA. *Can MA be encoded into the asynchronous π-calculus or CCS?*

In the tutorial we shall show that the answers to the previous questions are negative, i.e. those encodings do not exist under certain conditions (Section 2.3). The proofs are based on the possibility/impossibility of solving the symmetric leader election problem.

In encodings of languages that (do not) admit a solution for leader election problems, one important requirement is that the encoding preserves the original distribution among processes. This requirement aims at avoiding that the encoding may introduce a central coordinator [21, 23]. Therefore this condition makes the notion of encoding suitable to compare expressiveness of languages for distributed systems, where processes are expected to coordinate without the help of a centralised server.

The negative results mentioned above have been achieved in recent years as follows:

- Palamidessi [20, 21] established that π_m is strictly more expressive than π_s;
- Phillips and Vigliotti [24, 23, 31] proved a that small fragment of MA is not encodable in π_s.

Both those separation results are proved by considering the leader election problem in a fully connected (and symmetric) network. For instance, Palamidessi showed that the problem can be solved in the case of π_m, but not in the case of π_s. If there were an encoding from π_m to π_s, then the solution for π_m could be translated into one for π_s, provided that the encoding satisfied certain conditions (such as distribution—see Section 2.3). No such encoding can exist.

Moreover, finer-grained separation results are proved by considering the leader election problem in a network whose underlying graph is a ring. Those latter negative results have been achieved in recent years as follows:

- Palamidessi [20, 21] proved that CCS does not admit a solution to the leader election problem for certain symmetric rings, while π_m does. She deduced that there is no encoding from π_m into CCS.
- Phillips and Vigliotti [25] proved that a subcalculus of MA admits a solution to the leader election problem for symmetric rings. They concluded that this calculus cannot be encoded into CCS.

The tutorial is organised in three parts as follows: (1) A general part where we discuss leader election in distributed networks, and how to formalise the problem in process calculi (Section 2). In Section 3 we define the various calculi we shall consider. (2) A part where we deal with leader election problems in general symmetric networks (with no restriction on topology) (Section 4). We present solutions for various calculi, show that other calculi do not admit solutions, and derive separation results. (3) A part where we deal with leader election problems in rings (Section 5). We shall present positive and negative results for various calculi, and again derive separation results. We end the tutorial with a history of related work and conclusions.

2   Leader Election, Electoral Systems and Encodings

After first discussing leader election informally, we show how it can be formalised in the setting of process calculi and reduction semantics. We then discuss criteria for encodings between calculi.

2.1   Leader Election Problems in Distributed Systems

In this section we introduce leader election problems as described in the field of distributed systems. We talk of problems in the plural, because there are different settings that lead to diverse solutions (when solutions do exist). A network is informally a set of machines that run independently and that compute through communication. Abstractly we can think of them as processes. Processes have the same state, if they can perform intuitively the same actions. The essence of a symmetric leader election problem is to find an algorithm where, starting from a configuration (network) of processes in the *same state*, any possible computation reaches a configuration where *one* process is in the state of *leader* and the other processes are in the state *lost* (i.e. they have lost the election). In some cases a solution may be impossible, and in other cases there may be more than one algorithm, and then complexity measures can be used in order to compare the different solutions. In this tutorial, we shall not consider such issues.

The criteria common to all leader election problems are the following:

Symmetry. Each process in the network has to have the *same duties*. This is a necessary requirement in order not to trivialise the problem. In fact, in an asymmetric configuration of processes, one process can declare itself the winner. This is not possible in symmetric configurations, since if one process can declare itself the winner, every other process in the configuration can do the same. Thus, in symmetric networks, for the winner to be elected, the *initial symmetry* has to be somehow broken.

Distribution. The computation has to be *decentralised*, in the sense that the computation has to start from any subset of processes in the network or configuration. In general, leader election problems are run after a reconfiguration or crash of a system, to the end of establishing which process can start the initialisation. In this context, the configuration of processes has to be able to elect a leader without any help from outside.

Uniqueness of the leader. The processes in a network reach a *final configuration* from *any* computation. In the final configuration there is *one process only* that is elected the *winner* and the other processes in the configuration have lost.

Leader election problems may vary according to the following parameters:

Topology of the network. The network could be a *fully connected graph* or a *ring* or *tree* or any other graph or hyper-graph [1, 30, 11]. The topology of the network influences the construction of the algorithm, since it changes the information regarding the totality of the processes involved.

In this tutorial we look at general networks, where there is no restriction on topology, in Section 4, and at rings in Section 5. In the general case, our algorithms will assume that the network is fully connected, though of course this is not assumed when we state impossibility results.

Knowledge of size of the network. The number of processes can be known or unknown to the processes before starting the election [30]. This parameter also influences the construction of an algorithm. In this tutorial we shall implement algorithms where the size of the network is known.

Declaration of the leader. The leader could be announced by one process only, which could be the leader itself or any other process. Alternatively every process in the configuration has to be aware of the winner. The latter requirement is considered standard, although the weaker one (the former one) is also acceptable, since the winner could inform the other processes of the outcome of the election.

We shall adopt the weaker assumption in this tutorial for simplicity. Note that the original paper [21] uses the stronger requirement for her results.

We have described the leader election problem as presented in the field of distributed algorithms. In this field, it is common to reason on what is known as *pseudo-code* [18]. This means that proofs are given by using some form of 'general-enough-language', that is, a mixed ad-hoc Pascal-like language and natural language without any formalised semantics. Nestmann shows that this approach very often hides underpinning problems and assumptions. The formal and rigorous semantics of process algebra, as presented in this tutorial, is therefore an advantage in the description of leader election problems. Formal semantics is necessary when proving that either a given algorithm is the correct solution to a leader election problem, or that no algorithm exists.

2.2 Electoral Systems

In this section we formalise the leader election problem in process calculi using reduction semantics (unlabelled transitions). Milner and Sangiorgi [16] motivated the study of reduction semantics on the grounds that it is a uniform way of describing semantics for calculi that are syntactically different from each other. In fact, reduction semantics has been widely used for its simplicity and ability to represent uniformly simple process calculi such as CCS [14], first- and second-order name passing-calculi such as the π-calculus and the higher-order π-calculus [16, 28], and more complex calculi such as the Seal Calculus [6] and the Ambient Calculus [5]. Reduction semantics will provide a uniform framework for all calculi we shall consider.

In reduction semantics a process calculus L is identified with: (1) a set of processes; (2) a reduction relation; and (3) an observational predicate. First of all, we assume the existence of a set of names $\mathcal{N}$: the variables $m, n, x, y \ldots$ range over it. Names are meant to be atomic, and they are a useful abstraction to represent objects that in real life we do not want to view as separated, such as identifiers, sequences of bits, etc.

Some operators of a language are *binding*, in the sense that names that fall within their *scope* are called *bound*, and processes that differ in bound variables only are considered identical. Names that are not bound in a process are called *free*. These concepts will be explicitly defined for each concrete syntax considered later in this tutorial.

We assume that a language L contains at least the parallel composition operator $|$ and the restriction operator $\nu n\, P$. We assume that in each calculus $|$ is a fair operator, in the sense that it does not nondeterministically choose the right or the left-hand side process. This semantics will be common to all the calculi we shall consider in this tutorial. Restriction $\nu n\, P$ binds n; it makes the name n private in P. We write $\nu \tilde{n}$ instead of $\nu n_1 \ldots \nu n_k$ for some list of names $n_1, \ldots, n_k$ which is not relevant in the context.

The computational steps for a language can be captured by a simple relation over the set of processes called the *reduction relation*, written $\rightarrow$. To model visible behaviour of programs, an *observation relation* is defined between processes and names; $P \downarrow n$ means intuitively that the process P has the observable name n. We shall see in each concrete calculus how these notions are defined.

Networks are informally compositions of processes or processes composed with the operator $|$; the size of a network is the number of processes that can be "regarded as separate units". This means that a composition of processes can be seen as one process only in counting the size of the network. A *symmetric* network is a network where components differ only on their names. Components of a network are connected if they share names, using which they can engage in communication. *Rings* are networks where each process is connected just to its left-hand and right-hand neighbours. A network elects a leader by exhibiting a special name, and an *electoral system* is a network where every possible maximal computation elects a leader.

We now make these notions precise. We assume that $\mathcal{N}$ includes a set of *observables* $\mathsf{Obs} = \{\omega_i : i \in \mathbb{N}\}$, such that for all i, j we have $\omega_i \neq \omega_j$ if $i \neq j$. The observables will be used by networks to communicate with the outside world.

Definition 2.1. *Let P be a process. A computation $\mathcal{C}$ of P is a (finite or infinite) sequence $P = P_0 \rightarrow P_1 \rightarrow \cdots$. It is maximal if it cannot be extended, i.e. either $\mathcal{C}$ is infinite, or else it is of the form $P_0 \rightarrow \cdots \rightarrow P_h$ where $P_h \nrightarrow$.*

Definition 2.2. *Let* $\mathcal{C}$ *be a computation* $P_0 \rightarrow \cdots \rightarrow P_h \rightarrow \cdots$. *We define the observables of* $\mathcal{C}$ *to be* $\mathsf{Obs}(\mathcal{C}) = \{\omega \in \mathsf{Obs} : \exists h \ P_h \downarrow \omega\}$.

Networks are collections of processes running in parallel:

Definition 2.3. *A network* Net *of size* k *is a pair* $(A, \langle P_0, \ldots, P_{k-1} \rangle)$, *where* A *is a finite set of names and* $P_0, \ldots, P_{k-1}$ *are processes. The process interpretation* $\mathsf{Net}^\natural$ *of* Net *is the process* $\nu A \, (P_0 \mid \cdots \mid P_{k-1})$. *We shall always work up to structural congruence, so that the order in which the restrictions in* A *are applied is immaterial.*

Networks are to be seen as presentations of processes, showing how the global process is distributed to the k nodes of the network. We shall sometimes write $[P_0 \mid \cdots \mid P_{k-1}]$ instead of $\nu A \, (P_0 \mid \cdots \mid P_{k-1})$, when the globally restricted names do not need to be made explicit.

We shall tend to write networks in their process interpretation (i.e. as restricted parallel compositions), while still making it clear which process belongs to each node of the network.

Networks inherit a notion of computation from processes through the process interpretation: $\mathsf{Net} \rightarrow \mathsf{Net}'$ if $\mathsf{Net}^\natural \rightarrow \mathsf{Net}'^\natural$. Overloading notation, we shall let $\mathcal{C}$ range over network computations. Also, we define the observables of a network computation $\mathcal{C}$ to be the observables of the corresponding process computation: $\mathsf{Obs}(\mathcal{C}) = \mathsf{Obs}(\mathcal{C}^\natural)$.

The definitions that follow lead up to the formulation of symmetry in a network (Definition 2.7), capturing the notion that each process is the same apart from the renaming of free names.

Definition 2.4. *A permutation is a bijection* $\sigma : \mathcal{N} \rightarrow \mathcal{N}$ *such that* σ *preserves the distinction between observable and non-observable names, i.e.* $n \in \mathsf{Obs}$ *iff* $\sigma(n) \in \mathsf{Obs}$. *Any permutation* σ *gives rise in a standard way to a mapping on processes, where* $\sigma(P)$ *is the same as* P, *except that any free name* n *of* P *is changed to* $\sigma(n)$ *in* $\sigma(P)$, *with bound names being adjusted as necessary to avoid clashes.*

A permutation σ *induces a bijection* $\hat{\sigma} : \mathbb{N} \rightarrow \mathbb{N}$ *defined as follows:* $\hat{\sigma}(i) = j$ *where* $\sigma(\omega_i) = \omega_j$. *Thus for all* $i \in \mathbb{N}$, $\sigma(\omega_i) = \omega_{\hat{\sigma}(i)}$. *We use* $\hat{\sigma}$ *to permute the indices of processes in a network.*

Definition 2.5. *Let* $\mathsf{Net} = \nu \tilde{n} \, (P_0 \mid \cdots \mid P_{k-1})$ *be a network of size* k. *An automorphism on* Net *is a permutation* σ *such that (1)* $\hat{\sigma}$ *restricted to* $\{0, \ldots, k-1\}$ *is a bijection, and (2)* σ *preserves the distinction between free and bound names, i.e.* $n \in \tilde{n}$ *iff* $\sigma(n) \in \tilde{n}$. *If* $\hat{\sigma}$ *restricted to* $\{0, \ldots, k-1\}$ *is not the identity we say* σ *is non-trivial.*

Definition 2.6. *Let* σ *be an automorphism on a network of size* k. *For any* $i \in \{0, \ldots, k-1\}$ *the orbit* $\mathcal{O}_{\hat{\sigma}}(i)$ *generated by* $\hat{\sigma}$ *is defined as follows:*

$$\mathcal{O}_{\hat{\sigma}}(i) = \{i, \hat{\sigma}(i), \hat{\sigma}^2(i), \ldots, \hat{\sigma}^{h-1}(i)\}$$

where $\hat{\sigma}^j$ *represents the composition of* $\hat{\sigma}$ *with itself* j *times, and* h *is least such that* $\hat{\sigma}^h(i) = i$. *If every orbit has the same size then* σ *is well-balanced.*

Definition 2.7. *Let* Net $= \nu\vec{n}\,(P_0 \mid \cdots \mid P_{k-1})$ *be a network of size* k *and let* σ *be an automorphism on it. We say that* Net *is* symmetric with respect to σ *iff for each* $i = 0, \ldots, k-1$ *we have* $P_{\hat{\sigma}(i)} = \sigma(P_i)$.

We say that Net *is* symmetric *if it is symmetric with respect to some automorphism with a single orbit (which must have size* k *).*

Intuitively an electoral system is a network which reports a unique winner, no matter how the computation proceeds.

Definition 2.8. *A network* Net *of size* k *is an* electoral system *if for every maximal computation* $\mathcal{C}$ *of* Net *there exists an* $i < k$ *such that* $\mathsf{Obs}(\mathcal{C}) = \{\omega_i\}$.

2.3 Encodings

The concept of encoding is inherently associated to expressiveness. If there exists an encoding $[\![-]\!]$ from a source language S to a target language T, one could see the language T as 'mirroring' S. Thus, the model underpinning S is at least as expressive as the one underpinning T. At the highest level of abstraction, an encoding $[\![-]\!]$ is a function from a source language to a target language. However, not just any function $[\![-]\!]$ from source language to target language should be accepted as an encoding; some 'relevant' behaviour of the first language must be 'preserved'.

We appeal here to the intuitive meaning of the words 'relevant' and 'to preserve', but it remains to formalise the meaning of these words, by exhibiting the semantic properties that $[\![-]\!]$ must satisfy. There is no definitive list of properties that are relevant or that have to be satisfied by an encoding. We shall give below some of the most common ones. Assuming that $P \in S$, and that $\rightarrow^*$ means the reflexive and transitive closure of the reduction relation, we then have:

- Preservation of execution steps (completeness): if $P \rightarrow P'$ then $[\![P]\!] \rightarrow^*$ $[\![P']\!]$ [19, 13, 4];
- Reflection of execution steps (soundness): if $[\![P]\!] \rightarrow^* Q$ then there is P' such that $P \rightarrow^* P'$ and $Q \rightarrow^* [\![P']\!]$ [19, 13];
- Barb preservation (completeness): if $P \downarrow n$ then $[\![P]\!] \downarrow n$ [32];
- Barb reflection (soundness): if $[\![P]\!] \downarrow n$ then $P \downarrow n$ [32].

(Of course, other properties could be added.)

One might also add syntactic requirements on an encoding. To give a concrete example, assuming that $\mid$ and ν are two operators common to S and T, then the statements below express that $[\![-]\!]$ preserves bound names (restriction) and distribution (parallel composition). Clearly the list could be longer, according to the number of common operators in the source and the target language. Other syntactic properties specific to languages could be considered.

- Distribution preservation: $[\![P \mid Q]\!] = [\![P]\!] \mid [\![Q]\!]$ [21, 25, 23];
- Name preservation: $[\![\nu n \, P]\!] = \nu n \, [\![P]\!]$ [7];

- Substitution preservation: for all substitutions σ on S there exists a substitution θ on T such that $[\![\sigma(P)]\!] = \theta([\![P]\!])$ [21, 31];
- Link independence: if $fn(P) \cap fn(Q) = \emptyset$ then $fn([\![P]\!]) \cap fn([\![Q]\!]) = \emptyset$ [21, 25].

(Of course, other properties could be added.)

The list of properties given above is certainly not exhaustive, but it includes some common properties used by the scientific community [19, 5, 21, 23, 25, 32, 8].

In general, it is not required that all of the properties above are satisfied in order for a function to be called an encoding. More specifically, there is not even a subset of these properties that is regarded as *necessary*. In fact, the conditions regarded as relevant depend on the reasons why the encoding is sought in the first place. For instance one could show that some primitives are redundant in a calculus by showing an encoding from the full set of processes to an appropriate fragment. This could be very useful for implementation purposes. This is the case for the programming language Pict [26], which is based on the asynchronous π-calculus, where input-guarded choice can be implemented [19]. One could also show that one calculus can be encoded into another in order to 'inherit' some (possibly good) properties. For instance, from the encoding of the λ-calculus into the π-calculus one could derive easily the Turing completeness of the π-calculus.

In encodings of languages that admit a solution for leader election problems, one important requirement is that the encoding is homomorphic with respect to parallel composition, i.e. preserves distribution. This requirement aims at avoiding that the encoding introduces a trivial solution to such a problem [21, 23]. However, Nestmann [17] and Prasad [27] argue that this requirement is too strong for practical purposes. We would like to defend it, on the basis that it corresponds to requiring that the degree of distribution of the processes is maintained by the translation, i.e. no coordinator is added. This condition makes the notion of encoding suitable to compare expressiveness of languages for distributed systems, where processes are expected to coordinate without the help of a centralised control.

Although there is no unanimous agreement on what constitutes an encoding, it is clear that the judgment as to whether a function is an encoding relies on acceptance or rejection of the properties that hold for the encoding. That is, to give a meaning to the results that will be presented in this tutorial, the conditions on encodings we shall now present have to be accepted and considered 'reasonable'.

In dealing with leader election problems, an encoding must *preserve the fundamental criteria of the problem*, that is, the *conditions* for an encoding must preserve symmetric electoral systems without introducing a solution.

Definition 2.9. *Let L and L' be process languages. An encoding $[\![-]\!] : L \to L'$ is*

1. distribution-preserving *if for all processes P, Q of L, $[\![P \mid Q]\!] = [\![P]\!] \mid [\![Q]\!]$;*
2. permutation-preserving *if for any permutation of names σ in L there exists a permutation θ in L' such that $[\![\sigma(P)]\!] = \theta([\![P]\!])$ and the permutations are compatible on observables, in that for all $i \in \mathbb{N}$ we have $\sigma(\omega_i) = \theta(\omega_i)$, so that $\hat{\sigma}(i) = \hat{\theta}(i)$;*

3. observation-respecting *if for any P in L,*

(a) *for every maximal computation $\mathcal{C}$ of P there exists a maximal computation $\mathcal{C}'$ of $[\![P]\!]$ such that* $\mathsf{Obs}(\mathcal{C}) = \mathsf{Obs}(\mathcal{C}')$;

(b) *for every maximal computation $\mathcal{C}$ of $[\![P]\!]$ there exists a maximal computation $\mathcal{C}'$ of P such that* $\mathsf{Obs}(\mathcal{C}) = \mathsf{Obs}(\mathcal{C}')$.

The condition of preserving distribution is important in ruling out encodings which make use of a *central server*. That means that, if the target language does not admit a fully distributed solution to the leader election problem, the encoding cannot introduce a spurious solution. The second condition prevents a trivial solution from being introduced by collapsing all the set of natural numbers $\{0, 1, \ldots, k-1\}$ to a $j \in \mathbb{N}$. The first two items aim to map symmetric networks to symmetric networks of the same size and with the same orbits. The third item aims at preserving the uniqueness of the winner. The condition is on barbs because the winner in this framework is represented with a barb. The conditions of Definition 2.9 been formulated with the aim of achieving the following lemma, which says that symmetric electoral systems are preserved.

Lemma 2.10. *[24, 23] Let L and L' be process languages. Suppose $[\![-]\!] : L \to L'$ is a uniform observation-respecting encoding. Suppose that* Net *is a symmetric electoral system of size k in L with no globally bound names. Then* $[\![\mathsf{Net}]\!]$ *is a symmetric electoral system of size k in L'.*   □

3   Calculi

In this section we define the various calculi we shall consider.

3.1   The π-calculus with Mixed Choice

We assume the existence of names $n \in \mathcal{N}$ and co-names $\overline{n} \in \overline{\mathcal{N}}$. The set of process terms of the π-calculus with mixed choice (π_m) is given by the following syntax:

$$P, Q ::= \mathbf{0} \mid \sum_{i \in I} \alpha_i.P \mid P \mid Q \mid \nu n\, P \mid \,! P$$

where I is a finite set. The *prefixes* of processes, ranged over by α, are defined by the following syntax:

$$\alpha ::= m(n) \mid \overline{m}\langle n \rangle.$$

Summation $\sum_{i \in I} \alpha_i.P_i$ represents a finite choice among the different processes $\alpha_i.P$. This operator is also called *mixed choice*, since both input and output prefixes can be present in the same summation. The symbol $\mathbf{0}$, called *nil*, is the inactive process. Commonly in the π-calculus, $\mathbf{0}$ is an abbreviation for the empty choice. Although redundant, we introduce it here as a primitive for uniformity with the syntax of other calculi. *Replication* $! P$ simulates recursion by spinning off copies of P. *Parallel composition* of two processes $P \mid Q$ represents P and Q computing independently from each other. *Restriction* $\nu n\, P$ creates a new name n in P, which is bound. We shall feel free to omit trailing $\mathbf{0}$s. Thus we write α

instead of $\alpha.\mathbf{0}$. The notion of the *free names* $fn(P)$ of a term P is standard, taking into account that the only binding operators are input prefix and restriction. We write $P\{n/m\}$ to mean that each free occurrence of m is substituted by n in P. We reserve η for a bijection on I; we write $\sum_{\eta(i)\in I}$ for permutation on the sub-processes in the choice operator. The *reduction relation* over the processes of π_m is the smallest relation satisfying the following rules:

$$\text{(Pi Comm)} \quad (m(x).P + G) \mid (\overline{m}\langle n\rangle.Q + H) \to P\{n/x\} \mid Q$$

$$\text{(Par)} \quad \frac{P \to P'}{P \mid Q \to P' \mid Q} \qquad \text{(Res)} \quad \frac{P \to P'}{\nu n\, P \to \nu n\, P'}$$

$$\text{(Str)} \quad \frac{P \equiv Q \quad Q \to Q' \quad Q' \equiv P'}{P \to P'}$$

where G, H are summations. *Structural congruence* $\equiv$ allows rearrangement of processes; it is the smallest congruence over the set of processes that satisfies the following equations:

$$\begin{array}{ll} P \mid \mathbf{0} \equiv P & \nu n\, (P \mid Q) \equiv P \mid \nu n\, Q \quad \text{if } n \notin fn(P) \\ P \mid Q \equiv Q \mid P & \nu m\, \nu n\, P \equiv \nu n\, \nu m\, P \\ (P \mid Q) \mid R \equiv P \mid (Q \mid R) & !P \equiv P \mid !P \\ \nu n\, \mathbf{0} \equiv \mathbf{0} & \sum_{i\in I}\alpha_i.P_i \equiv \sum_{\eta(i)\in I}\alpha_{\eta(i)}.P_{\eta(i)} \end{array}$$

together with α-conversion of bound names. A process P *exhibits barb* n, written as $P \downarrow n$, iff $P \equiv \nu\vec{m}\,((\overline{n}\langle x\rangle.Q + G) \mid R)$ with $n \notin \vec{m}$. We only use barbs on outputs; input barbs are not needed, and we thereby obtain greater uniformity across the calculi we are considering.

3.2   The π-calculus with Separate Choice

The π-calculus with separate choice (π_s) [29] is the sub-calculus of π_m where summations cannot mix input and output guards. The set of processes is given by the following grammar:

$$P, Q ::= \mathbf{0} \mid \sum_{i\in I}\alpha_i^I.P_i \mid \sum_{i\in I}\alpha_i^O.P_i \mid !P \mid P|Q \mid \nu n\, P$$

$$\alpha^I ::= m(n) \qquad \alpha^O ::= \overline{m}\langle n\rangle$$

The semantics of this calculus is the same as for π_m taking into account the syntactic restrictions. One could regard π_s as having the same expressive strength as the asynchronous π-calculus [10, 2], in view of the results on encoding of separate choice [17].

3.3   CCS

In this paper we shall use the version of CCS presented in [14], with the addition of value passing. As well as names $n \in \mathcal{N}$, we use co-names $\overline{n} \in \overline{\mathcal{N}}$, a set $\mathcal{V}$ of values, ranged over by $v, \ldots$, and a set $\mathcal{W}$ of variables, ranged over by $x, \ldots$. The sets $\mathcal{N}$, $\overline{\mathcal{N}}$, $\mathcal{V}$ and $\mathcal{W}$ are mutually disjoint. Processes are defined as follows:

$$P, Q ::= \mathbf{0} \mid \sum_{i \in I} \pi_i.P_i \mid P \mid Q \mid \nu n\, P \mid A\langle m_1, \ldots, m_k \rangle$$

where I is a finite set. The *prefixes* of processes, ranged over by π, are defined by the following syntax:

$$\pi ::= n(x) \mid \overline{n}\langle v \rangle.$$

Here recursion is handled by process identifiers with parameters; each identifier A is equipped with a defining equation $A(\vec{m}) \stackrel{\text{df}}{=} P_A$. Structural congruence is the same as for π_{m}, except that the law for replication is omitted and we add the following rule for the identifiers:

$$A\langle \vec{n} \rangle \equiv P_A\{\vec{n}/\vec{m}\} \text{ if } A(\vec{m}) \stackrel{\text{df}}{=} P_A .$$

The reduction relation has the rule

$$(\text{CCS Comm}) \quad (n(x).P + G) \mid (\overline{n}\langle v \rangle.Q + H) \rightarrow P\{v/x\} \mid Q$$

(where G, H are summations) together with (Par), (Res) and (Str) as for π_{m}. The notion of the *free names* $fn(P)$ of a term P is standard, taking into account that the only binding operator on names is restriction. Barbs are much as for π_{m}: a process P *exhibits barb* n, written as $P \downarrow n$, iff $P \equiv \nu\vec{m}\,((\overline{n}\langle v \rangle.Q + G) \mid R)$ with $n \notin \vec{m}$.

The difference between CCS and π_{m} may be illustrated by the π_{m} process $P \stackrel{\text{df}}{=} a(x).\overline{x}\langle b \rangle$. This is not a valid CCS process, since x cannot be used as a name in CCS. Clearly, when P is composed with $Q \stackrel{\text{df}}{=} \overline{a}\langle c \rangle.Q'$, P can acquire a new name c that may be used for future communication.

3.4 Mobile Ambients

In the presentation of Mobile Ambients, we follow [5], except for communication, as noted below. Let $P, Q, \ldots$ range over processes and $M, \ldots$ over capabilities. We assume a set of names $\mathcal{N}$, ranged over by $m, n, \ldots$. Processes are defined as follows:

$$P, Q ::= \mathbf{0} \mid P \mid Q \mid \nu n\, P \mid \, !P \mid n[\,P\,] \mid M.P \mid (n).P \mid \langle n \rangle$$

We describe here only the operators specific to ambients: $n[\,P\,]$ is an ambient named n containing process P; $M.P$ performs capability M before continuing as P; and $(n).P$ receives input on an anonymous channel, with the input name replacing free occurrences of name n in P; and finally $\langle n \rangle$ is a process which outputs name n. Notice that output is *asynchronous*, that is, it has no continuation. Restriction and input are name-binding, which naturally yields the definition of the free names $fn(P)$ of a given process P.

Capabilities are defined as follows:

$$M ::= \text{in } n \mid \text{out } n \mid \text{open } n$$

Capabilities allow movement of ambients (in n and out n) and dissolution of ambients (open n).

We confine ourselves in this paper to communication of names, rather than full communication including capabilities (as in [5]). This serves to streamline the presentation; the results would also hold for full communication.

The *reduction* relation $\rightarrow$ is generated by the following rules:

(In)	$n[\text{in } m.P \mid Q] \mid m[R] \rightarrow m[n[P \mid Q] \mid R]$
(Out)	$m[n[\text{out } m.P \mid Q] \mid R] \rightarrow n[P \mid Q] \mid m[R]$
(Open)	$\text{open } n.P \mid n[Q] \rightarrow P \mid Q$
(MA Comm)	$\langle n \rangle \mid (m).P \rightarrow P\{n/m\}$

$$(\text{Amb}) \qquad \frac{P \rightarrow P'}{n[P] \rightarrow n[P']}$$

together with rules (Par), (Res) and (Str) as given for π_{m}. Structural congruence is the least congruence generated by the following laws:

$$
\begin{array}{lll}
P \mid Q \equiv Q \mid P & \nu n\, \nu m\, P \equiv \nu m\, \nu n\, P & \\
(P \mid Q) \mid R \equiv P \mid (Q \mid R) & \nu n\, (P \mid Q) \equiv P \mid \nu n\, Q & \text{if } n \notin \mathit{fn}(P) \\
P \mid \mathbf{0} \equiv P & \nu n\, m[P] \equiv m[\nu n\, P] & \text{if } n \neq m \\
!P \equiv P \mid !P & \nu n\, \mathbf{0} \equiv \mathbf{0} &
\end{array}
$$

together with α-conversion of bound names. The most basic observation we can make of an MA process is the presence of an unrestricted top-level ambient. A process P *exhibits barb* n, written as $P \downarrow n$, iff $P \equiv \nu\vec{m}\,(n[Q] \mid R)$ with $n \notin \vec{m}$.

4   Leader Election in General Symmetric Networks

We present solutions to the leader election problem for symmetric networks in a variety of calculi (Section 4.1), followed by results showing the impossibility of solutions in other calculi (Section 4.2). We conclude the section by using the preceding to obtain separation results (Section 4.3).

4.1   Calculi with Electoral Systems

In this section we present solutions to the leader election problem in symmetric networks of any finite size in some fragments of CCS, π_{m} and MA. The solutions are of course still valid in the full calculi. The solutions for CCS and π_{m} are the same, since CCS is a subcalculus of π_{m} and therefore once a solution is proposed for CCS it trivially implies that there is a solution for π_{m}.

Definition 4.1. *1. Let $\pi_{\mathsf{m}}^{-\nu}$ be π_{m} but without restriction (public π_{m}).*

2. Let $CCS^{-\nu}$ be CCS but without restriction (public CCS).

3. Let MA^{io} be MA without communication, restriction and the open capability (pure public boxed MA).

We start by defining a symmetric electoral system of size two in $CCS^{-\nu}$. Let a network Net be defined as follows:

$$P_0 \stackrel{\mathrm{df}}{=} x_0(y) + \overline{x_1}\langle z\rangle.\overline{w_0}\langle z\rangle \qquad P_1 \stackrel{\mathrm{df}}{=} x_1(y) + \overline{x_0}\langle z\rangle.\overline{w_1}\langle z\rangle \qquad \mathsf{Net} \stackrel{\mathrm{df}}{=} P_0 \mid P_1.$$

The network is symmetric with respect to a single-orbit automorphism σ which swaps 1 and 0, with σ the identity on all other names. There are only two possible computations. One is the following:

$$\mathcal{C} : \mathsf{Net} \rightarrow \overline{w_1}\langle z\rangle \qquad \mathsf{Obs}(\mathcal{C}) = \{\omega_1\}.$$

The other one is identical up to the renaming of σ. The values passed are just dummies, which can be omitted; there is a crucial use of mixed choice to break symmetry.

The previous solution can be generalised to networks of any size k. Before giving the formal definition, we provide an informal description of the algorithm. Successive pairs of processes fight each other. Winning an individual fight is achieved by sending a message to the loser. Each time, the loser drops out of the contest. Eventually only one process is left standing. It has defeated every other process and is therefore the winner. Each node is composed of two parts:

1. A process that either sends a message to another node and proceeds to fight the remaining processes, or receives a message and will no longer take part in the election process. In this latter case, it will announce to every other node that it has lost.
2. A counter, which collects all the messages of loss from the other processes, and after $k-1$ messages declares victory (so processes have to know the size of the network).

One important feature in this implementation is the use of mixed choice, in the description of the process that runs for the election. Let $\prod_{i<k} P_i$ stand for $P_0 \mid \cdots \mid P_{k-1}$.

Theorem 4.2. *For any $k \geq 1$, in $CCS^{-\nu}$ there exists a symmetric electoral system of size k defined by* $\mathsf{Net} \stackrel{\mathrm{df}}{=} \prod_{i<k} P_i$ *where*

$$P_i \stackrel{\mathrm{df}}{=} Elect_i \mid Counter_{i,0}^k$$
$$Elect_i \stackrel{\mathrm{df}}{=} \overline{n_i}.Elect_i + \sum_{0 \leq s < k, s \neq i} n_s.(\prod_{0 \leq t < k, t \neq i} \overline{lost_t})$$
$$Counter_{i,j}^k \stackrel{\mathrm{df}}{=} lost_i.Counter_{i,j+1}^k \quad (0 \leq j < k-1)$$
$$Counter_{i,k-1}^k \stackrel{\mathrm{df}}{=} \overline{w_i}. \qquad\qquad \square$$

Because $CCS^{-\nu}$ can be regarded as a subcalculus of $\pi_m^{-\nu}$, the algorithm written above is also a solution for $\pi_m^{-\nu}$. Hence:

Corollary 4.3. *For any $k \geq 1$, in $\pi_m^{-\nu}$ there exists a symmetric electoral system of size k.*

We now turn to showing the existence of symmetric electoral systems in MA. In fact we can make do with the fragment MA^{io}. Before presenting a solution for networks of arbitrary size, we present an electoral system of size two. Let

$$P_0 \stackrel{\mathrm{df}}{=} n_0[\,\text{in } n_1.\omega_0[\,\text{out } n_0.\text{out } n_1\,]\,] \qquad P_1 \stackrel{\mathrm{df}}{=} n_1[\,\text{in } n_0.\omega_1[\,\text{out } n_1.\text{out } n_0\,]\,]$$

$$\text{Net} \stackrel{\mathrm{df}}{=} P_0 \mid P_1 .$$

The network is symmetric with respect to a single-orbit automorphism σ which swaps 1 and 0. There are only two possible computations. We shall present the first one in detail:

$$\begin{aligned}
\mathcal{C} : n_0[\,\text{in } n_1.\omega_0[\,\text{out } n_0.\text{out } n_1\,]\,] \mid n_1[\,\text{in } n_0.\omega_1[\,\text{out } n_1.\text{out } n_0\,]\,] &\rightarrow \\
n_1[\,n_0[\,\omega_0[\,\text{out } n_0.\text{out } n_1\,]\,]\,] \mid \text{in } n_0.\omega_1[\,\text{out } n_1.\text{out } n_0\,]\,] &\rightarrow \\
n_1[\,\omega_0[\,\text{out } n_1\,]\,] \mid n_0[\,]\,] \mid \text{in } n_0.\omega_1[\,\text{out } n_1.\text{out } n_0\,]\,] &\rightarrow \\
\omega_0[\,]\,] \mid n_1[\,n_0[\,]\,]\,] \mid \text{in } n_0.\omega_1[\,\text{out } n_1.\text{out } n_0\,]\,]\,].
\end{aligned}$$

Thus we conclude $\mathsf{Obs}(\mathcal{C}) = \{\omega_0\}$. The other computation is identical up to renaming via σ. Notice that symmetry is broken by one ambient entering the other.

The general solution for a network of any size is more complex, and before introducing the technical solution we shall provide an informal description.

The basic idea of the algorithm is that winning the election is achieved by having all the opponents inside. Each process is composed of two ambients: one that runs for the election and the other that has the rôle of a counter. Any ambient entering another one has lost the election. It will release an ambient called *lose*, which will eventually appear at the top level, where the counters are. The winning ambient is left on its own, at the top level, while all the other ambients are inside the winner. The counter will declare the winner once every loser has entered.

Theorem 4.4. *[23] In MA^{io}, for any $k \geq 1$ there exists a symmetric electoral system of size k, defined by $\text{Net} \stackrel{\mathrm{df}}{=} \prod_{i<k} P_i$ where*

$$\begin{aligned}
P_i &\stackrel{\mathrm{df}}{=} n_i[\,\textstyle\prod_{j \neq i} \text{in } n_j.lose_i[\,Outn\,]\,] \mid c_i[\,C_{i,i+1}\,] \\
Outn &\stackrel{\mathrm{df}}{=} \textstyle\prod_{j<k} !\,\text{out } n_j \\
C_{i,i} &\stackrel{\mathrm{df}}{=} \omega_i[\,\text{out } c_i\,] \\
C_{i,j} &\stackrel{\mathrm{df}}{=} \text{in } lose_j.C'_{i,j} \qquad (j \neq i) \\
C'_{i,j} &\stackrel{\mathrm{df}}{=} \text{out } lose_j.C_{i,j+1} \qquad (j \neq i) \qquad\qquad \square
\end{aligned}$$

In the preceding theorem we use addition modulo k.

4.2   Calculi Without Electoral Systems

In this section we shall show that there are calculi that do not admit a symmetric electoral system. We shall see that certain operators are needed to break symmetry and for a solution to be possible. For π-calculus and CCS the crucial operator is the mixed choice operator. In fact, both π-calculus and CCS with separate choice cannot solve the problem of electing a leader in any graph. In the case of MA, the in capability is the symmetry-breaking operator.

The proof of the impossibility of symmetric leader election has different technical details according to the different formalisms, but there is a common structure. The basic idea is to construct one maximal computation which preserves, at some points, the invariant property of reaching a symmetric state. In fact, in symmetric states, election fails either because no one declares himself the winner or, if anybody declares himself a winner, the other processes in the network can do the same.

To make this more concrete we consider an example in π_s.

$$P_0 \stackrel{df}{=} \overline{n}_0.\omega_0 \mid n_1 \qquad P_1 \stackrel{df}{=} \overline{n}_1.\omega_1 \mid n_0 \qquad \text{Net} \stackrel{df}{=} P_0 \mid P_1.$$

The network of size two written above is symmetric with the standard automorphism that swaps 1 and 0, but it is not an electoral system. To see this it is sufficient to follow one maximal computation:

$$\mathcal{C}: \quad P_0 \mid P_1 \rightarrow \omega_0 \mid n_1 \mid \overline{n}_1.\omega_1 \rightarrow \omega_0 \mid \omega_1 \ .$$

This example shows that, after the initial step breaking symmetry made by P_0 in trying to declare himself the winner, P_1 can respond in a similar way, which leads to a symmetric network again. Finally, no leader is elected because there is more than one winner: $\text{Obs}(\mathcal{C}) = \{\omega_1, \omega_0\}$. The proof for the general case follows closely such reasoning; each time a step is made by a process (or pair of processes), the other processes can mimic this step, in such a way that symmetry is reached again, and no winner is possible.

There is no solution to the leader election problem in π_s:

Theorem 4.5. *[21] Let* Net $= [P_0 \mid \cdots \mid P_{k-1}]$ *with* $k \geq 2$ *be a symmetric network in* π_s. *Then* Net *cannot be an electoral system.* $\square$

A similar theorem could be stated for CCS with separate choice; however, unlike π_s, such a calculus has never been considered, and therefore we leave out the statement. It is clear that the mixed choice operator is the key for the expressiveness result in the π-calculus. In MA, the in capability is crucial in order to break the symmetry; in fact, if this is removed, the leader election problem cannot be solved in any graph.

Definition 4.6. *Let* MA^{-in} *denote MA without the* in *capability.*

Theorem 4.7. *[24, 23] Let* Net $= [P_0 \mid \cdots \mid P_{k-1}]$ *with* $k \geq 2$ *be a symmetric network in* MA^{-in}. *Then* Net *cannot be an electoral system.* $\square$

4.3   Separation Results

By Lemma 2.10, a uniform observation-respecting encoding maps symmetric electoral systems (with no globally bound names) to symmetric electoral systems.

So for instance we can now deduce that there can be no uniform observation-respecting encoding from π_m into π_s, since the former has a symmetric electoral system of at least size two (from Corollary 4.3) and the latter does not (Theorem 4.5).

We can tabulate the positive results of Section 4.1 and the negative results of Section 4.2 in the following diagram:

$$\frac{\mathrm{CCS}^{-\nu} \quad \pi_m^{-\nu} \quad \mathrm{MA}^{\mathrm{io}}}{\pi_s \quad \mathrm{MA}^{-\mathrm{in}}}$$

All calculi above the line have symmetric electoral systems for any finite size. Those below the line do not have symmetric electoral systems for any size greater than one. Therefore there is no uniform, observation-respecting encoding from any calculus above the line to any below the line, giving us many separation results.

5   Leader Election in Symmetric Rings

In distributed computing, one standard network topology is a ring, where each process can only communicate with its left-hand and right-hand neighbours. As far as leader election is concerned, this means that algorithms which assume that all processes are directly linked to all other processes (as considered in Section 4) will no longer work. In this section we examine whether enhanced leader election algorithms which can handle rings are available for the languages we are considering. This will enable us to separate some of the languages in the top row of the diagram in Section 4.3.

One possible way to conduct leader election in rings is what we shall call the *two-phase* method. This starts by using an algorithm to create links between all processes. Symmetry is preserved during this first (or *link-creation*) phase. Once this is done, in the second (or *election*) phase a leader election algorithm devised for fully connected networks (as in Section 4) can be used to produce the leader.

The π-calculus has the power to create new links; we shall see that the link-creation phase referred to above can be carried out in π_m (in fact it can be done in π_s). Since π_m can solve leader election for fully connected networks, it can therefore perform leader election on rings using the two-phase method. By contrast, CCS does not have the power to create new links; therefore CCS cannot perform leader election on rings with composite (non-prime) size.

We now consider the ambient world. In MA, the communication primitives have the same operational semantics as the π-calculus, except that they are *anonymous*, in the sense that there are no channels on which communication happens (in the π-calculus one would write $m(x).P$ for an input on the channel m, while in MA one would write $(x).P$ for an anonymous input). Thus, since the communication primitives in ambients are very similar to those of the π-calculus, it would be not surprising if the two-phase method could be formulated in MA, since MA can solve the leader election problem in fully connected networks.

However, the leader election problem for symmetric rings of any size is solved without the use of communication primitives. This means that link passing, in this case, is somehow simulated, since there is no explicit way of passing names in the absence of communication. The open capability is crucial in this setting. It is, in fact, the capability that simulates link passing, since it can be shown that MA, without the open capability does not admit a solution for leader election problems in rings of composite size.

5.1   Rings and Independence Preservation

We start by providing a general framework for leader election problems in rings, augmenting that presented in Section 2.2. Note that in our framework, unlike in the standard distributed systems literature, we do not distinguish between unidirectional rings, where messages are passed in one direction only, say from left-hand to right-hand neighbours or vice-versa, and bidirectional rings, where communication can flow in either direction.

Given a network $\mathsf{Net} = \nu\vec{n}\,(P_0 \mid \cdots \mid P_{k-1})$, we can associate a graph with Net by letting the set of nodes be $\{0,\ldots,k-1\}$ and letting $i,j < k$ be adjacent iff $\mathit{fn}(P_i) \cap \mathit{fn}(P_j) \neq \emptyset$. A network forms a ring if the processes can be arranged in a cycle, and each node i is adjacent to at most its two neighbours in the cycle.

Definition 5.1. *A ring is a network* $\mathsf{Net} = \nu\vec{n}\,(P_0 \mid \cdots \mid P_{k-1})$ *which has a single-orbit automorphism* σ *such that for all* $i,j < k$, *if* $\mathit{fn}(P_i) \cap \mathit{fn}(P_j) \neq \emptyset$ *then one of* $i = j$, $\hat{\sigma}(i) = j$ *or* $\hat{\sigma}(j) = i$ *must hold. A ring is* symmetric *if it is symmetric with respect to such an automorphism* σ.

Notice that the definition bans links between non-adjacent nodes in the ring, but does not require the existence of links between adjacent nodes. Thus a completely disconnected network is a ring.

Recall that an *independent set* in a graph is a set of nodes such that no two nodes of the set are adjacent.

Definition 5.2. *Two processes* P *and* Q *are* independent *if they do not share any free names:* $\mathit{fn}(P) \cap \mathit{fn}(Q) = \emptyset$.

Definition 5.3. *Let* σ *be an automorphism on a network* $\mathsf{Net} = \nu\vec{n}\,(P_0 \mid \cdots \mid P_{k-1})$. *Then* Net *is independent with respect to* σ *if every orbit forms an independent set, in the sense that if* $i,j < k$ *are in the same orbit of* $\hat{\sigma}$ *with* $i \neq j$, *then* P_i *and* P_j *are independent.*

Unlike in Section 4, in this section we shall consider encodings which map rings to rings. We therefore need a further property on top of uniformity and the preservation of the observables. This property will guarantee that the connectivity of the original network is not increased.

Definition 5.4. *An encoding is* independence-preserving *if for any processes* P, Q, *if* P *and* Q *are independent then* $[\![P]\!]$ *and* $[\![Q]\!]$ *are also independent.*

The property above states that such an encoding "does not increase the level of connectivity of the network".

Lemma 5.5. *[25] Suppose* $\llbracket - \rrbracket : L \to L'$ *is a uniform, observation-respecting and independence-preserving encoding. Suppose that* Net *is a symmetric ring of size* $k \geq 1$ *which is an electoral system. Then* $\llbracket$ Net $\rrbracket$ *is also a symmetric ring of size* k *which is an electoral system.*   □

5.2   Calculi with Electoral Systems for Rings

In this section we show that we can solve leader election on symmetric rings in π_m and in MA. We start with a solution to the leader election problem for rings in π_m. The algorithm has two phases. In phase one the processes pass names around the ring so that every process becomes directly connected to every other process. Here there is an essential use of the π-calculus, though without any use of choice.

We define a symmetric ring $P_0 \mid \cdots \mid P_{k-1}$ which is an electoral system. Suppose that process P_i has a channel n_i initially known only to itself, and can send messages to P_{i-1} along channel x_i. Then the names n_i are passed around the ring so that all processes share them and can use them in the election phase. We have to be careful that for each P_i the outputs occur in the same order as the inputs, so that names do not get confused. We therefore allocate to each P_i a "synchroniser" name y_i which ensures that each successive output is completed before the next one is enabled. We elide the dummy names passed along y_i.

For $0 \leq i \leq k$, we let $P_i \stackrel{\mathrm{df}}{=} P_i^0 \langle x_i, x_{i+1}, y_i, n_i \rangle$, where for $0 \leq j \leq k - 2$ we let

$$P_i^j(x_i, x_{i+1}, y_i, n_i, \ldots, n_{i+j})$$
$$\stackrel{\mathrm{df}}{=} \bar{x}_i \langle n_{i+j} \rangle . \bar{y}_i \mid x_{i+1}(n_{i+j+1}) . y_i . P_i^{j+1} \langle x_i, x_{i+1}, y_i, n_i, \ldots, n_{i+j+1} \rangle$$

and $P_i^{k-1}(x_i, x_{i+1}, y_i, n_i, \ldots, n_{i-1}) \stackrel{\mathrm{df}}{=} Q_i \langle n_i, \ldots, n_{i-1} \rangle$. Here Q_i is a process which has acquired all the n_i and is ready to carry out the election phase. Once Q_i is reached, the names x_i, x_{i+1} and y_i are no longer required.

For π_m, we have seen what the Q_i would look like in Theorem 4.2, and therefore we can state the following theorem:

Theorem 5.6. *(cf. [21]) For any* $k \geq 1$, *there is a symmetric ring of size* k *which is an electoral system in* $\pi_\mathsf{m}^{-\nu}$.   □

We now discuss the solution to the leader election problem for rings in pure public MA (i.e. MA without communication and restriction). We use the two-phase method. In the link-creation phase we send ambients round the ring which contain the appropriate capabilities. These are opened by their intended recipients, which then can exercise these capabilities. We already know how to carry out the election phase from Theorem 4.4, though in fact we use a different algorithm, which is easier to set up via the link-creation phase. We omit the precise details of the construction, as they are quite lengthy.

Theorem 5.7. *[25] For any* $k \geq 1$ *there is a symmetric ring of size* k *which is an electoral system in pure public MA.*   □

5.3 Calculi Without Electoral Systems for Rings

In this section, we consider the calculi that do not have electoral systems for symmetric rings. In this case, the failure of the election is not related to the ability of breaking the initial symmetry. In fact in CCS or MA^{io}, leader election problems can be solved in fully connected networks. The separation results say something regarding the possibility of creating new shared resources. In the π-calculus this phenomenon is present since channels can be values as well; in MA, this phenomenon is simulated via the open capability. Thus, CCS and boxed MA (i.e. MA without the open capability) do not admit a solution to the leader election problem in rings.

As in the case of general networks, the proofs for the negative results differ in their technical details in each formalism, but there is a common strategy. If a ring is of composite (non-prime) size, then it is symmetric with respect to a permutation with multiple independent orbits of the same size. The basic idea is to show that there is a maximal computation where, even though symmetry may be broken in the ring as a whole, symmetry is maintained within each orbit, and the nodes of each orbit remain independent. It remains an open problem whether the result presented below still holds in networks whose size is a prime number.

Theorem 5.8. *[21, 25] For any composite $k > 1$, CCS and boxed MA do not have a symmetric ring of size k which is an electoral system.* $\square$

5.4 Separation Results

By Lemma 5.5, we can now deduce that there can be no uniform, observation-respecting and independence-preserving encoding from π_m into CCS, since the former has a symmetric electoral system which is a ring of size four (from Theorem 5.6) and the latter does not (Theorem 5.8).

Much as in Section 4.3, we can tabulate the results of Sections 5.2 and 5.3 as follows:

$$\frac{\pi_m^{-\nu} \quad \text{pure public MA}}{\text{CCS} \quad \text{boxed MA}}$$

All calculi above the line have symmetric electoral systems which are rings for any finite size. Those below the line do not have symmetric electoral systems which are rings for composite sizes greater than one. Therefore there is no uniform, observation-respecting and independence-preserving encoding from either calculus above the line to either below the line.

6 Conclusions and Related Work

The first attempt to represent leader election problems in process algebra was made by Bougé [3]. He formalised the notion of leader election problem in symmetric networks for CSP [9]. The most remarkable achievements are the separation results between CSP with input and output guards and CSP with input guards only, and between the latter and CSP without guards, based on the notion of *symmetric reasonable implementation*.

A similar formalisation of the notion of leader election problem was made by Palamidessi [21] for the π-calculus. Palamidessi proves *formally* that any symmetric network in the π-calculus with separate choice admits a computation that never breaks the initial symmetry. This result is used to show that there is no encoding of the π-calculus with mixed choice into the π-calculus with separate choice. In her paper Palamidessi uses a graph framework, as in the tradition of distributed algorithms [11, 30, 1, 3], and she proves that CCS [12] does not admit a symmetric electoral system in a ring, as opposed to the π-calculus with mixed choice. Using a similar approach Ene and Muntean [7] show that the π-calculus with broadcasting primitives cannot be encoded in the standard π-calculus.

Finally, Phillips and Vigliotti used these proof techniques to separate MA from the separate-choice π-calculus and MA^{-in} [23], and mixed choice π-calculus and MA from CCS and boxed MA [25]. This work was carried out in the reduction semantics framework used also in this tutorial. This framework has the advantage of uniformity across a range of process calculi. Our results say nothing, with respect to leader election, on the relationship between the mixed choice π-calculus and MA, or between CCS and boxed MA. These are still open problems.

In this tutorial we have collected together results from different papers [20, 21, 24, 23, 25], given a uniform presentation and highlighted the similarities and differences between the various approaches to leader election problems. We have omitted proofs and lengthy details; however, those are available in the original papers.

Acknowledgements

The work of Catuscia Palamidessi and Maria Grazia Vigliotti has been partially supported by the INRIA/ARC project ProNoBiS. Maria Grazia Vigliotti thanks the Group MIMOSA at INRIA Sophia Antipolis for having allowed her to work as guest at their site. We also thank the anonymous referees for their comments.

References

[1] D. Angluin. Local and global properties in networks of processors. In *Proceedings of the 12th Annual ACM Symposium on Theory of Computing*, pages 82–93. ACM, 1980.

[2] G. Boudol. Asynchrony and the π-calculus. Technical Report 1702, INRIA Sophia-Antipolis, 1992.

[3] L. Bougé. On the existence of symmetric algorithms to find leaders in networks of communicating sequential processes. *Acta Informatica*, 25:179–201, 1988.

[4] L. Cardelli and A.D. Gordon. Anytime, Anywhere: Modal Logic for Mobile Ambients. In *Proceedings of the 27th ACM Symposium on Principles of Programming Languages*, pages 365–377, 2000.

[5] L. Cardelli and A.D. Gordon. Mobile ambients. *Theoretical Computer Science*, 240(1):177–213, 2000.

[6] G. Castagna, J. Vitek, and F. Zappa Nardelli. The Seal calculus. *Information and Computation*, 201(1):1–54, 2005.

[7] C. Ene and T. Muntean. Expressiveness of point-to-point versus broadcast communications. In *Proceedings of 12th International Symposium on Fundamentals of Computation Theory (FCT'99)*, volume 1684 of *Lecture Notes in Computer Science*, pages 258–268. Springer-Verlag, 1999.

[8] D. Gorla. On the relative expressive power of asynchronous communication primitives. In L. Aceto and A. Ingólfsdóttir, editors, *Proceedings of 9th International Conference on Foundations of Software Science and Computation Structures (FoSSaCS'06)*, volume 3921 of *Lecture Notes in Computer Science*, pages 47–62. Springer-Verlag, 2006.

[9] C.A.R. Hoare. *Communicating Sequential Processes*. Prentice-Hall, 1985.

[10] K. Honda and M. Tokoro. An object calculus for asynchronous communication. In *Proceedings of European Conference on Object-Oriented Programming (ECOOP'91)*, volume 512 of *Lecture Notes in Computer Science*, pages 133–147. Springer-Verlag, 1991.

[11] N. Lynch. *Distributed Algorithms*. Morgan Kaufmann, 1996.

[12] R. Milner. *Communication and Concurrency*. Prentice-Hall, 1989.

[13] R. Milner. Functions as processes. *Mathematical Structures in Computer Science*, 2(2):269–310, 1992.

[14] R. Milner. *Communicating and Mobile Systems: the π-Calculus*. Cambridge University Press, 1999.

[15] R. Milner, J. Parrow, and D. Walker. A calculus for mobile processes, parts I and II. *Information and Computation*, 100(1):1–77, 1992.

[16] R. Milner and D. Sangiorgi. Barbed Bisimulation. In *Proceedings of the 19th International Colloquium on Automata, Languages and Programming*, volume 623 of *Lecture Notes in Computer Science*, pages 685–695. Springer-Verlag, 1992.

[17] U. Nestmann. What is a 'good' encoding of guarded choice? *Information and Computation*, 156:287–319, 2000.

[18] U. Nestmann. Modeling consensus in a process calculus. In *Proceedings of CONCUR'03*, volume 2761 of *Lecture Notes in Computer Science*, pages 393–407. Springer-Verlag, 2003.

[19] U. Nestmann and B.C. Pierce. Decoding Choice Encodings. *Information and Computation*, 163(1):1–59, 2000.

[20] C. Palamidessi. Comparing the expressive power of the synchronous and the asynchronous π-calculus. In *Proceedings of the 25th ACM Symposium on Principles of Programming Languages*, pages 256–265. ACM, 1997.

[21] C. Palamidessi. Comparing the expressive power of the synchronous and the asynchronous π-calculi. *Mathematical Structures in Computer Science*, 13(5):685–719, 2003.

[22] I.C.C. Phillips. CCS with priority guards. In *Proceedings of 12th International Conference on Concurrency Theory, CONCUR 2001*, volume 2154 of *Lecture Notes in Computer Science*, pages 305–320. Springer-Verlag, 2001.

[23] I.C.C. Phillips and M.G. Vigliotti. Symmetric electoral systems for ambient calculi. Submitted.

[24] I.C.C. Phillips and M.G. Vigliotti. Electoral systems in ambient calculi. In *Proceedings of 7th International Conference on Foundations of Software Science and Computation Structures, FoSSaCS 2004*, volume 2987 of *Lecture Notes in Computer Science*, pages 408–422. Springer-Verlag, 2004.

[25] I.C.C. Phillips and M.G. Vigliotti. Leader election in rings of ambient processes. *Theoretical Computer Science*, 356(3):468–494, 2006.

[26] B.C. Pierce and D.N. Turner. Pict: A programming language based on the pi-calculus. In G. Plotkin, C. Stirling, and M. Tofte, editors, *Proof, Language and Interaction: Essays in Honour of Robin Milner*, pages 455–494. MIT Press, 2000.

[27] K.V.S. Prasad. Broadcast Calculus Interpreted in CCS up to Bisimulation. In *Proceedings of Express'01*, volume 52 of *Electronic Notes in Theoretical Computer Science*, pages 83–100. Elsevier, 2002.

[28] D. Sangiorgi. *Expressing Mobility in Process Algebra: First-Order and Higher-Order Paradigms*. PhD thesis, University of Edinburgh, 1993.

[29] D. Sangiorgi and D. Walker. *The π-Calculus: a Theory of Mobile Processes*. Cambridge University Press, 2001.

[30] G. Tel. *Distributed Algorithms*. Cambridge University Press, 2000.

[31] M.G. Vigliotti. *Reduction Semantics for Ambient Calculi*. PhD thesis, Imperial College London, 2004.

[32] N. Yoshida. Graph Types for Monadic Mobile Process Calculi. In *Proceedings of 16th FST/TCS*, volume 1180 of *Lecture Notes in Computer Science*, pages 371–386. Springer-Verlag, 1996.

Divide and Congruence: From Decomposition of Modalities to Preservation of Branching Bisimulation

Wan Fokkink[1,2], Rob van Glabbeek[3,4], and Paulien de Wind[1]

[1] Vrije Universiteit Amsterdam, Section Theoretical Computer Science, Amsterdam
[2] CWI, Department of Software Engineering, Amsterdam
[3] National ICT Australia, Sydney
[4] University of New South Wales, School of Computer Science and Engineering, Sydney
{wanf, pdwind}@cs.vu.nl, rvg@cs.stanford.edu

Abstract. We present a method for decomposing modal formulas for processes with the internal action τ. To decide whether a process algebra term satisfies a modal formula, one can check whether its subterms satisfy formulas that are obtained by decomposing the original formula. The decomposition uses the structural operational semantics that underlies the process algebra. We use this decomposition method to derive congruence formats for branching and rooted branching bisimulation equivalence.

1 Introduction

Structural operational semantics [20] provides process algebras and specification languages with an interpretation. It generates a labelled transition system, in which states are the closed terms over a (single-sorted, first-order) signature, and transitions between states may be supplied with labels. The transitions between states are obtained from a transition system specification, which consists of a set of proof rules called transition rules.

Labelled transition systems can be distinguished from each other by a wide range of behavioural equivalences, based on e.g. branching structure or decorated versions of execution sequences. VAN GLABBEEK [11] classified equivalences for processes that take into account the internal action τ. Here we focus on one such equivalence, called branching bisimulation [14].

In general a behavioural equivalence induced by a transition system specification is not a congruence, i.e. the equivalence class of a term $f(p_1, \ldots, p_n)$ need not be determined by the equivalence classes of its arguments $p_1, \ldots, p_n$. Being a congruence is an important property, for instance in order to fit the equivalence into an axiomatic framework. Syntactic formats for transition rules have been developed with respect to several behavioural equivalences, to ensure that such an equivalence is a congruence. These formats help to avoid repetitive congruence proofs. Several congruence formats were introduced for bisimulation, such as the De Simone format [21], the GSOS format [4], the tyft/tyxt format [16], and the ntyft/ntyxt format [15]. BLOOM [2] introduced congruence formats for

F.S. de Boer et al. (Eds.): FMCO 2005, LNCS 4111, pp. 195–218, 2006.
© Springer-Verlag Berlin Heidelberg 2006

weak and branching bisimulation and for rooted weak and branching bisimulation. These formats include so-called patience rules for arguments i of function symbols f, which imply that a term $f(p_1, \ldots, p_n)$ inherits the τ-transitions of its argument p_i. Furthermore, arguments of function symbols that contain running processes are marked, and this marking is used to restrict occurrences of variables in transition rules.

Behavioural equivalences can be characterised in terms of the observations that an experimenter could make during a session with a process. Modal logic captures such observations. A modal characterisation of an equivalence consists of a class C of modal formulas such that two processes are equivalent if and only if they make true the same formulas in C. For instance, Hennessy-Milner logic [17] is a modal characterisation of bisimulation.

LARSEN AND LIU [19] introduced a method for decomposing formulas from Hennessy-Milner logic for concrete processes, with respect to terms from a process algebra with a structural operational semantics in De Simone format. To decide whether a process algebra term satisfies a modal formula, one can check whether its subterms satisfy certain other formulas, obtained by decomposing the original formula. This method was extended by BLOOM, FOKKINK & VAN GLABBEEK [3] to ntyft/ntyxt format without lookahead, and by FOKKINK, VAN GLABBEEK & DE WIND [9] to tyft/tyxt format. In [3], the decomposition method was applied to obtain congruence formats for a range of behavioural equivalences. The idea is that given an equivalence and its modal characterisation C, the congruence format for this equivalence must ensure that decomposing a formula in C always produces formulas in C.

Here we extend the work of [3] to processes with τ-transitions. We present a method for decomposing formulas from modal logic for processes with τ-transitions. In order to minimise the complexity inherent in the combination of modal decomposition and the internal action τ, we apply the decomposition method to so-called abstraction-free TSSs, where only the patience rules contain the label τ in the conclusion. Furthermore, we use this decomposition method to obtain congruence formats for branching and rooted branching bisimulation. These formats include TSSs that are not abstraction-free, owing to the compositionality of the abstraction operator, which renames certain actions into τ. Our formats use two predicates on arguments of function symbols, to mark both running processes and processes that may have started running. Our congruence formats are more liberal than the simply BB and RBB cool formats from [2] and the RBB safe format from [7]. In Sect. 7 we will present a more in-depth comparison with congruence formats from [2,7,13].

In a companion paper [10], we derive congruence formats for η- and rooted η-bisimulation, with a reference to the current paper for the decomposition method. Thus we drive home the point that, in contrast to the ad hoc construction of congruence formats from the past, we can now systematically derive expressive congruence formats from the modal characterisations of behavioural equivalences.

2 Preliminaries

2.1 Equivalences on Labelled Transition Systems

A *labelled transition system (LTS)* is a pair $(\mathbb{P}, \rightarrow)$ with $\mathbb{P}$ a set of *processes* and $\rightarrow \subseteq \mathbb{P} \times (A \cup \{\tau\}) \times \mathbb{P}$ where τ is an *internal action* and A a set of *actions* not containing τ. We use α, β, γ for elements of $A \cup \{\tau\}$ and a, b for elements of A. We write $p \xrightarrow{\alpha} q$ for $(p, \alpha, q) \in \rightarrow$ and $p \xnrightarrow{\alpha}$ for $\neg\exists q \in \mathbb{P} : p \xrightarrow{\alpha} q$. Furthermore, $\xRightarrow{\epsilon}$ denotes the transitive-reflexive closure of $\xrightarrow{\tau}$.

Definition 1 ([14]). *A symmetric relation* $B \subseteq \mathbb{P} \times \mathbb{P}$ *is a* branching bisimulation *if* pBq *and* $p \xrightarrow{\alpha} p'$ *implies that either* $\alpha = \tau$ *and* $p' B q$, *or* $q \xRightarrow{\epsilon} q' \xrightarrow{\alpha} q''$ *for some* q' *and* q'' *with* pBq' *and* $p'Bq''$.

    Processes p, q *are* branching bisimilar, *denoted by* $p \mathbin{\underline{\leftrightarrow}}_b q$, *if there exists a* branching bisimulation B *with* pBq.

Branching bisimulation is not a congruence with respect to most process algebras from the literature, meaning that the equivalence class of a term $f(p_1, \ldots, p_n)$ is not always determined by the equivalence classes of its arguments $p_1, \ldots, p_n$. A rootedness condition remedies this imperfection.

Definition 2 ([14]). *A symmetric relation* $R \subseteq \mathbb{P} \times \mathbb{P}$ *is a* rooted branching bisimulation *if* pRq *and* $p \xrightarrow{\alpha} p'$ *implies that* $q \xrightarrow{\alpha} q'$ *for some* q' *with* $p' \mathbin{\underline{\leftrightarrow}}_b q'$.

    Processes p, q *are* rooted branching bisimilar, *denoted by* $p \mathbin{\underline{\leftrightarrow}}_{rb} q$, *if there exists a rooted branching bisimulation* R *with* pRq.

2.2 Modal Logic

Modal logic aims to formulate properties of processes in an LTS. Following [11], we extend Hennessy-Milner logic [17] with the modal connectives $\langle \epsilon \rangle \varphi$ and $\langle \hat{\tau} \rangle \varphi$.

Definition 3. *The class* $\mathbb{O}$ *of modal formulas is defined as follows, where* I *ranges over all index sets:*

$$\mathbb{O} \quad \varphi ::= \bigwedge_{i \in I} \varphi_i \mid \neg\varphi \mid \langle \alpha \rangle \varphi \mid \langle \epsilon \rangle \varphi \mid \langle \hat{\tau} \rangle \varphi$$

$p \models \varphi$ denotes that p satisfies φ. By definition, $p \models \langle \alpha \rangle \varphi$ if $p \xrightarrow{\alpha} p'$ with $p' \models \varphi$, $p \models \langle \epsilon \rangle \varphi$ if $p \xRightarrow{\epsilon} p'$ with $p' \models \varphi$, and $p \models \langle \hat{\tau} \rangle \varphi$ if either $p \models \varphi$ or $p \xrightarrow{\tau} p'$ with $p' \models \varphi$. We use abbreviations $\top$ for the empty conjunction, $\varphi_1 \wedge \varphi_2$ for $\bigwedge_{i \in \{1,2\}} \varphi_i$, $\varphi\langle\alpha\rangle\varphi'$ for $\varphi \wedge \langle\alpha\rangle\varphi'$, and $\varphi\langle\hat{\tau}\rangle\varphi'$ for $\varphi \wedge \langle\hat{\tau}\rangle\varphi'$. We write $\varphi \equiv \varphi'$ if $p \models \varphi \Leftrightarrow p \models \varphi'$ for any process p in any LTS.

Definition 4. *The subclasses* $\mathbb{O}_b$ *and* $\mathbb{O}_{rb}$ *of* $\mathbb{O}$ *are defined as follows:*

$$\mathbb{O}_b \quad \varphi ::= \bigwedge_{i \in I} \varphi_i \mid \neg\varphi \mid \langle\epsilon\rangle(\varphi\langle\hat{\tau}\rangle\varphi') \mid \langle\epsilon\rangle(\varphi\langle a\rangle\varphi')$$

$$\mathbb{O}_{rb} \quad \varphi ::= \bigwedge_{i \in I} \varphi_i \mid \neg\varphi \mid \langle\alpha\rangle\hat{\varphi} \mid \hat{\varphi} \ (\hat{\varphi} \in \mathbb{O}_b)$$

The classes $\mathbb{O}_b^{\equiv}$ *and* $\mathbb{O}_{rb}^{\equiv}$ *are the closures of* $\mathbb{O}_b$, *respectively* $\mathbb{O}_{rb}$, *under* $\equiv$.

The last clause in the definition of $\mathbb{O}_{rb}$ guarantees that $\mathbb{O}_b \subseteq \mathbb{O}_{rb}$, which will be needed in the proof of Prop. 4. If this clause were omitted, it would still follow that $\mathbb{O}_b^{\overline{\equiv}} \subseteq \mathbb{O}_{rb}^{\overline{\equiv}}$, using structural induction together with $\langle\epsilon\rangle\varphi \equiv \varphi \vee \langle\tau\rangle\langle\epsilon\rangle\varphi$ and $\langle\hat\tau\rangle\varphi \equiv \varphi \vee \langle\tau\rangle\varphi$. Note that if $\varphi \in \mathbb{O}_b^{\overline{\equiv}}$, then $\langle\epsilon\rangle\varphi \equiv \langle\epsilon\rangle(\varphi\langle\hat\tau\rangle\varphi) \in \mathbb{O}_b^{\overline{\equiv}}$.

For $L \subseteq \mathbb{O}$, we write $p \sim_L q$ if p and q satisfy the same formulas in L. Note that, trivially, $p \sim_{\mathbb{O}_b} q \Leftrightarrow p \sim_{\mathbb{O}_b^{\overline{\equiv}}} q$ and $p \sim_{\mathbb{O}_{rb}} q \Leftrightarrow p \sim_{\mathbb{O}_{rb}^{\overline{\equiv}}} q$.

Theorem 1. $p \underline{\leftrightarrow}_b q \Leftrightarrow p \sim_{\mathbb{O}_b} q$ and $p \underline{\leftrightarrow}_{rb} q \Leftrightarrow p \sim_{\mathbb{O}_{rb}} q$, for all $p, q \in \mathbb{P}$.

A proof of this theorem is presented in the appendix.

2.3   Structural Operational Semantics

Let V be an infinite set of variables, with typical elements x, y, z. A syntactic object is *closed* if it does not contain any variables. A *signature* is a set Σ of function symbols f with arity $ar(f)$. We always take $|\Sigma|, |A| \leq |V|$. The set $\mathbb{T}(\Sigma)$ of terms over Σ and V is defined as usual. t, u denote terms and p, q closed terms. $var(t)$ is the set of variables that occur in t. A substitution is a partial function from V to $\mathbb{T}(\Sigma)$. A closed substitution σ is a total function from V to closed terms.

Definition 5. A (positive or negative) literal *is an expression* $t \xrightarrow{\alpha} t'$ *or* $t \xrightarrow{\alpha}\!\!\!\!\!/\,$. A (transition) rule *is of the form* $\dfrac{H}{t \xrightarrow{\alpha} t'}$ *with* H *a set of literals called the premises.* $t \xrightarrow{\alpha} t'$ *is the* conclusion *and* t *the* source *of the rule. A rule* $\dfrac{\emptyset}{t \xrightarrow{\alpha} t'}$ *is also written* $t \xrightarrow{\alpha} t'$. *A transition system specification (TSS), written* (Σ, R), *consists of a signature* Σ *and a collection* R *of transition rules over* Σ.

Definition 6. *Let* $P = (\Sigma, R)$ *be a TSS. An* irredundant proof *from* P *of a rule* $\dfrac{H}{t \xrightarrow{\alpha} t'}$ *is a well-founded tree with the nodes labelled by literals and some of the leaves marked "hypothesis", such that the root has label* $t \xrightarrow{\alpha} t'$, H *is the set of labels of the hypotheses, and if* μ *is the label of a node that is not a hypothesis and* K *is the set of labels of the children of this node, then* μ *is positive and* $\dfrac{K}{\mu}$ *is a substitution instance of a rule in* R.

The proof of $\dfrac{H}{t \xrightarrow{\alpha} t'}$ is called irredundant because H must equal (instead of include) the set of labels of the hypotheses. This irredundancy will be crucial for the preservation of our congruence formats in Sect. 4.1 (see Prop. 2).

A TSS is meant to specify an LTS in which the transitions are closed positive literals. A TSS with only positive premises specifies an LTS in a straightforward way, but it is not so easy to associate an LTS to a TSS with negative premises. From [12] we adopt the notion of a well-supported proof of a closed literal. Literals $t \xrightarrow{\alpha} t'$ and $t \xrightarrow{\alpha}\!\!\!\!\!/\,$ are said to *deny* each other.

Definition 7. *Let* $P = (\Sigma, R)$ *be a TSS. A* well-supported proof *from* P *of a closed literal* μ *is a well-founded tree with the nodes labelled by closed literals, such that the root is labelled by* μ, *and if* ν *is the label of a node and* K *is the set of labels of the children of this node, then:*

1. *either ν is positive and $\frac{K}{\nu}$ is a closed substitution instance of a rule in R;*
2. *or ν is negative and for each set N of closed negative literals with $\frac{N}{\kappa}$ irre-dundantly provable from P and κ a closed positive literal denying ν, a literal in K denies one in N.*

$P \vdash_{ws} \mu$ *denotes that a well-supported proof from P of μ exists. P is complete if for each p and α, either $P \vdash_{ws} p \overset{\alpha}{\not\rightarrow}$ or $P \vdash_{ws} p \overset{\alpha}{\longrightarrow} p'$ for some p'.*

A complete TSS specifies an LTS, consisting of the *ws*-provable closed positive literals.

2.4 Notions Regarding Transition Rules

In this section we present terminology for syntactic restrictions on rules, originating from [3,15,16].

Definition 8. *An* ntytt *rule is a rule in which the right-hand sides of positive premises are variables that are all distinct, and that do not occur in the source. An* ntytt *rule is an* ntyxt *rule if its source is a variable, an* ntyft *rule if its source contains exactly one function symbol and no multiple occurrences of variables, and an* nxytt *rule if the left-hand sides of its premises are variables.*

Definition 9. *A variable in a rule is* free *if it occurs neither in the source nor in right-hand sides of premises. A rule has* lookahead *if some variable occurs in the right-hand side of a premise and in the left-hand side of a premise. A rule is* decent *if it has no lookahead and does not contain free variables.*

The ntyft/ntyxt and ready simulation formats [15,3] were originally introduced to guarantee congruence for bisimulation and ready simulation.

Definition 10. *A TSS is in* ntyft/ntyxt *format if it consists of ntyft and ntyxt rules, and in* ready simulation *format if moreover its rules do not have lookahead.*

A predicate $\aleph$ marks arguments of function symbols that contain running processes (cf. [3]). Typically, in process algebra, $\aleph$ holds for the arguments of the merge $\|$, but not for the arguments of alternative composition $+$.

Definition 11. *Let $\aleph$ be a unary predicate on $\{(f, i) \mid 1 \leq i \leq ar(f),\ f \in \Sigma\}$. If $\aleph(f, i)$, then argument i of f is* liquid; *otherwise it is* frozen. *An occurrence of x in t is at an $\aleph$-liquid position (or $\aleph$-liquid for short), if either $t = x$, or $t = f(t_1, \ldots, t_{ar(f)})$ and the occurrence is at an $\aleph$-liquid position in t_i for a liquid argument i of f; otherwise the occurrence is at an $\aleph$-frozen position.*

A patience rule for an argument i of a function symbol f expresses that term $f(p_1, \ldots, p_n)$ inherits the τ-transitions of argument p_i (cf. [2,7]). We will require the presence of patience rules for $\aleph$-liquid arguments.

Definition 12. *An ntyft rule is a patience rule for f if it is of the form*

$$\frac{x_i \xrightarrow{\tau} y}{f(x_1, \ldots, x_i, \ldots, x_{ar(f)}) \xrightarrow{\tau} f(x_1, \ldots, x_{i-1}, y, x_{i+1} \ldots, x_{ar(f)})}$$

It is an $\aleph$-patience rule if $\aleph(f, i)$.

An ntytt rule is $\aleph$-*patient* if it is irredundantly provable from the $\aleph$-patience rules. Such rules have the form $\frac{t \xrightarrow{\tau} y}{C[t] \xrightarrow{\tau} C[y]}$ with $C[]$ an $\aleph$-liquid context, meaning that the context symbol $[]$ occurs at an $\aleph$-liquid position.

Definition 13. *A TSS is abstraction-free with respect to $\aleph$ if only $\aleph$-patience rules have a conclusion of the form $t \xrightarrow{\tau} u$.*

In Section 4.2 we will obtain preservation results of modal formulas in $\mathbb{O}_b$ and $\mathbb{O}_{rb}$ on abstraction-free TSSs. We will lift these to congruence results for $\leftrightarrow_b$ and $\leftrightarrow_{rb}$ on general TSSs, using two facts: abstraction operators preserve $\leftrightarrow_b$ and $\leftrightarrow_{rb}$, and each TSS can be embedded in an abstraction-free TSS augmented with an abstraction operator.

2.5   Ruloids

To decompose modal formulas, we use a result from [3], where for any TSS P in ready simulation format a collection of decent nxytt rules, called P-*ruloids*, is constructed. We explain this construction on a rather superficial level; the precise transformation can be found in [3].

First P is converted to a TSS in decent ntyft format. In this conversion from [16], free variables in a rule are replaced by closed terms, and if the source is of the form x then this variable is replaced by a term $f(x_1, \ldots, x_n)$ for each $f \in \Sigma$. Next, using a construction from [8], left-hand sides of positive premises are reduced to variables. Roughly the idea is, given a premise $f(t_1, \ldots, t_n) \xrightarrow{\alpha} y$ in a rule r, and a rule $\frac{H}{f(x_1, \ldots, x_n) \xrightarrow{\alpha} t}$, to transform r by replacing the aforementioned premise by H, y by t, and the x_i by the t_i; this is repeated (transfinitely) until all positive premises with a non-variable left-hand side have disappeared. In the final transformation step, rules with a *negative* conclusion $t \xrightarrow{\alpha}$ are introduced. The motivation is that instead of the notion of well-founded provability in Def. 7, we want a more constructive notion like Def. 6, by making it possible that a negative premise is matched with a negative conclusion. A rule r with a conclusion $f(x_1, \ldots, x_n) \xrightarrow{\alpha}$ is obtained by picking one premise from each rule with a conclusion $f(x_1, \ldots, x_n) \xrightarrow{\alpha} t$, and including the denial of each of the selected premises as a premise of r. For this last transformation it is essential that rules do not have lookahead.

The resulting TSS, which is in decent ntyft format, is denoted by P^+. The notion of irredundant provability is adapted in a straightforward fashion to accommodate rules with a negative conclusion. In [3] it is established that $P \vdash_{ws} \mu$

if and only if μ is irredundantly provable from P^+, for all closed literals μ. P-ruloids are those decent nxytt rules that are irredundantly provable from P^+. The following correspondence result from [3] between a TSS and its ruloids plays a crucial role in the decomposition method employed here. It says that there is a well-supported proof from P of a transition $p \xrightarrow{a} q$, with p a closed substitution instance of a term t, if and only if there is a proof of this transition that uses at the root a P-ruloid with source t.

Proposition 1 ([3]). *Let P be a TSS in ready simulation format. Then $P \vdash_{ws} \sigma(t) \xrightarrow{\alpha} p$ if and only if there are a P-ruloid $\dfrac{H}{t \xrightarrow{\alpha} u}$ and a σ' with $P \vdash_{ws} \sigma'(\mu)$ for $\mu \in H$, $\sigma'(t) = \sigma(t)$ and $\sigma'(u) = p$.*

It is not hard to see that the notion of abstraction-freeness is preserved by the transformation to P-ruloids.

Lemma 1. *If a TSS P is abstraction-free with respect to some $\aleph$, then all P-ruloids with a conclusion of the form $t \xrightarrow{\tau} u$ are $\aleph$-patient.*

3   Decomposition of Modal Formulas

In this section we show how one can decompose formulas from $\mathbb{O}$. To each term t and formula φ we assign a set $t^{-1}(\varphi)$ of *decomposition mappings* $\psi : V \to \mathbb{O}$. Each of these mappings $\psi \in t^{-1}(\varphi)$ guarantees that $\sigma(t) \models \varphi$ if $\sigma(x) \models \psi(x)$ for $x \in var(t)$. Vice versa, whenever $\sigma(t) \models \varphi$, there is a decomposition mapping $\psi \in t^{-1}(\varphi)$ with $\sigma(x) \models \psi(x)$ for $x \in var(t)$. This is formalised in Thm. 2.

In order to minimise the complexity inherent in the combination of modal decomposition and the internal action τ, we apply the decomposition method to abstraction-free TSSs. In Sect. 4, where we will develop congruence formats on the basis of this decomposition method, we will be able to circumvent the restriction to abstraction-free TSSs, owing to the compositionality of the abstraction operator.

Definition 14. *Let P be a TSS in ready simulation format, which contains the $\aleph$-patience rules and is abstraction-free with respect to $\aleph$. We define $\cdot^{-1}$: $\mathbb{T}(\Sigma) \times \mathbb{O} \to \mathcal{P}(V \to \mathbb{O})$ as follows. Let t denote a univariate term, i.e. without multiple occurrences of the same variable.*

1. $\psi \in t^{-1}(\bigwedge_{i \in I} \varphi_i)$ iff for $x \in V$

$$\psi(x) = \bigwedge_{i \in I} \psi_i(x)$$

where $\psi_i \in t^{-1}(\varphi_i)$ for $i \in I$.
2. $\psi \in t^{-1}(\neg\varphi)$ iff there is a function $h : t^{-1}(\varphi) \to var(t)$ with

$$\psi(x) = \bigwedge_{\chi \in h^{-1}(x)} \neg\chi(x) \qquad \text{for } x \in V$$

3. $\psi \in t^{-1}(\langle \alpha \rangle \varphi)$ iff there is a P-ruloid $\dfrac{H}{t \xrightarrow{\alpha} u}$ and a $\chi \in u^{-1}(\varphi)$ with

$$\psi(x) = \begin{cases} \chi(x) \;\; \wedge \displaystyle\bigwedge_{x \xrightarrow{\beta} y \in H} \langle \beta \rangle \chi(y) \;\; \wedge \displaystyle\bigwedge_{x \xrightarrow{\gamma}\!\!\!\!\!/ \;\in H} \neg \langle \gamma \rangle \top & \text{if } x \in var(t) \\[4mm] \top & \text{if } x \notin var(t) \end{cases}$$

4. $\psi \in t^{-1}(\langle \epsilon \rangle \varphi)$ iff there is a $\chi \in t^{-1}(\varphi)$ with

$$\psi(x) = \begin{cases} \langle \epsilon \rangle \chi(x) & \text{if } x \text{ occurs } \aleph\text{-liquid in } t \\ \chi(x) & \text{otherwise} \end{cases}$$

5. $\psi \in t^{-1}(\langle \hat{\tau} \rangle \varphi)$ iff one of the following holds:
   (a) $\psi \in t^{-1}(\varphi)$, or
   (b) there is an $x_0 \in V$ that occurs $\aleph$-liquid in t and a $\chi \in t^{-1}(\varphi)$ such that

$$\psi(x) = \begin{cases} \langle \hat{\tau} \rangle \chi(x) & \text{if } x = x_0 \\ \chi(x) & \text{if } x \neq x_0 \end{cases}$$

6. $\psi \in \rho(t)^{-1}(\varphi)$ for $\rho : var(t) \to V$ not injective iff there is a $\chi \in t^{-1}(\varphi)$ with

$$\psi(x) = \bigwedge_{y \in \rho^{-1}(x)} \chi(y) \qquad \text{for } x \in V$$

It is not hard to see that if $\psi \in t^{-1}(\varphi)$, then $\psi(x) \equiv \top$ for $x \notin var(t)$.

To explain the idea behind Def. 14, we expand on two of its cases. Consider $t^{-1}(\neg \varphi)$, and let σ be any closed substitution. We have $\sigma(t) \not\models \varphi$ if and only if there is no $\chi \in t^{-1}(\varphi)$ such that $\sigma(x) \models \chi(x)$ for all $x \in var(t)$. In other words, for each $\chi \in t^{-1}(\varphi)$, $\psi(x)$ must contain a conjunct $\neg \chi(x)$, for some $x \in var(t)$.

Consider $t^{-1}(\langle \alpha \rangle \varphi)$, and let σ be any closed substitution. The question is under which conditions $\psi(x) \in \mathbb{O}$ on $\sigma(x)$, for $x \in var(t)$, there is a transition $\sigma(t) \xrightarrow{\alpha} q$ with $q \models \varphi$. According to Prop. 1, there is such a transition if and only if there is a closed substitution σ' with $\sigma'(t) = \sigma(t)$ and a P-ruloid $\dfrac{H}{t \xrightarrow{\alpha} u}$ such that (1) the premises in $\sigma'(H)$ are satisfied and (2) $\sigma'(u) \models \varphi$. The first condition is covered if for $x \in var(t)$, $\psi(x)$ contains conjuncts $\langle \beta \rangle \top$ for $x \xrightarrow{\beta} y \in H$ and conjuncts $\neg \langle \gamma \rangle \top$ for $x \xrightarrow{\gamma}\!\!\!\!/ \;\in H$. By adding a conjunct $\chi(x)$, and replacing each conjunct $\langle \beta \rangle \top$ by $\langle \beta \rangle \chi(y)$, for some $\chi \in u^{-1}(\varphi)$, the second condition is covered as well.

The following theorem will be the key to the forthcoming congruence results.

Theorem 2. *Given a complete TSS P in ready simulation format, which contains the $\aleph$-patience rules and is abstraction-free with respect to $\aleph$. For any term t, closed substitution σ and $\varphi \in \mathbb{O}$:*

$$\sigma(t) \models \varphi \;\Leftrightarrow\; \exists \psi \in t^{-1}(\varphi) \; \forall x \in var(t) : \sigma(x) \models \psi(x)$$

Proof. By structural induction on φ. First we treat the case where t is univariate.

- $\varphi = \bigwedge_{i \in I} \varphi_i$

  $\sigma(t) \models \bigwedge_{i \in I} \varphi_i \Leftrightarrow \forall i \in I : \sigma(t) \models \varphi_i \Leftrightarrow \forall i \in I \; \exists \psi_i \in t^{-1}(\varphi_i) \; \forall x \in var(t) :$
  $\sigma(x) \models \psi_i(x) \Leftrightarrow \exists \psi \in t^{-1}(\bigwedge_{i \in I} \varphi_i) \; \forall x \in var(t) : \sigma(x) \models \psi(x).$

- $\varphi = \neg\varphi'$

  $\sigma(t) \models \neg\varphi' \Leftrightarrow \sigma(t) \not\models \varphi' \Leftrightarrow \exists h : t^{-1}(\varphi') \to var(t) \; \forall \chi \in t^{-1}(\varphi') : \sigma(h(\chi)) \not\models$
  $\chi(h(\chi)) \Leftrightarrow \exists h : t^{-1}(\varphi') \to var(t) \; \forall x \in var(t) : \sigma(x) \models \bigwedge_{\chi \in h^{-1}(x)} \neg\chi(x) \Leftrightarrow$
  $\exists \psi \in t^{-1}(\neg\varphi') \; \forall x \in var(t) : \sigma(x) \models \psi(x).$

- $\varphi = \langle\alpha\rangle\varphi'$

  ($\Rightarrow$) Let $\sigma(t) \models \langle\alpha\rangle\varphi'$. Then $P \vdash_{ws} \sigma(t) \xrightarrow{\alpha} p$ with $p \models \varphi'$. By Prop. 1 there
  is a P-ruloid $\frac{H}{t \xrightarrow{\alpha} u}$ and a σ' with $P \vdash_{ws} \sigma'(\mu)$ for $\mu \in H$, $\sigma'(t) = \sigma(t)$, i.e.
  $\sigma'(x) = \sigma(x)$ for $x \in var(t)$, and $\sigma'(u) = p$. Since $\sigma'(u) \models \varphi'$, by induc-
  tion there is a $\chi \in u^{-1}(\varphi')$ with $\sigma'(z) \models \chi(z)$ for $z \in var(u)$. Furthermore,
  $\sigma'(z) \models \chi(z) \equiv \top$ for $z \notin var(u)$. Define $\psi \in t^{-1}(\langle\alpha\rangle\varphi')$ as in Def. 14.3, using
  $\frac{H}{t \xrightarrow{\alpha} u}$ and χ. Let $x \in var(t)$. For $x \xrightarrow{\beta} y \in H$, $P \vdash_{ws} \sigma'(x) \xrightarrow{\beta} \sigma'(y) \models \chi(y)$,
  so $\sigma'(x) \models \langle\beta\rangle\chi(y)$. Moreover, for $x \xrightarrow{\gamma} \not\in H$, $P \vdash_{ws} \sigma'(x) \xrightarrow{\gamma}\not\to$, so the consistency of $\vdash_{ws}$ (see [12]) yields $P \not\vdash_{ws} \sigma'(x) \xrightarrow{\gamma} q$ for all closed terms q, and
  thus $\sigma'(x) \models \neg\langle\gamma\rangle\top$. Hence $\sigma(x) = \sigma'(x) \models \psi(x)$.

  ($\Leftarrow$) Let $\psi \in t^{-1}(\langle\alpha\rangle\varphi')$ with $\sigma(x) \models \psi(x)$ for $x \in var(t)$. There is a P-ruloid

  $$\frac{\{x \xrightarrow{\beta_i} y_i \mid i \in I_x, \; x \in var(t)\} \cup \{x \xrightarrow{\gamma_j}\not\to \mid j \in J_x, \; x \in var(t)\}}{t \xrightarrow{\alpha} u}$$

  and a $\chi \in u^{-1}(\varphi')$ with $\psi(x) = \chi(x) \wedge \bigwedge_{i \in I_x} \langle\beta_i\rangle\chi(y_i) \wedge \bigwedge_{j \in J_x} \neg\langle\gamma_j\rangle\top$ for $x \in$
  $var(t)$. For $x \in var(t)$, $\sigma(x) \models \psi(x)$ yields, for $i \in I_x$, $P \vdash_{ws} \sigma(x) \xrightarrow{\beta_i} p_i$ with
  $p_i \models \chi(y_i)$ for some closed term p_i; moreover, for $j \in J_x$, $P \not\vdash_{ws} \sigma(x) \xrightarrow{\gamma_j} q$
  for all closed terms q, so by the completeness of P, $P \vdash_{ws} \sigma(x) \xrightarrow{\gamma_j}\not\to$. Define
  $\sigma'(x) = \sigma(x)$ and $\sigma'(y_i) = p_i$ for $x \in var(t)$ and $i \in I_x$. Here we use
  that the y_i are all different and do not occur in t. Then $\sigma'(z) \models \chi(z)$ for
  $z \in var(u)$, since $var(u) \subseteq \{x, y_i \mid x \in var(t), i \in I_x\}$. So by induction,
  $\sigma'(u) \models \varphi'$. Moreover, for $x \in var(t)$, $P \vdash_{ws} \sigma'(x) \xrightarrow{\beta_i} \sigma'(y_i)$ for $i \in I_x$,
  and $P \vdash_{ws} \sigma'(x) \xrightarrow{\gamma_j}\not\to$ for $j \in J_x$, so by Prop. 1, $P \vdash_{ws} \sigma'(t) \xrightarrow{\alpha} \sigma'(u)$. Hence
  $\sigma(t) = \sigma'(t) \models \langle\alpha\rangle\varphi'$.

- $\varphi = \langle\epsilon\rangle\varphi'$

  ($\Rightarrow$) We prove by induction on n: if $P \vdash_{ws} p_i \xrightarrow{\tau} p_{i+1}$ for $i \in \{0, \ldots, n-1\}$
  with $\sigma(t) = p_0$ and $p_n \models \varphi'$, then there is a $\psi \in t^{-1}(\langle\epsilon\rangle\varphi')$ with $\sigma(x) \models \psi(x)$
  for $x \in var(t)$.

  $n = 0$ Since $\sigma(t) = p_0 \models \varphi'$, by induction on formula size, there is a $\chi \in$
  $t^{-1}(\varphi')$ with $\sigma(x) \models \chi(x)$ for $x \in var(t)$. Define $\psi \in t^{-1}(\langle\epsilon\rangle\varphi')$ as in
  Def. 14.4, using χ. Then $\sigma(x) \models \psi(x)$ for $x \in var(t)$.

  $n > 0$ Since $P \vdash_{ws} \sigma(t) \xrightarrow{\tau} p_1$, by Prop. 1 there is a P-ruloid $\frac{H}{t \xrightarrow{\tau} u}$ and
  a σ' with $P \vdash_{ws} \sigma'(\mu)$ for $\mu \in H$, $\sigma'(t) = \sigma(t)$, i.e. $\sigma'(x) = \sigma(x)$ for
  $x \in var(t)$, and $\sigma'(u) = p_1$. Since $\sigma'(u) = p_1 \xrightarrow{\tau} \cdots \xrightarrow{\tau} p_n \models \langle\epsilon\rangle\varphi'$,
  by induction on n, there is a $\chi \in u^{-1}(\langle\epsilon\rangle\varphi')$ with $\sigma'(y) \models \chi(y)$ for
  $y \in var(u)$. Furthermore, $\sigma'(y) \models \chi(y) \equiv \top$ for $y \notin var(u)$. Since P

is abstraction-free, by Lem. 1, the P-ruloid $\frac{H}{t \stackrel{\tau}{\longrightarrow} u}$ must be $\aleph$-patient. Thus $H = \{x_0 \stackrel{\tau}{\longrightarrow} y_0\}$, where x_0 occurs $\aleph$-liquid in t and, since t is univariate, $u = t[y_0/x_0]$. Moreover, $y_0 \notin var(t)$, so u is also univariate. The occurrence of y_0 in u is $\aleph$-liquid, so according to Def. 14.4, $\chi(y_0)$ is of the form $\langle \epsilon \rangle \varphi''$. Let $\psi(x_0) = \chi(y_0)$, $\psi(y_0) = \chi(x_0) \equiv \top$, and $\psi(z) = \chi(z)$ otherwise. By alpha-conversion, $\chi \in u^{-1}(\langle \epsilon \rangle \varphi')$ implies $\psi \in t^{-1}(\langle \epsilon \rangle \varphi')$. For $x \in var(t) \backslash \{x_0\}$, $\sigma(x) = \sigma'(x) \models \chi(x) = \psi(x)$. Furthermore, $P \vdash_{ws} \sigma'(x_0) \stackrel{\tau}{\longrightarrow} \sigma'(y_0)$ and $\sigma'(y_0) \models \chi(y_0) = \psi(x_0)$; so since $\psi(x_0)$ is of the form $\langle \epsilon \rangle \varphi''$, $\sigma(x_0) = \sigma'(x_0) \models \psi(x_0)$.

($\Leftarrow$) Let $\psi \in t^{-1}(\langle \epsilon \rangle \varphi')$ with $\sigma(x) \models \psi(x)$ for $x \in var(t)$. Then there is a $\chi \in t^{-1}(\varphi')$ with $\psi(x) = \langle \epsilon \rangle \chi(x)$ if x occurs $\aleph$-liquid in t and $\psi(x) = \chi(x)$ otherwise. For each x that occurs $\aleph$-liquid in t, $\sigma(x) \models \psi(x) = \langle \epsilon \rangle \chi(x)$, i.e. $\sigma(x) \stackrel{\epsilon}{\Longrightarrow} p_x$ with $p_x \models \chi(x)$. Define $\sigma'(x) = p_x$ if x occurs $\aleph$-liquid in t and $\sigma'(x) = \sigma(x)$ otherwise. Due to the presence of the $\aleph$-patience rules and the fact that t is univariate, $\sigma(t) \stackrel{\epsilon}{\Longrightarrow} \sigma'(t)$. Furthermore, $\sigma'(x) \models \chi(x)$ for $x \in var(t)$, so by induction on formula size, $\sigma'(t) \models \varphi'$. Hence $\sigma(t) \models \langle \epsilon \rangle \varphi'$.

$- \varphi = \langle \hat{\tau} \rangle \varphi'$

($\Rightarrow$) Suppose $\sigma(t) \models \langle \hat{\tau} \rangle \varphi'$. Then either $\sigma(t) \models \varphi'$ or $P \vdash_{ws} \sigma(t) \stackrel{\tau}{\longrightarrow} p \models \varphi'$ for some closed term p. In the first case, by induction there is a $\psi \in t^{-1}(\varphi')$ such that $\sigma(x) \models \psi(x)$ for $x \in var(t)$; by Def. 14.5(a), $\psi \in t^{-1}(\langle \hat{\tau} \rangle \varphi')$, and we are done. In the second case, by Prop. 1 there is a P-ruloid $\frac{H}{t \stackrel{\tau}{\longrightarrow} u}$ and a closed substitution σ' with $P \vdash_{ws} \sigma'(\mu)$ for $\mu \in H$, $\sigma'(t) = \sigma(t)$, i.e. $\sigma'(x) = \sigma(x)$ for $x \in var(t)$, and $\sigma'(u) = p$. Since $\sigma'(u) \models \varphi'$, by induction there is a $\chi \in u^{-1}(\varphi')$ such that $\sigma'(y) \models \chi(y)$ for $y \in var(u)$. Furthermore, $\sigma'(y) \models \chi(y) \equiv \top$ for $y \notin var(u)$. Since P is abstraction-free, by Lem. 1, the P-ruloid $\frac{H}{t \stackrel{\tau}{\longrightarrow} u}$ must be $\aleph$-patient. Thus $H = \{x_0 \stackrel{\tau}{\longrightarrow} y_0\}$, where x_0 occurs $\aleph$-liquid in t and, since t is univariate, $u = t[y_0/x_0]$. Moreover, $y_0 \notin var(t)$, so u is also univariate. Let $\psi(x_0) = \langle \hat{\tau} \rangle \chi(y_0)$, $\psi(y_0) = \chi(x_0) \equiv \top$, and $\psi(x) = \chi(x)$ otherwise. By Def. 14.5(b) together with alpha-conversion, $\psi \in t^{-1}(\langle \hat{\tau} \rangle \varphi')$. For $x \in var(t) \backslash \{x_0\}$, $\sigma(x) = \sigma'(x) \models \chi(x) = \psi(x)$. Moreover, since $P \vdash_{ws} \sigma'(x_0) \stackrel{\tau}{\longrightarrow} \sigma'(y_0)$ and $\sigma'(y_0) \models \chi(y_0)$, it follows that $\sigma(x_0) = \sigma'(x_0) \models \langle \hat{\tau} \rangle \chi(y_0) = \psi(x_0)$.

($\Leftarrow$) Suppose $\psi \in t^{-1}(\langle \hat{\tau} \rangle \varphi')$ with $\sigma(x) \models \psi(x)$ for all $x \in var(t)$. If $\psi \in t^{-1}(\varphi')$, then by induction $\sigma(t) \models \varphi'$, so $\sigma(t) \models \langle \hat{\tau} \rangle \varphi'$, and we are done. Suppose that for some $\chi \in t^{-1}(\varphi')$ and some x_0 that occurs $\aleph$-liquid in t, $\psi(x) = \chi(x)$ for $x \neq x_0$ and $\psi(x_0) = \langle \hat{\tau} \rangle \chi(x_0)$. Then $\sigma(x) \models \chi(x)$ for $x \in var(t) \backslash \{x_0\}$. Furthermore, $\sigma(x_0) \models \psi(x_0) = \langle \hat{\tau} \rangle \chi(x_0)$, so either $\sigma(x_0) \models \chi(x_0)$ or $\sigma(x_0) \stackrel{\tau}{\longrightarrow} p \models \chi(x_0)$ for some closed term p. In the first case, by induction $\sigma(t) \models \varphi'$, so $\sigma(t) \models \langle \hat{\tau} \rangle \varphi'$, and we are done. In the second case, define $\sigma'(x) = \sigma(x)$ for $x \in var(t)$ and $\sigma'(y_0) = p$. Since $P \vdash_{ws} \sigma'(x_0) \stackrel{\tau}{\longrightarrow} \sigma'(y_0)$, and $\frac{x_0 \stackrel{\tau}{\longrightarrow} y_0}{t \stackrel{\tau}{\longrightarrow} t[y_0/x_0]}$ is an $\aleph$-patient P-ruloid, by Prop. 1, $P \vdash_{ws} \sigma'(t) \stackrel{\tau}{\longrightarrow} \sigma'(t[y_0/x_0])$. Furthermore, by induction $\sigma'(t[y_0/x_0]) \models \varphi'$. Hence $\sigma(t) = \sigma'(t) \models \langle \hat{\tau} \rangle \varphi'$.

Finally, suppose t is not univariate. Let $t = \rho(u)$ for some univariate u and $\rho : var(u) \rightarrow V$ not injective. $\sigma(\rho(u)) \models \varphi \Leftrightarrow \exists \chi \in u^{-1}(\varphi)\ \forall y \in var(u) :$ $\sigma(\rho(y)) \models \chi(y) \Leftrightarrow \exists \chi \in u^{-1}(\varphi)\ \forall x \in var(t) : \sigma(x) \models \bigwedge_{y \in \rho^{-1}(x)} \chi(y) \Leftrightarrow \exists \psi \in t^{-1}(\varphi)\ \forall x \in var(t) : \sigma(x) \models \psi(x)$. $\qquad\square$

The part of Thm. 2 that deals with the modalities $\bigwedge_{i \in I}$, $\neg$ and $\langle \alpha \rangle$ only has been established in [9]. There, a few examples are given showing how Def. 14 can be used to decompose a modal formula, as well as a counterexample showing that the completeness requirement in Thm. 2 cannot simply be skipped. The inclusion of the modalities $\langle \epsilon \rangle$ and $\langle \hat{\tau} \rangle$ is new. The following example illustrates the use of the decomposition method on a formula with the modality $\langle \epsilon \rangle$.

Example 1. Let $A = \{a\}$ and $P = (\Sigma, R)$, where Σ consists of a binary function symbol $\|$ with liquid arguments, and R contains the rules $\dfrac{x \xrightarrow{\alpha} x'}{x \| y \xrightarrow{\alpha} x' \| y}$ and $\dfrac{y \xrightarrow{\alpha} y'}{x \| y \xrightarrow{\alpha} x \| y'}$ for $\alpha \in \{a, \tau\}$. The TSS P is complete and in ready simulation format. Furthermore, it contains the two patience rules and is abstraction-free.

We compute $(x \| y)^{-1}(\langle \epsilon \rangle \langle a \rangle \top)$. By Def. 14.4, for each $\psi \in (x \| y)^{-1}(\langle \epsilon \rangle \langle a \rangle \top)$ we have $\psi(x) = \langle \epsilon \rangle \chi(x)$ and $\psi(y) = \langle \epsilon \rangle \chi(y)$ for some $\chi \in (x \| y)^{-1}(\langle a \rangle \top)$. According to Def. 14.3, $(x \| y)^{-1}(\langle a \rangle \top) = \{\chi_1, \chi_2\}$, where χ_1 and χ_2 are constructed from the only P-ruloids with a conclusion $x \| y \xrightarrow{a}$ _, namely $\dfrac{x \xrightarrow{a} x'}{x \| y \xrightarrow{a} x' \| y}$ and $\dfrac{y \xrightarrow{a} y'}{x \| y \xrightarrow{a} x \| y'}$, together with $\xi_1 \in (x' \| y)^{-1}(\top)$ resp. $\xi_2 \in (x \| y')^{-1}(\top)$:

$$\chi_1(x) = \xi_1(x) \wedge \langle a \rangle \xi_1(x') \equiv \langle a \rangle \top \qquad \chi_2(x) = \top$$
$$\chi_1(y) = \top \qquad\qquad\qquad\qquad\qquad \chi_2(y) = \xi_2(y) \wedge \langle a \rangle \xi_2(y') \equiv \langle a \rangle \top$$

Hence $(x \| y)^{-1}(\langle \epsilon \rangle \langle a \rangle \top) = \{\psi_1, \psi_2\}$ with ψ_1 and ψ_2 defined as follows:

$$\psi_1(x) = \langle \epsilon \rangle \chi_1(x) \equiv \langle \epsilon \rangle \langle a \rangle \top \qquad \psi_2(x) = \langle \epsilon \rangle \chi_2(x) = \langle \epsilon \rangle \top \equiv \top$$
$$\psi_1(y) = \langle \epsilon \rangle \chi_1(y) = \langle \epsilon \rangle \top \equiv \top \qquad \psi_2(y) = \langle \epsilon \rangle \chi_2(y) \equiv \langle \epsilon \rangle \langle a \rangle \top$$

4 Branching Bisimulation as a Congruence

We proceed to apply the decomposition method from the previous section to derive congruence formats for branching and rooted branching bisimulation equivalence. The idea is that the branching bisimulation format must guarantee that a formula from $\mathbb{O}_b$ is always decomposed into formulas from $\mathbb{O}_b^{\overline{\equiv}}$ (see Prop. 3). Likewise, the rooted branching bisimulation format must guarantee that a formula from $\mathbb{O}_{rb}$ is always decomposed into formulas from $\mathbb{O}_{rb}^{\overline{\equiv}}$ (see Prop. 4). This implies the desired congruence results (see Thm. 3 and Thm. 4). In the derivation of the congruence formats, we will circumvent the restriction in the decomposition method to abstraction-free TSSs, using compositionality of the abstraction operator.

4.1   Congruence Formats

We assume a second predicate Λ on arguments of function symbols, to denote that the processes they contain may have started running, but might currently be resting, in which case no patience rules are needed for these arguments. Always $\aleph \subseteq \Lambda$.

Definition 15. *Let* $\aleph \subseteq \Lambda$. *An ntytt rule* $\frac{H}{t \xrightarrow{\alpha} u}$ *is rooted branching bisimulation safe with respect to* $\aleph$ *and* Λ *if:*

1. *it has no lookahead,*
2. *right-hand sides of premises occur only* Λ-*liquid in* u, *and*
3. *if* x *occurs exactly once[1] in* t, *at a* Λ-*liquid position, then:*
   (a) *all occurrences of* x *in the rule are* Λ-*liquid,*
   (b) x *has no* $\aleph$-*liquid occurrences in left-hand sides of negative premises,*
   (c) x *has at most one* $\aleph$-*liquid occurrence in the left-hand side of one positive premise, and this premise has a label from* A, *and*
   (d) *if* x *occurs* $\aleph$-*frozen in* t, *then* x *does not occur* $\aleph$-*liquid in left-hand sides of premises.*

In case Λ *is the universal predicate, we say that the rule is* branching bisimulation safe *with respect to* $\aleph$.

Definition 16. *A TSS in ready simulation format is in* rooted branching bisimulation format *if, for some* $\aleph \subseteq \Lambda$, *it consists of the* $\aleph$-*patience rules and rules that are rooted branching bisimulation safe with respect to* $\aleph$ *and* Λ.

A TSS in ready simulation format is in branching bisimulation format *if, for some* $\aleph$, *it consists of the* $\aleph$-*patience rules and rules that are branching bisimulation safe with respect to* $\aleph$.

If a TSS P is in rooted branching bisimulation format then there are smallest predicates $\aleph_0$ and Λ_0 such that P consists of the $\aleph_0$-patience rules and rules that are rooted branching bisimulation safe with respect to $\aleph_0$ and Λ_0. Namely the Λ_0-liquid arguments are *generated* by requirements 2 and 3(a) of Def. 15; they are the smallest collection of arguments such that these two requirements are satisfied. Given Λ_0, $\aleph_0$ is the unique collection of arguments within Λ_0 for which patience rules exists. For any TSS P, $\aleph_0$ and Λ_0 can be calculated in this way, and whether P is in rooted branching bisimulation format then depends solely on whether requirements 1 and 3(b–d) of Def. 15 are satisfied.

When restricting to TSSs consisting of nxytt rules only, it becomes easier to reformulate the definition of the rooted branching bisimulation format without mentioning $\aleph$. Namely, requirements 3(b–d) of Def. 15, together with the existence of the patience rules required in Def. 16 then amount to

---

[1] For the rooted branching bisimulation format in Def. 16, only the requirements for rules in which t is univariate matter. The formulation of Def. 15 for general terms t paves the way for Prop. 2.

3. (b) x does not occur as the left-hand side of a negative premise,
   (c) x occurs at most once as the left-hand side of a positive premise, and this premise has a label from A, and
   (d) if within t, x occurs in an argument of an operator f for which there is no patience rule, then x does not occur in the left-hand side of premises.

A TSS is now in rooted branching bisimulation format if it consists of patience rules and rules that are rooted branching bisimulation safe with respect to Λ and that collection of patience rules.

Using this, it is not hard to see that the rooted branching bisimulation format strengthens the RBB safe format from [7].

In the definition of modal decomposition, we did not use the rules from the original TSS P, but the P-ruloids. Therefore we must verify that if P is in (rooted) branching bisimulation format, then so are the P-ruloids.

Proposition 2. *If a TSS P is in (rooted) branching bisimulation format with respect to some $\aleph$ (and Λ), then each P-ruloid is either $\aleph$-patient or (rooted) branching bisimulation safe with respect to $\aleph$ (and Λ).*

The proof of Prop. 2 is omitted here. The key part of the proof is to show that the decent (rooted) branching bisimulation format is preserved under irredundant provability. The adjective irredundant is essential here; this preservation result would fail if "junk" could be added to the premises of derived transition rules.

4.2 Preservation of Modal Characterisations

In this section we prove that given a TSS in rooted branching bisimulation format, if $\psi \in t^{-1}(\varphi)$ with $\varphi \in \mathbb{O}_b$, then $\psi(x) \in \mathbb{O}_{\overline{b}}^{\equiv}$ if x occurs only Λ-liquid in t. (That is why in the branching bisimulation format, Λ must be universal.) If $\varphi \in \mathbb{O}_{rb}$, then $\psi(x) \in \mathbb{O}_{rb}^{\equiv}$ for all variables x.

Proposition 3. *Let P be an abstraction-free TSS in rooted branching bisimulation format, with respect to some $\aleph$ and Λ. For any term t and variable x that occurs only Λ-liquid in t:*

$$\varphi \in \mathbb{O}_b \;\Rightarrow\; \forall \psi \in t^{-1}(\varphi) : \psi(x) \in \mathbb{O}_{\overline{b}}^{\equiv}$$

Proof. We apply structural induction on $\varphi \in \mathbb{O}_b$. Let $t \in \mathbb{T}(\Sigma)$ and $\psi \in t^{-1}(\varphi)$, and let x occur only Λ-liquid in t. First we treat the case where t is univariate. If $x \notin var(t)$, then $\psi(x) \equiv \top \in \mathbb{O}_{\overline{b}}^{\equiv}$. Suppose x occurs once in t.

- $\varphi = \bigwedge_{i \in I} \varphi_i$ with $\varphi_i \in \mathbb{O}_b$ for $i \in I$. By Def. 14.1, $\psi(x) = \bigwedge_{i \in I} \psi_i(x)$ with $\psi_i \in t^{-1}(\varphi_i)$ for $i \in I$. By induction, $\psi_i(x) \in \mathbb{O}_{\overline{b}}^{\equiv}$ for $i \in I$, so $\psi(x) \in \mathbb{O}_{\overline{b}}^{\equiv}$.
- $\varphi = \neg\varphi'$ with $\varphi' \in \mathbb{O}_b$. By Def. 14.2, there is a function $h : t^{-1}(\varphi') \to var(t)$ such that $\psi(x) = \bigwedge_{\chi \in h^{-1}(x)} \neg\chi(x)$. By induction, $\chi(x) \in \mathbb{O}_{\overline{b}}^{\equiv}$ for $\chi \in h^{-1}(x)$, so $\psi(x) \in \mathbb{O}_{\overline{b}}^{\equiv}$.

- $\varphi = \langle\epsilon\rangle(\varphi_1\langle\hat{\tau}\rangle\varphi_2)$ with $\varphi_1, \varphi_2 \in \mathbb{O}_b$. By Def. 14.4, either $\psi(x) = \langle\epsilon\rangle\chi(x)$ if x occurs $\aleph$-liquid in t, or $\psi(x) = \chi(x)$ if x occurs $\aleph$-frozen in t, for some $\chi \in t^{-1}(\varphi_1\langle\hat{\tau}\rangle\varphi_2)$. By Def. 14.1, $\chi(x) = \chi_1(x)\wedge\chi_2(x)$ with $\chi_1 \in t^{-1}(\varphi_1)$ and $\chi_2 \in t^{-1}(\langle\hat{\tau}\rangle\varphi_2)$. By Def. 14.5, either $\chi_2(x) = \langle\hat{\tau}\rangle\xi(x)$ and x occurs $\aleph$-liquid in t, or $\chi_2(x) = \xi(x)$, for some $\xi \in t^{-1}(\varphi_2)$. So $\psi(x)$ is of the form $\langle\epsilon\rangle(\chi_1(x)\langle\hat{\tau}\rangle\xi(x))$, $\langle\epsilon\rangle(\chi_1(x) \wedge \xi(x))$ or $\chi_1(x) \wedge \xi(x)$. By induction, $\chi_1(x), \xi(x) \in \mathbb{O}_b^{\equiv}$. Hence $\psi(x) \in \mathbb{O}_b^{\equiv}$.

- $\varphi = \langle\epsilon\rangle(\varphi_1\langle a\rangle\varphi_2)$ with $\varphi_1, \varphi_2 \in \mathbb{O}_b$. By Def. 14.4, either $\psi(x) = \langle\epsilon\rangle\chi(x)$ if x occurs $\aleph$-liquid in t, or $\psi(x) = \chi(x)$ if x occurs $\aleph$-frozen in t, for some $\chi \in t^{-1}(\varphi_1\langle a\rangle\varphi_2)$. By Def. 14.1, $\chi(x) = \chi_1(x) \wedge \chi_2(x)$ with $\chi_1 \in t^{-1}(\varphi_1)$ and $\chi_2 \in t^{-1}(\langle a\rangle\varphi_2)$. By induction, $\chi_1(x) \in \mathbb{O}_b^{\equiv}$. By Def. 14.3,

$$\chi_2(x) = \xi(x) \wedge \bigwedge_{x \xrightarrow{\beta} y \in H} \langle\beta\rangle\xi(y) \wedge \bigwedge_{x \xrightarrow{\gamma}\!\!\!\!\!/ \ \in H} \neg\langle\gamma\rangle\top$$

for some $\xi \in u^{-1}(\varphi_2)$ and P-ruloid $\frac{H}{t\xrightarrow{a}u}$. Since $a \neq \tau$, by Prop. 2, $\frac{H}{t\xrightarrow{a}u}$ is rooted branching bisimulation safe with respect to $\aleph$ and Λ. Since the occurrence of x in t is Λ-liquid, x occurs only Λ-liquid in u. Moreover, variables in right-hand sides of premises in H occur only Λ-liquid in u. So by induction, $\xi(x) \in \mathbb{O}_b^{\equiv}$ and $\xi(y) \in \mathbb{O}_b^{\equiv}$ for $x \xrightarrow{} y \in H$. We distinguish two cases.

CASE 1: The occurrence of x in t is $\aleph$-liquid. Then $\psi(x) = \langle\epsilon\rangle\chi(x)$. Since $\frac{H}{t\xrightarrow{a}u}$ is rooted branching bisimulation safe with respect to $\aleph$ and Λ and an nxytt rule, x does not occur in left-hand sides of negative premises in H, and at most once in the left-hand side of one positive premise in H, which is of the form $x \xrightarrow{b} y$ with $b \in A$. Hence either $\chi_2(x) = \xi(x)$ or $\chi_2(x) = \xi(x)\langle b\rangle\xi(y)$. Since $\psi(x) = \langle\epsilon\rangle(\chi_1(x) \wedge \chi_2(x))$, either $\psi(x) = \langle\epsilon\rangle(\chi_1(x) \wedge \xi(x)) \in \mathbb{O}_b^{\equiv}$ or $\psi(x) \equiv \langle\epsilon\rangle(\chi_1(x) \wedge \xi(x)\langle b\rangle\xi(y)) \in \mathbb{O}_b^{\equiv}$.

CASE 2: The occurrence of x in t is $\aleph$-frozen. Then $\psi(x) = \chi(x)$. Since $\frac{H}{t\xrightarrow{a}u}$ is rooted branching bisimulation safe with respect to $\aleph$ and Λ and an nxytt rule, x does not occur in left-hand sides of premises in H. So $\chi_2(x) = \xi(x)$, and thus $\psi(x) = \chi_1(x) \wedge \chi_2(x) = \chi_1(x) \wedge \xi(x) \in \mathbb{O}_b^{\equiv}$.

Finally, suppose t is not univariate. Then $t = \rho(u)$ for some univariate term u and $\rho : var(u) \to V$ not injective. By Def. 14.6, $\psi(x) = \bigwedge_{y \in \rho^{-1}(x)} \chi(y)$ for some $\chi \in u^{-1}(\varphi)$. Since u is univariate, and for each $y \in \rho^{-1}(x)$ the occurrence in u is Λ-liquid, $\chi(y) \in \mathbb{O}_b^{\equiv}$ for $y \in \rho^{-1}(x)$. Hence $\psi(x) \in \mathbb{O}_b^{\equiv}$. □

Proposition 4. *Let P be an abstraction-free TSS in rooted branching bisimulation format, with respect to some $\aleph$ and Λ. For any term t and variable x:*

$$\varphi \in \mathbb{O}_{rb} \Rightarrow \forall\psi \in t^{-1}(\varphi) : \psi(x) \in \mathbb{O}_{rb}^{\equiv}$$

Proof. We apply structural induction on $\varphi \in \mathbb{O}_{rb}$. Let $t \in \mathbb{T}(\Sigma)$ and $\psi \in t^{-1}(\varphi)$. We restrict attention to the case where t is univariate; the general case then follows just as at the end of the proof of Prop. 3. If $x \notin var(t)$, then $\psi(x) \equiv \top \in \mathbb{O}_{rb}^{\equiv}$. So suppose x occurs once in t.

– The cases $\varphi = \bigwedge_{i \in I} \varphi_i$ and $\varphi = \neg\varphi'$ proceed as in the proof of Prop. 3.

– $\varphi = \langle\alpha\rangle\varphi'$ with $\varphi' \in \mathbb{O}_b$. By Def. 14.3,

$$\psi(x) = \chi(x) \wedge \bigwedge_{x \xrightarrow{\beta} y \in H} \langle\beta\rangle\chi(y) \wedge \bigwedge_{x \xrightarrow{\gamma} \in H} \neg\langle\gamma\rangle\top$$

for some $\chi \in u^{-1}(\varphi')$ and P-ruloid $\frac{H}{t \xrightarrow{\alpha} u}$. By induction, $\chi(x) \in \mathbb{O}_{rb}^{\equiv}$. (Induction may be applied because $\varphi' \in \mathbb{O}_b \subseteq \mathbb{O}_{rb}$.) By Prop. 2, $\frac{H}{t \xrightarrow{\alpha} u}$ is either rooted branching bisimulation safe with respect to $\aleph$ and Λ or $\aleph$-patient. In either case, variables in right-hand sides of premises in H occur only Λ-liquid in u. By Prop. 3, $\chi(y) \in \mathbb{O}_{rb}^{\equiv}$ for $x \xrightarrow{\beta} y \in H$, so $\langle\beta\rangle\chi(y) \in \mathbb{O}_{rb}^{\equiv}$. Also $\neg\langle\gamma\rangle\top \in \mathbb{O}_{rb}^{\equiv}$. Hence $\psi(x) \in \mathbb{O}_{rb}^{\equiv}$.

– $\varphi \in \mathbb{O}_b$. If the occurrence of x in t is Λ-liquid, then $\psi(x) \in \mathbb{O}_{rb}^{\equiv}$ follows from Prop. 3. So we can assume that this occurrence is Λ-frozen, and hence $\aleph$-frozen. The cases $\varphi = \bigwedge_{i \in I} \varphi_i$ and $\varphi = \neg\varphi'$ proceed as before. We focus on the other two cases.

  * $\varphi = \langle\epsilon\rangle(\varphi_1\langle\hat{\tau}\rangle\varphi_2)$ with $\varphi_1, \varphi_2 \in \mathbb{O}_b \subseteq \mathbb{O}_{rb}$. Since the occurrence of x in t is $\aleph$-frozen, by Def. 14.4, $\psi(x) = \chi(x)$ for some $\chi \in t^{-1}(\varphi_1\langle\hat{\tau}\rangle\varphi_2)$. By Def. 14.1, $\chi(x) = \chi_1(x) \wedge \chi_2(x)$ with $\chi_1 \in t^{-1}(\varphi_1)$ and $\chi_2 \in t^{-1}(\langle\hat{\tau}\rangle\varphi_2)$. Since the occurrence of x in t is $\aleph$-frozen, by Def. 14.5, $\chi_2(x) = \xi(x)$ for some $\xi \in t^{-1}(\varphi_2)$. By induction, $\chi_1(x), \xi(x) \in \mathbb{O}_{rb}^{\equiv}$. Hence $\psi(x) \in \mathbb{O}_{rb}^{\equiv}$.
  * $\varphi = \langle\epsilon\rangle(\varphi_1\langle a\rangle\varphi_2)$ with $\varphi_1, \varphi_2 \in \mathbb{O}_b \subseteq \mathbb{O}_{rb}$. Since the occurrence of x in t is $\aleph$-frozen, by Def. 14.4, $\psi(x) = \chi(x)$ for some $\chi \in t^{-1}(\varphi_1\langle a\rangle\varphi_2)$. By Def. 14.1, $\chi(x) = \chi_1(x) \wedge \chi_2(x)$ with $\chi_1 \in t^{-1}(\varphi_1)$ and $\chi_2 \in t^{-1}(\langle a\rangle\varphi_2)$. By induction, $\chi_1(x), \chi_2(x) \in \mathbb{O}_{rb}^{\equiv}$. Hence $\psi(x) \in \mathbb{O}_{rb}^{\equiv}$. □

4.3 Congruence Results

Finally we are in a position to prove the promised congruence results.

Lemma 2. *Given a complete, abstraction-free TSS in branching bisimulation format, with respect to some $\aleph$. If $\sigma(x) \underline{\leftrightarrow}_b \sigma'(x)$ for $x \in var(t)$, then $\sigma(t) \underline{\leftrightarrow}_b \sigma'(t)$.*

Proof. By Thm. 1, $\sigma(x) \underline{\leftrightarrow}_b \sigma'(x)$ implies $\sigma(x) \sim_{\mathbb{O}_b^{\equiv}} \sigma'(x)$ for $x \in var(t)$. Let $\sigma(t) \models \varphi \in \mathbb{O}_b$. By Thm. 2 there is a $\psi \in t^{-1}(\varphi)$ with $\sigma(x) \models \psi(x)$ for $x \in var(t)$. Since Λ is universal, by Prop. 3, $\psi(x) \in \mathbb{O}_b^{\equiv}$ for $x \in var(t)$. Since $\sigma(x) \sim_{\mathbb{O}_b^{\equiv}} \sigma'(x)$, $\sigma'(x) \models \psi(x)$ for $x \in var(t)$. By Thm. 2, $\sigma'(t) \models \varphi$. Likewise, $\sigma'(t) \models \varphi \in \mathbb{O}_b$ implies $\sigma(t) \models \varphi$. So $\sigma(t) \sim_{\mathbb{O}_b} \sigma'(t)$. Hence $\sigma(t) \underline{\leftrightarrow}_b \sigma'(t)$. □

Theorem 3. *Given a complete TSS $P = (\Sigma, R)$ in branching bisimulation format, with respect to some $\aleph$. If $\sigma(x) \underline{\leftrightarrow}_b \sigma'(x)$ for $x \in var(t)$, then $\sigma(t) \underline{\leftrightarrow}_b \sigma'(t)$.*

Proof. Let P' be obtained from P, by changing in all rules, expect the $\aleph$-patience rules, conclusions of the form $t \xrightarrow{\tau} u$ into $t \xrightarrow{i} u$, for a fresh action $i \notin A \cup \{\tau\}$. By construction, P' is abstraction-free and in branching bisimulation format with respect to $\aleph$. So by Lem. 2, $\underline{\leftrightarrow}_b$ is a congruence for all operators of P'.

Let P'' be obtained from P' by adding a new operator τ_i with rules

$$\frac{x \xrightarrow{\alpha} y}{\tau_i(x) \xrightarrow{\alpha} \tau_i(y)} \quad (\alpha \neq i) \qquad \frac{x \xrightarrow{i} y}{\tau_i(x) \xrightarrow{\tau} \tau_i(y)}$$

This operator turns all i-labels into τ-labels. It is well-known and trivial to check that $\underline{\leftrightarrow}_b$ is a congruence for τ_i as well.

If follows trivially that for any operator $f \in \Sigma$ the behaviour of $\tau_i \circ f$ in P'' is the same as the behaviour of f in P. So as $\underline{\leftrightarrow}_b$ is a congruence for $\tau_i \circ f$ in P'', it must be a congruence for f in P. □

Lemma 3. *Given a complete, abstraction-free TSS in rooted branching bisimulation format, with respect to some $\aleph$ and Λ. If $\sigma(x) \underline{\leftrightarrow}_{rb} \sigma'(x)$ for $x \in var(t)$, then $\sigma(t) \underline{\leftrightarrow}_{rb} \sigma'(t)$.*

Theorem 4. *Given a complete TSS in rooted branching bisimulation format, with respect to some $\aleph$ and Λ. If $\sigma(x) \underline{\leftrightarrow}_{rb} \sigma'(x)$ for $x \in var(t)$, then $\sigma(t) \underline{\leftrightarrow}_{rb} \sigma'(t)$.*

The proof of Lem. 3 is similar to the one of Lem. 2, except that Prop. 4 is applied instead of Prop. 3. Likewise, the proof of Thm. 4 is similar to the one of Thm. 3.

5   Applications

In this section we present four applications of the rooted branching bisimulation format.

5.1   Basic Process Algebra

Basic process algebra BPA [1] assumes a collection Act of constants, called *atomic actions*, which upon execution terminate successfully. The signature of BPA moreover includes function symbols $\_+\_$ and $\_\cdot\_$ of arity two, called *alternative composition* and *sequential composition*, respectively. Intuitively, $t_1 + t_2$ executes either t_1 or t_2, while $t_1 \cdot t_2$ first executes t_1 and upon successful termination executes t_2. We assume a special atomic action $tick \in Act$, indicating the activity of successful termination upon executing the internal action τ, and a special constant *deadlock* δ, outside Act, which does not display any behaviour. These intuitions are made precise by means of the transition rules for BPA_δ^{tick} presented below. In these rules, ℓ ranges over Act, and α over $A = \{\ell, \ell_\sqrt{} \mid \ell \in Act\}$. The label $\ell_\sqrt{}$ denotes that upon execution of ℓ, the process terminates successfully.

$$\ell \xrightarrow{\ell_\sqrt{}} \delta \qquad \frac{x_1 \xrightarrow{\alpha} y}{x_1 + x_2 \xrightarrow{\alpha} y} \qquad \frac{x_2 \xrightarrow{\alpha} y}{x_1 + x_2 \xrightarrow{\alpha} y}$$

$$\frac{x_1 \xrightarrow{\ell} y}{x_1 \cdot x_2 \xrightarrow{\ell} y \cdot x_2} \qquad \frac{x_1 \xrightarrow{\ell_\sqrt{}} y}{x_1 \cdot x_2 \xrightarrow{\ell} x_2}$$

The label *tick* counts as internal action, and for this reason the labels *tick* and $tick_{\sqrt{}}$ can also be written τ and $\tau_{\sqrt{}}$, respectively. The label $\tau_{\sqrt{}}$ denotes termination and counts as a normal observable action. When this action occurs in the first component of a sequential composition, it changes into the internal action τ, so that this TSS is not abstraction-free. We do not have $a \underline{\leftrightarrow}_{rb} a \cdot tick$, as the former process performs one visible action and the latter two. For this reason we call the constant *tick* *tick*, rather than τ.

The TSS above is in rooted branching bisimulation format, if we take the arguments of alternative composition to be Λ-frozen, the first argument of sequential composition to be $\aleph$-liquid, and the second argument of sequential composition to be $\aleph$-frozen. For the sake of the application to the action refinement operator, in Sect. 5.4, we take the second argument of sequential composition to be Λ-liquid.

Corollary 1. *Rooted branching bisimulation is a congruence for* BPA_δ^{tick}.

5.2   Binary Kleene Star

The *binary Kleene star* $t_1{}^*t_2$ [18] repeatedly executes t_1 until it executes t_2. This operational behaviour is captured by the following rules, which are added to the rules for BPA_δ^{tick}.

$$\frac{x_1 \xrightarrow{\ell} y}{x_1{}^*x_2 \xrightarrow{\ell} y \cdot (x_1{}^*x_2)} \qquad \frac{x_1 \xrightarrow{\ell_{\sqrt{}}} y}{x_1{}^*x_2 \xrightarrow{\ell} x_1{}^*x_2} \qquad \frac{x_2 \xrightarrow{\alpha} y}{x_1{}^*x_2 \xrightarrow{\alpha} y}$$

The resulting TSS is in rooted branching bisimulation format, if we take the arguments of the binary Kleene star to be Λ-frozen.

Corollary 2. *Rooted branching bisimulation is a congruence for* BPA_δ^{tick} *with the binary Kleene star.*

5.3   Initial Priority

Initial priority is a unary function symbol that assumes an ordering on labels (which is usually defined on the level of atomic actions). The term $\theta(t)$ executes the transitions of t, with the restriction that an initial transition $t \xrightarrow{\alpha} t_1$ only gives rise to an initial transition $\theta(t) \xrightarrow{\alpha} t_1$ if there does not exist an initial transition $t \xrightarrow{\beta} t_2$ with $\alpha < \beta$. This intuition is captured by the rule for the initial priority operator below, which is added to the rules for BPA_δ^{tick}.

$$\frac{x \xrightarrow{\alpha} y \quad x \xrightarrow{\beta}\!\!\!\!\!/ \ \ \text{for } \alpha < \beta}{\theta(x) \xrightarrow{\alpha} y}$$

The resulting TSS is in rooted branching bisimulation format, if we take the argument of initial priority to be Λ-frozen.

Corollary 3. *Rooted branching bisimulation is a congruence for* BPA_δ^{tick} *with initial priority.*

5.4   Action Refinement

In the previous applications, it sufficed to take $\Lambda = \aleph$. In the following example, however, this is not possible.

The binary *action refinement* operator $t_1[\ell \leadsto t_2]$, for $\ell \in Act\backslash\{tick\}$, replaces each ℓ-transition in t_1 by t_2. Its transition rules, presented below, are added to the rules for BPA_δ^{tick}.

$$\frac{x_1 \xrightarrow{\alpha} y}{x_1[\ell \leadsto x_2] \xrightarrow{\alpha} y[\ell \leadsto x_2]} \quad (\alpha \neq \ell, \ell_{\sqrt{}})$$

$$\frac{x_1 \xrightarrow{\ell} y_1 \quad x_2 \xrightarrow{\ell'} y_2}{x_1[\ell \leadsto x_2] \xrightarrow{\ell'} y_2 \cdot (y_1[\ell \leadsto x_2])} \qquad \frac{x_1 \xrightarrow{\ell_{\sqrt{}}} y_1 \quad x_2 \xrightarrow{\ell'} y_2}{x_1[\ell \leadsto x_2] \xrightarrow{\ell'} y_2}$$

$$\frac{x_1 \xrightarrow{\ell} y_1 \quad x_2 \xrightarrow{\ell'_{\sqrt{}}} y_2}{x_1[\ell \leadsto x_2] \xrightarrow{\ell'} y_1[\ell \leadsto x_2]} \qquad \frac{x_1 \xrightarrow{\ell_{\sqrt{}}} y_1 \quad x_2 \xrightarrow{\ell'_{\sqrt{}}} y_2}{x_1[\ell \leadsto x_2] \xrightarrow{\ell'_{\sqrt{}}} y_2}$$

The resulting TSS is in rooted branching bisimulation format, if we take the first argument of action refinement to be $\aleph$-liquid and the second argument to be Λ-frozen. For the second rule to be rooted branching bisimulation safe, it is essential that the second argument of sequential composition is Λ-liquid, for else it would violate restriction 2 of Def. 15.

Corollary 4. *Rooted branching bisimulation is a congruence for BPA_δ^{tick} with action refinement.*

6   Counterexamples

This section presents a series of counterexamples of complete TSSs in ntyft/ntyxt format, to show that none of the syntactic restrictions of our congruence formats can be omitted. (Of course it remains possible that certain restrictions can be refined.) In [16] a series of counterexamples can be found showing that the syntactic restrictions of the ntyft/ntyxt format are essential as well. Furthermore, in [5] a counterexample is given to show that completeness (there called positive after reduction) is essential.

It is well-known that branching bisimulation is not a congruence for BPA_δ^{tick}. For instance, $a \leftrightarrow_b tick\cdot a$, but $a + c \not\leftrightarrow_b (tick\cdot a) + c$. Still we saw in Sect. 5.1 that the TSS for this process algebra is in rooted branching bisimulation format. This shows that universality of the predicate Λ cannot be omitted from the branching bisimulation format.

The examples in this section assume an action set $A = \{a, b, c\}$ and a TSS $P = \{\Sigma, R\}$, where the signature Σ contains the constant 0 and unary function symbols α_- for $\alpha \in A \cup \{\tau\}$, and R contains the rules $\alpha x \xrightarrow{\alpha} x$ for $\alpha \in A \cup \{\tau\}$. The argument of α_- is $\aleph$-frozen. Unlike before, in this section occurrences of

a, b, c as labels in rules are explicit action names, instead of parameters ranging over A.

Example 2. We extend P with the following rule:

$$\frac{x \xrightarrow{a} y \quad y \xrightarrow{b} z}{f(x) \xrightarrow{c} 0}$$

The rule above is not rooted branching bisimulation safe, because it contains lookahead, violating restriction 1 (of Def. 15). Clearly, $ab0 \leftrightarrow_{rb} a\tau b0$ (and thus $ab0 \leftrightarrow_b a\tau b0$). However, $f(ab0) \not\leftrightarrow_b f(a\tau b0)$ (and thus $f(ab0) \not\leftrightarrow_{rb} f(a\tau b0)$), since $f(ab0) \xrightarrow{c} 0$, while $f(a\tau b0) \not\xrightarrow{\alpha}$ for $\alpha \in \{c, \tau\}$.

Example 3. We extend P with the following rule:

$$\frac{x \xrightarrow{a} y}{f(x) \xrightarrow{a} f(y)}$$

The argument of f must be $\aleph$-frozen, in view of the restriction in Def. 16 that for each $\aleph$-liquid argument there is an $\aleph$-patience rule. The rule above is not rooted branching bisimulation safe. Namely, if the argument of f is Λ-frozen, then y occurs both as the right-hand side of a premise and Λ-frozen in the right-hand side of the conclusion, violating restriction 2. And if the argument of f is Λ-liquid, then x occurs Λ-liquid and $\aleph$-frozen in the source and $\aleph$-liquid in the left-hand side of the premise, violating restriction 3(d). We have $f(aa0) \not\leftrightarrow_b f(a\tau a0)$, since $f(aa0) \xrightarrow{a} f(a0) \xrightarrow{a} f(0)$, while $f(a\tau a0)$ can only do an a-transition to $f(\tau a0)$, and $f(\tau a0) \not\xrightarrow{\alpha}$ for $\alpha \in \{a, \tau\}$.

Example 4. We extend P with the following rules:

$$\frac{x \xrightarrow{\tau} y}{f(x) \xrightarrow{\tau} f(y)} \qquad \frac{x \xrightarrow{a} y}{f(x) \xrightarrow{a} f(y)} \qquad \frac{x \not\xrightarrow{a}}{f(x) \xrightarrow{c} 0}$$

The argument of f has to be Λ-liquid, for else the first and second rule would violate restriction 2. It even has to be $\aleph$-liquid, for otherwise these rules would violate requirement 3(d). However, with the argument of f $\aleph$-liquid, the third rule is not rooted branching bisimulation safe, because x occurs $\aleph$-liquid both in the source and in the left-hand side of the negative premise, violating restriction 3(b). We have $f(aa0) \not\leftrightarrow_b f(a\tau a0)$, since $f(a\tau a0) \xrightarrow{a} f(\tau a0) \xrightarrow{c} 0$, while $f(aa0)$ can only do an a-transition to $f(a0)$, and $f(a0) \not\xrightarrow{\alpha}$ for $\alpha \in \{c, \tau\}$.

Example 5. We extend P with the following rules:

$$\frac{x \xrightarrow{\tau} y}{f(x) \xrightarrow{\tau} f(y)} \qquad \frac{x \xrightarrow{a} y}{f(x) \xrightarrow{a} f(y)} \qquad \frac{x \xrightarrow{\tau} y}{f(x) \xrightarrow{c} 0}$$

As in the previous example, the argument of f has to be $\aleph$-liquid. The third rule is not rooted branching bisimulation safe, because x occurs $\aleph$-liquid both in the source and in the left-hand side of the positive premise with label τ, violating restriction 3(c). We have $f(aa0) \not\leftrightarrow_b f(a\tau a0)$, since $f(a\tau a0) \xrightarrow{a} f(\tau a0) \xrightarrow{c} 0$, while $f(aa0)$ can only do an a-transition to $f(a0)$, and $f(a0) \not\xrightarrow{\alpha}$ for $\alpha \in \{c, \tau\}$.

Example 6. We extend P with the following rules:

$$\eta \xrightarrow{a} 0 \qquad \zeta \xrightarrow{b} 0 \qquad \eta \xrightarrow{\tau} \zeta \qquad \zeta \xrightarrow{\tau} \eta \qquad \nu \xrightarrow{a} 0 \qquad \nu \xrightarrow{b} 0$$

$$\frac{x \xrightarrow{\tau} y}{f(x) \xrightarrow{\tau} f(y)} \qquad \frac{x \xrightarrow{a} y \quad x \xrightarrow{b} z}{f(x) \xrightarrow{c} 0}$$

Again, the argument of f is $\aleph$-liquid. The last rule is not rooted branching bisimulation safe, because x has an $\aleph$-liquid occurrence in the source, and two $\aleph$-liquid occurrences in the left-hand sides of the premises, violating restriction 3(c). Clearly, $\tau\nu \leftrightarrow_{rb} \tau\eta$. However, $f(\tau\nu) \not\leftrightarrow_b f(\tau\eta)$, since $f(\tau\nu) \xrightarrow{\tau} f(\nu) \xrightarrow{c} 0$, while $f(\tau\eta)$ only exhibits an infinite sequence of τ-transitions: $f(\tau\eta) \xrightarrow{\tau} f(\eta) \xrightarrow{\tau} f(\zeta) \xrightarrow{\tau} f(\eta) \xrightarrow{\tau} \cdots$.

Example 7. In the TSS from Example 6, we replace the last rule with the following rules:

$$f(x) \xrightarrow{\tau} g(x) \qquad \frac{x \xrightarrow{a} y \quad x \xrightarrow{b} z}{g(x) \xrightarrow{c} 0}$$

The argument of f is again $\aleph$-liquid, and the argument of g must be Λ-frozen, as otherwise the second rule would violate restriction 3(c). The first rule above is not rooted branching bisimulation safe, because x occurs $\aleph$-liquid (hence Λ-liquid) in the source and Λ-frozen in the right-hand side of the conclusion, violating restriction 3(a). We have $f(\tau\nu) \not\leftrightarrow_b f(\tau\eta)$, since $f(\tau\nu) \xrightarrow{\tau} f(\nu) \xrightarrow{\tau} g(\nu) \xrightarrow{c} 0$, while $f(\tau\eta)$ can only perform τ-transitions.

Example 8. In the TSS from Example 6, we replace the last rule with the following rules:

$$\frac{x \xrightarrow{a} y \quad x \xrightarrow{b} z}{g(x) \xrightarrow{c} 0} \qquad \frac{g(x) \xrightarrow{c} y}{f(x) \xrightarrow{c} 0}$$

As in the previous example, the argument of f must be $\aleph$-liquid, and the argument of g Λ-frozen. The last rule above is not rooted branching bisimulation safe, because x occurs $\aleph$-liquid in the source and Λ-frozen in the left-hand side of the premise, violating restriction 3(a). We have $f(\tau\nu) \not\leftrightarrow_b f(\tau\eta)$, since $f(\tau\nu) \xrightarrow{\tau} f(\nu) \xrightarrow{c} 0$, while $f(\tau\eta)$ can only perform τ-transitions.

7   Related Work

The first congruence formats for branching and rooted branching bisimulation were presented in [2], and reformulated in [13]. Those formats, which are contained in the GSOS format [4], distinguish so-called "principal" operators and "abbreviations". The latter can be regarded as syntactic sugar, adding nothing that could not be expressed with principal operators. Our formats are incomparable with the ones of [2,13]. However, our formats generalise the result of simplifying the formats of [2,13] by requiring all operators to be principal.

For the branching bisimulation format our generalisation consists of allowing transition rules outside the GSOS format; the simplified format of [2,13] is exactly the intersection of our branching bisimulation format and the GSOS format. However, the intersection of our rooted branching bisimulation format and the GSOS format is still a proper generalisation of the simplified format for rooted branching bisimulation of [2,13]. The latter can be described as the intersection of our rooted branching bisimulation format and the GSOS format in which all arguments of all operators that occur in right-hand sides of conclusions of transition rules are required to be Λ-liquid.

The format of [2,13] for rooted branching bisimulation distinguishes "tame" and "wild" function symbols. In terms of our approach, wild operators have only Λ-frozen arguments, and tame operators only Λ-liquid arguments. The idea to allow operators with both kinds of arguments stems from [7].

In [7] a format for rooted branching bisimulation was proposed that generalises the simplified format of [2,13]. Given that it applies to TSSs with predicates, it is incomparable with our current rooted branching bisimulation format. However, predicates can easily be encoded in terms of transitions, and when disregarding predicates, our current format is more general than the format of [7]. Still, the format of [7] strictly contains the intersection of our format with the GSOS format, and all applications of our work discussed in Sect. 5 fall within that intersection.

In [10] we apply the techniques of the current paper to derive congruence formats for η- and rooted η-bisimulation. These formats differ from the ones of the current paper only in restriction 2 of Def. 15. There it is required that right-hand sides of premises occur only $\aleph$-liquid in u, whereas here we merely require Λ-liquidity. That the rooted branching bisimulation format is essentially more general than the rooted η-bisimulation format is illustrated by the action refinement example of Sec. 5.4. BPA_δ^{tick} with action refinement falls outside the rooted η-bisimulation format, due to the fact that the second argument of sequential composition needs to be $\aleph$-liquid in order for the second action refinement rule to be rooted η-bisimulation safe. Indeed, this operator fails to be compositional for rooted η-bisimulation [14].

References

1. J.A. BERGSTRA & J.W. KLOP (1984): *Process algebra for synchronous communication. Information and Control* 60(1/3), pp. 109–137.
2. B. BLOOM (1995): *Structural operational semantics for weak bisimulations. Theoretical Computer Science* 146(1/2), pp. 25–68.
3. B. BLOOM, W.J. FOKKINK & R.J. VAN GLABBEEK (2004): *Precongruence formats for decorated trace semantics. ACM Transactions on Computational Logic* 5(1), pp. 26–78.

4. B. BLOOM, S. ISTRAIL & A.R. MEYER (1995): *Bisimulation can't be traced.* Journal of the ACM 42(1), pp. 232–268.
5. R.N. BOL & J.F. GROOTE (1996): *The meaning of negative premises in transition system specifications.* Journal of the ACM 43(5), pp. 863–914.
6. R. DE NICOLA & F.W. VAANDRAGER (1995): *Three logics for branching bisimulation.* Journal of the ACM 42(2), pp. 458–487.
7. W.J. FOKKINK (2000): *Rooted branching bisimulation as a congruence.* Journal of Computer and System Sciences 60(1), pp. 13–37.
8. W.J. FOKKINK & R.J. VAN GLABBEEK (1996): *Ntyft/ntyxt rules reduce to ntree rules.* Information and Computation 126(1), pp. 1–10.
9. W.J. FOKKINK, R.J. VAN GLABBEEK & P. DE WIND (2006): *Compositionality of Hennessy-Milner logic by structural operational semantics.* Theoretical Computer Science 354(3), pp. 421–440.
10. W.J. FOKKINK, R.J. VAN GLABBEEK & P. DE WIND (2005): *Divide and congruence applied to η-bisimulation.* In Proc. SOS'05, To appear, ENTCS. Elsevier.
11. R.J. VAN GLABBEEK (1993): *The linear time-branching time spectrum II: The semantics of sequential systems with silent moves.* In Proc. CONCUR'93, LNCS 715, pp. 66–81. Springer.
12. R.J. VAN GLABBEEK (2004): *The meaning of negative premises in transition system specifications II.* Journal of Logic and Algebraic Programming 60/61, pp. 229–258.
13. R.J. VAN GLABBEEK (2005): *On cool congruence formats for weak bisimulations (extended abstract).* In Proc. ICTAC'05, LNCS 3722, pp. 331–346. Springer.
14. R.J. VAN GLABBEEK & W.P. WEIJLAND (1996): *Branching time and abstraction in bisimulation semantics.* Journal of the ACM 43(3), pp. 555–600.
15. J.F. GROOTE (1993): *Transition system specifications with negative premises.* Theoretical Computer Science 118(2), pp. 263–299.
16. J.F. GROOTE & F.W. VAANDRAGER (1992): *Structured operational semantics and bisimulation as a congruence.* Information and Computation 100(2), pp. 202–260.
17. M.C.B. HENNESSY & R. MILNER (1985): *Algebraic laws for non-determinism and concurrency.* Journal of the ACM 32(1), pp. 137–161.
18. S.C. KLEENE: *Representation of events in nerve nets and finite automata.* In (C. Shannon and J. McCarthy, eds.) *Automata Studies*, pp. 3–41. Princeton University Press, 1956.
19. K.G. LARSEN & X. LIU (1991): *Compositionality through an operational semantics of contexts.* Journal of Logic and Computation 1(6), pp. 761–795.
20. G.D. PLOTKIN (2004): *A structural approach to operational semantics.* Journal of Logic and Algebraic Programming 60/61, pp. 17–139. Originally appeared in 1981.
21. R. DE SIMONE (1985): *Higher-level synchronising devices in* MEIJE–SCCS. Theoretical Computer Science 37(3), pp. 245–267.

A   Modal Characterisation of Branching Bisimulation

We prove the first part of Thm. 1, which states that $\mathbb{O}_b$ is a modal characterisation of branching bisimulation equivalence. The proof is based on [6]. We need to prove, given an LTS $(\mathbb{P}, \to)$, that $p \leftrightarrow_b q \Leftrightarrow p \sim_{\mathbb{O}_b} q$ for all $p, q \in \mathbb{P}$.

Proof. ($\Rightarrow$) Suppose $p \leftrightarrow_b q$, and $p \models \varphi$ for some $\varphi \in \mathbb{O}_b$. We prove $q \models \varphi$, by structural induction on φ. The reverse implication ($q \models \varphi$ implies $p \models \varphi$) follows by symmetry.

- $\varphi = \bigwedge_{i \in I} \varphi_i$. Then $p \models \varphi_i$ for $i \in I$. By induction $q \models \varphi_i$ for $i \in I$, so $q \models \bigwedge_{i \in I} \varphi_i$.
- $\varphi = \neg\varphi'$. Then $p \not\models \varphi'$. By induction $q \not\models \varphi'$, so $q \models \neg\varphi'$.
- $\varphi = \langle\epsilon\rangle(\varphi_1\langle\hat{\tau}\rangle\varphi_2)$. Then for some n there are $p_0, \ldots, p_n \in \mathbb{P}$ with $p_0 = p$, $p_i \xrightarrow{\tau} p_{i+1}$ for $i \in \{0, \ldots, n-1\}$, and $p_n \models \varphi_1\langle\hat{\tau}\rangle\varphi_2$. We apply induction on n.

  $n = 0$ Then $p \models \varphi_1$, so by induction on formula size, $q \models \varphi_1$. Furthermore, either (1) $p \models \varphi_2$ or (2) there is a $p' \in \mathbb{P}$ with $p \xrightarrow{\tau} p'$ and $p' \models \varphi_2$. In case (1), by induction on formula size, $q \models \varphi_2$, so $q \models \langle\epsilon\rangle(\varphi_1\langle\hat{\tau}\rangle\varphi_2)$. In case (2), since $p \leftrightarrow_b q$, by Def. 1 either (2.1) $p' \leftrightarrow_b q$ or (2.2) $q \xRightarrow{\epsilon} q' \xrightarrow{\tau} q''$ with $p \leftrightarrow_b q'$ and $p' \leftrightarrow_b q''$. In case (2.1), by induction on formula size, $q \models \varphi_2$. In case (2.2), by induction on formula size, $q' \models \varphi_1$ and $q'' \models \varphi_2$. In both cases, $q \models \langle\epsilon\rangle(\varphi_1\langle\hat{\tau}\rangle\varphi_2)$.

  $n > 0$ Since $p \xrightarrow{\tau} p_1$, and $p \leftrightarrow_b q$, according to Def. 1 there are two possibilities.

  1. Either $p_1 \leftrightarrow_b q$. Since $p_1 \models \langle\epsilon\rangle(\varphi_1\langle\hat{\tau}\rangle\varphi_2)$, by induction on n, $q \models \langle\epsilon\rangle(\varphi_1\langle\hat{\tau}\rangle\varphi_2)$.
  2. Or $q \xRightarrow{\epsilon} q' \xrightarrow{\tau} q''$ with $p_1 \leftrightarrow_b q''$. Since $p_1 \models \langle\epsilon\rangle(\varphi_1\langle\hat{\tau}\rangle\varphi_2)$, by induction on n, $q'' \models \langle\epsilon\rangle(\varphi_1\langle\hat{\tau}\rangle\varphi_2)$. Hence $q \models \langle\epsilon\rangle(\varphi_1\langle\hat{\tau}\rangle\varphi_2)$.

- $\varphi = \langle\epsilon\rangle(\varphi_1\langle a\rangle\varphi_2)$. Then for some n there are $p_0, \ldots, p_n \in \mathbb{P}$ with $p_0 = p$, $p_i \xrightarrow{\tau} p_{i+1}$ for $i \in \{0, \ldots, n-1\}$, and $p_n \models \varphi_1\langle a\rangle\varphi_2$. We apply induction on n.

  $n = 0$ Then $p \models \varphi_1$, and there is a $p' \in \mathbb{P}$ with $p \xrightarrow{a} p'$ and $p' \models \varphi_2$. Since $p \leftrightarrow_b q$, by Def. 1 $q \xRightarrow{\epsilon} q' \xrightarrow{a} q''$ with $p \leftrightarrow_b q'$ and $p' \leftrightarrow_b q''$. By induction on formula size, $q' \models \varphi_1$ and $q'' \models \varphi_2$. Hence $q \models \langle\epsilon\rangle(\varphi_1\langle a\rangle\varphi_2)$.

  $n > 0$ Since $p \xrightarrow{\tau} p_1$, and $p \leftrightarrow_b q$, according to Def. 1 there are two possibilities.

  1. Either $p_1 \leftrightarrow_b q$. Since $p_1 \models \langle\epsilon\rangle(\varphi_1\langle a\rangle\varphi_2)$, by induction on n, $q \models \langle\epsilon\rangle(\varphi_1\langle a\rangle\varphi_2)$.
  2. Or $q \xRightarrow{\epsilon} q' \xrightarrow{\tau} q''$ with $p_1 \leftrightarrow_b q''$. Since $p_1 \models \langle\epsilon\rangle(\varphi_1\langle a\rangle\varphi_2)$, by induction on n, $q'' \models \langle\epsilon\rangle(\varphi_1\langle a\rangle\varphi_2)$. Hence $q \models \langle\epsilon\rangle(\varphi_1\langle a\rangle\varphi_2)$.

We conclude that $p \sim_{\mathbb{O}_b} q$.

($\Leftarrow$) We prove that $\sim_{\mathbb{O}_b}$ is a branching bisimulation relation. The relation is clearly symmetric. Let $p \sim_{\mathbb{O}_b} q$. Suppose $p \xrightarrow{\alpha} p'$. If $\alpha = \tau$ and $p' \sim_{\mathbb{O}_b} q$, then the first condition of Def. 1 is fulfilled. So we can assume that either (i) $\alpha \neq \tau$ or (ii) $p' \not\sim_{\mathbb{O}_b} q$. We define two sets:

$$Q' = \{q' \in \mathbb{P} \mid q \xRightarrow{\epsilon} q' \wedge p \not\sim_{\mathbb{O}_b} q'\}$$
$$Q'' = \{q'' \in \mathbb{P} \mid \exists q' \in \mathbb{P} : q \xRightarrow{\epsilon} q' \xrightarrow{\alpha} q'' \wedge p' \not\sim_{\mathbb{O}_b} q''\}$$

For each $q' \in Q'$, let $\varphi_{q'}$ be a formula in $\mathbb{O}_b$ such that $p \models \varphi_{q'}$ and $q' \not\models \varphi_{q'}$. (Such a formula always exists because $\mathbb{O}_b$ is closed under negation $\neg$.) We define

$$\varphi = \bigwedge_{q' \in Q'} \varphi_{q'}$$

Similarly, for each $q'' \in Q''$, let $\psi_{q''}$ be a formula in $\mathbb{O}_b$ such that $p' \models \psi_{q''}$ and $q'' \not\models \psi_{q''}$. We define

$$\psi = \bigwedge_{q'' \in Q''} \psi_{q''}$$

Clearly, $\varphi, \psi \in \mathbb{O}_b$, $p \models \varphi$ and $p' \models \psi$. We distinguish two cases.

1. $\alpha \neq \tau$. Since $p \models \langle \epsilon \rangle(\varphi\langle\alpha\rangle\psi) \in \mathbb{O}_b$ and $p \sim_{\mathbb{O}_b} q$, also $q \models \langle\epsilon\rangle(\varphi\langle\alpha\rangle\psi)$. Hence $q \overset{\epsilon}{\Longrightarrow} q' \overset{\alpha}{\longrightarrow} q''$ with $q' \models \varphi$ and $q'' \models \psi$. By the definition of φ and ψ it follows that $p \sim_{\mathbb{O}_b} q'$ and $p' \sim_{\mathbb{O}_b} q''$.

2. $\alpha = \tau$ and $p' \not\sim_{\mathbb{O}_b} q$. Let $\tilde{\varphi} \in \mathbb{O}_b$ such that $p' \models \tilde{\varphi}$ and $p, q \not\models \tilde{\varphi}$. Since $p \models \langle\epsilon\rangle(\varphi\langle\hat{\tau}\rangle(\tilde{\varphi} \wedge \psi)) \in \mathbb{O}_b$ and $p \sim_{\mathbb{O}_b} q$, also $q \models \langle\epsilon\rangle(\varphi\langle\hat{\tau}\rangle(\tilde{\varphi} \wedge \psi))$. So $q \overset{\epsilon}{\Longrightarrow} q'$ with $q' \models \varphi\langle\hat{\tau}\rangle(\tilde{\varphi} \wedge \psi)$. By definition of φ it follows that $p \sim_{\mathbb{O}_b} q'$. Thus $q' \not\models \tilde{\varphi}$, so $q' \overset{\tau}{\longrightarrow} q''$ with $q'' \models \tilde{\varphi} \wedge \psi$. By the definition of ψ it follows that $p' \sim_{\mathbb{O}_b} q''$.

Both cases imply that the second condition of Def. 1 is fulfilled. We therefore conclude that $\sim_{\mathbb{O}_b}$ is a branching bisimulation relation. □

Using the first part of Thm. 1, which was proved above, it is not hard to derive the second part of Thm. 1, i.e. that $\mathbb{O}_{rb}$ is a modal characterisation of rooted branching bisimulation equivalence.

Abstraction and Refinement in Model Checking

Orna Grumberg

Computer Science Department
Technion
Haifa 32000, Israel

1 Introduction

In this paper we survey abstraction and refinement in model checking. We restrict the discussion to existential abstraction which over-approximates the behaviors of the concrete model. The logics preserved under this abstraction are the universal fragments of branching-time temporal logics as well as linear-time temporal logics. For simplicity of presentation, we also restrict the discussion to abstraction functions, rather then abstraction relations. Thus, every concrete state is represented by exactly one abstract state. An abstract state then represents a set of concrete states, which is disjoint from the sets represented by other abstract states.

Abstraction is identified by a set of abstract states $\widehat{S}$, an abstraction mapping h, that associates with each concrete state the abstract state which represents it, and a set of atomic propositions AP which label the concrete and abstract states. We present three types of abstractions which differ in the choice of $\widehat{S}$, h, and AP: predicate abstraction, visible-variable abstraction, and data abstraction. We also suggest how an abstraction can be extracted from a high-level description of a program.

We describe the CounterExample-Guided Abstraction-Refinement (CEGAR) methodology which suggests an iterative, automated approach to verification with abstraction. We comment on different possible implementations for constructing the abstract model and its refinements.

2 Preliminaries

2.1 Temporal Logics

Model checking algorithms typically use finite state transition systems to model the verified systems and propositional temporal logics to specify the desired properties. In this section we present the syntax and semantics of several subsets of the temporal logic CTL* [25].

Let AP be a set of atomic propositions. We define CTL* in *positive normal form*, in which negations are applied only to atomic propositions. This will facilitate the definition of universal and existential subsets of CTL* [29]. Since negations are not allowed, both conjunction and disjunction are required. Negations applied to the *next-time* operator **X** can be "pushed inwards" using the

F.S. de Boer et al. (Eds.): FMCO 2005, LNCS 4111, pp. 219–242, 2006.

logical equivalence $\neg(\mathbf{X}\,f) = \mathbf{X}\,\neg f$. The *unless* operator $\mathbf{V}$ (sometimes called the *release* operator), which is the dual of the *until* operator $\mathbf{U}$, is also added. Thus, $\neg(f\,\mathbf{U}\,g) = \neg f\,\mathbf{V}\,\neg g$.

Definition 1 (CTL*). *For a given set of atomic propositions AP, the logic CTL* is the set of state formulas, defined recursively by means of state formulas and path formulas as follows. State formulas are of the form:*

- *If $p \in AP$, then p and $\neg p$ are state formulas.*
- *If f and g are state formulas, then so are $f \wedge g$ and $f \vee g$.*
- *If f is a path formula, then $\mathbf{A}\,f$ and $\mathbf{E}\,f$ are state formulas.*

Path formulas are of the form:

- *If f is a state formula, then f is a path formula.*
- *If f and g are path formulas, then so are $f \wedge g$, and $f \vee g$.*
- *If f and g are path formulas, then so are $\mathbf{X}\,f$, $f\,\mathbf{U}\,g$, and $f\,\mathbf{V}\,g$.*

The abbreviations true, false and implication $\rightarrow$ are defined as usual. For path formula f, the following abbreviations are widely used. $\mathbf{F}\,f \equiv true\,\mathbf{U}\,f$ express the properties that sometimes in the future f holds. $\mathbf{G}\,f \equiv false\,\mathbf{V}\,f$ express the properties that f holds globally.

CTL [14] is a branching-time subset of CTL* in which every temporal operator is immediately preceded by a path quantifier. Thus, nesting of temporal operators with no path quantifier in between is not allowed. Formally, CTL (in positive normal form) is the set of state formulas defined by:

- If $p \in AP$, then p and $\neg p$ are CTL formulas.
- If f and g are CTL formulas, then so are $f \wedge g$ and $f \vee g$.
- If f and g are CTL formulas, then so are $\mathbf{AX}\,f$, $\mathbf{A}(f\,\mathbf{U}\,g)$, $\mathbf{A}(f\,\mathbf{V}\,g)$ and $\mathbf{EX}\,f$, $\mathbf{E}(f\,\mathbf{U}\,g)$, $\mathbf{E}(f\,\mathbf{V}\,g)$.

ACTL* is the *universal* subset of CTL* in which only $\mathbf{A}$ path quantifiers are allowed. Similarly, ECTL* is the *existential* subset of CTL*in which only $\mathbf{E}$ path quantifiers are allowed. ACTL and ECTL are the restriction of ACTL* and ECTL* to CTL.

LTL [49] can be defined as the subset of ACTL* consisting of formulas of the form $\mathbf{A}\,f$, where f is a path formula in which the only state subformulas permitted are Boolean combinations of atomic propositions. More precisely, f is defined (in positive normal form) by

1. If $p \in AP$ then p and $\neg p$ are path formulas.
2. If f_1 and f_2 are path formulas, then $f_1 \wedge f_2$, $f_1 \vee f_2$, $\mathbf{X}\,f_1$, $f_1\,\mathbf{U}\,f_2$, and $f_1\,\mathbf{V}\,f_2$ are path formulas.

We will refer to such f as an LTL *path formula*.

The semantics of CTL* is defined with respect to a finite state transition system called *Kripke structure*.

Definition 2 (Kripke structure). *Let AP be a set of atomic propositions. A Kripke structure M over AP is a four-tuple $M = (S, S_0, R, L)$, where*

- *S is a (finite) set of states;*
- *$S_0 \subseteq S$ is the set of initial states;*
- *$R \subseteq S \times S$ is the transition relation, which must be* total, *i.e., for every state $s \in S$ there is a state $s' \in S$ such that $R(s, s')$;*
- *$L : S \to \mathcal{P}(AP)$ is a function that labels each state with the set of atomic propositions true in that state.*

A *path* in M starting from a state s is an infinite sequence of states $\pi = s_0 s_1 s_2 \ldots$ such that $s_0 = s$, and for every $i \geq 0$, $R(s_i, s_{i+1})$. The suffix of π from state s_i is denoted π^i. The requirement that R is total simplifies the semantics of temporal logics over a Kripke structure since all paths are infinite. Several different semantics over finite paths can be found in [24].

We now consider the semantics of the logic CTL* with respect to a Kripke structure.

Definition 3 (Satisfaction of a formula). *Given a Kripke structure M, satisfaction of a state formula f by a model M at a state s, denoted $M, s \models f$, and of a path formula g by a path π, denoted $M, \pi \models g$, is defined as follows (where M is omitted when clear from the context).*

1. *$s \models p$ if and only if $p \in L(s)$; $s \models \neg p$ if and only if $p \notin L(s)$.*
2. *$s \models f \wedge g$ if and only if $s \models f$ and $s \models g$.*
   $s \models f \vee g$ if and only if $s \models f$ or $s \models g$.
3. *$s \models \mathbf{A} f$ if and only if for every path π from s, $\pi \models f$.*
   $s \models \mathbf{E} f$ if and only if there exists a path π from s such that $\pi \models f$.
4. *$\pi \models f$, where f is a state formula, if and only if the first state of π satisfies f.*
5. *$\pi \models f \wedge g$ if and only if $\pi \models f$ and $\pi \models g$.*
   $\pi \models f \vee g$ if and only if $\pi \models f$ or $\pi \models g$.
6. *(a) $\pi \models \mathbf{X} f$ if and only if $\pi^1 \models f$.*
   (b) $\pi \models f \mathbf{U} g$ if and only if for some $n \geq 0$, $\pi^n \models g$ and for all $i < n$, $\pi^i \models f$.
   (c) $\pi \models f \mathbf{V} g$ if and only if for all $n \geq 0$, if (for all $i < n$, $\pi^i \not\models f$) then $\pi^n \models g$.

$M \models f$ *if and only if for every $s \in S_0$, $M, s \models f$.*

In [25] it has been shown that CTL and LTL are incomparable in their expressive power, and that CTL* is more expressive than either of them.

2.2   Model Checking

Given a Kripke structure $M = (S, R, S_0, L)$ and a specification φ in a temporal logic such as CTL, the *model checking problem* is the problem of finding all states s such that $M, s \models \varphi$ and checking whether the initial states are included in those states.

When M does not satisfy φ, model checking can provide a *counterexample* which demonstrates why the specification does not hold in the model. Counterexamples are very helpful for debugging. However, most model checking tools provide them only in limited cases. Common counterexamples have the form of either a finite path or a "lasso", which is a finite path followed by a simple cycle. The former is suitable for demonstrating why a specification of the form **AG** p fails to hold. It provides a finite path to a state satisfying $\neg p$. The latter is suitable to demonstrate why **AF** p fails. It shows an infinite path in a "lasso" shape along which all states satisfy $\neg p$. For general specifications, a tree or even a general graph is needed. Counterexamples for ACTL formulas are defined in [19] and for full CTL in [53].

Model checking has been successfully applied in hardware verification, and is emerging as an industrial standard tool for hardware design . A partial list of tools for hardware verification includes SMV [41] and NuSMV [12], FormalCheck [31], RuleBase [2], and Forecast [26]. Recently, several tools for model checking of software have been developed as well and applied to non-trivial examples. A partial list consists of SPIN [34], Bandera [21], Java PathFinder [32], SLAM, Bebop, and Zing [1], Blast [3], Magic [9], and CBMC [16]. An extensive overview of model checking algorithms can be found in [13].

The main technical challenge in model checking is the *state explosion* problem which occurs if the system is a composition of several components or if the system variables range over large domains.

An explicit state model checker is a program which performs model checking directly on a Kripke structure. SPIN [33] is an example of a successful tool of that kind. Large models are often handled implicitly. Two widely used approaches are the BDD-based [8,42] and the SAT-based [4] model checking.

BDD-based model checking: Ordered Binary Decision Diagrams (BDDs) [7] are canonical representations of Boolean functions. They are often concise in their memory requirements. Furthermore, most operations needed for model checking can be defined in terms of Boolean functions and can be implemented efficiently with BDDs.

In BDD-based (also called *symbolic*) model checking, the transition relation of the Kripke structure is represented by a Boolean function, which in turn is represented by a BDD. Sets of states are also represented by Boolean functions. Fixpoint characterizations of temporal operators are applied to the Boolean functions representing the Kripke structure. BDDs are sometimes, but not always, exponentially smaller than explicit representation of the corresponding Boolean functions. In such cases, symbolic verification is successful.

Two operations are central to model checking. Given a set of states Q, *Image computation* computes the set of successors of states in Q:

$$Image(Q) := \{t \mid \exists s[R(s, t) \wedge Q(s)]\}.$$

Preimage computation computes the set of predecessors of states in Q:

$$Preimage(Q) := \{s \mid \exists t[R(s,t) \ \wedge \ Q(t)]\}.$$

Unfortunately, in contrast to pure Boolean operations, these operations are not efficiently computable [42], and their computation is a major bottleneck in symbolic model checking.

SAT-based model checking: Many problems, including some versions of model checking, can very naturally be translated into the *satisfiability* problem of propositional calculus. The satisfiability problem is known to be NP-complete. Nevertheless, modern SAT-solvers, developed in recent years, can handle formulas with several thousands of variables within a few seconds. SAT-solvers such as Grasp [39], Prover [52], Chaff [47], and Berkmin [27], and many others, are based on sophisticated learning techniques and data structures that accelerate the search for a satisfying assignment, if exists.

Below we describe a simple way to exploit satisfiability for bounded model checking of properties of the form $\mathbf{AG}\,p$, where p is a Boolean formula. *Bounded Model Checking* [5,4] accepts a model M, a natural number (a bound) k, and a formula $\mathbf{AG}\,p$ as above. It constructs a propositional formula $f_{M,k}$, describing all computations of M of length k. It also constructs a propositional formula $f_{\varphi,k}$, describing all paths of length k satisfying the property $\varphi = \neg\,\mathbf{AG}\,p = \mathbf{EF}\,\neg p$. Next, it sends $f_{M,k} \wedge f_{\varphi,k}$ to a SAT-solver to check for satisfiability. If the formula is satisfiable then $M \not\models \mathbf{AG}\,p$ and the satisfying assignment corresponds to a computation of M, leading to a state satisfying $\neg p$. This path is a *counterexample* for the checked formula. If $f_{M,k} \wedge f_{\varphi,k}$ is unsatisfiable then no counterexample of length k exists in M. The bound k is then increased and the check is repeated.

The method described above is mainly suitable for refutation. Verification is obtained only if k exceeds the length of the longest path among all shortest paths from an initial state to some state in M. In practice, it is hard to compute this bound and even when known, it is often too large to handle. Full verification with SAT is possible using other methods, such as interpolation [43,40], induction [51], and ALL-SAT [11,44,30]. However, these methods are more limited in their applicability to large systems. Bounded model checking can easily be extended for checking LTL formulas, interpreted over finite paths [5].

Many of the modern hardware verification tools such as NuSMV [12], Rule-Base [2], Forecast & Thunder [26,20], and FormalCheck [31] include both SAT and BDD methods and apply the one that is most successful in each case.

2.3   Equivalences and Preorders

In this section we define relations on Kripke structures that guarantee logic preservation. The relations are *structural*. That is, they are defined by means of states and transitions of the Kripke structures. The structural relations correspond to *logical* relations that guarantee preservation of truth of formulas between related structures. These relations are exploited in many of the approaches to avoiding the state explosion problem in model checking, such as, abstraction, modular model checking, symmetry, and partial-order reductions [13]. Instead of checking the full model of the system, a smaller model with guaranteed logic preservation is checked.

We define two structural relations: The *bisimulation relation* [48] and the *simulation preorder* [45]. Intuitively, two states are bisimilar if they are identically labeled and for every successor of one there is a bisimilar successor of the other. Similarly, one state is smaller than another by the simulation preorder if they are identically labeled and for every successor of the smaller state there is a corresponding successor of the greater one. The simulation preorder differs from bisimulation in that the greater state may have successors with no corresponding successors in the smaller state.

Let AP be a set of atomic propositions and let $M_1 = (S_1, S_{0_1}, R_1, L_1)$ and $M_2 = (S_2, S_{0_2}, R_2, L_2)$ be two structures over AP.

Definition 4. *A relation $B \subseteq S_1 \times S_2$ is a* bisimulation relation *[48] over M_1 and M_2 if the following conditions hold:*

1. *For every $s_1 \in S_{0_1}$ there is $s_2 \in S_{0_2}$ such that $B(s_1, s_2)$. Moreover, for every $s_2 \in S_{0_2}$ there is $s_1 \in S_{0_1}$ such that $B(s_1, s_2)$.*
2. *For every $(s_1, s_2) \in B$,*
   - $L_1(s_1) = L_2(s_2)$ *and*
   - $\forall t_1[\ R_1(s_1, t_1) \longrightarrow \exists t_2[\ R_2(s_2, t_2) \ \wedge \ B(t_1, t_2)\ ]].$
   - $\forall t_2[\ R_2(s_2, t_2) \longrightarrow \exists t_1[\ R_1(s_1, t_1) \ \wedge \ B(t_1, t_2)\ ]].$

We write $s_1 \cong s_2$ for $B(s_1, s_2)$. We say that M_1 and M_2 are *bisimilar* (denoted $M_1 \cong M_2$) if there exists a bisimulation relation B over M_1 and M_2.

Definition 5. *A relation $H \subseteq S_1 \times S_2$ is a* simulation relation *[46] over M_1 and M_2 if the following conditions hold:*

1. *For every $s_1 \in S_{0_1}$ there is $s_2 \in S_{0_2}$ such that $H(s_1, s_2)$.*
2. *For every $(s_1, s_2) \in H$,*
   - $L_1(s_1) = L_2(s_2)$ *and*
   - $\forall t_1[\ R_1(s_1, t_1) \longrightarrow \exists t_2[\ R_2(s_2, t_2) \ \wedge \ H(t_1, t_2)\ ]].$

We write $s_1 \preceq s_2$ for $H(s_1, s_2)$. M_2 *simulates* M_1 (denoted $M_1 \preceq M_2$) if there exists a simulation relation H over M_1 and M_2.

The following theorem relates bisimulation and simulation to the logics they preserve[1].

Theorem 1

- *[6] Let $M_1 \cong M_2$. Then for every CTL^* formula f (with atomic propositions in AP), $M_1 \models f$ if and only if $M_2 \models f$.*
- *[29] Let $M_1 \preceq M_2$. For every $ACTL^*$ formula f with atomic propositions in AP, $M_2 \models f$ implies $M_1 \models f$.*

---

[1] Bisimulation and simulation also preserve the μ-calculus logic [35] and its universal [37] subset, respectively. The discussion of μ-calculus is beyond the scope of this paper.

2.4   Programs and Their Models

We describe a simple syntactic framework to formalize programs. A *program* $\mathcal{P}$ has a finite set of variables $V = \{v_1, \cdots, v_n\}$ (sometimes also denoted as a tuple $\bar{v} = (v_1, \ldots, v_n)$), where each variable v_i has an associated domain D_{v_i}. The set of all possible states for program $\mathcal{P}$ is $D_{v_1} \times \cdots D_{v_n}$ which we denote by D. The value of a variable v in state s is denoted by $s(v)$. *Expressions* are built from variables in V, constants in D_{v_i}, and function symbols in the usual way, e.g. $v_1 + 3$. *Atomic formulas* are constructed from expressions and relation symbols, e.g. $v_1 + 3 < 5$. Similarly, *predicates* are composed of atomic formulas using negation ($\neg$), conjunction ($\wedge$), and disjunction ($\vee$). Thus, predicates are in fact quantifier-free first order formulas. Given a predicate p, Atoms(p) is the set of atomic formulas occurring in it. Let p be a predicate containing variables from V, and $d = (d_1, \ldots, d_n)$ be an element from D. Then we write $d \models p$ when the predicate obtained by replacing each occurrence of the variable v_i in p by the constant d_i evaluates to true.

Predicates are used to identify initial states of the program as well as conditions in program statements such as **if** and **while**.

A specification for a program $\mathcal{P}$ is an ACTL* formula φ whose atomic formulas are predicates over the program variable. Let Atoms(φ) be the set of atomic formulas appearing in the specification φ. Atoms($\mathcal{P}$) is the set of atomic formulas that appear in the definition of initial states or in the conditions in the program.

Each program $\mathcal{P}$ naturally corresponds to a Kripke structure $M = (S, S_0, R, L)$, where $S = D$ is the set of states, $S_0 \subseteq S$ is a set of initial states, $R \subseteq S \times S$ is a transition relation, and L is a labeling function given by $L(d) = \{f \in \text{Atoms}(\mathcal{P}) \mid d \models f\}$. Translating a program into a Kripke structure is straightforward and will not be described here.

3   Abstract Models

In this section we define an abstract model (Kripke structure) based on a given concrete one. The abstract model is guaranteed by construction to be greater than the concrete model by the simulation relation, thus preservation of universal logics is obtained. In practice, however, the concrete model is too large to fit into memory and therefore is never produced. The abstract models are in fact constructed directly from some high-level description of the system.

For simplicity we consider abstractions obtained by collapsing disjoint sets of concrete states (in S) into single abstract states (in $\widehat{S}$). We will not consider here non-disjoint sets, as is done for instance in *Abstract Interpretation* [37,22].

We use a function $h : S \to \widehat{S}$, called the *abstraction mapping*, to map each concrete state to the abstract state that represents it. The abstraction mapping h induces an equivalence relation $\equiv_h$ on the domain S in the following manner: Let s, t be states in S, then

$$s \equiv_h t \text{ iff } h(s) = h(t).$$

Since an abstraction can be represented either by an abstraction mapping h or by an equivalence relation $\equiv_h$, we sometimes switch between these representations. When the context is clear, we often write $\equiv$ instead of $\equiv_h$.

3.1   Existential Abstraction

We define abstract Kripke structures by means of *existential abstraction* [15]. Existential abstraction defines an abstract state to be an initial state if it represents an initial concrete state. Similarly, there is a transition from abstract states $\widehat{s}$ to abstract state $\widehat{s'}$ if there is a transition from a state represented by $\widehat{s}$ to a state represented by $\widehat{s'}$ (see Figure 1). Formally,

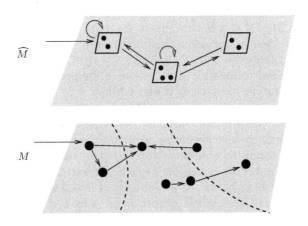

Fig. 1. Existential Abstraction. M is the original Kripke structure, and $\widehat{M}$ the abstracted one. The dotted lines in M indicate how the states of M are clustered into abstract states.

Definition 6. *Let* $M = (S, S_0, R, L)$ *be a (concrete) Kripke structure, let* $\widehat{S}$ *be a set of abstract states and* $h : S \to \widehat{S}$ *be an abstraction mapping. The abstract Kripke structure* $\widehat{M} = (\widehat{S}, \widehat{S_0}, \widehat{R}, \widehat{L})$ *generated by* h *for* M *is defined as follows:*

1. $\widehat{S_0}(\widehat{s})$ *iff* $\exists s\,(h(s) = \widehat{s} \ \wedge\ S_0(s))$.
2. $\widehat{R}(\widehat{s_1}, \widehat{s_2})$ *iff* $\exists s_1 \exists s_2\,(h(s_1) = \widehat{s_1} \ \wedge\ h(s_2) = \widehat{s_2} \ \wedge\ R(s_1, s_2))$.
3. $\widehat{L}(\widehat{s}) = \bigcap_{h(s)=\widehat{s}} L(s)$.

Having 'iff' in items 1 and 2 of the definition above results in the *exact* abstract model of M, with respect to h. Replacing 'iff' by 'if' results in a model with more initial states and more transitions, which still over-approximates the structure M. Such a model is sometimes easier to construct. The results below hold for any abstract Kripke structure constructed by existential abstraction, not only for the exact one.

Note that, $\widehat{s}$ is labeled by an atomic proposition if and only if all the states it represents are labeled by that proposition. We would like the abstract model to satisfy as many atomic propositions as possible. In order to achieve this, we introduce a condition on the abstraction mapping, guaranteeing that all concrete states in an equivalence class of $\equiv_h$ share the same labels.

An abstraction mapping h is *appropriate* for a specification φ if for all atomic formulas $f \in Atoms(\varphi)$, and for all states s and t in S such that $s \equiv_h t$ it holds that $s \models f \Leftrightarrow t \models f$.

Let M and φ be defined over AP and let h be appropriate for φ, then $s \equiv_h t$ implies $L(s) = L(t)$. Moreover, $h(s) = \widehat{s}$ implies $\widehat{L}(\widehat{s}) = L(s)$.

The following theorem shows that for ACTL*, specifications which are correct for $\widehat{M}$ are correct for M as well.

Theorem 2. *Let M be a Kripke structure and φ be an ACTL* formula, both defined over AP. Further, let h be appropriate for φ. Then $M \preceq \widehat{M}$. Consequently, $\widehat{M} \models \varphi$ implies $M \models \varphi$.*

Note that once $\widehat{S}$, h, and AP are given, $\widehat{S_0}$, $\widehat{R}$, and $\widehat{L}$ are uniquely determined. Thus, $\widehat{S}$, h, and AP uniquely determine $\widehat{M}$. Since h implicitly includes the information about $\widehat{S}$ and AP, we sometimes refer to h for identifying $\widehat{M}$. In the next subsections we will define different types of abstraction by means of their abstract states and abstraction mapping. Other abstraction types are also possible.

3.2   Abstraction Types

Let $\mathcal{P}$ be a program and let φ be an ACTL* formula. We describe several ways to define abstractions that are appropriate for checking φ on $\mathcal{P}$. They are all based on the existential abstraction. They differ from each other in their choice of abstract states, in the set of atomic propositions that label both concrete and abstract states and in the definition of the abstraction function h.

Predicate Abstraction: Predicate abstraction [28,50] is based on a set of predicates $\{P_1, \ldots, P_k\}$, defined over the program variables. Recall that predicates are quantifier-free first order formulas. Since our goal is to check a property φ on a program $\mathcal{P}$, $Atoms(\varphi)$, the set of predicates appearing in φ, must be included in the set of predicates. In addition, this set will contain some of the conditions in control statements in $\mathcal{P}$, and possibly other predicates.

In order to define the abstract state space, each predicate P_j is associated with a Boolean variable B_j. The set of abstract states are valuations of $\{B_1, \ldots, B_k\}$. Thus, $\widehat{S} = \{0,1\}^k$.

The predicates are also used to define the abstraction mapping h between the concrete and abstract state spaces. A concrete state s will be mapped to an abstract state $\widehat{s}$ through h if and only if the truth value of each predicate on s

equals the value of the corresponding Boolean variable in the abstract state $\widehat{s}$. Formally,

$$h(s) = \widehat{s} \;\Leftrightarrow\; \bigwedge_{1 \le j \le k} (P_j(s) \Leftrightarrow B_j(\widehat{s})). \tag{1}$$

The predicates also serve as the atomic propositions that label the states in the concrete and abstract models. That is, the set of atomic propositions is $AP = \{P_1, P_2, .., P_k\}$. A state in the concrete system will be labeled with all the predicates it satisfies. Note that, all concrete states mapped to the same abstract state $\widehat{s}$ agree on the values of all predicates P_j and also agree with $\widehat{s}$ on the value of the corresponding B_j. Thus, an abstract state will be labeled with predicate P_j if and only if the corresponding bit B_j is 1 in that state.

Note also that h is a function because each P_j can have one and only one value on a given concrete state and so the abstract state corresponding to the concrete state is unique. h is also appropriate for any ACTL* formula over AP, and in particular φ.

Once $\widehat{S}$, h, and AP have been determined, the rest of the abstract model is defined as explained before, by means of existential abstraction.

Example 1. We will exemplify some of the notions defined above on a simple example. Consider a program $\mathcal{P}$ with variables x, y over the natural numbers and a single transition $x := x + 1$. Let $AP = \{P_1, P_2, P_3\}$ where $P_1 = (x \le 1)$, $P_2 = (x > y)$, and $P_3 = (y = 2)$.

Let s and t be two concrete states such that $s(x) = s(y) = 0$, $t(x) = 1$ and $t(y) = 2$. Then, $L(s) = \{P_1\}$ and $L(t) = \{P_1, P_3\}$.

The abstract states are defined over valuations of the Boolean variable B_1, B_2, B_3. Thus, $\widehat{S} \subseteq \{0, 1\}^3$. The abstraction mapping h is: $h(s) = (1, 0, 0)$ and $h(t) = (1, 0, 1)$. Note that $\widehat{L}((1, 0, 0)) = L(s) = \{P_1\}$, where $\widehat{L}((1, 0, 1)) = L(t) = \{P_1, P_3\}$. The abstract transition relation can be represented by the following formula:

$$\widehat{R}(B_1, B_2, B_3, B_1', B_2', B_3') \Longleftrightarrow$$
$$\exists x, y, x', y' [\; P_1(x, y) \Leftrightarrow B_1 \;\wedge\; P_2(x, y) \Leftrightarrow B_2 \;\wedge\; P_3(x, y) \Leftrightarrow B_3 \;\wedge$$
$$x' = x + 1 \;\wedge\; y' = y \;\wedge$$
$$P_1(x', y') \Leftrightarrow B_1' \;\wedge\; P_2(x', y') \Leftrightarrow B_2' \;\wedge\; P_3(x', y') \Leftrightarrow B_3' \;].$$

If the program $\mathcal{P}$ is over a finite, relatively small state space, then BDDs can be used to compute $\widehat{R}$. For that, we will need a BDD representation of the concrete transition relation R (possibly in the form of a partitioned transition relation [13]). Further, we will need a BDD representation for h.

If the program is over a finite but large state space then SAT solvers will be more appropriate, while if its state space is infinite then theorem prover will have to be used [50].

The two other types of abstractions described next can both be defined by means of predicate abstraction. However, they are interesting special cases.

Abstraction based on visible and invisible variables: The visible-variables abstraction, also known as *localization reduction* [36], is based on a partition of the program variables into visible and invisible variables. It is a simpler special case of predicate abstraction and is widely used in model checking of hardware. The visible variables, denoted $\mathcal{V}$, are considered to be important for the checked property φ and hence are retained in the abstract model. This set includes, in particular, all variables that appear in φ. The rest of the variables, called *invisible*, are considered irrelevant for checking φ. Ideally, only a small subset of the variables will be considered visible.

Formally, given a set of variables $U = \{u_1, \ldots, u_p\}$, $U \subseteq V$, let s^U denotes the portion of s that corresponds to variables in U, i.e., $s^U = (s(u_1), \ldots, s(u_p))$

Let $\mathcal{V} = \{u_1, \ldots, u_q\} \subseteq V$ be the set of visible variables. Then, the set of abstract states is $\widehat{S} = D_{u_1} \times \ldots \times D_{u_q}$. The abstraction function $h : S \to \widehat{S}$ is defined as $h(s) = s^{\mathcal{V}}$. AP includes all atomic propositions in φ. Since all variables that appear in φ are visible, h is appropriate for φ.

A conservative choice of the set of visible variables is described below. Assume that each variable $v \in V$ is associated with a next-state function $f_v(V)$. Typically, f_v depends only on a subset of V. The Cone Of Influence (COI) [13] of a formula φ is defined inductively as follows. It includes all the variables in φ. In Addition, if v is in COI, then all variables on which f_v depends are also in COI.

Taking the COI of φ to be the set of visible variable, results in an abstract model which is *equivalent* to the concrete model with respect to φ. That is, the abstract model satisfies φ if and only if the concrete model satisfies it. As a result, refutation of φ on the abstract model implies refutation on the concrete model. This choice, however, is often not practical, since COI is typically too large.

Note that, in contrast to predicate abstraction, the visible-variables abstraction cannot retain any information on variables over infinite domain. Such variables must be considered invisible. This is because the domain of a visible variable is taken as is and no abstraction is applied to it. In the next section we present an abstraction that can abstract domains of individual variables.

Data abstraction: Another useful abstraction can be obtained by abstracting away some of the data information. *Data abstraction* [15,38] is done by choosing, for every variable in the system, an abstract domain that is typically significantly smaller than the original domain. The abstraction function maps concrete data domains to abstract data domains and induces an abstraction function from concrete states to abstract states.

Clearly, a property verified for the abstract model can only refer to the abstract values of the program variables. In order for such a property to be meaningful in the concrete model we label the concrete states by atomic formulas of the form $\widehat{v_i} = a$, where a is an element of the abstract domain of v_i. These atomic formulas indicate that the variable v_i has some value d that has been abstracted to a.

Let $\mathcal{P}$ be a program with variables $v_1, \ldots, v_n$. For simplicity we assume that all variables are over the same domain D. Thus, the concrete model of the system is defined over states s of the form $s = (d_1, \ldots, d_n)$ in $D \times \ldots \times D$, where d_i is the value of v_i in this state.

In order to build an abstract model for $\mathcal{P}$ we need to choose an abstract domain A and an variable-abstraction mapping $h : D \to A$. The abstract state space is then defined by

$$\widehat{S} = A \times \ldots \times A.$$

The abstraction mapping is an extension of the variable-abstraction mapping h to n-tuples in $D \times \ldots \times D$. By abuse of notion we denote the abstraction mapping by h as well.

$$h((d_1, \ldots, d_n)) = (h(d_1), \ldots, h(d_n)).$$

As before, an abstract state $(a_1, \ldots, a_n)$ of $\widehat{S}$ represents the set of all states $(d_1, \ldots, d_n)$ such that $h((d_1, \ldots, d_n)) = (a_1, \ldots, a_n)$.

The next step is to restrict the concrete model of $\mathcal{P}$ so that it reflects only the abstract values of its variables. This is done by defining the set of atomic propositions as follows:

$$AP = \{ \ \widehat{v_i} = a \mid i = 1, \ldots, n \ \text{ and } \ a \in A \ \}.$$

The notation $\widehat{v_i}$ is used to emphasize that we refer to the abstract value of the variable v_i. The labeling of a state $s = (d_1, \ldots, d_n)$ in the concrete model will be defined by

$$L(s) = \{ \ \widehat{v_i} = a_i \mid h(d_i) = a_i, \ i = 1, \ldots, n \ \}.$$

By restricting the state labeling we lose the ability to refer to the actual values of the program variables. However, many of the states are now indistinguishable and can be collapsed into a single abstract state.

Here again all states mapped to an abstract state agree on all atomic propositions. Thus, the abstraction mapping h is appropriate for every ACTL* formula defined over AP. The abstract labeling, defined according to the existential abstraction, can also be described as follows. Let $\widehat{s} = (a_1, \ldots, a_n)$. Then,

$$\widehat{L}(\widehat{s}) = \{ \ \widehat{v_i} = a_i \mid i = 1, \ldots, n \ \}.$$

Example 2. Let $\mathcal{P}$ be a program with a variable x over the integers. Let s, s' be two program states such that $s(x) = 2$ and $s'(x) = -7$. Following are two possible abstractions.

Abstraction 1:

$$A_1 = \{a_-, a_0, a_+\} \text{ and}$$

$$h_1(d) = \begin{cases} a_+ & \text{if } d > 0 \\ a_0 & \text{if } d = 0 \\ a_- & \text{if } d < 0 \end{cases}$$

Thus, $h(s) = (a_+)$ and $h(s') = (a_-)$. The set of atomic propositions is $AP_1 = \{ \ \widehat{x} = a_-, \ \widehat{x} = a_0, \ \widehat{x} = a_+ \ \}$.

The labeling of states in the concrete and abstract models induced by A_1 and h_1 is:

$L_1(s) = \widehat{L}(a_+) = \{\widehat{x} = a_+\}$ and $L_1(s') = \widehat{L}(a_-) = \{\widehat{x} = a_-\}$.

Abstraction 2:

$$A_2 = \{a_{even}, a_{odd}\} \text{ and}$$

$$h_2(d) = \begin{cases} a_{even} & \text{if } even(|d|) \\ a_{odd} & \text{if } odd(|d|) \end{cases}$$

Here $h(s) = (a_{even})$ and $h(s') = (a_{odd})$. The set of atomic propositions is $AP_2 = \{ \widehat{x} = a_{even}, \widehat{x} = a_{odd} \}$.
The labeling induced by A_2 and h_2 is:

$L_2(s) = \widehat{L}(a_{even}) = \{\widehat{x} = a_{even}\}$ and $L_2(s') = \widehat{L}(a_{odd}) = \{\widehat{x} = a_{odd}\}$.

4 Deriving Models from the Program Text

In the next section we explain how the exact and approximated abstract model for the system can be derived directly from a high-level description of a program. In order to avoid having to choose a specific programming language, we argue that the program can be described by means of first-order formulas. In this section we demonstrate how this can be done.

Let $\mathcal{P}$ be a program, and let $\overline{v} = (v_1, \ldots, v_n)$ and $\overline{v}' = (v'_1, \ldots, v'_n)$ be two copies of the program variables, representing the current and next state, respectively. The program will be given by two first-order formulas, $\mathcal{S}_0(\overline{v})$ and $\mathcal{R}(\overline{v}, \overline{v}')$, describing the set of initial states and the set of transitions, respectively. Let $\overline{d} = (d_1, \ldots, d_n)$ be a vector of values. The notation $\mathcal{S}_0[\overline{v} \leftarrow \overline{d}]$ indicates that for every $i = 1, \ldots, n$, the value d_i is substituted for the variable v_i in the formula $\mathcal{S}_0$. A similar notation is used for substitution in the formula $\mathcal{R}$.

Definition 7. *Let $S = D \times \ldots \times D$ be the set of states in a model M. The formulas $\mathcal{S}_0(\overline{v})$ and $\mathcal{R}(\overline{v}, \overline{v}')$ define the set of initial states S_0 and the set of transitions R in M as follows. Let $s = (d_1, \ldots, d_n)$ and $s' = (d'_1, \ldots, d'_n)$ be two states in S.*

- $S_0(s) \Leftrightarrow \mathcal{S}_0(\overline{v})[\overline{v} \leftarrow \overline{d}]$ *is true.*
- $R(s, s') \Leftrightarrow \mathcal{R}(\overline{v}, \overline{v}')[\overline{v} \leftarrow \overline{d}, \overline{v}' \leftarrow \overline{d}']$ *is true.*

The following example demonstrates how a program can be described by means of first-order formulas. A more elaborate explanation can be found in [13]. We assume that each statement in the program starts and ends with labels that uniquely define the corresponding locations in the program. The program locations will be represented in the formula by the variable pc (the *program counter*), which ranges over the set of program labels.

Example 3. Given a program with one variable x that starts at label l_0, in any state in which x is even, the set of its initial states is described by the formula:

$$\mathcal{S}_0(pc, x) = \quad pc = l_0 \,\wedge\, even(x).$$

Let $l : x := e \; l'$ be a program statement. the transition relation associated with this statement is described by the formula:

$$\mathcal{R}(pc, x, pc', x') = \quad pc = l \,\wedge\, x' = e \,\wedge\, pc' = l'.$$

Given the statement $l :$ if $x = 0$ then $l_1 : x := 1$ else $l_2 : x := x + 1 \; l'$, the transition relation associated with it is described by the formula:

$$\begin{aligned}
\mathcal{R}(pc, x, pc', x') = ((\; & pc = l \,\wedge\, x = 0 \,\wedge x' = x \wedge pc' = l_1) \vee \\
(\; & pc = l \,\wedge\, x \neq 0 \,\wedge x' = x \wedge pc' = l_2) \vee \\
(& pc = l_1 \wedge x' = 1 \wedge pc' = l') \vee \\
(& pc = l_2 \wedge x' = x + 1 \wedge pc' = l')).
\end{aligned}$$

Note that checking the condition of the *if* statement takes one transition, along which the value of the program variable is checked but not changed. If the program contains an additional variable y, then $y' = y$ will be added to the description of each of the transitions above. This captures the fact that variables that are not assigned a new value keep their previous value.

4.1   Deriving Abstract Models

Let $\mathcal{S}_0$ and $\mathcal{R}$ be the formulas describing a concrete model M. Let $\widehat{S}$ and h be the set of abstract states and the abstraction mapping, defining an abstract model $\widehat{M}$. We would like to define formulas $\widehat{\mathcal{S}_0}$ and $\widehat{\mathcal{R}}$ that describe the model $\widehat{M}$. We first define formulas that describe the *exact* abstract model. To emphasize that it is the exact model we will denote it by $\widehat{M}_e$. We then show how to construct formulas describing an *approximated* abstract model with possibly more initial states and more transitions. The latter formulas represent an abstract model which is less precise than the exact one, but is easier to compute.

Let $\widehat{S}$ be defined over the variables $(\widehat{v_1}, \ldots, \widehat{v_k})$, that is $\widehat{S}$ is the set of valuations of those variables. Further, let $h((v_1, \ldots, v_n))) = (\widehat{v_1}, \ldots, \widehat{v_k})$. Thus, h maps valuations over the concrete domain to valuations over the abstract domain. The new formulas that we construct for $\widehat{M}$ will be defined over the variables $(\widehat{v_1}, \ldots, \widehat{v_k})$. The formulas will determine for abstract states whether they are initial and whether there is a transition connecting them. For this purpose, we first define a derivation of a formula over variables $\widehat{v_1}, \ldots, \widehat{v_k}$ from a formula over $v_1, \ldots, v_n$.

Definition 8. *Let φ be a first-order formula over variables $v_1, \ldots, v_n$. The formula $[\varphi]$ over $\widehat{v_1}, \ldots, \widehat{v_k}$ is defined as follows:*

$$[\varphi](\widehat{v_1}, \ldots, \widehat{v_k}) = \exists v_1 \ldots v_n \left(h((v_1, \ldots, v_n))) = (\widehat{v_1}, \ldots, \widehat{v_k}) \wedge \varphi(v_1, \ldots, v_n) \right).$$

Lemma 1. *Let $\mathcal{S}_0$ and $\mathcal{R}$ be the formulas describing a model M. Then the formulas $\widehat{\mathcal{S}}_0 = [\mathcal{S}_0]$ and $\widehat{\mathcal{R}} = [\mathcal{R}]$ describe the exact model $\widehat{M}_e$.*

The lemma holds since $\widehat{M}_e$ is defined by existential abstraction (see Definition 6). This is directly reflected in $[\mathcal{S}_0]$ and $[\mathcal{R}]$.

Using $\widehat{\mathcal{S}}_0$ and $\widehat{\mathcal{R}}$ allows us to build the exact model $\widehat{M}_e$ without first building the concrete model M. However, the formulas $\mathcal{S}_0$ and $\mathcal{R}$ might be quite large. Thus, applying existential quantification to them might be computationally expensive. We therefore define a transformation $\mathcal{T}$ on first-order formulas. The idea of $\mathcal{T}$ is to push the existential quantification inwards, so that it is applied to simpler formulas.

Definition 9. *Let φ be a first-order formula in positive normal form. Then $\mathcal{T}(\varphi)$ is defined as follows:*

1. *If p is a predicate, then $\mathcal{T}(p(v_1,\ldots,v_n)) = [p](\widehat{v}_1,\ldots,\widehat{v}_k)$ and $\mathcal{T}(\neg p(v_1,\ldots,v_n)) = [\neg p](\widehat{v}_1,\ldots,\widehat{v}_k)$.*
2. *$\mathcal{T}(\varphi_1 \wedge \varphi_2) = \mathcal{T}(\varphi_1) \wedge \mathcal{T}(\varphi_2)$.*
3. *$\mathcal{T}(\varphi_1 \vee \varphi_2) = \mathcal{T}(\varphi_1) \vee \mathcal{T}(\varphi_2)$.*
4. *$\mathcal{T}(\forall v \varphi) = \forall \widehat{v} \mathcal{T}(\varphi)$.*
5. *$\mathcal{T}(\exists v \varphi) = \exists \widehat{v} \mathcal{T}(\varphi)$.*

We can now define an *approximated* abstract model $\widehat{M}$. It is defined over the same set of states as the exact model, but its set of initial states and set of transitions are defined using the formulas $\mathcal{T}(\mathcal{S}_0)$ and $\mathcal{T}(\mathcal{R})$. The following lemma ensures that every initial state of $\widehat{M}_e$ is also an initial state of $\widehat{M}$. Moreover, every transition of $\widehat{M}_e$ is also a transition of $\widehat{M}$.

Lemma 2. *For every first-order formula φ in positive normal form, $[\varphi]$ implies $\mathcal{T}(\varphi)$. In particular, $[\mathcal{S}_0]$ implies $\mathcal{T}(\mathcal{S}_0)$ and $[\mathcal{R}]$ implies $\mathcal{T}(\mathcal{R})$.*

Note that the other direction does not hold. Cases 2 and 4 of Definition 9 result in nonequivalent formulas.

Corollary 1. $M \preceq \widehat{M}_e \preceq \widehat{M}$.

By allowing $\widehat{M}$ to have more behaviors than $\widehat{M}_e$, we increase the likelihood that it will falsify ACTL* formulas that are actually true in the concrete model and possibly true in $\widehat{M}_e$. This reflects the tradeoff between the precision of the model and the ease of its computation.

In practice, there is no need to construct formulas in order to build the approximated model. Let p be a predicate associated with a basic action a in the program (e.g. conditions, assignments of mathematical expressions). The user should provide *abstract predicates* $[p]$ and $[\neg p]$ for every such action a. Based on these, the approximated model can be constructed automatically.

In [15,38], the construction of abstract models presented here has been developed and applied in the context of data abstraction.

5 Counterexample-Guided Abstraction Refinement

It is easy to see that, regardless of the type of abstraction we use, the abstract model $\widehat{M}$ contains less information than the concrete model M[2]. Thus, model checking the structure $\widehat{M}$ potentially produces incorrect results. Theorem 2 guarantees that if an ACTL* specification is true in $\widehat{M}$ then it is also true in M. On the other hand, the following example shows that if the abstract model invalidates an ACTL* specification, *the actual model may still satisfy the specification.*

Example 4. The US traffic light controller presented in Figure 2, is defined over atomic propositions $AP = \{state = red\}$. We would like to prove for it the formula $\psi = \mathbf{AG}\,\mathbf{AF}(state = red)$ using the abstraction mapping $h(red) = \widehat{red}$ and $h(green) = h(yellow) = \widehat{go}$. It is easy to see that $M \models \psi$ while $\widehat{M} \not\models \psi$. There exists an infinite abstract trace $\langle \widehat{red}, \widehat{go}, \widehat{go}, \dots \rangle$ that invalidates the specification. However no corresponding concrete trace exists.

Fig. 2. Abstraction of a US traffic light

When an abstract counterexample does not correspond to some concrete counterexample, we call it *spurious*. For example, $\langle \widehat{red}, \widehat{go}, \widehat{go}, \dots \rangle$ in the above example is a spurious counterexample.

Let us consider the situation outlined in Figure 3. We see that the abstract path does not have a corresponding concrete path. Whichever concrete path we go, we will end up in state D, from which we cannot go further. Therefore, D is called a *deadend state*. On the other hand, the *bad state* is state B, because it made us believe that there is an outgoing transition. Finally, state I is an *irrelevant state* since it is neither deadend nor bad. To eliminate the spurious path, the abstraction can be refined, for instance, as indicated by the thick line, separating deadend states from bad states.

5.1 The Abstraction-Refinement Framework for ACTL*

In this section we present the framework of *CounterExample-Guided Abstraction-Refinement* (CEGAR), for the logic ACTL* and existential abstraction. The main steps of the CEGAR framework are presented below:

1. Given a model M and an ACTL* formula φ, generate an initial abstract model $\widehat{M}$.

---

[2] From now on we will assume that $\widehat{M}$ is defined according to an abstraction mapping h which is appropriate for the checked property.

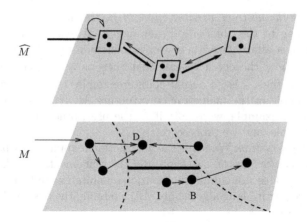

Fig. 3. The abstract path in $\widehat{M}$ (indicated by the thick arrows) is spurious. To eliminate the spurious path, the abstraction has to be refined as indicated by the thick line in M.

2. Model check $\widehat{M}$ with respect to φ [3]. If φ is true, then conclude that the concrete model satisfies the formula and stop. If a counterexample $\widehat{T}$ is found, check whether it is also a counterexample in the concrete model. If it is, conclude that the concrete model does not satisfy the formula and stop. Otherwise, the counterexample is spurious. Proceed to step 3.

3. Refine the abstract model, so that $\widehat{T}$ will not be included in the new, refined abstract model. Go back to step 2.

Suggesting an initial abstraction and refinements manually requires great ingenuity and close acquaintance with the verified system. Here we present a framework, developed in [17], in which both steps are done automatically. The initial abstraction is constructed based on the program text, and refinements are determined by spurious counterexamples.

5.2   Detailed Overview of CEGAR

We now describe in more detail the CEGAR framework for ACTL*. For a program $\mathcal{P}$ and an ACTL* formula φ, our goal is to check whether the Kripke structure M corresponding to $\mathcal{P}$ satisfies φ. The CEGAR methodology consists of the following steps.

1. *Generate the initial abstraction:* We generate an initial abstraction mapping h by examining the program text. We consider the conditions used in control statements such as **if**, **while**, and **case**, and also the atomic formulas in φ. The initial abstraction is an existential abstraction, constructed according to one of the abstractions described in Section 3.2.

---

[3] Most existing model checking tools handle CTL or LTL which are subsets of ACTL*.

2. *Model-check the abstract structure:* Let $\widehat{M}$ be the abstract Kripke structure corresponding to the abstraction mapping h. We check whether $\widehat{M} \models \varphi$. If the check is affirmative, then we can conclude that $M \models \varphi$ (see Theorem 2). Suppose the check reveals that there is a counterexample $\widehat{T}$. We ascertain whether $\widehat{T}$ is an actual counterexample, i.e., it corresponds to a counterexample in the unabstracted structure M. If $\widehat{T}$ turns out to be an actual counterexample, we report it to the user, otherwise $\widehat{T}$ is a spurious counterexample, and we proceed to step 3.

3. *Refine the abstraction:* We refine the abstraction mapping h by partitioning a *single equivalence class* of $\equiv$ so that after the refinement, the refined abstract structure $\widehat{M}$ does not admit the spurious counterexample $\widehat{T}$. We will not discuss here partitioning algorithms. After refining the abstraction mapping, we return to step 2.

The refinement can be accelerated in the cost of faster increase of the abstract model if the criterion obtained for partitioning one equivalence class (e.g. a new predicate) is used to partition all classes.

Depending on the type of h and the size of M, the initial abstract model (i.e., abstract initial states and abstract transitions) can be built using BDDs, SAT solvers or theorem provers. Similarly, the partitioning of abstract states, performed in the refinement, can be done using BDDs (e.g. as in [17]), SAT solvers (e.g. as in [10]), or linear programming and machine learning (e.g. as in [18]).

5.3   BDD-Based CEGAR

In this section we describe a BDD-based implementation of the CEGAR framework, in which the initial abstraction and the refinements are computed and represented symbolically, using BDDs.

Model Checking the Abstract Model. We use standard symbolic model checking procedures to determine whether $\widehat{M}$ satisfies the specification φ. If it does, then by Theorem 2 we can conclude that the original Kripke structure also satisfies φ. Otherwise, assume that the model checker produces a counterexample $\widehat{T}$ corresponding to the abstract model $\widehat{M}$. In the rest of this section, we will focus on counterexamples which are *finite paths*. In [17], counterexamples consisting of a finite path followed by a loop are also considered. In [19], tree-like counterexamples for all of ACTL are considered.

5.4   Identification of Spurious Path Counterexamples

Assume the counterexample $\widehat{T}$ is a path $\langle \widehat{s_1}, \cdots, \widehat{s_n} \rangle$. Given an abstract state $\widehat{s}$, the set of concrete states s such that $h(s) = \widehat{s}$ is denoted by $h^{-1}(\widehat{s})$,

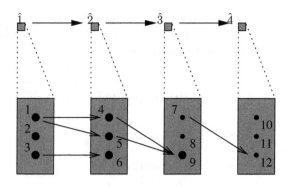

Fig. 4. An abstract counterexample

i.e., $h^{-1}(\widehat{s}) = \{s|h(s) = \widehat{s}\}$. We extend h^{-1} to sequences in the following way: $h^{-1}(\widehat{T})$ is the set of concrete paths defined as follows:

$$h^{-1}(\widehat{T}) = \{\langle s_1, \cdots, s_n \rangle | \bigwedge_{i=1}^{n} h(s_i) = \widehat{s}_i \ \wedge \ S_0(s_1) \ \wedge \ \bigwedge_{i=1}^{n-1} R(s_i, s_{i+1})\}.$$

Next, we give a *symbolic* algorithm to compute $h^{-1}(\widehat{T})$. Let $S_1 = h^{-1}(\widehat{s}_1) \cap S_0$. For $1 < i \leq n$, we define S_i in the following manner: $S_i := Image(S_{i-1}) \cap h^{-1}(\widehat{s}_i)$. Recall that, $Image(S_{i-1})$ is the set of successors of states in S_{i-1}. The sequence of sets S_i is computed symbolically using BDDs and the standard image computation algorithm. The following lemma establishes the correctness of this procedure.

Lemma 3. *The following are equivalent:*

(i) The path $\widehat{T}$ corresponds to a concrete counterexample.
(ii) The set of concrete paths $h^{-1}(\widehat{T})$ is non-empty.
(iii) For all $1 \leq i \leq n$, $S_i \neq \emptyset$.

Suppose that condition (iii) of Lemma 3 is violated, and let i be the largest index such that $S_i \neq \emptyset$. Then $\widehat{s}_i$ is called the *failure state* of the spurious counterexample $\widehat{T}$. It follows from Lemma 3 that if $h^{-1}(\widehat{T})$ is empty (i.e., if the counterexample $\widehat{T}$ is spurious), then there exists a minimal i ($2 \leq i \leq n$) such that $S_i = \emptyset$.

Example 5. In this example we apply data abstraction. Consider a program with only one variable with domain $D = \{1, \cdots, 12\}$. Assume that the abstraction mapping h maps $d \in D$ to $\lfloor (d-1)/3 \rfloor + 1$. There are four abstract states corresponding to the equivalence classes $\{1, 2, 3\}$, $\{4, 5, 6\}$, $\{7, 8, 9\}$, and $\{10, 11, 12\}$. We call these abstract states $\widehat{1}$, $\widehat{2}$, $\widehat{3}$, and $\widehat{4}$. The transitions between states in the concrete model are indicated by the arrows in Figure 4; small dots denote non-reachable states. Suppose that we obtain an abstract counterexample

$\widehat{T} = \langle \widehat{1}, \widehat{2}, \widehat{3}, \widehat{4} \rangle$. It is easy to see that $\widehat{T}$ is spurious. Using the terminology of Lemma 3, we have $S_1 = \{1, 2, 3\}$, $S_2 = \{4, 5, 6\}$, $S_3 = \{9\}$, and $S_4 = \emptyset$. Notice that S_4 is empty. Thus, $\widehat{s_3}$ is the failure state.

Algorithm SplitPATH($\widehat{T}$)

$$S := h^{-1}(\widehat{s_1}) \cap S_0$$
$$j := 1$$
while $(S \neq \emptyset$ and $j < n)$ {
$$\quad j := j + 1$$
$$\quad S_{\text{prev}} := S$$
$$\quad S := Image(S) \cap h^{-1}(\widehat{s_j}) \quad \}$$
if $S \neq \emptyset$ **then** output "counterexample exists"
else output j-1, S_{prev}

Fig. 5. SplitPATH checks if an abstract path is spurious

The symbolic Algorithm **SplitPATH** in Figure 5 computes the index of the failure state and the set of states S_{i-1}; the states in S_{i-1} are called *dead-end* states. After the detection of the dead-end states, we proceed to the refinement step. On the other hand, if the conditions stated in Lemma 3 are true, then **SplitPATH** will report a "real" counterexample and we can stop.

5.5   Refining the Abstraction

In this section we explain how to refine an abstraction to eliminate the spurious counterexample. In order to simplify the discussion we assume that the abstract model is exact (see the discussion following Definition 6). Less precise abstract models can also be handled. Recall the discussion concerning Figure 3 in Section 5.1 where we identified deadend states, bad states, and irrelevant states. The refinement should suggest a partitioning of equivalence classes, that will separate the deadend states S_D from the bad states S_B.

We already have the deadend states. S_D is exactly the set S_{prev}, returned by the algorithm **SplitPATH($\widehat{T}$)**. The algorithm also returns $j - 1$, the index in the counterexample where the failure state has been encountered. We can now compute the bad states symbolically as follows:

$$S_B = PreImage(h^{-1}(\widehat{s_{j+1}})) \cap h^{-1}(\widehat{s_j}).$$

$h^{-1}(\widehat{s_j})$ should now be partitioned to separate these two sets of states. This can be done in different ways. For example, if we work directly with BDDs, then we can add a new abstract state $\widehat{s_j'}$ to $\widehat{S}$ and update the BDD for h so that states in S_D are now mapped to the new state $\widehat{s_j'}$. Of course, now $\widehat{R}$, $\widehat{S_0}$ and $\widehat{L}$ should be updated.

Our refinement procedure continues to refine the abstraction mapping by partitioning equivalence classes until a real counterexample is found, or the property is verified. If the concrete model is finite, then the partitioning procedure is guaranteed to terminate.

6 Conclusion

We surveyed abstractions based on over-approximation and preserving truth results of universal branching-time logics from the abstract model to the concrete model.

We did not cover many other approaches to abstraction. Those are usually based on more elaborated models. Such models allow, for instance, for abstract states to represent non-disjoint sets of concrete states. Others allow two types of transitions that over- or under-approximate the concrete transition relation and thus preserve the truth of full branching-time logics. Others allow to interpret formulas over 3-valued semantics, and can preserve both truth and falsity of full branching-time logics.

A relevant question for the abstraction-refinement framework is whether every infinite-state model has a finite-state abstraction (sometimes referred to as completeness). This question has been discussed for branching-time logics in, e.g., [23]. It turns out that some notion of fairness is needed in order to guarantee completeness. It should be noted that for a finite model this question does not arise since it can always serve as its own abstraction. It should also be noted that even for complete abstraction the iterative process of abstraction-refinement is not guaranteed to terminate since there is no constructive way to construct the abstraction.

References

1. T. Ball and S. Rajamani. Checking temporal properties of software with boolean programs. In *In Proceedings of the Workshop on Advances in VErification (WAVE)*, July 2000.
2. I. Beer, S. Ben-David, C. Eisner, and A. Landver. RuleBase: an industry-oriented formal verification tool. In *proceedings of the 33rd Design Automation Conference (DAC'96)*, pages 655–660. IEEE Computer Society Press, June 1996.
3. Dirk Beyer, Thomas A. Henzinger, Ranjit Jhala, and Rupak Majumdar. Checking memory safety with blast. In *Proceedings of the International Conference on Fundamental Approaches to Software Engineering (FASE)*, volume 3442 of *Lecture Notes in Computer Science*, pages 2–18, 2005.
4. A. Biere, A. Cimatti, E. M. Clarke, M. Fujita, and Y. Zhu. Symbolic model checking using SAT procedures instead of BDDs. In *proceedings of the 36rd Design Automation Conference (DAC'99)*. IEEE Computer Society Press, June 1999.
5. A. Biere, A. Cimatti, E. M. Clarke, and Y. Zhu. Symbolic model checking without bdds. In *International Conference on Tools and Algorithms for the Construction and Analysis of Systems (TACAS'99)*, number 1579 in Lecture Notes in Computer Science. Springer-Verlag, 1999.

6. M. C. Browne, E. M. Clarke, and O. Grumberg. Characterizing finite kripke structures in propositional temporal logic. *Theor.Comp.Science*, 59(1–2), July 1988.
7. R. E. Bryant. Graph-based algorithms for boolean function manipulation. *IEEE Transaction on Computers*, pages 35(8):677–691, 1986.
8. J. R. Burch, E. M. Clarke, and K. L. McMillan. Symbolic model checking: 10^{20} states and beyond. *Information and Computation*, 98:142–170, 1992.
9. Sagar Chaki, Edmund Clarke, Alex Groce, Somesh Jha, and Helmut Veith. Modular verification of software components in C. In *International Conference on Software Engineering (ICSE)*, pages 385–395, 2003.
10. P. Chauhan, E.M. Clarke, J. Kukula, S. Sapra, H. Veith, and D.Wang. Automated abstraction refinement for model checking large state spaces using SAT based conflict analysis. In *Formal Methods in Computer Aided Design (FMCAD)*, November 2002.
11. Pankaj Chauhan, Edmund M. Clarke, and Daniel Kroening. Using SAT based image computation for reachability analysis. Technical Report CMU-CS-03-151, Carnegie Mellon University, School of Computer Science, 2003.
12. A. Cimatti, E. Clarke, F. Giunchiglia, and M. Roveri. NuSMV: a new symbolic model checker. *Software Tools for Technology Transfer*, 1998.
13. E. Clarke, O. Grumberg, and D. Peled. *Model Checking*. MIT Publishers, 1999.
14. E. M. Clarke and E. A. Emerson. Synthesis of synchronization skeletons for branching time temporal logic. In D. Kozen, editor, *Logic of Programs: Workshop, Yorktown Heights, NY, May 1981*, volume 131 of *Lecture Notes in Computer Science*. Springer-Verlag, 1981.
15. E. M. Clarke, O. Grumberg, and D. E. Long. Model checking and abstraction. In *Proceedings of the Nineteenth Annual ACM Symposium on Principles of Programming Languages*. Association for Computing Machinery, January 1992.
16. Edmund Clarke and Daniel Kroening. Hardware verification using ANSI-C programs as a reference. In *Proceedings of ASP-DAC 2003*, pages 308–311. IEEE Computer Society Press, January 2003.
17. E.M. Clarke, O. Grumberg, S. Jha, Y. Lu, and H. Veith. Counterexample-guided abstraction refinement. *J. ACM*, 50(5):752–794, 2003.
18. E.M. Clarke, A. Gupta, J. Kukula, and O. Strichman. SAT based abstraction-refinement using ILP and machine leraning techniques. In *Proc. of Conference on Computer-Aided Verification (CAV)*, volume 2404 of *Lecture Notes in Computer Science*, pages 137–150, Copenhagen, Denmark, July 2002. Springer-Verlag.
19. E.M. Clarke, S. Jha, Y. Lu, and H. Veith. Tree-like counterexamples in model checking. In *Seventeenth Annual IEEE Symposium on Logic In Computer Science (LICS)*, Copenhagen, Denmark, July 2002.
20. F. Copty, L. Fix, R. Fraer, E. Giunchiglia, G. Kamhi, A. Tacchella, , and M. Y. Vardi. Benefits of bounded model checking at an industrial setting. In *13th International Conference on Computer Aided Verification (CAV'01)*, volume 2102 of *LNCS*, Paris, France, July 2001.
21. J. C. Corbett, M. B. Dwyer, J. Hatcliff, S. Laubach, C. S. Pasareanu, Robby, and H. Zheng. Bandera: extracting finite-state models from java source code. In *International Conference on Software Engineering*, pages 439–448, 2000.
22. D. Dams, R. Gerth, and O. Grumberg. Abstract interpretation of reactive systems. *ACM Transactions on Programming Languages and System (TOPLAS)*, 19(2), 1997.
23. Dennis Dams and Kedar S. Namjoshi. The existence of finite abstractions for branching time model checking. In *Logic in Computer Science (LICS)*, pages 335–344, 2004.

24. Cindy Eisner, Dana Fisman, John Havlicek, Yoad Lustig, Anthony McIsaac, and David Van Campenhout. Reasoning with temporal logic on truncated paths. In *15th International Conference on Computer Aided Verification (CAV'03)*, volume 2725 of *Lecture Notes in Computer Science*, pages 27–39, Boulder, CO, USA, July 2003.

25. E. A. Emerson and J. Y. Halpern. "Sometimes" and "Not Never" revisited: On branching time versus linear time. *J. ACM*, 33(1):151–178, 1986.

26. R. Fraer, G. Kamhi, Z. Barukh, M.Y. Vardi, and L. Fix. Prioritized traversal: Efficient reachability analysis for verification and falsification. In *12th International Conference on Computer Aided Verification (CAV'00)*, volume 1855 of *LNCS*, Chicago, USA, July 2000.

27. E. Goldberg and Y. Novikov. Berkmin: A fast and robust SAT-solver. In *DATE*, 2002.

28. Sussanne Graf and Hassen Saidi. Construction of abstract state graphs with PVS. In *Proc. of Conference on Computer-Aided Verification (CAV)*, volume 1254 of *Lecture Notes in Computer Science*, pages 72–83. Springer-Verlag, June 1997.

29. O. Grumberg and D.E. Long. Model checking and modular verification. *ACM Trans. on Programming Languages and Systems*, 16(3):843–871, 1994.

30. O. Grumberg, A. Schuster, and A. Yadgar. Reachability using a memory-efficient all-solutions sat solver. In *Fifth Inernation Conference on Formal Methods in Computer-Aided Design (FMCAD'04)*, November 2004.

31. Z. Har'El and R. P. Kurshan. Software for analytical development of communications protocols. *AT&T Technical Journal*, 69(1):45–59, Jan.–Feb. 1990.

32. K. Havelund and T. Pressburger. Model checking JAVA programs using JAVA PathFinder. *International Journal on Software Tools for Technology Transfer*, 2(4):366–381, 2000.

33. G. Holzmann. *Design and Validation of Computer Protocols*. Prentice-Hall International Editors, 1991.

34. G. Holzmann. Logic verification of ansi-c code with SPIN. In *Proceedings of the 7th international SPIN workshop*, volume 1885 of *LNCS*, pages 131–147, 2000.

35. D. Kozen. Results on the propositional μ-calculus. *TCS*, 27, 1983.

36. R. P. Kurshan. *Computer-Aided Verification of coordinating processes - the automata theoretic approach*. Princeton University Press, Princeton, New Jersey, 1994.

37. C. Loiseaux, S. Graf, J. Sifakis, A. Bouajjani, and S. Bensalem. Property preserving abstractions for the verification of concurrent systems. *Formal Methods in System Design*, 6:11–45, 1995.

38. D. E. Long. *Model Checking, Abstraction, and Compositional Reasoning*. PhD thesis, Carnegie Mellon University, 1993.

39. J.P. Marques-Silva and Karem A. Sakallah. GRASP: A search algorithm for propositional satisfiability. *IEEE Transactions on Computers*, 48(5):506–521, 1999.

40. K. McMillan. Applications of craig interpolation to model checking. In *11th International Conference on Tools and Algorithms for the Construction and Analysis of Systems (TACAS)*, Lecture Notes in Computer Science, pages 1–12, Edinburgh, Scotland, April 2005. Springer.

41. K. L. McMillan. *Symbolic Model Checking: An Approach to the State Explosion Problem*. PhD thesis, Carnegie Mellon University, 1992.

42. K. L. McMillan. *Symbolic Model Checking*. Kluwer Academic Publishers, 1993.

43. K. L. McMillan. Interpolation and SAT-based model checking. In *CAV*, volume 2725 of *Lecture Notes in Computer Science*, 2003.

44. Ken L. McMillan. Applying SAT methods in unbounded symbolic model checking. In *Computer Aided Verification*, 2002.
45. R. Milner. An algebraic definition of simulation between programs. In *Proc. 2nd Int. Joint Conf. on Artificial Intelligence*, pages 481–489. BCS, 1971.
46. R. Milner. An algebraic definition of simulation between programs. In *Proceedings of the Second Internation Joint Conference on Artificial Intelligence*, pages 481–489, September 1971.
47. M.W. Moskewicz, C.F. Madigan, Y. Zhao, L. Zhang, and S. Malik. Chaff: engineering an efficient SAT solver. In *39th Design Aotomation Conference (DAC'01)*, 2001.
48. D. Park. Concurrency and automata on infinite sequences. In *5th GI-Conference on Theoretical Computer Science*, pages 167–183. Springer-Verlag, 1981. LNCS 104.
49. A. Pnueli. The Temporal Semantics of Concurrent Programs. *Theoretical Computer Science*, 13:45–60, 1981.
50. Hassen Saidi and Natarajan Shankar. Abstract and model check while you prove. In *Proceedings of the eleventh International Conference on Computer-Aided Verification (CAV99)*, Trento, Italy, July 1999.
51. M. Sheeran, S. Singh, and G. Staalmarck. Checking safety properties using induction and a sat-solver. In *Third International Conference on Formal methods in Computer-Aided Design (FMCAD'00)*, Austin, Texas, November 2000.
52. M. Sheeran and G. Staalmarck. A tutorial on stalmarck's proof procedure for propositional logic. *Formal Methods in System Design*, 16(1), January 2000.
53. Sharon Shoham and Orna Grumberg. A game-based framework for CTL counterexamples and 3-valued abstraction-refinemnet. In *Proceedings of the 15th International Conference on Computer Aided Verification (CAV'03)*, volume 2725 of *Lecture Notes in Computer Science*, pages 275–287, Boulder, CO, USA, July 2003. Springer.

Program Compatibility Approaches

Edmund Clarke[1], Natasha Sharygina[1,2], and Nishant Sinha[1]

[1] Carnegie Mellon University
[2] Universita della Svizzera Italiana

Abstract. This paper is a survey of several techniques that have proven useful in establishing compatibility among *behaviorally similar* programs (e.g., system upgrades, object sub- and supertypes, system components produced by different vendors, etc.). We give a comparative analysis of the techniques by evaluating their applicability to various aspects of the compatibility problem[1].

1 Introduction

Component-based development aims to facilitate the construction of large-scale applications by supporting the composition of simple building blocks into complex applications. The use of off-the-shelf components offers a great potential for: (1) significantly reducing cost and time-to-market of large-scale and complex software systems, (2) improving system maintainability and flexibility by allowing new components to replace old ones, and (3) enhancing system quality by allowing components to be developed by those who are specialized in the application area. Despite the advantages of the component-based approach, the use of commercial off-the-shelf software–especially when delivered as black-box components–has raised a number of technical issues. One of the fundamental problems relates to guaranteeing the safety of replacement of older components by their newer or upgraded counterparts. This problem is a particular instance of a more general task of checking compatibility between behaviorally similar program components. Among many approaches for component-based specification and design developed over the years (see an excellent overview in [25]), assessment of compatibility between different components remains a challenging task.

A limited answer to the component compatibility problem can be given by traditional type systems. It is well known [19], however, that type checking, while very useful, captures only a small part of what it means for a program to be correct. Instead it is necessary to establish a stronger requirement that ensures the behavioral correctness of components.

This paper provides a selective overview of several techniques that ensure the requirement of behavioral compatibility among components. The paper is organized as follows. Section 2 gives an overview of the interface automata formalism and describes the notions of compatiblity and substitutability as defined in this formalism. Section 3 presents a technique to check if upgrades to one or more components in a component

---

[1] The work described in section on substitutability check is based on a 2005 *Formal Methods* paper, *Dynamic Component Substitutability*, Lecture Notes in Computer Science 3582, 2005 by the same authors.

F.S. de Boer et al. (Eds.): FMCO 2005, LNCS 4111, pp. 243–258, 2006.

assembly are compatible with the other components in the assembly. Section 4 outlines ideas of behavioral subtyping which ensure that subtype objects preserve properties of their supertypes. Section 5 presents an automated and compositional procedure to solve the component substitutability problem in the context of evolving software systems. Finally, Section 6 provides a comparative evaluation of the presented techniques.

2   Interface Automata Compatibility

Interface automata [10] were proposed by Alfaro et al. for capturing the temporal input-output (I/O) behaviors of software component interfaces. Given a software component, these automata model both input assumptions about the temporal order of inputs and output guarantees about generation of outputs for the component. In contrast to similar formalisms like I/O automata [20], the interface automata approach handles both *composition* and *refinement* of automata differently. Two automata are said to be compatible if there exists *some* environment that can provide inputs so that the illegal states of the product automaton are avoided. Composition of two interface automata is defined only if they are mutually compatible. One interface automaton refines another if it has weaker input assumptions and stronger output guarantees. Both concepts are formally defined using game theory semantics. More specifically, they are defined in terms of a game between Input and Output players, which model the environment and the component interface automata, respectively.

The interface automata formalism relies on an optimistic approach to component composition. Composing two interface automata could lead to error states where one automaton generates an output that is an illegal input for the other automaton. However, the optimistic composition approach steers clear of the error states by checking if there exists a legal environment that does not lead the composed system to an error state. As opposed to the I/O automata approach [20] which allows an arbitrary input environment (which may lead the composed system to an illegal state), the interface automata assumes a helpful environment while computing the reachable states of the composed automaton. Algorithmically, such a composition is obtained by solving a game between the product automaton of the components (which attempts to get to an error state) and the environment (which attempts to avoid error states).

The following provides formal description of the interface automata formalism and the notions of the component composition and refinement.

An interface automaton is a tuple, $P = \langle V_P, V_P^{init}, A_P^I, A_P^O, A_P^H, T_P \rangle$, where :

- V_P is a set of states.
- $V_P^{init} \subseteq V_P$ is a set of initial states, having at most one state.
- A_P^I, A_P^O, A_P^H are mutually disjoint sets of input, output and internal actions. The set of all actions $A_P = A_P^I \cup A_P^O \cup A_P^H$.
- $T_P \subseteq V_P \times A_P \times V_P$ is a set of steps.

P is said to be *closed* if it has only internal actions, i.e., $A_P^I = A_P^O = \emptyset$, otherwise it is said to be *open*. If $(v, a, v') \in T_P$, then action a is said to be enabled at state v. The set $A_P^I(v)$ of enabled input actions specifies which inputs are accepted at the state v; the other inputs in $A_P^I \setminus A_P^I(v)$ are *illegal* inputs at that state.

2.1   Composition

Composition of two interface automata is defined only if their actions are disjoint, except that an input action of one component may coincide with the output action of another component, in which case it is called a shared action. Two automata synchronize on shared actions, and asynchronously interleave on all other actions.

Formally, two automata P and Q are composable if $A_P^I \cap A_Q^I = \emptyset$, $A_P^O \cap A_Q^O = \emptyset$, $A_Q^H \cap A_P = \emptyset$ and $A_P^H \cap A_P = \emptyset$. The shared actions $shared(P, Q)$ of the two automata are given by the expression $(A_P^I \cap A_Q^O) \cup (A_P^O \cap A_Q^I)$. If P and Q are composable interface automata, their product $P \otimes Q$ is the interface automaton defined by: $V_{P \otimes Q} = V_P \times V_Q$, $V_{P \otimes Q} = V_P^{init} \times V_Q^{init}$, $A_{P \otimes Q}^I = (A_P^I \cup A_Q^I) \setminus shared(P, Q)$, $A_{P \otimes Q}^O = (A_P^O \cup A_Q^O) \setminus shared(P, Q)$ and $A_{P \otimes Q}^H = A_P^H \cup A_Q^H \cup shared(P, Q)$. The transitions $T_{P \otimes Q}$ are obtained by synchronizing P and Q on shared actions and asynchronously interleaving all other action steps. A state (v, u) in $P \otimes Q$ is said to be *illegal* if there exists a shared action $a \in P \otimes Q$, such that a is enabled in P at state v but is not enabled in Q at state u or vice-versa.

Compatibility. If the product $P \otimes Q$ is closed, then P and Q are compatible if no illegal state of $P \otimes Q$ is reachable from an initial state. When $P \otimes Q$ is open, then P and Q can be compatible if there exists a *legal* environment interface automaton E (composable with $P \otimes Q$) that can provide inputs to $P \otimes Q$ such that no illegal state is reachable in the composition $E \otimes (P \otimes Q)$. Alternatively, two interface automata P and Q are compatible iff (a) they are composable and (b) their composition is non-empty. If P and Q are compatible, then their composition can be computed by a polynomial time algorithm [10]. Composition of compatible interface automata is associative and hence can be computed in an iterative manner.

Intuitively, an interface automaton for a system component represents both assumptions about the environment and guarantees (or the observed outputs) of the specified component. Two assumptions are made about the environment: (i) each output step of the component must be accepted by the environment as an input and (ii) if an input action is not enabled at a state of a component, then the environment does not provide it as an input. The component guarantees consist of the behavior sequences and choices of input, output and internal actions at each state of the automaton. A drawback of this formalism is that one can construct trivial legal environments to show compatibility of components; an environment that generates no inputs for $P \otimes Q$ can trivially avoid the illegal states of $P \otimes Q$. In other words, the formalism can not express the fact that specific inputs must be present in the environment.

2.2   Refinement

The refinement relation formalizes the relation between abstract and concrete versions of the same component. The usual approaches to check refinement are based on the trace containment or simulation preorder relations. It is argued that the former notions are only suitable for input-enabled systems, where all input actions at each state are always enabled. In contrast, for non-input-enabled systems like interface automata, a refinement check based on checking *alternating simulation* [10] is proposed. The key idea here is that, in the non-input-enabled setting, the implementation must allow *more* legal inputs and exhibit *fewer* outputs, than the specification.

Intuitively, an interface automaton Q refines another interface automaton P (written $Q \preccurlyeq P$), if there exists an alternating simulation relation $\preccurlyeq$ between Q and P, i.e., all input steps of P can be simulated by Q and all output steps of Q can be simulated by P. Moreover, $A_P^I \subseteq A_Q^I$ and $A_Q^O \subseteq A_P^O$. Note that both P and Q may also have internal steps, which are independent from each other. Therefore, the definition of alternating simulation is extended to handle internal steps. Given a state v of an interface automaton P, $\epsilon - closure_P(v)$ is defined to be the set of states (including v) that are reachable from v in P via internal actions. Given a state u in Q, $\epsilon - closure_Q(u)$ is defined similarly. Let $I_P(v)$ and $I_Q(u)$ denote the set of input steps enabled at *all* states in $\epsilon - closure_P(v)$ and $\epsilon - closure_Q(u)$, respectively. Similarly, let $O(v)$ and $O(u)$ denote the set of output steps enabled at *some* state in $\epsilon - closure_P(v)$ and $\epsilon - closure_Q(u)$, respectively. Also let $S_P(v, a)$ denote the set of all successors v'' in P such that for some $v' \in \epsilon - closure_P(v)$, $(v', a, v'') \in T_P$. $S_Q(u, a)$ is defined similarly.

Now, a binary relation $\preccurlyeq \subseteq V_Q \times V_P$ is an alternating simulation from Q to P if for all states $v \in V_P$ and $u \in V_Q$ such that $u \preccurlyeq v$, the following conditions hold:

1. $I(v) \subseteq I(u)$ and $O(u) \subseteq O(v)$.
2. For all $a \in I(v) \cup O(u)$ and all states $u'' \in S_Q(u, a)$, there is a state $v'' \in S_P(v, a)$ such that $u'' \preccurlyeq v''$.

Finally, Q is said to refine P, if there exist states $v \in V_P^{init}$ and $u \in V_Q^{init}$ such that $u \preccurlyeq v$ and both $A_P^I \subseteq A_Q^I$ and $A_Q^O \subseteq A_P^O$ hold. Refinement between interface automata is a preorder, i.e., reflexive and transitive.

This notion of refinement has two useful properties:

– *Substitutivity.* If Q refines P and is connected to the environment by the same inputs, then we can always replace P by Q in a larger system. Note that Q must have no more inputs than P since incompatibilities may occur when environment presents those inputs to Q.
– *Compositionality.* In order to check if $Q \parallel Q' \preccurlyeq P \parallel P'$, it is sufficient to check $Q \preccurlyeq P$ and $Q' \preccurlyeq P'$, separately.

Interface automata, as defined above, execute asynchronously. The formalism has been extended to synchronous interfaces [6]. A general formalism relating components and their interface models has been developed [11] using the notion of interface automata.

3   Checking Compatibility of Upgrades

McCamant and Ernst present a technique [21] to check if upgrades to one or more components in a component assembly (also referred to as an *application*) are compatible with the other components in the assembly. More precisely, their work seeks to identify unanticipated interactions among software components as a result of an upgrade, before the older components are replaced by the upgraded ones. Their approach is based on computing a summary (a set of pre- and post-condition pairs on interface variables) of the observed behavior of the old and new components as well as a summary of the environment components that interact with the old component. An upgrade is permitted only if these summaries for the old and new components are compatible; otherwise, a warning is issued together with a witness that illustrates the incompatibility. The technique uses a large number of input test sequences and valid executions of components to compute the summary of the input/output behavior of a component and its environment. The compatibility check procedure crucially depends on the computed summaries and the authors have used it successfully to detect incompatibilities during upgrade of the Linux C library.

3.1 Single Component Upgrade

We now describe their approach for the case of a single component upgrade in an application. It is assumed that the application is observed to function properly with some version of the component and the verification task is to validate that the application will function correctly after upgrading the component to a new version. The upgrade compatibility check technique first computes an operational abstraction (summary) of the behaviors of the old component that are used by the rest of the system. The summary is computed using the tool Daikon [14] for automatically inferring program invariants from a representative set of program behaviors and consists of pre- and post-condition tuples for the component. The new component vendor also computes this observation summary for the new component, based on the test suite for the component and provides the summary to the compatibility check procedure. The procedure then compares the old and the new operational abstractions to test if the new abstraction is stronger than the older one. More precisely, the procedure checks if the new abstraction is able to accept as many inputs and produces no more outputs than the old abstraction. This check is performed using the Simplify theorem prover [12].

If the test succeeds, then the new component can be safely used in all situations where the old component was used. Otherwise, the check provides feedback about the incompatibility in terms of specific procedure pre- and post-conditions. In spite of an incompatibility being present, it may still be the case that the new component is acceptable. The final decision is made by examining the feedback manually.

3.2 Multiple Component Upgrades

Handling upgrades for components with persistent state (e.g., due to variables in object-oriented programs) or callbacks is more difficult. Similarly, handling simultaneous upgrades for multiple components requires more sophisticated analysis. For this analysis, an application is sub-divided into *modules* with the assumption that any upgrade affects one or more complete modules. Now, the upgrade compatibility check technique not only computes an observational summary of each upgraded module in the context of its environment modules, but also computes a summary of the behavior of environment modules, as observed by that module.

The observational summaries consist of three types of relations. (1) *Call and return relations* represent the procedure call dependencies between modules. (2) *Internal data-flow relations* represent how the output of a module depends on the module's inputs. This relation is stored as logical formula on input and output variables of a module and generalizes upon the observed behaviors of the module during testing. (3) *External summary relations* represent how each input to the module might depend on the behavior of the rest of the system and any previous outputs of the module. These relations may be considered to be dual of the internal data-flow relations and represent assumptions about how the module is used in the application.

In the event of an upgrade of multiple modules, it is assumed that each upgraded module is accompanied by sets of new data-flow and external summary relations. The compatibility check is then performed by checking if the new summary relations obey the old relations. This check is performed using the notion of a *feasible subgraph* [21] for a summary relation, which captures a subset of system executions over which the summary relation should hold. An upgrade is considered to be safe if it allows each summary relation to hold over every corresponding feasible subgraph. Several optimizations are presented aimed at reducing the number of feasible subgraphs to be re-validated for each summary relation.

As an example, consider an application with two modules, U and C, where C is supplied by a vendor and provides a procedure f and U calls f. The calls and returns to f are denoted by f and f', respectively. The summary relation associated with C consists of two parts: (i) the preconditions of f (assumptions on external components) represented by $\overline{C}(f)$ and (ii) a data-flow relation $C(f|f')$ describing the postconditions of f. Both these relations are based on the vendor's testing of C. Similarly, the relations associated with U are as follows: $U(f)$ consists of a set of preconditions describing how U calls f and $\overline{U}(f|f')$ describes the postconditions U expects from the call. In order to verify that the new component C may be safely substituted for the old one in the above application, the following checks are performed:

$$U(f) \implies \overline{C}(f) \quad (U(f) \wedge C(f'|f)) \implies \overline{U}(f'|f)$$

Here, the first check makes sure that all preconditions $\overline{C}(f)$ of f in C are met by postconditions $U(f)$ of U and the second check ensures that the return values from call to f satisfy the expectation of the module U. This procedure has been extended to handle upgrades for modules with internal state and callbacks and also for simultaneous upgrades of multiple modules.

3.3   Case Studies

The authors evaluate their technique on upgrades of the GNU C library distributed with Linux systems. The library provides the C standard library functions and wrappers around the low-level system calls and is used by a large number of commonplace applications on Linux. It contains multiple versions of some procedures in order to maintain backward compatibility and the linker is responsible for compiling the correct versions together. The authors subverted the version compatibility checks and checked if the procedures marked as incompatible can be used without error by the client applications and whether differences between procedures marked with the same version can cause errors. Binary versions of the applications and the C library were used together with a wrapper around the C library, which keeps track of the arguments to and from each function call in the library.

The authors compare two versions of the C library and used the set of common Linux applications as a "test suite" for constructing the observational summaries. Of the selected 76 procedures in the library, the tool correctly warns of 10 behavioral differences and approves 57 upgrades as compatible. For the remaining 9 procedures, an (spurious) incompatibility is detected with respect to summaries computed with one or more test applications. A different experiment examined two incompatible upgrades of another set of procedures from the C library, where the tool was able to detect the incompatibilities.

4   Preservation of Program Properties by Behavioral Subtyping

The problem of behavioral consistency among various versions of programs is also addressed in the work of Liskov and Wing [19]. This work explores ideas of behavioral subtyping using invariants and constraints. It defines the subtype relation that ensures that subtype objects preserve properties of their supertypes. The properties are the formal specifications of the sub- and supertypes.

Liskov and Wing define an object's type not only by the object's legal values (as in traditional type checking) but also by its interface with environment (by means of the object's methods). Therefore, the properties of the subtype relations are both the supertype's values and its methods. Thus, altogether, the behavioral subtyping is defined to preserve the behavior of supertype methods and also all invariant properties of its supertype.

4.1   Subtype Relation

The formalization of the subtype relation is given in Figure 1. It uses the model of a type that is defined as a triple, $\langle O, V, M \rangle$, where O is a set of objects, V is a set of values for an object, and M is a set of methods that provide the means to manipulate the object. A *computation*, i.e., program execution, is a sequence of alternating states and transitions starting in some initial state. The formalization of types uses type invariants and constraints (for example, type σ can refer to its invariant I_σ and constraint, C_σ). Methods of each type are denoted by m (for example, methods of type τ are denoted as m_τ.

Subtyping is enforced by the invariant checking that is essentially established as an abstraction function. Additionally, a renaming map is defined. The rest of the section provides the formalization of this approach as presented in [19].

The subtype relation relates two types σ and τ. Each type's specifications preserve their invariants, I_σ and I_τ, and satisfy their constraints, C_σ and C_τ, respectively. In the rules, since x is an object of type σ, its value (x_{pre} or x_{post}) is a member of S (set of values of type σ) and therefore cannot be used directly in the predicates about objects of the supertype τ (which are in terms of values in T). Therefore, an abstraction function A is used to translate these values using the system predicates from subtype to supertype values. This approach requires that an abstraction function be defined for all legal values of the subtype (although it need not be defined for values that do not satisfy the subtype invariant). Moreover, it must map legal values of the subtype to legal values of the supertype.

The first clause (cf. Figure 1) addresses the need to relate inherited methods of the subtype to those of the supertype. The first two signature rules are the standard contra/covariance rules [4,3]. The exception rule says that m_σ may not throw more exceptions (the exceptions concept is taken from object-oriented programming) than m_τ, since a caller of a method on a supertype object should not expect to handle an unknown exception. The pre- and post-condition rules are the intuitive counterparts to the contravariant and covariant rules for method signatures. The pre-condition rule ensures the subtype's method can be called in any state required by the supertype. The post-condition rule says that the subtype method's post-condition can be stronger than the supertype method's post-condition; hence, any property that can be proved based on the supertype method's post-condition also follows from the subtype's method's post-condition.

The second clause addresses preserving program-independent properties. The invariant rule and the assumption that the type specification preserves the invariant suffices to argue that invariant properties of a supertype are preserved by the subtype. This approach does not include the invariant in the methods (or constraint) rule directly.

Definition of the subtype relation, $\preceq$: $\sigma = \langle O_\sigma, S, M \rangle$ is a *subtype* of $\tau = \langle O_\tau, T, N \rangle$ if $\exists A : S \rightarrow T$, and a renaming map, $R : M \rightarrow N$, such that:

1. Subtype methods preserve the supertype methods behavior. If m_τ of τ is the corresponding renamed method m_σ of σ, the following rules must hold:

Signature Rule.

— *Contravariance of arguments.* m_τ and m_σ have the same number of arguments. If the list of argument types of m_τ is α and that of m_σ is β, then $\forall i. \alpha_i \preceq \beta_i$.
— *Covariance of result.* Either both m_τ and m_σ have a result or neither has. If there is a result, let m_τ's result type be α and and m_σ's be β. Then $\beta \preceq \alpha$.
— *Exception rule.* The exceptions thrown during execution of m_σ are contained in the set of exceptions thrown during execution of m_τ.

Methods Rule. For all $(x : \sigma)$, the following holds:

— *Pre-condition rule.* $m_\tau.pre[A(x_{pre})/x_{pre}] \Rightarrow m_\sigma.pre$.
— *Post-condition rule.* $m_\sigma.post \Rightarrow m_\tau.post[A(x_{pre})/x_{pre}, A(x_{post})/x_{post}]$

2. Subtypes preserve supertype properties. For all computations c, and all states ρ and ψ in c such that ρ precedes ψ, and for all $(x : \sigma)$, the following holds :

— *Invariant Rule.* Subtype invariants ensure supertype invariants. $I_\sigma \Rightarrow I_\tau[A(x_\rho)/x_\rho]$
— *Constraint Rule.* Subtype constraints ensure supertype constraints.
$C_\sigma \Rightarrow C_\tau[A(x_\rho)/x_\rho, [A(x_\psi)/x_\psi]$

Fig. 1. Definition of the subtype relation [19]

4.2   Pragmatics of the Subtype Relation Approach

The definition of the subtype relation by Liskov and Wing captures the intuition of programmers for designing type hierarchies in object-oriented languages. The major contribution is that it provides precise definitions to capture it. As a result systems become amenable to formal analysis of ensuring behavioral compatibility between super- and subtype objects. Liskov and Wing report a number of successful examples where the subtype relation was useful in validating several benchmarks.

5   Substitutability Check

Our own earlier work [5] gives an automated and compositional procedure to solve the substitutability problem in the context of evolving software systems. Checking substitutability is defined as verifying whether (i) any updated portion of software continues to provide all services provided by it earlier counterpart, and (ii) all previously established system correctness properties remain valid after the upgrades. A component is essentially a C program communicating with other components via blocking message passing. A component assembly consists of collection of such concurrent components. In the following, $\mathcal{I}$ denotes the set of indices of the upgraded components in the assembly.

The procedure consists of two phases, namely, containment and compatibility. The containment phase checks locally if any useful behavior has been lost during upgrade of a component in the assembly and relies on simultaneous use of over- and under-approximations of the evolved software component. The compatibility phase checks if the added behaviors of the upgraded component violate any global safety specifications. This phase uses a dynamic assume-guarantee reasoning algorithm, wherein previously generated assumptions before upgrades are reused efficiently to re-validate the new assembly. The framework uses iterative abstraction/refinement paradigm [2,8,17] for both containment and compatibility phases. This approach enabled extraction of relatively simple finite-state models from complex C code. State-event automata (finite automata with both state and edges labeled) are used to represent these abstractions. Moreover, simultaneous upgrade of multiple components are allowed in this framework.

5.1   Containment Check

The containment step verifies for each $i \in \mathcal{I}$, that $C_i \sqsubseteq C_i'$, i.e., every behavior of C_i is also a behavior of C_i'. If $C_i \not\sqsubseteq C_i'$, we also generate a counterexample behavior in $Behv(C_i) \setminus Behv(C_i')$ which will be subsequently provided as feedback. This containment check is performed iteratively and component-wise as depicted in Figure 2 (CE refers to the counterexample generated during the verification phase). For each $i \in \mathcal{I}$, the containment check proceeds as follows:

1. Abstraction. Construct finite models M and M' such that the following conditions **C1** and **C2** hold:

$$\textbf{(C1)}\ C_i \sqsubseteq M \qquad \textbf{(C2)}\ M' \sqsubseteq C_i'$$

Here M is an *over-approximation* of C_i and can be constructed by standard predicate abstraction [15]. M' is constructed from C_i' via a modified predicate abstraction which produces an *under-approximation* of its input C component. We now describe the details of the abstraction steps.

Suppose that C_i comprises of a set of C statements $Stmt = \{st_1, \ldots, st_k\}$. Let V be the set of variables in the C_i. A valuation of all the variables in a program corresponds to a concrete state of the given program. We denote it by $\bar{v}$.

Predicates are functions that map a concrete state $\bar{v} \in S$ into a Boolean value. Let $\mathcal{P} = \{\pi_1, \ldots, \pi_k\}$ be the set of predicates over the given program. On evaluating the set of predicates in $\mathcal{P}$ in a particular concrete state $\bar{v}$, we obtain a vector of boolean values $\bar{b}$, where $b_i = \pi_i(\bar{v})$. The boolean vector $\bar{b}$ represents an abstract state and we denote this operation by an abstraction function α: $\bar{b} = \alpha(\bar{v})$.

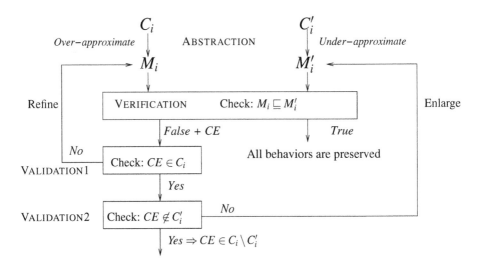

Fig. 2. The containment phase of the substitutability framework

May Predicate Abstraction: Over-approximation. This step corresponds to the standard predicate abstraction. Each statement (or basic block) St in C_i is associated with a transition relation $T(\bar{v}, \bar{v}')$. Here, $\bar{v}$ and $\bar{v}'$ represent a concrete state before and after execution of St, respectively. Given the set of predicates $\mathcal{P}$ and associated vector of Boolean variables $\bar{b}$ as before, we compute an abstract transition relation $\hat{T}(\bar{b}, \bar{b}')$ as follows:

$$\hat{T}(\bar{b}, \bar{b}') = \exists \bar{v}, \bar{v}' \ : \ T(\bar{v}, \bar{v}') \wedge \bar{b} = \alpha(\bar{v}) \wedge \bar{b}' = \alpha(\bar{v}') \tag{1}$$

$\hat{T}$ is an existential abstraction of T and is also referred to as its *may* abstraction $\hat{T}_{may}$ [24]. We compute this abstraction using the weakest precondition (WP) transformer [13,18] on predicates in $\mathcal{P}$ along with an automated theorem prover [15].

Must Predicate Abstraction: Under-approximation. The modified predicate abstraction constructs an under-approximation of the concrete system via universal or *must* abstraction. Given a statement St in the modified component C'_i and its associated transition relation $T(\bar{v}, \bar{v}')$ as before, we compute its must abstraction with respect to predicates $\mathcal{P}$ as follows:

$$\hat{T}(\bar{b}, \bar{b}') = \forall \bar{v}, \exists \bar{v}' \; : \; T(\bar{v}, \bar{v}') \wedge \bar{b} = \alpha(\bar{v}) \wedge \bar{b}' = \alpha(\bar{v}') \qquad (2)$$

We use $\hat{T}_{must}$ to denote the above relation. Note that $\hat{T}_{must}$ contains a transition from an abstract state $\bar{b}$ to $\bar{b}'$ iff for every concrete state $\bar{v}$ corresponding to $\bar{b}$, there exists a concrete transition to a state $\bar{v}'$ corresponding to $\bar{b}'$ [24]. Further, it has been shown [24] that the concrete transition relation T simulates the abstract transition relation $\hat{T}_{must}$. Hence, $\hat{T}_{must}$ is an under-approximation of T. Again, we compute $\hat{T}_{must}$ using the WP transformer on the predicates together with a theorem prover. At the end of this phase, we obtain M as an over-approximation of C_i and M' as an under-approximation of C'_i.

2. Verification. Verify if $M \sqsubseteq M'$ (or alternatively $M \setminus B \sqsubseteq M'$ if the upgrade involved some bug fix and the bug was defined as a SE automata B). If so then from **(C1)** and **(C2)** (cf. **Abstraction**) above we know that $C_i \sqsubseteq C'_i$ and we terminate with success. Otherwise we obtain a counterexample CE.

3. Validation 1. Check if CE is a real behavior of C_i. To do this we first compute the set S of concrete states of C_i that are reachable by simulating CE on C_i. This is done via symbolic simulation and the result is a formula ϕ that represents S. Then CE is a real behavior of C_i iff $S \neq \emptyset$, i.e., iff ϕ is satisfiable. If CE is a real behavior of C_i, we proceed to the next step. Otherwise we refine model M (remove spurious CE) by constructing a new set of predicates $\mathcal{P}'$ and repeat from Step 2.

4. Validation 2. Check if CE is *not* a real behavior of C'_i. To do this we first symbolically simulate CE on C'_i to compute the reachable set S' of concrete states of C'_i. This is done as in the previous validation step and the result is again a formula ϕ that represents S'. Then CE is not a real behavior of C'_i iff $S' = \emptyset$, i.e., iff ϕ is unsatisfiable. If CE is not a real behavior of C'_i, we know that $CE \in Behv(C_i) \setminus Behv(C'_i)$. We add CE to the feedback step and stop. Otherwise we enlarge M' (add CE) by constructing a new set of predicates $\mathcal{P}'$ and repeat from Step 2. This step is an antithesis of standard abstraction-refinement since it *adds* the valid behavior CE back to M'. However it is conceptually similar to standard abstraction-refinement and we omit its details in this article.

Figure 2 depicts the individual steps of this containment check. The check is either successful (all behaviors of C_i are verified to be present in C'_i) or returns an actual diagnostic behavior CE as a feedback to the developers.

5.2 Compatibility Check

The compatibility check ensures that the upgraded system satisfies global safety specification. The check relies on an automated assume-guarantee reasoning procedure [9], where the key idea is to generate an environment assumption for a component automatically and then verify if the rest of the system satisfies the assumption. An algorithm for learning regular sets, L^* [1,23], is used to automatically generate these assumptions assisted by a modelchecker [7]. It is assumed that appropriate assumptions have been generated by performing automated A-G reasoning over the assembly before an upgrade occurs. Upon an upgrade, the compatibility check procedure reuses the previously generated assumptions and locally modifies them in order to re-validate the upgraded component assembly. Similar to the containment phase, this check is performed on finite-state state-event (SE) automaton abstractions from the C components.

Automated Assume-Guarantee Reasoning. Assume-guarantee (A-G) based reasoning [22] is a well-known compositional verification technique. The essential idea here is to model-check each component independently by making an assumption about its environment, and then discharge the assumption on the collection of the rest of the components. Given a set of component SE automata $M_1, \ldots, M_n$ obtained after abstraction and a specification SE automata φ, consider the following non-circular A-G rule (called AG-NC) for n components:

$$\frac{M_1 \parallel A_1 \sqsubseteq \varphi \quad M_2 \parallel \cdots \parallel M_n \sqsubseteq A_1}{M_1 \parallel \cdots \parallel M_n \sqsubseteq \varphi}$$

In the above, A_1 is a deterministic SE automata representing the assumption about the environment under which M_1 is expected to operate correctly. The second premise is itself an instance of the top-level proof-obligation with $n - 1$ component SE automata. Therefore, AG-NC can be recursively applied to the rest of the components so that every rule premise contains exactly one component automaton. The assumptions are generated using L^* together with a model checker for SE automata in an iterative fashion, in a manner similar to the technique proposed by Cobleigh et al. [9]. In order to show that a component satisfies a global property, the technique first iteratively learns an assumption automaton that must be satisfied by its environment components. However, this initial assumption may be too strong to hold on its environment. Therefore, the assumption is gradually weakened by model checking it alternately against the component and its environment, and using the counterexamples generated.

The compatibility check makes use of AG-NC in the above form to first generate $n - 1$ assumptions and then perform re-validation of upgrades. This re-validation may involve modifying several previously generated assumptions. The compatibility check avoids re-generating all such assumptions from scratch by proposing a technique to effectively reuse the previous assumptions by re-validating them first. A dynamic L^* algorithm is proposed that first re-validates the previously stored set of samples with respect to the upgraded assembly and then continues to learn in the usual fashion. This gives rise to a dynamic procedure for A-G reasoning over component assemblies across upgrades, also called as dynamic A-G.

Compatibility check with Dynamic A-G. The central idea in the compatibility check algorithm is to use dynamic L^* for learning assumptions as opposed to the original L^* algorithm. This allows the check to fully reuse the previous verification results, and in particular, contributes to its locally efficient nature.

Suppose we have a component assembly $\mathcal{C}$ consisting of n components and a given index set $\mathcal{I}$, identifying the upgraded components. We assume that a set of $n - 1$ assumptions are available from a compatibility check before the upgrade took place. Now, suppose that the component assembly goes through an upgrade and the behaviors of one or more SE automata M_i ($1 \leq i \leq n$) change. Note that the previous compatibility check provides us with a set of assumptions A_j ($1 \leq j < n$). The dynamic compatibility check procedure **DynamicCheck** learns new assumptions required for the verification of the upgraded assembly while reusing the previous set of assumptions A_j by first re-validating them, if necessary.

We present an overview of the algorithm **DynamicCheck** for two SE automata. The complete details of the generalization of the algorithm to an arbitrary collection of SE automata can be found in [5]. Suppose we have two old SE automata M_1, M_2 and a property SE automaton φ. We assume that we previously verified $M_1 \parallel M_2 \sqsubseteq \varphi$ using **DynamicCheck**. The algorithm **DynamicCheck** uses dynamic L^* to learn appropriate assumptions that can discharge the premises of AG-NC. In particular suppose that while trying to verify $M_1 \parallel M_2 \sqsubseteq \varphi$, **DynamicCheck** generated an assumption A, with an observation table $\mathcal{T}$.

Now suppose we have new versions M_1', M_2' for M_1, M_2 where at least one of the M_i is different from M_i'. **DynamicCheck** will now reuse $\mathcal{T}$ and invoke the dynamic L^* algorithm to automatically learn an assumption A' such that: (i) $M_1' \parallel A' \sqsubseteq \varphi$ and (ii) $M_2' \sqsubseteq A'$. More precisely, **DynamicCheck** proceeds iteratively as follows:

1. It checks if $M_1 = M_1'$. If this holds, then it follows from the definition of AG-NC that the corresponding assumption language remains the same. Therefore, the algorithm starts learning from the previous table $\mathcal{T}$ itself, i.e., it sets $\mathcal{T}' := \mathcal{T}$. Otherwise it re-validates $\mathcal{T}$ against M_1' to obtain a new table $\mathcal{T}'$.

2. The algorithm then derives a conjecture A' from $\mathcal{T}'$ and checks if $M_2' \sqsubseteq A'$. If this check passes, then the procedure terminates with TRUE and a new assumption A'. Otherwise, a counterexample CE is obtained.

3. The counterexample CE is analyzed to see if CE corresponds to a real counterexample to $M_1' \parallel M_2' \sqsubseteq \varphi$ (same as a membership query with M_1'). If so, the algorithm constructs such a counterexample and terminates with FALSE. Otherwise it updates $\mathcal{T}'$ using CE.

4. $\mathcal{T}'$ is closed by making membership queries and the algorithm repeats from Step 2.

5.3   Case Studies

The compatibility check phase for checking component substitutability was implemented in the COMFORT [16] framework. COMFORT extracts abstract component SE models from C programs using predicate abstraction and performs automated A-G reasoning on them. If the compatibility check returns a counterexample, the counterexample validation and abstraction-refinement modules of COMFORT are employed to check for spuriousness and perform refinement, if necessary. The evaluation benchmarks consist of an assembly having seven components, which implement an interprocess communication (IPC) protocol.

Both single and simultaneous upgrades of the *write-queue* and the *ipc-queue* components in the IPC assembly were used. The upgrades had both missing and extra behaviors as compared to the original system. A set of properties describing behaviors of the verified portion of the IPC protocol were used. It was observed that the compatibility check required much less time for re-validation (due to reuse of previously generated assumptions) as compared to time for compositional verification of the original system.

6   Comparative Analysis

We have presented four techniques each of which addresses a problem of behavioral consistency among programs. While the techniques address similar problems of the program compatibility, they differ greatly in the specification formalisms and algorithmic approaches. This makes it difficult to conduct comparative analysis among the techniques. To overcome this difficulty, we chose one of the techniques as a reference point against which we compared the other three approaches. Specifically, we compared the automata interface approach, the observation summary approach of McCamant and Ernst, and the behavioral subtyping technique to our own work on component substitutability.

6.1   Interface Automata Formalism

In the interface automata formalism, substitution check corresponds to a refinement check, which ensures that the newer component exhibits fewer outputs and accepts more inputs than the old component. Our approach, however, differentiates between the refinement and substitution checks. We believe that the refinement check is too strong to be used as a substitution check since it is not adequate to check substitution locally without taking into account the exact behaviors of the environment components.

Given two interface automata M and N, checking alternating refinement [10] between M and N ($N \preceq M$, cf. Section 2) is an effective way to *locally* check for substitution of M by N. However, this refinement check assumes that the environment components remain the same, i.e., they continue to stimulate all inputs of M and are capable of responding to no more than the present outputs of M. Note that in case of multiple component upgrades, it is possible that the new environment for the component is more *supportive*, i.e., on one hand, it does not stimulate all inputs of M and on the other it is able to respond to even more outputs from M. If the new environment is more supportive, then it is possible that $N \npreceq M$ but is still substitutable. In other words, even though some inputs of N may be absent in M, M may still substitute N since the absent inputs are no longer stimulated by the new environment. Therefore a substitutability check must take account of the new environment precisely rather than identifying it on basis of input and output behaviors of the previous component M. These criteria becomes even more important if multiple components in an assembly are upgraded and as a consequence, the environment for several components changes simultaneously.

6.2   Observation-Based Compatibility of Upgrades

McCamant et al. [21] suggest a technique for checking compatibility of multi-component upgrades. They derive consistency criteria by focusing on input/output component behavior only and abstract away the temporal information. Even though they state that their abstractions are unsound in general, they report success in detecting important errors on GNU C library upgrades. In contrast, our work on component substitutability uses abstractions that preserve temporal information about component behavior and are always sound. Moreover, they need to recompute the external observational summaries for each upgrade from scratch while our compatibility check procedure is able to reuse the previous verification proofs to re-validate the upgraded system.

6.3   Behavioral Subtype Checking

Conceptually, the subtype relation-based approach is similar to our work not only in that it is based on establishing the behavioral consistency among system components, but also in that it handles changes among versions of programs. The subtype check approach handles mutable objects and allows subtypes to have more methods than their supertypes. The component substitutability approach allows removal and addition of behaviors to the upgraded component as compared to its earlier counterpart.

The subtype relation is established as an invariant check. It requires defining an abstraction function that is a restricted form of the simulation relation between the subtype and supertype objects. Our work, uses the language containment approach and thus is more expensive computationally. However, our framework allows checking general safety properties, while work of Liskov and Wing handles only a restricted set of safety properties.

References

1. Dana Angluin. Learning regular sets from queries and counterexamples. In *Information and Computation*, volume 75(2), pages 87–106, November 1987.
2. T. Ball and S. Rajamani. Boolean programs: A model and process for software analysis. *TR-2000-14*, 2000.
3. A. Black, A. Hutchinson, N. Jul, E. Levy, and L. Carter. Distribution and abstract types in emerald. *IEEE TSE*, 13(1):65–76, 1987.
4. L. Cardelli. A semantics of multiple inheritance. *Information and Computation*, 76:138–164, 1988.
5. Sagar Chaki, Edmund Clarke Natasha Sharygina, and Nishant Sinha. Dynamic component substitutability analysis. In *Proc. of Conf. on Formal Methods*, volume 3582 of *Lecture Notes in Computer Science*, pages 512–528. Springer Verlag, 2005.
6. Arindam Chakrabarti, Luca de Alfaro, Thomas A. Henzinger, and Freddy Y. C. Mang. Synchronous and bidirectional component interfaces. In *CAV*, pages 414–427, 2002.
7. E. Clarke, O. Grumberg, and D. Peled. *Model Checking*. MIT Press, December 1999.
8. Edmund M. Clarke, Orna Grumberg, Somesh Jha, Yuan Lu, and Helmut Veith. Counterexample-guided abstraction refinement. In E. Allen Emerson and A. Prasad Sistla, editors, *Proceedings of the 12th International Conference on Computer Aided Verification (CAV '00)*, volume 1855 of *Lecture Notes in Computer Science*, pages 154–169. Springer-Verlag, July 2000.

9. J. M. Cobleigh, Dimitra Giannakopoulou, and Corina S. Păsăreanu. Learning assumptions for compositional verification. In Hubert Garavel and John Hatcliff, editors, *Proceedings of the 9th International Conference on Tools and Algorithms for the Construction and Analysis of Systems (TACAS '03)*, volume 2619 of *Lecture Notes in Computer Science*, pages 331–346. Springer-Verlag, April 2003.

10. Luca de Alfaro and Thomas A. Henzinger. Interface automata. In *FSE*, 2001.

11. Luca de Alfaro and Thomas A. Henzinger. Interface theories for component-based design. In *EMSOFT*, pages 148–165, 2001.

12. David Detlefs, Greg Nelson, and James B. Saxe. Simplify: a theorem prover for program checking. *J. ACM*, 52(3):365–473, 2005.

13. Edsger Dijkstra. *A Discipline of Programming*. Prentice-Hall, 1976.

14. M.D. Ernst, J. Cockrell, W.G. Griswold, and D. Notkin. Dynamically discovering likely program invariants to support program evolution. In *International Conference on Software Engineering (ICSE'99)*, pages 213–224, 1999.

15. Susanne Graf and Hassen Saïdi. Construction of abstract state graphs with PVS. In Orna Grumberg, editor, *Proceedings of the 9th International Conference on Computer Aided Verification (CAV '97)*, volume 1254 of *Lecture Notes in Computer Science*, pages 72–83. Springer-Verlag, June 1997.

16. James Ivers and Natasha Sharygina. Overview of ComFoRT: A model checking reasoning framework. *CMU/SEI-2004-TN-018*, 2004.

17. Robert Kurshan. *Computer-Aided Verification of Coordinating Processes: The Automata-Theoretic Approach*. Princeton University Press, 1994.

18. K. Rustan M. Leino. Efficient weakest preconditions. *Inf. Process. Lett.*, 93(6):281–288, 2005.

19. B. Liskov and J. Wing. Behavioral subtyping using invariants and constraints. *Formal Methods for Distributed Processing, an Object Oriented Approach*, pages 254–280, 2001.

20. N. Lynch and M. Tuttle. Hierarchical correctness proofs for distributed algorithms. 1987.

21. Stephen McCamant and Michael D. Ernst. Early identification of incompatibilities in multi-component upgrades. In *ECOOP Conference*, Olso, Norway, 2004.

22. A. Pnueli. In transition from global to modular temporal reasoning about programs. In *Logics and models of concurrent systems*. Springer-Verlag New York, Inc., 1985.

23. Ronald L. Rivest and Robert E. Schapire. Inference of finite automata using homing sequences. In *Information and Computation*, volume 103(2), pages 299–347, 1993.

24. Sharon Shoham and Orna Grumberg. Monotonic abstraction-refinement for CTL. In *TACAS*, pages 546–560, 2004.

25. Clemens Szyperski, Dominik Gruntz, and Stephan Murer. *Component Software - Beyond Object-Oriented Programming*. Addison-Wesley, ACM Press, 2002.

Cluster-Based LTL Model Checking
of Large Systems

Jiří Barnat, Luboš Brim, and Ivana Černá*

Department of Computer Science, Faculty of Informatics
Masaryk University, Brno, Czech Republic

Abstract. In recent years a bundle of parallel and distributed algorithms for verification of finite state systems has appeared. We survey distributed-memory enumerative LTL model checking algorithms
designed for networks of workstations communicating via MPI. In the
automata-based approach to LTL model checking the problem is reduced to the accepting cycle detection problem in a graph. Distributed
algorithms, in opposite to sequential ones, cannot rely on depth-first
search postorder which is essential for efficient detection of accepting
cycles. Therefore, diverse conditions that characterise the existence of
cycles in a graph have to be employed in order to come up with efficient
and practical distributed algorithms. We compare these algorithms both
theoretically and experimentally and determine cases where particular
algorithms can be successful.

1 Introduction

With the increase in complexity of computer systems, it becomes more important
to develop formal methods for ensuring their quality and reliability. Various techniques for automated and semi-automated analysis and verification have been
successfully applied to real-life computer systems. However, these techniques
are computationally hard and memory intensive in general and their applicability to extremely large systems is limited. The major hampering factor is the
state space explosion problem due to which large industrial models cannot be
efficiently handled by a single state-of-the-art computer.

Much attention has been focused on the development of approaches to battle
the state space explosion problem. Many techniques, such as abstraction, state
compression, state space reduction, symbolic state representation, etc., are used
to reduce the size of the problem to be handled allowing thus a single computer to process larger systems. There are also techniques that purely focus on
increasing the amount of available computational power. These are, for example, techniques to fight memory limits with efficient utilisation of an external
I/O device [1,24,34,40], or techniques that introduce cluster-based algorithms to
employ aggregate power of network-interconnected computers.

---

* Supported in part by grant no. GACR 201/06/1338.

F.S. de Boer et al. (Eds.): FMCO 2005, LNCS 4111, pp. 259–279, 2006.

Cluster-based algorithms perform their computation simultaneously on a number of workstations that are allowed to communicate and synchronise themselves by means of message passing. Cluster-based algorithms can thus be characterised as parallel algorithms performing in a distributed memory environment. The algorithms prove their usefulness in verification of large-scale systems. They have been successfully applied to symbolic model checking [29,30], analysis of stochastic [31] and timed [7] systems, equivalence checking [10] and other related problems [8,11,28].

In this tutorial paper we focus on LTL model checking and we survey all the known cluster-based algorithms for enumerative LTL model checking, compare them, discuss their advantages and disadvantages, and determine cases in which individual algorithms are more appropriate than the others.

2   Distributed LTL Model Checking

Model checking is one of the major techniques used in the formal verification [21]. It builds on an automatic procedure that takes a model of the system and decides whether it satisfies a given property. In case the property is not satisfied, the procedure gives a counterexample, i.e. a particular behaviour of the model that violates the verified property.

Linear temporal logic LTL [37] is a widely used language for specification of properties of concurrent programs. An efficient automata-based procedure to decide LTL model checking problem was introduced in [42]. The approach exploits the fact that every set of executions expressible by an LTL formula is an ω-regular set and can be described by a *Büchi automaton*. In particular, the approach suggests to express all system executions by a *system automaton* and all executions not satisfying the formula by a *property* or *negative claim automaton*. These automata are combined into their synchronous product in order to check for the presence of system executions that violate the property expressed by the formula. The language recognised by the *product automaton* is empty if and only if no system execution is invalid.

The language emptiness problem for Büchi automata can be expressed as an *accepting cycle detection problem* in a graph. Each Büchi automaton can be naturally identified with an *automaton graph* which is a directed graph $G = (V, E, s, A)$ where V is the set of vertices ($n = |V|$), E is a set of edges ($m = |E|$), s is an initial vertex, and $A \subseteq V$ is a set of accepting vertices. We say that a reachable cycle in G is accepting if it contains an accepting vertex. Let $\mathcal{A}$ be a Büchi automaton and $G_{\mathcal{A}}$ the corresponding automaton graph. Then $\mathcal{A}$ recognises a nonempty language iff $G_{\mathcal{A}}$ contains an accepting cycle. The LTL model-checking problem is thus reduced to the accepting cycle detection problem in automaton graphs.

The best known enumerative sequential algorithms for detection of accepting cycles are the *Nested DFS* algorithm [22,33] (implemented, e.g., in the model checker SPIN [32]) and *SCC-based algorithms* originating in Tarjan's algorithm for the decomposition of the graph into strongly connected components

(SCCs) [41]. While Nested DFS is more space efficient, SCC-based algorithms produce shorter counterexamples in general. For a survey on sequential algorithms see [25].

An important criterion for a model checking algorithm is whether it works *on-the-fly*. On-the-fly algorithms generate the automaton graph gradually as they explore vertices of the graph. An accepting cycle can thus be detected before the complete set of vertices is generated and stored in memory. On-the-fly algorithms usually assume the graph to be given implicitly by the function F_{init} giving the initial vertex and by the function F_{succ} which returns immediate successors of a given vertex.

Cluster-based algorithms we describe in this paper work with implicit graph representation and use the so called *partition function* in order to exploit the distributed memory. The partition function distributes vertices of the graph among the participating workstations so that every workstation maintains only a part of the graph. In particular, when immediate successors of a vertex are generated, they are classified according to partition function into *local* and *remote* vertices. The local vertices are stored and further processed locally while the remote vertices are sent over the network for local processing on the owning workstations. In this manner the workstations generate the graph in parallel.

As the state space generation and reachability analysis are easily parallelised, their cluster-based implementations appeared as extension modules within a few model checking tools, see e.g. [35,28,7]. However, accepting cycle detection algorithms cannot be parallelised as easily. In [3] the authors showed that cluster-based version of Nested DFS may produce incorrect results. The reason for this is the crucial dependency of sequential accepting cycle detection algorithms on depth-first search postorder. Reif showed that computing depth-first search postorder is P-complete [39], hence unamenable to parallelisation.

A few fundamentally different cluster-based techniques for accepting cycle detection appeared though. They typically perform repeated reachability over the graph. Unlike the postorder problem, reachability is a graph problem which can be well parallelised.

The first cluster-based algorithm for full LTL model checking was presented in [3] and further improved in [6]. The algorithm introduces a new data structure to detect split cycles (Section 7). In [12,13] the LTL model checking problem is reduced to the negative cycle problem (Section 5). Set-based approach is put to use in the algorithm presented in [18] (Section 4). Algorithmic solution based on breadth-first search (BFS) is given in [2,5] (Section 6). Algorithm described in [14,16] employs ordering of vertices to solve the LTL model checking problem.

The purpose of this survey paper is to provide a unifying presentation of the above mentioned cluster-based LTL model checking algorithms with the aim to better understand their principles and to learn about the strengths and weaknesses of individual techniques. For each algorithm we first explain its underlying idea, then we present the algorithm using a high-level pseudo-code and conclude by some comments about the complexity and other interesting issues related to the algorithm. For details the reader is asked to consult the respective papers.

3   Maximal Accepting Predecessor

Fundamentals

A vertex u is a predecessor of a vertex v if there is a non-trivial path from u to v. The main idea behind the algorithm is based on the fact that each accepting vertex lying on an accepting cycle is its own predecessor. Instead of expensive computing and storing of all accepting predecessors for each (accepting) vertex, the algorithm computes a single representative accepting predecessor for each vertex. We presuppose a linear ordering $\prec$ of vertices (given e.g. by their memory representation) and choose the *maximal accepting predecessor*. For a vertex u we denote its maximal accepting predecessor in the graph G by $map_G(u)$. Clearly, if an accepting vertex is its own maximal accepting predecessor ($map_G(u) = u$), it lies on an accepting cycle. Unfortunately, the opposite does not hold in general. It can happen that the maximal accepting predecessor for an accepting vertex on a cycle does not lie on the cycle. This is exemplified on the graph given in Figure 1. The accepting cycle $\langle 2, 1, 3, 2 \rangle$ is not revealed due to the greater accepting vertex 4 outside the cycle. However, as vertex 4 does not lie on *any* cycle, it can be safely deleted from the set of accepting vertices and the accepting cycle still remains in the resulting graph. This idea is formalised as a *deleting transformation*. Whenever the deleting transformation is applied to automaton graph G with $map_G(v) \neq v$ for all $v \in V$, it shrinks the set of accepting vertices by those vertices that do not lie on any cycle.

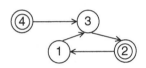

Fig. 1. Undiscovered cycle

Definition 1. *Let $G = (V, E, s, A)$ be an automaton graph and map_G its maximal accepting predecessor function. A deleting transformation (del) is defined as $del(G) = (V, E, s, \overline{A})$, where $\overline{A} = A \setminus \{u \in A \mid map_G(u) \prec u\}$.*

As the set of accepting vertices can change after the deleting transformation has been applied, maximal accepting predecessors must be recomputed. It can happen that even in the graph $del(G)$ the maximal accepting predecessor function is still not sufficient for cycle detection. However, after a finite number of applications of the deleting transformation an accepting cycle is certified. For $i \in \mathbb{N}$ let us define a graph G^i inductively as $G^0 = G$ and $G^{i+1} = del(G^i)$.

Theorem 1. *Let $G = (V, E, s, A)$ be an automaton graph. The graph G contains an accepting cycle if and only if there is a natural $i \in \mathbb{N}$ and a vertex $v \in V$ such that $map_{G^i}(v) = v$.*

For an automaton graph without accepting cycles the repetitive application of the deleting transformation results in an automaton graph with an empty set of accepting vertices.

Algorithmics

The algorithm (for pseudo-code see Figure 2) iteratively computes maximal accepting predecessors and modifies the set of accepting vertices. The MAP procedure always starts by initialising the map value of the initial vertex to nil, all the other vertices are assigned the undefined initial map value, denoted by $\perp$. Every time a vertex receives a new (greater) map value, the vertex is pushed into a $waiting$ queue and the new map value is propagated to all its successors. If an accepting vertex is reached for the first time (line 14) the vertex is inserted into the set $shrinkA$ of vertices to be removed from A by the deleting transformation. However, if the accepting vertex is reached from a greater accepting vertex (lines 15 and 16) this value will be propagated to all its successors and the vertex is removed from the set $shrinkA$.

```
1  proc MAIN(V, E, s, A)
2     while A ≠ ∅ do
3         MAP(V, E, s, A)
4         A := A \ shrinkA
5     od
6     report (NO ACCEPTING CYCLE exists)
7  end

8  proc MAP(V, E, s, A)
9     foreach u ∈ V do map(u) := ⊥ od
10    map(s) := nil
11    waiting.push(s)
12    while waiting ≠ ∅ do
13        u := waiting.pop()
14        if u ∈ A then if map(u) ≺ u then propag := u; shrinkA.add(u)
15                             else propag := map(u);
16                                  shrinkA.remove(u) fi
17                 else propag := map(u)
18        fi
19        foreach (u, v) ∈ E do
20            if propag = v then report (ACCEPTING CYCLE found) fi
21            if propag ≻ map(v) then map(v) := propag
22                                    waiting.push(v) fi
23        od
25    od
26 end
```

Fig. 2. Maximal Accepting Predecessor

We do not explicitly describe the actual distribution of the algorithm as this is quite direct. The very basic operation is the propagation of map values which can be done in any order and thus also in parallel.

The distributed algorithm implements several improvements of the above given basic algorithm. The most important one is based on the observation that accepting cycle in G can be formed from vertices with the same maximal accepting predecessor only. A graph induced by the set of vertices having the same maximal accepting predecessor is called *predecessor subgraph*. It is clear that every strongly connected component (hence every cycle) in the graph is completely included in one of the predecessor subgraphs. Therefore, after applying the deleting transformation, the new *map* function can be computed separately and independently for every predecessor subgraph. This allows for speeding up the computation (values are not propagated to vertices in different subgraphs) and for an efficient parallelisation of the computation. Every predecessor subgraph is identified through the accepting vertex which is the common maximal accepting predecessor for all vertices in the subgraph. Once an accepting cycle is detected, the predecessor subgraphs are effectively used to output a reachable accepting cycle representing an invalid execution of the system.

Comments

Time complexity of the distributed Maximal Accepting Predecessor algorithm is $\mathcal{O}(a^2 \cdot m)$, where a is the number of accepting vertices. Here the factor $a \cdot m$ comes from the computation of the *map* function and the factor a relates to the number of iterations.

Experimental evaluation demonstrates that accepting cycles are typically detected in very early iterations. On the other hand, if there is no accepting cycle in the graph, the number of iterations is typically very small comparing to the size of the graph (up to 40-50). Thus, the algorithm exhibits nearly linear performance.

One of the key aspects influencing the overall performance of the algorithm is the underlying ordering of vertices used by the algorithm. In order to optimise the complexity one aims to decrease the number of iterations by choosing an appropriate vertex ordering. Ordering $\prec$ is *optimal* if the presence of an accepting cycle can be decided in one iteration. It can be easily shown that for every automaton graph there is an optimal ordering. Moreover, an optimal ordering can be computed in linear time.

An example of an optimal ordering is depth-first search postorder. Unfortunately, the *optimal ordering problem*, which is to decide for a given automaton graph and two accepting vertices u, v whether u precedes v in *every* optimal ordering of graph vertices, is P-complete [14] hence unlikely to be computed effectively in a distributed environment. Therefore, several heuristics for computing a suitable vertex ordering are used. The trivial one orders vertices lexicographically according to their bit-vector representations. The more sophisticated heuristics relate vertices with respect to the order in which they were traversed. However, experimental evaluation has shown that none of the heuristics significantly outperforms the others. On average, the most reliable heuristic is the one based on breadth-first search followed by the one based on (random) hashing.

4   Strongly Connected Components

Fundamentals

The accepting cycle detection problem can be directly reformulated as a question whether the automaton graph contains a nontrivial accepting strongly connected component.

A *strongly connected component* (SCC) of $G = (V, E, s, A)$ is a maximal (with respect to set inclusion) set of vertices $C \subseteq V$ such that for each $u, v \in C$, the vertex v is reachable from u and vice versa. The *quotient graph* of G, $Q(G)$, is a graph (W, H) where W is the set of the SCCs of G and $(C_1, C_2) \in H$ if and only if $C_1 \neq C_2$ and there exist $r \in C_1, s \in C_2$ such that $(r, s) \in E$. The *height* of the graph G, $h(G)$, is the length of the longest path in the quotient graph of G (note that the quotient graph is acyclic). A strongly connected component is *trivial* if it has no edges, *initial* if it has no predecessor in the quotient graph, and *accepting* if it contains an accepting vertex.

Decomposition into SCCs can be solved in linear time by Tarjan's algorithm [41]. Once a graph is decomposed to its SCCs, the accepting cycle problem is easily answered by testing the particular components for acceptance. However, Tarjan's algorithm is based on depth-first search postorder and its transformation into a cluster setting is difficult.

The inspiration for the distributed SCC-based algorithm for detection of accepting cycles is taken from symbolic algorithms for cycle detection, namely from SCC hull algorithms. SCC hull algorithms compute the set of vertices containing all accepting components. Algorithms maintain the approximation of the set and successively remove non-accepting components until they reach a fixpoint. Different strategies to remove non-accepting components lead to different algorithms. An overview, taxonomy, and comparison of symbolic algorithms can be found in independent reports [26] and [38].

As the base for the distributed enumerative algorithm presented here the *One Way Catch Them Young* strategy [26] has been chosen. The enumerative algorithm works on individual vertices rather than on sets of vertices as is the case in symbolic approach. A component is removed by removing its vertices. The algorithm employs two rules to remove vertices of non-accepting components:

- if a vertex is not reachable from any accepting vertex then the vertex does not belong to any accepting component and
- if a vertex has in-degree zero then the vertex does not belong to any accepting component.

Note that an alternative set of rules can be formulated as

- if no accepting vertex is reachable from a vertex then the vertex does not belong to any accepting component and
- if a vertex has out-degree zero then the vertex does not belong to any accepting component.

This second set of rules results in an algorithm which works in a *backward* manner and we will not describe it explicitly here.

Algorithmics

The basic scheme is given in Figure 3. The function *Reachability*(A) computes the set of all vertices that are reachable from A (including A) in $G(S)$. The function *Elimination*(S) eliminates those vertices that have zero in-degree in

$G(S)$. When starting the computation of $Elimination(S)$ only vertices from A can have zero in-degree $G(S)$, however by their elimination in-degree of their successors can be decreased. The computation of $Elimination(S)$ is performed by successive removal of vertices that do not have predecessors in $G(S)$.

```
proc SCC((V, E, s, A))
    S := V;
    S := Reachability(A);
    old := ∅;
    while (S ≠ old) do
        old := S;
        S := Reachability(A);
        S := Elimination(S);
    od
    if (S = ∅) then report (NO ACCEPTING CYCLE exists)
               else report (ACCEPTING CYCLE found) fi
end
```

Fig. 3. SCC-based Algorithm

The assignment $S := Reachability(A)$ removes from the graph $G(S)$ all initial non-accepting components (in fact only SCCs reachable from an accepting component are left in $G(S)$). The assignment $S := Elimination(S)$ removes from the graph $G(S)$ all initial trivial components (in fact a trivial SCC is left in $G(S)$ only if it is reachable from an accepting component in $G(S)$). Thus each iteration of the **while** cycle (so called *external iteration*) removes initial unfair components of $Q(G)$ until the fixpoint is reached.

The actual distribution of the algorithm is quite direct as the very basic operations are reachability, which is well distributable, and a local testing of vertex in-degree.

Comments

The presented SCC-based algorithm in its forward version does not work on-the-fly and the entire automaton graph has to be generated first. The same is true for the backward version. Moreover, the backward version actually needs to store the edges to be able to perform backward reachability. This is however payed out by relaxing the necessity to compute successors, which is in fact a very expensive operation in practise.

Time complexity of the SCC-based algorithm is $\mathcal{O}(h \cdot m)$ where $h = h(G)$. Here the factor m comes from the computation of *Reachability* and *Elimination* functions and the factor h relates to the number of external iterations. In practise, the number of external iterations is very small (up to 40-50) even for large graphs. This observation is supported by experiments in [26] with the symbolic implementation and hardware circuits problems. Similar results are communicated in [36] where heights of quotient graphs were measured for several models. As reported, 70% of the models has height smaller than 50.

A positive aspect of SCC-based distributed algorithms is their effectiveness for *weak automaton graphs*. A graph is weak if each SCC component of G is either fully contained in A or is disjoint with A. For weak graphs one iteration of the SCC-based algorithm is sufficient to decide accepting cycles. The studies of temporal properties [23,19] reveal that verification of up to 90% of LTL properties leads to weak automaton graphs.

Last but not least, SCC-based algorithms can be effortlessly extended to automaton graphs for other types of nondeterministic word automata like generalised Büchi automata and Streett automata.

5   Negative Cycles

Fundamentals

The general idea behind the next approach is to reduce the accepting cycle detection problem to another one which admits better parallelisation. A suitable problem is the negative cycle detection problem. The reduction assigns lengths to automaton graph edges in such a way that all edges outgoing from accepting vertices have length -1 and all the other edges have length 0. Under this assignment negative length cycles coincide with accepting cycles. The negative cycle problem is closely related to the single-source shortest path (SSSP) problem. In fact, the presented algorithm solves the SSSP problem and can be seen as a distributed version of the Bellman-Ford method [9,27].

The method maintains for every vertex v its distance label $d(v)$, parent vertex $p(v)$, and status $S(v) \in \{unreached, labelled, scanned\}$. Initially, $d(v) = \infty$, $p(v) = nil$, and $S(v) = unreached$ for every vertex v. The method starts by setting $d(s) = 0$, $p(s) = nil$ and $S(s) = labelled$, where s is the initial vertex. At every step a *labelled* vertex is selected and scanned. When scanning a vertex u, all its outgoing edges are *relaxed*. Relaxation of an edge (u, v) means that if $d(v) > d(u) + l(u, v)$ then $d(v)$ is set to $d(u) + l(u, v)$ and $p(v)$ is set to u. The status of u is changed to *scanned* while the status of v is changed to *labelled*. If all vertices are either *scanned* or *unreached* then d gives the shortest path lengths. Moreover, the *parent graph* G_p is the graph of shortest paths. More precisely, the parent graph is a subgraph G_p of G induced by edges $(p(v), v)$ for all v such that $p(v) \neq nil$.

Different strategies for selecting a labelled vertex to be scanned lead to different algorithms. The Bellman–Ford algorithm employs FIFO strategy to select vertices and runs in $\mathcal{O}(m \cdot n)$ time in the worst case. For graphs with negative edge lengths there is no shortest path to the vertices on a negative length cycle and the scanning method must be modified to recognise negative cycles. The cluster-based algorithm employs the *walk to root* strategy which traverses a *parent graph*. The walk to root strategy is based on the fact (see e.g. [20]) that any cycle in parent graph G_p corresponds to a negative cycle in the automaton graph.

The walk to root method tests whether G_p is acyclic. Suppose the parent graph G_p is acyclic and an edge (u, v) is relaxed, i.e. $d(v)$ is decreased. This operation creates a cycle in G_p if and only if v is an ancestor of u in the current G_p. Before applying the operation, we follow the parent pointers from u until we reach either v or s. If we stop at v a negative cycle is detected. Otherwise the relaxation does not create a cycle. However, since the path to the initial vertex can be long, the cost of edge relaxation becomes $\mathcal{O}(n)$ instead of $\mathcal{O}(1)$. In order to optimise the overall computational complexity, amortisation is used to pay the cost of checking G_p for cycles. More precisely, the parent graph G_p is tested only after the underlying shortest paths algorithm performs $\Omega(n)$ relaxations. The running time is thus increased only by a constant factor.

Algorithmics

Each workstation performs repeatedly the basic scanning operation on vertices with status *labelled*. To relax a cross-edge (u, v), where u and v belong to different workstations, a message is sent to the owner of v. For negative cycle detection a procedure *Walk to Root* (WTR) is used in an amortised manner. A workstation starts the detection only after it has relaxed n edges. WTR tries to identify a cycle in the parent graph by following the parent pointers from a current vertex.

As the relaxation of edges is performed in parallel and the cycle detection is not initiated after every change in the parent graph, it can happen that even if the relaxation of an edge (u, v) does not create a cycle in the parent graph G_p there can be a cycle in G_p on the way from u to the initial vertex s. In order to recognise such a cycle a value *walk(x)* is associated with every vertex x. Its initial value is *nil*. Once procedure *WTR* that started at a vertex *origin*, passes through a vertex v, the value *walk(v)* is set to *origin*. Reaching a vertex already marked with the value *origin* clearly indicates a cycle in the parent graph.

However, it can happen that more than one procedure *WTR* is active at the same time. Consequently, *WTR* initiated in vertex *origin* can get to a vertex marked with a value different from *origin* indicating that some other *WTR* is active. Such a collision is resolved in favour of the procedure which has started at the greater vertex (with respect to a linear ordering on vertices). *WTR* started at the lower vertex is terminated. Another situation that could happen is that *WTR* started at *origin* gets to a vertex already marked with *origin*, but this mark has been introduced by a previous *WTR* initiated at *origin*. This would lead to a false detection of a cycle. To guarantee correctness the algorithm in fact marks every vertex with two values: *origin* and *stamp*. The value *stamp* is equal to the number of *WTR* procedures initiated by the particular workstation. This value allows to distinguish among vertices marked by current and some previous *WTRs* started at the same vertex.

Comments

The worst case time complexity of the algorithm is $\mathcal{O}(n \cdot m)$, i.e. it is the same as that of Bellman-Ford algorithm. Experiments have shown that the algorithm is of great use for models without errors where the computation stabilises in the early stages. Several other strategies (see [20] for their survey) to detect negative cycles in the parent graph were implemented and experimentally evaluated in [17] with the conclusion that the walk to root strategy in most cases outperforms the others.

6   Back-Level Edges

Fundamentals

The algorithm builds on breadth-first search (BFS) exploration of the graph. BFS is typically used in graph algorithms that work with distances and distances can also be used to characterise cycles in a graph.

Distance of a vertex $u \in V$, $d(u)$, is the length of a shortest path from the initial vertex to the vertex u. The set of vertices with the same distance is called *level*. An edge $(u, v) \in E$ is called a *back-level edge* if $d(u) \geq d(v)$.

The key observation connecting the cycle detection problem with the back-level edge concept is that every cycle contains at least one back-level edge. A parallel level-synchronised breadth-first search is performed to discover back-level edges. Back-level edges are used as triggers which start a cycle detection. However, it is too expensive to test every back-level edge for being a part of a cycle. The algorithm therefore integrates several optimisations and heuristics to decrease the number of tested edges and speed-up the cycle test.

Algorithmics

Breadth-first search systematically explores edges of G starting from the initial vertex s. It expands the *frontier* between discovered and undiscovered vertices uniformly across the breadth of the graph. When a new vertex is generated, its owner is computed, and the vertex is sent for exploration to the workstation where it belongs. Relating this approach to breadth-first search, the main problem is that the breadth-first search frontier can get split, i.e., there might be a vertex that is expanded prematurely with respect to breadth-first search order.

The algorithm for back-level edge detection (see the pseudo-code in Figure 4) builds on preventing the breadth-first search frontier from getting split. In particular, every workstation participating in the computation organises vertices from its part of the global BFS frontier into two queues, the current level queue (CLQ) and the next level queue (NLQ). Only vertices stored in CLQ are processed. Newly generated vertices are inserted into respective NLQs. Workstations participating in computation synchronise as soon as all their CLQs are empty. After that, each workstation moves vertices from NLQ to CLQ and continues with exploration vertices from CLQ.

Note that it is difficult to compute the distance for a newly generated vertex if its relevant predecessor is not local. In such a case the workstation cannot access the distance value of the predecessor. However, in level-synchronised breadth-first search the distance of a vertex can be computed by counting the number of synchronisations. A similar problem arises when a back-level edge needs to be reported. In sequential breadth-first search, a back-level edge is detected when its destination vertex[1] is reached. In the distributed setting, the initial vertex of the edge may be remote and thus locally inaccessible. To solve this problem the contents of CLQ and NLQ are slightly modified. While in the sequential

---

[1] Destination vertex of an oriented edge (u, v) is the vertex v.

```
proc DISTRIBUTED-BL-EDGE-DETECTION(netid)
  CLQ := ∅; NLQ := ∅; Visited := ∅; Level := 0
  initvertex := F_init(); finished := false
  if (netid = Partition(initvertex))
    then enqueue(NLQ, (−, initvertex))
  fi
  while (¬finished) do
        swap(NLQ, CLQ)
        while (CLQ ≠ ∅) do
              (p, v) := dequeue(CLQ)
              if (v ∉ Visited)
                then Visited := Visited ∪ {v}
                     d(v) := Level;
                     foreach t ∈ F_succs(v) do
                           if (Partition(t) ≠ netid)
                             then SendTo(Partition(t),
                                         enqueue(NLQ, (v, t)))
                             else enqueue(NLQ, (v, t))
                           fi
                     od
                else if (d(v) < Level)
                        then Report back-level edge (u, v)
                     fi
              fi
        od
        Synchronize(finished := (all NLQ = ∅))
        Level := Level + 1
  od
end
```

Fig. 4. BFS-based cycle detection algorithm – back-level edge detection

algorithm the objects enqueued to queues are vertices to be explored, in the distributed algorithm the objects enqueued to queues are edges to be explored. Each edge is actually a pair of vertices that contains a vertex to be explored and its predecessor.

In general, a sufficient technique to decide about the presence of a cycle is to check each vertex for its *self-reachability* in a separate reachability procedure. The back-level edge based algorithm builds on the self-reachability approach, but limits the number of self-reachability tests. The idea is that it is enough to perform a self-reachability test for only one vertex on a cycle. Every cycle contains at least one back-level edge and if the self-reachability test is performed for all back-level edge initial vertices then no cycle can be missed. Thus, the algorithm alternates between two phases. In the first phase it discovers all back-level edges from the current level and in the second phase it performs all self-reachability tests.

Each self-reachability test is restricted to vertices with distances less or equal to the distance of the vertex to be reached. In this way it can happen that a path to the vertex to be reached remains undetected. However, every cycle in the graph is detected when the self-reachability test is started in a vertex with maximal distance among vertices forming the cycle.

The goal of each self-reachability test (see Figure 5) is to hit the initial vertex of back-level edge from which it was initiated (the so-called *target*). If at least one test succeeds then the presence of a cycle is ensured and the algorithm is terminated. Otherwise, it continues with the exploration of the next level. Since there are many self-reachability procedures performed concurrently, the target of each nested procedure cannot be maintained in a single variable (as it is in the case of the Nested DFS algorithm) but has to be propagated by the nested procedures.

```
proc CHECK-BL-EDGES(netid)
    while (¬Synchronize() ∨ BLQ ≠ ∅) do
        if (BLQ ≠ ∅)
            then (target, q) := dequeue(BLQ)
                if d(q) < Level
                    then if (q = target)
                            then Report cycle
                         fi
                         foreach t ∈ F_{succs}(q) do
                            if (Partition(t) ≠ netid)
                                then SendTo(Partition(t),
                                            enqueue(BLQ, (target, t)))
                                else enqueue(BLQ, (target, t))
                            fi
                         od
                fi
        fi
    od
end
```

Fig. 5. BFS-based cycle detection algorithm – self-reachability test

When checking vertex u for self-reachability, the corresponding test procedure may revisit every vertex v that is reachable from vertex u and satisfies $d(u) \geq d(v)$ as many times as there are different paths leading from u to v. Therefore the algorithm includes several improvements to decrease the number of re-visits.

To distinguish accepting and non-accepting cycles, the nested procedure is modified to maintain an additional *accepting* bit. This accepting bit is used to indicate that the self-reachability test has passed through an accepting vertex.

Comments

The algorithm performs well on graphs with small number of back-level edges. In such cases the performance of the algorithm approaches the performance of reachability analysis, although, the algorithm performs full LTL model checking. On the other hand, a drawback shows up when a graph contains many back-level edges. In such a case, frequent revisiting of vertices in the second phase of the algorithm causes the time of the computation to be high.

The level-synchronised BFS approach also allows to involve BFS-based Partial Order Reduction (POR) technique [21] in the computation. POR technique prevents some vertices of the graph from being generated while preserving result of the verification. Therefore, it allows analysis of even larger systems. The standard DFS-based POR technique strongly relies on DFS stack and as such it is inapplicable to cluster-based environment [15].

7 Dependency Graph

Fundamentals

Local cycles in a distributed graph can be detected using standard sequential techniques, therefore, the real problem in cluster-based detection of accepting cycles is the detection of cycles that are split among workstations. The idea of the last algorithm is to construct a smaller graph by omitting those parts of the original graph that are irrelevant for the detection of split cycles.

By a *split cycle* we mean a cycle that contains at least one *cross-edge*. An edge (u, v) is a cross-edge if vertices u and v are owned by two different workstations. Vertex v is called a *transfer vertex* if there is a cross-edge (u, v). Let $G = (V, E, s, A)$ be a graph, we call graph $G_{dep} = (V_{dep}, E_{dep})$ a *dependency graph* if V_{dep} contains the initial vertex, all accepting vertices, and all transfer vertices of the product automaton graph, and the reachability relation induced by reflexive and transitive closure of E_{dep} is a subset of the reachability relation induced by reflexive and transitive closure of E. Directly from the definition we have that there is an accepting cycle in G_{dep} if and only if there is a split accepting cycle in G.

The cluster-based algorithm stores the dependency graph explicitly in a distributed manner. In particular, vertices of the dependency graph are distributed among the workstations by the same partition function as used for the original graph. To maintain consistency of the dependency graph in a distributed environment, the graph is implemented using a particular data structure called *dependency structure*.

Definition 2. *Let workstations be identified by numbers* $1, \ldots, n$. *Let* $\mathcal{DS}$ *be a collection of graphs* $\{(S_1, T_1), \ldots, (S_n, T_n)\}$ *where every* S_i *is the set of initial, accepting and transfer vertices owned by workstation* i, *and a set of (transfer) vertices reachable through a cross-edge from vertices owned by workstation* i, *and* $T_i \subseteq S_i \times S_i$ *is a set of transitions.* $\mathcal{DS}$ *is called a* dependency structure *if the graph* (S, T), *where* $S = \cup_{i=1}^n S_i$ *and* $T = \cup_{i=1}^n T_i$, *has the following properties:*

- $v \in S \implies (s, v) \in T^*$
- $u, v \in S \land u \leadsto_G v \land Partition(u) \neq Partition(v) \implies (u, v) \in T^*$
- $u, v \in S \land u \not\leadsto_G v \implies (u, v) \notin T^*$.

where T^* *is the reflexive and transitive closure of* T, *s is the initial vertex of the graph,* $\leadsto_G$ ($\not\leadsto_G$) *correspond to the standard reachability (un-reachability) relation in the graph* G, *and function* $Partition$ *is used to determine the owning workstation for a given vertex.*

An example of a partitioned graph and a corresponding dependency structure is depicted in Figure 6.

Algorithmics

The algorithm employing dependency structure performs its task in two global steps [3,6]. In the first step it explores the given graph in order to construct

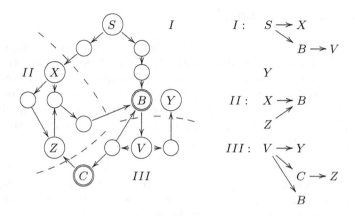

Fig. 6. Example of dependency structures

the dependency structure and detect local accepting cycles. If no local accepting cycle is detected, the algorithm continues with the second step. Vertices that have no successors in the dependency structure are *recursively* removed from it as they cannot lie on a split cycle. If all vertices are removed from the structure, there is no split cycle in the original graph. In the other case, the presence of a split cycle is detected. Note that a split cycle must be accepting if it belongs to a *fully accepting component* of the graph (see Section 8). In the case of *partially accepting components*, the algorithm employs sequential techniques to distinguish accepting and non-accepting cycles.

The purpose of the first step is to compute the dependency structure. Therefore, for each local vertex v the procedure has to explore all paths starting at v and leading to a transfer vertex or vertex already stored in the local part of the dependency structure. Thus, the complexity of the local computation is $O(n!)$, where n is the number of local vertices. Note that exploring all local paths starting at v is sufficient for detection of local accepting cycles reachable from v.

Comments

The algorithm was historically the first cluster-based algorithm for detection of accepting cycles, hence for the full LTL model checking. The original idea of the algorithm builds on backward elimination of vertices with no successors (see Section 4) from the dependency structure. However, any cluster-based algorithm presented in this survey can be combined with the dependency structure in order to detect split accepting cycles. The worst case complexity of $O(n!)$ has never been encountered in numerous practical experiments. The only disadvantages of the approach are thus the additional space needed for storing the dependency structure and a small inconvenience caused by sequential distributed-memory computation in the case of partially accepting components.

8   Preserving Cycle Locality

Technique presented in this Section should be viewed as a problem decomposition technique rather than a cluster-based algorithm. In the case of automata-based approach to LTL model checking the product automaton originates from synchronous product of the property and system automata. Hence, vertices of product automaton graph are ordered pairs. An interesting observation formalised in Lemma 1 is that every cycle in a product automaton graph emerges from cycles in system and property automaton graphs.

Lemma 1. *Let A, B be Büchi automata and $A \otimes B$ their synchronous product. If C is a strongly connected component in the automaton graph of $A \otimes B$, then A-projection of C and B-projection of C are (not necessarily maximal) strongly connected components in automaton graphs of A and B, respectively.*

As the property automaton origins from the LTL formula to be verified, it is typically quite small and can be pre-analysed. In particular, it is possible to identify all strongly connected components of the property automaton graph. Respecting strongly connected components of the property automaton a partition function preserving cycle locality can be defined. The partitioning strategy is to assign all vertices that project to the same strongly connected component of the property automaton graph to the same workstation. Since no cycle is split it is possible to employ localised Nested DFS algorithm to perform local accepting cycle detection simultaneously on all participating workstations.

Yet another interesting information can be drawn from the property automaton graph decomposition. Maximal strongly connected components can be classified into three categories:

Type F:(*Fully Accepting*) Any cycle within the component contains at least one accepting vertex. (There is no non-accepting cycle within the component.)
Type P: (*Partially Accepting*) There is at least one accepting cycle and one non-accepting cycle within the component.
Type N: (*Non-Accepting*) There is no accepting cycle within the component.

Realising that vertex of a product automaton graph is accepting only if the corresponding vertex in the property automaton graph is accepting it is possible to characterise types of strongly connected components of product automaton graph according to types of components in the property automaton graph. Classification of components into types N, F, and P is useful in other cluster-based algorithms presented in this paper.

9   Experiments

To experimentally evaluate the presented cluster-based model checking algorithms a series of experiments was conducted [43]. All experiments were performed on a cluster of homogeneous Linux workstations equipped with 1GB RAM and 2.6 GHz Pentium 4 CPU using verification tool DiVinE [4].

Table 1. Comparison of cluster-based LTL model checkers

20 workstations	PLC	Anders	Bakery1	Bakery2	MCS1	MCS2
Negative Cycle	2.4	**142.1**	5.3	53.4	**75.2**	1.0
Forward SCC elimination	1408.1	528.0	11.1	1.8	253.4	137.7
Backward SCC elimination	868.8	159.2	3.7	2.1	85.2	50.2
Max Accepting Preds	**0.7**	411.3	1.2	**0.9**	126.6	**0.4**
Localised Nested DFS	0.8	919.9	**0.2**	12.7	465.5	2.7
Back Level Edges	5.1	TE	41.6	4.7	31211.6	1.8
Dependency Structure	1.0	ME	4.2	4.4	ME	1436.7

	Peterson	LUP1	LUP2	Elevator1	Elevator2	Phils
Negative Cycle	86.7	197.8	52.8	2004.1	1477.4	**1.7**
Forward SCC Elimination	291.2	527.8	398.7	1715.3	4138.3	2083.9
Backward SCC Elimination	113.9	**174.6**	126.6	ME	ME	ME
Max Accepting Preds	43.3	481.6	64.9	ME	ME	ME
Localised Nested DFS	**2.9**	1785.4	**4.7**	ME	**0.8**	84.0
Back Level Edges	98.0	14077.1	514.4	**41.6**	ME	9.9
Dependency Structure	454.0	ME	338.9	ME	ME	3.7

10 workstations	PLC	Anders	Bakery1	Bakery2	MCS1	MCS2
Negative Cycle	1.9	**180.7**	5.0	33.8	**90.8**	**0.3**
Forward SCC Elimination	1627.6	670.6	12.2	1.6	336.0	186.8
Backward SCC Elimination	955.3	207.3	3.9	1.0	110.8	73.7
Max Accepting Preds	0.6	693.9	1.0	**0.6**	239.6	1.0
Localised Nested DFS	**0.1**	1964.6	**0.1**	9.5	530.5	2.3
Back Level Edges	3.2	TE	41.8	2.7	TE	0.5
Dependency Structure	0.7	ME	5.1	2.9	ME	3100.8

	Peterson	LUP1	LUP2	Elevator1	Elevator2	Phils
Negative Cycle	274.0	254.4	15.6	3539.1	1934.9	ME
Forward SCC Elimination	376.2	679.3	508.3	**2555.0**	ME	3157.9
Backward SCC Elimination	166.2	**227.3**	172.2	ME	ME	ME
Max Accepting Preds	104.2	732.5	106.2	ME	ME	ME
Localised Nested DFS	**2.2**	2155.6	**3.7**	ME	**0.6**	45.5
Back Level Edges	289.7	16909.1	947.4	ME	ME	2.1
Dependency Structure	464.3	ME	433.5	ME	ME	**0.3**

Graphs used in experiments were both with and without accepting cycles, and their size ranged from 10^5 vertices and 10^6 edges (Bakery2) to 10^8 vertices and 10^9 edges (Elevator2). The graphs were distributed among workstation using the default partition function as implemented in DiVinE. The function distributes states among workstations randomly preserving even distribution.

In Table 1 runtimes in seconds are given. The names of algorithms should be self-explanatory. Values "ME" and "TE" stand for memory and time (10 hours) limit exceed, respectively.

10 Conclusions

The paper surveys cluster-based algorithms for verification of LTL properties of large systems. The cluster-based approach to LTL model checking widens the set of systems and LTL formulae that can be verified within reasonable time and space limits. This was conclusively demonstrated by the experiments performed. However, the cluster-based approach brings only linearly increasing computational resources and as such it cannot solve the state explosion problem completely.

Another contribution of the cluster-based approach observed during the experimental evaluation relates to the verification of middle-sized systems. These are such systems that can still be verified sequentially using the Nested DFS algorithm, but whose verification requires a nontrivial amount of time. This is surprisingly not a rare situation as a single workstation manages to store automaton graphs with up to ten millions of vertices. In that case cluster-based LTL model checker can be faster.

In model checking applications, the existence of an accepting cycle indicates an invalid behaviour. In such a case, it is essential that the user is given an accepting cycle as a *counterexample*, typically presented in the form of a finite stem followed by a cycle. The counterexample should be as short as possible to facilitate debugging. The great advantage of the presented cluster-based techniques is that due to their the breadth-first search nature, the counterexamples are very short in comparison to those computed by depth-first search algorithms.

The overall complexity of cluster-based algorithms strongly depends on the graph partition. As the graph is given implicitly, we cannot pre-compute an optimal partition. The experiments with various static partitions indicate that a random partition is in this situation the best choice.

As indicated by numerous experiments, no single cluster-based LTL model checking algorithm has the edge over the others in any application area. Moreover, it is very difficult to determine a priori which technique is the most suitable for a given verification problem. It is thus sensible to apply different techniques to the same problem.

References

1. T. Bao and M. Jones. Time-Efficient Model Checking with Magnetic Disks. In *Proc. Tools and Algorithms for the Construction and Analysis of Systems*, volume 3440 of *LNCS*, pages 526–540. Springer-Verlag, 2005.
2. J. Barnat, L. Brim, and J. Chaloupka. Parallel Breadth-First Search LTL Model-Checking. In *Proc. 18th IEEE International Conference on Automated Software Engineering*, pages 106–115. IEEE Computer Society, 2003.
3. J. Barnat, L. Brim, and J. Stříbrná. Distributed LTL model-checking in SPIN. In *Proc. SPIN Workshop on Model Checking of Software*, volume 2057 of *LNCS*, pages 200–216. Springer-Verlag, 2001.
4. J. Barnat, L. Brim, I. Černá, and P.Šimeček. DiVinE – The Distributed Verification Environment. In *Proceedings of 4th International Workshop on Parallel and Distributed Methods in verifiCation*, pages 89–94, 2005.

5. J. Barnat and I. Černá. Distributed Breadth-First Search LTL Model Checking. *Formal Methods in System Design*, 2006. to appear.
6. Jiří Barnat. *Distributed Memory LTL Model Checking*. PhD thesis, Faculty of Informatics, Masaryk University Brno, 2004.
7. G. Behrmann, T. S. Hune, and F. W. Vaandrager. Distributed Timed Model Checking – How the Search Order Matters. In *Proc. Computer Aided Verification*, volume 1855 of *LNCS*, pages 216–231. Springer, 2000.
8. A. Bell and B. R. Haverkort. Sequential and distributed model checking of petri net specifications. *Int J Softw Tools Technol Transfer*, 7(1):43–60, 2005.
9. R. Bellman. On a Routing Problem. *Quarterly of Applied Mathematics*, 16(1):87–90, 1958.
10. S. Blom and S. Orzan. A Distributed Algorithm for Strong Bisimulation Reduction Of State Spaces. *Int J Softw Tools Technol Transfer*, 7(1):74–86, 2005.
11. B. Bollig, M. Leucker, and M. Weber. Parallel Model Checking for the Alternation Free μ-Calculus. In *Proc. Tools and Algorithms for the Construction and Analysis of Systems*, volume 2031 of *LNCS*, pages 543 – 558. Springer-Verlag, 2001.
12. L. Brim, I. Černá, P. Krčál, and R. Pelánek. Distributed LTL Model Checking Based on Negative Cycle Detection. In *Proc. Foundations of Software Technology and Theoretical Computer Science*, volume 2245 of *LNCS*, pages 96–107. Springer-Verlag, 2001.
13. L. Brim, I. Černá, P. Krčál, and R. Pelánek. How to Employ Reverse Search in Distributed Single-Source Shortest Paths. In *Proc. Theory and Practice of Informatics (SOFSEM)*, volume 2234 of *LNCS*, pages 191–200. Springer-Verlag, 2001.
14. L. Brim, I. Černá, P. Moravec, and J. Šimša. Accepting Predecessors are Better than Back Edges in Distributed LTL Model-Checking. In *Formal Methods in Computer-Aided Design (FMCAD 2004)*, volume 3312 of *LNCS*, pages 352–366. Springer-Verlag, 2004.
15. L. Brim, I. Černá, P. Moravec, and J. Šimša. Distributed Partial Order Reduction. *Electronic Notes in Theoretical Computer Science*, 128:63–74, 2005.
16. L. Brim, I. Černá, P. Moravec, and J. Šimša. How to Order Vertices for Distributed LTL Model-Checking Based on Accepting Predecessors. In *4th International Workshop on Parallel and Distributed Methods in verifiCation (PDMC'05)*, July 2005.
17. L. Brim, I. Černá, and L. Hejtmánek. Distributed Negative Cycle Detection Algorithms. In *Proc. Parallel Computing: Software Technology, Algorithms, Architectures & Applications*, volume 13 of *Advances in Parallel Computing*, pages 297–305. Elsevier, 2004.
18. I. Černá and R. Pelánek. Distributed Explicit Fair cycle Detection (Set Based Approach). In *Model Checking Software. 10th International SPIN Workshop*, volume 2648 of *LNCS*, pages 49–73. Springer-Verlag, 2003.
19. I. Černá and R. Pelánek. Relating Hierarchy of Temporal Properties to Model Checking. In *Proc. Mathematical Foundations of Computer Science*, volume 2747 of *LNCS*, pages 318–327. Springer-Verlag, 2003.
20. B. V. Cherkassky and A. V. Goldberg. Negative-Cycle Detection Algorithms. *Mathematical Programming*, 85:277–311, 1999.
21. E.M. Clarke, O. Grumberg, and D.A. Peled. *Model Checking*. MIT, 1999.
22. C. Courcoubetis, M.Y. Vardi, P. Wolper, and M. Yannakakis. Memory-Efficient Algorithms for the Verification of Temporal Properties. *Formal Methods in System Design*, 1:275–288, 1992.

23. M. B. Dwyer, G. S. Avrunin, and J. C. Corbett. Property Specification Patterns for Finite-State Verification. In *Proc. Workshop on Formal Methods in Software Practice*, pages 7–15. ACM Press, 1998.

24. S. Edelkamp and S. Jabbar. Large-Scale Directed Model Checking LTL. In *Model Checking Software: 13th International SPIN Workshop*, volume 3925 of *LNCS*, pages 1–18. Springer-Verlag, 2006.

25. J. Esparza and S. Schwoon. A note on on-the-fly verification algorithms. In *Proc. Tools and Algorithms for the Construction and Analysis of Systems*, volume 3440 of *LNCS*, pages 174–190. Springer-Verlag, 2005.

26. K. Fisler, R. Fraer, G. Kamhi, M. Y. Vardi, and Z. Yang. Is there a best symbolic cycle-detection algorithm? In *Proc. Tools and Algorithms for the Construction and Analysis of Systems*, volume 2031 of *LNCS*, pages 420–434. Springer-Verlag, 2001.

27. L.R. Ford. Network Flow Theory. Rand Corp., Santa Monica, Cal., 1956.

28. H. Garavel, R. Mateescu, and I. Smarandache. Parallel State Space Construction for Model-Checking. In *Proc. SPIN Workshop on Model Checking of Software*, volume 2057 of *LNCS*, pages 216–234. Springer-Verlag, 2001.

29. O. Grumberg, T. Heyman, N. Ifergan, and A. Schuster. "achieving speedups in distributed symbolic reachability analysis through asynchronous computation". In *Correct Hardware Design and Verification Methods, 13th IFIP WG 10.5 Advanced Research Working Conference, CHARME 2005*, Lecture Notes in Computer Science, pages 129–145. Springer, 2005.

30. O. Grumberg, T. Heyman, and A. Schuster. Distributed Model Checking for μ-calculus. In *Proc. Computer Aided Verification*, volume 2102 of *LNCS*, pages 350–362. Springer-Verlag, 2001.

31. B. R. Haverkort, A. Bell, and H. C. Bohnenkamp. On the Efficient Sequential and Distributed Generation of Very Large Markov Chains From Stochastic Petri Nets. In *Proc. 8th Int. Workshop on Petri Net and Performance Models*, pages 12–21. IEEE Computer Society Press, 1999.

32. G. J. Holzmann. *The Spin Model Checker: Primer and Reference Manual*. Addison-Wesley, 2003.

33. G. J. Holzmann, D. Peled, and M. Yannakakis. On Nested Depth First Search. In *Proc. SPIN Workshop on Model Checking of Software*, pages 23–32. American Mathematical Society, 1996.

34. S. Jabbar and S. Edelkamp. Parallel External Directed Model Checking with Linear I/O. In *Verification, Model Checking, and Abstract Interpretation: 7th International Conference, VMCAI 2006*, volume 3855 of *LNCS*, pages 237–251. Springer-Verlag, 2006.

35. F. Lerda and R. Sisto. Distributed-Memory Model Checking with SPIN. In *Proc. SPIN Workshop on Model Checking of Software*, number 1680 in LNCS, pages 22–39. Springer-Verlag, 1999.

36. R. Pelánek. Typical Structural Properties of State Spaces. In *Proc. of SPIN Workshop*, volume 2989 of *LNCS*, pages 5–22. Springer-Verlag, 2004.

37. A. Pnueli. The Temporal Logic of Concurrent Programs. *Theoretical Computer Science*, 13:45–60, 1981.

38. K. Ravi, R. Bloem, and F. Somenzi. A Comparative Study of Symbolic Algorithms for the Computation of Fair Cycles. In *Proc. Formal Methods in Computer-Aided Design*, volume 1954 of *LNCS*, pages 143–160. Springer-Verlag, 2000.

39. J. Reif. Depth-first Search is Inherently Sequential. *Information Proccesing Letters*, 20(5):229–234, 1985.

40. U. Stern and D.L. Dill. Using magnetic disc instead of main memory in the murφ verifier. In *Proc. of Computer Aided Verification*, volume 1427 of *LNCS*, pages 172 – 183. Springer-Verlag, 1998.

41. R. Tarjan. Depth First Search and Linear Graph Algorithms. *SIAM Journal on Computing*, pages 146–160, Januar 1972.

42. M.Y. Vardi and P. Wolper. An automata-theoretic approach to automatic program verification. In *Proc. IEEE Symposium on Logic in Computer Science*, pages 322–331. Computer Society Press, 1986.

43. Pavel Šimeček. DiVinE – Distributed Verification Environment. Master's thesis, Masaryk Univeristy Brno, 2006.

Safety and Liveness
in Concurrent Pointer Programs

Dino Distefano[1], Joost-Pieter Katoen[2,3], and Arend Rensink[3]

[1] Dept. of Computer Science, Queen Mary, University of London, United Kingdom
[2] Software Modeling and Verification Group, RWTH Aachen, Germany
[3] Formal Methods and Tools, University of Twente, The Netherlands

Abstract. The incorrect use of pointers is one of the most common source of software errors. Concurrency has a similar characteristic. Proving the correctness of concurrent pointer manipulating programs, let alone algorithmically, is a highly non-trivial task. This paper proposes an automated verification technique for concurrent programs that manipulate linked lists. Key issues of our approach are: automata (with fairness constraints), heap abstractions that are tailored to the program and property to be checked, first-order temporal logic, and a tableau-based model-checking algorithm.

1 Introduction

Pointers are an indispensable part of virtually all imperative programming languages, be it implicitly (like in Java or "pure" object-oriented languages) or explicitly (like in the C family of languages). However, programming with pointers is known to be error-prone, with potential pitfalls such as dereferencing null pointers and the creation of memory leaks. This is aggravated by aliasing, which may easily give rise to unwanted side-effects because apparently unaffected variables may be modified by changing a shared memory cell — the so-called *complexity of pointer swing*. The analysis of pointer programs has been a topic of continuous research interest since the early seventies [10,15]. The purpose of this research is twofold: to assess the correctness of pointer programs, or to identify the potential values of pointers at compile time so as to allow more efficient memory management strategies and the use of code optimization.

The problems of pointer programming become even more pressing in a concurrent setting where memory is *shared* among threads. Since the mainstream object-oriented languages all offer shared-memory concurrency, this setting is in fact quite realistic. Concurrent systems are difficult enough to analyze in the absence of pointers; the study of this area has given rise to techniques such as process algebra [30,6], temporal logic [35] and comparative concurrency theory [23]. Techniques for analyzing programs that feature both concurrency and pointers are scarce indeed.

Properties of pointer programs. Alias analysis, i.e., checking whether pairs of pointers can be aliases, has received much attention (see, e.g., [13,26]) initially.

F.S. de Boer et al. (Eds.): FMCO 2005, LNCS 4111, pp. 280–312, 2006.
© Springer-Verlag Berlin Heidelberg 2006

[16] introduced and provided algorithms to check the class of so-called position-dependent alias properties, such as "the n-th cell of v's list is aliased to the m-th cell of list w". Recently, extensions of predicate calculus to reason about pointer programs have become en vogue: e.g., *BI* [24], separation logic [37], pointer assertion logic (*PAL*) [25], alias logic [8,9], local shape logic [36] and extensions of spatial logic [11]. These approaches are almost all focused on verifying pre- and postconditions in a Hoare-style manner.

Since our interest is in concurrent (object-oriented) programs and in expressing properties over dynamically evolving pointer (i.e., object reference) structures, we use first-order linear-time temporal logic (LTL) as a basis and extend it with pointer assertions on single-reference structures, such as aliasing, position-dependent aliasing, as well as predicates to reason about the birth and death of cells. This results in an extension of propositional logic, which we call *NTL* (Navigation Temporal Logic), similar in nature to that proposed in Evolution Temporal Logic (*ETL*) [40] — see below for a more detailed comparison. The important distinguishing feature of these logics with respect to "plain old" propositional logic is that *quantification occurs outside the temporal modalities*; in other words, we can reason about the evolution of entities over time. This type of logic is known as *quantified modal logic*; see, e.g., [21,3]. This is in contrast to *PAL*, which contains similar pointer assertions as *NTL* (and goes beyond lists), but has neither primitives for the birth and death of cells nor temporal operators.

In the semantics of *NTL* (in contrast to *ETL*, which uses 3-valued logical structures) we follow the traditional automata-based approach: models of *NTL* are infinite runs that are accepted by Büchi automata where states are equipped with a representation of the heap. (In terms of quantified modal logic, our models have variable domains and are non-rigidly designating.) Evolving heaps have been lately used to model mobile computations. In that view *NTL* combines both spatial and temporal features as the ambient logic introduced in [11]. In fact in [17] one of the authors has shown how to use the *NTL* model to analyze mobile ambients.

Heap abstraction. Probably the most important issue in analyzing pointer programs is the choice of an appropriate representation of the heap. As the number of memory cells for a program is not known a priori and in general is undecidable, a concrete representation is inadequate. Analysis techniques for pointer programs therefore typically use abstract representations of heaps such as, e.g., location sets [39] (that only distinguish between single and multiple cells), k-limiting paths [26] (allowing up to k distinct cells for some fixed k), or summary nodes [38] in shape graphs. This paper uses an abstract representation that is tailored to unbounded linked list structures. The novelty of our abstraction is its parameterization in the pointer program as well as in the formula. Cells that represent up to M elements, where M is a formula-dependent constant, are exact whereas unbounded cells (akin to summary nodes) represent longer lists. The crux of our abstraction is that it guarantees each unbounded cell to be preceded by a chain of at least L exact cells, where L is a program-dependent constant.

Parameters L and M depend on the longest pointer dereferencing in the program and formula, respectively. In contrast with the k-limiting approach, where an adequate general recipe to determine k is lacking, we show how (minimal bounds on) the parameters L and M can be determined by a simple static analysis.

Pointer program analysis. Standard type-checking is not expressive enough to establish properties of pointer programs such as (the absence of) memory leaks and dereferencing null pointers. Instead, existing techniques for analyzing pointer programs include abstract interpretation [16], deduction techniques [8,22,24,33,37,25,32], design by derivation *a la* Dijkstra [28], and shape analysis [38], or combinations of these techniques.

We pursue a fully automated verification technique, and for that reason we base our approach on model checking. Our model-checking algorithm is a nontrivial extension of the tableau-based algorithm for LTL [27], tailored to the variable-domain models described above. For a given *NTL*-formula Φ, this algorithm is able to check whether Φ is valid in the automaton-model of the concurrent pointer program at hand. The algorithm, like in any approach based on abstraction, is approximative: in our case this means that it suffers from false negatives, i.e., a verification may wrongly conclude that the program refutes a formula. In such a case, however, diagnostic information can be provided (unlike *ETL*, and as for *PAL*) that may be used for further analysis. Besides, by incrementing the parameters M and L, a more concrete model is obtained that is guaranteed to be a correct refinement of the (too coarse) abstract representation. This contrasts with the *ETL* approach where manually-provided instrumentation predicates are needed. As opposed to the *PAL* approach, which is fully automated only for sequential loop-free programs, our technique is fully automated for concurrent pointer programs that may include loops.

Main contributions. Summarizing, the main contributions of this paper are:

1. A quantified temporal logic (with some second-order features) that contains pointer assertions as well as predicates referring to the birth or death of memory cells;
2. An automaton-based model for pointer programs where states are abstract heap structures and transitions represent the dynamic evolving of these heaps; the model deals finitely with unbounded allocations.
3. A program analysis that automatically derives an over-approximation of the invariant of concurrent programs manipulating lists. This analysis is sound and it is guaranteed to terminate.
4. A control on the degree of *concreteness* of abstract heap structures, in the form of two parameters that are obtained by a straightforward static analysis of the program and formula at hand. On incrementing these parameters, refined heap structures are automatically obtained. Vice-versa, by decrementing them more abstract models are derived. Hence the process of abstraction-refinement of the analysis is reduced to only tuning these two numeric parameters.

5. A model checking algorithm to verify safety and liveness properties (expressed by formulae in our logic) against abstract representations of pointer programs.

This results in a push-button technique: given a program and a temporal logic property, the abstract automaton as well as the verification result for the property are determined completely algorithmically. Moreover, to our knowledge, we are the first to develop model-checking techniques for (possibly) unbounded evolving heaps of the kind described above. (Recently, regular model checking has been applied to check properties of linked lists [7])

Our current approach deals with single outgoing pointers only. This still allows us to consider many interesting structures such as acyclic, cyclic, shared and unbounded lists (as in [28] and [16]), as well as hierarchies (by back-pointers). Besides, several *resource managers* such as memory managers only work with lists [34]. Moreover, several kernel routines and device drivers uses lists. Our abstract heap structures can also model mobile ambients [17].

Related work. Above we have already mentioned many sources of related work. Two of them, however, deserve a more detailed discussion: *shape analysis* and *separation logic.*

In [38], a framework for the generation of a family of shape analysis algorithms based on 3-valued logic and abstract interpretation is presented. This very general framework can be instantiated in different ways to handle different kinds of data structures at different levels of precision and efficiency.

The similarity between the analysis in [38] and ours is mostly in the use of summary nodes in order to obtain finite states representation of the invariant of the program. However, our summaries are only used (and tailored) to abstract lists whereas in [38] they can be more general. In fact, since in [38] states are represented by 3-valued logical structures, the abstraction is done by the partitioning induced by the predicate values (canonical abstraction). In contrast, our abstraction is technically implemented by means of morphisms which keep a strong correspondence between the abstract heap and the concrete ones it represents.

Among the differences between the two approaches, we have that [38] gives a collecting semantics of the program. We use an automata semantics which allows us to apply temporal reasoning and verify a wide range of safety and liveness properties. Also, the framework of [38] makes use of instrumentation predicates to refine the analysis whereas the refinement in our case is done by tuning two numerical parameters. Moreover using morphisms, the soundness of the new refined model is automatically guaranteed and therefore there is no need to provide a proof of the equivalence for the two models.

The closest extension of [38] to our work is the aforementioned [40] on a first-order modal (temporal) logic (called *ETL*) for allocation and deallocation of objects and threads as well as for the specification of properties related to the evolution of the heap. Although the aims of that paper and ours are surprisingly close (for example in the kind of properties expressible in *NTL* and *ETL*), the technical machinery has those differences mentioned above between our work and the setting of [38]. Moreover, [40] uses a trace semantics where each trace is encoded by first-order logical structure. Formulae of *ETL* are then translated in first-order logic with transitive closure for the evaluation on a trace. We use Büchi automata to generate traces and verify *NTL* by an extension of the LTL model-checking algorithm.

Separation logic [37,24,34] is an extension of Hoare logic able to prove heap-manipulating programs in a concise and modular manner. At the core of separation logic there is a new operator $*$ called *separating conjunction*. The formula $P * Q$ holds if P and Q hold in disjoint parts of memory. The $*$ operator stands at the foundation of local reasoning in separation logic: it allows one to focus only on the cells that are accessed by the program without the need to keep track of possible aliases. Lately a lot of attention has been devoted in the design of decision procedures and tools for program analysis that uses separation logic as an effective model [4,5].

Although separation logic uses the random access memory model, it seems that it would be possible to give a graph-based semantics for the logic. Interestingly, for subsets of separation logic working only on lists, many features, of this model would be very similar to the heaps we have introduced in this paper. For example, our unbounded entities would correspond to the predicate listseg(x, y) indicating a pure list segment from x to y. It would be interesting to see if the *frame rule* of separation logic, which allows modular reasoning about heap manipulating programs, can be proved sound for such graph model.

Outline of the paper. This paper is, in a sense, a companion to [18] and a summary (and partial revision) of [19], where we presented the technical details of the automata, logic and (to some degree) the model checking algorithm. Here we focus more on the usability aspects. We present the concurrent pointer language in Section 2 and discuss a number of examples. Section 3 presents a concrete semantics for the language. In Section 4 we define the operational semantics on the basis of the abstract automata described above; in Section 5 we introduce the logic and its semantics, and discuss it on the basis of the examples given in Section 2. We also (quite briefly) discuss the principles of the model checking algorithm, in Section 6. Details of the model checking algorithm and all proofs can be found in [19].

2   Concurrent Pointer-Manipulating Programs

This section introduces a simple concurrent programming language dealing with pointer structures. It incorporates means to create and destroy heap cells (referred to by pointers), and operations to manipulate them. A concurrent producer-consumer problem and an in-place reversal program are used to illustrate the kind of programs that can be written. In the discussion of these programs, some relevant temporal properties will be introduced. Later on in the paper, the formal specification and verification of these properties is treated.

2.1   Programming Language

Let PV be a set of program variables with $v, v_i \in PV$. Each program variable is assumed to denote a memory cell, where the constant *nil* is treated as a special cell. A program variable is said to be undefined in case it is not pointing to any cell. The syntax of programs is given by the following grammar:

$$p ::= \mathbf{var}\ v_1, \ldots, v_n : (s_1 \parallel \cdots \parallel s_k)$$

$$s ::= \mathsf{new}(\ell)\ \Big|\ \mathsf{dispose}(\alpha)\ \Big|\ \ell := \alpha\ \Big|\ \mathsf{skip}\ \Big|\ s; s\ \Big|\ \mathbf{if}\ (b)\{\,s\,\}\{\,s\,\}\ \Big|$$

$$\qquad \mathbf{while}\ (b)\{\,s\,\}\ \Big|\ \langle s \rangle\ \Big|\ \mathsf{error}$$

$$\alpha ::= nil\ \Big|\ v\ \Big|\ \alpha{\uparrow}$$

$$\ell ::= v\ \Big|\ \ell{\uparrow}$$

$$b ::= \alpha = \alpha\ \Big|\ \mathsf{undef}(\alpha)\ \Big|\ b \vee b\ \Big|\ \neg b$$

Thus, a program p is a parallel composition of a finite number of statements preceded by the declaration of a finite number of global variables. Statements have the following intuitive interpretation.

- new(ℓ) creates (i.e., allocates) a new cell that will be referred to by ℓ. The old value of ℓ is lost. Thus, if ℓ is the only pointer to cell e, say, then after the execution of new(ℓ), e has become "unreachable". In this case, e is automatically garbage collected together with the entities that are only reachable from e.
- dispose(α) destroys (i.e., deallocates) the cell associated to α, and makes α and every other pointer referring to it undefined. For the sake of simplicity, new and dispose create, respectively destroy, a single entity only; generalizations in which several entities are considered simultaneously can be added in a straightforward manner.
- The assignment $\ell := \alpha$ assigns a reference to the cell denoted to by α to ℓ. (Note that *nil* cannot occur as left-hand side of an assignment.) Again, the cell that ℓ was referring to might become unreferenced, in which case it is removed by garbage collection.
- Sequential composition, while, skip and if have the standard interpretation. The statement $\langle s \rangle$ denotes an atomic region, i.e., all statements in s are executed atomically, without possible interference of any other concurrent statement.
- α stands for a *pointer expression* whereas ℓ stands for a *location*. The suffix $\uparrow$ in both cases expresses dereferencing, or following the single outgoing pointer. We denote $x{\uparrow}^0 = x$ and $x{\uparrow}^{n+1} = (x{\uparrow}^n){\uparrow}$.
- The expression undef(α) yields true if and only if α is undefined (which can for instance happen as a consequence of dispose(β) if originally $\beta = \alpha$). Obviously, this is different from testing for $\alpha = nil$. The capability of testing for undefinedness within the language can be useful if we want to express behavior on the level of system programs.

Statements containing meaningless but legal expressions, such as dispose(nil) and $nil\!\uparrow$, will result in a run-time error (as defined by our semantics later on). The halting of a statement due to such error is indicated by the construct error. This construct is thus a semantical one, and cannot be part of any program.

2.2 Some Example Programs

Producer-consumer programs. Consider the concurrent producer-consumer problem that consists of three concurrent processes. The producer process repeatedly generates new items by allocating new memory cells referred to by the global program variable p. It does so only when p is undefined. A one-place buffer process copies the memory cell referred to by p (if any) and makes p undefined. As soon as an item is available in the buffer, the consumer process is able to empty the buffer by disposing the memory cell. Typical properties that the producer-consumer program should satisfy are:

- absence of memory leaks, i.e., any produced item is eventually consumed
- first-in first-out property, i.e., items are consumed in the order of production
- unboundedness of the number of produced items

The first and last are typical liveness property, whereas the second is a safety property.

To show the intricacy of the producer-consumer problem, we present several programs that are slight variants of each other, and discuss their properties. A first producer-consumer program that realizes the sketched approach is:

$$
\begin{aligned}
&\textbf{var } c, p, w : && // \text{ program variables}\\
&(\quad \textbf{while } (\mathit{true}) \textbf{ if } (\mathsf{undef}(p)) \ \{\mathsf{new}(p); \} && // \text{ producer}\\
&\ ||\ \textbf{while } (\mathit{true}) \textbf{ if } (\neg\mathsf{undef}(p)) \ \{c := p; p := w; \} && // \text{ buffer}\\
&\ ||\ \textbf{while } (\mathit{true}) \textbf{ if } (\neg\mathsf{undef}(c)) \ \{\mathsf{dispose}(c); \} && // \text{ consumer}\\
&)
\end{aligned}
$$

This first program clearly suffers from a memory leak, as it allows produced cells to be never consumed. This can be expressed by "possibly, a produced entity is never referred to by c". This stems from the fact that the producer can put a new item in the buffer before the consumer retrieves the previous one. The following variant avoids this problem by exploiting the auxiliary variable w (which was used before just to make p undefined). The buffer process thus becomes:

$$\textbf{while } (\mathit{true}) \textbf{ if } (\neg\mathsf{undef}(p)) \ \{w := p; p := c; c := w; \}$$

whereas the producer and consumer processes remain as before. This program indeed has no memory leak — provided that the consumer process is scheduled infinitely often — but violates the order-preservation property; i.e., items may be consumed in a different order than they are produced. This occurs for instance in Fig. 1, which represents an example run of the program.

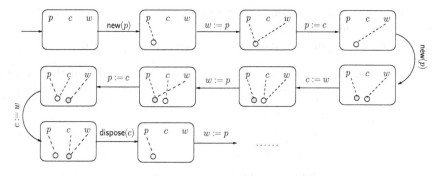

Fig. 1. The order of consumption $\neq$ the order of production

To overcome this problem, the guard of the buffer process is strengthened such that the producer is only allowed to put a new item into the buffer whenever the previous item has been retrieved. This yields the following buffer process:

$$\textbf{while } (\textit{true}) \textbf{ if } (\neg\mathsf{undef}(p) \wedge \mathsf{undef}(c)) \; \{w := p; p := c; c := w; \}$$

The producer and consumer process are as before. It can be shown that this program indeed satisfies all properties: it guarantees that memory leaks cannot occur (assuming process fairness), the order of production is preserved, and an unbounded number of items is produced.

Although the discussed programs can in the course of time produce an unbounded number of items, the buffer capacity is still finite. This is no longer valid for the following variant. Rather than modeling the buffer as a separate process, we consider the buffer to be realized as a global linked list of unbounded length. The producer adds entities to the tail tl of the buffer, whereas the consumer process removes and consumes them from the head hd of the buffer.

> **var** $hd, tl, t :$
> $(\quad \mathsf{new}(tl); hd := tl; \textbf{while } (\textit{true}) \; \{\mathsf{new}(tl\uparrow); tl := tl\uparrow \}$ ⠀⠀⠀⠀ // producer
> $\|\; \textbf{while } (\textit{true}) \textbf{ if } (hd \neq tl) \; \{t := hd; hd := hd\uparrow; \mathsf{dispose}(t) \}$ // consumer
> $)$

In addition to the previously mentioned properties, it is desirable that during the execution of this program, the tail of the buffer never gets disconnected from the head.

In-place list reversal. As a final example we consider a classical sequential list-manipulating problem, viz. reversing the direction of a list. We show two solutions, one of which is actually incorrect. Both programs try to establish reversal in a destructive (or so-called *in-place*) manner as they reuse the cells of the original list, as initially pointed to by program variable v, to built the reversed list. Properties of interest for this problem include, for instance:

- v's list will be (and remains to be) reversed;
- none of the elements in v's list will ever be deleted;
- v and w always point to distinct lists (heap non-interference).

Here, w is an auxiliary variable that is used in the construction of the reversed list. The following program is taken from [2], but violates the first property.

$$
\begin{aligned}
&\textbf{var } v, w, t, z : \\
&\textbf{if } (v \neq nil) \; \{ \\
&\quad t := v{\uparrow}; w := nil; \\
&\quad \textbf{while } (t \neq nil) \; \{ \\
&\qquad z := t{\uparrow}; v{\uparrow} := w; w := v; v := t; t := z \\
&\quad \} \\
&\}
\end{aligned}
$$

The problem in this erroneous program is that one pointer is missing in the reversed list. Before continue reading, the reader is invited to find the error in the program.

The following list-reversal program (see, e.g., [8,37,38]) reverses the list in a correct manner, i.e., this program satisfies the three aforementioned properties:

$$
\begin{aligned}
&\textbf{var } v, w, t : \\
&w := nil; \\
&\textbf{while } (v \neq nil) \; \{ \\
&\quad t := w; w := v; v := v{\uparrow}; w{\uparrow} := t \\
&\}
\end{aligned}
$$

2.3   The Topic of This Paper

To check properties like the ones in the previous examples in a *fully automated* manner is the challenge that is faced in this paper. We advocate an automata-based model-checking approach in which states are equipped with (abstract) heap representations. As property-specification language we propose to use a first-order variant of linear temporal logic. Before explaining the heap abstraction mechanism, we provide the concrete (and infinite-state) semantics of our example programming language. This is characterized by the fact that each cell and pointer is represented explicitly.

3   Concrete Semantics

We assume a universe of entities, Ent, including a distinguished element nil, used to represent a canonical entity without outgoing references. We let $PV \subseteq Ent$, i.e., program variables are assumed to correspond to special entities that exist throughout the entire computation.

Configurations. Automata will be used as semantical model for our programming language. States (called configurations) of these automata are equipped with information about the current entities, their pointer structure, and the current set of fresh entities.

Definition 1 (configuration). *A configuration is a tuple* $c = \langle E, \prec, N \rangle$ *such that:*

- $E \subseteq Ent$ *is a finite set of entities, with* $nil \in E$.
- $\prec \subseteq E \times E$ *is a binary relation over* E, *such that:*

$$outdegree_\prec(e) \leqslant 1 \text{ for all } e \in E \quad and \quad outdegree_\prec(nil) = 0$$

- $N \subseteq E$ *is the set of fresh entities*

c is called reachable *if for all* $e \in E$, *there is some* $e' \in PV \cap E$ *such that* $e' \prec^* e$ *(where* $\prec^*$ *is the reflexive and transitive closure of* $\prec$).

A configuration is used to model the heap of a program. Note that in general these concrete heaps can grow unboundedly. The only data structure allowed is a cell with at most a single pointer to another cell. The cells are modeled by entities and the pointers by the binary relation $\prec$. Note the restriction on the $\prec$-outdegree, which implies that any entity has at most one $\prec$-successor. The derived partial function $succ : E \rightharpoonup E$ is defined by:

$$succ(e) = e' \quad \text{if} \quad e \prec e' \quad .$$

Example 1. In Fig. 1, the configurations are depicted as ovals, program variables stand for the entities representing them, and the dashed lines between variables and entities represent the pointers from e_v to $succ(e_v)$. The entity *nil* is not depicted in these configurations. If in cells the outgoing pointer is not depicted then it is dangling. The fresh entities in a configuration are the entities that are absent in the previous configuration. They typically arise as a result of executing the new statement.

Interpreting navigation expressions. The semantics of navigation expression α in configuration $c = \langle E, \prec, N \rangle$ is given by:

$$[\![nil]\!]_c^{\text{exp}} = nil$$
$$[\![v]\!]_c^{\text{exp}} = succ(v)$$
$$[\![\alpha{\uparrow}]\!]_c^{\text{exp}} = succ\left([\![\alpha]\!]_c^{\text{exp}}\right)$$

where *succ* is assumed to be strict, i.e., $succ(\bot) = \bot$. We omit the subscript c from $[\![\ ]\!]_c^{\text{exp}}$ in case the configuration is clear from the context. The semantics of left-hand sides of assignments is defined as:

$$[\![v]\!]_c^{\text{loc}} = v$$
$$[\![\ell{\uparrow}]\!]_c^{\text{loc}} = succ\left([\![\ell]\!]_c^{\text{loc}}\right)$$

Note that $[\![v]\!]^{\text{loc}}$ equals the entity denoting v in case v occurs as left-hand side of an assignment (or as argument of new), whereas $[\![v]\!]^{\text{exp}}$ is the cell referred to by v whenever v occurs as right-hand side (or as argument of dispose).

Heap manipulations. The following operations on configurations are useful to define the operational semantics of operations such as new, dispose and assignment. All operations manipulate the heap, and yield a new heap that is obtained by either adding or deleting entities, or by changing pointers. Assume w.l.o.g. that *Ent* is totally ordered by some arbitrary natural ordering; this is convenient for selecting a fresh entity in a deterministic way. The following operations require $\llbracket \ell \rrbracket^{\mathsf{loc}}$ and $\llbracket \alpha \rrbracket^{\mathsf{exp}}$ to be different from $\bot$ and *nil*.

- The operation $add(c, \ell)$ extends the configuration $c = \langle E, \prec, N \rangle$ with a fresh entity e referred to by the expression ℓ:

$$add(c, \ell) = \langle E \cup \{e\}, \prec', \{e\} \rangle \text{ with } e = \min(Ent \setminus E)$$
$$\prec' = \prec \setminus \{(\llbracket \ell \rrbracket^{\mathsf{loc}}, \llbracket \ell \rrbracket^{\mathsf{exp}})\} \cup \{(\llbracket \ell \rrbracket^{\mathsf{loc}}, e)\}$$

- The operation $cancel(c, \alpha)$ deletes the entity denoted by the navigation expression α from the configuration c:

$$cancel(c, \alpha) = \langle E', \prec \cap (E' \times E'), \varnothing \rangle, \text{ with } E' = E \setminus \{\llbracket \alpha \rrbracket^{\mathsf{exp}}\}$$

Note that in the resulting configuration, every pointer to $\llbracket \alpha \rrbracket^{\mathsf{exp}}$ becomes undefined.

- Finally, the operation $modify(c, \ell, \alpha)$ changes the configuration c such that the entity denoted by ℓ points to the entity referred to by α:

$$modify(c, \ell, \alpha) = \langle E, \prec', \varnothing \rangle \text{ with } \prec' = \prec \setminus \{(\llbracket \ell \rrbracket^{\mathsf{loc}}, \llbracket \ell \rrbracket^{\mathsf{exp}})\}$$
$$\cup \{(\llbracket \ell \rrbracket^{\mathsf{loc}}, \llbracket \alpha \rrbracket^{\mathsf{exp}})\}$$

Stated in words, the outgoing pointer of the entity denoted by ℓ is redirected to the entity denoted by α.

The final operation on heap structures that is needed for the semantics is garbage collection. This is done by explicitly determining the entities in a configuration that are "reachable" (via the pointer structure) from some program variable. We define:

$$gc(c) = \langle E', \prec \cap (E' \times E'), N \cap E' \rangle \text{ with } E' = \{e \mid \exists e' \in PV. e' \prec^* e\}$$

Example applications of the heap manipulations are provided in Fig. 2.

Pointer automata. The semantics of the programming language is given by a pointer automaton, in fact an automaton that accepts infinite sequences of configurations according to a generalized Büchi acceptance condition. Each state in the pointer automaton is equipped with a concrete configuration that represents the current heap content.

Definition 2 (pointer automaton). *A pointer automaton A is a tuple $(Q, cf, \rightarrow, I, \mathcal{F})$ where:*

- *Q is a non-empty, denumerable set of states*
- *$cf : Q \rightarrow Cnf$ is a mapping associating a configuration with every state*

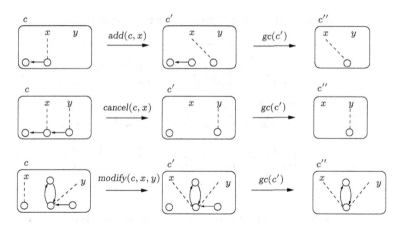

Fig. 2. Example heap manipulations

- $\rightarrow \, \subseteq Q \times Q$ *is a transition relation*
- $I \subseteq Q$ *is a set of initial states, and*
- $\mathcal{F} \subseteq 2^Q$ *is a generalized Büchi acceptance condition.*

We write $q \rightarrow q'$ instead of $(q, q') \in \, \rightarrow$. According to the generalized Büchi acceptance condition, $q_0 q_1 q_2 \cdots$ is an accepting *run* of A if $q_i \rightarrow q_{i+1}$ for all $i \geqslant 0$, $q_0 \in I$ and $|\{i \mid q_i \in F\}| = \omega$ for all $F \in \mathcal{F}$. That is, each accept set $F \in \mathcal{F}$ needs to be visited infinitely often. Let $runs(A)$ denote the set of runs of A. Run $q_0 q_1 q_2 \cdots$ accepts the sequence of configurations $cf(q_0)\, cf(q_1)\, cf(q_2) \cdots$. The language $\mathcal{L}(A)$ denotes the set of configuration sequences that is accepted by some run of A.

Note that here and in the sequel we will implicitly interpret all configuration sequences *up to isomorphism*, where a sequence $c_0\, c_1\, c_2 \cdots$ is isomorphic to $c_0'\, c_1'\, c_2' \cdots$ if each c_i is isomorphic to c_i', in the natural sense of having a bijective mapping $\psi_i : E_i \rightarrow E_i'$ that both preserves and reflects structure, and, moreover, $\psi_i(e) = \psi_{i+1}(e)$ for $e \in E_i \cap E_{i+1}$.

Operational semantics. Let *Par* denote the compound statements, i.e., the statements generated by $r ::= s \mid r \parallel s$ with s a program statement as defined in Section 2. The compound statements constitute the states of the pointer automaton that will be associated to a program. We first provide the inference rules for those statements that might affect the heap structure, cf. Table 1. Any manipulation on an undefined navigation expression results in a run-time error, denoted by the process **error**. Any attempt to delete, create or assign a value to the constant *nil* fails too. These errors are considered to be local, i.e., the process attempting to execute these statements aborts, but this does not affect other concurrent processes. This will become clear from the rules for parallel composition.

The semantics of the other control structures is defined by the rules in Table 2. The rules for the alternative and sequential composition as well as

Table 1. Operational rules for heap manipulations

$$\frac{[\![\ell]\!]^{\mathsf{loc}} \notin \{\bot, nil\}}{\mathsf{new}(\ell), c \rightarrow \mathsf{skip}, gc \circ add(c, \ell)} \qquad \frac{[\![\ell]\!]^{\mathsf{loc}} \in \{\bot, nil\}}{\mathsf{new}(\ell), c \rightarrow \mathsf{error}, c}$$

$$\frac{[\![\alpha]\!]^{\mathsf{exp}} \notin \{\bot, nil\}}{\mathsf{dispose}(\alpha), c \rightarrow \mathsf{skip}, gc \circ cancel(c, \alpha)} \qquad \frac{[\![\alpha]\!]^{\mathsf{exp}} \in \{\bot, nil\}}{\mathsf{dispose}(\alpha), c \rightarrow \mathsf{error}, c}$$

$$\frac{[\![\ell]\!]^{\mathsf{loc}} \notin \{\bot, nil\}}{\ell := \alpha, c \rightarrow \mathsf{skip}, gc \circ modify(c, \ell, \alpha)} \qquad \frac{[\![\ell]\!]^{\mathsf{loc}} \in \{\bot, nil\}}{\ell := \alpha, c \rightarrow \mathsf{error}, c}$$

Table 2. Operational rules for the control structures

$$\frac{[\![b]\!]^{\mathsf{exp}} = true}{\mathbf{if}\ (b)\{s_1\}\{s_2\}, c \rightarrow s_1, c} \qquad \frac{[\![b]\!]^{\mathsf{exp}} = false}{\mathbf{if}\ (b)\{s_1\}\{s_2\}, c \rightarrow s_2, c}$$

$$\frac{s_1, c \rightarrow s_1', c' \wedge s_1' \notin \{\mathsf{skip}, \mathsf{error}\}}{s_1\ ;\ s_2, c \rightarrow s_1'\ ;\ s_2, c'} \qquad \frac{s_1, c \rightarrow \mathsf{skip}, c'}{s_1\ ;\ s_2, c \rightarrow s_2, c'} \qquad \frac{s_1, c \rightarrow \mathsf{error}, c}{s_1\ ;\ s_2, c \rightarrow \mathsf{error}, c}$$

$$\frac{}{\mathbf{while}\ (b)\{s\}, c \rightarrow \mathbf{if}\ (b)\{\ s\ ;\ \mathbf{while}\ (b)\{s\}\ \}\{\ \mathsf{skip}\ \}, c} \qquad \frac{}{\langle s \rangle, c \rightarrow \mathsf{atomic}\ s', c'}$$

$$\frac{s, c \rightarrow s', c' \wedge s' \notin \{\mathsf{skip}, \mathsf{error}\}}{\mathsf{atomic}\ s, c \rightarrow \mathsf{atomic}\ s', c'} \qquad \frac{s, c \rightarrow s', c' \wedge s' \in \{\mathsf{skip}, \mathsf{error}\}}{\mathsf{atomic}\ s, c \rightarrow s', c'}$$

$$\frac{s_j, c \rightarrow s_j', c' \wedge s_j' \neq \mathsf{error} \wedge (\forall i \neq j.\, s_i \neq \mathsf{atomic}\ s_i')}{s_1\ \|\ \cdots\ \|\ s_j\ \|\ \cdots\ \|\ s_k, c \rightarrow s_1\ \|\ \cdots\ \|\ s_j'\ \|\ \cdots\ \|\ s_k, c'}$$

$$\frac{s_j, c \rightarrow \mathsf{error}, c \wedge (\forall i \neq j.\, s_i \neq \mathsf{atomic}\ s_i')}{s_1\ \|\ \cdots\ \|\ s_j\ \|\ \cdots\ \|\ s_k, c \rightarrow s_1\ \|\ \cdots\ \|\ \mathsf{error}\ \|\ \cdots\ \|\ s_k, c}$$

$$\frac{\forall 0 < j \leqslant k.\, s_j \in \{\mathsf{skip}, \mathsf{error}\}}{s_1\ \|\ \cdots\ \|\ s_k, c \rightarrow s_1\ \|\ \cdots\ \|\ s_k, c}$$

for iteration are straightforward. Note that the boolean expression $\mathsf{undef}(\alpha)$ yields true whenever $[\![\alpha]\!]^{\mathsf{exp}} = \bot$, and false otherwise. The semantics of the other boolean expressions is standard (where equality is assumed to be strict) and is omitted here. The semantics of atomic regions are determined by three rules. On entering an atomic region, the process s is marked as "being in control"; this is indicated by the prefix atomic. This mark is lost once the atomic region is left, or whenever an error occurs. Once marked as being atomic, the process has control and is allowed to complete its atomic region without any possible interference of any other process. This is established by the first two rules for parallel composition. Once all processes are finished or aborted, the program loops. This is established by the last inference rule, and is exploited to impose fairness constraints. As a result, all runs of any pointer program are infinite.

Definition 3. *The concrete semantics of program*

$$p = \text{decl } v_1, \ldots, v_n : (s_1 \parallel \cdots \parallel s_k)$$

is the pointer automaton $\llbracket p \rrbracket^{\text{conc}} = (Q, cf, \rightarrow, I, \mathcal{F})$ *such that:*

- $Q \subseteq Par \times Cnf$ with $cf(r, c) = c$
- $\rightarrow\ \subseteq Q \times Q$ *is the smallest relation satisfying the rules in Table 1 and 2;*
- $I = \{(s_1 \parallel \cdots \parallel s_k, \langle \{v_1, \ldots, v_n\}, \varnothing, \varnothing \rangle)\}$
- $\mathcal{F} = \{\widehat{\mathcal{F}}_i \mid 0 \leqslant i < k\} \cup \{\widetilde{\mathcal{F}}_i \mid 0 \leqslant i < k\}$ *where:*

$$\widehat{\mathcal{F}}_i = \{(s_1' \parallel \cdots \parallel s_k', c) \in Q \mid s_i' = \text{skip} \vee s_i' = \text{error} \vee s_i' = \text{while}(b)\{s\}; s''\}$$
$$\widetilde{\mathcal{F}}_i = \{(s_1' \parallel \cdots \parallel s_k', c) \in Q \mid s_i' = \text{skip} \vee s_i' = \text{error} \vee s_i' = s; \text{while}(b)\{s\}; s''\}.$$

A few remarks are in order. For state $(r, c) \in Q$, r is the compound statement to be executed and c is a reachable (concrete) configuration, i.e., it only contains the entities reachable from some program variable in the program p. $\llbracket p \rrbracket^{\text{conc}}$ has a single initial state $s_1 \parallel \cdots \parallel s_k$ together with a heap that initially contains a cell for each program variable only. The set of accept states for the i-th sequential component s_i consists of all states in which the component i has either terminated ($s_i = \text{skip}$), aborted ($s_i = \text{error}$), or is processing a loop (which could be infinite). Note that according to this acceptance condition, processes that consist of an infinite loop are executed in a fair manner. This applies, e.g., to both processes in the producer-consumer example.

Example 2. Consider the example programs provided in Section 2. It can be checked that Fig. 1 indeed is a possible run that is allowed by the semantics of the second producer-consumer program. The transition labels are provided for convenience only. The initial part of the (infinite-state) pointer automaton that is obtained for the producer-consumer program with the shared list is given in Fig. 3.

4   Heap Abstractions

The most obvious way to model pointer structures is to represent each entity and each pointer individually as we did in the previous section. For most programs, like, e.g., the producer/consumer program with the shared linked list, this will give rise to infinite pointer automata. To obtain more abstract (and compact) views of pointer structures, chains of cells will be aggregated and represented by one (or more) cells. We consider the abstraction of *pure chains* (and not of arbitrary graphs) in order to be able to keep the "topology" of pointer structures invariant in a more straightforward manner.

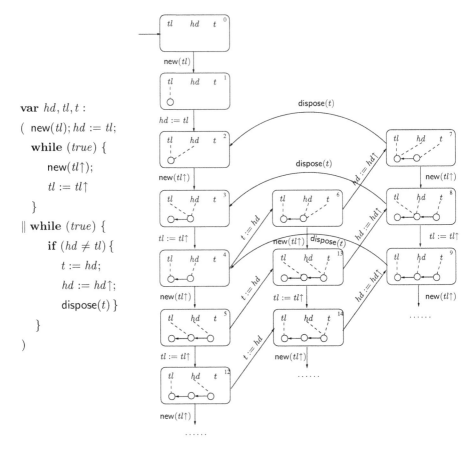

var hd, tl, t :

(new(tl); $hd := tl$;
  while ($true$) {
    new($tl\uparrow$);
    $tl := tl\uparrow$
  }
|| while ($true$) {
    if ($hd \neq tl$) {
      $t := hd$;
      $hd := hd\uparrow$;
      dispose(t) }
  }
)

Fig. 3. Fragment of the automaton for the producer-consumer program

4.1   Abstracting Pure Chains

Pure chains. A sequence $e_1, \ldots, e_k$ of entities in a configuration is a chain (of length k) if $e_i \prec e_{i+1}$, for $0 < i < k$. The non-empty set E of entities is a chain of length $|E| = k$ iff there exists a bijection $f : \{1, \ldots, k\} \to E$ such that $f(1), \ldots, f(k)$ is a chain; let *first*$(E) = f(1)$ and *last*$(E) = f(k)$. E is a *pure chain* if *indegree*$_\prec(e) = 1$ for all $e \in f(2), f(3), \ldots, f(k)$ and f is unique (which may fail to be the case if the chain is a cycle). Note that chains consisting of a single element are trivially pure.

Abstracting pure chains. An abstract entity may represent a pure chain of "concrete" entities. The concrete representation of abstract entity e is indicated by its *cardinality* $\mathcal{C}(e) \in \mathbb{M} = \{1, \ldots, M\} \cup \{*\}$, for some fixed constant $M > 0$. Entity e for which $\mathcal{C}(e) = m \leqslant M$ represents a chain of m "concrete" entities; if $\mathcal{C}(e) = *$, e represents a chain that is longer than M. (Such entities are similar to summary nodes [38], with the specific property that they always abstract from pure chains.) The special cardinality function $\mathbf{1}$ yields one for each entity. The precision of the abstraction is improved on increasing M (because more configurations are distinguished); moreover, as we will discuss in the next section, to model check a given temporal property, M has to be large enough to at least evaluate all atomic predicates in the property with certainty.

Definition 4 (abstract configuration). *An* abstract configuration *is a tuple* $c = \langle E, \prec, N, \mathcal{C} \rangle$ *such that* $\langle E, \prec, N \rangle$ *is a configuration and* $\mathcal{C} : E \to \mathbb{M}$ *is a mapping associating a cardinality to each* $e \in E$, *such that* $\mathcal{C}(e) = 1$ *if* $e \in N \cup PV$.

Evidently, each concrete configuration (cf. Def. 1) is an abstract configuration such that $\mathcal{C} = \mathbf{1}$.

Configurations representing pure chains at different abstraction levels are related by *morphisms*, defined as follows. Let Cnf denote the set of all configurations ranged over by c and c', and $\mathcal{C}(\{e_1, \ldots, e_n\}) = \mathcal{C}(e_1) \oplus \ldots \oplus \mathcal{C}(e_n)$ denote the number of concrete cells represented by e_1 through e_n, where $n \oplus m = n+m$ if $n+m \leqslant M$ and $*$ otherwise.

Definition 5 (morphism). *For* $c, c' \in Cnf$, *a morphism from* c *to* c' *is a surjective function* $h : E \to E'$ *such that:*

1. *for all* $e \in E'$, $h^{-1}(e)$ *is a pure chain and* $\mathcal{C}'(e) = \mathcal{C}(h^{-1}(e))$
2. $e \prec' e' \Rightarrow last(h^{-1}(e)) \prec first(h^{-1}(e'))$
3. $e \prec e' \Rightarrow h(e) \preceq' h(e')$ *where* $\preceq'$ *denotes the reflexive closure of* $\prec'$
4. $h(e) \in N'$ *if and only if* $e \in N$.

According to the first condition only pure chains may be abstracted by a single entity, while keeping the cardinalities invariant. The second and third condition enforce the preservation of the pointer structure under h. The last condition asserts that the notion of freshness should be preserved. Intuitively speaking, by means of a morphism the abstract shape of the pointer dependencies represented by the two related configurations is maintained. The identity function id is a morphism and morphisms are closed under composition.

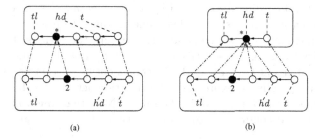

(a)   (b)

Fig. 4. Morphisms between configurations of the producer-consumer program at different abstraction levels

Example 3. Fig. 4(a) shows two configurations of the producer-consumer program with a shared list as buffer, at two levels of abstraction. It is assumed that $M=2$. The top configurations are abstractions of the bottom ones. Open circles denote concrete entities and filled circles denote abstract entities; their cardinality is indicated next to them. The morphism is indicated by dashed arrows. An alternative abstraction of the same configuration is depicted in Fig. 4(b). Although the indicated mapping is indeed a morphism in the sense of Def. 5, it is clear that this abstraction is too coarse as there is no way to distinguish between the cells pointed to by hd and $hd\uparrow$, expressions that both occur in the producer-consumer program.

Evolving pointer structures. Morphisms relate configurations that model the pointer structure at distinct abstraction levels. They do not model the dynamic evolution of such linking structures. To reflect the execution of pointer-manipulating statements, such as either the creation or deletion of entities, or the change of pointers — the so-called "pointer swing" —by assignments (e.g., $x := x\uparrow\uparrow$), we use *reallocations*.

Definition 6 (reallocation). *For $c, c' \in Cnf$, $\lambda : (E^\perp \times E'^\perp) \to \mathbb{M}$ is a reallocation if:*

1. *(a)* $\mathcal{C}(e) = \bigoplus_{e' \in E'^\perp} \lambda(e, e')$ *and (b)* $\mathcal{C}'(e') = \bigoplus_{e \in E^\perp} \lambda(e, e')$
2. *(a) for all $e \in E$, $\{e' \mid \lambda(e, e') \neq 0\}$ is a chain, and*
   (b) for all $e' \in E'$, $\{e \mid \lambda(e, e') \neq 0\}$ is a chain
3. *for all $e \in E$, $|\{e' \mid \lambda(e, e') = *\}| \leqslant 1$*
4. *$\{e \mid \lambda(\perp, e) > 0\} = N'$*

Let Λ denote the set of reallocations, and $c \overset{\lambda}{\rightsquigarrow} c'$ denote that there exists a reallocation λ between c and c'.

We explicitly use the undefinedness symbol $\perp$ to model birth (allocation) and death (deallocation) of entities: $\lambda(\perp, e) = n \neq 0$ denotes the birth of (n instances of) e whereas $\lambda(e, \perp) = n \neq 0$ denotes the death of (n instances of) e. The conditions express that reallocation λ redistributes cardinalities on E to E' such that (1a) the total cardinality sent by λ from a source entity $e \in E$ equals $\mathcal{C}(e)$ and (1b) the total cardinality received by a target entity $e' \in E'$ equals $\mathcal{C}'(e')$; also, (2a) the entities that send at least one instance to a given target entity $e' \in E'$ form a chain in the source, and likewise, (2b) the entities that receive at least one entity from a given source $e \in E$ form a chain in the target. Moreover, (3) for each source entity e, at most one target entity e' receives unboundedly many instances. Finally (4) expresses the correlation between the birth of entities and the freshness of those entities in the target. Note that, due to $\mathcal{C}'(e') = 1$ for $e' \in N'$ (see 4) and condition (1b) it follows that $\lambda(\perp, e') = 1$ and $\lambda(e, e') = 0$ for all $e \in E$.

In some cases we can derive a reallocation λ_R between abstract configurations unambiguously from a binary relation R between the sets of entities. In the lemma below we use $R(e)$ to denote $\{e' \mid (e, e') \in R\}$ and $R^{-1}(e')$ to denote $\{e \mid (e, e') \in R\}$.

Lemma 1. *Let c, c' be two abstract configurations, and let $R \subseteq E \times E'$ be a binary relation. We call R predictable if it satisfies the following conditions for all $(e, e') \in R$:*

- *either $|R(e)|=1$ and $\mathcal{C}(R^{-1}(e'))=\mathcal{C}'(e')$ or $|R^{-1}(e')|=1$ and $\mathcal{C}'(R(e))=\mathcal{C}(e)$;*
- *$R(e)$ is a $\prec'$-chain and $R^{-1}(e')$ is a $\prec$-chain;*
- *$e'' \in R(e)$ implies either $e'' = e'$ or $\mathcal{C}'(e') = 1$ or $\mathcal{C}'(e'') = 1$;*
- *$e' \notin N'$.*

If R is predictable, there is exactly one reallocation λ_R between c and c' with:

- *$R = \{(e, e') \in E \times E' \mid \lambda(e, e') > 0\}$;*
- *$\lambda(\bot, e') > 0$ if and only if $R^{-1}(e') = \varnothing$;*
- *$\lambda(e, \bot) > 0$ if and only if $R(e) = \varnothing$.*

Note that, in particular, any one-to-one relation between c and c' for which $\mathcal{C}(e) = \mathcal{C}'(e')$ if $(e, e') \in R$, is predictable. A special class are the so-called *functional reallocations*, which leave all cardinalities unchanged.

It is straightforward to check that, for any configuration c, the "identity" function that maps each pair (e, e) for $e \in E_c$ onto $\mathcal{C}_c(e)$ is a reallocation.

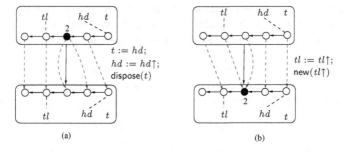

(a)   (b)

Fig. 5. Reallocations for evolution in the producer-consumer program

Example 4. Fig. 5(a) shows how an abstract configuration of the producer-consumer program (for $M=2$) evolves on performing two assignments and a disposal. The corresponding reallocation is depicted by dashed arrows between the configurations. Fig. 5(b) shows the reversed transition and its reallocation. Note that in (a) a cell is disposed (the one without outgoing dashed arrow), whereas in (b) a cell is created (the one without incoming dashed arrow).

The concept of reallocation can be considered as a generalization of the idea of identity change as, for instance, present in history-dependent automata [31]: besides the possible change of the abstract identity of concrete entities, it allows for the evolution of pointer structures. Reallocations allow "extraction" of concrete entities from abstract entities by a redistribution of cardinalities between entities. Extraction is analogous to *materialization* [38]. Reallocations ensure that entities that are born do not originate from any other entity. Moreover, entities that die can only be reallocated to $\bot$. This is the way in which birth and death of cells is modeled.

Pointer automata. In order to model the dynamic evolution of programs manipulating abstract representations of linked lists, we use (abstract) pointer automata. These are the same structures as before, except that each transition is now indexed with a reallocation, and states are equipped with abstract (rather than concrete) configurations.

Definition 7 (abstract pointer automaton). *An abstract pointer automaton $A = \langle Q, cf, \rightarrow, I, \mathcal{F} \rangle$ with Q, cf, I and $\mathcal{F}$ as before (cf. Def 2), and transition relation $\rightarrow \subseteq Q \times \Lambda \times Q$, indexed by reallocations, such that:*

$$q \xrightarrow{\lambda} q' \quad \text{implies that} \quad \lambda \text{ is a reallocation from } cf(q) \text{ to } cf(q')$$

Runs of abstract pointer automata are alternating sequences of states and reallocations, i.e., $q_0 \lambda_0 q_1 \lambda_1 q_2 \cdots$ such that $q_i \xrightarrow{\lambda_i} q_{i+1}$ for all $i \geqslant 0$, $q_0 \in I$, and each accept set in $\mathcal{F}$ is visited infinitely often. Each run can be said to accept sequences of *concrete* configurations that are compatible with the reallocations, in a way to be defined below.

4.2 Symbolic Semantics

Although the concrete semantics is rather simple and intuitive, it suffers from the problem that it easily results in an infinite state space. To circumvent this problem, we provide a semantics in terms of abstract pointer automata.

Informal idea of the symbolic semantics. As a start, we determine by means of a syntactic check through the program p under consideration, the "longest" navigation expression that occurs in it and fix constant L_p such that

$$L_p > \max\{n \mid v{\uparrow}^n \text{ occurs in program } p\}$$

Besides the formula-dependent constant M, the program-dependent constant L_p can be used to tune the precision of the symbolic representation, i.e., by increasing L_p the model becomes less abstract. Unbounded entities (i.e., those with cardinality $*$) will be exploited in the semantics to keep the model finite. The basic intuition of our symbolic semantics is that unbounded entities should always be preceded by a chain of at least L_p concrete entities. Such states (or configurations) are called *safe*. This principle allows us to precisely determine the concrete entity that is referred to by any navigation expression in the program.[1] As assignments may yield unsafe configurations (due to program variables that are "shifted" too close to an unbounded entity), these statements require some special treatment (as we will see).

Definition 8 (safe configuration). *For fixed $L > 0$, configuration c is L-safe if:*

$$\forall e \in PV. \forall e' : d(e, e') \leqslant L \Rightarrow \mathcal{C}(e') = 1$$

where $d(e, e') = n$ if $e' = succ^n(e)$, and $d(e, e') = \perp$ if $e \not\rightarrow^* e'$.

---

[1] This is the sense in which the configuration is safe. The reader should not confuse the idea of safe configuration we use here with other concepts such as memory safety.

Here, $succ^0(e) = e$ and $succ^{n+1}(e) = succ(succ^n(e))$. That is to say, in an L-safe configuration, all entities within distance L of a program variable are concrete.

Example 5. The upper configuration in Fig. 4(a) is 2-safe, since each program variable is at distance at least two from the abstract entity, but not 3-safe. (Recall that each program variable is an entity.) The upper configuration in Fig. 4(b) is not 1-safe. It follows by easy verification that all states in the concrete pointer automaton $[\![p]\!]^{conc}$ for program p are L-safe for any $L > 0$.

Normal form. For the symbolic semantics we consider configurations that, up to isomorphism, uniquely represent a set of "safe" states that may be related by morphisms. Such configurations are said to be in *normal form*. The notion of normal form is based on compactness:

Definition 9 (compact configuration). *For fixed $L > 0$, configuration c is L-compact if for any entity e:*

$$indegree_{\prec}(e) > 1 \quad or \quad d(e', e) \leqslant L+1 \text{ for some } e' \in PV$$

Configuration c is thus called *L-compact* if non-trivial pure chains appear within at most distance $L+1$ from some program variable. Cells that belong to a cycle and that are "entrances" to the cycle are compact, i.e., these cells will not be abstracted from.

Example 6. The upper configuration in Fig. 4(a) is 2-compact, as all entities are within distance at most three from a program variable. The following L-safe configuration (for any $L > 0$), on the other hand, is not L-compact for $L < 3$:

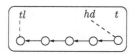

as two concrete cells are "too far" from a program variable, and thus need to be represented in a more compact way.

Definition 10 (normal-form configuration). *For fixed $L > 0$, configuration c is in L-normal form whenever it is L-safe and L-compact.*

Given that the number of program variables is finite, and that we only consider cells that are reachable from program variables, it follows that:

Theorem 1. *There are only finitely many L-normal form configurations.*

The fact that the normal form of an L-safe configuration is unique follows from the following:

Theorem 2. *For $c \in Cnf$: if c is L-safe and reachable, then there is a unique L-normal $c' \in Cnf$ and a unique morphism between c and c'.*

Intuitively speaking, configurations in L-normal form are the most compact representations of L-safe configurations. The normal form of L-safe configuration c is denoted $nf(c)$, and $h_{nf}(c)$ denotes the corresponding unique morphism between c and $nf(c)$.

Example 7. Let $M{=}2$. In the following figure, the right hand configuration is the L-normal form of left hand one for $L{=}2$:

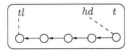   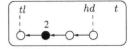

In the following figure, the right hand configuration is the L-normal form of left hand one for $L{=}1$:

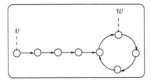   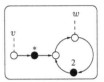

For normal form configurations, we define the following relation between abstract reallocations and pairs of concrete configurations.

Definition 11 (encoding). *Let c, c' be in L-normal form (for some L) and let λ be a reallocation between c and c'. λ is said to encode a concrete pair of reallocations c_1, c_1' if $c = nf(c_1)$ and $c' = nf(c_1')$ with normal form morphisms h_{nf} and h'_{nf}, respectively, and for all $e \in E$ and $e' \in E'$:*

$$\lambda(e, \bot) = |h_{nf}^{-1}(e) \setminus E_1'|$$

$$\lambda(\bot, e') = |h'^{-1}_{nf}(e') \setminus E_1|$$

$$\lambda(e, e') = |h_{nf}^{-1}(e) \cap h'^{-1}_{nf}(e')|$$

(where the cardinalities on the right hand side are interpreted modulo M, i.e., they turn into $*$ if the cardinality exceeds M).

For an abstract pointer automaton A whose configurations are all in normal form, such as the ones we will use below to give a finite-state semantics to our language, using this notion of encoding we can define what it means for A to *simulate* a concrete automaton (see Sect. 4.3), as well as the *language* of A. In particular, for the latter, we consider that a run $q_0 \lambda_0 q_1 \lambda_1 q_2 \cdots$ of A accepts a sequence of concrete configurations $c_0\, c_1\, c_2\, \cdots$ if each λ_i encodes the pair c_i, c_{i+1}, and we define $\mathcal{L}(A)$ to be the set of configuration sequences accepted by some run of A.

Safe expansions. As argued above, performing an assignment to an L-safe state may lead to a state that is not L-safe due to program variables that are moved too close to an unbounded entity. This happens, for instance, when variable

v is assigned an entity further down in the list originally pointed to by v. To overcome this difficulty, the semantics of assignment yields a *set* of possible successor configurations that are related to each other in some sense. This is the main source of nondeterminism (i.e., over-approximation). These configurations, together with the morphisms that relate them to the configuration c in which the assignment is executed, are the *safe expansions* of c.

Definition 12 (safe expansion). *For fixed $L > 0$ and configuration c, Υc is the set of pairs (c', h) such that c' is L-safe and h is a morphism from c' to c with shrink factor at most L.*

The shrink factor of morphism h is defined as $\max\{|h^{-1}(e)| - 1 \mid e \in E'\}$. It is important to note that Υc is finite (up to isomorphism).

Operational semantics. With the use of safe expansions we are now in a position to define the symbolic semantics of our programming language. A key observation is that the definitions of $add(c, \ell)$, $cancel(c, \alpha)$ and $modify(c, \ell, \alpha)$ can also be applied if c is abstract, provided it is L-safe for some L no smaller than the number of consecutive dereferencing operations in ℓ and α — so that $[\![\ell]\!]^{\text{loc}}$, $[\![\ell]\!]^{\text{exp}}$ and $[\![\alpha]\!]^{\text{exp}}$ all point to a uniquely determined, concrete entity. For that reason we can use the relation $\rightarrow$ as derived according to Tables 1 and 2 over abstract configurations, as long as we ensure L-safety for sufficiently large L. Furthermore, if we derive a transition $s, c \rightarrow s', c'$ using these rules, then the identity relation $\{(e, e) \mid e \in E \cap E'\}$ is predictable in the sense of Lemma 1.

Definition 13. *The symbolic semantics of the program*

$$p = \text{decl } v_1, \ldots, v_n : (s_1 \parallel \cdots \parallel s_k)$$

is the (abstract) pointer automaton $[\![p]\!]^{\text{symb}} = \langle Q, cf, \rightarrow, I, \mathcal{F} \rangle$ where Q, cf, I and $\mathcal{F}$ are defined as for the concrete semantics (see Def. 3) and $\rightarrow \subseteq Q \times \Lambda \times Q$ is the smallest relation satisfying:

$$\frac{s, c \rightarrow s', c' \;\wedge\; (c'', h) \in \Upsilon c'}{s, c \rightarrow_{\lambda_R} s', nf(c'')} \quad \text{where} \quad R = h_{nf} \circ h^{-1} \circ id_{E \cap E'} \ .$$

Let us explain this rule. The idea is that, by construction, all abstract configurations generated by the semantics are in L-normal form, implying that they are L-safe for sufficiently large L, so that we can indeed apply the concrete operational semantics (as discussed above). The abstract configuration thus derived, however, is no longer in L-normal form; therefore we take all safe expansions (introducing non-determinism) and normalize them. These steps (derivation–expansion–normalization) are accompanied by, respectively, a one-to-one identity relation or partial function $(id_{E \cap E'})$, an inverse morphism (h^{-1}) and a morphism (h_{nf}). By the definition of safe expansion it follows that $h(e) = h(e')$ for distinct e, e' implies (i) either e or e' has cardinality 1, and (ii) $h_{nf}(e) \neq h_{nf}(e')$. From this and the fact that both h and h_{nf} are morphisms, it can be deduced that $h_{nf} \circ h^{-1} \circ id_{E \cap E'}$ is predictable in the sense of Lemma 1, and hence λ_R is well-defined.

It is noteworthy that the safe expansion step is only really necessary if the original, concrete transition has been caused by an underlying $modify()$ operation (i.e., is the result of an assignment): the $add()$ and $cancel()$ operations cannot result in unsafe configurations, and hence no expansion is necessary afterwards. It is, therefore, only assignment statements that cause non-determinism in the abstract semantics.

Example 8. Consider the producer-consumer program where the buffer is modeled as a shared (unbounded) list:

var hd, tl, t :

(new(tl); $hd := tl$; **while** (*true*) {new($tl\uparrow$); $tl := tl\uparrow$ }   // producer

|| **while** (*true*) **if** ($hd \neq tl$) {$\langle t := hd$; $hd := hd\uparrow\rangle$; dispose(t) } // consumer

)

An initial fragment of the (abstract) pointer automaton for this program has already been provided in Example 2. For $L=2$ and $M=1$, Fig. 6 illustrates the part of the abstract pointer automaton in which abstraction plays a role. (The entire pointer automaton has 30 states.) With respect to the version given before, we have introduced atomicity in the consumer, which now atomically takes an item from the list and shifts the hd of the buffer. To avoid cluttering up the figure, the reallocations and the program statements are omitted, as are the accept states. The same applies to the intermediate states of the atomic regions.

Note that a collector cell is introduced as soon as two concrete cells can be "summarized" without violating the 2-safeness constraint. This happens, e.g., when performing the assignment $tl := tl\uparrow$ in configuration 22. A case of nondeterminism that arises from considering safe expansions for assignments are the two transitions, both labeled with the statement $\langle t := hd$; $hd := hd\uparrow\rangle$, emanating from configuration 28. As the source configuration contains a collector cell, this cell represents a list of two or more cells. Both possibilities are considered: for a list of exactly two elements, configuration 22 results; the other case corresponds to configuration 26.

4.3   Properties of the Semantics

The symbolic semantics gives us an analysis that by itself already yields some useful information on the program, such as the possibility of memory violation (e.g., if one of the parallel components of the program in a reachable state equals error). This analysis has two important properties: it is sound since it represents an over-approximation of the concrete semantics; and it is finite, and therefore computable.

In more detail, the concrete and abstract pointer automata generated by the concrete and symbolic semantics of a given program, respectively, are related by a forward simulation defined using the notion of encoding in Def. 11. Let q be

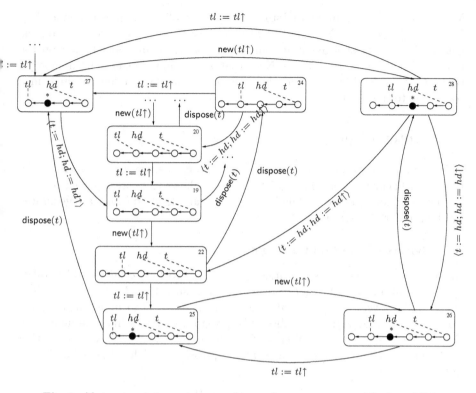

Fig. 6. Abstract pointer automaton for producer-consumer with shared list

a state in the concrete automaton. The abstract state q_{abs} is said to simulate q whenever

(i) $cf(q_{abs}) = nf(cf(q))$, and
(ii) for every transition $q \rightarrow q'$, there exists a reallocation λ that encodes the pair $cf(q)$, $cf(q')$, such that $q_{abs} \rightarrow_\lambda q'_{abs}$ and q'_{abs} simulates q'.

Pointer automaton A^{symb} simulates A^{conc}, denoted $A^{\mathsf{conc}} \sqsubseteq A^{\mathsf{symb}}$, whenever there exists a forward simulation relation satisfying (i) and (ii) for all pairs (c, c_{abs}) in the relation, such that initial states and accept states correspond. The following is then straightforward to prove:

Theorem 3. *If $A^{\mathsf{conc}} \sqsubseteq A^{\mathsf{symb}}$, then $\mathcal{L}(A^{\mathsf{conc}}) \subseteq \mathcal{L}(A^{\mathsf{symb}})$.*

The relation between the concrete and symbolic semantics can be expressed in terms of this notion of forward simulation (for details see [18]):

Theorem 4. *For any program p: $[\![p]\!]^{\mathsf{conc}} \sqsubseteq [\![p]\!]^{\mathsf{symb}}$.*

Moreover, we have the following crucial property of the symbolic semantics:

Theorem 5. *For any program p: $[\![p]\!]^{\mathsf{symb}}$ is finite state.*

More specifically, the number of states of the symbolic semantics is bounded by $k \cdot 2^K \cdot \sum_{n=0}^{K} (n+1)^n \cdot \sum_{n=0}^{K} (M+1)^n$ where k is a constant dependent on the length of the longest sequential component and K is an upper-bound on the number of entities in each state. Note that K is bounded since the number of program variables is finite, and there cannot be an infinite-length chain in a state, due to normal form.

5 Pointer Logic

To express properties of concurrent pointer programs, we use a first-order extension of linear temporal logic [35]. The logic allows to express properties over sequences of configurations. The intention is that these sequences are generated by the pointer automata.

5.1 Syntax of the Pointer Logic

In the logic, heap cells (i.e., entities) are referred to by *logical* variables, taken from a countable set LV, ranged over by x, y, z, such that $LV \cap PV = \varnothing$. The connection between logical variables and cells is established by a partial valuation, meaning that logical variables, like program variables, may be undefined. Logical variables are a special case of pointer expressions, i.e., expressions that refer to heap cells. The syntax of pointer expressions is defined as before by the grammar:

$$\alpha ::= nil \mid x \mid \alpha\uparrow$$

where *nil* denotes the special entity in *Ent*, x denotes the cell assigned by the current valuation (which may be *nil* or undefined), and $\alpha\uparrow$ denotes the entity referred to by (the entity denoted by) α (if any). Thus, $x\uparrow^n$ denotes the $(n+1)$-st cell in the list referred to by x.

The syntax of the logic *Navigation Temporal Logic* (NTL, for short) is defined by the grammar:

$$\Phi ::= \alpha = \alpha \mid \alpha \leadsto \alpha \mid \mathsf{undef}\,\alpha \mid \mathsf{new}\,\alpha \mid \exists x.\,\Phi \mid \Phi \wedge \Phi \mid \neg\Phi \mid \bigcirc\Phi \mid \Phi\,\mathsf{U}\,\Phi$$

The proposition $\alpha = \beta$ states that α and β are aliases. Here, equality is strict. Proposition $x\uparrow^2 = y\uparrow^3$, for example, denotes that the third cell in x's list is also the fourth cell in y's list. The proposition $\alpha \leadsto \beta$ expresses that (the cell denoted by) β is reachable from (the cell denoted by) α via the pointer structure. Thus, $x \leadsto y\uparrow^3$ expresses that in the current state the fourth cell in y's list can be reached by following the pointer structure from the cell denoted by x. Proposition $\mathsf{undef}\,\alpha$ states that α is dangling (i.e., undefined), and $\mathsf{new}\,\alpha$ asserts that the cell referred to by α is fresh. The existential quantification $\exists x.\Phi$ is valid if an appropriate cell for x can be found such that Φ holds. The boolean connectives, and the linear temporal connectives $\bigcirc$ (next) and U (until) have the usual interpretation. We denote $\alpha \neq \beta$ for $\neg(\alpha = \beta)$, $\alpha \not\leadsto \beta$ for $\neg(\alpha \leadsto \beta)$, $\mathsf{alive}\,\alpha$ for $\neg(\mathsf{undef}\,\alpha)$, and $\forall x.\,\Phi$ for $\neg(\exists x.\,\neg\Phi)$. The other boolean connectives (such as disjunction, implication and equivalence) and the temporal operators $\Diamond$ (eventually) and $\Box$ (always) are obtained in the standard way.

Note that *NTL* is in fact a *quantified modal logic* (see, e.g., [3,21]) as quantification and temporal operators can be mixed arbitrarily. In particular, temporal operators can be used inside quantification.

Example 9. We illustrate the expressiveness of the logic NTL by a number of example properties that are frequently encountered for pointer manipulating programs.

- The third cell in x's list and the head of y's list eventually become aliases:

$$\Diamond(x{\uparrow}{\uparrow} = y).$$

- $x{\uparrow}$ will never be dangling:

$$\Box(\text{alive}\, x{\uparrow}).$$

- Eventually, v will be part of a non-empty cycle:

$$\Diamond(\exists x.\, x \neq v \,\wedge\, x \leadsto v \,\wedge\, v \leadsto x)$$

- Every cell reachable from v will be eventually disposed:

$$\forall x.\, (v \leadsto x \Rightarrow \Diamond\text{undef}\, x)$$

- Whenever y is a cell in x's list, y and x can only become disconnected when y is disposed:

$$(\forall x.\, \forall y.\, x \leadsto y \Rightarrow (\Box\text{alive}\, y \,\vee\, (x \leadsto y)\, \mathsf{U}\, \text{undef}\, y))$$

- An unbounded number of cells will be created:

$$\Box\Diamond(\exists x.\, \text{new}\, x)$$

- Cells are disposed in the order of creation:

$$\Box\, (\forall x.\, \text{new}\, x \,\Rightarrow\, \Box\, (\forall y.\, \text{new}\, y \,\Rightarrow\, (\text{alive}\, y\, \mathsf{U}\, \text{undef}\, x)))$$

This can be understood as follows: any entity x that is fresh in the current state will be dead before (or at the same time as) any younger entity y (fresh in some later state) dies.

Program variables. To enable reasoning over program variables (rather than just logical ones), we introduce for each relevant program variable v a logical variable x_v, which always evaluates to the entity $v \in E$. We then use v in the logic as syntactic sugar for $x_v{\uparrow}$, so that it has the expected value. Furthermore, when we write $\exists x.\, \Phi$ we really mean $\exists x.\, (x \neq x_{v_1} \wedge \ldots \wedge x \neq x_{v_n}) \,\Rightarrow\, \Phi$, where $\{v_1, \ldots, v_n\}$ is the set of program variables occurring in the program.

Example 10. Consider the list-reversal program (cf. Section 2) that intends to reverse the list initially pointed to by variable v. Properties of interest of this program include, for instance:

– v and w always point to distinct lists (heap non-interference):

$$\Box(\forall x.\, v \rightsquigarrow x \;\Rightarrow\; w \not\rightsquigarrow x)$$

– v's list will be (and remains to be) reversed and the resulting list will be given to w [2]:

$$\forall x.\forall y.\, ((v \rightsquigarrow x \;\wedge\; x{\uparrow} = y) \;\Rightarrow\; \Diamond\Box(y{\uparrow} = x \wedge w \rightsquigarrow y))$$

Note that the previous formula expresses the precise specification of the list reversal program. In particular, it implies that the reversed list contains precisely the same elements of the original list and that their pointers are properly reversed. This property is not usually verifiable by shape analyses that do not keep track of the evolution of entities during the program computation.

– none of the cells in v's list will ever be deleted:

$$\forall x.\, (v \rightsquigarrow x \;\Rightarrow\; \Box\mathsf{alive}\, x)$$

Properties for the producer-consumer program with a shared list are:

– every element in the buffer is eventually consumed:

$$\Box(hd \neq tl \;\Rightarrow\; \exists x.\, (x = hd \;\wedge\; \Diamond\mathsf{undef}\, x))$$

(Note that this is *not* the same as $\Box(hd \neq tl \Rightarrow \Diamond\mathsf{undef}\ hd)$; in the former property, x is frozen to the value of hd in the state where it is bound, and so the property expresses that *that* particular entity dies; the latter expresses that hd itself may become undefined.)

– the tail is never deleted nor disconnected from the head:

$$\Box(\mathsf{alive}\ tl \;\wedge\; hd \rightsquigarrow tl)$$

Taking into account the semantics of the logic, to be defined below, from Fig. 6 it can be observed that both formulae are valid in the abstract pointer automaton that models the producer-consumer program. Using Theorem 4 and Corollary 1, we conclude that the original program (as represented in the concrete semantics) also exhibits these properties. The same applies to the ordering property that requires elements to be consumed in the order of production.

---

[2] If one is interested in only checking whether v's list is reversed at the end of the program, program locations can be added and referred to in the standard way.

5.2   Semantics of the Pointer Logic

Logical formulae are interpreted over infinite sequences of configurations. We need a function θ that is a partial valuation of the logical variables, i.e., $\theta(x)$ is either undefined or equals some cell, which is then the value of x — as we shall see, this is always an entity in the initial configuration of the sequence under consideration.

The semantics of navigation expression α is given by:

$$[\![nil]\!]_{\prec,\theta} = nil$$
$$[\![x]\!]_{\prec,\theta} = \theta(x)$$
$$[\![\alpha\!\uparrow]\!]_{\prec,\theta} = succ\,([\![\alpha]\!]_{\prec,\theta})$$

Let $\sigma = c_0\,c_1\,c_2\cdots$ be a sequence of concrete configurations. The semantics of NTL-formulae is defined by the satisfaction relation $\sigma, \theta \models \Phi$, defined as follows:

$$\sigma, \theta \models \alpha = \beta \quad \text{iff} \quad [\![\alpha]\!]_{\prec_0,\theta} = [\![\beta]\!]_{\prec_0,\theta}$$
$$\sigma, \theta \models \alpha \rightsquigarrow \beta \quad \text{iff} \quad \exists k \geqslant 0.\,[\![\alpha\!\uparrow^k]\!]_{\prec_0,\theta} = [\![\beta]\!]_{\prec_0,\theta}$$
$$\sigma, \theta \models \mathsf{undef}\,\alpha \quad \text{iff} \quad [\![\alpha]\!]_{\prec_0,\theta} = \bot$$
$$\sigma, \theta \models \mathsf{new}\,\alpha \quad \text{iff} \quad [\![\alpha]\!]_{\prec_0,\theta} \in N_0$$
$$\sigma, \theta \models \exists x.\,\Phi \quad \text{iff} \quad \exists e \in E_0 : \sigma, \theta\{e/x\} \models \Phi$$
$$\sigma, \theta \models \Phi \wedge \Psi \quad \text{iff} \quad \sigma, \theta \models \Phi \text{ and } \sigma, \theta \models \Psi$$
$$\sigma, \theta \models \neg\Phi \quad \text{iff} \quad \sigma, \theta \not\models \Phi$$
$$\sigma, \theta \models \bigcirc\Phi \quad \text{iff} \quad \sigma^1, \tilde{\theta}_1 \models \Phi$$
$$\sigma, \theta \models \Phi\,\mathsf{U}\,\Psi \quad \text{iff} \quad \exists i.\,(\sigma^i, \tilde{\theta}_i \models \Psi \text{ and } \forall j < i.\,\sigma^j, \tilde{\theta}_j \models \Phi).$$

Here, $\tilde{\theta}_i$ is defined by $\tilde{\theta}_0 = \theta$ and $\tilde{\theta}_{i+1} = \tilde{\theta}_i(x) \cap (LV \times E_{i+1})$; i.e., as soon as an entity is deallocated in the sequence (at some step $j \leqslant i$), it can no longer occur as an image in θ_i. The substitution $\theta\{e/x\}$ is defined as usual, i.e., $\theta\{e/x\}(x) = e$ and $\theta\{e/x\}(y) = \theta(y)$ for $y \neq x$. σ^i denotes the suffix of σ that is obtained by erasing the first i items from σ. Note that the proposition $\alpha \rightsquigarrow \beta$ is satisfied if $[\![\beta]\!] = \bot$ and $[\![\alpha]\!]$ can reach some cell with an undefined outgoing reference.

5.3   Properties

For pointer automaton A and NTL-formula Φ, $A \models \Phi$ holds whenever for *all* allocation sequences σ of configurations in $\mathcal{L}(A)$ we have $\sigma, \theta \models \Phi$. The following is then an immediate consequence of Theorem 3.

Corollary 1. *For any NTL-formula Φ and pointer automata A and A':*

$$A \sqsubseteq A' \;\Rightarrow\; (A' \models \Phi \;\Rightarrow\; A \models \Phi)$$

In particular, as for any program p we have that $[\![p]\!]^{\mathsf{conc}} \sqsubseteq [\![p]\!]^{\mathsf{symb}}$ (Theorem 4), it follows that any NTL-formula Φ that is valid for (the finite-state!) $[\![p]\!]^{\mathsf{symb}}$, it holds that Φ is valid in the (possibly infinite-state) program p. As this applies to all NTL-formulae, this includes safety and liveness properties.

6 Model Checking Pointer Logic

For the setup proposed in this paper we have developed a model checking algorithm, using tableau graphs as in [27] to establish whether or not a formula Φ is valid on a given (finite) abstract pointer automaton A. The algorithm is described in detail in [19]; here we give a brief summary.

The parameters M and L. In the previous section, we have stressed that the precision of automaton A is ruled by two parameters: L, which controls the distance between entities before they are collected into unbounded entities, and M, which controls the information we have about unbounded entities. As described in Sect. 4, L is used in the generation of models from programs; it is no longer of importance in the model checking stage (where we supposed to have the model already). M, on the other hand, is a formula-dependent constant that must exceed $\sum_{x \in \Phi} \max\{i \mid x{\uparrow}^i \text{ occurs in } \Phi\}$ *for the formula Φ that we want to check on the model A.* This may mean that the A at hand is not (yet) suitable for checking a given formula Φ, namely if M for that model does not meet this lower bound. In that case we have to *stretch* the model.

Example 11. Consider, for instance, the model depicted in Fig. 6. If we want to check whether the buffer may have size 5, this can be expressed by the formula $\Diamond(hd{\uparrow}^5 \leadsto tl)$; but in states where entities of the buffer have been collected into an unbounded entity (states 25–29 in the figure), it is not clear whether $hd{\uparrow}^5$ is pointing to (some entity within) that unbounded entity, or to some entity following it, in particular to tl.

To overcome this problem, we can stretch a given model without loss of information (but with loss of compactness, and hence increase of complexity of the model checking). Let, $\mathcal{C}(A)$ be the maximal concrete cardinality of some entity in A. In [19], the operation $A \Uparrow \widehat{M}$ is defined, which stretches A such that $\mathcal{C}(A \Uparrow \widehat{M})$ is $\widehat{M}$. The resulting pointer automaton copies each state in A that contains an unbounded entity e, such that for each materialization of e from $M, M{+}1, \ldots, \widehat{M}$ and $*$ a state exists. We then have the following result:

Theorem 6. *For all abstract pointer automata A such that $\mathcal{C}(A) < \widehat{M}$: $\mathcal{L}(A) = \mathcal{L}(A \Uparrow \widehat{M})$.*

The automaton $A \Uparrow \widehat{M}$ is a factor $n^{\widehat{M}-M}$ times as large as A, where n is the maximum number of unbounded entities in the abstract configurations of A.

The tableau graph. The next step is to construct a *tableau graph* $G_A(\Phi)$ for Φ from a given pointer automaton A, assuming that stretching has been done, so M satisfies the given lower bound for Φ. $G_A(\Phi)$ enriches A, for each of its states q, with information about the collections of formulae relevant to the validity of Φ that possibly hold in q. These "relevant formulae" are essentially subformulae of Φ and their negations; they are collected into the so-called *closure* of Φ. For instance, the closure of the formula $tl\,\mathsf{alive} \Rightarrow \Box(tl\,\mathsf{alive})$ which expands to $\neg\Psi \vee \neg(true \cup \neg\Psi)$ with $\Psi = tl\,\mathsf{alive}$, is the set

$$true \quad \Psi \quad true \cup \neg\Psi \quad \bigcirc(true \cup \neg\Psi) \quad \bigcirc\neg(true \cup \neg\Psi) \quad \Phi$$
$$\neg true \quad \neg\Psi \quad \neg(true \cup \neg\Psi) \quad \neg\bigcirc(true \cup \neg\Psi) \quad \neg\bigcirc\neg(true \cup \neg\Psi) \quad \neg\Phi \ .$$

In general, the size of the closure is linear in the size of the formula (as in [27]). The states of $G_A(\Phi)$ are called *atoms* (q, D) where q is a state of A and D a consistent and complete set of valuations of formulae from the closure of Φ on (the entities of) q. Consistency and completeness approximately mean that, for instance, if Ψ_1 is in the closure then exactly one of Ψ_1 and $\neg\Psi_1$ is "included in" D (i.e., D contains a valuation for it), and if $\Psi_1 \vee \Psi_2$ is in the closure then it is "in" D iff Ψ_1 or Ψ_2 is "in" D, etc. For the precise definition we refer to [19]. For any q, the number of atoms on q is exponential in the size of the closure and in the number of entities in q.

A transition from (q, D) to (q', D') exists in the tableau graph $G_A(\Phi)$ if $q \rightarrow_\lambda q'$ in A and, moreover, to the valuation of each sub-formula $\bigcirc\Psi$ in D there exists a corresponding valuation of Ψ in D' — where the correspondence is defined modulo the reallocation λ.

A *fulfilling path* in $G_A(\Phi)$ is then an infinite sequence of transitions, starting from an initial state, that also satisfies all the "until" sub-formulae $\Psi_1 \cup \Psi_2$ in the atoms, in the sense that if a valuation of $\Psi_1 \cup \Psi_2$ is in a given atom in the sequence, then a corresponding valuation of Ψ_2 occurs in a later atom — where correspondence is the same notion as above, but now modulo a sequence of reallocations. We have the following result:

Proposition 1. *$A \models \Phi$ iff there does not exist a fulfilling path in $G_A(\neg\Phi)$.*

Hence the validity of the formula Φ is related to the existence of a fulfilling path in the graph $G_A(\neg\Phi)$. To decide this, we seek for the existence of a *self-fulfilling strongly connected sub-component* (SCS) of the tableau graph that is *reachable from an initial state through some prefix trace*. This gives a necessary criterion for the existence of a fulfilling path. In particular, if we use $Inf(\pi)$ to denote the set of atoms that occur infinitely often in an (arbitrary) infinite path π in $G_A(\Phi)$, then we have:

Proposition 2. *$Inf(\pi)$ is not a self-fulfilling SCS $\Rightarrow$ π is not a fulfilling path.*

Since the number of SCSs of any finite tableau graph is finite, and the property of self-fulfillment is decidable, this gives rise to a mechanical procedure for verifying the validity of formulae. This is formulated in the following theorem:

Theorem 7. *For any finite abstract pointer automaton A, it is possible to verify mechanically whether $A \models \Phi$.*

This, combined with Th. 4, implies that, for any concrete automaton A^{conc} of which A is an abstraction, it is also possible to verify mechanically whether $A^{\mathsf{conc}} \models \Phi$. Note that although this theorem leaves the possibility of *false negatives* (as usual in model checking in the presence of abstraction), it does not produces false positives. This applies to both safety and liveness properties. Having false negatives means that if the algorithm fails to show $A \models \Phi$ then it cannot be concluded that Φ is *not* satisfiable (by some run of A). However, since such a failure is always accompanied by a "prospective" fulfilling path of $\neg\Phi$, further analysis or testing may be used to come to a more precise conclusion.

The algorithm is summarized in Table 3.

Table 3. Procedure for validity of Φ in A

procedure valid(A, Φ)
begin
   construct $G_A(\neg\Phi)$;
   construct the set Π of reachable self-fulfilling SCS
     satisfying the accept condition on $\mathcal{F}_A$;
   if $\Pi = \varnothing$
   then return: "Φ is valid in A";
   else return $G' \in \Pi$ with its prefix as a (possible) counterexample;
   fi
end

7 Concluding Remarks

In this paper, we have introduced a sound analysis of concurrent programs manipulating heap-allocated linked lists. The analysis is based on an automaton model where states are equipped with abstract heap representations and transitions with mappings that allow to model the evolution of heap during the program computation. Moreover, the analysis is parametric in two constants. This latter feature reduces the process of abstraction-refinement to simply increasing/decreasing these parameters.

Furthermore, we define a temporal logic called *NTL* with pointer assertions as well as predicates referring to the birth or death of memory cells. Although *NTL* is essentially a first-order logic, it contains two second-order features: the reachability predicate $\alpha \leadsto \beta$ (which computes the transitive closure of pointers), and the freshness predicate new α (which expresses membership of the *set* of fresh entities).

For *NTL*, we introduce a sound (but not complete) model-checking algorithm to verify formulae against our automata models. Thus, safety and liveness properties of heap mutating programs can be verified. We like to mention that for the (much) simpler framework in which pointers are ignored, it is possible to check dynamic properties such as the creation and disposal of heap cells in a sound *and complete* manner, as described in [20].

References

1. S. Bardin, A. Finkel, and D. Nowak. Towards symbolic verification of programs handling pointers. In: *AVIS 2004*.
2. A. Barr. *Find the Bug in this Java Program*. Addison-Wesley, 2005.

3. D. Basin, S. Matthews and L. Vigano. Labelled modal logics: quantifiers. *J. of Logic, Language and Information*, **7**(3);237–263, 1998.
4. J. Berdine, C. Calcagno, P.W. O'Hearn. A decidable fragment of separation logic. In: *FSTTCS*, LNCS 3328, pp. 97-109, 2004.
5. J. Berdine, C. Calcagno, P.W. O'Hearn. Symbolic execution with separation logic. *APLAS*, LNCS 3780, pp. 52-68, 2005.
6. J. Bergstra, A. Ponse and S.A. Smolka (editors). *Handbook of Process Algebra.* Elsevier, 2001.
7. A. Bouajjani, P. Habermehl, P. Moro and T. Vojnar. Verifying programs with dynamic 1-selector-linked list structures in regular model checking. In: *TACAS*, LNCS 3440, pp. 13–29, 2005.
8. M. Bozga, R. Iosif, and Y. Lakhnech. Storeless semantics and alias logic. In: *PEPM*, pp. 55–65. ACM Press, 2003.
9. M. Bozga, R. Iosif and Y. Lakhnech. On logics of aliasing. In: *SAS*, LNCS 3148, pp. 344-360, 2004.
10. R. Burstall. Some techniques for proving correctness of programs which alter data structures. *Machine Intelligence* **6**: 23–50, 1971.
11. L. Cardelli, P. Gardner, and G. Ghelli. A spatial logic for querying graphs. In: *ICALP*, LNCS 2380, pp. 597–610. Springer, 2002.
12. L. Cardelli and A.D. Gordon. Anytime, anywhere: modal logics for mobile ambients. In: *POPL*, pp. 365–377. ACM Press, 2000.
13. D.R. Chase, M. Wegman and F. Zadeck. Analysis of pointers and structures. In: *PLDI*, pp. 296–310. ACM Press, 1990.
14. S. Chong and R. Rugina. Static analysis of accessed regions in recursive data structures. In: *SAS*, LNCS 2694, pp. 463–482, 2003.
15. S.A. Cook and D. Oppen. An assertion language for data structures. In: *POPL*, pp. 160–166. ACM Press, 1975.
16. A. Deutsch. Interprocedural may-alias analysis for pointers: beyond k-limiting. In: *PLDI*, pp. 230–241. ACM Press, 1994.
17. D. Distefano. A parametric model for the analysis of mobile ambients. In: *APLAS*, LNCS 3780, pp. 401–417, 2005.
18. D. Distefano, J.-P. Katoen, and A. Rensink. Who is pointing when to whom? – On the automated verification of linked list structures In: *FSTTCS*, LNCS 3328, pp. 250–262, 2004.
19. D. Distefano, A. Rensink and J.-P. Katoen. Who is pointing when to whom? – On the automated verification of linked list structures CTIT Tech. Rep. 03-12, 2003.
20. D. Distefano, A. Rensink, and J.-P. Katoen. Model checking birth and death. In: *TCS*, pp. 435–447. Kluwer, 2002.
21. M. Fitting. On quantified modal logic. *Fundamenta Informatica*, **39**(1):5–121, 1999.
22. P. Fradet, R. Gaugne, and D. Le Métayer. Static detection of pointer errors: an axiomatisation and a checking algorithm. In: *ESOP*, pp. 125–140, LNCS 1058, 1996.
23. R.J. van Glabbeek. The linear time-branching time spectrum I. In [6], Chapter 1, pp. 3–101, 2001.
24. S. Ishtiaq and P.W. O'Hearn. BI as an assertion language for mutable data structures. In: *POPL*, pp. 14–26, ACM Press, 2001.
25. J. Jensen, M. Jørgensen, M. Schwartzbach and N. Klarlund. Automatic verification of pointer programs using monadic second-order logic. In: *PLDI*, pp. 226–236. ACM Press, 1997.

26. N.D. Jones and S.S. Muchnick. Flow analysis and optimization of Lisp-like structures. In S.S. Muchnick and N.D. Jones, editors, *Program Flow Analysis: Theory and Applications*, Chapter 4, pp. 102-131, Prentice-Hall, 1981.

27. O. Lichtenstein and A. Pnueli. Checking that finite state concurrent programs satisfy their linear specification. In: *POPL*, pp. 97–107. ACM Press, 1985.

28. G. Nelson. Verifying reachability invariants of linked structures. In: *POPL*, pp. 38–47. ACM Press, 1983.

29. R. Manevich, E. Yahav, G. Ramalingam, and M. Sagiv. Predicate abstraction and canonical abstraction for singly-linked lists. In: *VMCAI*, LNCS 3385, pp. 181–198, 2005.

30. R. Milner. *A Calculus of Communicating Systems*. LNCS 92, Springer, 1980.

31. U. Montanari and M. Pistore. An introduction to history-dependent automata. *ENTCS* **10**, 1998.

32. A. Møller and M. Schwartzbach. The pointer assertion logic engine. In: *PLDI*, pp. 221–213. ACM Press, 2001.

33. J. Morris. Assignment and linked data structures. In: *Th. Found. of Progr. Meth.*, pp. 25–34. Reidel, 1981.

34. P.W. O'Hearn, H. Yang, and J.C. Reynolds. Separation and information hiding. In: *POPL*, pp. 268–280. ACM Press, 2004.

35. A. Pnueli. The temporal logic of programs. In: *FOCS*, pp. 46–57. IEEE CS Press, 1977.

36. A. Rensink. Canonical graph shapes. In: *ESOP*, LNCS 2986, pp. 401–415. Springer, 2004.

37. J.C. Reynolds. Separation logic: A logic for shared mutable data structures. In: *LICS*, pp. 55–74. IEEE CS Press, 2002.

38. M. Sagiv, T. Reps, and R. Wilhelm. Solving shape-analysis problems in languages with destructive updating. *ACM TOPLAS*, **20**(1): 1–50, 1998.

39. L. Séméria, K. Sato and G. de Micheli. Resolution of dynamic memory allocation and pointers for the behavioural synthesis from C. In: *DATE*, pp. 312–319. ACM Press, 2000.

40. E. Yahav, T. Reps, M. Sagiv, and R. Wilhelm. Verifying temporal heap properties specified via evolution logic. In: *ESOP*, LNCS 2618, pp. 204–222. Springer, 2003.

41. T. Yavuz-Kahveci and T. Bultan. Automated verification of concurrent linked lists with counters. In: *SAS*, LNCS 2477, pp. 69–82, 2002.

Modular Specification of Encapsulated Object-Oriented Components

Arnd Poetzsch-Heffter and Jan Schäfer

Technische Universität Kaiserslautern, Germany
poetzsch@informatik.uni-kl.de

Abstract. A well-defined boundary of components allows to encapsulate internal state and to distinguish between internal calls that remain
inside the component and external calls that have target objects outside
the component. From a static point of view, such boundaries define the
programmer's interface to the component. In particular, they define the
methods that can be called on the component. From a dynamic point of
view, the boundaries separate the component state and those parts of
the program state outside the component.
   In this tutorial paper, we investigate encapsulated components that
are realized based on object-oriented concepts. We define a semantics
that captures a flexible notion of hierarchical encapsulation with confined references. The semantics generalizes the encapsulation concepts
of ownership types. It is used as a foundation for modular behavioral
component specifications. In particular, it allows to provide a simple semantics for invariants and an alternative solution for the frame problem.
We demonstrate this new specification methodology by typical programming patterns.

1 Introduction

Component-based software is developed by linking components or by building
new components from existing ones. A key issue in component-based software
development is to specify the component interfaces in an implementation independent way so that components can be used relying only on their specifications.
The often cited component definition by Szyperski [36], p. 41, says: "A software
component is a unit of composition with contractually specificied interfaces and
explicit context dependencies only (...)." In this tutorial paper, we investigate
behavioral specification techniques for encapsulated object-oriented components
that we call *boxes*. A box instance is a runtime entity that encapsulates a number
of objects. Some of these objects are confined to the box, that is, they may not
be referenced from outside the box. Other objects of the box may be referenced
from the outside. The box model is a generalization of programming models
underlying ownership type systems. It simplifies the semantics of specification
constructs and handles complex program patterns. In particular, we consider
reentrant calls and components with multiple ingoing references. According to
the tutorial character of the paper, conveying the general concepts will be favored
over technical rigour.

F.S. de Boer et al. (Eds.): FMCO 2005, LNCS 4111, pp. 313–341, 2006.
© Springer-Verlag Berlin Heidelberg 2006

Component specifications are used as documentation and to improve program development and understanding. They can support program testing and runtime checks. Furthermore, they simplify static analysis and are a prerequisite for the verification of program properties. A central goal for specification techniques in all these areas is *modularity*. A modular specification technique allows showing that a component implementation satisfies its specification by only knowing the modules implementing the component and by only using specified properties of referenced components. In particular, knowledge about the application context of a component is not necessary. Modularity is a very important requirement for the scalability of a specification technique, because components can be checked once and for all independent of future application contexts. Unfortunately, due to aliasing and subtyping, modularity is difficult to achieve in an object-oriented setting, in particular if components consist of collaborating objects.

In the remainder of this section, we introduce the programming model underlying boxes (Subsect. 1.1), explain the challenges of modularity in more detail, and shortly describe our approach (Subsect. 1.2). In Sect. 2, we present the box model and its semantic foundations. Section 3 describes the developed specification technique along with its application. A discussion of our approach and its relation to existing work is contained in Sect. 4. The paper is completed by conclusions and topics for future work in Sect. 5.

1.1   Programming Model Based on Boxes

In this subsection, we informally introduce the *box model* consisting of the new concept "Box" and the underlying programming model. We build on the general object-oriented model with classes, objects, (object) references, object-local state represented by instance variables, methods to define behavior, and a type system with subtyping. We use notations from Java and C# (see [14,22]). Throughout the paper, we make two simplifying assumptions: We only consider *single-threaded* programs with *terminating* methods[1].

A *box instance* or *box*, for short, is a runtime entity. Like an object, a box is created, has an identity and a local state. However, a box is in general realized by several objects. A prominent example — often discussed in work on ownership and alias control — is a linked list object with iterators (see e.g. [2]). Figure 1 shows such a list box, indicated by a rounded rectangle with a dashed line. A box and its state is characterized by:

- an *owner* object that is created together with the box (the IterList-object in Fig. 1); the owner is one of the boundary objects;
- other *boundary* objects, that is, objects that can be accessed from outside the box (the two Iterator-objects in Fig. 1);

---

[1] These assumptions focus the paper, they are not necessary requirements. On the contrary, one major motivation for the development of the box model is a higher-level model for synchronization in multi-threaded programs.

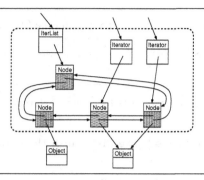

Fig. 1. A box encapsulating the implementation of a linked list

- so-called *confined* objects that may not be accessed from outside the box (the Node-objects in Fig. 1);
- so-called *external* objects that are referenced from within the box (the objects outside the dashed line in Fig. 1).

The *concrete state* of a box changes if the state of one of its objects changes or if a new object is created within the box. As part of the concrete state of a box may be hidden, clients of a box usually see only an abstraction of the concrete state, the so-called *abstract state*. Clients use the functionality of a box by calling methods on the owner or the other boundary objects. Thus, to work with a box, a client has to know the constructor and public interface of the owner object and the public interfaces of the other boundary objects. In addition, it is helpful to know the public interfaces of external objects passed to the box, because this is the only way a box can influence the state outside the box, the so-called *box environment*. Figure 2 presents the interfaces of the IterList-box.

The interfaces in Fig. 2 use two notations that go beyond Java or C#. Interfaces marked with the keyword **box** provide a box constructor (IterList in Fig. 2). Thus, a box interface is similar to the public interface of a class without public fields. The annotion of arguments and results by the keyword **external** indicates that such arguments and results may refer to objects in the

```
box interface IterList {                 interface Iterator {
  IterList ();                             boolean hasNext();
  external Object get( int index );        external Object next();
  void add( external Object x );           void     remove();
  external Object remove( int index );   }
  boolean contains(external Object x);
  Iterator  listIterator ();             interface Object {
}                                          boolean equals(external Object x);
                                         }
```

Fig. 2. Interfaces of lists with iterators

box interface SecretHolder {	**box interface** Stranger {
SecretHolder();	Stranger();
void invite(**external** Stranger x);	void doMeAFavor(**external** Object x);
}	}

Fig. 3. Exporting objects by calls to external references

box environment. More precisely, we distinguish three different kinds of arguments and results:

1. *Data objects* are considered global values of the system that can be arbitrarily passed around. They are either of a primitive type like `boolean` or `int` or of a so-called `pure` type. A pure type has only immutable objects and its methods have no side-effects (see [18]). A typical example for a pure type is the type `String` in Java. We assume that types are declared as pure so that it is known whether a type is pure or not.
2. *Boundary objects* are the internal objects of a box that may be *exposed* to the box environment either as a result of a method or by passing them as a parameter to a method called on an external object. Arguments or results that are not pure and have no annotation are considered boundary objects.
3. *External objects* are objects that are passed into the box. Usually, these objects are objects from outside the box. For flexibility reasons, we allow as well to pass boundary objects as external objects into a box. (The semantic details will be treated in Sect. 2.)

Component Categories. Based on the box model, we can categorize components according to their behavior at the boundary. For example, lists with iterators have the following characteristic features:

1. They have a nontrivial encapsulated state that can be manipulated from the outside by "handles", like e.g. iterators (below, we will see that an iterator can change the state of the list and of the other iterators).
2. They import external references only by methods called on boundary objects.
3. They do not call methods with side-effects on external references (below we see, that a call of method `contain` in `IterList` leads to external calls of method `equals`).

The list with iterator example is often used in the literature, because its features are shared by other components, for example by complex data structures with iterators for special traversals or, on a more conceptual level, by file systems with file handlers. Although many specification and verification frameworks already have problems handling components with these feature, we believe for two reasons that we have to cover a larger class of components. One reason is that more general components are used in practice. We will look at a representative example, namely an instance of the observer pattern, in the next subsection.

The other reason is that we would like to use the model to analyse, specify, or exclude more complex component interaction. As an example, consider the boxes in Fig. 3. At first sight, secret holders will keep their secret. There is no method returning anything. However, a secret holder can reference a Stranger-object and it can do the stranger a favor, passing some object to the stranger. Accidentally, it might pass an object of type Secret representing a secret. The stranger could cast the received object down to a Secret-object and extract the secret. Two aspects that have motivated design decision of the box model can be learned from this example:

- External calls should be explicit in specifications.
- Downcasts of external objects should not be allowed.

Before we present the semantic basis for the box model, we look at the main motivation for the model, that is, the challenges of modular specification.

1.2 Specification and Modularity

Component specifications express different kinds of properties of components. *Functional* properties relate method results to method arguments. *Structural* properties describe invariants on the reference structure between objects. For example, in the box model, we guarantee that all reference chains from an object outside the box to an object inside the box go through a boundary object. *Frame* properties state the effects of a method call and what is not affected by a call, often called the *non-effects*. The treatment of non-effects is very important in an object-oriented setting, because a method call $X.m(Y,Z)$ can potentially affect all objects that are reachable from X, Y, Z via reference chains.

In this subsection, we explain what modularity means for box specifications and describe the challenges of modularity.

Box Specifications and Modularity. For the definition of modularity, we have to make some assumptions about the implementation of a box B and need some terminology. In a first step, we assume that an implementation of B consists of a set of classes and interfaces. One of the classes implements B and has a public constructor with the same argument types as the constructor in the box interface of B (the external annotations are not considered). An implementation of a box is called a *box class*. Boxes with such implementations are called *simple*. For an interface I, the *minimally type-closed* set of interfaces containing I, denoted by $MTC(I)$, is the smallest set satisfying the properties:

- $I \in MTC(I)$
- if $J \in MTC(I)$ and T is an argument or result type of J, then T is primitive or $T \in MTC(I)$

An *interface specification* consists of annotations specifying properties of the interface. Our interface specification technique is explained in Sect. 3. An example of an interface specification for IterList is shown in Fig. 11, p. 333.

For a box B, we distinguish between three not necessarily disjoint subsets of $MTC(B)$:

- The *exposed* interfaces describe the interfaces of boundary objects including the interface of B.
- The *referenced* interfaces describe the interfaces of external objects.
- The *additional* interfaces are the interfaces in $MTC(B)$ that are neither exposed nor referenced.

A *box specification* consists of the exposed interface specifications and uses the referenced and additional interface specifiations. In many cases, some of the exposed interfaces already exist when a new box class is developed.

Definition (Modularity). A specification technique for simple boxes or box-like components is called *modular* if one can show that the box class satisfies its specification by using only

- the referenced and additional interface specifications, and
- the classes and interfaces of the implementation.

Before we analyse the challenges of modularity, we slightly generalize our implementation concept and, together with it, the notion of modularity. The implementation of a *compound* box may use other boxes. Whereas — from an implementation point of view — this merely structures the complete set of classes and interfaces an implementation consists of, it generalizes the notion of modularity. The implementation of a compound box B consists of a set of classes and interfaces, and a set of box specifications not containing B.[2] The classes can use the specified boxes. As these boxes are encapsulated in B, we call them *inner* boxes of B.

For compound boxes or similar hierarchical components, modularity allows the use of inner box specification, but not of their implementation. Compound boxes have a flavor of composition. However, the box model does not support direct composition without glue code. Box classes are composed by additional program parts that link the box instances at runtime and provide further functionality or adaption.

Challenges of Modularity. Every modular specification and verification framework for object-oriented components with method call semantics is confronted with three main challenges:

1. *Control of specification scope*: The specification of a component C may only express properties that are under full control of C. Otherwise, these properties might be invalidated by other components or program parts that are not known when C's specification is checked.

---

[2] We claim that even recursive boxes can be allowed, but do not consider it here, because we have not yet investigated it in detail.

2. *Underspecification and reentrance*: A component C can reference another component D through an interface I with a very weak specification. That is, C knows almost nothing about the behavior of D. In particular, methods called from C on D might cause reentrant calls on C that are not specified in I.

3. *Frame problem*: Specifications have to be sufficiently expressive w.r.t. effects and non-effects to the enviroment. For example, if a component C uses components D and E for its implementation, it has to know whether a method call on D causes a side-effect on E or not. Otherwise, it has no information about the state of E after the call.

To illustrate these main challenges of modularity, we consider a simplified instance of the observer pattern. An observable game is a two-player game with alternative moves where a human plays against the computer. One player plays white, the other black. The interfaces of this example are given in Fig. 4. Method move allows the human to make a move that is internally answered by the computer, method swapPlayers swaps the players, and method readPos reads and returns the current position on the board. MoveDescr and Position are pure types. Method register registers observers of the game. The interface of box GameObserver describes a simple observer.

To both box interfaces in Fig. 4, we have already added ghost and model variables expressing the box state. The ghost variable gameObs in interface ObservableGame captures the set of referenced observers of a game, variable obsGame holds the observed game of a game observer. The model variables currentPos, player, and displayedPos hold the current position of a game, the color of the human player, and the displayed position of an observer respectively. (More details are given in Sect. 3.)

```
box interface ObservableGame {
    references Observer* gameObs;
    model Position currentPos;
    model Color player;
    ObservableGame();
    void move( MoveDescr md );
    void swapPlayers();
    Position readPos();
    void register (external Observer go);
}

interface Observer {GameObserver
    void stateChanged()
}
```

```
box interface GameObserver
            extends Observer {
    references ObservableGame obsGame;
    model Position displayedPos;
    GameObserver(
        external ObservableGame g );
    void stateChanged();

invariant
    // out of control:
        forall( o in obsGame.gameObs ){
            o instanceof GameObserver
        }
    // problematic:
        this in obsGame.gameObs
}
```

Fig. 4. Interfaces of ObservableGame and GameObserver

Control of Specification Scope. The scope of a specification depends on the component model and encapsulation discipline. In our case, the scope is related to the box. The situation is simple if specifications only depend on the local state of the box, because this state can be controlled. It is less clear if a specification depends on state of referenced boxes. For example, the first invariant of box GameObserver, stating that the referenced game has only game observers of type GameObserver in Fig. 4, is not locally verifiable, because the interface of ObservableGame allows to register observers of other types. The second invariant is more interesting. If the specification of ObservableGame guarantees a reasonable behavior of register and allows us to prove that the set of game observes is only growing and if we can verify that the constructor GameObserver does registration correctly, one might be able to verify the second invariant in a modular way (cf. [4] for a detailed discussion).

Underspecification and Reentrance. In a typical observer scenario, the observed subject has only very little information about the observers. For example, the box ObservableGame only knows that observers have a method stateChanged. It knows nothing about the behavior of stateChanged. Now, let us assume we want to prove that the implementation of method move does not swap the players. As method move changes the position, it will call method stateChanged. Figure 5 shows a scenario in which a somewhat malicious observer calls swapPlayers before returning from stateChanged. Thus, we can only prove the "non-swapplayers" property in a modular way if the specification of ObservableGame can restrict reentrant calls. More generally, a modular specification technique has to provide mechanisms to control reentrant calls.

Frame Problem. To illustrate the frame problem, we consider a gaming system that uses ObservableGame and GameObserver as inner boxes, that is, modular verification has to rely on their specification. A central invariant of the gaming system would be that the current observers currObs of the system display the current position of their observed games:

forall(o in currObs){ o.displayPos == o.obsGame.currentPos }

This invariant can only be shown if the specification of move guarantees that all registered observers are notified. More generally, a method specification must

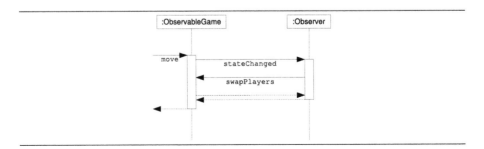

Fig. 5. An observer modifying the state of the game by a reentrant call

describe its side-effects. Furthermore, we want to know what is left unchanged by a method execution. For example, it should be derivable from the specifications that a move in one game does not affect the state of another game (if this is the case).

Approach. Our specification approach is based on the encapsulation properties of the box model. The box model is semantically founded in the programming language. This is different from most other approaches to modular specification, where the structuring and encapsulation techniques are only part of the specification framework. Having a clear foundation in the language semantics provides a more expressive basis to develop a specification technique. This is important for our goal to separate the behavioral specifications from the implementation.

The remainder of this tutorial paper presents central parts of our approach. In Sect. 2, we demonstrate how the box model can be integrated into the semantics of a simple class-based language. To keep the presentation focused, the language supports only a subset of the constructs that we use in the specification examples. In Sect. 3, we explain the main concepts of our specification technique and show how the specifications profit from the box model.

2   Encapsulated Object-Oriented Components

Heap encapsulation can be achieved by different techniques. We propose here a semantic-based approach, that is, an approach in which the structuring of the heap is part of the programming language semantics.

It is helpful to compare the general approach with the step from untyped to typed languages. Typed languages provide an additional notion, the types, to formulate certain desirable program properties. Types have a clear foundation in the language semantics (e.g. the type of an object is needed for casts). They avoid runtime errors (e.g. situations where a target object of a call does not have an appropriate method), but most of the checks can be done at compile time so that runtime overhead can be kept small. Our goals are similar. We provide a notion of encapsulation, namely the boxes. Our box model has the following features:

1. They hierarchically structure the heap. In particular, this structure can be used to define the meaning of interface specifications.
2. They distinguish between internal and external calls. This is important for partitioning systems into components.
3. They provide a notion of object confinement. This supports the programmer management of alias control and is important for modular verification.

In this section, we show how boxes can be founded in the language semantics. We believe that the presented approach can be extended to object-oriented programming languages like e.g. Java and C#. Techniques for static checking are shortly discussed in Sect. 4.

$P \in$ **Program**	::= $\overline{D}$	
$D \in$ **TypeDecl**	::= $ID \mid BD \mid CD$	
$ID \in$ **IntfDecl**	::= interface I extends $\overline{I}$ { $\overline{G}$ }	
$BD \in$ **BoxDecl**	::= box interface B extends $\overline{I}$ { $\overline{G}$ }	
$CD \in$ **ClassDecl**	::= class C implements $\overline{S}$ { $\overline{T}\ \overline{f};\ \overline{M}$ }	
$A \in$ **Annotation**	::= boundary | external	
$m \in$ **MethodName**		
$G \in$ **AbstractMeth**	::= $A\ S\ m(\ \overline{A}\ \overline{S}\ \overline{x}\ )$	
$M \in$ **MethodDecl**	::= $T\ m(\ \overline{T}\ \overline{x}\ )$ { e }	
$e \in$ **Expr**	::= $x \mid (T)\ e \mid$ new $lm\ em\ R(\overline{e}) \mid e.f \mid e.f = e \mid e.m(\overline{e}) \mid$	
	let $x = e$ in $e \mid\ \ldots$	
$lm \in$ **LocModifier**	::= local | global	
$em \in$ **ConfModifier**	::= confined | exposable	
$x, y \in$ **Variable**		
$I \in$ **InterfaceName**	$R \in$ **BoxName** $\cup$ **ClassName**	
$B \in$ **BoxName**	$S \in$ **InterfaceName** $\cup$ **BoxName**	
$C \in$ **ClassName**	$T \in$ **InterfaceName** $\cup$ **BoxName** $\cup$ **ClassName**	

Fig. 6. Syntax of OBO

A Simple OO-Language with Boxes. We present a simple OO-language supporting the box model, called *OBO*. The language is similar to other OO-kernel languages ([13,16]). To focus on the central issues, we make the following simplifications:

- OBO supports subtyping, but not inheritance. In particular, the root type Object is an interface (see Fig. 2).
- OBO supports only default constructors.
- OBO has no exception handling mechanism. If a runtime error occurs, that is, if there is no applicable semantic rule, we assume that the program aborts.
- In OBO, all pure types, including String, are predefined. They have appropriate box interfaces and are treated as external types. That is, in OBO interfaces, we only distinguish between boundary and external types.

Figure 6 shows the syntax of OBO. Within the syntax, lists are denoted by an overline. A program consists of a list of interfaces, box interface, and class declarions, including a startup class Main of the form:

```
class Main {  String main( String arg ){ e } }
```

Interfaces and box interfaces are as explained in Subsect. 1.1. For each box interface B in a program, there has to be exactly one class implementing B. This class is denoted by $class(B)$ in the semantics below. Context conditions are essentially like in Java, in particular the typing rules apply. The subtype relation is denoted by $\preceq$.

The creation expression starting with keyword new deserves consideration. It allows to create instances of a class or box. The instance can be created locally

$$
\begin{aligned}
b &\in \textbf{Box} &::=&\ bc \mid \texttt{globox} \\
o &\in \textbf{Object} &::=&\ (b, C, j; em) \\
r &\in \textbf{Reference} &::=&\ \langle o, T, rk \rangle \\
rk &\in \textbf{RefKind} &::=&\ \texttt{intn} \mid \texttt{extn} \\
v &\in \textbf{Value} &::=&\ null \mid r \\
OS &\in \textbf{ObjState} &::=&\ \langle \bar{v} \rangle \\
BS &\in \textbf{BoxState} &::=&\ \{o : OS\} \\
H &\in \textbf{Heap} &::=&\ \{b : BS\} \\
F &\in \textbf{StackFrame} &::=&\ \{x : v\} \\
j &\in \textbf{ObjId} \\
bc &\in \textbf{CreatedBox}
\end{aligned}
$$

Fig. 7. Dynamic entities of OBO

or globally. Within a program, global creation is only allowed for the predefined pure types of OBO. That is, all other creations take place in the box of the this-object. A more general creation scheme is desirable for programmers, but would complicate our kernel language and is beyond the scope of this presentation. Instances can be created as confined or exposable. References to confined instances may not leave the box in which the instance is created whereas exposable instances may be passed out. More precise explanations of the expressions are given together with the semantics.

Semantics. A box could be represented by the owner object that is created together with the box. This is certainly an appropriate solution for implementations and is essentially the idea of Boogie where ownership is represented by ghost variables. Here, we use an approach with explicit box instances. As formalized in Fig. 7, a box is either the predefined global box $\texttt{globox}$ or a *created* box. A created box has a *parent* box from which it was created. The transitive reflexive closure of the child-parent relation is called the inclusion relation, denoted by $\subseteq$. In particular, we have for any created box b: $b \subset parent(b) \subseteq \texttt{globox}$. The creation of boxes is formalized similar to object creation. We assume that there is a sufficiently large set of boxes from which we choose and allocate a box. Details are described together with the operational semantics below.

Each box b is confined in one of its ancestors. This so-called *confining* box is denoted by $confIn(b)$. The meaning of the confinement is that boundary objects of b may not be accessed from outside $confIn(b)$. The confining box will be determined at box creation. We assume that we can create new boxes for any given parent with an appropriate confining box.

An object is represented as a triple consisting of its box, its class, and an identifier to distinguish objects of the same class in a box. Furthermore, an object carries the information whether it is confined to its box b or whether it can be exposed (see Fig. 7). In the latter case, it is confined to $confIn(b)$. To distinguish between internal and external calls, we access objects over explicitly modeled references. A reference is a triple consisting of the referenced object,

$box : \textbf{Object} \to \textbf{Box}$
$box\,(b, \_, \_; \_) = b$

$thisBox : \textbf{StackFrame} \to \textbf{Box}$
$thisBox(F) = box(F(this))$

$receivingBox : \text{lm} \times \textbf{StackFrame} \to \textbf{Box}$
$receivingBox(global, F) = \texttt{globox}$
$receivingBox(local, F) \;\; = thisBox(F)$

$passable : \textbf{Value} \times \textbf{Box} \times \textbf{A} \to \textbf{Bool}$
$passable(null, b_r, a) \qquad\qquad\qquad = true$
$passable(\langle(b, C, \_; conf), \_, \_\rangle, b_r, external) = (br \le b)$
$passable(\langle(b, C, \_; expo), \_, \_\rangle, b_r, external) = (br \le confIn(b))$
$passable(\langle(b, C, \_; conf), \_, \rangle, b_r, boundary) = (b = br)$
$passable(\langle(b, C, \_; expo), \_, \_\rangle, b_r, boundary) = (br \le confIn(b) \wedge b \le br)$

$adapt : \textbf{Value} \times \textbf{S} \times \textbf{Box} \times \textbf{A} \to \textbf{Value}$
$adapt(null, S, br, a) \qquad\qquad\qquad\qquad = null$
$adapt(\langle o, \_, \_\rangle, S, br, external) \qquad\qquad\;\; = \langle o, S, extn\rangle$
$adapt(\langle(b, C, j; em), \_, \_\rangle, S, br, boundary) = \langle(b, C, j; em), C, intn\rangle$ if $br = b$
$\qquad\qquad\qquad\qquad\qquad\qquad\qquad\qquad = \langle(b, C, j; em), S, extn\rangle$ otherwise

Fig. 8. OBO's auxiliary functions

a type, and a reference kind. The type is a supertype of the object type and is used to prevent illegal downcasts. The reference kind distinguishes between internal objects, and objects that are considered external. (Notice, that this is similar to external references in JavaCard applets [34]; see as well Sect. 4).

Figure 7 contains as well the definitions of heaps and stack frames. Heaps map boxes to box-local state reflecting the structuring of the store. Figure 9 presents the big-step operational semantics for OBO. The underlying judgment $H, F \vdash e \Rightarrow v, H'$ expresses that the evaluation of an expression e in a state with heap H and stack frame F has v as result and H' as resulting heap. The semantics uses auxiliary functions from Fig. 8. In the following, we discuss the interesting rules.

Rule (E-CAST OBJ) shows how the distinction between references and objects is used to restrict downcasts. A downcast is only allowed to the type of the reference, not to the type of the object.

Rule (E-NEW BOX) captures the creation of a box instance b together with its owner object o. A possible approach would have been to make the functions *parent* and *confIn* part of the state and enlarge their domain whenever a box is allocated. As our core language does not support modification of the box structure after box creation, we use a simpler formalization that avoids this. We assume a rich box structure with an infinite carrier set $\textbf{CreatedBox} \cup \{\texttt{globox}\}$ and functions *parent* and *confIn* having the following properties:

(E-VAR)

$$\frac{F(x) = v}{H, F \vdash x \Rightarrow v, H}$$

(E-CAST NULL)

$$\frac{H, F \vdash e \Rightarrow null, H_0}{H, F \vdash (T)\, e \Rightarrow null, H_0}$$

(E-CAST OBJ)

$$\frac{H, F \vdash e \Rightarrow r, H_0 \qquad r = \langle \_, T_1, \_\rangle \qquad T_1 \preceq T}{H, F \vdash (T)\, e \Rightarrow r, H_0}$$

(E-NEW BOX)

$$\frac{\begin{array}{c} b \notin dom(H) \qquad b_0 = receivingBox(lm, F) \qquad parent(b) = b_0 \\ confIn(b) = \text{if } em = conf \text{ then } b_0 \text{ else } confIn(b_0) \qquad class(B) = C \\ o = (b, C, j; expo) \qquad fields(C) = \overline{T}\,\overline{f} \qquad BS = \{o \mapsto \langle \overline{null}\rangle\} \text{ with } |\overline{null}| = |\overline{f}| \end{array}}{H, F \vdash \mathbf{new}\ lm\ em\ B() \Rightarrow \langle o, B, \mathbf{extn}\rangle, H[b \mapsto BS]}$$

(E-NEW OBJ)

$$\frac{\begin{array}{c} b = thisBox(F) \qquad o = (b, C, j, em) \\ o \notin dom(H(b)) \qquad fields(C) = \overline{T}\,\overline{f} \qquad BS = H(b)[o \mapsto \langle \overline{null}\rangle] \text{ with } |\overline{null}| = |\overline{f}| \end{array}}{H, F \vdash \mathbf{new}\ \mathbf{local}\ em\ C() \Rightarrow \langle o, C, \mathbf{intn}\rangle, H[b \mapsto BS]}$$

(E-FIELD)

$$\frac{H, F \vdash e \Rightarrow \langle o, C, \mathbf{intn}\rangle, H_0 \qquad fields(C) = \overline{T}\,\overline{f} \qquad H_0(box(o))(o) = \overline{v}}{H, F \vdash e.f_i \Rightarrow v_i, H_0}$$

(E-FIELDUP)

$$\frac{\begin{array}{c} H, F \vdash e_0 \Rightarrow \langle o, C, \mathbf{intn}\rangle, H_0 \qquad fields(C) = \overline{T}\,\overline{f} \\ b = box(o) \qquad H_0(b)(o) = \overline{v} \qquad H_0, F \vdash e_1 \Rightarrow v, H_1 \qquad BS = H_1(b)[o \mapsto [v/v_i]\overline{v}] \end{array}}{H, F \vdash e_0.f_i = e_1 \Rightarrow v, H_1[b \mapsto BS]}$$

(E-INVK INTN)

$$\frac{\begin{array}{c} H, F \vdash e \Rightarrow \langle o, C, \mathbf{intn}\rangle, H_0 \qquad H_0, F \vdash e_1 \Rightarrow v_1, H_1 \cdots H_{n-1}, F \vdash e_n \Rightarrow v_n, H_n \\ mbody(m, C) = \overline{x}.e_b \qquad H_n, \{this \mapsto \langle o, C, \mathbf{intn}\rangle, \overline{x} \mapsto \overline{v}\} \vdash e_b \Rightarrow v_m, H_m \end{array}}{H, F \vdash e.m(\overline{e}) \Rightarrow v_m, H_m}$$

(E-INVK EXTN)

$$\frac{\begin{array}{c} H, F \vdash e \Rightarrow \langle o_0, S, \mathbf{extn}\rangle, H_0 \\ o_0 = (b_r, C, \_; em) \qquad a_m\ S_m\ m(a_1\ S_1, \ldots, a_n\ S_n)\ signatureOf\ m\ in\ S \\ H_0, F \vdash e_1 \Rightarrow v_1, H_1 \qquad \cdots \qquad H_{n-1}, F \vdash e_n \Rightarrow v_n, H_n \\ passable(v_1, b_r, a_1) \qquad \cdots \qquad passable(v_n, b_r, a_n) \qquad mbody(m, C) = \overline{x}.e_b \\ H_n, \{this \mapsto \langle o_0, C, \mathbf{intn}\rangle, \overline{x} \mapsto adapt(v_i, T_i, b_r, a_i)\} \vdash e_b \Rightarrow v_m, H_m \\ passable(v_m, thisBox(F), \mathbf{external}) \end{array}}{H, F \vdash e.m(\overline{e}) \Rightarrow adapt(v_m, T_m, thisBox(F), a_m), H_m}$$

(E-LET)

$$\frac{H, F \vdash e_0 \Rightarrow v_0, H_0 \qquad H_0, F[x \mapsto v_0] \vdash e \Rightarrow v, H_1}{H, F \vdash \mathbf{let}\ x = e_0\ \mathbf{in}\ e \Rightarrow v, H_1}$$

Fig. 9. Rules of OBO's operational semantics

1. *parent* defines a tree structure on **CreatedBox** with root `globox`.
2. For all nodes b and all ancestor nodes b_a of b, the set of b's children with $confIn(b) = b_a$ is infinite (where the ancestor relation is the transitiv reflexive closure of the parent relation).

Box creation means to choose a box b from the box structure that is not yet part of the heap. Let b_0 be the receiving box which is either the global box (recall that this is only allowed for pure types) or the box of the current this-object. The new box b is chosen such that its parent is b_0 and its owner is confined either in b_0 or in $confIn(b_0)$ depending on the encapsulation modifier *em*. The second property above guarantees that such a new box always exists. Rule (E-NEW OBJ) shows the creation of objects. Objects may only be created locally.

Rules (E-FIELD) and (E-FIELDUP) show that read and write accesses are only allowed through internal references. Below we show that expressions only evaluates to internal references, if the referenced object is in the same box as the current this-object.

Rules (E-INVK INTN) and (E-INVK EXTN) describe internal and external calls. An internal call is an ordinary dynamically bound method call. The function *mbody* yields the parameters and body of method m in class C. The receiver object of an external call might belong to a different box than the current this-object. Thus, values can be passed from one box to another. The value *null* can always be passed. To check whether a reference r is passable, we distinguish two cases:

- r is considered external in the receiving box b_r: Then the confined box of r's object has to include b_r (otherwise, confinement is violated).
- r should be boundary in the receiving box b_r: Then, it has to be checked that r's object is included in b_r (otherwise it cannot be a boundary object of b_r) and that the confined box of r's object includes b_r (otherwise, confinement is violated).

If a reference is passable, it has to be adapted to the new box. The adapted reference is an internal reference if the parameter annotation is `boundary` and the receiving box is equal to the box of the referenced object. Otherwise, it is an external reference.

Execution of an OBO program starts with a configuration containing an object X of class `Main` in the global box and a stack frame F for executing method `main` with $F(this) = X$ and $F(arg)$ referencing the input string. The result of executing the expression in the body of `main` is the result of the program execution.

Properties. The box semantics has two central properties: Internal references never leave their box, and objects are never referenced from outside their confining box. To formulate these properties precisely, we interpret each semantic rule as a recursive procedure that takes the heap, stack frame, and expression as parameters and returns the expression value and heap as results. The antecedents of the rule constitute the body of the procedure, a sequence of checks and recursive calls. Execution of an OBO program corresponds to a call tree of these recursive procedures. A *pre-configuration* consists of the input heap and stack frame and the value null, a *post-configuration* consists of the result heap, the input stack frame, and the result value. A configuration is either a pre- or post-configuration. For all configurations (H, F, v) of a OBO program execution the following holds:

- Internal references never leave their box, that is:
  if $H(b)(o_0) = \overline{v}$ with $v_i = \langle o, T, intn \rangle$, then $box(o) = b$;
  if $thisBox(F) = b$ and $F(x) = \langle o, T, intn \rangle$, then $box(o) = b$;
  if $thisBox(F) = b$ and $v = \langle o, T, intn \rangle$, then $box(o) = b$.
- An object o is never referenced from outside its confining box $b_{cf(o)}$:
  if $H(b)(o_0) = \overline{v}$ with $v_i = \langle o, \_, \_ \rangle$, then $b \subseteq b_{cf(o)}$;
  if $thisBox(F) = b$ and $F(x) = \langle o, \_, \_ \rangle$, then $b \subseteq b_{cf(o)}$;
  if $thisBox(F) = b$ and $v = \langle o, \_, \_ \rangle$, then $b \subseteq b_{cf(o)}$.

A proof sketch of these properties is contained on the appendix. A further discussion of the box model is given in Sect. 4.

3 Modular Specification of Box Interfaces

We have seen that a box is a generalization of an object. Consequently, we reuse language concepts for class specifications, in particular from JML [18], and for refinement of object-oriented programs, in particular from [7]. Our contributions in this area are the extension of such techniques to the box model and full implementation independence which is important in a component setting. We present the specification technique along with the examples introduced in Sect. 1 and explain central aspects of box specifications.

The specification technique is concerned with the internal state of the box, with access to a box from the enviroment, and with accesses of the box to the enviroment. A box specification addresses four aspects:

- Declarative object-oriented models that are used to express box state and method behavior in an implementation independent way.
- Specification of encapsulation aspects consisting of method argument and result annotations and a mechanism to keep track of the references that are exposed to the environment and that refer to external objects.
- The internal state of a box as described by model variables of its boundary objects. Model variables are specification only variables that are visible to the client of the box. The initial state of a box is described together with the constructor. The state space can be restricted by invariants.
- The behavior of methods contained in exposed interfaces. In addition to declarative pre-post specifications, the technique supports abstract statements and a simple approach to achieve modularity in the context of reentrant calls.

In the following, we first introduce declarative models. Then, we explain specifications for boxes that can only be accessed through their owner, focusing on the specification of external calls. Finally, we show how multiple-access boxes can be handled.

3.1   Declarative Models

To be applicable to components, specifcations should not refer to implementation parts. We achieve implementation independency by using declarative models. A declarative model provides the types, values, and mathematical functions to explain the state space of a box. A specification framework usually provides standard models for datatypes like sets and lists. Other models may be component specific and must be developed by the component developer. For the following, we assume the parametric datatypes `Set<A>` and `List<A>` as standard models. We use Java-like notation for the interfaces and indicate by the keyword `pure` that method calls of these types have no side-effects.

```
pure interface Set<T> {
    static  Set<T> empty();
    boolean contains(T elem);
    Set<T>  insert(T elem);
    Set<T>  delete(T elem);
}
```

```
pure interface List<T> {
    static  List<T> empty();
    boolean contains(T elem);
    T       nth(int index);
    int     length();
    List<T> appendLast(T elem);
    List<T> delete(T elem);
    Set<T>  toSet();
}
```

As an example for a component specific model, we consider the declarative model the `ObservableGame` interface of Fig. 4. Moves are described by a string and are checked and converted to values of type `MoveDescr` by a function `mkMoveDescr`. The type `Position` models the positions of the game and provides functions for the initial position, for checking whether a move is legal in a position, and for yielding the new position after a move.

```
pure interface Color {
    static Color WHITE = new Color();
    static Color BLACK = new Color();
    Color other();
    // WHITE.other() == BLACK
    // BLACK.other() == WHITE
}
```

```
pure interface Position {
    static   Position initial ();
    boolean  legal( MoveDescr md );
    Position doMove(MoveDescr md);
    // if this. legal (md),
    //    return position after move,
    // else return this
}
```

```
pure interface MoveDescr {
    static MoveDescr mkMvDescr(String s);
}
```

Different techniques can be used to specify declarative models. As declaritive models are simpler than state-based models with side-effects, an informal description is often sufficient. JML uses functional programming [17]. The Larch approach uses abstract datatypes ([15]). We applied logic-based specification techniques in previous work ([31]).

3.2 Specifying Single-Access Boxes

A box that can only be accessed through its owner is called a *single-access box*. Such a box exposes only one reference to clients, that is, it essentially behaves like one object (of course, it can be implemented by many objects). We explain the specification technique along with the specification of `ObservableGame` in Fig. 10.

Encapsulation. As explained in Sect. 2, encapsulation is based on the box model of the underlying programming language. From the method signatures in Fig. 10, one can see that only the contructor exposes a reference, namely the owner, and that only method `register` imports external non-pure references to the box. To keep track of imported references, the specification technique supports the declaration of specification-only ghost variables using the keyword `references`. The variables are either of a type T or of a type $T*$ where T is a reference type. In the latter case, the variable stores sets of references of type T (we do not use type `Set<T>` to distinguish between references to sets of T and sets of references to T-objects).

Box State. The state of a box consists of the internal state of the box and the set of external and exposed references. For single access boxes, the internal box state can be associated with the owner. The state space is expressed by so-called *model variables*. Model variables are similar to instance variables, but are specification-only variables. As shown in Fig. 10, the state of `ObservableGame`-boxes is captured by two model variables. Variable `currentPos` holds the current position of the game and variable `player` records the color of the human player.

The initial state of a box after termination of the constructor is described together with the constructor (cf. Fig. 10). The techniques for specifying constructors are the same as those for methods and are explained below.

Method Behavior. According to the semantics of Sect. 2, the general execution behavior of a method m on box B can be described by a list of execution segments. A *segment* is either internal or external. Internal segments consist of box internal execution actions not containing an external call. External segments correspond to external calls. They are indexed by the receiver object and the sent message. External segments are called *simple* if they do not cause a reentrant call to B. Otherwise each call back to B is again described by a list of execution segments. The specification of a method should describe:

- the precondition, if any[3],
- the *local effects*, that is, the modifications of the box state,
- the *frame effects*, that is, the external calls to the box environment, and
- restrictions on reentrant calls.

---

[3] A missing precondition is equivalent to precondition `true`.

```
box interface ObservableGame
{
  references Observer* gameObs;
  model Color player;
  model Position currentPos;

  ObservableGame()
    ensures  player == Color.WHITE && currentPos == Position.initial()
        &&  gameObs == Set.empty() ;

  pure Position readPos()
    ensures  result  == currentPos ;

  void register( external Observer go )
    requires go != null
    ensures  gameObs == pre(gameObs).insert(go)
        &&  unchanged([currentPos,player]) ;

  void move( MoveDescr md )
    behavior if( currentPos.legal(md) ) {
                currentPos = currentPos.doMove(md);
                foreach( o in gameObs ){ o.stateChanged(); }
                forsome( cmd : currentPos.legal(cmd) ){
                  currentPos = currentPos.doMove(cmd);
                  foreach( o in gameObs ){ o.stateChanged(); }
                }
              }
    ensures  unchanged([player,gameObs]) ;
    invokable this.readPos() ;

  void swapPlayers()
    behavior player = other(player);
                forsome( cmd : currentPos.legal(cmd) ){
                  currentPos = currentPos.doMove(cmd));
                  foreach( o in gameObs ){ o.stateChanged(); }
                }
    ensures  unchanged([gameObs]) ;
    invokable this.readPos() ;
}

interface Observer {
  void stateChanged()
    behavior arbitrary ;
}
```

Fig. 10. Behavioral specification of box ObservableGame

The new aspect of our technique is the treatment of effects and frame properties. We distinguish between local and external effects. Local effects may be underspecified. That is, a method may modify more than the specification reveals. For external effects, it is the other way round. A method may only perform external calls that are mentioned in the specification. Thus, a specification provides a guarantee that no effects or only certain effects can happen.

We use language constructs from precondition-postcondition-style specifications and from refinement-style specifications. The precondition, indicated by the keyword **requires**, is given by a boolean expression (e.g. the precondition of method **register** in Fig. 10 requires that the argument is non-null). Methods that do not change the box state and have no effects on the box environment can be declared as pure (e.g. the method **readPos** in Fig. 10 is a pure method). The local and frame effects of a method are specified by an ensures clause or a behavior clause.

As usual, an *ensures clause* is expressed by a boolean expression. It may use the prestate values of *box-local variables*, denoted by an application of the operator **pre** to the variable name, and their poststate values as well as the return value of the method, denoted by the identifier **result**. As abbreviation, we use the operator **unchanged** taking a list of variables and stating that the value of the variables is the same in pre- and poststate (the specification of **register** illustrates its use).

A *behavior clause* consists of an abstract statement describing the internal segments of the method and when external calls happen. Abstract statements might be nondeterministic. For example, the specification of **move** in Fig. 10 calls method **stateChanged** for each registered observer. The order of the calls is not fixed by the foreach-statement (compare [7]). We support as well a nondeterministic forsome-statement: If there exists an element satisfying the given predicate, one such element is chosen and the body is executed. Otherwise, the body is not executed. The completely unknown behavior is denoted by arbitrary (the specification of **stateChanged** provides a typical example).

A method execution satisfies a behavior clause if it implements one of the possible behaviors. The order of internal actions is not relevant as long as the specified state before an external call is correct. An ensures clause may be added to a behavior clause, to explicitly state properties that can be derived from the behavior clause. It is not allowed to specify additional properties. Methods **move** and **swapPlayers** show a combination of behavior and ensures clauses.

In connection with the box model, specifications based on abstract statements provide a new solution to the frame problem. The effects of a method are seperated into two parts: the box-local effects and the external effects. Local effects may be underspecified, that is, the behavior clauses need not completely determine the state changes. In particular, subboxes (not treated in this paper) can refine the local effects, for example w.r.t. extended state. We could have used modifies clauses to express what remains unchanged within a box. However, as the abstract state space of the box is known, one can as well simply list what remains unchanged (see for example the ensures clause of method **move** in Fig. 10).

The real difference between our approach and the modifies-clause approach to the frame problem concerns the modifications to the environment. In our approach, a method specification has to define all possible external calls. In particular, if no external call is specified, it is a guarantee that there are no effects to the environment. In the case of external modifications, the modifies-clause approach needs to describe the unknown effected state by some abstract variables and later specify the dependencies between the abstract variables and the concrete environment. This is often a difficult task. On the other hand, the verification techniques for modifies clauses are more advanced than for our approach based on external calls.

Finally, a method specification can limit the acceptable reentrant calls. Without an invokable clause, all reentrant calls are allowed. If an invokable clause is given, like, for example, in the specification of the methods move and swapPlayers in Fig. 10, only the listed reentrant calls are acceptable. If the client of the box does not prevent inacceptable reentrant calls, the box need no longer satisfy its contract. As shown in Subsect. 1.2, the restriction on reentrant calls is needed for modularity.

3.3   Specifying Multiple-Access Boxes

Boxes with multiple boundary objects and boundary objects of different types provide additional specification challenges. We will focus here on three aspects:

1. Control of the exposed references to boundary objects.
2. Box state with multiple objects and invariants.
3. Internal method calls in specifications.

We explain these aspects along with the IterList example (see Fig. 11 and 12). The specification essentially formulates the behavior of the Java class LinkedList (see [35]).

Controling Exposed References. In addition to its owner, a box can expose other boundary objects. Similar to the outgoing references (e.g., variable elems keeps track of outgoing references in the specification of Fig. 11[4]), a specification has to control exposed references in special ghost variables declared with the keyword exposes. For example, the IterList specification captures the set of exposed iterators in variable iters (see Fig. 11). Updates of the exposes variables are described in the method specifications; we say that exposed references are *registered*. An implementation satisfies an exposes specification if only registered references are exposed.

---

[4] We enforce that all outgoing, non-pure references are registered. We investigate whether it is sufficient to register only references that are used in external calls. That could reduce the specification overhead; in particular, the ghost variable elems would become dispensable.

```
box interface IterList  {
  exposes    Iterator ∗ iters ;
  references Object∗ elems;
  model List<Object> value;

  IterList ()
    ensures value==List.empty() && iters==Set.empty() && elems==Set.empty();

  invariant
    forall( it1,  it2 in iters ){  (it1.pos<=it2.pos && !it1.valid) ==> !it2.valid }

  pure external Object get( int index )
    requires 0 <= index && index < value.length();
    ensures   result  == value.nth(index);

  void add( external Object x )
    behavior foreach( it in iters ){
                if( it.pos == value.length() ) it.valid = false;
             }
             value = value.appendLast(x);
             elems = toSet(value);

  external Object remove( int index )
    requires 0 <= index && index < value.length()
    behavior foreach( it in iters ){
                if( it.pos >= index ) it.valid = false;
             }
             result = value.nth(index);
             value  = value.delete(index);
             elems  = value.toSet();

  pure boolean contains ( external Object x )
    behavior if( x == null ) {
                result = value.contains(null);
             } else {
             result = false;
             foreach( y in value ) {
               if( x.equals(y) ) {
                  result = true; break;
             } } }

  Iterator  listIterator ()
    ensures !pre( iters ).contains( result )   && iters .contains( result )
            && result .myList == this       && result .pos == 0
            && result . valid == true        && result .hasCurrent == false ;
}
```

Fig. 11. Behavioral specification of box IterList

```
interface Iterator
{
  model IterList myList;
  model int pos;
  model boolean valid;
  model boolean hasCurrent;


  invariant
    ( 0 <= pos ) && ( valid ==> pos <= myList.value.length() )

  pure boolean hasNext()
    requires valid
    ensures  result == (pos < myList.value.length())

  external Object next()
    requires valid && (pos < myList.value.length())
    behavior result = myList.get(pos);
             pos++;
             hasCurrent = true;

  void remove()
    requires valid && hasCurrent
    behavior myList.remove(pos);
}
```

Fig. 12. Behavioral specification of interface `Iterator`

Box State Revisited. Whereas in single-access boxes the box state can be associated with the owner object, this is not appropriate for multiple-access boxes. For a client of the box, it is more natural to distribute the box state over the boundary objects, in particular, because newly created boundary objects often make it necessary to extend the state space. For the `IterList` example, distributing the state means that part of the box state is associated with the owner (namely the represented list, see model variable `value` in Fig. 11) and other parts are associated with the iterators (namely the current iterator position in the list and the information whether an iterator is valid and has a current element; see model variables `pos`, `valid`, and `hasCurrent` in Fig. 12).

In addition to the state of the boundary objects, the relationship between boundary objects has to be modeled. As demonstrated by the model variable `myList` in Fig. 12, references between boundary objects can be used. It is allowed to access the state of referenced objects in specifications, because the references are encapsulated within the box. For example, the invariant of the `Iterator` interface accesses the value of the associated list and the invariant of the `IterList` interface accesses the exposed iterators.

The box model provides a fairly straightforward semantics for invariants. The invariants of a box B have to hold whenever execution is outside B, that is, in any configuration with $box(F(this)) \not\subseteq B$. In particular, they have to hold before outgoing calls. Note that there may as well be reentrant calls from inner boxes (although, one can argue that this is bad programming style). However, these calls are under the control of the box designer. To achieve modularity, invariants may only refer to box local state. This is for example true for the invariants given in Fig. 11 and 12. The requirement is not satisfied by the invariants given in Fig. 4. The references clause in GameObserver states that the observed game obsGame is outside the box. Thus, its fields may not be used in the invariants. To handle such invariants and the one given on page 320 in our approach, one has to define a box GamingSystem that encapsulate ObservableGame and GameObserver. This can be a very lightweight box providing only methods for creating observable games and game observers. It would be a multiple-access box having observable games and game observers as boundary objects. The invariants in question would become part of the box specification of GamingSystem.

Internal Calls. Whereas the support of external calls is necessary to handle effects and non-effects to the environment in an abstract way, internal calls are important to structure interface specifications and to improve reuse. A good example is the remove method of the iterator in Fig. 12. The behavior is simply described by an internal call to the remove method of the list. If this was not allowed, one would have had to describe the complex behavior of the latter method twice. Notice that the specification of the remove method in IterList demonstrates as well how the exposes variables can be used to describe effects to all boundary objects.

Distributing the box state and supporting internal calls over the boundary objects has the additional advantage that interface specifications can be used for different boxes. For example the Iterator-specification of Fig. 12 could be used for different collection boxes if the model variable myList is generalized to a more abstract type.

4   Discussion and Related Work

In this section, we relate the presented techniques to existing work and shortly discuss our design decisions. The section is structured according to the main aspects of the specification technique.

Encapsulation. Encapsulation is a central technique to achieve modularity ([26] discusses the relation between encapsulation- and visibility-based modularity). The current techniques for object-based encapsulation build on ownership concepts (see [9,8]). The basic idea is to guarantee the owner-as-dominator property: All reference chains from an object in the global context to an object X in a non-global context go through X's owner. The box model incorporates two extensions to the original ownership model:

- In [6,8], objects of inner classes are allowed as boundary objects. We generalized this to arbitrary boundary objects. At the moment, we do not have a checking technique for our full model. In particular, we cannot support programs in which boundary objects are passed back into a box as explicit parameters. Our currently developed checking approach (see [33]) builds on a variant of ownership domains [2].
- The universe type system [23,24] realizes a slightly different discipline (see [11]) and controls references leaving a context. Such references have to be read-only in the universe model.

There are different approaches to specify and check ownership. Most of the work cited above uses type systems. Many aspects of our approach are inspired by the assertion-based ownership technique of Boogie [5]. Within Boogie, each object X has a ghost variable referencing X's owner. These ghost variables can be used for specification and verification purposes and support ownership transfer [19].

Our work was also inspired by techniques for applet isolation in Java Card. To control accesses from other applets, Java Card allows such external accesses only through so-called shareable interfaces. Dynamic checks enforce this condition at runtime [34]. The semantics that was used in a paper on static checking of applet isolation has already separated references and objects and supported context information in the references [12]. The distinction between internal and external references is also motivated by role models for objects, in particular those described in [28].

Invariants and Reentrant Calls. Invariants are a central specification technique, for both hidden implementation aspects and visible properties of the abstract state of a component. Unfortunately, it is fairly difficult to provide a modular semantics for them in object-oriented programming. In [26], Müller et al. investigate the most common semantic approach based on so-called visible states. The visible state semantics requires that invariants have to hold in pre- and post-states of all calls to public methods. They show that a naive visible state semantics does not work for layered objects structures and provide a refined version. This so-called relevant invariant semantics inspired our approach in which box invariants have to hold whenever execution is outside the box. Our semantics is simpler as it does not enforce invariants to hold in pre- and poststates of internal method calls.

The Boogie methodology supports a more dynamic approach. The execution points at which invariants have to hold are expressed by special specification constructs ([5,27]) that are placed in the program. This makes the approach difficult to use for an implementation independent setting. A very strong feature of the Boogie approach is its flexible support for inheritance.

To extend our box-based invariant semantics and our basic mechanism to exclude unwanted reentrant calls, we can build on work on typestates [10] and on friend concepts [4]. Typestates can be used to represent sets of invokable methods that allow reentrance under certain specified conditions. The friends concept would enable us to support invariants that access state outside the box (like the invariants in Fig. 4).

Frame Problem. The specification of frame properties is a notoriously difficult problem. The main source of the problem for object-oriented programming is the weak knowledge about the effects or non-effects in the context of extendible state and virtual methods (recall the `ObservableGame` example from Fig. 4). Most existing solutions are based on abstraction techniques and lists of variables that might be modified ([20,23,21,25]). Specifications based on abstract statements do not explicitly list the modifiable variables, but associate modifications with methods ([7]). As described in Subsect. 3.2, we use the same approach for external effects.

5   Conclusions and Future Work

We presented an object-oriented kernel language OBO that supports a notion of dynamically created encapsulation regions called boxes. The implementation of a box can create and encapsulate other boxes. The box model distinguishes between internal and external references and supports object confinement.

In this paper, we used boxes as a semantic foundation for object-oriented software components. We described a behavioral specification technique for component instances that supports dynamically created interface objects and external modifying calls that might lead to reentrance.

In summary, we consider the presented work a further step to close the gap between specification techiques for programs and implementation independent specifications for components. Directions of future work include:

- the extension to all features of object-orientation; in particular, a behavioral subtype relation between box interfaces is needed;
- the development of powerful checking techniques;
- the adaption of existing verification techniques to the box model;
- the exploitation of boxes for higher-level concurrency models.

In addition, we are interested in more theoretical aspects like representation indepence (cf. [3]), calculi for OO-programming [1] and components [32], and questions related to specification completeness.

Acknowledgement. We thank the reviewers and Ina Schaefer for their helpful comments on previous versions of this paper.

References

1. Erika Ábrahám, Marcello M. Bonsangue, Frank S. de Boer, Andreas Grüner, and Martin Steffen. Observability, connectivity, and replay in a sequential calculus of classes. In Frank S. de Boer et. al., editors, *Formal Methods for Components and Objects, FMCO 2004*, volume 3657 of *LNCS*, pages 296–316. Springer-Verlag, 2005.
2. Jonathan Aldrich and Criag Chambers. Ownership domains: Separating aliasing policy from mechanism. In Odersky [29], pages 1–25.

3. Anindya Banerjee and David A. Naumann. Representation independence, confinement and access control. In *Proceedings of the 29th ACM SIGPLAN-SIGACT Symposium on Principles of Programming Languages (POPL'02)*, pages 166–177. ACM Press, January 2002.

4. Michael Barnett and David A. Naumann. Friends need a bit more: Maintaining invariants over shared state. In Dexter Kozen and Carron Shankland, editors, *Mathematics of Program Construction, 7th International Conference, MPC 2004*, volume 3125 of *Lecture Notes in Computer Science*, pages 54–84. Springer-Verlag, 2004.

5. Mike Barnett, Robert DeLine, Manuel Fähndrich, K. Rustan M. Leino, and Wolfram Schulte. Verification of object-oriented programs with invariants. *Journal of Object Technology*, 3(6), 2004.

6. Chandrasekhar Boyapati, Robert Lee, and Martin Rinard. Ownership types for safe programming: Preventing data races and deadlocks. In OOPSLA'02 [30], pages 211–230.

7. Martin Büchi. *Safe Language Mechanisms for Modularization and Concurrency*. PhD thesis, Turku Centre for Computer Science, May 2000.

8. Dave Clarke. *Object Ownership and Containment*. PhD thesis, University of New South Wales, July 2001.

9. Dave Clarke, John Potter, and James Noble. Ownership types for flexible alias protection. In *Proceedings of the 13th ACM SIGPLAN Conference on Object-Oriented Programing, Systems, Languages, and Applications (OOPSLA'98)*, pages 48–64. ACM Press, October 1998.

10. Robert DeLine and Manuel Fähndrich. Typestates for objects. In Odersky [29], pages 465–490.

11. Werner Dietl and Peter Müller. Universes: Lightweight ownership for JML. *Journal of Object Technology*, 4(8):5–32, 2005.

12. Werner Dietl, Peter Müller, and Arnd Poetzsch-Heffter. A type system for checking applet isolation in Java Card. In *Construction and Analysis of Safe, Secure and Interoperable Smart devices (CASSIS 2004)*, volume 3362 of *Lecture Notes in Computer Science*. Springer-Verlag, March 2004.

13. Matthew Flatt, Shriram Krishnamurthi, and Matthias Felleisen. A programmer's reduction semantics for classes and mixins. *Formal Syntax and Semantics of Java*, 1523:241–269, 1999.

14. James Gosling, Bill Joy, Guy Steele, and Gilad Bracha. *The Java^{TM} Language Specification – Second Edition*. Addison-Wesley, June 2000.

15. J. V. Guttag and J. J. Horning. *Larch: Languages and Tools for Formal Specification*. Texts and Monographs in Computer Science. Springer-Verlag, 1993.

16. Atsushi Igarashi, Benjamin C. Pierce, and Philip Wadler. Featherweight Java: A minimal core calculus for Java and GJ. *ACM Transactions on Programming Languages and Systems (TOPLAS)*, 23(3):396–450, May 2001.

17. Gary T. Leavens, Albert L. Baker, and Clyde Ruby. JML: A notation for detailed design. In Haim Kilov, Bernhard Rumpe, and Ian Simmonds, editors, *Behavioral Specifications of Businesses and Systems*, chapter 12, pages 175–188. Kluwer, 1999.

18. Gary T. Leavens, Albert L. Baker, and Clyde Ruby. Preliminary design of JML. Technical Report No. 98-06z, Iowa State University, 2004.

19. K. R. M. Leino and P. Müller. Object invariants in dynamic contexts. In Odersky [29], pages 491–516.

20. K. Rustan M. Leino and Greg Nelson. Data abstraction and information hiding. *ACM Transactions on Programming Languages and Systems (TOPLAS)*, 24(5):491–553, 2002.

21. K. Rustan M. Leino, Arnd Poetzsch-Heffter, and Yunhong Zhou. Using data groups to specify and check side effects. In *Proceedings of the ACM SIGPLAN 2002 Conference on Programming language design and implementation (PLDI'02)*, pages 246–257. ACM Press, June 2002.
22. Microsoft. *C# Language Specification*. 2001.
23. Peter Müller. *Modular Specification and Verification of Object-Oriented Programs*, volume 2262 of *Lecture Notes in Computer Science*. Springer-Verlag, 2002.
24. Peter Müller and Arnd Poetzsch-Heffter. Universes: A type system for alias and dependency control. Technical Report 279–1, Fernuniversität Hagen, 2001.
25. Peter Müller, Arnd Poetzsch-Heffter, and Gary T. Leavens. Modular specification of frame properties in JML. *Concurrency and Computation: Practice and Experience*, 15(2):117–154, 2003.
26. Peter Müller, Arnd Poetzsch-Heffter, and Gary T. Leavens. Modular invariants for layered object structures. Technical Report 424, ETH Zürich, Chair of Software Engineering, 2005.
27. David A. Naumann. Assertion-based encapsulation, object invariants and simulations. In Frank S. de Boer, Marcello M. Bonsangue, Susanne Graf, and Willem P. de Roever, editors, *Formal Methods for Components and Objects, Third International Symposium, FMCO 2004*, volume 3657 of *Lecture Notes in Computer Science*, pages 251–273. Springer-Verlag, 2005.
28. James Noble, Jan Vitek, and John Potter. Flexible alias protection. In Eric Jul, editor, *Proceedings of the 12th European Conference on Object-Oriented Programming (ECOOP'98)*, volume 1445 of *Lecture Notes in Computer Science*, pages 158–185. Springer-Verlag, July 1998.
29. Martin Odersky, editor. *Proceedings of the 18th European Conference on Object-Oriented Programming (ECOOP'04)*, volume 3086 of *Lecture Notes in Computer Science*. Springer-Verlag, June 2004.
30. *Proceedings of the 17th ACM SIGPLAN Conference on Object-Oriented Programing, Systems, Languages, and Applications (OOPSLA'02)*. ACM Press, November 2002.
31. Arnd Poetzsch-Heffter. Specification and verification of object-oriented programs. Habilitationsschrift, Technische Universität München, 1997.
32. Riccardo Pucella. Towards a formalization for COM part I: the primitive calculus. In OOPSLA'02 [30], pages 331–342.
33. Jan Schäfer and Arnd Poetzsch-Heffter. Simple fuzzy ownership domains. Unpublished. Preliminary version. Available at http://softech.informatik.uni-kl.de/~janschaefer.
34. Sun Microsystems, Inc., Palo Alto, CA. *Java Card^{TM} 2.1.1 Virtual Machine Specification*, May 2000.
35. Sun Microsystems, Inc. *Java^{TM} 2 Platform, Standard Edition, v 1.4.2 API Specification*, 2003. http://java.sun.com/j2se/1.4.2/docs/api/.
36. Clemens Szyperski, Dominik Gruntz, and Stephan Murer. *Component Software — Beyond Object-Oriented Programming*. Addison-Wesley, second edition, 2002.

Appendix

The appendix present proof sketches for the properties given in Sect. 2.

Definition (Configuration). A *configuration* is a triple $\langle H, F, v \rangle$, consisting of a heap H, a stack frame F and a value v.

Definition (Intern-Closed Configuration). A configuration (H, F, v) is called *intern-closed*, denoted by $(H, F, v) \vdash \nabla$, if the following conditions hold:

1. If $H(b)(o_0) = \overline{v}$ with $v_i = \langle o, \_, \texttt{intn} \rangle$, then $box(o) = b$
2. If $thisBox(F) = b$ and $F(x) = \langle o, \_, \texttt{intn} \rangle$, then $box(o) = b$
3. If $thisBox(F) = b$ and $v = \langle o, \_, \texttt{intn} \rangle$, then $box(o) = b$

Theorem 1. *If* $(H, F, null) \vdash \nabla$ *and* $H, F \vdash e \Rightarrow v, H_0$ *then* $(H_0, F, v) \vdash \nabla$

Note that initial configurations appearing in premises of evaluation rules are all *intern-closed*, which is (and needs to be) shown in the proof below.

Proof. Suppose $(H, F, null) \vdash \nabla$ and $H, F \vdash e \Rightarrow v, H_0$. We show that $(H_0, F, v) \vdash \nabla$. As F does not change, we only have to show conditions (1) and (3) of the intern-closed definition. We do an induction on the evaluation rules.

(E-VAR) Immediate.

(E-CAST NULL) By the induction hypothesis.

(E-CAST OBJ) By the induction hypothesis.

(E-NEW BOX) (1) follows by assumption $(H, F, null) \vdash \nabla$ and the fact that $H(b)(o) = \overline{null}$. (3) follows because $v = \langle o, B, \texttt{extn} \rangle$.

(E-NEW OBJ) (1) follows by assumption $(H, F, null) \vdash \nabla$ and the fact that $H(b)(o) = \overline{null}$. (3) follows from the premises $b = thisBox(F)$ and $o = (b, C, j, em)$.

(E-FIELD) By the induction hypothesis.

(E-FIELDUP) By the induction hypothesis we get $(H_0, F, \langle o, C, \texttt{intn} \rangle) \vdash \nabla$ and $(H_1, F, v) \vdash \nabla$. With the premise $b = box(o)$ it follows $thisBox(F) = b$. Let $v = \langle o_1, \_, \texttt{intn} \rangle$. Hence $thisBox(F) = box(o_1)$ and so $b = box(o_1)$. Thus $(H_1[b \mapsto BS], F, v) \vdash \nabla$.

(E-INVK INTN) By the induction hypothesis we get $(H_0, F, \langle o, C, \texttt{intn} \rangle) \vdash \nabla$. Hence $thisBox(F) = box(o)$. By repeated application of the induction hypothesis we get $(H_i, F, v_i) \vdash \nabla$, for $0 < i \leq n$. Let $F_m = \{this \mapsto o, \overline{x} \mapsto \overline{v}\}$. Hence $thisBox(F_m) = thisBox(F)$ and so $(H_n, F_m, null) \vdash \nabla$. Applying the induction hypothesis leads to $(H_m, F_m, v_m) \vdash \nabla$. And finally, $(H_m, F, v_m) \vdash \nabla$.

(E-INVK EXTN) By repeated application of the induction hypothesis we get $(H_0, F, \langle o_0, S, \texttt{extn} \rangle) \vdash \nabla$ and $(H_i, F, v_i) \vdash \nabla$, for $0 < i \leq n$. Let $F_m = \{this \mapsto \langle o_0, C, \texttt{intn} \rangle, \overline{x} \mapsto \overline{adapt(v_i, T_i, b, a_i)}\}$. Note that $thisBox(F_m) = b$. We have to show that $\forall x$ with $F_m(x) = \langle o_x, T_x, \texttt{intn} \rangle$. $box(o_x) = b$. The *adapt* function turns all references into \texttt{extn} references, except for the case, where $a_i = \texttt{boundary}$. In that case, however, $b = box(o_x)$. Hence $(H_n, F_m, null) \vdash \nabla$. By the induction hypothesis, $(H_m, F_m, v_m) \vdash \nabla$. Let $v_r = adapt(v_m, T_m, thisBox(F), a_m)$. The adapt function only returns an \texttt{intn} reference if $thisBox(F) = box(v_m)$, thus $(H_m, F, v_r) \vdash \nabla$.

(E-LET) By the induction hypothesis.   □

Definition. $cf(o)$ is defined as follows.

cf : **Object** $\to$ **Box**
$cf(b, C, k; \texttt{confined})$ $= b$
$cf(b, C, k; \texttt{exposable}) = confIn(b)$

Definition (Confined Configuration). A configuration (H, F, v) is called *confined*, denoted by $(H, F, v) \vdash \triangle$, if the following conditions hold:

1. If $H(b)(o_0) = \overline{v}$ with $v_i = \langle o, \_, \_ \rangle$, then $b \subseteq cf(o)$
2. If $thisBox(F) = b$ and $F(x) = \langle o, \_, \_ \rangle$, then $b \subseteq cf(o)$
3. If $thisBox(F) = b$ and $v = \langle o, \_, \_ \rangle$, then $b \subseteq cf(o)$

Theorem 2. *If* $(H, F, null) \vdash \triangle$ *and* $H, F \vdash e \Rightarrow v, H_0$ *then* $(H_0, F, v) \vdash \triangle$

Like above, the proof also shows that all initial configurations of rule premises are confined.

Proof. Suppose $(H, F, null) \vdash \triangle$ and $H, F \vdash e \Rightarrow v, H_0$. We show that $(H_0, F, v) \vdash \triangle$. As F does not change, we only have to show conditions (1) and (3) of the confinedness definition. We do an induction on the evaluation rules.

(E-VAR) Immediate.
(E-CAST NULL) By the induction hypothesis.
(E-CAST OBJ) By the induction hypothesis.
(E-NEW BOX) (1) follows by the fact that $H(b)(o) = \overline{null}$. (3): Depending on e_m, $confIn(b)$ is either b_0 or $confIn(b_0)$. Hence $cf(o)$ is either b, b_0, or $confIn(b_0)$. As $parent(b) = b_0$, it follows $b \subset b_0$. In addition, $b \subseteq confIn(b_0)$. Thus $b \subseteq cf(o)$.
(E-NEW OBJ) (1) follows by the fact that $H(b)(o) = \overline{null}$. (3): From the premise $box(o) = b$ we get $cf(o) \in \{b, confIn(b)\}$. Hence $b \subseteq cf(o)$.
(E-FIELD) (1) by the induction hypothesis. (3): Let $thisBox(F) = b$, for some b. By Theorem 1, $b = box(o)$. Hence $b \subseteq cf(o)$.
(E-FIELDUP) Let $thisBox(F) = b_1$, for some b_1. By Theorem 1, $b_1 = box(o)$. Hence by the premise $b = box(o)$, it follows $b_1 = b$. Let $v = \langle o_v, \_, \_ \rangle$. Hence, by Theorem 1, $box(o_v) = b$. Hence $b \subseteq cf(o_v)$. Thus $(H_1[b \mapsto BS], F, v) \vdash \triangle$.
(E-INVK INTN) By repeated application of the induction hypothesis we get $(H_i, F, v_i) \vdash \triangle$, for $0 < i \leq n$. Let $F_m = \{this \mapsto \langle o, C, \texttt{intn} \rangle, \overline{x} \mapsto \overline{v}\}$. Hence, $thisBox(F) = thisBox(F_m)$. Hence, $(H_n, F_m, null) \vdash \triangle$. We can apply the induction hypothesis and get $(H_m, F_m, v_m) \vdash \triangle$. Thus, $(H_m, F, v_m) \vdash \triangle$.
(E-INVK EXTN) By repeated application of the induction hypothesis we get $(H_i, F, v_i) \vdash \triangle$, for $0 < i \leq n$. Let $F_m = \{this \mapsto \langle o_0, C, \texttt{intn} \rangle, \overline{x} \mapsto adapt(v_i, T_i, b, a_i)\}$. The $passable(v_i, b, a_i)$ premises ensure that $b \subseteq box(v_i)$. Hence it follows $(H_n, F_m, null) \vdash \triangle$. We can apply the induction hypothesis and get $(H_m, F_m, v_m) \vdash \triangle$. Let $adapt(v_m, T_m, thisBox(F), \texttt{external}) = \langle o_r, \_, \_ \rangle$. We must show that $thisBox(F) \subseteq cf(o_r)$ But this is ensured by the premise $passable(v_m, T_m, thisBox(F), \texttt{external})$. Thus $(H_m, F, \langle o_r, \_, \_ \rangle) \vdash \triangle$.
(E-LET) By the induction hypothesis. $\square$

Beyond Assertions: Advanced Specification and Verification with JML and ESC/Java2

Patrice Chalin[1], Joseph R. Kiniry[2],
Gary T. Leavens[3], and Erik Poll[4]

[1] Concordia University, Montréal, Québec, Canada
[2] University College Dublin, Ireland
[3] Iowa State University, Ames, Iowa, USA
[4] Radboud University Nijmegen, the Netherlands

Abstract. Many state-based specification languages, including the Java Modeling Language (JML), contain at their core specification constructs familiar to most undergraduates: e.g., assertions, pre- and postconditions, and invariants. Unfortunately, these constructs are not sufficiently expressive to permit formal modular verification of programs written in modern object-oriented languages like Java. The necessary extra constructs for specifying an object-oriented module include (perhaps the less familiar) frame properties, datagroups, and ghost and model fields. These constructs help specifiers deal with potential problems related to, for example, unexpected side effects, aliasing, class invariants, inheritance, and lack of information hiding. This tutorial paper focuses on JML's realization of these constructs, explaining their meaning while illustrating how they can be used to address the stated problems.

1 Introduction

Textbooks on program verification typically explain the notions of pre- and postconditions, loop invariants, and so on for toy programming languages. The goal of this paper is to explain some of the more advanced concepts that are necessary in order to allow the formal modular verification of (sequential) programs written in a popular mainstream object-oriented language: Java. The Java Modeling Language (JML) [BCC+05, LBR06, LPC+06], a Behavioral Interface Specification Language (BISL) [Win90] for Java, will be our notation of choice for expressing specifications.

The reader is assumed to be familiar with the basics of Design by Contract (DBC) [Mey97] or Behavioral Interface Specifications (BISs) and the central role played by assertions in these approaches. Readers without this background may wish to consult one of several books or articles offering tutorials on the subject [Hoa69, LG01, MM02, Mey92, Mey97, Mor94]. A tutorial that explains these basic ideas using JML is also available [LC05].

F.S. de Boer et al. (Eds.): FMCO 2005, LNCS 4111, pp. 342–363, 2006.

1.1   Approaches to Verification

Tools useful for checking that JML annotated Java modules meet their specifications fall into two main categories:[1]

- runtime assertion checking (RAC) tools, and
- static verification (SV) tools.

These categories also represent two complementary forms of assertion checking,
the foundations of which were laid out before the 1950s in the pioneering work
of Goldstine, von Neumann and Turing [Jon03]. Runtime assertion checking
involves the testing of specifications during program execution; any violations
result in special errors being reported. The idea of checking *contracts* at runtime
was popularized by Eiffel [Mey97] as of the late 80s; other early work includes
Rosenblum's APP annotation language for C [Ros92, Ros95]. The main RAC
tool for JML is jmlc [CL02]. RAC support for JML is also planned for the next
release of the Jass tool [BFMW01].

In static verification, logical techniques are used to prove, before runtime,
that no violations of specifications will take place at runtime. The adjective
static emphasizes that verification happens by means of a static analysis of the
code, i.e., without running it. Program verification tools supporting JML include
JACK [BRL03], KeY [ABB+05], Krakatoa [MPMU04], LOOP [BJ01], and Jive
[MPH00]. In this paper we will focus on ESC/Java2 [CK04], the main (extended)
static checker for JML.

RAC and SV tools have complementary strengths. Compared to runtime assertion checking, static verification often provides stronger guarantees and it can
give them earlier. However, these advantages come at a price: SV tools generally
require fairly complete specifications not only for the module being checked, but
also for the modules and libraries that it depends on. Furthermore, in order to be
effective and keep false positives to a minimum, SV tools require specifications
to make use of some of the advanced features described in this paper.

1.2   Outline

The remainder of the paper is organized as follows. The basic notation used
in JML for method contracts and invariants is covered in Section 2. Section 3
explains frame properties, and Section 4 model fields. The treatment of behavioral subtyping is given in Section 5. Section 6 explains ghost fields. Section 7
introduces the JML notations that deal with ownership and aliasing. Finally,
conclusions and related work are given in Section 8.

2   JML Basics: Pre- and Postconditions, and Invariants

This section examines the specification and implementation of various kinds of
clocks. In doing so, we review basic concepts such as method contracts and class
invariants and introduce their JML notation.

---

[1] There are also several other kinds of tool available for use with JML [BCC+05].

2.1   Method Contracts

We begin with the specification of a `TickTockClock` as given in Fig. 1. This specification illustrates basic method contracts formed by:

- preconditions (introduced by the `requires` keyword), and
- postconditions (`ensures`).

An example of such a contract is found in the specification of the method `getSecond()` on lines 23–24. The JML specification for each method is written in front of the method itself, and is found in stylized Java comments that begin with an at-sign ('@').

A method contract without an explicit `requires` clause has an implicit precondition of *true*. Thus, such a method imposes no requirements on its callers. This default means that the `requires` clause written for `getHour()` could have been omitted entirely. Similarly, the default postcondition when none is explicitly given in an `ensures` clause is also *true*, which says that the method makes no guarantees to its caller. The constructor (on lines 12–15) and the method `getMinute()` (on lines 21–22) are examples of class members with implicit `requires` clauses.

Note that assertion expressions appearing in `requires` and `ensures` clauses are written using a Java-like syntax. In postconditions of (non-`void`) methods, `\result` can be used to refer to the value being returned by the method. The only other JML specific operator used in this clock specification is the `\old()` operator, which is used in an `ensures` clause of `tick` (on lines 29–31). The expression `\old(`e`)` refers to the value of e in the method's pre-state, i.e., the state just before the method is executed.

Preconditions and postconditions are often split over multiple `requires` and `ensures` clauses, as illustrated for the postcondition of `getSecond()` (on lines 23–24). Multiple `ensures` clauses, or multiple `requires` clauses, are equivalent to a single clause consisting of the conjunction (`&&`) of their respective assertions.

Method contracts, like the contract of `tick()` on lines 27–37 of Fig. 1, are written as one or more *specification cases* combined with the keyword `also`. Each specification case is a "mini-contract" in itself, having a precondition and postcondition (either explicit or implicit) as well as other clauses that are covered below. Use of specification cases allows developers to structure their specifications and to (literally) break it up into (generally) distinct cases.

The contract for `tick()`, which is somewhat contrived for illustrative purposes, highlights to clients that its behavior essentially has two cases of interest. Either

- seconds are less than 59 and the seconds are incremented by one, or
- seconds are at 59 and they will be wrapped back to 0.

We note in passing that the specification of `tick()` is incomplete, as it might be during the development of the `TickTockClock` class. Informal comments, like the one on line 36, are useful for remembering what remains to be formalized or to avoid formalization (e.g., if it is too costly), although they do not help in verification.

```
1   public class TickTockClock {
2     //@ public model JMLDataGroup _time_state;
3
4     //@ protected invariant 0 <= hour && hour <= 23;
5     protected int hour; //@ in _time_state;
6     //@ protected invariant 0 <= minute && minute <= 59;
7     protected int minute; //@ in _time_state;
8     //@ protected invariant 0 <= second && second <= 59;
9     protected int second; //@ in _time_state;
10
11    //@ ensures getHour() == 12 && getMinute() == 0 && getSecond() == 0;
12    public /*@ pure @*/ TickTockClock() {
13        hour = 12; minute = 0; second = 0;
14    }
15
16    //@ requires true;
17    //@ ensures 0 <= \result && \result <= 23;
18    public /*@ pure @*/ int getHour() { return hour; }
19
20    //@ ensures 0 <= \result && \result <= 59;
21    public /*@ pure @*/ int getMinute() { return minute; }
22
23    //@ ensures 0 <= \result;
24    //@ ensures \result <= 59;
25    public /*@ pure @*/ int getSecond() { return second; }
26
27    /*@ requires   getSecond() < 59;
28     @ assignable hour, minute, second; // NB for expository purposes only
29     @ assignable _time_state;
30     @ ensures    getSecond() == \old(getSecond() + 1) &&
31     @                getMinute() == \old(getMinute()) &&
32     @                getHour() == \old(getHour());
33     @ also
34     @ requires   getSecond() == 59;
35     @ assignable _time_state;
36     @ ensures    getSecond() == 0;
37     @ ensures    (* hours and minutes are updated appropriately *);
38     @*/
39    public void tick() {
40        second++;
41        if (second == 60) { second = 0; minute++; }
42        if (minute == 60) { minute = 0; hour++; }
43        if (hour == 24)   { hour = 0; }
44    }
45  }
```

Fig. 1. JML specification for TickTockClock. The datagroup _time_state, the associated **assignable** clauses and **in** clauses are explained later, in Section 3

2.2   Purity

In the DBC approach, only query methods can be used in assertion expressions because they are required to be side-effect free [Mey97]. The corresponding concept in JML is known as method *purity*; pure methods are not allowed to have side effects, and pure constructors can only assign to the fields of the object they are initializing. Purity is statically checked by the JML tools. The restriction that only methods declared as `pure` can be used in assertion expressions is also checked statically. E.g., since the method `getSecond()` is declared `pure`, it is legal to make use of it in the postcondition of `tick()`.

Notice that the `TickTockClock` constructor is declared as `pure` despite the fact that it assigns to the fields `hour`, `minute` and `second`. Such instance field assignments are permitted inside the bodies of constructors because they are benevolent side-effects—i.e., that have no observable effect on clients. On the other hand, a pure constructor would not be permitted to assign to a static field. Purity, and particularly variants in the strength (restrictiveness) of its definition are a subject of active research—e.g., a stronger notion of purity than that of JML has been proposed by Darvas and Müller [DM05]. On the other hand, purity is often too strong [LCC+05], and so a notion of "observational purity" that permits benevolent side effects (such as updates to caches) is also under consideration [BSS04, Nau05].

2.3   Lightweight vs. Heavyweight

JML actually has two kinds of specification cases: lightweight and heavyweight. Lightweight specification cases are useful when giving partial specifications, and in practice are often used with ESC/Java2. To convey that one is intending to give a complete specification for some precondition, one would use a heavyweight specification case. Such heavyweight specification cases are often used with runtime assertion checking.

The specification cases of the `tick()` method are lightweight. An example use of heavyweight specification cases is found on the `setTime()` method of the `SettableClock` class given in Fig. 2. A heavyweight specification case is easily recognized by the use of a "behavior" keyword at the beginning of the case. The contract of `setTime()` illustrates the two kinds of heavyweight specification cases most often used. The first specification case uses the `normal_behavior` keyword and it describes the intended behavior of the method when it returns normally. The second specification case uses the `exceptional_behavior` keyword and it describes the intended behavior of the method when the method raises an exception. The latter case is described at greater length in Section 2.4. Notice that the heavyweight specification cases of `setTime()` start with `public`. This means that the specification cases are visible to clients, and hence, for example, will be included as a part of client visible documentation generated using JmlDoc [BCC+05]. It also means that these specification cases cannot refer to `private` or `protected` fields.

```
1   class SettableClock extends TickTockClock {
2
3       // ...
4
5       /*@ public normal_behavior
6        @    requires    0 <= hour && hour <= 23 &&
7        @                0 <= minute && minute <= 59;
8        @    assignable _time_state;
9        @    ensures     getHour() == hour &&
10       @                getMinute() == minute && getSecond() == 0;
11       @ also
12       @  public exceptional_behavior
13       @    requires    !(0 <= hour && hour <= 23 &&
14       @                0 <= minute && minute <= 59);
15       @    assignable  \nothing;
16       @    signals     (IllegalArgumentException e) true;
17       @    signals_only IllegalArgumentException;
18       @*/
19      public void setTime(int hour, int minute) {
20          if (!(0 <= hour & hour <= 23 & 0 <= minute & minute <= 59)) {
21              throw new IllegalArgumentException();
22          }
23          this.hour = hour;
24          this.minute = minute;
25          this.second = 0;
26      }
27  }
```

Fig. 2. JML specification for SettableClock

Contracts built from lightweight specification cases have fewer keywords and mandatory clauses. In particular, the visibility of a lightweight specification case cannot be given explicitly since, by definition, its visibility is the same as the visibility of the method it is attached to. The method contracts in TickTockClock are all examples of lightweight method specifications.

2.4 Exceptions and Exceptional Postconditions

JML distinguishes two kinds of postcondition:

- normal postconditions, expressed by means of **ensures** clauses, that must hold when a method terminates normally, and
- exceptional postconditions, expressed by means of **signals** clauses, that must hold when a method terminates with an exception.

The exceptional specification case of SettableClock.setTime() is interpreted as follows: if hour and minute are not within their valid ranges, then the method will raise an IllegalArgumentException and the system state will be left unchanged.

Notice that in the TickTockClock class there are no Java throws clauses. Still, Java permits the constructor and any of the methods of this class to throw a RuntimeException—one commonly raised runtime exception is NullPointerException. JML is more strict when it comes to declaring runtime exceptions: whereas Java allows any constructor or method to throw a runtime exception, JML only allows this if the exception is listed in the method's throws clause, or in the method contract's signals_only clause. SettableClock.setTime() illustrates use of the latter. Therefore, constructors or methods without an explicit throws clause have an implicit exceptional postcondition of signals (Exception) false. So the specification in Fig. 1 rules out the generation of any runtime exceptions, making the specification much stronger than it might appear at first sight. However, JML, like Java, makes a distinction between exceptions and errors; since Java's type Error is not a subtype of Exception, JML specifications do not say anything about virtual machine errors, such as running out of memory [PH97].

2.5   Instance and Static Invariants (and the Callback Problem)

A JML invariant clause declared with a static modifier is called a *static invariant*. Static invariants express properties which must hold of the static attributes of a class. An assertion that appears in a non-static invariant clause is called a *instance invariant* or an *object invariant*. Note that while this terminology is contrary to the literature, it is more accurate with respect to the nomenclature of Java. In this paper, an unqualified use of the term "invariant" will refer to an "object invariant."

The semantics of object invariants is more involved than most specifiers expect, especially for newcomers to the field of object-oriented specification. Hence, while this issue has been widely known for quite some time [Szy98], we believe it is worth a brief explanation. Intuitively, an object invariant:

- has to be established by constructors—i.e., it is implicitly included in the postcondition of constructors;
- can be assumed to hold on entry to methods, but methods must also reestablish it on exit. Hence, the invariant is implicitly included in the preconditions, and (normal and exceptional) postconditions of methods.

This intuition may suggest that the notion of object invariant is not really necessary, but rather that it just provides a convenient shorthand. This idea is a common misconception, as there is more to the notion of invariant than the intuitions summarized above. One difference is that invariants apply to all subtypes through specification inheritance (Section 5), whereas predicates that just happen to appear in all pre-and post conditions are not inherited as part of the specification of any new methods that may be added in a subtype.

One other issue is related to callbacks. For example, suppose that the `tick` method called another method at a program point where its invariant is broken, such as the call to `canvas.paint()` in the following:

```
public void tick() {
  second++;
  // object invariant might no longer hold
  canvas.paint();
  /* ... */
}
```

It would then be reasonable for the canvas to invoke, e.g., the `getSecond()` method of the current clock object, performing a so-called callback. However, since the invariant of this clock object is broken, its behavior is unconstrained, in particular because the preconditions of all methods (which implicitly include the object invariant) are all false.

To avoid such problems, the invariant not only has to be re-established at the end of each method, but also at those program points where a (non-helper) method is invoked. These program points—i.e., all program points at which a method invocation starts or ends—are called the *visible states*. The visible state semantics for invariants says that all invariants of all objects must hold at these visible states. This semantics is very strong and in many cases overly restrictive. Less restrictive, but still sound, approaches are still a hot topic of ongoing research. A more thorough discussion of this problem and a proposed solution for JML is given in [MPHL05]; alternative solutions are explored elsewhere [BDF+04, HK00, JLPS05, MHKL05].

3 Frame Properties

In traditional specifications that give pre- and postcondition for methods (or procedures) one often uses the convention that any variables not mentioned in the postcondition have not been changed. This approach is *not* workable for realistic object-oriented programs. For example, consider the method `tick()` in Fig. 1. This method may modify the three private fields `second`, `minute` and `hour`, but these do not appear in the postcondition. Rewriting the specification so it does mention these fields is clearly not what we would want, since in the specification of this public method we do not want to refer to private fields.

A JML `assignable` clause is used in a method contract to specify which parts of the system state *may* change as the result of the method execution. This is the so-called *frame property* [BMR95]. Any location outside the frame property is guaranteed to have the same value after the method has executed (called the post-state) as it did before the method executed (in the pre-state). The notion of *datagroup* [Lei98] allows us to abstract away from private implementation details in frame properties and provides flexibility in specifications. This section explains these notions and the need for them.

An `assignable` clause specifies that a method may change certain fields without having to specify how they might change. So the specification of the method `tick()` could include

```
assignable hour, minute, second;
```

to state that it may modify these three fields, without having to mention the fields in the postcondition. If no `assignable` clause is given for a non-pure method, then it has the default frame condition `assignable \everything`. However, pure methods (Section 2.2) have a default frame of `assignable \nothing`.

Object-oriented languages such as Java require some means for abstraction in assignable clauses. E.g., the first `assignable` clause for `tick()` given above leaves a lot to be desired. Firstly, it exposes implementation details, because it mentions the names of protected fields. Secondly, the specification is overly restrictive for any future subclasses. By the principle of *behavioral subtyping*, discussed in more detail in Section 5, the implementation of `tick()` in any future subclass of `TickTockClock` has to meet the specification given in `TickTockClock`. This means that the method body can only assign to the three fields of `TickTockClock`, which is far too restrictive in practice. To give a concrete example, suppose we introduce a subclass `TickTockClockWithDate` of `TickTockClock` that, in addition to keeping the time, also keeps track of the current date. Clearly such a subclass will introduce additional fields to record the date and `tick` will have to modify these fields when the end of a day is reached; however, the assignable clause given above will not allow these fields to be changed, as they are not explicitly listed.

Datagroups [Lei98] provide a solution to this problem. The idea is that a datagroup is an abstract piece of an object's state that may still be extended by future subclasses. The specification in Fig. 1 declares a (public) datagroup `_time_state` and declares that the three (private) fields belong to this datagroup. This datagroup is (partially) used to specify `tick()`. This avoids exposing any private implementation details, and subclasses of `TickTockClock` may extend the datagroup with additional fields it introduces.

Datagroups may be nested by using the `in` clause to say that one datagroup is part of another one. The JML specification for `java.lang.Object` declares a datagroup named `objectState`. Since this datagroup is inherited by all other classes, as a convention one can use `objectState` in any class to describe what constitutes the 'state' of an object of that class. Had we followed this convention then, e.g., we would have declared the `_time_state` datagroup to be in `objectState`.

Finally we note that, although `assignable` clauses are needed when doing program verification, they are *not* currently used during runtime assertion checking. (The RAC tool checks `assignable` clauses statically and does not check them at runtime.)

```
1   public class Clock {
2     //@ public model long _time;
3     //@ private represents _time = second + minute*60 + hour*60*60;
4
5     //@ public invariant _time == getSecond()+ getMinute()*60 + getHour()*60*60;
6     //@ public invariant 0 <= _time && _time < 24*60*60;
7
8     //@ private invariant 0 <= hour && hour <= 23;
9     private int hour; //@ in _time;
10    //@ private invariant 0 <= minute && minute <= 59;
11    private int minute; //@ in _time;
12    //@ private invariant 0 <= second && second <= 59;
13    private int second; //@ in _time;
14
15    //@ ensures _time == 12*60*60;
16    public /*@ pure @*/ Clock() { hour = 12; minute = 0; second = 0; }
17
18    //@ ensures 0 <= \result && \result <= 23;
19    public /*@ pure @*/ int getHour() { return hour; }
20
21    //@ ensures 0 <= \result && \result <= 59;
22    public /*@ pure @*/ int getMinute() { return minute; }
23
24    //@ ensures 0 <= \result && \result <= 59;
25    public /*@ pure @*/ int getSecond() { return second; }
26
27    /*@ requires   0 <= hour && hour <= 23;
28      @ requires   0 <= minute && minute <= 59;
29      @ assignable _time;
30      @ ensures    _time == hour*60*60 + minute*60;
31      @*/
32    public void setTime(int hour, int minute) {
33      this.hour = hour; this.minute = minute; this.second = 0;
34    }
35
36    //@ assignable _time;
37    //@ ensures _time == \old(_time + 1) % 24*60*60;
38    public void tick() {
39      second++;
40      if (second == 60) { second = 0; minute++; }
41      if (minute == 60) { minute = 0; hour++; }
42      if (hour == 24)   { hour = 0; }
43    }
44  }
```

Fig. 3. Example JML specification illustrating the use of model fields

4   Model Fields

Model fields [CLSE05] are closely related to the notion of data abstraction proposed by Hoare [Hoa72]. A model field is a specification-only field that provides
an abstraction of (part of) the concrete state of an object. The specification in
Fig. 3 illustrates the use of a model field. It abstracts away from the particular concrete representation of time by using a model field _time that represents
the number of seconds past midnight. Notice how this abstraction allows for a
brief but complete specification of the method tick(). The represents clause
of line 3 relates the model field to its concrete representation, in this case as a
function of hour, minute and second. Hence, the represents clause defines the
representation function of _time. (In its most general form, JML also permits
represents clauses that are relational [LPC+06], but we do not discuss these
here.)

   Note that the _time model field is public, and hence visible to clients, though
its representation is not. The represents clause must be declared private, because it refers to private fields. For every model field there is an associated
datagroup, so that the model field can also be used in assignable clauses. In
fact, a field of type JMLDataGroup is a degenerate model field that holds no
information.

   A difference between model fields for objects and the traditional notion of
abstract value for abstract data types is that an object can have several model
fields, providing abstractions of different aspects of the object. For instance, the
specification of AlarmClock (a subclass of Clock, given in Fig. 4) uses two model
fields, one for the current time, which it inherits from Clock, and one for the
alarm time.

   Model fields are especially useful in the specification of Java interfaces, as
interfaces do not contain any concrete representation we can refer to in specifications. We can declare model fields in a Java interface then every class that
implements the interface can define its own represents clause relating this
abstract field to its concrete representation. For a more extensive discussion
of model fields see [CLSE05]. Cok discusses how model fields are treated in
ESC/Java2 [Cok05], while Leino and Müller have recently worked on handling
model fields in the context of verification [LM06].

5   Behavioral Subtyping and Specification Inheritance

JML enforces *behavioral subtyping* [Ame90, DL96, LD00, LW95, LW94, Mey97]:
instances of a given type T must meet the specifications of each of type T's
supertypes. This ensures Liskov's "substitution principle" [Lis88], i.e., it ensures
that using an object of a subclass in a place where an object of the superclass
is expected does not cause any surprises, ensuring that the introduction of new
subclasses does not break any existing code. This idea is also known as supertype
abstraction [Lea90, LW95].

For example, consider the class `AlarmClock` in Fig. 4. Because `AlarmClock` is a subtype of `Clock`, it inherits all the specifications of `Clock`, i.e., all invariants specified for `Clock` also apply to `AlarmClock`, and any (overriding) method in `AlarmClock` has to meet the specification for the corresponding method in `Clock`. For example, the overriding `AlarmClock` method `tick()` has to meet the specification given for it in `Clock`. Note that any methods which are not overridden have to be re-verified, to ensure that they maintain any additional invariants of the subclass. ([RL00] investigates ways to avoid some of this re-verification.)

When it comes to method specifications, behavioral subtyping requires that the specification of an overriding method m must refine that of its supertypes in the sense that whenever a supertype's precondition for m is satisfied, then the supertype's postcondition for m must hold. It follows that the preconditions of an overriding method may only be weaker. Furthermore, whenever an overridden method's precondition is satisfied then the postcondition of the overriding method must imply the postcondition of the overridden method. One way to achieve this is would be to allow a subtype to give a new specification for a method—effectively overriding the one in the supertype—and then prove the necessary refinement relationship. Instead, JML uses the principle of *specification inheritance* for method specifications [DL96]: all specification cases written for an overriding method are "conjoined" (using `also`) with the specification cases of the method(s) being overridden. Specification inheritance guarantees that the overriding method obeys all the inherited specification cases and thus that the method satisfies a refinement of the inherited specifications. This automatically makes all subtypes behavioral subtypes and thus validates the principle of supertype abstraction.

The meaning of specification cases conjoined by `also` can be a bit subtle. However, it is easiest to just keep in mind that all specification cases of all inherited methods have to each be obeyed by a method. If, for a given method, the subtype and supertypes all specify the same precondition and assignable clause, then the conjoined specification will be equivalent to a single specification case whose precondition and assignable clause are the same as in the individual specification cases, and with a postcondition that is the conjunction of the postconditions in the individual specification cases. If different preconditions are given in a sub- and supertype the meaning of the conjoined specification cases is more involved: the precondition of the conjoined specification will effectively be the disjunction of the preconditions from the individual specification cases, and the postcondition of the conjoined specification will effectively be a conjunction of implications, where each precondition (wrapped in `\old()`) implies the corresponding postcondition. This effective postcondition is slightly weaker than the conjunction of the postconditions, since each postcondition only has to apply in case the corresponding precondition was satisfied [DL96].

Before closing this section we point out that the `alarm` field (line 13) and `alarm` parameter (line 15) of the `AlarmClock` class are explicitly declared to be

```
1   class AlarmClock extends Clock {
2     //@ public model int _alarmTime;
3     //@ private represents _alarmTime = alarmMinute*60 + alarmHour*60*60;
4
5     //@ public ghost boolean _alarmOn = false; //@ in _time;
6
7     //@ private invariant 0 <= alarmHour && alarmHour <= 23;
8     private int alarmHour; //@ in _alarmTime;
9
10    //@ private invariant 0 <= alarmMinute && alarmMinute <= 59;
11    private int alarmMinute; //@ in _alarmTime;
12
13    private /*@ non_null @*/ AlarmInterface alarm;
14
15    public /*@ pure @*/ AlarmClock(/*@ non_null @*/ AlarmInterface alarm) {
16      this.alarm = alarm;
17    }
18
19    /*@ requires   0 <= hour && hour <= 23;
20      @ requires   0 <= minute && minute <= 59;
21      @ assignable _alarmTime;
22      @*/
23    public void setAlarmTime(int hour, int minute) {
24      alarmHour = hour;
25      alarmMinute = minute;
26    }
27
28    // spec inherited from superclass Clock
29    public void tick() {
30      super.tick();
31      if (getHour() == alarmHour & getMinute() == alarmMinute & getSecond() == 0) {
32        alarm.on();
33        //@ set _alarmOn = true;
34      }
35      if ((getHour() == alarmHour & getMinute() == alarmMinute+1 & getSecond() == 0) ||
36          (getHour() == alarmHour+1 & alarmMinute == 59 & getSecond() == 0)) {
37        alarm.off();
38        //@ set _alarmOn = false;
39      }
40    }
41  }
```

Fig. 4. Example JML specification illustrating the concepts of specification inheritance and ghost fields

non-null instances of **AlarmInterface**. While this is unnecessary (since declarations of reference types are non-null by default in JML [LCC+05, Cha06]), it is also harmless and can in fact be helpful to JML newcomers. Though we will not have the need in our examples, declarations that may be null must be annotated with the **nullable** modifier.

```
1  public interface AlarmInterface {
2    public void on();
3    public void off();
4  }
```

Fig. 5. Interface of the alarm used in `AlarmClock`

6 Ghost Fields

Like model fields, ghost fields are specification-only fields, so they cannot be referred to by Java code. While a model field provides an abstraction of the existing state, a ghost field can provide some additional state, which may—or may not—be related to the existing state. Unlike a model field, a ghost field can be assigned a value. This is done by a special `set` statement that must be given in a JML annotation. Before we discuss the difference between model and ghost fields in more detail, let us first look at an example of the use of a ghost field.

Suppose that we want to convince ourselves that the implementation of `AlarmClock` will not invoke the method `alarm.on()` twice in a row, or the method `alarm.off()` twice in a row, but that it will always call `alarm.on()` and `alarm.off()` alternately. (One could add JML contracts to `AlarmInterface` to specify this requirement, but we will not consider that here.)

The state of an `AlarmClock` object does not record if the associated `alarm` is ringing or not, nor does it record which method it has last invoked on `alarm`. For the purpose of understanding the behavior of the `AlarmClock`, and possibly capturing this understanding in additional JML annotations, it may be useful to add an extra boolean field to the state that records if the associated alarm is ringing. In Fig. 4, we have declared a boolean ghost field `_alarmRinging`. Two assignments to this field are included in the method `tick()`. The assignments ensure that the field is true when the alarm ringing and false otherwise. A subtle issue here is that `_alarmRinging` has to be included in the datagroup associated with `_time`. This is because—by the principle of specification inheritance—the method `tick()` is only allowed to have side effects on `_time`. Since `tick()` assigns to `_alarmRinging`, the field has to be included in this datagroup. (As was mentioned in Section 3, we could have instead declared `_time` to be in `objectState`, and used `objectState` in the assignable clause of `tick()`. It then would have been more natural to declare `_alarmRinging` to be in `objectState`.)

One can now try to capture the informal requirement that "the alarm will ring for the minute that follows the specified alarm time," by formulating invariants relating the new ghost field `_alarmRinging` to the 'real' state of the `AlarmClock`. There are many ways to express such a relation, for instance using the following as the invariant:

```
_alarmRinging <==> _alarmTime <= _time && _time < alarmTime + 60;
```

Verification by ESC/Java2 will immediately point out that these invariants may be violated, namely by invocations of `setTime` and `setAlarmTime`. This highlights a potential weakness in the implementation: relying on the comparison of the current time and the alarm time in the decision to turn the alarm off might result in unwanted behavior. The alarm could be turned on twice in a row, or turned off twice in a row. Also, the alarm could ring for longer than 60 seconds, if one of these times is changed while the alarm is ringing.

An improvement in the implementation is to count down the number of seconds left until the alarm is disabled and use this count as a basis for switching off the alarm, rather than relying on a comparison of the current time and the alarm time.

```
/** The number of seconds remaining to keep ringing the alarm.
 * If zero, the alarm is silent (off). */
//@ private invariant 0 <= alarmSecondsRemaining &&
//@                        alarmSecondsRemaining <= 60;

/*@ private invariant _alarmRinging
 @                        <==> alarmSecondsRemaining > 0; @*/
private int alarmSecondsRemaining = 0; //@ in _time;
...

public boolean tick() {
  super.tick();
  if (alarmSecondsRemaining > 0) {
    alarmSecondsRemaining--;
    if (alarmSecondsRemaining == 0) {
      alarm.off();
      //@ set _alarmRinging = false;
    }
  } else if (getHour() == alarmHour &
             getMinute() == alarmMinute) {
             alarm.on();
             alarmSecondsRemaining = 60 - getSecond();
             //@ set _alarmRinging = true;
  }
}
```

Now that we have a close correspondence between the ghost field `_alarmRinging` and the field `alarmSecondsRemaining`, one could choose to replace the ghost field by a model field:

```
/*@ public model boolean _alarmRinging; in _time;
 @ private represents _alarmRinging
 @                        <- alarmSecondsRemaining > 0;
 @*/
```

Of course, one could also choose to turn the ghost field into a real field. This would make the implementation simpler to understand.

Ghost vs. model fields. To recap, the crucial difference between a ghost and a model field is that a ghost field extends the state of an object, whereas a model field is an abstraction of the existing state of an object. A ghost field may be assigned to in annotations using the special `set` keywords. A model field cannot be assigned to, but changes value automatically whenever some of the state that it depends on changes, as laid down by the representation relation.

Since ghost fields are only changed by `set` statements, they are only changed under program control. Model fields, however, potentially change their values whenever the concrete fields they depend on change. As Leino and Müller recently noted [LM06], such instantaneous changes to model fields are not necessarily sensible, because the computation of the model fields may assume that various invariants hold.

7   Aliasing

The potential of aliasing is a major complication in program verification, and indeed a major source of bugs in programs. To illustrate the issue, Fig. 6 shows `DigitalDisplayClock`, which uses an integer array `time` of length 6 to represent time (line 13). For the correct functioning of the clock it will be important that this array is not aliased by a field outside of the class. If the array is aliased, code outside of this class could alter `time` and break the invariants for the array [NVP98]. Indeed, the fact that the (private) invariants depends on the array `time` already suggest that the field needs to be alias-protected.

By inspecting the entire code of the class, it is easy to convince oneself that references to this array are not leaked. However, this does not guarantee that a subclass does not introduce ways to leak references to `time`. For example, the subclass `BrokenDigitalDisplayClock` in Fig. 7 breaks the guarantee that `time` will not be aliased.

There has been considerable work on extending programming languages with some form of ownership (also known as confinement). JML includes support for the universe type system [MPHL03] as a way to specify and enforce ownership constraints. As is illustrated in Fig. 6 line 13, the `time` array is declared as a `rep`-field[2] hence forbidding `time` from being aliased outside the object. The typechecker incorporated in the JML compiler will, e.g., warn that the class `BrokenDigitalDisplayClock` in Fig. 7 is not well-typed because it breaks the guarantee that `time` will not be aliased outside this class. Verification with ESC/Java2 does not yet take universes into account and this is still the subject of ongoing work.

---

[2] `rep` is short for representation.

```
1   public class DigitalDisplayClock {
2     //@ public model long _time;
3     //@ private represents _time = getSecond()+getMinute()*60+getHour()*60*60;
4
5     //@ protected invariant time.length == 6;
6     //@ protected invariant 0 <= time[0] && time[0] <= 9; // sec
7     //@ protected invariant 0 <= time[1] && time[1] <= 5; // sec
8     //@ protected invariant 0 <= time[2] && time[2] <= 9; // min
9     //@ protected invariant 0 <= time[3] && time[3] <= 5; // min
10    //@ protected invariant 0 <= time[4] && time[4] <= 9; // hr
11    //@ protected invariant 0 <= time[5] && time[5] <= 2; // hr
12    //@ protected invariant time[5] == 2 ==> time[4] <= 3; // hr
13    protected /*@ non_null rep @*/ int[] time; // NB rep modifier
14    /*@ pure @*/ public DigitalDisplayClock() {
15      { time = new rep int [6]; }   // NB rep modifier
16
17    //@ ensures 0 <= \result && \result <= 23;
18    public /*@ pure @*/ int getHour() { return  time[5]*10 + time[4]; }
19
20    //@ ensures 0 <= \result && \result <= 59;
21    public /*@ pure @*/ int getMinute() { return time[3]*10 + time[2]; }
22
23    //@ ensures 0 <= \result && \result <= 59;
24    public /*@ pure @*/ int getSecond() { return time[1]*10 + time[0]; }
25
26    /*@ requires   0 <= hour && hour <= 23 && 0 <= minute && minute <= 59;
27      @ assignable _time;
28      @ ensures    getHour()==hour && getMinute()==minute && getSecond()==0;
29      @*/
30    public void setTime(int hour, int minute) {
31      time[5] = hour / 10;    time[4] = hour % 10;
32      time[3] = minute % 10;  time[2] = minute % 10;
33      time[1] = 0 ;           time[0] = 0;
34    }
35
36    //@ assignable _time;
37    //@ ensures _time == (\old(_time)+1) % 24*60*60;
38    public void tick() {
39      time[0]++;
40      if (time[0] == 10) { time[0] = 0; time[1]++; }
41      if (time[1] == 6)  { time[1] = 0; time[2]++; } // minute passed
42      if (time[2] == 10) { time[2] = 0; time[3]++; }
43      if (time[3] == 6)  { time[3] = 0; time[4]++; } // hour passed
44      if (time[4] == 10) { time[4] = 0; time[3]++; }
45      if (time[5] == 2 & time[4] == 4)
46        { time[5] = 0; time[4] = 0; } // day passed
47    }
48  }
```

Fig. 6. Clock implementation using an array and the universe type system to ensure that references to this array are not leaked outside the current object

```
1  class BrokenDigitalDisplayClock extends DigitalDisplayClock {
2    //@ requires time.length == 6;
3
4    public BrokenDigitalDisplayClock( /*@ non_null @*/ int[] time) {
5      this.time = time; // illegal!
6    }
7
8    public /*@ pure @*/ int[] expose() { return time; } // illegal!
9  }
```

Fig. 7. A subclass of `DigitalDisplayClock` which breaks encapsulation of the private array `time`, both by its constructor, which imports a potentially aliased reference, and the method `expose`, which exports a reference to `time`

8 Conclusions

Preconditions, postconditions and invariants alone are insufficient to accurately specify object-oriented programs. This paper has illustrated some of the more advanced specification constructs of the JML specification language, notably: frame conditions, datagroups, model and ghost fields, and support for alias control.

A language extension to C# that is similar in purpose and scope to JML is the Spec# specification language [BLS04]. Like JML, Spec# enjoys tool support for runtime checking and static verification, the latter being provided by the Boogie program verifier. Spec# and JML share similar basic and advanced language constructs, although details vary. In particular, Spec# provides a novel methodology to cope with object invariants [BDF+04].

As a final note, we point out that the question of which constructs are necessary and sufficient for the specification of mainstream object-oriented programs is far from settled. Even the semantics for some of the basic, let alone advanced, features discussed in this paper are still the subject of active research as is clear from the references given to very recent work.

Acknowledgments. Thanks to David Cok of Eastman Kodak Company for his comments and feedback on this paper. The work of Joseph Kiniry and Erik Poll is funded in part by the Information Society Technologies programme of the European Commission, Future and Emerging Technologies under the IST-2005-015905 MOBIUS project. The work of Gary Leavens was funded by the US National Science Foundation under grants CCF-0428078 and CCF-0429567. Patrice Chalin was funded in part by the Natural Sciences and Engineering Research Council of Canada under grant 261573-03.

References

[ABB+05]   W. Ahrendt, Th. Baar, B. Beckert, R. Bubel, M. Giese, R. Hähnle, W. Menzel, W. Mostowski, A. Roth, S. Schlager, and P. H. Schmitt. The KeY tool. *Software and System Modeling*, 4:32–54, 2005.

[Ame90]   P. America. Designing an object-oriented language with behavioural subtyping. In J.W. de Bakker, W.P. de Roever, and G. Rozenberg, editors, *Foundations of Object-Oriented Languages*, number 489 in LNCS, pages 60–90. Springer-Verlag, 1990.

[BCC+05]   Lilian Burdy, Yoonsik Cheon, David R. Cok, Michael Ernst, Joseph R. Kiniry, Gary T. Leavens, K. Rustan M. Leino, and Erik Poll. An overview of JML tools and applications. *International Journal on Software Tools for Technology Transfer (STTT)*, 7(3):212–232, 2005.

[BDF+04]   Mike Barnett, Robert DeLine, Manuel Fähndrich, K. Rustan M. Leino, and Wolfram Schulte. Verification of object-oriented programs with invariants. *Journal of Object Technology*, 3(6):27–56, 2004.

[BFMW01]   D. Bartetzko, C. Fischer, M. Möller, and H. Wehrheim. Jass — Java with assertions. In *Workshop on Runtime Verification at CAV'01*, 2001. Published in *ENTCS*, K. Havelund and G. Rosu (eds.), 55(2), 2001.

[BJ01]   Joachim van den Berg and Bart Jacobs. The LOOP compiler for Java and JML. In T. Margaria and W. Yi, editors, *TACAS'01*, number 2031 in Lecture Notes in Computer Science, pages 299–312. Springer-Verlag, 2001.

[BLS04]   Mike Barnett, K. Rustan M. Leino, and Wolfram Schulte. The Spec# programming system: An overview. In *Construction and Analysis of Safe, Secure and Interoperable Smart devices (CASSIS)*, volume 3362 of *Lecture Notes in Computer Science*, pages 49–69. Springer-Verlag, 2004.

[BMR95]   Alex Borgida, John Mylopoulos, and Raymond Reiter. On the frame problem in procedure specifications. *IEEE Transactions on Software Engineering*, 21(10):785–798, October 1995.

[BRL03]   Lilian Burdy, Antoine Requet, and Jean-Louis Lanet. Java applet correctness: A developer-oriented approach. In D. Mandrioli K. Araki, S. Gnesi, editor, *FME 2003*, volume 2805 of *Lecture Notes in Computer Science*, pages 422–439. Springer-Verlag, 2003.

[BSS04]   Mike Barnett, David A. Naumann Wolfram Schulte, and Qi Sun. 99.44% pure: Useful abstractions in specification. In *Formal Techniques for Java-like Programs (FTfJP'2004)*, pages 11–19, May 2004. http://www.cs.ru.nl/ftfjp/2004/Purity.pdf.

[Cha06]   Patrice Chalin. Towards support for non-null types and non-null-by-default in Java. In *Formal Techniques for Java-like Programs (FTfJP)*, 2006. To appear.

[CK04]   David R. Cok and Joseph R. Kiniry. ESC/Java2: Uniting ESC/Java and JML. Technical report, University of Nijmegen, 2004. NIII Technical Report NIII-R0413.

[CL02]   Yoonsik Cheon and Gary T. Leavens. A runtime assertion checker for the Java Modeling Language (JML). In Hamid R. Arabnia and Youngsong Mun, editors, *the International Conference on Software Engineering Research and Practice (SERP '02)*, pages 322–328. CSREA Press, June 2002.

[CLSE05]   Yoonsik Cheon, Gary T. Leavens, Murali Sitaraman, and Stephen Edwards. Model variables: Cleanly supporting abstraction in design by contract. *Software:Practice and Experience*, 35(6):583–599, May 2005.

[Cok05]   David R. Cok. Reasoning with specifications containing method calls in JML. *Journal of Object Technology*, 4(8):77–103, 2005.

[DL96]   Krishna Kishore Dhara and Gary T. Leavens. Forcing behavioral subtyp-
             ing through specification inheritance. In *18th International Conference
             on Software Engineering*, pages 258–267. IEEE Computer Society Press,
             1996.

[DM05]   Á. Darvas and P. Müller. Reasoning about method calls in JML Specifi-
             cations. In *Formal Techniques for Java-like Programs (FTfJP)*, 2005.

[HK00]   K. Huizing and R. Kuiper. Verification of object-oriented programs us-
             ing class invariants. In E. Maibaum, editor, *Fundamental Approaches to
             Software Engineering*, volume 1783 of *Lecture Notes in Computer Science*,
             pages 208–221. Springer-Verlag, 2000.

[Hoa69]   C.A.R. Hoare. An axiomatic basis for computer programming. *Commu-
             nications of the ACM*, 12(10):576–583, October 1969.

[Hoa72]   C.A.R. Hoare. Proof of correctness of data representations. *Acta Infor-
             matica*, 1(4):271–281, 1972.

[JLPS05]   Bart Jacobs, K. Rustan M. Leino, Frank Piessens, and Wolfram Schulte.
             Safe concurrency for aggregate objects with invariants. In *IEEE Interna-
             tional Conference on Software Engineering (SEFM 2005)*, pages 137–147.
             IEEE Computer Society, 2005.

[Jon03]   Cliff B. Jones. The early search for tractable ways of reasoning about
             programs. *IEEE Annals of the History of Computing*, 25(2):26–49, 2003.

[LBR06]   Gary T. Leavens, Albert L. Baker, and Clyde Ruby. Preliminary design
             of JML: A behavioral interface specification language for Java. Technical
             Report 98-06-rev29, Iowa State University, Department of Computer Sci-
             ence, January 2006. To appear in *ACM SIGSOFT Software Engineering
             Notes*.

[LC05]   Gary T. Leavens and Yoonsik Cheon. Design by Contract with JML.
             Draft, available from jmlspecs.org., 2005.

[LCC⁺05]   Gary T. Leavens, Yoonsik Cheon, Curtis Clifton, Clyde Ruby, and
             David R. Cok. How the design of JML accommodates both runtime asser-
             tion checking and formal verification. *Science of Computer Programming*,
             55(1–3):185–208, March 2005.

[LD00]   Gary T. Leavens and Krishna Kishore Dhara. Concepts of behav-
             ioral subtyping and a sketch of their extension to component-based sys-
             tems. In Gary T. Leavens and Murali Sitaraman, editors, *Foundations
             of Component-Based Systems*, chapter 6, pages 113–135. Cambridge Uni-
             versity Press, 2000.

[Lea90]   Gary T. Leavens. Modular verification of object-oriented programs
             with subtypes. Technical Report 90–09, Department of Computer Sci-
             ence, Iowa State University, Ames, Iowa, 50011, July 1990. Available
             by anonymous ftp from `ftp.cs.iastate.edu`, and by e-mail from al-
             manac@cs.iastate.edu.

[Lei98]   K. Rustan M. Leino. Data groups: Specifying the modification of extended
             state. In *OOPSLA '98 Conference Proceedings*, volume 33(10) of *ACM
             SIGPLAN Notices*, pages 144–153. ACM, October 1998.

[LG01]   Barbara Liskov and John Guttag. *Program Development in Java*. The
             MIT Press, Cambridge, Mass., 2001.

[Lis88]   Barbara Liskov. Data abstraction and hierarchy. *ACM SIGPLAN Notices*,
             23(5):17–34, May 1988. Revised version of the keynote address given at
             OOPSLA '87.

[LM06]   K. Rustan M. Leino and Peter Müller. A verification methodology
            for model fields. In *ESOP'2006*, Lecture Notes in Computer Science.
            Springer-Verlag, 2006. To appear.

[LPC+06]   Gary T. Leavens, Erik Poll, Curtis Clifton, Yoonsik Cheon, Clyde Ruby,
            David R. Cok, Peter Müller, Joseph R. Kiniry, and Patrice Chalin. JML
            Reference Manual. Department of Computer Science, Iowa State Univer-
            sity. Available from http://www.jmlspecs.org, January 2006.

[LW94]   Barbara Liskov and Jeannette Wing. A behavioral notion of subtyping.
            ACM Transactions on Programming Languages and Systems, 16(6):1811–
            1841, November 1994.

[LW95]   Gary T. Leavens and William E. Weihl. Specification and verification of
            object-oriented programs using supertype abstraction. *Acta Informatica*,
            32(8):705–778, November 1995.

[Mey92]   Bertrand Meyer. Applying "Design by Contract". *Computer*, 25(10):40–
            51, October 1992.

[Mey97]   Bertrand Meyer. *Object-oriented Software Construction*. Prentice Hall,
            New York, NY, second edition, 1997.

[MHKL05]   Ronald Middelkoop, Cornelis Huizing, Ruurd Kuiper, and Erik Luit.
            Cooperation-based invariants for OO languages. In *Proceedings of
            the International Workshop on Formal Aspects of Component Software
            (FACS'05)*, 2005.

[MM02]   Richard Mitchell and Jim McKim. *Design by Contract by Example*.
            Addison-Wesley, Indianapolis, IN, 2002.

[Mor94]   Carroll Morgan. *Programming from Specifications: Second Edition*. Pren-
            tice Hall International, Hempstead, UK, 1994.

[MPH00]   J. Meyer and A. Poetzsch-Heffter. An architecture for interactive program
            provers. In S. Graf and M. Schwartzbach, editors, *Tools and Algorithms
            for the Construction and Analysis of Systems*, volume 1785 of *LNCS*,
            pages 63–77. Springer-Verlag, 2000.

[MPHL03]   Peter Müller, Arnd Poetzsch-Heffter, and Gary T. Leavens. Modular spec-
            ification of frame properties in JML. *Concurrency, Computation Practice
            and Experience.*, 15:117–154, 2003.

[MPHL05]   Peter Müller, Arnd Poetzsch-Heffter, and Gary T. Leavens. Modular in-
            variants for layered object structures. Technical Report 424, ETH Zurich,
            March 2005.

[MPMU04]   C. Marché, C. Paulin-Mohring, and X. Urbain. The KRAKATOA tool for
            certification of Java/JavaCard programs annotated in JML. *Journal of
            Logic and Algebraic Programming*, 58(1–2):89–106, 2004.

[Nau05]   David A. Naumann. Observational purity and encapsulation. In *Fun-
            damental Aspects of Software Engineering (FASE)*, 2005. Obtained from
            the author.

[NVP98]   James Noble, Jan Vitek, and John Potter. Flexible alias protection. In
            Eric Jul, editor, *ECOOP '98 – Object-Oriented Programming, 12th Eu-
            ropean Conference, Brussels, Belgium*, volume 1445 of *Lecture Notes in
            Computer Science*, pages 158–185. Springer-Verlag, July 1998.

[PH97]   Arnd Poetzsch-Heffter. Specification and verification of object-oriented
            programs. Habilitation thesis, Technical University of Munich, January
            1997.

[RL00]   Clyde Ruby and Gary T. Leavens. Safely creating correct subclasses without seeing superclass code. In *OOPSLA 2000 Conference on Object-Oriented Programming, Systems, Languages, and Applications, Minneapolis, Minnesota*, volume 35(10) of *ACM SIGPLAN Notices*, pages 208–228, October 2000.

[Ros92]   D. S. Rosenblum. Towards a method of programming with assertions. In *Proceedings of the 14th International Conference on Software Engineering*, pages 92–104, May 1992.

[Ros95]   David S. Rosenblum. A practical approach to programming with assertions. *IEEE Transactions on Software Engineering*, 21(1):19–31, January 1995.

[Szy98]   C. Szyperski. *Component Software*. Addison-Wesley, 1998.

[Win90]   Jeannette M. Wing. A specifier's introduction to formal methods. *Computer*, 23(9):8–24, September 1990.

Boogie: A Modular Reusable Verifier for Object-Oriented Programs

Mike Barnett[1], Bor-Yuh Evan Chang[2], Robert DeLine[1],
Bart Jacobs[3], and K. Rustan M. Leino[1]

[1] Microsoft Research, Redmond, Washington, USA
{mbarnett, rdeline, leino}@microsoft.com
[2] University of California, Berkeley, California, USA
bec@cs.berkeley.edu
[3] Katholieke Universiteit Leuven, Belgium
bartj@cs.kuleuven.be

Abstract. A program verifier is a complex system that uses compiler
technology, program semantics, property inference, verification-condition
generation, automatic decision procedures, and a user interface. This
paper describes the architecture of a state-of-the-art program verifier for
object-oriented programs.

1 Introduction

A program verifier is built from a number of complex pieces of technology: a
source programming language, its usage rules and formal semantics, a logical
encoding suitable for automatic reasoning, abstract domains for program analysis and property inference, decision procedures for discharging proof obligations,
and a user interface that lets a user understand the results of the verification
process. Dealing with these complexities, like other software engineering problems, requires a modular architecture with well established interface boundaries.

In this paper, we describe the architecture of Boogie, a state-of-the-art
program verifier for verifying Spec# programs in the object-oriented .NET
framework. Internally, Boogie is structured as a pipeline performing a series
of transformations from the source program to a verification condition (VC) to
an error report (see Fig. 1). The novel aspects of the Boogie architecture include
the following:

1. *Design-Time Feedback.* Boogie (together with the Spec# compiler) is integrated with Microsoft Visual Studio to provide design-time feedback in the
   form of red underlinings that highlight not only syntax and typing errors
   but also semantic errors like precondition violations.
2. *Distinct Proof Obligation Generation and Verification Phases.* The Boogie
   pipeline is centered around intermediate representations in BoogiePL [DL05],
   a language tailored for expressing proof obligations and assumptions (Sec. 4).
   BoogiePL serves a critical role in separating the generation of proof obligations from the semantic encoding of the source program and the proving

F.S. de Boer et al. (Eds.): FMCO 2005, LNCS 4111, pp. 364–387, 2006.

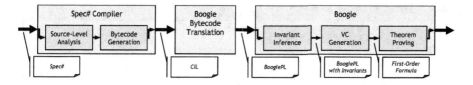

Fig. 1. The Boogie pipeline

of those obligations. This separation has been critical in the simultaneous development of the object-oriented program verification methodology and the core verification technology.

3. *Abstract Interpretation and Verification Condition Generation.* Boogie performs loop-invariant inference using abstract interpretation (Sec. 6) and generates verification conditions to be passed (Sec. 7) to an automatic theorem prover. This combination allows Boogie to utilize both the precision of verification condition generation (that must necessarily be lost in an abstraction) and the inductive invariant inference of abstract interpretation (that simply cannot be obtained with a concrete model).

2   Overview

In this introductory section, we give an overview of Boogie's architecture. The rest of the paper provides more details of each architectural component.

Source Language. The Spec# language is a superset of C#, adding specification features (i.e., *contracts*) such as pre- and postconditions and object invariants [BLS04]. Spec# prescribes static type checks beyond those prescribed by C# and introduces dynamic checks for the specified contracts. The compiler performs the static type checking and emits the dynamic checks as part of the target code. Boogie makes use of the type properties enforced by the compiler and attempts statically to prove that the dynamic checks will always succeed. Boogie thus checks for error conditions defined by the virtual machine, such as array bounds errors and type cast errors, and error conditions specified by user supplied contracts, such as precondition violations. To ensure soundness of the verification, Boogie additionally checks for error conditions defined by the programming methodology [BDF+04, LM04, BN04, LM05, LM06].

As depicted in Fig. 1, Spec# programs are compiled into CIL, the executable format of the .NET virtual machine. Boogie starts with an abstract syntax tree (AST) for this CIL, which it either gets directly from the compiler or reconstructs from reading a compiled .dll or .exe file. The latter is the more conventional mode of a program verifier and allows batch processing. The former allows Boogie to run as part of compilation, which enables a clean integration with Microsoft Visual Studio to provide design time feedback. This feedback shows up as red underlinings (fondly known as "red squigglies") in the program text, and the user can get further information by rolling the cursor over these underlinings,

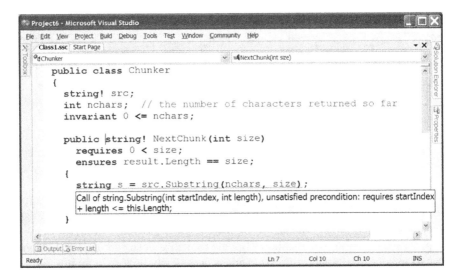

Fig. 2. Design time feedback of verification errors within Microsoft Visual Studio 2005. The red squiggly under the call to *Substring* indicates an error. The hover text shows the error to be a precondition violation.

which brings up some hover text that explains the problem (as shown in Fig. 2). To our knowledge, Boogie is the first program verifier to provide such interactive design-time feedback.

Intermediate Language. The generation of verification conditions from source code involves a great number of verifier design decisions. By staging this process by first translating CIL into BoogiePL, the Boogie architecture separates the concerns of deciding how to encode source language features and their usage rules from the concerns of how to reason about control flow in the program. BoogiePL provides **assert** statements that encode proof obligations stemming from the source program, to be checked by the program verifier, and **assume** statements that encode properties guaranteed by the source language and verification process, available for use in the proof by the program verifier. The architectural layering of verification condition generation via an intermediate program notation was used by ESC/Modula-3 [DLNS98] (cf. [Lei95]), which made use of *guarded commands* whose semantics is given by *weakest preconditions* [Dij76]. This architecture was sharpened by ESC/Java [FLL+02], which defined and staged the translation further [LSS99].

Verification condition generation involves not just the executable program statements in the source language, but also other declarations of the source program and properties guaranteed by the source language. In the aforementioned ESC tools, the logical encoding of these additional properties, called the *background predicate*, was produced separately from the intermediate program notation and fed directly to the theorem prover. BoogiePL innovates further by allowing the background predicate to be encoded as part of the intermediate program. That is, BoogiePL includes declarations for mathematical functions and axioms. Consequently, the translation of CIL culminates in a BoogiePL program that encodes the entire proof task—in fact, properties of Spec# and the source program are no longer used after this point in Boogie's pipeline, except when mapping errors back to line numbers in the source text.

Like other languages, BoogiePL can be printed as and parsed from a textual representation. This feature has been the most important vehicle in debugging and experimenting with our semantic encoding of Spec#. For example, it is often convenient to manually perform small changes to the BoogiePL program without having to modify the Spec# compiler and/or the bytecode translator.

This strong interface boundary between the bytecode translation and the rest of Boogie's pipeline also makes it possible for other program verifiers to reuse Boogie's VC generation, simply by encoding their proof obligations as BoogiePL programs. As such, BoogiePL can also be viewed as a high-level front-end to a theorem prover.

Inferred Properties. BoogiePL programs are turned into first-order verification conditions, a process which requires loop invariants. While these can come from the source programs, many loop invariants can be "boring" or "obvious" to the programmer, in which case the task of manually supplying these is onerous and having them as part of the source text provides more clutter than insight. Sometimes, the loop invariants are even impossible to express in the source language, as is the case when the invariant needs to refer to variables or functions of the BoogiePL encoding of the source program. Therefore, Boogie includes a framework for abstract interpretation [CC77], which can infer loop invariants of the BoogiePL program. These inferred invariants are inserted as **assume** statements into the loop heads of the BoogiePL program, so that they can be assumed by the VC to hold at the start of each loop iteration.

To modularly combine abstract domains and to support the use of object references that dereference the heap in the source program, Boogie innovates by connecting its abstract domains to a special abstract domain that, essentially, symbolically names locations in the heap, names that then are used by the other abstract domains [CL05].

Verification Conditions. After generating loop invariants, Boogie generates verification conditions from the resulting BoogiePL program. There are many logically equivalent ways of expressing the verification conditions, and which way is chosen can have a dramatic impact on the performance of the underlying theorem prover. Boogie performs a series of transformations on the program, essentially producing one snippet of the verification condition from each basic block of the BoogiePL procedure implementation being verified [BL05]. The verification condition is represented as a formula in first-order logic and arithmetic. It is then passed to a first-order automated theorem prover to determine the validity of the verification condition (and thus the correctness of the program).

```
public class Example {
  int x;
  string! s;
  invariant s.Length >= 12;

  public Example(int y) requires y > 0; { ... }
  public static void M(int n) {
    Example e = new Example(100/n);
    int k = e.s.Length;
    for (int i = 0; i < n; i++) { e.x += i; }
    assert k == e.s.Length;
  }
}
```

Fig. 3. An example Spec# class. Its BoogiePL translation is shown in Fig. 4.

The verification conditions are encoded in such a way as to make it possible to reconstruct from a failed proof an error trace (i.e., an execution path through the procedure leading to a proof obligation that the theorem prover is unable to establish [LMS05]). The bytecode translator performs enough bookkeeping to map the BoogiePL error trace back into a Spec# error trace, much like a compiler performs enough bookkeeping for a source-level debugger to operate from compiled code. Typically, a failed proof indicates an error in the program or some missing condition in a contract, but due to incompleteness in the theorem prover, there is also the possibility of spurious error reports. If the theorem prover runs out of some limited resource, such as the allotted time or space, that event is reported.

Theorem Prover. Boogie can generate verification conditions for the off-the-shelf theorem prover Simplify [DNS05], as well as for Zap [BLM05], a set of decision procedures developed at Microsoft Research. At the moment, most of our Boogie experience has been with Simplify, but we expect to shift our use toward Zap. The Boogie architecture makes it fairly easy to retarget the final step of the VC generation to a new theorem prover.

3   Spec#

Figure 3 shows a synthetic example program to highlight some of the features of Spec#; a more detailed introduction is found in the Spec# overview paper [BLS04]. The example shows one class, called *Example*, which contains two fields, an object invariant, a con-

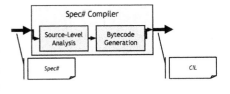

structor, and a method. The body of the method allocates a new *Example* object. The actual argument to the constructor, $100/n$, contains a potential division-by-zero error. The loop repeatedly increments the x field of the newly allocated object by various amounts. The code also saves the length of the string $e.s$ and later checks, using an assert statement, that it is unchanged by the loop.

Spec# incorporates a non-null type system [FL03]; the type string! means the field s can never hold the value null. We have found this to be the most common specification in object-oriented programming.

The Spec# compiler generates standard .NET assemblies. A .NET assembly contains bytecode in the form of method bodies within type definitions and *meta-data* for describing extra-runtime features of the types and their members. The meta-data format allows *custom attributes*, which are arbitrary user-defined data that we use to encode specifications. Due to the limitations of the meta-data format, we persist specifications as *serialized ASTs*. We use the same meta-data format to store *out-of-band* specifications. These are Spec# specifications for types and methods that are already defined in third-party assemblies. For instance, the Spec# distribution [Spe06] provides out-of-band contracts for the two most central assemblies in the .NET Base Class Library (BCL), mscorlib.dll and System.dll. Both the Spec# compiler and Boogie have the ability to weave together an assembly and its out-of-band specification so that it appears as if the contracts were natively present in the original assembly. One of the key benefits is that client code, which generally is heavily dependent on the BCL, receives warnings/errors related to incorrect usage of the library APIs. This feature has been critical in obtaining a usable development system with contracts.

4   BoogiePL

BoogiePL [DL05] is an effective intermediate language for verification condition generation of object-oriented programs because it lacks the complexities of a full-featured object-oriented programming language, while also introducing features of the target logic. As a result, it distributes the complexity of verification condition generation over two well-defined phases, each of which is significantly less complex than the whole. Compared with Spec#, BoogiePL retains the following features: procedures (but not methods), mutable variables, and pre- and postconditions. On the other hand, it lacks the following complications: expressions with side effects, a heap with objects, classes and interfaces, call-by-reference parameter passing, and structured control-flow. It introduces the following features for modeling: constants, function symbols, axioms, non-deterministic control-flow, and the notion of "going wrong".

Figure 4 shows the translation of the Spec# example given in Fig. 3. While we give details on how this translation is obtained in Sec. 5, we observe some salient features of BoogiePL here. BoogiePL looks somewhat like a high-level assembly language in that the control-flow is unstructured but the notions of statically-scoped locals and procedural abstraction are retained; however, intraprocedural control-flow is given by a non-deterministic **goto**. Also, observe that the heap has been made explicit with the global variable *Heap* and similarly the implicit receiver object of the method is now an explicit parameter *this*.

const *System.Object* : **name**;
const *Example* : **name**;
axiom *Example* <: *System.Object*;
function *typeof*(*obj* : **ref**) **returns** (*class* : **name**);

const *allocated* : **name**;
const *Example.x* : **name**;
const *Example.s* : **name**;

var *Heap* : [**ref**, **name**]**any**;

function *StringLength*(*s* : **ref**) **returns** (*len* : **int**);

procedure *Example..ctor*(*this* : **ref**, *y* : **int**);
   requires ... ∧ *y* > 0;   **modifies** *Heap*;   **ensures** ...;

procedure *Example.M*(*n* : **int**);
   requires ...;   **modifies** *Heap*;   **ensures** ...;

implementation *Example.M*(*n* : **int**)
{
   var *e* : **ref** **where** *e* = **null** ∨ *typeof*(*e*) <: *Example*;
   var *k* : **int**, *i* : **int**, *tmp* : **int**, *PreLoopHeap* : [**ref**, **name**]**any**;

   Start :
      assert *n* ≠ 0;
      tmp := 100/*n*;
      havoc *e*;
      assume *e* ≠ **null** ∧ *typeof*(*e*) = *Example* ∧ *Heap*[*e*, *allocated*] = **false**;
      Heap[*e*, *allocated*] := **true**;
      call *Example..ctor*(*e*, *tmp*);

      assert *e* ≠ **null**; *k* := *StringLength*(**cast**(*Heap*[*e*, *Example.s*], **ref**));
      i := 0;
      PreLoopHeap := *Heap*;
      goto *LoopHead*;

   LoopHead :
      goto *LoopBody*, *AfterLoop* :

   LoopBody :
      assume *i* < *n*;
      assert *e* ≠ **null**;
      Heap[*e*, *Example.x*] := **cast**(*Heap*[*e*, *Example.x*], **int**) + *i*;
      i := *i* + 1;
      goto *LoopHead*;

   AfterLoop :
      assume ¬(*i* < *n*);
      assert *e* ≠ **null**; **assert** *k* = *StringLength*(**cast**(*Heap*[*e*, *Example.s*], **ref**));
      return;
}

Fig. 4. A simplified version of the BoogiePL resulting from translation of the *Example* class in Fig. 3. The *Length* property of strings is translated specially as a BoogiePL function. The local variable *PreLoopHeap*, which stores a copy of the entire heap, is later used by the invariant inference.

A BoogiePL *program* consists of a *theory* that is used to encode the semantics of the source language, followed by an *imperative part*. We show the abstract syntax for BoogiePL; for punctuation and other concrete details, see [DL05].

$$program ::= typedecl^* \; symboldecl^* \; axiom^* \; vardeclstmt^* \; proc^* \; impl^*$$

We use the meta-level symbols $*, ^+, ^?$ to indicate a sequence, a nonempty sequence, and an optional syntactic entity, respectively, use | for alternatives, and use $\langle \cdot \rangle$ for grouping.

A theory consists of *type declarations*, *symbol declarations*, and *axioms*.

$typedecl ::= $ **type** *typename* ;
$symboldecl ::= constdecl \mid functiondecl$
$constdecl ::= $ **const** *var* : *type* ;
$type ::= $ **bool** | **int** | **ref** | **name** | **any** | *typename* | *arraytype*
$arraytype ::= [\; type \; , \; type \;] \; type$
$functiondecl ::= $ **function** *function* (*type**) **returns** (*type*) ;
$axiom ::= $ **axiom** *expr* ;

BoogiePL has types and the type checker enforces that every expression is properly typed. However, all type information is erased during the translation into verification conditions. The reason for having the types is to improve readability by expressing intent and to catch simple errors. However, any expression may be cast to type **any** and thence to any other type; just as types are erased in verification conditions, so are casts. In addition to built-in types like **bool** and **int**, BoogiePL supports user-defined types (*typename*) and arrays (*arraytype*). The types used to index into arrays can be any types, not just integers (we might therefore have called arrays maps). For brevity, we show only 2-dimensional arrays.

BoogiePL's expressions include boolean, reference, and integer literals and arithmetic and first-order logical operators:

$expr ::= literal \mid var \mid unop \; expr \mid expr \; binop \; expr \mid expr \; [\; expr \; , \; expr \;]$
$\qquad \mid funapp \mid quant \mid $ **cast** (*expr* , *type*) | **old** (*expr*)
$literal ::= $ **false** | **true** | **null** | *integer*
$binop ::= \Leftrightarrow \mid \Rightarrow \mid \vee \mid \wedge \mid <: \mid \leqslant \mid < \mid \neq \mid = \mid + \mid - \mid * \mid / \mid \%$
$unop ::= - \mid \neg$
$funapp ::= function \; (\; expr^* \;)$
$quant ::= (\forall \; vardecl^* \; trigger^* \; \bullet \; expr \;) \mid (\exists \; vardecl^* \; trigger^* \; \bullet \; expr \;)$
$vardecl ::= var : type \; \langle $**where** $expr \rangle^?$
$trigger ::= \{ \; expr^+ \; \}$

For use in procedure postconditions and implementations, the expression **old**(E) refers to the value of E in the procedure's pre-state. The **where** clause in a variable declaration postulates a unary constraint on the variable's value (like a type qualifier). Triggers are for use by the underlying theorem prover in deciding how to instantiate universal quantifiers [DNS05].

The imperative part of a BoogiePL program consists of global variable declarations, procedure headers (*procedures*), and procedure implementations (*implementations*).

$vardeclstmt ::= \textbf{var}\ vardecl^*\ ;$
$proc ::= \textbf{procedure}\ procname\ (\ vardecl^*\ )\ \langle\textbf{returns}\ (\ vardecl^*\ )\rangle^?$
$\quad \langle\textbf{free}^?\ \textbf{requires}\ expr\ ;\rangle^*\ \langle\textbf{modifies}\ var^*\ ;\rangle^*\ \langle\textbf{free}^?\ \textbf{ensures}\ expr\ ;\rangle^*$
$\quad implbody^?$
$impl ::= \textbf{implementation}\ procname\ (\ vardecl^*\ )\ \langle\textbf{returns}\ (\ vardecl^*\ )\rangle^?$
$\quad implbody$
$block ::= label:\ cmd^*\ transfercmd$
$implbody ::= \{\ vardeclstmt\ block^+\ \}$

As a syntactic sugar, a procedure header can have an optional implementation body, which has the same effect as an implementation declaration with the same name. While many languages have named out-parameters and an anonymous return value, BoogiePL simply allows multiple return values; they are all named as out-parameters in the **returns** clause.

An implementation body consists of a sequence of local variable declarations, followed by a sequence of *blocks*. An implementation starts at the block listed first, in a state where the procedure's preconditions hold and where global and local variables and in-parameters have values that satisfy their respective **where** clauses.

A block has a label and a sequence of commands, followed by a control transfer command.

$cmd ::= passive\ |\ assign\ |\ call$
$passive ::= \textbf{assert}\ expr\ ;\ |\ \textbf{assume}\ expr\ ;$
$assign ::= \textbf{var}\ \langle[expr\ ,\ expr\ ]\rangle^?\ :=\ expr\ ;\ |\ \textbf{havoc}\ var^+\ ;$
$call ::= \textbf{call}\ var^*\ :=\ procname\ (\ expr^*\ )\ ;$
$transfercmd ::= \textbf{goto}\ label^+\ ;\ |\ \textbf{return}\ ;$

The **assert** and **assume** commands indicate conditions to be checked or used, respectively, in the verification. If the given expression evaluates to **true**, then each of these commands proceeds like a no-op. If the condition evaluates to **false**, the assert command *goes wrong*, which is a terminal failure. For the assume command, if the condition evaluates to **false**, one is freed of all subsequent proof obligations, thus indicating a terminal success. The assume command, which is known as a *partial command* [Nel89] or *miracle* (cf. [BvW98]), is a crucial ingredient when encoding verification problems as programs (cf. [Lei95]). The **havoc** command assigns an arbitrary value to each indicated variable; when present, the variable's **where** clause constrains this value. The **goto** command jumps non-deterministically to one of the indicated blocks. The **return** command ends the implementation. It goes wrong if the procedure's non-**free** postconditions are not satisfied; otherwise, the procedure implementation terminates successfully.

The **call** command is defined in terms of the specification of the procedure being called. It goes wrong if the procedure's non-**free** preconditions do not hold.

Otherwise, the state after the **call** command satisfies the procedure's postconditions and the **where** clauses of the procedure's out-parameters. Specifically, it is not assumed that the procedure implementation that gets executed is one of the implementations declared in the program.

Free pre- and postconditions, like **where** clauses, are used for encoding properties guaranteed by the source language. For the most part, these features are just for convenience, because they encapsulate the many assumptions that would otherwise have to be sprinkled in many places. However, in the VC generation for loops (see Sec. 7), **where** clauses are essential for maintaining enough information about loop targets.

5   Translating CIL to BoogiePL Programs

In this section, we describe some key issues and design choices for the bytecode translator. These issues include encoding the heap, allocation, and fields, axiomatizing the Spec# type system, translating call-by-reference parameters, translating methods and method calls, and generating frame conditions.

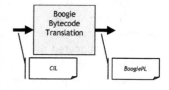

The bytecode translator first transforms a method body, consisting of CIL instructions, into a *normalized AST*, which is essentially an enriched object model that augments CIL with contract features: non-null type annotations, **assert** and **assume** statements, loop invariants, method contracts, object invariants, and various custom attributes for the programming methodology. In a normalized AST, as in CIL, a method body contains no structured programming constructs such as **if** statements or **while** statements. Rather, a method body contains a sequence of labeled blocks, each of which contains a sequence of statements, some of which may be conditional or unconditional branch statements that specify the label of the target block.

One of the differences between a normalized AST and BoogiePL is that in the former, a statement may contain expressions that may have side effects and that may go wrong (such as method calls). For this reason, Boogie transforms the normalized AST into a *flattened AST*, where the values of expressions are assigned to evaluation stack slots and only evaluation stack slots appear as operands of expressions and statements. A flattened AST is suitable for walking the sequence of statements and generating BoogiePL commands based on the kind of statement, though we do need a dataflow analysis to provide some flow-sensitive contextual information necessary for the translation of some statements.

In addition to inferring the CIL type of each local variable and evaluation stack slot, the analysis attempts to track the following information:

- managed pointers (i.e., reference parameters or arguments for reference parameters or the pointers used when dealing with structs)
- method pointers (which appear when creating a delegate instance)

- type tokens and *System.Type* objects (which appear when reflecting over types)
- booleans (for which CIL code uses integers)

Encoding the Heap, Allocation, and Fields. Recall that BoogiePL has no built-in notion of a heap, object allocation, or fields. The translation models the heap as a BoogiePL global two-dimensional array, named *Heap*, that maps an object reference o and a field name f to the current value of $o.f$ (as shown in Fig. 4) [Bur72]. Field names encountered during translation are emitted as unique constants, whose names are qualified by the name of the declaring class. We use a 2-dimensional heap [PH97] rather than one 1-dimensional "heap" per field (cf. [DLNS98, Lei95]), because the encoding of our modular verification methodology quantifies over field names (see frame conditions below).

Object allocation is modeled by adding an extra boolean field called allocated to each object, which indicates whether the object has been allocated. Allocating an object consists of choosing an object that has not yet been allocated and setting its allocated bit, see Fig. 4 (cf. [HW73, DLNS98, Lei95]). In managed code like Spec#, all objects reachable from the program are allocated. This property is important for proving that newly allocated objects are distinct from previously allocated objects, which is crucial for reasoning about object state updates. Allocatedness information is emitted in the form of procedure preconditions, frame conditions, and loop invariants, as well as axioms that state that objects reachable from allocated objects are allocated (cf. [LN02]). This statement is complicated somewhat by the fact that a path between two objects may pass through one or more structs.

Static fields are stored in the heap, just like instance fields. In particular, fields are translated as follows:

$o.f$ translates to $Heap[o, C\_f]$
$C.g$ translates to $Heap[\text{TypeObject}(C), C\_g]$

where fields f and g are declared by class C and o is an expression of type C. A major advantage of storing static fields in the heap as opposed to, for example, separate global variables, is that one frame condition can govern both static and instance fields. It also allows a more uniform treatment of both kinds of fields by the modular verification methodology.

Axiomatizing the Spec# Type System. In order to model the semantics of Spec# type tests and typecasts, an axiomatization of the subtype relation on reference types is required. This axiomatization additionally helps in deriving object distinctness results, which reduces the number of inequalities that users need to include in method contracts, object invariants, loop invariants, etc.

It turns out to be a challenge to author a type axiomatization that is queried efficiently by our theorem prover, so we are considering adding a decision procedure specifically for this purpose. Unfortunately, this choice would probably require that BoogiePL be made aware of the Spec# type system.

Translating Call-By-Reference Parameters. Both C# and Spec# support call-by-reference argument passing (reference parameters are marked **ref**). A call-by-reference parameter of type T takes as an argument not a value of type T but a pointer to a variable of type T. Accesses to the parameter are thus dereferences of the pointer.

BoogiePL does not support call-by-reference parameters directly. Since it does support both in- and out-parameters, we model reference parameters by performing copy-in/copy-out for the purposes of verification. In the Spec# program, when a variable x is passed as an argument to a reference parameter p, then in the BoogiePL program the value of x is passed as an argument to an in-parameter. At the start of the body of the callee, the in-parameter is copied into a local variable. Accesses to p in the Spec# program are translated into accesses of the local variable in the BoogiePL program. When the procedure completes, the local variable is copied into an out-parameter and at the call site the out-parameter is copied back into x.

Translating from IL introduces a snag: accesses to reference parameters appear as pointer dereferences, and the pointers being dereferenced are read from the parameter in some preceding instruction. As a result, it is impossible to tell by looking at the instruction itself which reference parameter is being referred to. This problem is solved by the bytecode translator's dataflow analysis mentioned above.

Using copy-in/copy-out is sound only if there is no aliasing amongst the actual arguments for reference parameters. Therefore, we disallow such aliasing in Spec#. (This is not yet implemented in the compiler, but we intend to impose enough restrictions on actual arguments that a simple syntactic check suffices to forbid such aliasing, cf. [Rey78].)

Translating Methods and Method Calls. For each declaration of a method or method override, the bytecode translation generates a BoogiePL procedure. For each method implementation, it also generates a BoogiePL implementation. Having a separate procedure per override permits specification refinement in subclasses.

For translating method calls, we distinguish two cases. When we can determine the exact target of a call (that is, the call is statically bound, such as for a non-virtual method or a base call), it is translated into a call to the associated procedure. When the call is dynamically bound, we translate the call into a call of an additional BoogiePL procedure that we generate for virtual methods. This gives us the flexibility to use a slightly different specification for such calls, as used by our methodology [BDF$^+$04].

Method Framing. In BoogiePL, the effect of a procedure is framed by its **modifies** clause. Specifically, a procedure may assign to a global variable only if the variable appears in the procedure's **modifies** clause. As mentioned above, the Spec# heap is modeled in BoogiePL as a global variable (observe the **modifies** clauses in Fig. 4 for *Heap*). Since almost all methods may potentially modify the heap (by creating a new object or assigning to a field), the heap appears in almost every procedure's **modifies** clause. However, this is clearly an overapproximation. Therefore, additional framing information is encoded in the BoogiePL program in the form of an extra postcondition on the procedure. This postcondition is known as the *frame condition*. The precise form of the frame condition depends on the modular verification methodology used; for example, for the original Boogie methodology [BDF+04], each procedure gets a frame condition of the following form:

$$(\forall o: \mathbf{ref}, f: \mathbf{name} \bullet$$
$$(o, f) \notin W \wedge \mathbf{old}(Heap[o, \mathsf{allocated}] \wedge \neg Heap[o, \mathsf{committed}])$$
$$\Rightarrow Heap[o, f] = \mathbf{old}(Heap[o, f]))$$

where W are the locations listed in the Spec# method's **modifies** clause, and $Heap[o, \mathsf{committed}]$ is a special field introduced by the modular verification methodology related to an ownership model [BDF+04]. Essentially, the frame condition says that unless a given location satisfies certain criteria, it is guaranteed not to incur a net modification by the method call.

The frame conditions generated by Boogie's bytecode translation are more complicated than the one we have shown here, but we lack the space to describe them in further detail.

Loop Framing. In order to generate verification conditions [BL05] for a loop, such as the following:

$$LoopHead: \mathbf{assert}\ I;\quad S;\quad \mathbf{goto}\ LoopHead;$$

it must be transformed into acyclic control flow that abstracts the behaviors of the loop (for soundness). Specifically, we transform the loop above into the following sequence of statements:

$$x_1^0 := x_1;\ \dots\ x_n^0 := x_n;\quad \mathbf{assert}\ I;$$
$$\mathbf{havoc}\ x_1, \dots, x_n;\quad \mathbf{assume}\ I;$$
$$S;\quad \mathbf{assert}\ I;\quad \mathbf{assume\ false};$$

where S is the loop body (which may include commands that jump out of the loop), $x_1, \dots, x_n$ are the variables (global or local) updated by S, and $x_1^0, \dots, x_n^0$ are fresh local variables. The predicate I serves as a loop invariant.

The transformation causes the loop body (as well as code paths that exit the loop) to be verified in all possible states that satisfy the loop invariant. The **assume false**; command indicates that a code path that does not exit the loop can be considered to reach terminal success at the end of the loop body, provided that the loop invariant has been re-established.

When the loop body updates the heap (which is the typical situation), the heap is **havoc**ed (i.e., assigned an arbitrary value) on entry to a loop. This abstraction results in a sound but gross overapproximation of the set of heap locations that may be modified by loop body executions. Some of the lost precision must necessarily be recovered by inference (see Sec. 6), but we can also emit *loop frame conditions* that increase the precision of the verification and are guaranteed by the verification methodology. For example, one loop frame condition that is always added states that all objects that were allocated on entry to the loop are still allocated at the start of the current iteration:

$$(\forall o: \mathbf{ref} \bullet \; Heap^0[o, allocated] \Rightarrow Heap[o, allocated])$$

6   Invariant Inference

Compared with other static analysis techniques, verification-condition generation offers a high degree of precision. However, a well-known issue with producing first-order verification conditions is the need for loop

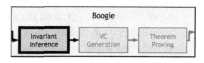

invariants. Loop invariants may be specified by the user in BoogiePL or Spec#, but while some loop invariants are key ideas in the verification of a program and thus useful to incorporate in the source, others—in particular, those that state which heap locations are left untouched by the loop body—are often boring or unintuitive to the programmer. To mitigate the need for user-supplied loop invariants, we use *abstract interpretation* [CC77], which systematically computes overapproximations of sets of reachable states, to infer some loop invariants before generating the verification condition.

Currently, the interaction between the abstract interpretation and the theorem proving is exceedingly simple: the abstract interpreter instruments the input BoogiePL program with the invariants it can infer using the selected abstract domains and passes the instrumented BoogiePL program to the verification-condition generator to produce a formula for the theorem prover. Particularly, there is no feedback from the theorem prover to the abstract interpreter, though we have some evidence that such an interaction may be beneficial [LL05].

In this section, we first discuss the design goals for our abstract interpretation framework used in Boogie and then show how these goals are achieved. Finally, we sketch the kinds of invariants that can be obtained and are particularly important for Boogie to infer.

A Generic Abstract Interpretation Framework. Because we would like to use the abstract interpretation in different settings and with varying configurations (e.g., to trade-off precision for efficiency), we heavily modularize the abstract interpretation framework. In particular, when we design the abstract domains, which capture the kind of invariants we can infer, we want to ignore the following concerns:

1. *Exploration Strategies.* We want to separate out the efficiency concerns in how the (abstract) state space is explored. As is standard, we use a generic fixed point engine.
2. *The Abstract Transition Relation.* The abstract transition relation defines how program statements affect abstract states; that is, given an abstract

state at the program point before a given statement, what are the abstract successor states that conservatively approximate the effect of the statement. We want to be agnostic to the input language when designing the abstract domains, and we want to be able to define different abstract transition relations over the same abstract domains easily (e.g., for both intra- and interprocedural analyses). To achieve this goal, we fix some generic operators on abstract domains that can be easily combined to define various abstract transition relations.

3. *Combining Abstract Domains.* It is well-known that a combined analysis can be more precise than the separate sub-analyses working independently. We would like to design and implement logically separate abstract domains independently but obtain the precision of the combined analysis easily. In other words, we want an easy way to construct *reduced product* analyses [CC79].

Expressions. For goals 2 and 3 above, we fix a common language of expressions for communicating with or among abstract domains. In implementation, this language is defined using a Spec# interface hierarchy, which is implemented by the BoogiePL AST classes. This setup makes it easy to use the abstract domains with other tools, as one simply needs to implement the abstract interpretation framework interfaces with the AST classes for the language of interest (instead of writing translation routines).

Expressions are simply variables, λ-expressions (for variable binding), and function symbols applied to expressions:

expressions	Expr	$e, p ::= x \mid \lambda x.\, e \mid f(e^*)$
variables	Var	$x, y, ...$
function symbols	FunSym	f

A *constraint* is any boolean-valued expression, and the set of function symbols include the usual operators from first-order logic: $\neg$, $\wedge$, $\vee$, $\Rightarrow$, $\Leftrightarrow$, $\forall$, and $\exists$.

Abstract Domains. An abstract domain must implement the signature shown in Fig. 5. Each abstract domain defines a type `Elt`, which represent the elements of the domain. The concretization function γ yields the predicate that corresponds to the given element. (In the literature, the concrete domain is usually phrased in terms of sets of machine states, rather than state predicates.) When analyzing a program, we do not need to evaluate the corresponding abstraction function α, so we have omitted it from the signature. As usual, we require a partial ordering on domain elements, a

```
type Elt
val γ            : Elt → Expr
val ⊤            : Elt
val ⊥            : Elt
val ⊑            : Elt × Elt → bool
val ⊔            : Elt × Elt → Elt
val ▽            : Elt × Elt → Elt
val Constrain : Elt × Expr → Elt
val Eliminate : Elt × Var → Elt
val Rename     : Elt × Var × Var → Elt
```

Fig. 5. Abstract domains

greatest element, and a least element, which are given by $\sqsubseteq$, $\top$, and $\bot$, respectively; $\top$ is required to correspond to **true** and $\bot$ to **false**. We also need join $\sqcup$ and widen ∇ upper bound operators for the fixed point engine to handle control-flow join points: $\sqcup$ is usually the least upper bound operator and ∇ must have the stabilizing property.

The final three operations provide a generic interface for implementing abstract transition relations. The `Constrain` operation adds (i.e., conjoins) a constraint to an element, `Eliminate` existentially quantifies (i.e., projects out) a variable, and `Rename` renames a free variable. For example, we might define the abstract transition relation on an assignment statement as follows:

$$\downarrow A$$

$$\boxed{x := e}$$

$$\downarrow \quad \texttt{Rename(Eliminate(Constrain}(A, x' = e), x), x', x)$$
$$\text{(for a fresh variable } x')$$

which says if A is the state before the assignment, the successor state is obtained by constraining A with $x' = e$ for a fresh variable x', then eliminating the old variable x, and finally renaming x' to x.

Base Domains. Typically, the elements of an abstract domain can be viewed as constraints of a particular form on a set of variables (that is, on independent coordinates). For example, the polyhedra abstract domain [CH78] can represent linear-arithmetic constraints like $x + y \leqslant z$. We have implementations for a number of such standard abstract domains, which we call *base domains*. For inferring linear-arithmetic constraints, we have an implementation of the polyhedra domain [CH78], though we do not currently have implementations of any cheaper numerical domains (e.g., intervals or octagons [Min01]). We also have various basic abstract domains for constant propagation and dynamic type analysis. Finally, we have an important base domain that tracks what parts of the heap are preserved across updates (the *heap succession domain*) [CL05].

Combining Abstract Domains. Often, the constraints of interest involve function and relation symbols that are not all supported by any single abstract domain. For example, a constraint of possible interest in the analysis of a Spec# program is $\mathsf{sel}(H, o, \mathsf{x}) + k \leqslant \mathsf{length}(a)$ where H denotes the current heap, $\mathsf{sel}(H, o, \mathsf{x})$ represents the value of the x field of an object o in the heap H (written $o.x$ in Spec# and written $H[o, \mathsf{x}]$ is our BoogiePL encoding), and $\mathsf{length}(a)$ gives the length of an array a. A constraint like this cannot be represented directly in the polyhedra domain because the polyhedra domain does not support the functions sel and length. Rather than building support for these functions into polyhedra, our framework includes a coordinating abstract domain that hides such *alien expressions* from base domains like polyhedra. This coordinating abstract domain, called the *congruence-closure domain*, is parameterized by the various base domains and tracks equalities and performs congruence-closure in order transparently to extend the base domains to work with alien expressions (i.e., expressions it does not understand and should be treated as uninterpreted) [CL05]. Such a modularization is particularly important. For example, including the heap succession domain as a base domain enables other base domains to obtain more precise properties of fields that depend on knowing that parts of the heap are preserved (without requiring the other base domains to know anything about heap updates).

Inferred Invariants. To get an idea of the kinds of invariants inferred by Boogie, consider again the example shown in Fig. 4. Using a standard polyhedra base domain (or in fact an interval domain would suffice) with the congruence-closure domain, we get the loop invariant $0 \leqslant i$ that gives the range of i. Using the heap succession domain with the congruence-closure domain, we infer the following important frame condition loop invariant (here shown in a simplified form):

$$(\forall o: \textbf{ref}, f: \textbf{name} \bullet$$
$$(o \neq this \lor f \neq \textsf{Example.x}) \Rightarrow Heap[o, f] = PreLoopHeap[o, f])$$

This loop invariant is not only "boring" to the user but cannot even be specified at the source-level, since it quantifies over all objects and field names; however, it is necessary to be able to verify the assertion at the end of the method body in Fig. 3. The inferred loop invariants are inserted into the BoogiePL program in Fig. 4 as assume statements at the beginning of block $LoopHead$.

7   Verification Condition Generation

A BoogiePL program encodes sets of program traces and proof obligations in those traces. Verification condition generation turns those proof obligations into first-order formulas. As already described, BoogiePL is

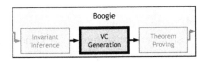

intentionally *not* a structured programming language. That is, a BoogiePL program is a somewhat high-level way of specifying a control-flow graph whose nodes are *basic blocks*. Since our verification conditions are computed using the standard weakest-precondition calculus [Dij76, Nel89], we had to develop a method for computing first-order weakest preconditions of an unstructured program.

Our method, which we have described in detail elsewhere [BL05], produces one VC for every BoogiePL procedure implementation. It starts by transforming the implementation into some loop-free BoogiePL code that over-approximates the loops in the original. It then performs a *single assignment* transformation (cf. [CFR+91, FS01]), resulting in only *passive* code, that is, code without state changes. Finally, to encode the unstructured nature of the control flow, we introduce for every block A a boolean variable A_{ok}, defined to be *true* if every execution starting from A is correct (i.e., does not go wrong). For a block:

$A: PassiveCommands; \textbf{goto } B, C;$

the *block equation* that defines A_{ok} is:

$$A_{ok} \;\Leftarrow\; \mathfrak{wp}(PassiveCommands,\; B_{ok} \wedge C_{ok})$$

where $\mathfrak{wp}$ computes the weakest precondition of *PassiveCommands* with respect to the postcondition $B_{ok} \wedge C_{ok}$. The VC is then:

$$Axioms \;\wedge\; BlockEqs \;\Rightarrow\; Start_{ok}$$

where *Axioms* is the conjunction of the axioms in the BoogiePL program, *BlockEqs* is the conjunction of block equations (which thus encode the semantics of the passive BoogiePL code), and *Start* is the implementation's start block.

While translating the BoogiePL program into a verification condition, the back-end phase builds up a table mapping labeled subformulas to BoogiePL program elements. The back-end phase uses this table to translate the label output from the theorem prover into an error message in terms of the BoogiePL program [LMS05]. Similarly, the front-end bytecode translation creates a table mapping BoogiePL program elements to Spec# program elements. This table allows it to take an error message on a BoogiePL program and generate an error message on the original Spec# program in terms that the programmer can understand.

Currently, Boogie produces verification conditions for the Simplify theorem prover [DNS05], which has a successful history of being used in program verifiers, starting with ESC/Modula-3 [DLNS98] for which it was first developed. A crucial ingredient in this success is the generation of VCs that allow the theorem prover to find concise proofs, essentially. Simplify uses what it calls the *goal property heuristic* [DNS05], which thrives on the kind of formulas generated by ESC/Modula-3 and, especially, by ESC/Java [FS01, Lei05]. However, Boogie's VCs represent the program's control flow in a different (and more compact) way than was used in ESC/Java, which sometimes causes Simplify to be slower than we would like. In addition, we have found that the formulas we use to axiomatize the Spec# class and interface subtypes are unexpectedly causing the prover to spend too much time in unfruitful ways. Finally, our heavy use of quantifiers in expressing certain changes in the heap sometimes causes Simplify to run out of steam (in particular, it reaches its "matching depth" [DNS05]). We are looking forward to addressing these issues in the further use and development of Zap [BLM05], but at present, Zap is not able to match the utility of Simplify.

8   Related Work

The body of previous work in program verification is enormous. In this section, we mention some of the tools that are most closely related to Boogie.

Three static program verifiers for the object-oriented language Java are LOOP, JIVE, and KeY. LOOP [BJ01, JP03] takes Java plus contracts written in the Java Modeling Language (JML) [LBR99, LBR03]. It uses the interactive theorem prover PVS [ORR+96], for which it generates proof obligations that look like Hoare triples [Hoa69, JP01]. It also provides some automation by a weakest-precondition tactic [Jac04]. JIVE [MMPH97] also uses a Hoare-like logic [PH97] and its custom-built interactive theorem prover operates at the level of Hoare triples (as opposed to first-order VCs generated from the programs). The KeY tool [ABB+05] offers several specification notations, including JML and dynamic logic, and targets several proof engines. The main differences between these three tools and Boogie are that they address a more limited subset of the source language and that they are not automatic.

Program verification technology has also been used in tools that find some program errors without promising to find all errors. These include the Extended Static Checkers for Modula-3 and Java [DLNS98, FLL+02, Lei00, KC04], JACK [BRL03], Krakatoa [MPMU04], and Cadeuces [FM04]. The automation in these tools rivals that of Boogie, and they all support the Simplify [DNS05] theorem prover. In addition, JACK supports PVS and the interactive prover of the Atelier B toolkit. Like Boogie, Krakatoa and Cadeuces generate verification conditions via an intermediate language, called Why [Fil03]. Though developed independently, Why and BoogiePL are more similar than they are different. The Why tool currently supports six different theorem provers, both interactive and automatic, but does not support property inference like Boogie's.

A number of programming languages have built-in specifications or were designed with verification in mind. Among these are Gypsy [AGB+77], Euclid [LHL+81], APP [Ros95], and others mentioned in the Spec# overview paper [BLS04]. The languages SPARK Ada [Bar03], B [Abr96], ACL2 [KMM00], Perfect Developer [Esc06], and C0 [LPP05] include verifiers with interactive theorem provers. The Eiffel language [Mey92] is well known for its pioneering combination of object-orientation and dynamically checked contracts, but it does not yet offer static verification.

9   Conclusion

In summary, Boogie is an automatic program verifier for modern object-oriented programs. Its architecture helps tame the complexity of the program verification task. Providing design-time feedback, Boogie moves the program verifier closer to the developer, while still hiding the theorem prover and other verification machinery from the developer. Designed around an intermediate programming notation, BoogiePL, it separates the semantic encoding of the source program from the analysis of this encoding. Since Boogie can also read BoogiePL programs directly, it offers the possibility for others to write program verifiers by encoding their proof obligations in BoogiePL.

We have applied Boogie to a growing number of small (300–1500 lines) programs, and we are applying Boogie to parts of its own implementation (which is written in Spec#). We also are supporting an experiment in using Boogie on production code. This experience constantly demands support for more programming idioms, more targeted default specifications, better explanations of error messages (especially those having to do with violations of the ownership-based alias-confinement regime), and higher performance.

Boogie can be run as part of compilation, where the compiler provides its in-memory data structures to Boogie for verification. The verification results of Boogie could be used by the compiler's code optimizer to produce better performing code (cf. [Van94, FKR⁺00]). However, this is not part of the current Boogie architecture. The prospects of including this feedback in the architecture seem promising, but also contains some research questions such as how and to what degree to rely on specifications of code that may not have been verified.

The Spec# compiler produces both metadata and compiled code from Spec# contracts like preconditions. Lately, we have considered the possibility of using only stylized patterns of compiled code. Under such a design, Boogie would reconstruct the contracts from the stylized patterns of CIL instructions, and special method stubs would have to be created to support contracts on abstract methods. The advantage of such a design would be to make it possible to write contracts in .NET languages without contract features, by manually coding the stylized precondition checks. Boogie could then be applied to other .NET languages, too.

In developing Boogie's abstract interpretation framework, we found on numerous occasions the need to determine whether or not a given predicate holds. This functionality is readily available in the theorem prover, so we have wished that the abstract interpreter and the theorem prover would be more closely related. Indeed, there is already overlap between these two components. For example, both deal with linear arithmetic, both deal with uninterpreted function symbols, and both deal with the heap. Unlike the abstract interpreter, the theorem prover supports quantifiers and therefore provides a simple way to extend its reasoning to special domains; and unlike the theorem prover, the abstract interpreter computes fixpoints, rather than just answering boolean queries. We see the combination of these two components as a possible improvement in the Boogie architecture and as an exciting and important research area.

Acknowledgments. This work would not have been possible without the efforts of the rest of the Spec# team: Manuel Fähndrich, Wolfram Schulte, and Herman Venter. We are especially grateful for the persistence and patience that Herman Venter has shown as he pioneers the use of Boogie in production code. We thank Peter Müller and Arnd Poetzsch-Heffter for performing case studies and diagnosing bugs in the system, and Francesco Logozzo for writing part of the abstract interpretation code. We are indebted to the Spec# user community and also to the anonymous reviewers.

References

[ABB⁺05]   Wolfgang Ahrendt, Thomas Baar, Bernhard Beckert, Richard Bubel, Martin Giese, Reiner Hähnle, Wolfram Menzel, Wojciech Mostowski, Andreas Roth, Steffen Schlager, and Peter H. Schmitt. The KeY tool. *Software and System Modeling*, 4(1):32–54, February 2005.

[Abr96]   Jean-Raymond Abrial. *The B-Book: Assigning Programs to Meanings.* Cambridge University Press, August 1996.

[AGB⁺77]   Allen L. Ambler, Donald I. Good, James C. Browne, Wilhelm F. Burger, Richard M. Cohen, Charles G. Hoch, and Robert E. Wells. GYPSY: A language for specification and implementation of verifiable programs. *SIGPLAN Notices*, 12(3):1–10, March 1977.

[Bar03]   John Barnes. *High Integrity Software: The SPARK Approach to Safety and Security.* Addison Wesley, 2003.

[BDF⁺04]   Michael Barnett, Robert DeLine, Manuel Fähndrich, K. Rustan M. Leino, and Wolfram Schulte. Verification of object-oriented programs with invariants. *Journal of Object Technology*, 3(6):27–56, 2004.

[BJ01]   Joachim van den Berg and Bart Jacobs. The LOOP compiler for Java and JML. In Tiziana Margaria and Wang Yi, editors, *Tools and Algorithms for the Construction and Analysis of Systems (TACAS)*, volume 2031 of *Lecture Notes in Computer Science*, pages 299–312. Springer, 2001.

[BL05]   Mike Barnett and K. Rustan M. Leino. Weakest-precondition of unstructured programs. In *Workshop on Program Analysis for Software Tools and Engineering (PASTE)*, pages 82–87, 2005.

[BLM05]   Thomas Ball, Shuvendu Lahiri, and Madanlal Musuvathi. Zap: Automated theorem proving for software analysis. Technical Report MSR-TR-2005-137, Microsoft Research, October 2005.

[BLS04]   Mike Barnett, K. Rustan M. Leino, and Wolfram Schulte. The Spec# programming system: An overview. In *Construction and Analysis of Safe, Secure, and Interoperable Smart devices (CASSIS)*, volume 3362 of *Lecture Notes in Computer Science*, pages 49–60. Springer, 2004.

[BN04]   Mike Barnett and David A. Naumann. Friends need a bit more: Maintaining invariants over shared state. In Dexter Kozen and Carron Shankland, editors, *Mathematics of Program Construction (MPC)*, volume 3125 of *Lecture Notes in Computer Science*, pages 54–84. Springer, 2004.

[BRL03]   L. Burdy, A. Requet, and J.-L. Lanet. Java applet correctness: a developer-oriented approach. In Keijiro Araki, Stefania Gnesi, and Dino Mandrioli, editors, *FME 2003: Formal Methods, International Symposium of Formal Methods Europe*, volume 2805 of *Lecture Notes in Computer Science*, pages 422–439. Springer, September 2003.

[Bur72]   Rod M. Burstall. Some techniques for proving correctness of programs which alter data structures. *Machine Intelligence*, 7:23–50, 1972.

[BvW98]   Ralph-Johan Back and Joakim von Wright. *Refinement Calculus: A Systematic Introduction.* Graduate Texts in Computer Science. Springer-Verlag, 1998.

[CC77]   Patrick Cousot and Radhia Cousot. Abstract interpretation: A unified lattice model for static analysis of programs by construction or approximation of fixpoints. In *Fourth ACM Symposium on Principles of Programming Languages (POPL)*, pages 238–252, January 1977.

[CC79]   Patrick Cousot and Radhia Cousot. Systematic design of program analysis frameworks. In *Sixth ACM Symposium on Principles of Programming Languages (POPL)*, pages 269–282, January 1979.

[CFR⁺91]   Ron Cytron, Jeanne Ferrante, Barry K. Rosen, Mark N. Wegman, and F. Kenneth Zadeck. Efficiently computing static single assignment form and the control dependence graph. *ACM Transactions on Programming Languages and Systems*, 13(4):451–490, October 1991.

[CH78]   Patrick Cousot and Nicolas Halbwachs. Automatic discovery of linear re-
            straints among variables of a program. In *Fifth ACM Symposium on Prin-
            ciples of Programming Languages (POPL)*, pages 84–96, January 1978.

[CL05]   Bor-Yuh Evan Chang and K. Rustan M. Leino. Abstract interpretation
            with alien expressions and heap structures. In Radhia Cousot, editor,
            Verification, Model Checking, and Abstract Interpretation (VMCAI), vol-
            ume 3385 of *Lecture Notes in Computer Science*, pages 147–163. Springer,
            2005.

[Dij76]   Edsger W. Dijkstra. *A Discipline of Programming*. Prentice Hall, Engle-
            wood Cliffs, NJ, 1976.

[DL05]   Robert DeLine and K. Rustan M. Leino. BoogiePL: A typed procedural
            language for checking object-oriented programs. Technical Report MSR-
            TR-2005-70, Microsoft Research, March 2005.

[DLNS98]   David L. Detlefs, K. Rustan M. Leino, Greg Nelson, and James B. Saxe.
            Extended static checking. Research Report 159, Compaq Systems Re-
            search Center, December 1998.

[DNS05]   David Detlefs, Greg Nelson, and James B. Saxe. Simplify: a theorem
            prover for program checking. *Journal of the ACM*, 52(3):365–473, May
            2005.

[Esc06]   Escher Technologies. Perfect Developer. http://eschertech.com/, 2006.

[Fil03]   Jean-Christophe Filliâtre. Verification of non-functional programs using
            interpretations in type theory. *The Journal of Functional Programming*,
            13(4):709–745, July 2003.

[FKR⁺00]   Robert Fitzgerald, Todd B. Knoblock, Erik Ruf, Bjarne Steensgaard, and
            David Tarditi. Marmot: An Optimizing Compiler For Java. *Software—
            Practice and Experience*, 30(3):199–232, 2000.

[FL03]   Manuel Fähndrich and K. Rustan M. Leino. Declaring and checking
            non-null types in an object-oriented language. In Ron Crocker and Guy
            L. Steele Jr., editors, *Object-Oriented Programming Systems, Languages
            and Applications (OOPSLA)*, pages 302–312. ACM, 2003.

[FLL⁺02]   Cormac Flanagan, K. Rustan M. Leino, Mark Lillibridge, Greg Nelson,
            James B. Saxe, and Raymie Stata. Extended static checking for Java. In
            Programming Language Design and Implementation (PLDI), pages 234–
            245, 2002.

[FM04]   Jean-Christophe Filliâtre and Claude Marché. Multi-prover verification
            of C programs. In Jim Davies, Wolfram Schulte, and Michael Barnett,
            editors, *Formal Engineering Methods (ICFEM)*, volume 3308 of *Lecture
            Notes in Computer Science*, pages 15–29. Springer, 2004.

[FS01]   Cormac Flanagan and James B. Saxe. Avoiding exponential explo-
            sion: Generating compact verification conditions. In *POPL 2001: The
            28th ACM SIGPLAN-SIGACT Symposium on Principles of Programming
            Languages*, pages 193–205. ACM, January 2001.

[Hoa69]   C. A. R. Hoare. An axiomatic basis for computer programming. *Com-
            munications of the ACM*, 12(10):576–580,583, October 1969.

[HW73]   C. A. R. Hoare and N. Wirth. An axiomatic definition of the programming
            language PASCAL. *Acta Informatica*, 2(4):335–355, 1973.

[Jac04]   Bart Jacobs. Weakest pre-condition reasoning for Java programs with
            JML annotations. *Journal of Logic and Algebraic Programming*, 58(1–
            2):61–88, January–March 2004.

386 M. Barnett et al.

[JP01]   Bart Jacobs and Erik Poll. A logic for the Java Modeling Language JML.
           In H. Hussmann, editor, *Fundamental Approaches to Software Engineer-
           ing (FASE)*, volume 2029 of *Lecture Notes in Computer Science*, pages
           284–299. Springer, 2001.
[JP03]   Bart Jacobs and Erik Poll. Java program verification at Nijmegen: Devel-
           opments and perspective. In *Software Security—Theories and Systems,
           Second Mext-NSF-JSPS International Symposium, ISSS 2003*, pages 134–
           153, November 2003.
[KC04]   Joseph R. Kiniry and David R. Cok. ESC/Java2: Uniting ESC/Java and
           JML: Progress and issues in building and using ESC/Java2, including a
           case study involving the use of the tool to verify portions of an Internet
           voting tally system. In *Construction and Analysis of Safe, Secure, and
           Interoperable Smart devices (CASSIS)*, volume 3362 of *Lecture Notes in
           Computer Science*, pages 108–128. Springer, 2004.
[KMM00]   Matt Kaufmann, Panagiotis Manolios, and J Strother Moore. *Computer-
           Aided Reasoning: An Approach*. Kluwer Academic Publishers, June 2000.
[LBR99]   Gary T. Leavens, Albert L. Baker, and Clyde Ruby. JML: A notation for
           detailed design. In Haim Kilov, Bernhard Rumpe, and Ian Simmonds,
           editors, *Behavioral Specifications of Businesses and Systems*, pages 175–
           188. Kluwer Academic Publishers, Boston, 1999.
[LBR03]   Gary T. Leavens, Albert L. Baker, and Clyde Ruby. Preliminary design
           of JML: A behavioral interface specification language for Java. Technical
           Report 98-06u, Iowa State University, Department of Computer Science,
           April 2003.
[Lei95]   K. Rustan M. Leino. *Toward Reliable Modular Programs*. PhD thesis,
           CalTech, 1995. Available as Technical Report Caltech-CS-TR-95-03.
[Lei00]   K. Rustan M. Leino. Extended static checking: A ten-year perspective. In
           Reinhard Wilhelm, editor, *Informatics—10 Years Back, 10 Years Ahead*,
           volume 2000 of *Lecture Notes in Computer Science*. Springer, 2000.
[Lei05]   K. Rustan M. Leino. Efficient weakest preconditions. *Information
           Processing Letters*, 93(6):281–288, March 2005.
[LHL⁺81]   Butler W. Lampson, James J. Horning, Ralph L. London, James G.
           Mitchell, and Gerald J. Popek. Report on the programming language
           Euclid. Technical Report CSL-81-12, Xerox PARC, October 1981. An
           earlier version of this report appeared as volume 12, number 2 in *SIG-
           PLAN Notices*. ACM, February 1977.
[LL05]   K. Rustan M. Leino and Francesco Logozzo. Loop invariants on demand.
           In Kwangkeun Yi, editor, *Asian Symposium on Programming Languages
           and Systems (APLAS)*, volume 3780 of *Lecture Notes in Computer Sci-
           ence*, pages 119–134. Springer, 2005.
[LM04]   K. Rustan M. Leino and Peter Müller. Object invariants in dynamic con-
           texts. In Martin Odersky, editor, *European Conference on Object-Oriented
           Programming (ECOOP)*, volume 3086 of *Lecture Notes in Computer Sci-
           ence*, pages 491–516. Springer-Verlag, 2004.
[LM05]   K. Rustan M. Leino and Peter Müller. Modular verification of static
           class invariants. In John Fitzgerald, Ian J. Hayes, and Andrzej Tarlecki,
           editors, *Symposium on Formal Methods Europe (FM)*, volume 3582 of
           Lecture Notes in Computer Science, pages 26–42. Springer, 2005.

[LM06]   K. Rustan M. Leino and Peter Müller. A verification methodology for model fields. In Peter Sestoft, editor, *European Symposium on Programming (ESOP)*, volume 3924 of *Lecture Notes in Computer Science*, pages 115–130. Springer, 2006.

[LMS05]   K. Rustan M. Leino, Todd Millstein, and James B. Saxe. Generating error traces from verification-condition counterexamples. *Science of Computer Programming*, 55(1–3):209–226, March 2005.

[LN02]   K. Rustan M. Leino and Greg Nelson. Data abstraction and information hiding. *ACM Transactions on Programming Languages and Systems*, 24(5):491–553, September 2002.

[LPP05]   Dirk Leinenbach, Wolfgang Paul, and Elena Petrova. Towards the formal verification of a C0 compiler: Code generation and implementation correctness. In Bernhard K. Aichernig and Bernhard Beckert, editors, *Third IEEE International Conference on Software Engineering and Formal Methods (SEFM 2005)*, pages 2–12. IEEE Computer Society, September 2005.

[LSS99]   K. Rustan M. Leino, James B. Saxe, and Raymie Stata. Checking Java programs via guarded commands. In *Formal Techniques for Java Programs*, Technical Report 251. Fernuniversität Hagen, May 1999. Also available as Technical Note 1999-002, Compaq Systems Research Center.

[Mey92]   Bertrand Meyer. *Eiffel: The Language*. Object-Oriented Series. Prentice Hall, 1992.

[Min01]   Antoine Miné. The octagon abstract domain. In *Working Conference on Reverse Engineering (WCRE)*, pages 310–319, 2001.

[MMPH97]   Peter Müller, Jörg Meyer, and Arnd Poetzsch-Heffter. Programming and interface specification language of JIVE—specification and design rationale. Technical Report 223, Fernuniversität Hagen, 1997.

[MPMU04]   Claude Marché, Christine Paulin-Mohring, and Xavier Urbain. The KRAKATOA tool for certification of JAVA/JAVACARD programs annotated in JML. *Journal of Logic and Algebraic Programming*, 58(1–2):89–106, January–March 2004.

[Nel89]   Greg Nelson. A generalization of Dijkstra's calculus. *ACM Transactions on Programming Languages and Systems*, 11(4):517–561, October 1989.

[ORR⁺96]   Sam Owre, S. Rajan, John M. Rushby, Natarajan Shankar, and Mandayam K. Srivas. PVS: Combining specification, proof checking, and model checking. In Rajeev Alur and Thomas A. Henzinger, editors, *Computer-Aided Verification (CAV)*, volume 1102 of *Lecture Notes in Computer Science*, pages 411–414. Springer, 1996.

[PH97]   Arnd Poetzsch-Heffter. Specification and verification of object-oriented programs. Habilitationsschrift, Technische Universität München, 1997.

[Rey78]   John C. Reynolds. Syntactic control of interference. In *Fifth ACM Symposium on Principles of Programming Languages (POPL)*, pages 39–46, January 1978.

[Ros95]   David S. Rosenblum. A practical approach to programming with assertions. *IEEE Transactions on Software Engineering*, 21(1):19–31, January 1995.

[Spe06]   Spec# homepage. `http://research.microsoft.com/specsharp`, 2006.

[Van94]   Mark T. Vandevoorde. *Exploiting Specifications to Improve Program Performance*. PhD thesis, Massachusetts Institute of Technology, February 1994. Available as Technical Report MIT/LCS/TR-598.

On a Probabilistic Chemical Abstract Machine and the Expressiveness of Linda Languages

Alessandra Di Pierro[1], Chris Hankin[2], and Herbert Wiklicky[2]

[1] Dipartimento di Informatica, University of Pisa, Italy
[2] Department of Computing, Imperial College London, UK

Abstract. The Chemical Abstract Machine (CHAM) of Berry and Boudol provides a commonly accepted, uniform framework for describing the operational semantics of various process calculi and languages, such as for example CCS, the π calculus and coordination languages like Linda. In its original form the CHAM is purely non-deterministic and thus only describes what reactions are *possible* but not how long it will take (in the average) before a certain reaction takes place or its *probability*. Such quantitative information is however often vital for "real world" applications such as systems biology or performance analysis. We propose a probabilistic version of the CHAM. We then define a linear operator semantics for the probabilistic CHAM which exploits a tensor product representation for distributions over possible solutions. Based on this we propose a novel approach towards comparing the expressive power of different calculi via their encoding in the probabilistic CHAM. We illustrate our approach by comparing the expressiveness of various Linda Languages.

1 Introduction

The chemical reaction metaphor was introduced in [1]. Gamma is a declarative programming language that supports massive parallelism. A Gamma program consists of a *shared data space* – a multiset – and a collection of *conditional rewrite rules*. The chemical metaphor is of molecules reacting in a solution under physical laws; the condition in a Gamma rule is normally referred to as the *reaction* condition, whilst the non-conditional part of the rule is referred to as the *action*. A major principle in Gamma is that of local action: rules consume a small number of elements from the multiset and produce a small number of elements into the multiset; the conditional application of rules is determined by predicates over the consumed elements – there is no global state. Rules potentially compete for elements from the multiset. The "program" terminates when no further rules are enabled. This process is described in [2] in the following way: computation is "the global result of the successive applications of local, independent, atomic reactions".

One motivation for the model was that the standard data types used in declarative languages, for example the ubiquitous list, were over-constraining for parallel systems. For example, a Gamma rule for computing primes is:

$$x, y \to x \Leftarrow multiple(x, y)$$

F.S. de Boer et al. (Eds.): FMCO 2005, LNCS 4111, pp. 388–407, 2006.

where *multiple* is a predicate which is true whenever y is a multiple of x (the reader should compare this with the usual sieve solution). When this rule is combined with the solution $\{2, 3, 4, 5, 6, 7, 8\}$, the program will terminate with $\{2, 3, 5, 7\}$. There are a number of different reduction sequences that lead to this result; for example, one sequence might include the parallel execution of:

$$2, 4 \to 2 \text{ and } 3, 6 \to 3$$

There have been a number of later developments of Gamma; for example to introduce more structure to the multiset but without constraining the execution [3] and to add higher-order features [4]. The shared data space concept has proved to be a powerful principle in coordination programming [5]. More importantly from the perspective of this paper, Gamma provided inspiration for Berry and Boudol's Chemical Abstract Machine [6].

The CHAM was introduced to provide an abstract machine-based operational semantics for process calculi. It has been used for a variety of calculi including CCS, π-calculus and Linda-based coordination languages. The solution in a CHAM is again a multiset which may be structured using the notion of membranes – to encapsulate a sub-multiset – and airlocks – to expose part of a sub-multiset for interaction with the rest of the solution. A CHAM specification is then a collection of rules. Rules are either *specific* or *general*. Specific rules are similar to our primes example from above; however, the CHAM rules generally rely on sophisticated pattern matching rather than reaction conditions – this is sufficient to match input channels and output channels in the typical synchronous communication of CCS. The general rules provide for the "compatible closure" of the specific rules – allowing computation inside membranes and also in the presence of other elements in the solution.

The main contributions of this paper are twofold:

- to adapt the CHAM model to allow probabilistic computation; we believe this to be important not only to provide a formal semantics for the burgeoning number of probabilistic process calculi but also because probabilities will be essential for the more advanced modelling of biological and chemical systems.
- to use the structure of particular CHAMs to compare the expressiveness of different calculi.

The rest of this paper is structured as follows: in Section 2 we introduce the probabilistic CHAM; we then present a linear operator semantics for the pCHAM in Section 3; Section 4 presents a number of properties of the pCHAM; we describe the process of encoding various calculi in the pCHAM in Section 5 — this is relatively straightforward and follows the classical CHAM encodings; Section 6 concerns expressiveness; and we conclude in Section 7.

2 A Probabilistic CHAM

The idea of the *probabilistic CHAM* (pCHAM) is to "quantify" the likelihood or probability of executing an applicable rule. This allows us to resolve any non-deterministic choice in a reaction (sequence) probabilistically. We define the semantics of the pCHAM in terms of a Probabilistic Transition System (PTS) where the state space is represented by multisets of molecules. We recall the general definition of a (labelled) PTS as given in [7, Def 2].

Definition 1. *A probabilistic transition system is a tuple* $(S, A, \longrightarrow, \pi_0)$, *where:*

- *S is a non-empty, countable set of* states,
- *A is a non-empty, finite set of* actions,
- *$\longrightarrow \subseteq S \times A \times Dist(S)$ is a* transition relation, *and*
- *$\pi_0 \in Dist(S)$ is an* initial distribution *on S.*

A PTS $(S, A, \longrightarrow, \pi_0)$ is called *generative* if the transition relation is a partial function $\longrightarrow: S \hookrightarrow Dist(S \times A)$.

The semantics of a pCHAM is defined by a generative unlabelled PTS, i.e. a PTS with a single, anonymous label $\tau \in A$ (which we simply omit). We will concentrate on finite state spaces S, although we will occasionally also remark on the general countable case.

2.1   State Space

The probabilistic CHAM has the same basic state space as the classical CHAM, namely *solutions*, i.e. multisets of molecules. We denote by $\mathcal{T}$ the set of possible molecules, i.e. terms in some formal algebra or language, and by $\mathcal{M} = \mathcal{M}(\mathcal{T})$ the set of multisets of molecules in $\mathcal{T}$, i.e. functions of the form $S : \mathcal{T} \to \mathbb{N}$ for which we will usually use the common notation $\{\!\!\{ \ldots \}\!\!\}$.

We will assume a finite set of possible molecules in $\mathcal{T} = \{m_1, \ldots, m_t\}$, i.e. $t = |\mathcal{T}| < \infty$ and a finite (strict) upper bound s for the multiplicity of any molecule, i.e. $\max_{m_i \in \mathcal{T}} S(m_i) < s < \infty$. We will denote the set of possible multiplicities by $\mathcal{N} = \{1, \ldots, s - 1\} \subseteq \mathbb{N}$. These finiteness conditions can be relaxed relatively easily. However, they allow us for the time being a clearer presentation of the basic elements of the pCHAM; we can, for example, work with distributions in place of general measures, etc.

We will refer to distributions over solutions, i.e. over $\mathcal{M} = \mathcal{M}(\mathcal{T})$, as *ensembles* of molecules in $\mathcal{T}$ and denote them by:

$$\mu = \{\langle \{\!\!\{ m_{11}, \ldots, m_{1i_1} \}\!\!\}, p_1 \rangle, \ldots, \langle \{\!\!\{ m_{j1}, \ldots, m_{ji_j} \}\!\!\}, p_j \rangle\}$$

where i_k is the cardinality and p_k the probability of the multiset $\{\!\!\{ m_{k1}, \ldots, m_{ki_k} \}\!\!\}$. For the sake of simplicity of notation we use m_{ji} instead of the the more correct notation m_{j_i}. Moreover, in order to make the representation of ensembles more compact, we do not list multisets with zero probability.

A pCHAM with molecules in $\mathcal{T}$ and with an initial solution $S_0 \in \mathcal{M}(\mathcal{T})$ defines a probabilistic transition system $(\mathcal{M}, \Longrightarrow_p, \mu_0)$ with the point distribution $\mu_0 = \{\langle S_0, 1 \rangle\}$.

2.2   Specific Rules

The transition relation $\Longrightarrow_p$ for the PTS $(\mathcal{M}, \Longrightarrow_p, \mu_0)$ representing a pCHAM is specified via a certain set $\mathcal{R}$ of *specific rules* or — as with the non-deterministic CHAM in order to avoid "multiset matching" — by *rule schemata*. These rules are expressions of the form:

$$m_{i1}, \ldots, m_{ik} \longrightarrow_p m_{j1}, \ldots, m_{jl}$$

where $m_{i'j'}$ are molecules (or variables, cf [6]). These rules specify an individual pCHAM by describing possible rewriting steps together with a *probability p*.

It is important (in the context of the pCHAM) to distinguish between rules, for which we use the notation $\longrightarrow_p$, and the probabilistic transition relation on $\mathcal{M}$ which defines the multiset rewriting and for which we use the notation $\Longrightarrow_p$.

Probabilities are associated with rules not molecules. However, the rules of a specific pCHAM can exploit information contained in the molecules in order to obtain the intended probability p.

Example 2. We can also introduce probabilistic information as part of a molecule, e.g. $m'_i = p_i : m_i$, i.e. we can annotate standard molecules by providing information about their "reactiveness". Rules like $m_1, m_2 \longrightarrow m_3$ then would become, for example, something like:

$$p_1 : m_1, p_2 : m_2 \longrightarrow_{p_1 \cdot p_2} \max(p_1, p_2) : m_3$$

Example 3. Another possibility could be to provide "position information" and make the reaction probability of two molecules proportional to their "spatial" closeness, e.g.:

$$m_1@(x_1, y_1), m_2@(x_2, y_2) \longrightarrow_{d(m_1, m_2)} m_3@((x_1 + x_2)/2, (y_1 + y_2)/2)$$

with $d(m_1, m_2) = \sqrt{(x_1 - x_2)^2 + (y_1 - y_2)^2}$ the "Euclidean distance" between m_1 and m_2.

Example 4. The "spatial" information can also be generalised to "allocation environments" — similar to the notion in KLAIM [8], i.e. we can specify a sub-(multi)set $\{m_1, \ldots, m_k\}$ of molecules a given molecule m_0 can react with, i.e. the (multi)set of its "neighbours".

A further generalisation could introduce "probabilistic allocation environments" which specifies not just the possibility of reactions between certain molecules, but also their probability. Allocation environments can be used to simulate membranes of sub-solutions and probabilistic allocation environments allow the introduction of "soft membranes".

Example 5. Any non-deterministic CHAM can be lifted to a pCHAM by replacing the specific rule $m_{i1}, \ldots, m_{ik} \longrightarrow m_{j1}, \ldots, m_{jl}$ by $m_{i1}, \ldots, m_{ik} \longrightarrow_1 m_{j1}, \ldots, m_{jl}$. The 'standard probability' $p = 1$ will be renormalised (see below) to obtain a uniform distribution over all possible transformations of a multiset. Note that this is only one of the many possible ways a nondeterministic specific rule can be *implemented* as a probabilistic rule in order to specify an individual pCHAM. We will make the relationship between non-deterministic and probabilistic CHAM more precise in Section 4.2.

2.3 General Laws

A concrete pCHAM is defined by specifying its set of possible molecules $\mathcal{T}$, specific rules $\mathcal{R}$ and (optionally) an initial solution $S_0 \in \mathcal{M}$. The rules of the pCHAM can be extended and translated into the transition relation $\Longrightarrow_p$ of the corresponding probabilistic transition system $(\mathcal{M}, \Longrightarrow_p, \mu_0)$, with $\mu_0 = \{\langle S_0, 1 \rangle\}$, via four *general laws* which are straightforward generalisations of the laws of the non-deterministic CHAM, cf [6, Sect 3].

Reaction Law. This provides the essential mechanism which translates or lifts specific pCHAM rules to multiset rewritings. It also renormalises the (intended) transition probabilities p such that the probabilities associated to the transitions from any given multiset add up to one.

$$\frac{m_{i1}, \ldots, m_{ik} \longrightarrow_p m_{j1}, \ldots, m_{jl}}{\{|m_{i1}, \ldots, m_{ik}|\} \Longrightarrow_{\tilde{p}} \{|m_{j1}, \ldots, m_{jl}|\}}$$

where $\tilde{p}$ is the normalised probability $\tilde{p} = \frac{p}{P}$ with P the sum over all possible rewritings of $\{|m_{i1}, \ldots, m_{ik}|\}$.

This law is *non-local* as the normalisation has to take into account all the other transitions which could be applied to a given multiset/solution. However, as we will see later, we can actually avoid normalisation until we reach, for example, a terminal solution.

Chemical Law. The remaining general laws of the pCHAM extend the specific rules. The Chemical Law allows us to apply a rule in any context:

$$\frac{m_{i1}, \ldots, m_{ik} \longrightarrow_p m_{j1}, \ldots, m_{jl}}{m_{i1}, \ldots, m_{ik}, m'_1, \ldots, m'_n \longrightarrow_p m_{j1}, \ldots, m_{jl}, m'_1, \ldots, m'_n}$$

where $m'_1, \ldots, m'_n$ is any (maybe empty) collection of molecules.

This means that if we state a specific rule like $m_{i1}, \ldots, m_{ik} \longrightarrow_p m_{j1}, \ldots, m_{jl}$ for a pCHAM we also can use rules like $m_{i1}, \ldots, m_{ik}, m_0 \longrightarrow_p m_{j1}, \ldots, m_{jl}, m_0$, and $m_{i1}, \ldots, m_{ik}, m_0, m_3 \longrightarrow_p m_{j1}, \ldots, m_{jl}, m_0, m_3$, etc.

Membrane Law. For solutions with solutions as molecules we extend the set of specific rules such that a sub-solution can develop on its own.

$$\frac{m_{i1}, \ldots, m_{ik} \longrightarrow_p m_{j1}, \ldots, m_{jl}}{m'_1, \ldots, m'_n, \{|m_{i1}, \ldots, m_{ik}|\} \longrightarrow_p m'_1, \ldots, m'_n, \{|m_{j1}, \ldots, m_{jl}|\}}$$

If we define a *context* $C[]$ as usual as a multiset with a "hole", i.e. as a multiset $\{m_1, \ldots, m_n, []\}$ with a distinguished "hole" molecule $[]$ which can be replaced by any multiset S then we obtain the corresponding law of the general CHAM:

$$\frac{\{m_{i1}, \ldots, m_{ik}\} \Longrightarrow_p \{m_{j1}, \ldots, m_{jl}\}}{\{m'_1, \ldots, m'_n, \{m_{i1}, \ldots, m_{ik}\}\} \Longrightarrow_{\tilde{p}} \{m'_1, \ldots, m'_n, \{m_{j1}, \ldots, m_{jl}\}\}}$$

or more concisely:

$$\frac{S \Longrightarrow_p S'}{\{C[S]\} \Longrightarrow_{\tilde{p}} \{C[S']\}}$$

where $\tilde{p}$ is obtained by (re)normalising p.

Airlock Law. The "partial activation" of a sub-solution providing an 'airlock' to the surrounding solution is realised via:

$$m, m_1, \ldots, m_n \longrightarrow_{h(T)} m \lhd \{m_1, \ldots, m_n\}$$
$$m \lhd \{m_1, \ldots, m_n\} \longrightarrow_{f(T)} m, m_1, \ldots, m_n$$

The probabilities $h(T)$ and $f(T)$ specify the chances of "heating" up or "freezing" down airlocks. It could be the case that $h(T) = f(T)$, i.e. that the two rewritings happen with the same probability, but it could also be that one happens more frequently. Furthermore, it is also possible to change the probabilities depending on a control parameter T (*temperature*).

Considering the multiset rewrites which this universal rule justifies we get the following "probabilistic version" of the corresponding classical law:

$$\{m\} \uplus S \Longrightarrow_{\tilde{h}(T)} \{m \lhd S\} \quad \text{and} \quad \{m \lhd S\} \Longrightarrow_{\tilde{f}(T)} \{m\} \uplus S.$$

2.4 An Example

Consider (a finite version) of a CHAM which implements the well known sieve method for finding prime numbers. The initial solution is in this case the set of natural numbers $\{2, 3, \ldots, n\}$ or in general a multiset of numbers. The specific reaction rules are as follows:

If i and j are in solution such that there exists a $k \neq 1$ such that $j = i \cdot k$ then eliminate j from solution.

or as a simple rule schemata:

$$i, j \longrightarrow j \text{ iff } \exists k \neq 1.ik = j$$

An execution of this CHAM leads, for example, to the following reductions:

$$\{2, 3, 4, 5, 6, 7, 8, 9\} \longrightarrow \{2, 3, 5, 6, 7, 8, 9\}$$
$$\longrightarrow \{2, 3, 5, 7, 8, 9\}$$
$$\longrightarrow \{2, 3, 5, 7, 8\}$$
$$\longrightarrow \{2, 3, 5, 7\}$$

It is easy to see that we will always end up with the (multi)set of primes up to n. However, it is left open how fast we will reach this state, or how long it will take in the average until a certain non-prime number is eliminated.

A probabilistic version of the CHAM in this example needs to specify the probabilities for rule applications. A rather simple, maybe somewhat uninspired, way to this is to assume each rule will fire with the same probability, i.e.

$$i, j \longrightarrow_1 j \text{ iff } \exists k \neq 1.ik = j$$

One possible sequence of reductions for this pCHAM is then:

$$\{\!\{2, 3, 4, 5, 6, 7, 8, 9\}\!\} \Longrightarrow_{\frac{1}{6}} \{\!\{2, 3, 5, 6, 7, 8, 9\}\!\}$$
$$\Longrightarrow_{\frac{1}{4}} \{\!\{2, 3, 5, 7, 8, 9\}\!\}$$
$$\Longrightarrow_{\frac{1}{2}} \{\!\{2, 3, 5, 7, 8\}\!\}$$
$$\Longrightarrow_1 \{\!\{2, 3, 5, 7\}\!\}$$

Again, it is easy to see that this pCHAM will always end up with a multiset containing only primes. However, (despite the uniform distribution of probabilities to rules) we observe certain execution paths or traces with different probabilities, e.g. the one above with probability $\frac{1}{6}\frac{1}{4}\frac{1}{2} = \frac{1}{48}$.

3   Linear Operator Semantics of the pCHAM

As in the theory of stochastic processes, in particular of Markov Chains, we encode the probabilistic transition relation $\Longrightarrow_p$ as a linear operator $\mathbf{T}$ on the vector spaces $\mathcal{V}(\mathcal{M})$. Suppose we have an enumeration of the solutions in $\mathcal{M}$. The fact that $S_i \Longrightarrow_{p_{ij}} S_j$ will then be reflected by the fact that the entry $\mathbf{T}_{ij} = p_{ij}$. The advantage of the linear operator semantics is that it not only encodes the probability of transitions between solutions but also canonically extends to a relation between ensembles, i.e. distributions over solutions.

3.1   State Space

The first question we have to address is how many possible solutions are there in $\mathcal{M}$; this means that we have to determine the reachable set, i.e. the state space of possible configurations of the pCHAM. Unfortunately, the general situation requires an exponentially growing space to represent it: Assume that we have t different types of molecules and that their multiplicity is restricted by s, i.e. a given molecule/term type can appear with multiplicities 0 (not at all), 1, 2, etc. up to $s - 1$.

A finite multiset representing such a solution can be defined as a map from the set of all possible molecules $\mathcal{T} = \{m_1, m_2, \ldots, m_t\}$ to the set of multiplicities $\mathcal{N} = \{0, 1, \ldots, s-1\}$. The cardinality of the set of all maps $\mathcal{T} \to \mathcal{N}$ is $|\mathcal{N}|^{|\mathcal{T}|} = s^t$.

Ensembles correspond to particular vectors in the vector space of (formal) linear combinations of multisets:

$$\mathcal{V}(\mathcal{M}) = \left\{ \sum_i x_i S_i \mid x_i \in \mathbb{R} \text{ and } S_i \in \mathcal{M} \right\}$$

which, concentrating on the *coordinates* x_i, we can also identify with the space of tuples in $\mathbb{R}^{|\mathcal{M}|}$. A distribution over solutions of the pCHAM is a positive vector with 1-norm one, i.e. $x_i \geq 0$ for all i and $\sum_i |x_i| = 1$. The vector space containing all ensembles thus is unfortunately extremely large: $\mathcal{V}(\mathcal{M}(\mathcal{T})) = \mathbb{R}^{s^t}$.

3.2 Tensor Product Representations

The state space of size s^t is prohibitively large but at the same time unavoidable; a priori we cannot exclude any of the s^t possible molecular solutions and in principle it is possible that rules governing the dynamics of the pCHAM specify transitions from any of the s^t configurations to any other.

However, we can exploit the "structure" of the state space. If we consider for the moment only a single type of molecules, i.e. $t = 1$, then we have only to consider the bounding multiplicity s. The state space of this type of pCHAM has $s^1 = s$ possible states; ensembles thus are vectors in $\mathbb{R}^s = \mathcal{V}(\{0, \ldots, s-1\}) = \mathcal{V}(\mathcal{N})$. Considering two types of molecules, i.e. $t = 2$, requires that we keep track of the multiplicity of each of the two types of molecules. We thus get the state space of possible solutions as the Cartesian product $\mathcal{N} \times \mathcal{N}$. The possible ensembles, i.e. distributions of this space, are then elements of the tensor product: $\mathcal{V}(\mathcal{N} \times \mathcal{N}) = \mathcal{V}(\mathcal{N}) \otimes \mathcal{V}(\mathcal{N})$.

As an example, let us consider an ensemble on $\mathcal{T} = \{m_1, m_2, m_3\}$ which is given by $\{\langle S_1, \frac{1}{3}\rangle, \langle S_2, \frac{2}{3}\rangle\}$ with $S_1 = \{\!|m_1, m_1, m_3|\!\}$ and $S_2 = \{\!|m_1, m_2|\!\}$. The two multisets are represented by the vectors (taking as bound $s = 2$ for the multiplicities) in $\mathbb{R}^{3^3} = (\mathbb{R}^3)^{\otimes 3} = \mathbb{R}^{27}$: $(0, 0, 1) \otimes (1, 0, 0) \otimes (0, 1, 0)$ — which specifies the multiplicity of m_1 to be 2, the one for m_2 as 0 and of m_3 to be 1 — and $(0, 1, 0) \otimes (0, 1, 0) \otimes (1, 0, 0)$ — which expresses the fact that molecules m_1 and m_2 have a multiplicity one, while m_3 does not appear — and which we denote by μ_1 and μ_2. For both solution the three factors in the tensor product describe the multiplicity of each of the three molecules m_1, m_2 and m_3; the entries in these factors (p_0, p_1, p_2) specify that the molecule is missing with probability p_0, that there is one copy with probability p_1, and that its multiplicity is two with probability p_2. The original ensemble is represented by the weighted vector sum

$$\frac{1}{3}\mu_1 + \frac{2}{3}\mu_2 = \frac{1}{3}(0, 0, 1) \otimes (1, 0, 0) \otimes (0, 1, 0) + \frac{2}{3}(0, 1, 0) \otimes (0, 1, 0) \otimes (1, 0, 0).$$

Generalising this construction gives us an alternative description of the state-space of a pCHAM with t types of molecules and bounding multiplicity s:

$$\mathcal{V}(\mathcal{N}^t) = \mathcal{V}(\mathcal{N})^{\otimes t} = (\mathbb{R}^s)^{\otimes t} = \mathbb{R}^{s^t}$$

where $\mathcal{V}^{\otimes t}$ denotes the t-fold tensor product of $\mathcal{V}$, i.e. $\mathcal{V} \otimes \mathcal{V} \otimes \ldots \otimes \mathcal{V}$.

Although this representation (obviously) does not reduce the dimension of the state space of the pCHAM it "partitions" it in a certain way which will allow us to describe "local" rules in a more efficient way.

3.3   Representation of Rules

The encoding of a specific rule of a concrete pCHAM is straightforward and purely syntax-directed. Given a rule of the form:

$$m_{i_1}, \ldots, m_{i_k} \longrightarrow_p m_{j_1}, \ldots, m_{j_l}$$

we can translate it into a linear operator on the ensemble space $\mathcal{V}(\mathcal{M}) = (\mathbb{R}^s)^{\otimes t}$.

We first need to consider a *creation operator* $\mathbf{C} = \mathbf{C}_s$ and a *destruction operator* $\mathbf{D} = \mathbf{D}_s$ on each tensor component of $\mathcal{V}(\mathcal{M})$, i.e. on $\mathcal{V}(\mathcal{N}) = \mathbb{R}^s$ represented by the following matrices which increase or decrease the multiplicity of certain molecules, i.e.

$$(\mathbf{C})_{ij} = \begin{cases} 1 \text{ for } j = i+1 \\ 0 \text{ otherwise} \end{cases} \quad \text{and} \quad (\mathbf{D})_{ij} = \begin{cases} 1 \text{ for } j = i-1 \\ 0 \text{ otherwise} \end{cases}$$

These creation and destruction operators link the semantics of the pCHAM closely to so-called "Birth-and-Death processes" in probability theory, cf. e.g. [10].

Using these operators we can increase and decrease the multiplicity of every molecule m_k in a solution. To increase, for example, the multiplicity of the molecule m_2 by two in a solution made up of (at most) four different molecules we have to apply $(\mathbf{I} \otimes \mathbf{C} \otimes \mathbf{I} \otimes \mathbf{I}) \cdot (\mathbf{I} \otimes \mathbf{C} \otimes \mathbf{I} \otimes \mathbf{I}) = (\mathbf{I} \otimes \mathbf{CC} \otimes \mathbf{I} \otimes \mathbf{I})$ with $\mathbf{I}$ the identity operator/matrix on $\mathcal{V}(\mathcal{N})$, to the vector representing a given solution. In general, we can define the following two operators on $\mathcal{M}$:

$$\mathbf{G}_k = \bigotimes_{i=1}^{k-1} \mathbf{I} \otimes \mathbf{C} \otimes \bigotimes_{i=k+1}^{t} \mathbf{I} \quad \text{and} \quad \mathbf{K}_k = \bigotimes_{i=1}^{k-1} \mathbf{I} \otimes \mathbf{D} \otimes \bigotimes_{i=k+1}^{t} \mathbf{I}$$

which increase (generate) or decrease (kill) the multiplicity of the molecule m_k.

The last thing we need in order to define the encoding of rules is a test operator which checks whether there exists a certain molecule in the current solution. The local version of this existence operator $\mathbf{E}$ and its obvious extension $\mathbf{E}^{\geq \min}$ are given by:

$$(\mathbf{E})_{ij} = \begin{cases} 1 \text{ for } i = j \geq 1 \\ 0 \text{ otherwise} \end{cases} \quad \text{and} \quad (\mathbf{E}^{\geq \min})_{ij} = \begin{cases} 1 \text{ for } i = j \geq \min \\ 0 \text{ otherwise} \end{cases}$$

Note that $\mathbf{E}^n \neq \mathbf{E}^{\geq n}$. Using these local tests we can construct a global one:

$$\mathbf{E}_k = \bigotimes_{i=1}^{k-1} \mathbf{I} \otimes \mathbf{E} \otimes \bigotimes_{i=k+1}^{t} \mathbf{I} \quad \text{and} \quad \mathbf{E}_k^{\geq \min} = \bigotimes_{i=1}^{k-1} \mathbf{I} \otimes \mathbf{E}^{\geq \min} \otimes \bigotimes_{i=k+1}^{t} \mathbf{I}$$

A specific rule of a pCHAM $m_{i_1}, \ldots, m_{i_k} \longrightarrow_p m_{j_1}, \ldots, m_{j_l}$ is now represented by the operator product:

$$\mathbf{E}_{i_1}^{\geq S(m_{i_1})} \cdots \mathbf{E}_{i_k}^{\geq S(m_{i_k})} \cdot \mathbf{K}_{i_1}^{S(m_{i_1})} \cdots \mathbf{K}_{i_k}^{S(m_{i_k})} \cdot \mathbf{G}_{j_1}^{S(m_{j_1})} \cdots \mathbf{G}_{j_l}^{S(m_{j_l})}$$

where $S(m_k)$ is the multiplicity of each molecule on the left and right-hand side of the rule. The encoding simply tests if enough molecules are present such that the rule can be applied, then it destroys the molecules mentioned on the left-hand side of the rule, and finally it generates all molecules on the right-hand side. Of course, one can think of optimising the encoding by only destroying molecules which do not re-appear on the right-hand side, etc.

3.4   Representation of pCHAMs

After we have represented all specific rules we finally can present the encoding of a concrete pCHAM $(\mathcal{M}, \mathcal{R}, \mu_0)$. We first have to construct the operators $\mathbf{R}_i$ of all specific rules in $\mathcal{R}$ together with all the extended rules we obtain by the Chemical, Membrane and Airlock Laws. We denote the extended set of rules by $\mathcal{R}'$. Each of these rules comes with a probability p_i (either inherited from a more specific version if the Chemical, Membrane or Airlock Law was involved or directly from the specification of the specific rules).

The execution of the pCHAM now simply corresponds to choosing one of the applicable rule operators with the corresponding probability and applying it to the vector representing the current solution or more generally ensemble. This is achieved by considering the operator:

$$\mathbf{T} = \mathcal{N} \left(\sum_{R_i \in \mathcal{R}'} p_i \mathbf{R}_i \right)$$

where the *normalisation* operation $\mathcal{N}$ is defined by:

$$\mathcal{N}(\mathbf{T})_{ij} = \begin{cases} \frac{\mathbf{T}_{ij}}{T_j} & \text{if } T_j = \sum_i \mathbf{T}_{ij} \neq 0 \\ 1 & \text{if } T_j = \sum_i \mathbf{T}_{ij} = 0 \text{ and } i = j \\ 0 & \text{otherwise.} \end{cases}$$

The test operators $\mathbf{E}$ in the definitions of the $\mathbf{R}_i$s "filter" out all those rules which are not applicable, the p_i's weight the chances of each reaction according to the specific rules, and the normalisation $\mathcal{N}$ computes the correct probabilities $\tilde{p}_i$. If a solution is inactive, normalisation adds a one on the diagonal which preserves the current solution without changing anything.

The linear operator $\mathbf{T}$ encodes the probabilistic transition relation $\Longrightarrow_p$ of the probabilistic transition system $(\mathcal{M}, \Longrightarrow_p, \mu_0)$ defining the operational semantics of the pCHAM $(\mathcal{M}, \mathcal{R}, \mu_0)$ as stated by the following proposition.

Proposition 6. *Given a pCHAM $(\mathcal{M}, \mathcal{R}, \mu_0)$, let $\Longrightarrow_p$ be the probabilistic transition relation on $\mathcal{M}$ of the associated probabilistic transition system, and let $\mathbf{T}$ be the linear operator on $\mathcal{V}(\mathcal{M})$ associated to $\mathcal{R}$. Then, for all $S_i, S_j \in \mathcal{M}$*

$$S_i \Longrightarrow_p S_j \text{ iff } \mathbf{T}_{ij} = p.$$

In order to implement the execution of a pCHAM $(\mathcal{M}, \mathcal{R}, \mu_0)$ we have only to compute the iterated applications of the operator to the vector representing the initial ensemble, i.e. $\mathbf{T}^n(\mu_0)$, which realises a discrete time Markov Chain. Depending on the questions we are interested in we can investigate, for example, the long run average of this Markov Chain, or other features commonly studied in the theory of stochastic processes.

4   Properties of the pCHAM

Let us next discuss some of the properties and aspects of the pCHAM and its linear operator semantics. This is not an exhaustive study but merely attempts to address some of the more interesting features.

4.1   Completeness of the Linear Operator Semantics

In the previous section we have shown that the linear operator semantics allows us to encode any transformation of ensembles of a set of molecules $\mathbf{T}$, that is any pCHAM. The following proposition shows that the reverse also holds.

Proposition 7. *For every linear operator $\mathbf{T}$ on a finite-dimensional vector space $\mathcal{V}$ there exists a set of molecules $\mathcal{T}$ with $|\mathcal{T}| = t$ and multiplicity bounded by s and a pCHAM $(\mathcal{M}, \mathcal{R}, \mu_0)$ over $\mathcal{T}$, such that $\mathcal{V} = \mathcal{V}(\mathcal{M}(\mathcal{T}))$, i.e. the tensor product $(\mathbb{R}^s)^{\otimes t}$, and $\mathbf{T}$ is represented by a linear combination of the rule operators $\mathbf{R}_i$.*

Proof. It is sufficient to show that all *matrix units* $\mathbf{B}_{ij}$, i.e. matrices with a single 1 at row i and column j and all other entries 0, for each tensor factor $\mathcal{V}(\mathcal{N})$ can be represented as $\mathbf{E}^{\geq \max} \cdot \mathbf{D}^n \cdot \mathbf{C}^m$.

One can show that $\mathbf{B}_{ij} = \mathbf{E}^{\geq i} \mathbf{D}^{i-1} \mathbf{C}^j$. Operationally this corresponds to filtering out all situations where the multiplicity of a molecule is too small, then by destroying all additional copies and then creating the needed j copies.

Any element in $\mathcal{V}(\mathcal{N})^{\otimes t}$ can then be represented by a linear combination of matrix units in $\mathcal{V}(\mathcal{N})^{\otimes t}$ which in turn are represented as the tensor product of certain matrix units in each $\mathcal{V}(\mathcal{N})$. □

This result proves that any Markov Chain on $\mathcal{V}(\mathcal{M}(\mathcal{T}))$ can be represented by a pCHAM, i.e. whatever (memoryless, discrete time) random process one chooses, it is always possible to define the rules of a particular pCHAM which implements this behaviour.

It is interesting to note that the proof of this fact is not by giving an explicit construction of this pCHAM but by arguing that the dimension of the space generated by the "rule operators" is as large, i.e. has the same dimension, as $\mathcal{L}(\mathcal{V}(\mathcal{M}(\mathcal{T})))$ — where $\mathcal{L}(\mathcal{V})$ denotes the set of all linear operators on $\mathcal{V}$ — and that we therefore can construct a representation of any possible random "behaviour" as a linear combination of the basic operators $\mathbf{C}$, $\mathbf{D}$ and $\mathbf{E}$. We will utilise a similar reasoning when we compare the expressiveness of calculi in Section 6.

4.2 Non-deterministic vs Probabilistic CHAMs

An obvious issue concerns the relation between the classical CHAM and its probabilistic version. In order to clarify this relation it may help to discuss the role non-determinism plays in a specification as opposed to the role of probability. The following example illustrates the difference.

Example 8. Consider two types of molecules: a and d. We think of the first one as "active" elements which can spontaneously produce a d molecule or turn itself into a d molecule; the other one is "dead", i.e. it decays immediately.

The specification of such a behaviour via a non-deterministic CHAM can be given using the following specific rules.

$$a \longrightarrow a, d \qquad a \longrightarrow d \qquad d \longrightarrow$$

A concrete pCHAM with the same behaviour might have the following rules:

$$a \longrightarrow_{\frac{1}{2}} a, d \qquad a \longrightarrow_{\frac{1}{2}} d \qquad d \longrightarrow_1$$

or a general specification of pCHAMs with this behaviour could utilise 'unspecified' probabilities, i.e. with $p \in [0,1]$:

$$a \longrightarrow_p a, d \qquad a \longrightarrow_{1-p} d \qquad d \longrightarrow_1$$

If we assume *fairness* in the CHAM case and $p \in (0,1)$, i.e. $p \neq 0$ and $p \neq 1$ then we could expect that we get the same long time behaviour if we start with $\{a\}$ in the case of the CHAM and pCHAM formulation.

It is easy to see that in the case of the CHAM it is possible to obtain after n steps the solution $\{a\}$ as well as $\{a, d, \ldots, d\} = \{a, d^k\}$ for $k \leq n$, as well as the empty solution $\{\}$. However, in the case of the pCHAM, we will — after n steps — quite likely have the empty solution. More precisely, the probability of obtaining $\{a, d^k\}$ tends to vanish for increasing n.

In some sense the probabilistic specification reflects more closely than the non-deterministic specification the real situation as it discards the most unlikely solution. As the classical example of the Gambler's Ruin (cf. e.g. [9]) shows: In real life it is not enough to state that it is *possible* that one will win the lottery; we need to say how *probable* this is.

Essentially we can simulate a non-deterministic CHAM by a pCHAM by "forgetting" about the concrete probabilities which describe the ensembles $\mathbf{T}^n(\mu)$.

Given a non-deterministic CHAM $(\mathcal{M}, \mathcal{R}, \mu_0)$ we can construct a corresponding pCHAM $(\mathcal{M}, \mathcal{R}', \mu_0)$ by attaching to each classical rule in $\mathcal{R}$ some non-zero probability in order to obtain the set of probabilistic rules $\mathcal{R}'$. Vice versa we can also construct a non-deterministic CHAM for every given pCHAM by dropping the probabilities related to the rules. A pCHAM gives rise to a unique CHAM, but there are several pCHAM which correspond to any given CHAM.

Proposition 9. *Given a CHAM $(\mathcal{M}, \mathcal{R}, S_0)$ and a corresponding pCHAM represented by the operator $\mathbf{T}$ on $\mathcal{V}(\mathcal{M}(\mathcal{T})) = \mathcal{V}(\mathcal{M})^{\otimes t}$, a solution $S \in \mathcal{M}$ is reachable in n reaction steps in $(\mathcal{M}, \mathcal{R}, S_0)$ if and only if $\mathbf{T}^n(\{\langle S_0, 1 \rangle\})$ has a non-zero component corresponding to S.*

4.3   Locality of Rules of the pCHAM

Several people have argued that the need for normalisation imposes a severe non-locality constraint on probabilistic models of computations. This is only partly true as one can postpone the normalisation under certain circumstances. More precisely, if we start with a point distribution μ, i.e. if we know exactly with which chemical solution we start, then instead of normalising $\mathbf{T}$ we can normalise the $\mathbf{T}(\mu)$ — extending the normalisation to positive vectors in the obvious way by dividing them by their 1-norm $\|.\|_1$, i.e. the sum of all their coordinates.

Proposition 10. *Given a pCHAM* $(\mathcal{M}, \mathcal{R}, \mu_0)$ *and its operator* $\mathbf{T} = \mathcal{N}(\mathbf{T}')$ *with* $\mathbf{T}' = \sum_i p_i \mathbf{R}_i$ *on* $\mathcal{V}(\mathcal{M}(\mathcal{T})) = \mathcal{V}(\mathcal{N})^{\otimes t}$ *and an ensemble* $\mu = \{\langle \mu, 1 \rangle\}$ *then we have:*

$$\mathbf{T}(\mu) = \begin{cases} \mathcal{N}(\mathbf{T}'(\mu)) & \textit{if } \mathcal{N}(\mathbf{T}'(\mu)) \neq o \\ \mu & \textit{otherwise} \end{cases} \quad \textit{with } \mathcal{N}(\mu) = \begin{cases} \frac{\mu}{\|\mu\|_1} & \textit{if } \|\mu\|_1 \neq 0 \\ \mu & \textit{otherwise.} \end{cases}$$

We have for a single step and a point-ensemble essentially that $\mathbf{T}'$ and $\mathcal{N}$ commute, i.e. $\mathcal{N}(\mathbf{T}')(\mu) = \mathcal{N}(\mathbf{T}'(\mu))$ — only in the case of "blocked" solutions, which result in the zero vector o, we have to complicate things by 're-producing' the original vector.

In other words, if we consider the probabilities along a certain execution path we do not need to normalise the complete operator $\mathbf{T}'$. We can start with a point-ensemble, compute the probabilities of its successors in the above way by $\mathcal{N}(\mathbf{T}'(\mu))$, pick a *single* successor ensemble and repeat the application of the non-normalised $\mathbf{T}'$. Non-locality problems only arise when we consider $\mathbf{T}^n(\mu)$. The reason for this is that in this case we do not compute (the probabilities of) a *single* computational path but of *all* possible paths at the same time. This obviously implies the need to "distribute" the available probability non-locally between them by normalising $\mathbf{T}'$.

The operator $\mathbf{T}'$ encodes the rules $\longrightarrow_p$ while $\mathbf{T} = \mathcal{N}(\mathbf{T}')$ represents the rewrite steps $\Longrightarrow_p$. The possibility to postpone normalisation has also important consequences for the Linear Operator Semantics and its tensor product representation which can be treated in a "lazy" fashion. The only time we have to compute the tensor product effectively is when we normalise $\mathbf{T}'$, as long as we work with the original $\mathbf{T}'$ we can apply it component-wise to a given vector as for a distribution $\mu = \sum_i x_i \mu_i$ with $\mu_i = \bigotimes_j \mu_{ij}$ the application of $\mathbf{T} = \sum_k p_k \mathbf{R}_k$ with $\mathbf{R}_k = \bigotimes_j \mathbf{R}_{kj}$ is obtained as:

$$\mathbf{T}(\mu) = \sum_k p_k \sum_i (\bigotimes_j \mathbf{R}_{kj})(\bigotimes_j \mu_{ij}) = \sum_k p_k \sum_i \bigotimes_j \mathbf{R}_{kj}(\mu_{ij})$$

4.4   Finite vs Infinite pCHAMs

In the foregoing sections we have assumed that the multiplicity of molecules is bounded. However we can drop this finiteness condition and work instead with infinite matrices $\mathbf{E}$, $\mathbf{C}$ and $\mathbf{D}$. These correspond to so called *projections* ($\mathbf{E}$), and *shift operators* ($\mathbf{C}$ and $\mathbf{D}$).

We can consider instead of $\mathcal{V}(\mathcal{N})$ the (Banach) space of infinite sequences with bounded p-norm, i.e.

$$\ell^p(\mathcal{M}) = \left\{ \sum_{i=0}^{\infty} x_i S_i \mid x_i \in \mathbb{R}, S_i \in \mathcal{M}, (\sum_{i=0}^{\infty} |x_i|^p)^{\frac{1}{p}} < \infty \right\} \subseteq \mathcal{V}(\mathbb{N})$$

The infinite matrices $\mathbf{E}$, $\mathbf{C}$ and $\mathbf{D}$ represent bounded (and therefore continuous) operators. In particular, we can take the Hilbert space $\ell^2(\mathcal{M})$ and directly recast our finite-dimensional framework in this setting. To a certain degree this framework is even more convenient than the finite-dimensional one; for example we have $\mathbf{CD} = \mathbf{I}$, which is not the case in finite dimensions.

The construction of $\mathbf{T}$ follows the same recipe as before. We also observe that if we start with any initial solution μ_0 which can be represented by a vector in $\ell^2(\mathcal{M})$ — which is obviously the case for a point distribution — we can guarantee that the iterations $\mathbf{T}^n(\mu)$ will stay in $\ell^2(\mathcal{M})$.

5   Encoding Probabilistic Linda Languages

The CHAM model can be used to describe the operational semantics of various calculi like CCS, the π-calculus, and the Linda calculus which is at the base of several coordination languages, see e.g. [2]. Probabilistic versions of such calculi can be modelled via the pCHAM. We will concentrate here on the encoding of probabilistic Linda-like languages which we will then use as a base for demonstrating our approach to define and measure language expressiveness.

We consider a family of languages $\mathcal{L}(X)$ which differ from one another for the set X of communication primitives used. These primitives correspond to the basic Linda primitives for adding a token to a shared data-space, getting it from the data-space, and checking for its presence or absence in the data-space. The languages $\mathcal{L}(X)$ also include standard prefix and a probabilistic choice operator.

The syntax of $\mathcal{L}(X)$ is formally defined by the following grammar:

$$P ::= \mathbf{stop} \mid C.P \mid P \mid P \mid P +_p P$$
$$C ::= \mathbf{ask}(t) \mid \mathbf{tell}(t) \mid \mathbf{get}(t)$$

where t is a generic element called *token* in a denumerable set $\mathcal{D}$, P is a process and C a communication action (or prefix); we denote by $\mathcal{P}$ the set of all processes. The parameter X defining a Linda-like language $\mathcal{L}(X)$ is a subset of the primitives defined by C.

A program in $\mathcal{L}(X)$ is therefore either an inactive, trivial program $\mathbf{stop}$, or a sequential composition $C.P$ or a probabilistic choice $P +_p P$. As usual we omit a trailing $\mathbf{stop}$ if it is prefixed by a non-empty sequence of basic actions C.

A pCHAM encoding for $\mathcal{L}(X)$ is defined by specifying the set of molecules as $\mathcal{D} \cup \mathcal{P}$ and the following molecule transformation, i.e. specific rules (cf also [11]):

(i) $P_1 \mid P_2 \longrightarrow_1 P_1, P_2$ (v) **stop** $\longrightarrow_1$ **stop**

(ii) $P_1, P_2 \longrightarrow_1 P_1 \mid P_2$ (vi) **tell**$(t).P \longrightarrow_1 P, t$

(iii) $P_1 +_p P_2 \longrightarrow_p P_1$ (vii) **ask**$(t).P, s \longrightarrow_1 P, s$ if $t = s$

(iv) $P_1 +_p P_2 \longrightarrow_{1-p} P_2$ (viii) **get**$(t).P, s \longrightarrow_1 P$ if $t = s$

As with any pCHAM these rules give rise to a set of *rule operators* $\mathbf{R}_i$. All possible executions of $\mathcal{L}(X)$ programs are choices between or sequential application of these rules. In other words, all possible "behaviours" of $\mathcal{L}(X)$ programs are linear combinations and products of the rule operators $\mathbf{R}_i$. The possibilities of programs in a language $\mathcal{L}(X)$ are thus reflected in the structure of the algebra $\mathcal{A}(X)$ which is generated by (linear combinations and products of) the rule operators $\mathbf{R}_i$ of the pCHAM for $\mathcal{L}(X)$.

Example 11. To illustrate this let us construct the algebra $\mathcal{A}(\mathbf{tell}, \mathbf{ask}, \mathbf{get})$ for a "bounded" version version of the language $\mathcal{L}(\mathbf{tell}, \mathbf{ask}, \mathbf{get})$. We will allow only one type of token t, i.e. $\mathcal{D} = \{t\}$, which appears only with multiplicity $0, 1$ or 2.

The linear operator semantics of this language is given by operators on $\mathcal{V}(\mathcal{P}) \otimes \mathcal{V}(\{\{\emptyset\}, \{t\}, \{t, t\}\})$. To keep things as simple as possible we will concentrate only on the behaviour of the store, i.e. the possible transformations on $\mathcal{V}(\{\{\emptyset\}, \{t\}, \{t, t\}\})$ and ignore how the processes themselves change.

The operators corresponding to the rules for **tell** and **get** and the guard in the **ask** rule are given by:

$$\mathbf{T} = \begin{pmatrix} 0\,1\,0 \\ 0\,0\,1 \\ 0\,0\,1 \end{pmatrix} \qquad \mathbf{G} = \begin{pmatrix} 1\,0\,0 \\ 1\,0\,0 \\ 0\,1\,0 \end{pmatrix} \qquad \mathbf{A} = \begin{pmatrix} 0\,0\,0 \\ 0\,1\,0 \\ 0\,0\,1 \end{pmatrix}$$

The **stop** rule is implemented by the identity matrix $\mathbf{I}$. The other four rules do not directly influence the store component. However, they allow the combination of basic operators via linear combination (the choice rules) and product (via the parallel rules). The possible "behaviours" are therefore linear combination and products of these basic operators, i.e. we have to look at the algebras generated by some subset of $\{\mathbf{A}, \mathbf{G}, \mathbf{T}, \mathbf{I}\}$.

We can show that $\{\mathbf{A}, \mathbf{G}, \mathbf{T}, \mathbf{I}\}$ generate the full 3×3 matrix algebra $M(3)$. To do this it is sufficient to show that we can construct all matrix units (cf. proof of Proposition 7) in $M(3)$ using the basic matrices $\mathbf{A}$, $\mathbf{G}$, $\mathbf{T}$ and $\mathbf{I}$. Any other matrix in $M(3)$ is then a linear combination of the matrices $\mathbf{E}_{nm}$. For example one can easily check that the following holds:

$\mathbf{B}_{11} = \mathbf{I} - \mathbf{A}$, $\mathbf{B}_{12} = (\mathbf{I} - \mathbf{A})\mathbf{T}$, $\mathbf{B}_{13} = (\mathbf{I} - \mathbf{A})\mathbf{T}\mathbf{T}$

$\mathbf{B}_{21} = (\mathbf{I} - \mathbf{G})\mathbf{A}\mathbf{T}\mathbf{G}\mathbf{G}$, $\mathbf{B}_{22} = (\mathbf{I} - \mathbf{G})\mathbf{A}\mathbf{T}\mathbf{G}$, $\mathbf{B}_{23} = (\mathbf{I} - \mathbf{G})\mathbf{A}\mathbf{T}$

$\mathbf{B}_{31} = \mathbf{G}\mathbf{A}\mathbf{G}$, $\mathbf{B}_{32} = \mathbf{G}\mathbf{A}$, $\mathbf{B}_{33} = \mathbf{G}\mathbf{A}\mathbf{T}$

It might be worth noting that we extensively used the negative of $\mathbf{A}$, i.e. the testing for the absence of the token. One might therefore argue that the algebra $\mathcal{A}(X)$ contains not only the effective behaviours of programs in $\mathcal{L}(X)$ but also artificial ones. However, for the method for comparison of the expressiveness of languages we introduce in the next section, $\mathcal{A}(X)$ is a useful approximation.

6   Expressiveness

The pCHAM provides a uniform encoding for several probabilistic languages and calculi, in that it is a common abstract semantics on the base of which the observable behaviour of programs/processes in different languages/calculi can be specified. It is therefore reasonable to utilise such an encoding to compare the expressive power of one language relative to another. The idea is similar to the notion of embedding introduced in [12] and later refined in [13]: given two probabilistic languages Γ_1 and Γ_2 we first define their associated pCHAMs and then we compare them by checking whether or not one can "simulate" the other. The difference with the original notion of embedding is that we do not need to specify any particular observation criteria nor to compile a program in a language into a program in the other language; rather we encode both languages into the same kind of abstract semantics and compare "how many" computations can be performed by the first abstract machine which cannot be performed by the second. In fact, the linear operator semantics of the pCHAM also allows us to determine the "size" of the space of "behaviours" generated by a certain set of specific rules and thus provide obstructions which prevents the embedding or simulation of one pCHAM into another without constructing a counter-example.

This approach can also be adopted to compare the expressive power of non-probabilistic languages: we just need to consider the restriction of our linear operators to point distributions.

Example 12. Assume a finite set of molecules $\{m_1, \ldots, m_t\}$ without a bound on the multiplicity s. If the specific rules of a (p)CHAM are of the form:

$$m_{i1}, \ldots, m_{ik} \longrightarrow m_{j1}, \ldots, m_{jl} \text{ or } m_{i1}, \ldots, m_{ik} \longrightarrow_p m_{j1}, \ldots, m_{jl}$$

such that $l > k$ it is immediately clear that in each reaction the size of the solution is monotonically increasing. Such a (p)CHAM therefore is unable to, for example, purge a solution from all multiples of a certain molecule $\{m_1, m_1, m_1\} \Longrightarrow \{m_1\}$. It is also unable to embed a (p)CHAM whose specific rules include a rule like $m_2, m_4 \longrightarrow m_2$.

Let Γ be a probabilistic calculus and consider an operational semantics for Γ defined via a set of states $\mathcal{C}(\Gamma)$ and a transition relation $\rightarrow_p$ on $\mathcal{C}(\Gamma)$. By an *encoding* e of Γ into a pCHAM $pCHAM(\Gamma) = (\mathcal{M}, \mathcal{R}, \mu_0)$ we mean a (total) function:

$$e : \mathcal{C}(\Gamma) \to \mathcal{M}$$

which associates to every state of Γ a solution of $pCHAM(\Gamma)$ such that transitions in Γ correspond to transitions in $pCHAM(\Gamma)$, i.e. $C_1 \rightarrow_p C_2$ implies $e(C_1) \Longrightarrow_p e(C_2)$. We omit a more formal definition (which might impose additional constraints and correctness conditions on e) as we will consider here only the encoding of the Linda-like languages we presented in Section 5.

In order to compare the expressiveness of languages we could, on one hand, introduce a notion of an *embedding of languages* following directly Shapiro's approach [12,13]. Our idea, on the other hand, is to compare languages on the base of the possible behaviours of their associated pCHAMs. In order to do this one could develop a general notion of *pCHAM embeddings*, or a bit more concretely, address the question when pCHAMs, which are the result of the encoding of calculi or programming languages, can simulate each others behaviour. However, we will go one step further and base our notion of embedding not on the pCHAMs themselves but instead on the linear operator semantics. Our notion of embedding is illustrated by the following diagram:

$$\Gamma_1 \xrightarrow{\quad e_1 \quad} pCHAM(\Gamma_1) \approx\approx\approx \mathcal{A}(\Gamma_1)$$

$$\uparrow N$$

$$\Gamma_2 \xrightarrow{\quad e_2 \quad} pCHAM(\Gamma_2) \approx\approx\approx \mathcal{A}(\Gamma_2)$$

where e_1 and e_2 are the pCHAM *encodings* of Γ_2 and Γ_1 respectively, $\mathcal{A}(\Gamma_1)$ and $\mathcal{A}(\Gamma_2)$ are the linear algebras generated from the rules in $pCHAM(\Gamma_1)$ and $pCHAM(\Gamma_2)$ respectively, and N is a map $N : \mathcal{A}(\Gamma_2) \to \mathcal{A}(\Gamma_1)$ which implements the embedding.

In principle this embedding could be as complicated as one wants. If the two pCHAMs in question encode Turing complete calculi then it is always possible to encode one in the other in some way. However, we will consider only "reasonable" encodings which respect the structure of the calculi and their pCHAMs, i.e. encodings which are somehow compositional (on the molecular level). We will therefore concentrate our attention only on particular linear maps N between $\mathcal{A}(\Gamma_2)$ and $\mathcal{A}(\Gamma_1)$.

Definition 13. *A linear embedding of a linear algebra $\mathcal{A}_1$ into a linear algebra $\mathcal{A}_2$ is an injective algebra homomorphism, i.e. a linear and product preserving map $N : \mathcal{A}_1 \to \mathcal{A}_2$.*

A linear embedding of a calculus Γ_1 into another one Γ_2 is given by a linear embedding of the corresponding algebras $\mathcal{A}(\Gamma_1)$ into $\mathcal{A}(\Gamma_2)$.

There are further restrictions one could impose, e.g. that the pCHAMs and their algebras reflect the structure of the calculi in a particular way, etc. A particular situation is the comparison of sub-calculi of a given calculus; in this case e_1 and e_2 are the same function.

Example 14. A language $\mathcal{L}(X)$ can be embedded into a language $\mathcal{L}(Y)$ iff $\mathcal{A}(X)$ can be embedded in $\mathcal{A}(Y)$, cf also [14]. A simple property of the algebras $\mathcal{A}(X)$ and $\mathcal{A}(Y)$ like their dimension can give us a criterion to decide whether $\mathcal{A}(X)$ can be embedded into $\mathcal{A}(Y)$: if $\dim(\mathcal{A}(X)) > \dim(\mathcal{A}(Y))$ then it is impossible to embed $\mathcal{A}(X)$ into $\mathcal{A}(Y)$. However, it is not correct to conclude the opposite, i.e. $\dim(\mathcal{A}(X)) \leq \dim(\mathcal{A}(Y))$ does not necessarily imply that there is a "reasonable" embedding of $\mathcal{L}(X)$ into $\mathcal{L}(Y)$.

Considering the Linda-like languages from the previous section we can show, for example, that $\dim(\mathcal{A}(\textbf{tell}, \textbf{ask})) > \dim(\mathcal{A}(\textbf{tell}))$ and $\dim(\mathcal{A}(\textbf{tell}, \textbf{get})) > \dim(\mathcal{A}(\textbf{tell}))$ which means that it is impossible to embed either $\mathcal{L}(\textbf{tell}, \textbf{get})$

nor $\mathcal{L}(\textbf{tell}, \textbf{ask})$ in $\mathcal{L}(\textbf{tell})$. More concretely, one can show that $\mathcal{L}(\textbf{tell}, \textbf{ask})$ generates only the sub-algebra of upper triangular 3×3 matrices $U(3)$. We can embed this sub-algebra into the full matrix algebra $M(3)$ by taking $\textbf{N}$ the identity restricted to the sub-algebra $U(3)$, but not vice versa. An obstruction against the embeddability of $M(3)$ into $U(3)$ is the fact that the dimensions are incompatible, i.e. $\dim(M(3)) = 9$ while $\dim(U(3)) = 6$.

This is consistent with the hierarchy of languages in, e.g., [14]:

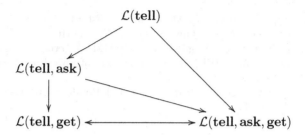

7   Conclusions

We presented a probabilistic version of the Chemical Abstract Machine. The CHAM and its probabilistic version pCHAM provide a basic and simple framework for comparing various probabilistic (or quantitative) calculi. The pCHAM model is based on a particular, discrete time Markov Chain (DTMC) model in which a scheduler decides at each time step on the probability that any of the applicable rules or reactions gets executed.

It will be interesting to investigate different, perhaps more general execution models for a pCHAM: For example, one could allow the scheduler to execute at each time step not only a single rule but any number of rules as long as they are not in "conflict"; this makes it necessary to develop a probabilistic mechanism for resolving such conflicts. Another line of further work will be devoted to the formulation of a continuous time Markov Chain (CTMC) model which we can define via so-called $\textbf{Q}$ matrices which themselves generate transition matrices as $\textbf{T}_t = \exp(t\textbf{Q})$; in this model the chance that any two rules "fire" simultaneously is zero and conflicts between rules are therefore not a problem.

Finally, we plan a closer investigation of the relation between (general) discrete and continuous time models and of expressiveness issues regarding the pCHAM encodings of synchronous versus asynchronous calculi, see e.g. [15].

References

1. Banâtre, J.P., Le Métayer, D.: The gamma model and its discipline of programming. Science of Computer Programming **15** (1990) 55–77
2. Banâtre, J.P., Fradet, P., Le Métayer, D.: Gamma and the chemical reaction model: Fifteen years after. In Calude, C., ed.: Multiset Processing. Volume 2235 of Lecture Notes in Computer Science., Springer Verlag (2001) 17–44

3. Fradet, P., Le Métayer, D.: Structured gamma. Science of Computer Programming **31** (1998) 263–289
4. Le Métayer, D.: Higher-order multiset programming. In: DIMACS workshop on specifications of parallel algorithms. Volume 18 of Dimacs series in Discrete Mathematics., American Mathematical Society (1994)
5. Andreoli, J.M., Hankin, C., Le Métayer, D.: Coordination Programming. Imperial College Press, London (1996)
6. Berry, G., Boudol, G.: The chemical abstract machine. Theoretical Computer Science **96** (1992) 217–248
7. Jonsson, B., Yi, W., Larsen, K.: 11. In: Probabilistic Extensions of Process Algebras. Elsevier Science, Amsterdam (2001) 685–710 see [16].
8. De Nicola, R., Ferrari, G., Pugliese, R.: KLAIM: A kernel language for agents interaction and mobility. IEEE Transactions on Software Engineering **24** (1998) 315–330
9. Grimmett, G., Stirzaker, D.: Probability and Random Processes. second edn. Clarendon Press, Oxford (1992)
10. Parzen, E.: Stochastic Processes. second edn. Classics in Applied Mathematics. SIAM (1999)
11. Ciancarini, P., Jensen, K., Yankelevich, D.: On the operational semantics of a coordination language. In Ciancarini, P., Nierstrasz, O., Yonezawa, A., eds.: ECOOP Workshop. Volume 924 of Lecture Notes in Computer Science., Springer Verlag (1995) 77–106
12. Shapiro, E.: Embeddings among concurrent programming languages. In Cleaveland, W.R., ed.: Proceedings CONCUR 92, Stony Brook, NY, USA. Volume 630 of Lecture Notes in Computer Science., Springer-Verlag (1992) 486–503
13. de Boer, F.S., Palamidessi, C.: Embedding as a tool for language comparison. Information and Computation **108** (1994) 128–157
14. Brogi, A., Di Pierro, A., Wiklicky, H.: Linear embedding for a quantitative comparison of language expressiveness. In: QAPL'01 — ACM Workshop on Quantitative Aspects of Programming Languages. Volume 59:3 of ENTCS., Elsevier (2002)
15. Palamidessi, C.: Comparing the expressive power of the synchronous and the asynchronous pi-calculus. Mathematical Structures in Computer Science **13** (2003) 685–719
16. Bergstra, J., Ponse, A., Smolka, S., eds.: Handbook of Process Algebra. Elsevier Science, Amsterdam (2001)
17. Palmer, T.: Banach Algebras and The General Theory of ∗-Algebras – Volume I: Algebras and Banach Algebras. Volume 49 of Encyclopedia of Mathematics and Its Applications. Cambridge University Press, Cambridge – New York (1994)
18. Kadison, R., Ringrose, J.: Fundamentals of the Theory of Operator Algebras: Volume I — Elementary Theory. Volume 15 of Graduate Studies in Mathematics. American Mathematical Society, Providence, Rhode Island (1997) reprint from Academic Press edition 1983.
19. Fillmore, P.A.: A User's Guide to Operator Algebras. John Wiley & Sons, New York — Chicester (1996)
20. Wegge-Olsen, N.: K-Theory and C^*-Algebras — A Friendly Approach. Oxford University Press, Oxford (1993)

A   Tensor Products

The tensor product plays a central role in our discussion. For the convenience of the reader we therefore recall some of the important facts about the tensor product of vectors, (Hilbert) spaces, operators, etc.

Let $\mathcal{V}_1, \mathcal{V}_2, \ldots, \mathcal{V}_n$ and $\mathcal{W}$ be linear spaces. A map $f : \mathcal{V}_1 \times \mathcal{V}_2 \times \ldots \times \mathcal{V}_n \to \mathcal{W}$ is called *multi-linear* if f is linear in each of its arguments. We denote by $\mathcal{L}(\mathcal{V}_1, \mathcal{V}_2, \ldots, \mathcal{V}_n; \mathcal{W})$ the set of multi-linear maps. The algebraic tensor product of vector spaces is defined via a universal property as follows (see e.g. Definition 1.10.1 in [17]).

Definition 15. *The algebraic tensor product of vector spaces $\mathcal{V}_1, \mathcal{V}_2, \ldots, \mathcal{V}_n$ is given by a vector space $\bigotimes_{i=1}^{n} \mathcal{V}_i$ and a map $p = \otimes_{i=1}^{n} \in \mathcal{L}(\mathcal{V}_1, \mathcal{V}_2, \ldots, \mathcal{V}_n; \bigotimes_{i=1}^{n} \mathcal{V}_i)$ such that if $\mathcal{W}$ is any vector space and $f \in \mathcal{L}(\mathcal{V}_1, \mathcal{V}_2, \ldots, \mathcal{V}_n; \mathcal{W})$ then there exists a unique map $h : \bigotimes_{i=1}^{n} \mathcal{V}_i \to \mathcal{W}$ satisfying $f = h \circ p$.*

This algebraic construction is sufficient for finite dimensional vector spaces. It is easy to show that in the finite dimensional case we have: $\mathcal{V}(X \times X) \cong \mathcal{V}(X) \otimes \mathcal{V}(X)$. In the infinite dimensional case one has to consider also topological aspects; for example, the algebraic tensor product of Hilbert spaces does not form in general a Hilbert space. Without going into the details — see for example [18], [19] or Appendix T in [20] — it is however possible to construct from the algebraic tensor product of Hilbert spaces $\mathcal{H}_1, \mathcal{H}_2, \ldots, \mathcal{H}_n$, a Hilbert space which is the tensor product $\bigotimes_{i=1}^{n} \mathcal{H}_i$.

The following results summarise important properties of the tensor product:

Proposition 16. *If $\mathcal{H}_1, \ldots, \mathcal{H}_n$ are Hilbert spaces and $\mathbf{A}_i \in \mathcal{B}(\mathcal{H}_i)$ with $i = 1, \ldots, n$ bounded linear operators, then there exists a unique bounded linear operator $\mathbf{A} \in \mathcal{B}(\mathcal{H}_1 \otimes \ldots \otimes \mathcal{H}_n)$ such that:*

$$\mathbf{A}(x_1 \otimes \ldots \otimes x_n) = \mathbf{A}_1(x_1) \otimes \ldots \otimes \mathbf{A}_n(x_n).$$

for all $x_i \in \mathcal{H}_i$ and we write $\mathbf{A} = \mathbf{A}_1 \otimes \ldots \otimes \mathbf{A}_n$.

Proposition 17. *The tensor product of (bounded) linear operators $\mathbf{A}_1, \mathbf{A}_2, \ldots, \mathbf{A}_n$ (on Hilbert spaces) is associative and has the following properties:*

(i) $(\mathbf{A}_1 \otimes \ldots \otimes \mathbf{A}_n)(\mathbf{B}_1 \otimes \ldots \otimes \mathbf{B}_n) = (\mathbf{A}_1 \mathbf{B}_1 \otimes \ldots \otimes \mathbf{A}_n \mathbf{B}_n)$

(ii) $\mathbf{A}_1 \otimes \ldots \otimes (\alpha \mathbf{A}_i) \otimes \ldots \otimes \mathbf{A}_n = \alpha(\mathbf{A}_1 \otimes \ldots \otimes \mathbf{A}_i \otimes \ldots \otimes \mathbf{A}_n)$

(iii) $\mathbf{A}_1 \otimes \ldots \otimes (\mathbf{A}_i + \mathbf{B}_i) \otimes \ldots \otimes \mathbf{A}_n = \mathbf{A}_1 \otimes \ldots \otimes \mathbf{A}_i \otimes \ldots \otimes \mathbf{A}_n + \mathbf{A}_1 \otimes \ldots \otimes \mathbf{B}_i \otimes \ldots \otimes \mathbf{A}_n$

(iv) $(\mathbf{A}_1 \otimes \ldots \otimes \mathbf{A}_n)^* = \mathbf{A}_1^* \otimes \ldots \otimes \mathbf{A}_n^*$

(v) $\|\mathbf{A}_1 \otimes \ldots \otimes \mathbf{A}_n\| = \|\mathbf{A}_1\| \ldots \|\mathbf{A}_n\|$

For a proof of these properties see e.g. discussions and remarks following Proposition 2.6.12 in [18].

Partial Order Reduction for Markov Decision Processes: A Survey

Marcus Groesser* and Christel Baier**

Institut für Informatik I
Römerstrasse 164
53117 Bonn
groesser@cs.uni-bonn.de
baier@cs.uni-bonn.de

Abstract. In the past, several model checking algorithms have been proposed to verify probabilistic reactive systems. In contrast to the non-probabilistic setting where various techniques have been suggested and successfully applied to combat the state space-explosion problem in the context of model checking the techniques used for probabilistic systems have mainly concentrated on symbolic methods with variants of decision diagrams or abstraction methods. Only recently results have been published that give criteria on applying partial order reduction for verifying quantitative linear time properties as well as branching time properties for probabilistic systems. This paper summarizes the results that have been established so far about partial order reduction for Markov decision processes. We present the different reduction conditions and provide a comparison of the corresponding results.

1 Introduction

Model checking is a technique that allows for the fully automatic verification of a property (often specified in a temporal logic) against a given system (e.g. modelled as a Kripke-structure (a labelled directed graph)). It supports the analysis of qualitative properties such as "every request is eventually answered". As the systems get very large (the so-called state space-explosion problem), a variety of techniques have been developed to tackle this problem. These include symbolic model checking with binary decision diagrams, partial order reduction, abstraction techniques and reasoning with symmetries, see e.g. [10] for an overview. The partial order reduction [39,32,19,34] is based on the observation that the execution order of concurrent operations does not necessarily change the validity of a property. Therefore, fixing one particular order of interleaving operations (without generating the others) helps to reduce the number of states and transitions that need to be explored while preserving the properties of interest. Over

---

* Supported by the DFG-NWO-Project "VOSS II" and the DFG-Project "SYANCO".
** Supported by the DFG-NWO-Project "VOSS II" and the DFG-Projects "PROB-POR" and "SYANCO".

F.S. de Boer et al. (Eds.): FMCO 2005, LNCS 4111, pp. 408–427, 2006.

the years model checking has been extended to probabilistic system, such as labelled Markov chains and labelled Markov decision processes (MDPs). The latter arise as natural operational models for e.g. randomized distributed algorithms and communication or security protocols, where the nondeterminism is used to model the interleaving of concurrent activities, the interaction with an uncertain environment (e.g. a user) or for abstraction purposes, whereas the probabilism serves to model e.g. coin tossing actions. The properties to be verified are of the kind "with probability 1, every request will eventually be granted" or "access is granted with a probability of at least 97%". Verification of such properties relies not only on graph algorithms (to explore the state space) but also on numerical methods to solve linear equation systems or linear programming problems [43,44,11,35,12,15]. Thus the state space-explosion problem is at least as relevant (or even more) than in the non-probabilistic setting. In the probabilistic setting, research on methods that combat the state space-explosion problem has mainly concentrated on symbolic techniques with variants of decision diagrams [22,2,8,23,31,29]. Moreover there is a range of results about state-aggregation with (formula-independent) bisimulation-like equivalences [4,9] and various abstraction techniques [13,26,27,18]. Only recently results have been published on partial order reduction for MDPs [5,14,3]. All of those publications extend a particular instance of partial order reduction, the so-called ample-set-method to MPDs. This paper gives a summary and comparison of those results.

Organization of the paper. Section 2 briefly summarizes the preliminaries concerning our model (Markov decision processes) and partial order reduction. In Section 3 the basic schema of the ample-set-method for linear time properties and non-probabilistic systems is presented. Section 4 provides the various results for partial order reduction on Markov decision processes. In Section 5, we explain the connections between the several reduction criteria and process equivalences. The paper ends with a brief conclusion in Section 6.

2 Preliminaries

In an MDP any state s might have several outgoing action-labeled transitions, each of them is associated with a probability distribution which yields the probabilities for the successor states. As in [36,30,15] we assume here that for any state s, the outgoing transitions of s have different action labels. (This corresponds to the so-called reactive model in the classification of [42].) In addition we assume here a labelling function that attaches to any state s a set of atomic propositions that are assumed to be fulfilled in state s. The atomic propositions will serve as atoms to formulate the desired properties in a temporal logical framework.

Definition 1. (Probability distribution) *Given a set T, a probability distribution on T is a function*

$$\mu \ : \ T \ \longrightarrow \ [0,1]$$

such that $\sum_{t \in T} \mu(t) = 1$. The support of μ is denoted by $supp(\mu) = \{t \in T : \mu(t) > 0\}$ and the set of probability distributions on T is denoted by $Distr(T)$. Given $t \in T$, μ_t denotes the Dirac distribution that assigns probability 1 to t. □

Definition 2. (Markov decision process (MDP), e.g. [36]) *An MDP is a tuple* $\mathcal{M} = (S, \mathsf{Act}, \mathsf{P}, s_{init}, \mathsf{AP}, \mathsf{L})$, *where*

- S *is a finite set of states,*
- Act *is a finite set of actions,*
- $\mathsf{P} : (S \times \mathsf{Act} \times S) \to [0, 1]$ *is the probability matrix,*
- $s_{init} \in S$ *is the initial state,*
- AP *is a finite set of atomic propositions and*
- $\mathsf{L} : S \to 2^{\mathsf{AP}}$ *is a labeling function.*

$\mathsf{Act}(s)$ *denotes the set of actions that are enabled in state* s, *i.e. the set of actions* $\alpha \in \mathsf{Act}$ *such that* $\mathsf{P}(s, \alpha, t) > 0$ *for some state* $t \in S$. *For any state* $s \in S$, *we require that* $\mathsf{Act}(s) \neq \emptyset$ *and* $\sum_{s' \in S} \mathsf{P}(s, \alpha, s') = 1$ *for any action* $\alpha \in \mathsf{Act}(s)$, *that is* $\mathsf{P}(s, \alpha, .)$ *is a probabilitiy distribution over* S. *(In particular, we assume that* $\mathcal{M}$ *does not have terminal states.)* □

The intuitive operational behavior of an MDP is as follows. If s is the current state then first one of the actions $\alpha \in \mathsf{Act}(s)$ is chosen non-deterministically. Afterwards action α is executed leading to state t with probability $\mathsf{P}(s, \alpha, t)$.

We refer to t as an α-successor of s if $\mathsf{P}(s, \alpha, t) > 0$. Action α is called a *probabilistic action* if it has a random effect, i.e., if there is at least one state s where α is enabled and that has two or more α-successors. Otherwise α is called non-probabilistic. In particular, if all actions in Act are non-probabilistic then our notion of an MDP reduces to an ordinary transition system with at most one outgoing α-transition per state and action α. When modelling realistic systems, most actions α will be non-probabilistic in the sense that they yield unique successor states.

Paths. An infinite path in an MDP is a sequence

$$\varsigma = s_0, \alpha_1, s_1, \alpha_2, \ldots \in (S \times \mathsf{Act})^{\omega}$$

such that $\alpha_i \in \mathsf{Act}(s_{i-1})$ and $\mathsf{P}(s_{i-1}, \alpha_i, s_i) > 0$ for any $i \geq 1$. We write paths in the form

$$\varsigma = s_0 \xrightarrow{\alpha_1} s_1 \xrightarrow{\alpha_2} s_2 \xrightarrow{\alpha_3} \ldots$$

$\mathsf{first}(\varsigma) = s_0$ denotes the starting state of ς and $\mathsf{trace}(\varsigma) = \mathsf{L}(s_0), \mathsf{L}(s_1), \mathsf{L}(s_2), \ldots$ the word over the alphabet 2^{AP} obtained by the projection of ς to the state labels. Finite paths (denoted by the greek letter σ) are finite prefixes of infinite paths that end in a state. We use the notations $\mathsf{first}(\sigma)$ and $\mathsf{trace}(\sigma)$ as for infinite paths, $\mathsf{last}(\sigma)$ for the last state of σ and $|\sigma|$ for the length (number of actions).

Schedulers. A scheduler denotes an instance that resolves the nondeterminism in the states, and thus yields a Markov chain and a probability measure on the paths. We consider here history dependent, randomized schedulers (briefly called schedulers) which are given by a function D that assigns to any finite path σ a probability distribution over $\mathsf{Act}(\mathsf{last}(\sigma))$. For a formal definition see

[36,5]. Intuitively a scheduler takes as input the "history" of a computation (formalized by a finite path σ) and chooses the next action α randomly, according to the probabilities specified by the distribution $D(\sigma)$. Given a scheduler D, the behavior of $\mathcal{M}$ under D can be formalized by a (possibly infinite-state) Markov chain. We write $\mathsf{Pr}^{D,s}$ or simply Pr^D to denote the standard probability measure on the Borel field of the infinite paths ς with $\mathsf{first}(\varsigma) = s$.

In Section 4 we will need the notion of *end components* which can be seen as the MDP-counterpart to terminal strongly connected components in Markov chains. An end component consists of a state-set $T \subseteq S$ and an action-set $A(t)$ for each state $t \in T$ such that, once T is entered and only actions in $A(t)$ are chosen, T will not be left and any state of T can be visited from any other state in T.

End Components [15,16]. Formally, an *end component* of $\mathcal{M}$ is a pair (T, A) consisting of a state-set $T \subseteq S$ and a function $A : T \to 2^{\mathsf{Act}}$ such that :

(1) $\emptyset \neq A(t) \subseteq \mathsf{Act}(t)$ for all states $t \in T$
(2) $\sum_{t' \in T} \mathsf{P}(t, \alpha, t') = 1$ for all $\alpha \in A(t)$ and $t \in T$
(3) The directed graph $(T, \longrightarrow_A)$ is strongly connected.

Here, $\longrightarrow_A$ denotes the edge-relation induced by A, i.e., $t \longrightarrow_A t'$ iff $\mathsf{P}(t, \alpha, t') > 0$ for some action $\alpha \in A(t)$.

The observation [15,16] that under each scheduler D almost all paths "end" in an end component can be formalized as follows:

$$\mathsf{Pr}^D\big\{\varsigma \in \mathsf{Paths}(s) : \mathsf{Limit}(\varsigma) \text{ is an end component }\big\} = 1$$

Here, for an infinite path $\varsigma = s_0 \xrightarrow{\alpha_1} s_1 \xrightarrow{\alpha_2} \ldots$, $\mathsf{Limit}(\varsigma)$ is the pair (T, A) where T is the set of states t that occur infinitely often in ς and $A(t)$ the set of actions $\alpha \in \mathsf{Act}(t)$ such that $s_i = t$ and $\alpha_{i+1} = \alpha$ for infinitely many indices i.

The correctness of partial order reduction criteria w.r.t temporal properties is typically formulated by means of an equivalence that identifies those paths whose traces (i.e., words obtained from the paths by projection on the state labels) agree up to stuttering. In this context stuttering refers to the repetition of the same state-labels.

Stutter equivalence. Two infinite words θ_1 and θ_2 over the alphabet 2^{AP} are called *stutter equivalent*,

$$\theta_1 \equiv_{st} \theta_2$$

iff there is an infinite word $\ell_1, \ell_2, \ldots$ over the alphabet 2^{AP} such that

$$\theta_1 = \ell_1^{k_1}, \ell_2^{k_2}, \ldots \quad \text{and} \quad \theta_2 = \ell_1^{n_1}, \ell_2^{n_2}, \ldots,$$

where $k_i, n_i \geq 1$. Two infinite paths ς_1 and ς_2 in a MDP are called stutter equivalent iff the induced words $\mathsf{trace}(\varsigma_1)$ and $\mathsf{trace}(\varsigma_2)$ over 2^{AP} are stutter equivalent.

For the partial order reduction we shall need the concept of *stutter actions*, i.e., actions that have no effect on the state-labels, no matter in which state they are taken.

Stutter actions. Formally action α of an MDP $\mathcal{M}$ is called a stutter action iff for all states $s, t \in S$ we have:

$$P(s, \alpha, t) > 0 \quad \text{implies} \quad \mathsf{L}(s) = \mathsf{L}(t).$$

We refer to $s \xrightarrow{\beta} t$ as a non-probabilistic stutter step if $\beta \in \mathsf{Act}(s)$ is a non-probabilistic stutter action and t the unique β-successor of s.

The main ingredient of any partial order reduction technique in the probabilistic or non-probabilistic setting is an adequate notion for the independence of actions. The rough idea is a formalization of actions belonging to different processes that are executed in parallel and do not affect each other, e.g. as they only refer to local variables and do not require any kind of synchronization.

Independence of actions. The formal definition for the independence of actions α and β in the composed transition system (which captures the semantics of the parallel composition of all processes that run in parallel) relies on recovering the interleaving diamonds. In non-probabilistic systems independence of two actions α and β means that for any state s where both α and β are enabled the execution of α does not affect the enabledness of β (i.e., the α-successor of s has an outgoing β-transition), and vice versa, and in addition the action sequences $\alpha\beta$ and $\beta\alpha$ lead to the same state. In the probabilistic setting the additional requirement that $\alpha\beta$ and $\beta\alpha$ have the same probabilistic effect is made:

Definition 3. (Independence of actions, cf. [14,5]) *Two actions* α, β *with* $\alpha \neq \beta$ *are called independent (in $\mathcal{M}$) iff for all states* $s \in S$ *with* $\{\alpha, \beta\} \subseteq \mathsf{Act}(s)$:

(1) $P(s, \alpha, t) > 0$ *implies* $\beta \in \mathsf{Act}(t)$,
(2) $P(s, \beta, u) > 0$ *implies* $\alpha \in \mathsf{Act}(u)$
(3) for all states $w \in S$: $\sum_{t \in S} P(s, \alpha, t) \cdot P(t, \beta, w) = \sum_{u \in S} P(s, \beta, u) \cdot P(u, \alpha, w)$

Two different actions α *and* β *are called dependent iff* α *and* β *are not independent. If* $\mathsf{A} \subseteq \mathsf{Act}$ *and* $\alpha \in \mathsf{Act} \setminus \mathsf{A}$ *then* α *is called independent from* A *iff for all actions* $\beta \in \mathsf{A}$, α *and* β *are independent. Otherwise* α *is called dependent on* A. □

Applying the above definition to non-probabilistic actions α and β (i.e., where $P(s, \alpha, t)$, $P(s, \beta, t) \in \{0, 1\}$ for all states s, t) yields the standard definition of independence of actions in ordinary transition systems.

Example 1. Fig. 1 shows a fragment of an MDP $\mathcal{M}_1$ representing the parallel execution of independent actions α and β. For example, α might stand for the outcome of the experiment of tossing a "one" with a dice, while β stands for tossing a fair coin. In general, whenever α and β stand for stochastic experiments that are independent in the classical sense then α and β viewed as actions of an MDP are independent. However, there are also other situations where two actions can be independent that do not have a fixed probabilistic branching pattern. E.g., actions α and β in the MDP $\mathcal{M}_2$ in Fig. 1 are independent. First notice that only in state s both α and β are enabled. The α-successors t, s of

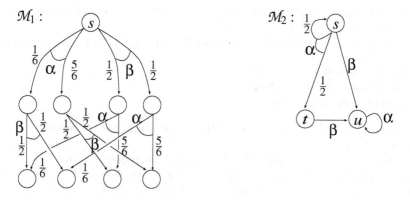

Fig. 1. Examples for independent actions

s have a β-transition to state u, while the β-successor u has a α-transition to itself. The effect under the action sequences $\alpha\beta$ and $\beta\alpha$ is the same as in either case state u is reached with probability 1.   □

Weight functions [28]. Let S, S' be finite sets and $\mathcal{R} \subseteq S \times S'$. If μ and μ' are probability distributions on S and S' respectively then a weight function for (μ, μ') with respect to $\mathcal{R}$ denotes a function $w : S \times S' \to [0,1]$ such that

- $w(s, s') > 0$ implies $(s, s') \in \mathcal{R}$,
- $\sum_{s' \in S'} w(s, s') = \mu(s)$ for all $s \in S$ and $\sum_{s \in S} w(s, s') = \mu'(s')$ for all $s' \in S'$.

We write $\mu \sqsubseteq_{\mathcal{R}} \mu'$ to denote the existence of a weight function for (μ, μ') w.r.t. $\mathcal{R}$ and refer to $\sqsubseteq_{\mathcal{R}}$ as the lifting of $\mathcal{R}$ to distributions.

3 Partial Order Reduction: The Ample Set Method

Several partial order reduction techniques have been developed from 1990 to 1995, [20,21,25,32,33,34,39,40,41]. In this paper we concentrate on one instance of partial order reduction techniques, the so-called ample set method which was developed by Doron Peled [32,33].

Given a transition system $\mathcal{T}$, either non-probabilistic (Kripke-structure) or probabilistic (MDP), the rough idea of the ample set method is to assign to any reachable state s of $\mathcal{T}$ an action-set ample$(s) \subseteq$ Act(s) and to construct a reduced system $\widehat{\mathcal{T}}$ that results by using the action-sets ample(s) instead of Act(s). The reduced system should be equivalent to the original system in some sense

$$\widehat{\mathcal{T}} \equiv \mathcal{T},$$

e.g. simulation equivalent or bisimulation equivalent, etc. Depending on the desired equivalence the defined ample-sets have to fulfill certain conditions. In the remainder of this chapter we will explain the conditions that Doron Peled [33] proposed to ensure stutter equivalence for a given non-probabilistic system $\mathcal{T}$ and its reduced system $\hat{\mathcal{T}}$.

In Section 4 we will show how these conditions can be extended to ensure

- stutter equivalence,
- simulation equivalence, resp.
- bisimulation equivalence

for a given MDP $\mathcal{M}$ and the reduced MDP $\hat{\mathcal{M}}$ and suitable notions of simulation and bisimulation.

We will now give the formal definition of the reduced system. As a non-probabilistic system $\mathcal{T}$ can be seen as a MDP with $P(s, \alpha, t) \in \{0, 1\}$ for all states s, t and actions α, we restrict our definition to the general case of an MDP.

Reduced system. Given an MDP $\mathcal{M} = (S, \mathsf{Act}, \mathbf{P}, s_{init}, \mathsf{AP}, \mathsf{L})$ and given a function $\mathsf{ample} : S \to 2^{\mathsf{Act}}$ with $\mathsf{ample}(s) \subseteq \mathsf{Act}(s)$ for all states s, the state space of the reduced MDP

$$\hat{\mathcal{M}} = (\hat{S}, \mathsf{Act}, \hat{\mathsf{P}}, s_{init}, \mathsf{AP}, \hat{\mathsf{L}})$$

induced by ample is the smallest set $\hat{S} \subseteq S$ that contains s_{init} and any state t where $\mathsf{P}(s, \alpha, t) > 0$ for some $s \in \hat{S}$ and $\alpha \in \mathsf{ample}(s)$. The labeling function $\hat{\mathsf{L}} : \hat{S} \to 2^{\mathsf{AP}}$ is the restriction of the original labeling function L to the state-set $\hat{S}$. The transition probability matrix of $\hat{\mathcal{M}}$ is given by:

$$\hat{\mathsf{P}}(s, \alpha, t) = \mathsf{P}(s, \alpha, t)$$

if $\alpha \in \mathsf{ample}(s)$ and 0 otherwise. State s is called fully expanded if $\mathsf{ample}(s) = \mathsf{Act}(s)$.

How is stutter equivalence between transition systems defined in the non-probabilistic setting? It means, that given a path from one of the systems, the other system must be able to produce a stutter equivalent path, where two paths are called stutter equivalent, if and only if their traces are stutter equivalent words over 2^{AP}.

Stutter equivalence. Given two non-probabilistic systems

$$\mathcal{T}_i = (S_i, \mathsf{Act}_i, \mathsf{P}_i, s_{init}^i, \mathsf{AP}_i, \mathsf{L}_i)^1, \qquad i = 1, 2$$

we call $\mathcal{T}_1$ and $\mathcal{T}_2$ stutter equivalent,

$$\mathcal{T}_1 \quad \equiv_{st} \quad \mathcal{T}_2,$$

if and only if for each path $\varsigma_1 = s_{init}^1 \xrightarrow{\alpha_1} s_1^1 \xrightarrow{\alpha_2} s_2^1 \xrightarrow{\alpha_3} \ldots$ of $\mathcal{T}_1$ there exists a path $\varsigma_2 = s_{init}^2 \xrightarrow{\beta_1} s_1^2 \xrightarrow{\beta_2} s_2^2 \xrightarrow{\beta_3} \ldots$ of $\mathcal{T}_2$ such that $\mathsf{trace}(\varsigma_2) \equiv_{st} \mathsf{trace}(\varsigma_1)$ and vice versa.

---

[1] $\mathsf{P}_i(s_i, \alpha_i, t_i) \in \{0, 1\}$ for all states $s_i, t_i \in S_i$ and all actions $\alpha_i \in \mathsf{Act}_i$.

(A0) **(Nonemptiness-condition)** For all states $s \in S$, $\emptyset \neq$ ample$(s) \subseteq$ Act(s).

(A1) **(Stutter-condition)** If $s \in \hat{S}$ and ample$(s) \neq$ Act(s) then all actions $\alpha \in$ ample(s) are stutter actions.

(A2) **(Dependence-condition)** For each path $\sigma = s \xrightarrow{\alpha_1} s_1 \xrightarrow{\alpha_2} \ldots \xrightarrow{\alpha_n} s_n \xrightarrow{\gamma}$ $\ldots$ in $\mathcal{M}$ where $s \in \hat{S}$ and γ is dependent on ample(s) there exists an index $i \in \{1, \ldots, n\}$ such that $\alpha_i \in$ ample(s).

(A3) **(Cycle-condition)** On each cycle $s \xrightarrow{\alpha_1} s_1 \xrightarrow{\alpha_2} \ldots \xrightarrow{\alpha_n} s_n = s$ in $\hat{\mathcal{M}}$ there exists a state s_i which is fully expanded, i.e., ample$(s_i) =$ Act(s_i).

Fig. 2. Conditions for the ample-sets

Note that given a stutter insensitive linear time property E, it holds that

$$T_1 \models E \quad \text{if and only if} \quad T_2 \models E.^2$$

Here, by stutter insensitive we mean a linear time property which can not distinguish between stutter equivalent paths, that is given two stutter equivalent paths ς_1 and ς_2, it holds that

$$\text{trace}(\varsigma_1) \in E \quad \text{if and only if} \quad \text{trace}(\varsigma_2) \in E.$$

A particular type of stutter insensitive linear time properties are specifications which are described by a formula of the Next Step free fragment of Linear Time Logic (LTL$_{\backslash X}$). Thus given a LTL$_{\backslash X}$ formula φ and two stutter equivalent systems T_1 and T_2 it holds that

$$T_1 \models \varphi \quad \text{if and only if} \quad T_2 \models \varphi.$$

Criteria for stutter equivalence. To gain stutter equivalence between the given non-probabilistic system T and the reduced system $\hat{T}$ (and therefore to preserve stutter insensitive linear time properties) the conditions shown in Figure 2 have been proposed in [33] where the following result has been shown :

Given a system $T = (S, \text{Act}, \text{P}, s_{init}, \text{AP}, \text{L})$ and a function ample : $S \rightarrow$ Act that satisfies the conditions (A0)-(A3) in Figure 2, it holds that

$$T \equiv_{st} \hat{T}.$$

In the following we will explain each of the conditions which will roughly sketch the proof.

(A0) Condition (A0) ensures that the reduced system is a sub-MDP of the original one and has no terminal states (as the original one).

---

[2] $T \models E$ means that for all paths ς of T, trace$(\varsigma) \in E$.

Thus each path of $\widehat{\mathcal{T}}$ is also a path of $\mathcal{T}$. We now have to show that for any path ς of $\mathcal{T}$ there is a stutter equivalent path $\hat{\varsigma}$ of $\widehat{\mathcal{T}}$. Let

$$\varsigma = s \xrightarrow{\alpha_1} s_1 \xrightarrow{\alpha_2} s_2 \xrightarrow{\alpha_3} \dots$$

be a path of $\mathcal{T}$. We explain how to construct a stutter equivalent path ς_1 starting in s such that its first action is an ample action of s. If $\alpha_1 \in \mathsf{ample}(s)$, let ς_1 be ς. If $\alpha_1 \notin \mathsf{ample}(s)$, let n be the smallest number such that $\alpha_n \in \mathsf{ample}(s)^3$. Assume that n is finite.

(A1) As s is not fully expanded and $\alpha_n \in \mathsf{ample}(s)$, (A1) ensures that α_n is a stutter action.

(A2) As α_n is the first ample-action of s that occurs along ς, (A2) ensures that α_n is independent from $\{\alpha_1, \dots, \alpha_{n-1}\}$.

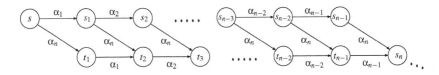

Hence we may replace the action sequence $\alpha_1 \dots \alpha_{n-1}\alpha_n$ by the action sequence $\alpha_n\alpha_1 \dots \alpha_{n-1}$ to obtain a path

$$\varsigma_1 = s \xrightarrow{\alpha_n} t_1 \xrightarrow{\alpha_1} \dots \xrightarrow{\alpha_{n-2}} t_{n-1} \xrightarrow{\alpha_{n-1}} s_n \xrightarrow{\alpha_{n+1}} s_{n+1} \xrightarrow{\alpha_{n+2}} \dots$$

which is stutter equivalent to ς.

If $n = \infty$, by similar arguments one can replace ς by a stutter equivalent path ς_1 with the same starting state $\mathsf{first}(\varsigma)$ and the action sequence $\beta\alpha_1\alpha_2 \dots$ where β is an arbitrary action in $\mathsf{ample}(\mathsf{first}(\varsigma))$.

In either case we obtain a path ς_1 that starts with a transition in the reduced system $\widehat{\mathcal{T}}$. We now may apply the same technique to the path ς_1 (more precisely, to the suffix of ς_1 that starts in the second state) to obtain a stutter equivalent path ς_2 whose first two transitions are transitions in $\widehat{\mathcal{T}}$. We continue in this way until the path ς of $\mathcal{T}$ is "transformed" into a path $\hat{\varsigma}$ in $\widehat{\mathcal{T}}$. Although conditions (A0)-(A2) are sufficient to guarantee the stutter equivalence of ς and the paths $\varsigma_1, \varsigma_2, \dots$, the cycle condition (A3) is needed to ensure the stutter equivalence of ς and $\hat{\varsigma}$.

4   The Ample Set Method for MDPs

We have just explained how the conditions (A0)-(A3) work to establish a stutter equivalence between the given system $\mathcal{T}$ and the reduced system $\widehat{\mathcal{T}}$. Given a path ς of $\mathcal{T}$ with the underlying action sequence $\alpha_1, \alpha_2, \dots$ where $\alpha_1 \notin \mathsf{ample}(\mathsf{first}(\varsigma))$, the main idea is to permute the first ample action of $\mathsf{first}(\varsigma)$ to the front of

---

[3] If none of the α_i is an ample-action of s, let n be ∞.

the action sequence. We gain a new stutter equivalent path ς_1 and repeat this procedure ad infinitum.

When dealing with MDPs, a problem arises. A scheduler for a given MDP $\mathcal{M}$ might schedule a non-ample action of the starting state. As this action can be probabilistic there might be several successors. For each of those the scheduler is able to schedule different ample actions of the starting state. Which of those should be choosen to be permuted to the front? In fact, a scenario as above must be forbidden. That is why in the probabilistic setting, we need an additional branching condition (A4) to make the ample set method work.

4.1   Establishing a Probabilistic Stutter Equivalence

In this paragraph we present the results of [5] which show how the ample set conditions can be extended to gain stutter equivalence between a given MDP $\mathcal{M}$ and the reduced MDP $\hat{\mathcal{M}}$.

First of all, we give the definition of stutter equivalence for MDPs.

Stutter equivalence for MDPs. Given two MDPs

$$\mathcal{M}_i = (S_i, \mathsf{Act}_i, \mathsf{P}_i, s^i_{init}, \mathsf{AP}_i, \mathsf{L}_i), \qquad i = 1, 2$$

we call $\mathcal{M}_1$ and $\mathcal{M}_2$ stutter equivalent ($\mathcal{M}_1 \equiv_{st} \mathcal{M}_2$), if and only if for each measurable, stutter insensitive linear time property E and each scheduler D_1 of $\mathcal{M}_1$ there is a scheduler D_2 of $\mathcal{M}_2$ such that

$$\mathsf{Pr}^{D_1}_{s^1_{init}} (\{\varsigma \text{ path of } \mathcal{M}_1 : \mathsf{trace}(\varsigma) \in E\}) = \mathsf{Pr}^{D_2}_{s^2_{init}} (\{\varsigma \text{ path of } \mathcal{M}_2 : \mathsf{trace}(\varsigma) \in E\})$$

and vice versa. As already mentioned in section 3, a formula of the Next Step free fragment of LTL (Linear Time Logic) specifies a stutter insensitive linear time property. Thus given a $\mathrm{LTL}_{\backslash X}$ formula φ and a probability bound $p \in [0, 1]$, the following holds for stutter equivalent MDPs $\mathcal{M}_1$ and $\mathcal{M}_2$:

$$\mathcal{M}_1 \models (\varphi, \bowtie p) \quad \text{if and only if} \quad \mathcal{M}_2 \models (\varphi, \bowtie p),\, [4]$$

where $\bowtie \in \{<, \leq, >, \geq\}$ is a comparison operator.

That means that given a qualitative $\mathrm{LTL}_{\backslash X}$ specification, it suffices to model check $\hat{\mathcal{M}}$ instead of $\mathcal{M}$ if we can garantuee the stutter equivalence between a given MDP and the reduced system. As $\hat{\mathcal{M}}$ is in general smaller than $\mathcal{M}$ this yields a possible speedup of the analysis. Of course the algorithmic construction of appropriate ample sets together with the construction and analysis of $\hat{\mathcal{M}}$ should be more efficient than model checking the full system $\mathcal{M}$. As you will see in the following, the partial order reduction criteria for the probabilistic setting are rather strong and might often lead to a minor savings of states. Nevertheless even a reduction that cannot shrink the state space of an MDP but only

---

[4] $\mathcal{M} \models (\varphi, \bowtie p)$ holds, if and only if under each scheduler of $\mathcal{M}$, the set of paths satisfying φ has measure $\bowtie p$.

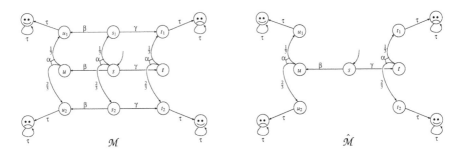

Fig. 3. (A0)-(A3) and (A4') do not establish stutter equivalence

the number of transitions can increase the efficiency of the probabilistic model checking procedure. The latter relies on solving linear programs where the number of linear (in)equalities for any state s is given by the number of outgoing transitions from s. Thus removing certain transitions via efficient reduction algorithms that e.g. operate on syntactic descriptions of the processes simplifies the linear program to be solved, and can therefore yield a speed-up of the analysis.

Why is it that conditions (A0)-(A3) can not ensure the stutter equivalence of a given MDP $\mathcal{M}$ and its reduced MDP $\hat{\mathcal{M}}$. A counterexample is depicted in Figure 3, which shows a MDP $\mathcal{M}^5$ and its reduced MDP for the following ample sets: $\mathsf{ample}(s) = \{\beta, \gamma\}$ and $\mathsf{ample}(s') = \mathsf{Act}(s')$ for all other states s'. It is easy to see that conditions (A0)-(A3) are satisfied (we assume that the labeling is given by ☺ and ⊗). But

$$\hat{\mathcal{M}} \quad \not\equiv_{st} \quad \mathcal{M},$$

as the maximum probability of eventually reaching ☺ in $\mathcal{M}$ is 1 (by choosing first α and then β in state s_1 and γ in state s_2). It is instead $\frac{2}{3}$ in $\hat{\mathcal{M}}$. The problem that arises is the following. The scheduler of $\mathcal{M}$ schedules a probabilistic non-ample action of the starting state s. Depending on the outcome (moving to state s_1 or s_2), the scheduler chooses different ample actions (of s). Thus choosing α first postpones the real nondeterministic decision between the ample actions β and γ. The reduced system $\hat{\mathcal{M}}$ is not able to mimic such a behaviour as it has to decide for a particular ample action of s in its first step (before the outcome of α is known). This decision is fixed from then on. It is exactly this behaviour that one has to forbid to gain stutter equivalence between the given system $\mathcal{M}$ and its reduced sytem. That means that if the system can branch probabilistically with non-ample actions (w.r.t. the starting state) then there should be only one ample action of the starting state.

The auhors of [5] proposed condition

(A4') (Branching-condition à la [5]) If $\sigma = s \xrightarrow{\alpha_1} s_1 \xrightarrow{\alpha_2} \ldots \xrightarrow{\alpha_n} s_n \xrightarrow{\gamma}$ ... is a path in $\mathcal{M}$ where $s \in \hat{S}$, $\alpha_1, \ldots, \alpha_n, \gamma \notin \mathsf{ample}(s)$ and γ is probabilistic then $|\mathsf{ample}(s)| = 1$.

---

[5] Note that α is the only probabilistic action of $\mathcal{M}$.

and showed that given a MDP $\mathcal{M}$ and ample sets that satisfy conditions (A0)-(A3) and (A4'), then

$$\hat{\mathcal{M}} \quad \equiv_{st} \quad \mathcal{M}.$$

Remark

- One should notice that condition (A4') is irrelevant for non-probabilistic systems. Thus the extended ample set method falls back to the original one, if applied to non-probabilistic systems.
- The authors of [5] were actually able to replace condition (A3) by a weaker condition

    (A3') **(End component-condition)** In each end component (T, A) in $\hat{\mathcal{M}}$ there exists a state $s \in T$ which is fully expanded, i.e., ample$(s) =$ Act(s).

    that uses the concept of de Alfaro's end components [15,16]. Again, if applied to non-probabilistic systems, condition (A3') is equivalent to condition (A3). However condition (A3') also allows for certain cycles violating the cycle-condition (A3). For instance, for the MDP $\mathcal{M}_2$ in Fig. 1, (A3') allows to choose ample$(s) = \{\alpha\}$ (provided that α is a stutter-action), as state s is not contained in an end component.

4.2 Establishing a Simulation Equivalence

In this paragraph we present the results of [14] which show how the ample set condition (A4') can be strengthened to gain some kind of simulation equivalence between a given MDP $\mathcal{M}$ and the reduced MDP $\hat{\mathcal{M}}$.

D'Argenio and Niebert noted in [14] that "the interplay between nondeterminism and probabilism is comparable to that of existential and universal quantification." Thus they followed the approach by Gerth et al [19] to ensure CTL$_{\setminus X}$ (the Next Step free fragment of computation tree logic) equivalence between a given non-probabilistic system $\mathcal{T}$ and its reduced system $\hat{\mathcal{T}}$. They proposed condition

(A4") **(Branching-condition à la [14])** For any state s in $\hat{S}$: ample$(s) =$ Act(s) or ample(s) is a singleton.

to ensure that the interplay between nondeterministic and probabilistic choices is preserved : either the unique nondeterministic choice is safe (hence $|$ample$(s)| = 1$) or all branching is preserved (ample$(s) =$ Act(s)).

Before we present the results of [14] the reader should notice that [14] required a stronger underlying structure for the given MDP. They assumed each action to have a fixed probabilistic branching pattern, i.e. if $\alpha \in$ Act(s) and there are numbers $x_1, \ldots, x_n \in (0, 1]$ and mutual distinct successor states $s_1, \ldots, s_n$ such that $P(s, \alpha, s_i) = x_i$ and $\sum_{i=1}^{n} x_i = 1$ then for all states t such that $\alpha \in$ Act(t) there exist mutual distinct states $t_1, \ldots, t_n$ such that $P(t, \alpha, t_i) = x_i, i = 1, \ldots, n$.

[14] established a (probabilistic weak) complete forward simulation equivalence between a given MDP $\mathcal{M}$ and the reduced MDP $\hat{\mathcal{M}}$. There a state of $\mathcal{M}$

is not simulated by one state of $\hat{\mathcal{M}}$, but by a probability distribution over the states of $\hat{\mathcal{M}}$.

To define this simulation we need the notion of probabilistic weak transitions which is given below.

Probabilistic weak transition

$$\frac{\alpha \in \mathsf{Act}(s)}{s \stackrel{\alpha}{\Longrightarrow} \mathsf{P}(s,\alpha,.)} \qquad \frac{\beta \in \mathsf{Act}(s), \beta \text{ stutter action and } \forall r \in supp(\mathsf{P}(s,\beta,.)) : r \stackrel{\alpha}{\Longrightarrow} \mu_r}{s \stackrel{\alpha}{\Longrightarrow} \sum_{r \in supp(\mathsf{P}(s,\beta,.))} \mathsf{P}(s,\beta,r) \cdot \mu_r}$$

Thus there is a probabilistic weak transition $s \stackrel{\alpha}{\Longrightarrow} \mu$, if there is a probabilistic directed tree starting in s, such that μ is the probability of reaching its leaves and only stutter actions occur in this tree except for the last action (leading to a leave), which must be α. Then let

$$s \stackrel{\hat{\alpha}}{\Longrightarrow} \mu \qquad \text{iff} \qquad s \stackrel{\alpha}{\Longrightarrow} \mu \quad \text{or} \quad (\alpha \text{ is a stutter action and } \mu = \mu_s{}^6).$$

Complete forward simulation (cfs)

Given two MDPs $\mathcal{M} = (S, \mathsf{Act}, \mathsf{P}, s_{init}, \mathsf{AP}, \mathsf{L})$ and $\mathcal{M}' = (S', \mathsf{Act}', \mathsf{P}', s'_{init}, \mathsf{AP}, \mathsf{L}')$ with the same set of atomic propositions and a binary relation $\mathcal{R} \subseteq S \times Distr(S')$. Then $\mathcal{R}$ is called a complete forward simulation for $\mathcal{M}$ and $\mathcal{M}'$, if $(s_{init}, \mu_{s'_{init}}) \in \mathcal{R}$ and for any pair (s, μ) in $\mathcal{R}$ the following two conditions are fulfilled.

(1) $\mathsf{L}(s) = \mathsf{L}'(s') \ \forall s' \in supp(\mu)$
(2) For any action $\alpha \in \mathsf{Act}(s)$ it holds that :

  (2.1) $\forall r \in supp(\mu) \ \exists \mu_r : r \stackrel{\hat{\alpha}}{\Longrightarrow} \mu_r$ and
  (2.2) $\exists \nu \in Distr(Distr(\mathcal{M}'))$ such that $\mathsf{P}(s,\alpha,.) \sqsubseteq_{\mathcal{R}} \nu$ and
  $\sum_{r \in supp(\mu)} \mu(r) \cdot \mu_r = \sum_{\mu' \in supp(\nu)} \nu(\mu') \cdot \mu'$

We call $\mathcal{M}$ and $\mathcal{M}'$ *complete forward simulation equivalent* if there are complete forward simulations for $\mathcal{M}$ and $\mathcal{M}'$ as well as for $\mathcal{M}'$ and $\mathcal{M}$. We write $\mathcal{M} \approx_{\mathrm{cfs}} \mathcal{M}'$ iff $\mathcal{M}$ and $\mathcal{M}'$ are complete forward simulation equivalent.

The authors of [14] showed that given a MDP $\mathcal{M}$ and ample sets satisfying conditions (A0)-(A3) and (A4") then

$$\hat{\mathcal{M}} \quad \approx_{\mathrm{cfs}} \quad \mathcal{M}.$$

As complete forward simulation is stronger than forward simulation which is known to preserve trace distribution [38], the authors of [14] argue that a given MDP $\mathcal{M}$ and its reduced MDP $\hat{\mathcal{M}}$ are trace distribution equivalent if conditions (A0)-(A3) and (A4") are satisfied. Therefore the reduction preserves the maximum probability of reaching a particular set of states.

We will now give an example for a complete forward simulation. Consider the MDPs $\mathcal{M}$ and $\hat{\mathcal{M}}$ in Figure 4 (α and β are stutter actions). Starting with the

---

[6] Recall that μ_s denotes the Dirac distribution that assigns probability 1 to the state s.

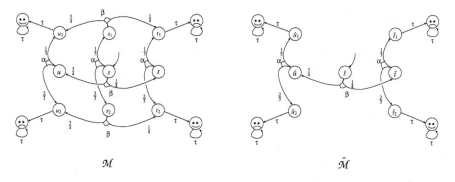

Fig. 4. Example for complete forward simulation

MDP $\mathcal{M}$ and choosing ample$(s) = \{\beta\}$, we obtain that (A0)-(A3) and (A4") are satisfied and $\hat{\mathcal{M}}$ is the reduced MDP. Then action α in state s has no "direct" match in state $\hat{s}$. But $\hat{\mathcal{M}}$ can execute first β and then α. How are the states s_1 and s_2 related to states of $\hat{\mathcal{M}}$? The state s_1 is simulated by the distribution μ_1 and s_2 is simulated by the distribution μ_2, where

$$\mu_1(\hat{u}_1) = \frac{3}{4}, \quad \mu_1(\hat{t}_1) = \frac{1}{4} \quad \text{and} \quad \mu_2(\hat{u}_2) = \frac{3}{4}, \quad \mu_2(\hat{t}_2) = \frac{1}{4}.$$

If $\mathcal{M}$ performs action β in state s_1 then $\hat{\mathcal{M}}$ does not perform any action, but matches the action of $\mathcal{M}$ with offering states $\hat{u}_1$ and $\hat{t}_1$ with the needed probabilities. Thus μ_1 and μ_2 "record" probabilistic choices that have already been made in $\hat{\mathcal{M}}$, but not yet in $\mathcal{M}$ (in this case, this is the execution of β).

Remark: Conditions (A0)-(A3) together with (A4") are exactly the conditions that Gerth et al[19] proposed to ensure CTL$_{\backslash X}$ (the Next Step free fragment of computation tree logic) equivalence between a given non-probabilistic system $\mathcal{T}$ and its reduced system $\hat{\mathcal{T}}$. In contrast to this both [14] as well as [5] mention that conditions (A0)-(A3) and (A4") are not sufficient to gain PCTL$_{\backslash X}$ [7] (the Next Step free fragment of probabilistic computation tree logic) equivalence between a given MDP $\mathcal{M}$ and the reduced MDP $\hat{\mathcal{M}}$ as the example in Figure 5 shows. In Figure 5, a and b are atomic propositions. As β is a stutter action which is independent from α, conditions (A0)-(A3) and (A4") are satisfied when choosing the singleton ample set $\{\beta\}$ in the initial state. However, the PCTL$_{\backslash X}$-formula

$$\mathbf{P}_{=1}\big[\Box\big((a \wedge \neg b) \rightarrow (\mathbf{P}_{=1}[\Diamond b] \vee \mathbf{P}_{=1}[\Diamond \neg a])\big)\big]$$

holds for $\hat{\mathcal{M}}$, but not for $\mathcal{M}$ (where $\Box$ stands for "always", $\Diamond$ stands for "eventually" and $\mathbf{P}_{=1}[\varphi]$ requires that under all schedulers the set of paths satisfying φ has measure 1).

Note that in a probabilistic forward simulation, state s of $\mathcal{M}$ would be simulated by a uniform distribution over the "a" states of $\hat{\mathcal{M}}$.

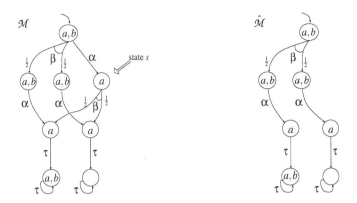

Fig. 5. (A0)-(A3), (A4") are not sufficient for PCTL$_{\backslash X}$

4.3   Establishing a Bisimulation Equivalence

Why is it that conditions (A0)-(A3) and (A4") are not enough for PCTL$_{\backslash X}$ equivalence. To gain CTL$_{\backslash X}$ equivalence for a non-probabilistic system $\mathcal{T}$ and its reduced system $\widehat{\mathcal{T}}$ one has to eliminate the possibility that a state of the reduced system can reach (in one step) several, but not all of its successors of the original system. This is done by condition (A4") stating that each state in the reduced system $\widehat{\mathcal{T}}$ is either fully expanded, or its ample set is a singleton. This suffices to preserve branching properties. Dealing with MDPs condition (A4") is not enough, as if a state s is not fully expanded and its ample set ample(s) = $\{\alpha\}$ is a singleton then α might be probabilistic. This means that the set of successors of s in $\hat{\mathcal{M}}$ can be a proper subset of the set of successor of s in $\mathcal{M}$ and contains more than a single state (see Figure 5, the example in Figure 5 is a probabilistic variant of the counterexample given in [19]). Thus a stronger condition is needed to ensure that a state which is not fully expanded has only one successor.

In this paragraph we present the results of [3] which show how the ample set condition (A4") can be strengthened to gain bisimulation equivalence between a given MDP $\mathcal{M}$ and the reduced MDP $\hat{\mathcal{M}}$. The notion of bisimulation is that of probabilistic visible bisimulation which is defined in the following.

Probabilistic visible bisimulation (pvb)
Given two MDPs $\mathcal{M} = (S, \text{Act}, \text{P}, s_{init}, \text{AP}, \text{L})$ and $\mathcal{M}' = (S', \text{Act}', \text{P}', s'_{init}, \text{AP}, \text{L}')$ with the same set of atomic propositions and a binary relation $\mathcal{R} \subseteq S \times S'$. Then $\mathcal{R}$ is called a probabilistic visible simulation if $(s_{init}, s'_{init}) \in \mathcal{R}$ and for any pair (s, s') in $\mathcal{R}$ the following three conditions are fulfilled.

(1) $\text{L}(s) = \text{L}'(s')$
(2) For any action $\alpha \in \text{Act}(s)$ at least one of the following two conditions holds:
    (2.1) α is a non-probabilistic stutter action such that $(t, s') \in \mathcal{R}$ for the unique α-successor t of s,

(2.2) There is a finite path σ' of the form $\sigma' = s'_0 \xrightarrow{\beta_0} s'_1 \ldots \xrightarrow{\beta_{n-1}} s'_n$ in $\mathcal{M}'$ s.t.[7]

  – $\beta_0, \ldots, \beta_{n-1}$ are non-probabilistic stutter actions,
  – $(s, s'_i) \in \mathcal{R}$ for $1 \le i \le n$,
  – $\alpha \in \mathsf{Act}'(s'_n)$ and $\mathsf{P}(s, \alpha, \cdot) \sqsubseteq_\mathcal{R} \mathsf{P}'(s'_n, \alpha, \cdot)$ [8].

(3) If there is an infinite path ς of the form $\varsigma = t_0 \xrightarrow{\beta_0} t_1 \xrightarrow{\beta_1} t_2 \xrightarrow{\beta_2} t_3 \xrightarrow{\beta_3} \ldots$ in $\mathcal{M}$ consisting of non-probabilistic stutter actions $\beta_0, \beta_1, \beta_2, \ldots$ and such that $(t_i, s') \in \mathcal{R}$, $i = 0, 1, 2, \ldots$ then there is a finite path σ' of the form $\sigma' = t'_0 \xrightarrow{\gamma_0} t'_1 \xrightarrow{\gamma_1} \ldots \xrightarrow{\gamma_{j-1}} t'_j \xrightarrow{\gamma_j} t'_{j+1}$ in $\mathcal{M}'$ such that $(s, t'_i) \in \mathcal{R}$, $i = 0, 1, \ldots, j$, $(t_1, t'_{j+1}) \in \mathcal{R}$, and $\gamma_0, \gamma_1, \ldots, \gamma_{j-1}, \gamma_j$ are non-probabilistic stutter actions.

$\mathcal{R}$ is called a probabilistic visible bisimulation for $(\mathcal{M}, \mathcal{M}')$ if $\mathcal{R}$ is a probabilistic visible simulation for $(\mathcal{M}, \mathcal{M}')$ and $\mathcal{R}^{-1}$ is a probabilistic visible simulation for $(\mathcal{M}', \mathcal{M})$. We write $\mathcal{M} \approx_{\mathrm{pvb}} \mathcal{M}'$ iff there exists a probabilistic visible bisimulation for $(\mathcal{M}, \mathcal{M}')$.

[3] argue that two probabilistic visible bisimilar MDPs $\mathcal{M}$ and $\mathcal{M}'$ satisfy the same $\mathrm{PCTL}^*_{\setminus X}$ state formulas. As already mentioned above, to gain $\mathrm{PCTL}^*_{\setminus X}$ equivalence between a MDP $\mathcal{M}$ and its reduced MDP $\hat{\mathcal{M}}$, we have to forbid that a state which is not fully expanded has more than a single successor. Thus [3] proposed condition

A4"' (Branching-condition à la [3]) For any state s in $\hat{S}$: $\mathsf{ample}(s) = \mathsf{Act}(s)$ or $\mathsf{ample}(s) = \{\alpha\}$, where α is a non-probabilistic action

and showed that given a MDP $\mathcal{M}$ and ample sets satisfying conditions (A0)-(A3) and (A4"') then

$$\hat{\mathcal{M}} \quad \approx_{\mathrm{pvb}} \quad \mathcal{M}.$$

Remark

  – One should notice that condition (A4"') is equivalent to (A4") if applied to non-probabilistic system. Thus (A4"') is a conservative adaption of condition (A4") suggested by Gerth et al. [19] to establish a visible bisimulation between a given non-probabilistic system T and its reduced system $\hat{T}$.
  – To handle branching time properties, the cycle-condition (A3) could also be replaced with the weaker end component condition (A3'). However, in combination with (A4"'), conditions (A3') and (A3) are equivalent. This follows from the fact that for any end component in $\hat{\mathcal{M}}$ where none of its states is fully expanded, the ample-sets of all its states are singletons consisting of a non-probabilistic action. Thus the end component under consideration is a cycle.

---

[7] The case $n = 0$, i.e., $\sigma' = s'$, is allowed.

[8] Note, that $P(s, \alpha, \cdot) \sqsubseteq_\mathcal{R} P'(s'_n, \alpha, \cdot)$ denotes the existence of a weight function for $(P(s, \alpha, \cdot), P'(s'_n, \alpha, \cdot))$ w.r.t. $\mathcal{R}$ (as introduced in section 2).

5   Partial Order Reduction Versus Process Equivalences

In this section we give a brief summary of the results presented in Section 4. With suitable notions of stutter equivalence, simulation and bisimulation equivalence we obtain:

(a) If conditions (A0)-(A3) and (A4') hold then $\mathcal{M}$ and $\hat{\mathcal{M}}$ are stutter equivalent (see Section 4.1), but in general $\hat{\mathcal{M}}$ does not simulate $\mathcal{M}$.
(b) If conditions (A0)-(A3) and (A4'') hold then $\mathcal{M}$ and $\hat{\mathcal{M}}$ are simulation equivalent (see Section 4.2), but in general not bisimilar.
(c) If conditions (A0)-(A3) and (A4''') hold then $\mathcal{M}$ and $\hat{\mathcal{M}}$ are probabilistic visible bisimilar (see Section 4.3).

In particular, stutter equivalent MDPs satisfy the same quantitative $\text{LTL}_{\setminus X}$ properties and probabilistic visible bisimilar MDPs satisfy the same $\text{PCTL}^*_{\setminus X}$ properties.

We will now give examples for the statements in (a) and (b). Figure 6 illustrates a reduction satisfying (A0)-(A3) and (A4') where $\hat{\mathcal{M}}$ does not simulate $\mathcal{M}$ (as stated in (a)). Here $\mathcal{M}$ and $\hat{\mathcal{M}}$ do not contain probabilistic actions, and hence can be viewed as ordinary transition systems. The intuitive argument why $\hat{\mathcal{M}}$ does not simulate $\mathcal{M}$ is that there is no possibility to mimic the nondeterministic choice in state t via a probabilistic choice over the two a-states in $\hat{\mathcal{M}}$. Note that the schedulers for $\mathcal{M}$ in the upper a-state t might choose β and γ (and thus combine the two lower a-states) with arbitrary probabilities while probabilistic forward simulation would require a *fixed* probability distribution over the two lower a-states to mimic the possible behaviors of t (which is not possible).

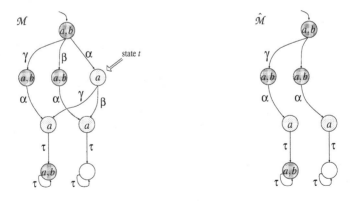

Fig. 6. (A0)-(A3) and (A4') hold, but $\hat{\mathcal{M}}$ does not simulate $\mathcal{M}$

For the example in Figure 5, $\mathcal{M}$ and $\hat{\mathcal{M}}$ are simulation equivalent. The intuitive argument why $\hat{\mathcal{M}}$ can simulate $\mathcal{M}$ is that state s is simulated by the probability distribution that assigns probability $1/2$ to the two a-states in $\hat{\mathcal{M}}$. But in Figure 5, $\mathcal{M}$ and $\hat{\mathcal{M}}$ are not bisimilar because there is *no state* in $\hat{\mathcal{M}}$ that corresponds to state s in $\mathcal{M}$. Thus Figure 5 yields an example for a reduction satisfying (A0)-(A3) and (A4") where $\mathcal{M}$ and $\hat{\mathcal{M}}$ are not bisimilar (as stated in (b)).

6 Conclusion

In this paper we gave an overview of results for partial order reduction with respect to Markov decision processes. This includes partial order criteria proposed by [5] that preserve quantitative linear time properties (see Section 4.1) as well as criteria proposed by [3] that preserve probabilistic branching time properties (see Section 4.3). It is worth noting that these criteria are the natural extension of the known reduction criteria for non-probabilistic systems and linear time properties, resp. branching time properties. Moreover in Section 4.2 we presented the criteria of [14] which establish a simulation equivalence between the given system and the reduced system. We are not aware of any theoretical consideration of partial order reduction criteria for MDPs other than [5,14,3], but we expect that more work will be done in this area in the future. Further directions include an investigation of other partial order techniques such as Valmari's *stubborn sets* [39,41] and Godefroid's *persistent sets* [20].

On the practical side our group is currently implementing the forthcoming model checker LiQuor [1] for quantitative LTL where the partial order criteria presented in Section 4.2 are implemented. Although these criteria are rather strong, first experimental results are promising as good reductions can be obtained. Moreover, while model checking probabilistic systems, even minor savings of states and transitions are desirable as the probabilistic model checking procedure relies not only on graph exploring algorithms (as in the non-probabilistic case), but also on solving linear programs where the number of linear inequalities for any state s is given by the number of outgoing transitions from s.

References

1. C. Baier, F. Ciesinski, and M. Groesser. Quantitative analysis of distributed randomized protocols. In *Proc. of the tenth International Workshop on Formal Methods for Industrial Critical Systems (FMICS 05)*, 2005.
2. C. Baier, E. Clarke, V. Hartonas-Garmhausen, M. Kwiatkowska, and M. Ryan. Symbolic model checking for probabilistic processes. In *Proc. International Colloquium on Automata, Languages and Programming (ICALP)*, volume 1256 of *Lecture Notes in Computer Science*, pages 430–440, 1997.
3. C. Baier, P. D'Argenio, and M. Größer. Partial order reduction for probabilistic branching time. In *Proc. QAPL*, 2005.
4. C. Baier, B. Engelen, and M. Majster-Cederbaum. Deciding bisimularity and similarity for probabilistic processes. *Jounal of Computer and System Sciences*, 60:187–231, 2000.
5. C. Baier, M. Größer, and F. Ciesinski. Partial order reduction for probabilistic systems. In QEST 2004 [37], pages 230–239.

6. C. Baier, B. Haverkort, H. Hermanns, J.-P. Katoen, and M. Siegle, editors. *Validation of Stochastic Systems*, volume 2925 of *Lecture Notes in Computer Science*, 2003.
7. A. Bianco and L. de Alfaro. Model checking of probabilistic and nondeterministic systems. In *Proc. Foundations of Software Technology and Theoretical Computer Science (FST & TCS)*, volume 1026 of *Lecture Notes in Computer Science*, pages 499–513, 1995.
8. M. Bozga and O. Maler. On the Representation of Probabilities over Structured Domains. In *Proc. International Conference on Computer Aided Verification (CAV)*, volume 1633 of *Lecture Notes in Computer Science*, pages 261–273, 1999.
9. S. Cattani and R. Segala. Decision algorithms for probabilistic bisimulation. In *Proc. International Conference on Concurrency Theory (CONCUR)*, volume 2421 of *Lecture Notes in Computer Science*, pages 371–385, 2002.
10. E. Clarke, Orna Grumberg, and Doron Peled. *Model Checking*. MIT Press, 1999.
11. C. Courcoubetis and M. Yannakakis. Markov decision processes and regular events (extended abstract). In *Proc. 17th on International Colloquium Automata, Languages and Programming (ICALP)*, volume 443 of *Lecture Notes in Computer Science*, pages 336–349, 1990.
12. C. Courcoubetis and M. Yannakakis. The complexity of probabilistic verification. *Journal of the ACM*, 42(4):857–907, 1995.
13. P. d' Argenio, B. Jeannet, H. Jensen, and K. Larsen. Reachability analysis of probabilistic systems by successive refinements. In [17], pages 57–76, 2001.
14. P.R. D'Argenio and P. Niebert. Partial order reduction on concurrent probabilistic programs. In QEST 2004 [37], pages 240–249.
15. L. de Alfaro. *Formal Verification of Probabilistic Systems*. PhD thesis, Stanford University, Department of Computer Science, 1997.
16. L. de Alfaro. Stochastic transition systems. In *Proc. 9th International Conference on Concurrency Theory (CONCUR)*, volume 1466 of *Lecture Notes in Computer Science*, pages 423–438, 1998.
17. L. de Alfaro and S. Gilmore, editors. *Proc. 1st Joint Int. Workshop Process Algebra and Probabilistic Methods, Performance Modeling and Verification (PAPM-PROBMIV)*, volume 2399 of *Lecture Notes in Computer Science*. Springer, 2001.
18. H. Fecher, M. Leuker, and V. Wolf. Don't know in probabilistic systems. In *Proceedings of 13th International SPIN Workshop on Model Checking of Software (SPIN'06)*, 2006.
19. R. Gerth, R. Kuiper, D. Peled, and W. Penczek. A partial order approach to branching time logic model checking. In *Proc. 3rd Israel Symposium on the Theory of Computing Systems (ISTCS'95)*, pages 130–139. IEEE Press, 1995.
20. P. Godefroid. *Partial Order Methods for the Verification of Concurrent Systems: An Approach to the State Explosion Problem*, volume 1032 of *Lecture Notes in Computer Science*. Springer-Verlag, 1996.
21. P. Godefroid, D. Peled, and M. Staskauskas. Using partial-order methods in the formal validation of industrial concurrent programs. In *Proc. International Symposium on Software Testing and Analysis*, pages 261–269. ACM Press, 1996.
22. G. Hachtel, E. Macii, A. Pardo, and F. Somenzi. Probabilistic Analysis of Large Finite State Machines. In *31st ACM/IEEE Design Automation Conference (DAC)*. San Diego Convention Center, 1994.
23. H. Hermanns, M. Kwiatkowska, G. Norman, D. Parker, and M. Siegle. On the use of MTBDDs for performability analysis and verification of stochastic systems. *Journal of Logic and Algebraic Programming: Special Issue on Probabilistic Techniques for the Design and Analysis of Systems*, 56:23–67, 2003.

24. H. Hermanns and R. Segala, editors. *Proc. 2nd Joint Int. Workshop Process Algebra and Probabilistic Methods, Performance Modeling and Verification (PAPM-PROBMIV)*, volume 2399 of *Lecture Notes in Computer Science*. Springer, 2002.

25. G. Holzmann and D. Peled. An improvement in formal verification. In *Proc. Formal Description Techniques, FORTE94*, pages 197–211, Berne, Switzerland, October 1994. Chapman & Hall.

26. M. Huth. Possibilistic and probabilistic abstraction-based model checking. In [24], pages 115–134, 2002.

27. M. Huth. Abstraction and probabilities for hybrid logics. In *Proc. 2nd workshop on Quantitative Aspects of Programming Languages*, 2004.

28. B. Jonsson and K. Larsen. Specification and refinement of probabilistic processes. In *Proc. LICS*, pages 266–277. IEEE CS Press, 1991.

29. M. Kwiatkowska, G. Norman, and D. Parker. Probabilistic symbolic model checking with PRISM: A hybrid approach. *International Journal on Software Tools for Technology Transfer (STTT)*,, 2004.

30. K. Larsen and A. Skou. Bisimulation through probabilistic testing. *Information and Computation*, 94(1):1–28, 1991.

31. A. Miner and D. Parker. Symbolic representations and analysis of large probabilistic systems. In [6], 2003.

32. D. Peled. All from one, one for all: On model checking using representatives. In *Proc. 5th International Computer Aided Verification Conference (CAV)*, volume 697 of *Lecture Notes in Computer Science*, pages 409–423, 1993.

33. D. Peled. Partial order reduction: Linear and branching time logics and process algebras. In [34], pages 79–88, 1996.

34. D. Peled, V. Pratt, and G. Holzmann, editors. *Partial Order Methods in Verification*, volume 29(10) of *DIMACS Series in Discrete Mathematics and Theoretical Computer Science*. American Mathematical Society, 1997.

35. A. Pnueli and L. D. Zuck. Probabilistic verification. *Information and Computation*, 103(1):1–29, 1993.

36. M. L. Puterman. *Markov Decision Processes—Discrete Stochastic Dynamic Programming*. John Wiley & Sons, Inc., New York, 1994.

37. *Proceedings of the 1st International Conference on Quantitative Evaluation of Systems (QEST 2004)*. Enschede, the Netherlands. IEEE Computer Society Press, 2004.

38. R. Segala. *Modeling and Verification of Randomized Distributed Real-Time Systems*. PhD thesis, Massachusetts Institute of Technology, 1995.

39. A. Valmari. A stubborn attack on state explosion. *Formal Methods in System Design*, 1:297–322, 1992.

40. A. Valmari. State of the art report: Stubborn sets. *Petri-Net Newsletters*, 46:6–14, 1994.

41. A. Valmari. Stubborn set methods for process algebras. In [34], pages 79–88, 1996.

42. R. van Glabbeek, S. Smolka, B. Steffen, and C. Tofts. Reactive, generative, and stratified models of probabilistic processes. In *Proc. 5th Annual Symposium on Logic in Computer Science (LICS)*, pages 130–141. IEEE Computer Society Press, 1990.

43. M. Vardi. Automatic verification of probabilistic concurrent finite-state programs. In *Proc. 26th IEEE Symposium on Foundations of Computer Science (FOCS)*, pages 327–338, 1985.

44. M. Vardi and P. Wolper. An automata-theoretic approach to automatic program verification (preliminary report). In *Proc. 1st Annual Symposium on Logic in Computer Science (LICS)*, pages 332–344. IEEE Computer Society Press, 1986.

Author Index

Lecture Notes in Computer Science

For information about Vols. 1–4011

please contact your bookseller or Springer